U.S. Restaurants
2011

Informed Reviews of 1800 of the Top Places to Eat in the Country

Compiled & written by

Steve Plotnicki

BOOKS

BOOKS

A Division of SJP Media LLC, P.O. Box 388, Holbrook, NY 11741

Opinionated About U.S. Restaurants 2011

Editor Troy Segal
Design Associate & Tech Consulting John Kern
Additional Design Susan Welt
Researchers Caroline Bollinger, Ellen McCurtin
Copyeditors Patricia Fogarty, Tom Holton, Stacey Peltz

Production Consulting gonzalez-defino
Maps Spatial Graphics, Inc.
Cover Photos of Asselina, Monument Lane and Walle provided cour-
tesy of Noah Fecks ©2011; Chilled Vegetable Minestrone at the Town
House by John Sconzo MD, provided courtesy of Docsconz. LLC
Back cover photo of Steve Plotnicki at Eleven Madison Park by Noah
Fecks.

Special thanks to Perri Defino for the role she played in helping to
design this book, to contributors Rowan Jacobsen, Tia Keenan, Mike
Sweeney, and to all of the dining enthusiasts who contributed reviews
to this guide.

For information about sales of this book please contact
info@opinionatedabout.com

Proudly Manufactured in the U.S.A.

ISBN-13: 978-09815650-1-9
ISBN-13: 978-09815650-2-6 (ebook)

Visit us on the web at www.opinionatedabout.com

Contents

continued

From the Publisher

EVER SINCE I WAS OLD ENOUGH TO TAKE THE SUBWAY INTO
Manhattan from my parents' home in Queens, New York
and began to discover the culinary wonders the world has to
offer, I've been passionate about dining. What started out as a
search for the best hamburger or the most succulent Chinese
dumplings evolved over time into a full-blown love affair that
now takes me all over the United States and Europe to eat at
some of the world's greatest restaurants. In the course of my
culinary odyssey, I've developed many friendships with people
who share my passion. Invariably, our discussions turn to the
subject of dining guides – the qualities that make them useful
and the flaws that render them less so. This book is the result
of those discussions and an attempt to correct the flaws.

One of our criticisms focuses on the failure of most guides to
properly calibrate their ratings among different geographic
locations. This is true of both survey-based guides, which
weave a series of opinions contributed by amateur enthusiasts into a single conclusion, and guides written by a staff of
professional reviewers. Survey-based guides are plagued by
results that give higher ratings to less-deserving places rather
than ones that experienced diners feel are important restaurants. Meanwhile, guides written by professionals all too often
demonstrate a bias toward a particular style of dining or the
restaurants in a specific region or country. And both types
of guides can be reluctant to demote once-great restaurants
even after years of poor performance.

I spent a number of years trying to figure out how to correct
these flaws. As I thought about what makes a good guide
tick, I came to the conclusion that it was a matter of opinion.

No, not the subjective meaning of the word "opinion," which is the way that most people use it. I am talking about the difference between good opinions and bad ones. If I could distinguish between the two and determine when a consensus was reached, it would be a new way of quantifying taste. As it turns out, differentiating between good and bad opinions was easy. More difficult was figuring out how to evaluate two opinions that reached different conclusions but that were equally valuable.

So after a number of years of poking, prodding, tweaking, refining and constantly recalibrating my methodology, I am proud to publish our first full guide to U.S. restaurants. I believe it accomplishes what it set out to achieve: an expression, in both numerical and editorial terms, of the state of dining in America as shaped by a set of informed opinions. I am confident that it is an improvement on the guides that are already on the market, and I hope you enjoy using it as much as I enjoyed creating it.

Steve Plotnicki

About This Guide

The American Diner Comes of Age

If we had to identify one of the most important trends in American dining, it would be the phenomenon of the chef returning to his roots – literally. Peoria, Illinois, Fredericksburg, Maryland, Smithville, Missouri and Findlay, Ohio, are not places where one expects to find a top restaurant. But in 2011, a place that is recommended in this guide exists in each of those cities, something that would have been impossible a decade ago.

A few things have factored into this phenomenon. First, as the American economy becomes less dependent on industrial production, there is a renewed interest in agriculture, with more areas reclaiming long-dormant farmlands and reviving agrarian activities. A second factor is a desire of many young chefs to run a first-rate kitchen, but also to start a family and have a home life. So, after apprenticeships in big-city restaurants, they're opening their own establishments in smaller towns – often their hometowns, where parents or in-laws furnish a built-in support system. A third factor is cost: It's a lot cheaper to open a restaurant in Peoria than it is in Chicago.

The theory is, "If you build it, they will come." Of course, that only works if people understand and appreciate what you are building. So add a fourth factor to this phenomenon, one that's at its very heart: the coming-of-age of the American diner. Each day, more and more people who were once happy subsisting on a diet of steaks and frozen lobster tails are showing interest in cuisine that utilizes local and sustainable ingredients and that is prepared by chefs who have trained at some of the best restaurants in the country.

How did this happen? Like any other aspect of life, progress is driven by the public having access to better information. Whether from cooking shows on television, regional magazines that spotlight local ingredients, farmers and cooks, a proliferation of farmers markets or a national food press that is more tuned in to the ways eating is changing, American diners are more receptive to the ways of the modern table than they have ever been. As a result, young chefs are now able to open restaurants in places that would have been unheard of in the past.

We believe this trend will continue, and in the years to come, we expect that our guides will recommend additional restaurants in what are now unexpected locations. And it wouldn't surprise us if, 10 or 15 years from now, the American dining scene resembles what food enthusiasts enjoyed in France during its culinary heyday: a beautiful mosaic of dining opportunities in which each region has one or two important restaurants that everyone needs to visit, while many of the cities and towns en route have restaurants that offer an honest version of the local cuisine.

continued

Our Restaurant Scale

Fine Dining

98.0-100	Worth Planning a Trip Around
95.0-97.9	An Important Destination
92.0-94.9	Highly Recommended
90.0-91.9	Recommended
88.0-89.9	Top Local Choice
85.0-87.9	Acceptable
75.0-84.9	Other Restaurants Mentioned

Cheap Eats

8.1-10.0	Uniquely Delicious
7.0-7.9	Recommended
Below 7.0	Other Places Mentioned

A Sample Review

Restaurant Name

Restaurant Score

Not Your Average Restaurant

92.0

Our reviewers love this restaurant, with its "ingredients, cuisine, wine list, service, décor and overall ambience that are all above average." Chef Auguste Savarin's CV includes cooking at the Hotel Pas de Luxe, as well as stints as the private chef for dignitaries on all seven continents (in Antarctica, guests were melting from his menu based on locally sourced ice). Not only does Savarin offer an above-average experience, on average it takes less time to get there than it takes to get to the average restaurant. "I wish more restaurants were like it," said one reviewer, who lamented, "though if other restaurants were more like it, it would merely become average. But I guess that'd be a good thing, since then they'd have to try even harder not to be average."

Eastern European | Informal | Moderate | BAYSIDE | 1776 Bell Blvd. | 718 -479-4738 | www.defintelynotyouraveragerestaurant.com | Dinner Fri only

What the Panelists Say

Cuisine | Atmosphere | Price Range | Locale | Address | Phone | Website | Hours

How Restaurants Are Rated

Panelists who participate in the survey are asked to rate restaurants on the following scale:

Must Go

Recommended +++

Recommended ++

Recommended +

Recommended

Acceptable

Can't Recommend

The ratings are then converted to numerical scores ranging from 75 to 105. Restaurants in the Cheap Eats category are converted to numerical scores ranging from 4 to 10.

Who Rated the Restaurants for this Guide

This guide was written by people who are passionate about dining out. When I say passionate, I don't mean people who just enjoy restaurants on a regular basis. I am talking about people who make dining a hobby: the gourmet equivalent of the type of person who is willing to fly from St. Paul to St. Andrews in order to play golf, or to travel from Miami to Milan to see his favorite soprano perform at La Scala. This is a guide for people who regularly travel long distances solely for the purpose of eating at interesting restaurants.

This community of devoted hobbyists, made up of people often referred to as destination diners, has been the heart and soul of the dining experience for the past century. For most of that time, they relied on the traditional press (newspapers, magazines and dining guides that employed professional reviewers) for news and information. This changed during the 1980s, when the survey-based guide came onto the scene. But while such guides offered a more democratic method of evaluating restaurants, their results were often questionable because they valued every opinion in the same way.

Then the Internet came along, and discussion forums and blogs gave the members of the destination-dining community a place where they could express themselves in public. No longer did we have to wait for the local newspaper to review a restaurant; now when a new place came along, an online review typically appeared the day after it opened. Soon the most fervent hobbyists – those who visited restaurants for which little or no information existed or those who could proffer an interesting take on a restaurant – saw their status change from mere enthusiast to one of enthusiast/tastemaker.

In the past, in order to access the treasure trove of knowledge possessed by this group, you'd have to spend endless hours browsing the Internet. And then you would have to figure out how to differentiate between good and bad opinions. But Opinionated About – a new type of survey that asks participants to describe how strongly they'd recommend a restaurant, while at the same time assigning a value to each participant's opinion – has changed that. In short, this guide accurately captures that community's opinion.

continued

I believe this new type of guide, one that gives everyone a voice but that calibrates opinions according to experience, results in ratings and reviews that are more reliable than those in other guides. I hope the narrative about the contemporary dining experience it provides will take its rightful place among the various forms of restaurant criticism currently available on the market.

Restaurant Weighting

Our online survey covers approximately 9,000 restaurants. Each restaurant is initially assigned a weight based on its price point, with more expensive restaurants assigned a higher weight than inexpensive ones. Once a restaurant qualifies for a rating, it is assigned a new weight based on that rating. So while a formal French restaurant starts out with a higher weight than a pizzeria, if it gets consistently bad reviews and the pizzeria gets rave reviews, the pizzeria can end up with a higher weight than the French restaurant.

Panelist Weighting

Each person who participates in the survey is assigned a weight based on the number and quality of restaurants he or she has reviewed. So if we take two reviewers – one who reviewed the survey's 100 highest-rated restaurants and a second who reviewed the 100 lowest-rated – the first person would have a greater impact on the final results. This approach in effect ends up rewarding participants whose dining experience extends beyond the city, and even the country, they live in – a result of the fact that when people travel to other cities, they tend to eat at the more highly rated places (do you know anyone who goes out of his way to eat at bad restaurants?). In addition, the formula for calculating participant and restaurant weights is dynamic: Each time new reviews are added to the database, the results are recast based on the new data.

Panel Experience Factor

Not surprisingly, the highest-rated restaurants, which are often destination places, have little trouble attracting experienced diners. But there are also many restaurants that attract only local diners, ones who do not have the same level of experience as our well-traveled reviewers. So, for every restaurant that qualifies, we check whether its panel of reviewers has a sufficient level of experience. If it has failed to attract enough experienced diners, we assume that the rating is too high and the restaurant is penalized. This helps to correct the local bias that typically plagues survey-based guides, while also allowing us to calibrate the ratings across the entire country, rather than just within a specific city.

Our Reviews

Our goal in tabulating ratings and comments is to establish an editorial slant on each restaurant. In doing so, we consider how a restaurant fared with reviewers relative to its reputation in the general dining community. This more nuanced approach allows us to tell you when a highly rated restaurant is on the decline, when a young chef might be in the ascendancy, when a famous chef is cashing in on his or her reputation and when opinions about a restaurant are genuinely split. When it comes to surveys, there is almost never true unanimity: Even the very top restaurants attract negative reviews. But what we can try to do is to tell you when we think those opinions are outliers (outside of the mainstream) and when they might demonstrate a trend line that we expect to continue.

The OAD Philosophy

Is Taste Objective or Subjective? Because personal choice plays such a big role in the dining experience, standards of quality and skill often get buried under the din of subjective opinion. For example: Two chefs from competing restaurants each purchase corn from a local farmer who sells two grades of corn, with one a superior crop that fetches a 20% premium over the other. One of the two chefs is happy to pay the premium, because his customers notice the better quality and are willing to spend more for it. But the second chef's customers are less discerning, so he buys the cheaper corn, puts the farmer's name on his menu and charges the same higher price as the other chef – in effect, pocketing the premium for himself.

So what are we to make of the diner who can't discern the difference in quality and who prefers the cheaper corn, arguing to the death that it's better than the one that goes for a premium? Well, putting aside the possibility of informed dissent – that he has actually come up with a better method of gauging corn quality – the reality is that his opinion is an outlier: If we were to survey the issue and graph the results, his view would fall outside of the areas that represent the majority view.

This book is about trying to deal with such conundrums, drawing a distinction between individual taste, which within the context of the story is subjective, and the concept of good taste, a more objective view shaped via a consensus of informed opinions. So when you hear us describe the consensus view as being right and the outlier as being wrong, don't be surprised.

Dining from a Historical Perspective Like other arts and crafts, dining is constantly evolving. Changes in quality of ingredients and culinary technique are obvious and easy to talk about. But changes in why people eat out and what they expect from the dining experience are much more subtle and not talked about as much. For almost the entire 20th century, there was a strong correlation between eating well and flaunting wealth. As a result, the dining experience was loaded up with luxury ingredients like foie gras, truffles and lobster. Even the less-costly bistro experience was often about roasts and braises with thick sauces or other preparations intended to make the dish appear more elaborate.

But in the last decade or so, there's been a change. Dining has shifted towards a more cerebral experience, and chefs are less reliant on luxury ingredients. Rather, they use science to try to get us to think about what an ingredient really tastes like. One chef cooks an egg for 45 minutes at 70 degrees centigrade, and another cooks it for 30 minutes at 75 degrees – each one trying to express the essence of the egg in an individual manner. Another pairs two different ingredients that previously were thought impossible to pair, and does it in a way that changes the way we think about those ingredients forever. Of course, this doesn't mean that lobster swimming in a butter-laden shellfish broth has disappeared from the contemporary dinner table, but for many diners, it doesn't hold the same level of importance it did 20 years ago.

Why Eat Out if I Can Cook Like That at Home? We used to relish the opportunity to travel to France to eat traditional French dishes. Take the Alsatian dish choucroute – something we'd be sure to eat whenever we visited Paris. But these days, with the help of cookbooks and cooking shows on TV, the version we make at home is every bit as good as what they serve in the typical Parisian brasserie. Likewise, there was a time when finding a delicacy like sautéed foie gras on a restaurant's menu would send us into a state of ecstasy. But now, with so many American chefs having trained at top kitchens in Europe, the dish has become so commonplace that it wouldn't surprise us if there are a dozen restaurants along any given mile in Manhattan that serve it.

Take the vast amount of talent working in American restaurants, combine it with better access to artisanal ingredients and the general public's increased knowledge of cuisine, and the result is that expectations have changed since our love affair with dining began. And while choucroute and sautéed foie gras are still on the menu, their mere presence is no longer enough; in order to attract attention, chefs need to make these dishes more interesting. Otherwise the only reason for going out to dinner is to save the effort of having to shop, cook and clean up. That wouldn't make dining much of a hobby, would it?

Technique versus Ingredients There has long been a debate about what plays a more important role in fine cuisine: technique or quality of ingredients. To some people, eating well is solely about eating the highest-quality food (prepared competently and correctly, of course). But others are more interested in how chefs treat and manipulate ingredients. In our opinion, the people on the ingredients side of the debate seem to have the weaker argument.

Let's assume that the quality of the ingredients that chefs use has been static since the beginning of the 20th century. If that's the case, how do you explain that Escoffier cooked them one way and Fernand Point another, and that the techniques that Paul Bocuse, Michel Guérard, Joël Robuchon and Alain Passard employed were so unusual that they each changed the course of cooking forever? This progression of culinary technique and theory explains why there are instances when a restaurant earned a lower rating than it had earned in the past, despite the fact that it continues to prepare the highest-quality ingredients in the same manner. So while it is important for us to tell you which restaurants source the very best ingredients, the goal of a restaurant guide is to catalog the way culinary philosophy and technique change over time.

Does Size Matter? There is a strong correlation between a restaurant's rating and the number of guests it serves daily: The fewer the people, the better the odds are that the rating will be higher than similar restaurants'. Understanding why is simple. Say one place employs a staff of 50 in order to serve 50 diners, while a second employs a staff of 25 to serve 150 diners. Now do some math: How much time and effort can a kitchen employee at the first restaurant spend in order to complete a task, compared to an employee at the second restaurant?

While we realize that most diners aren't normally focused on staff size, if you come upon a restaurant in this guide that has a lower rating than you expected, there's a good chance that their capacity is the culprit. This is especially true for restaurants we refer to as being in the "upper middle" category – venues (usually in major cities) set up to serve a large number of tables with a smaller staff, which allows them to charge lower prices than a true fine-dining establishment. And while these restaurants are capable of turning out a good meal, the attention to detail that you find at the very top restaurants is often missing.

Modern versus Classic Culinary Technique Much has been written on which is better: modern or traditional cooking techniques? To be honest, most of the debate focuses on less-important aspects like the use of foam or putting things like Pop Rocks into food. What modern culinary technique is truly about is applying science to the traditional craft of cooking. Consider the aforementioned boiled egg. Going back to the time of the caveman, three minutes in boiling water has resulted in a soft-boiled egg; 15 minutes means a hard-boiled one. But modern technology has allowed chefs to look at an egg in a different light – and the result is an entirely different cooked egg than the one the Flintstones ate.

Something else that is rarely discussed: how modern technology allows chefs to cook without using butter and oil as lubricants, resulting in food that is typically cleaner and healthier. Take your mother's pot roast: In order to make it tender, she browned it in fat and then braised it for hours so the meat fibers would break down. But these days, chefs cook fatty cuts of meat at low temperatures for long periods of time, and the meat becomes tender without losing fibers (and nutrients). That means the final product tastes only of the meat itself, not of the impurities created during all that braising. It also means plenty of light, natural juices to supplement the meat – no need for the thick, viscous, flour-enhanced gravies that came with Mom's pot roast.

It's a Matter of Style Thirty years ago, there was a good chance that a top French restaurant would be serving at least one dish *en croûte* (wrapped in pastry). But in this day and age, the practice has pretty much disappeared. Why? Quite simply, because in dining, as in fashion, styles change. And just like the bowler hat – a once-commonplace article that these days is worn only by the doorman at The Ivy restaurant in London – a dish *en croûte* has gone the way of the dodo: It used to be something served at important restaurants, but it's been banished to the takeout section of your local gourmet market.

This isn't to say that we've heard the last of pastry-wrapped food, and I am certain that in the future, some chef will revive the tradition. But, as they say in fashion circles, a style may come back, but it never comes back the same way twice. The revived *en croûte* will be connected to the original concept in principle, but ultimately it will be different enough to be considered modern.

So, in Conclusion . . . Our aim in publishing this guide is to encourage people to practice dining as a hobby. And while we understand that there is no single way to do that, we hope we have set out a few parameters. As far as we're concerned, any way you want to practice it is fine with us. But what we do ask is that you tell us about it, because people who disagree with our conclusions are as important to our survey as the people who are part of the consensus. The more complete the data, the better we can understand how taste and trends in dining are changing. After all, we don't set the standards – you do. Our job is merely to report on the dining experience, according to the way you see it.

Tips on Dining Out

Diners are always asking us whether the meals they will be served at a restaurant are going to be as good as the meals professional restaurant reviewers are served or meals that they read about elsewhere. It's a fair question and, to be honest, as much as everyone would like to think otherwise, not all diners are treated equally. This might come as a shock, but restaurants make an extra effort to make their regular customers happy, and they simply do not have the manpower or resources to offer the same treatment to every customer.

This uptick in quality manifests itself in a number of ways: The kitchen may source special ingredients for regular customers, or it might hold back the best-quality ingredients in order to make sure they go to a regular rather than to someone visiting for the first time. For a favored customer, the chef might prepare a dish or a series of dishes that are not on the menu, or the sommelier might even propose wines that are not on the printed list. If we had to put a number on it, "special" customers eat around 20 percent better than everyone else, which can be a huge increment at this level of quality.

Ask the Chef to Choose Here's a little secret that is guaranteed to improve your dining experience in most restaurants. When you go to a restaurant for the first time, say these nine simple words to your captain or waiter, "We would like the kitchen to cook for us." That is the secret handshake used in the dining community to communicate that you are serious about dining out and that you want to be accorded whatever special treatment the restaurant holds in reserve for regulars and other serious diners. Of course, you will be consulted on things like the number of courses in the meal, and you will be able to tell the kitchen to avoid specific ingredients you might dislike or are allergic to, but otherwise you just sit back and let the chef perform his or her magic for you.

I know it sounds counterintuitive – ceding control of the meal to the kitchen and letting it choose your dinner – but if you think about it for a second, it makes perfect sense. Let's say on the morning of your visit, the restaurant received shipments of pork and beef and the pork looked especially spectacular. Well, would you know that from reading the printed menu? Of course not. But by telling the kitchen that you would like to be considered a more serious diner than the average Joe, you increase the odds that the best the house can offer will come your way. Of course, there is a price for this style of dining, as the cost of the meal will reflect the unique treatment, but in our experience, it's a price that is well worth paying for those who are serious about dining.

Trust the Sommelier What's true for the meal is true for the wine. If you're a novice oenophile, your best chance of drinking well is to put yourself in the hands of the sommelier. Sure, we occasionally run into one of those old-fashioned sommeliers who snarl at you when you don't know your way around the list (this occurs mostly at old-line restaurants in France), but the new generation of sommeliers is user-friendly and trained to make you feel comfortable.

When it comes to budgeting for wine at a restaurant, there is no set rule about how much to spend. In general, if you are willing to pay between 50 to 100 percent of the cost of the food, the quality of the wine will usually match the quality of the food. We would also like to dissuade you from ordering elaborate wine pairings, in which the sommelier matches different wines to each course. In our experience, the quality you get when you allocate funds to a single bottle is significantly higher than the quality of wine you usually find in pairings.

Bring Your Own Wine One of the easiest ways to improve your meal is to bring your own wine. Many restaurants allow you to do so but charge a corkage fee for the privilege of opening your bottle, providing stemware and the services of the sommelier, who will handle your bottle with the same care and professionalism as if you had purchased a bottle from the restaurant's list. We prefer to give our business to restaurants that see the practice as a service issue. Corkage fees can range from nothing to as much as $85 per bottle in the very top restaurants.

List of Notable Restaurants

Most Important Restaurants in the U.S.
Worth Planning a Trip Around • An Important Destination
• Highly Recommended • Recommended

Top Inexpensive Dining
Uniquely Delicious • Recommended

Top Restaurants by Region
Boston & New England • New York Metropolitan & Upstate
• Washington DC & the Mid-Atlantic • Atlanta & the South
• Chicago & the Midwest • Las Vegas & the Southwest •
Los Angeles, Southern California & Hawaii • San Francisco,
Northern California & the Pacific Northwest

Top Restaurants by Category
Ethnic Cuisine (Fine Dining) • French • Italian/Mediterranean/
Greek • Japanese • New American • Progressive Cuisine
• Steak & Seafood (Traditional) • Top Moderately Priced
Restaurants • Top Inexpensive Dining–Artisanal • Top
Inexpensive Dining–Non-Artisanal • Bakeries • Barbecue &
Southern • Coffee Shops & Diners • Dessert • Hot Dogs &
Hamburgers • Pizzerias • Sandwiches • Seafood

continued

ψ Most Important Restaurants in the U.S.*

Worth Planning a Trip Around

1.	French Laundry, The	Yountville, CA	100.0
2.	Per Se	New York, NY	100.0
3.	Manresa	Los Gatos, CA	100.0
4.	Masa	New York, NY	100.0
5.	Alinea	Chicago, IL	100.0
6.	Jean Georges	New York, NY	100.0
7.	Urasawa	Beverly Hills, CA	99.3
8.	Le Bernardin	New York, NY	98.6
9.	Sushi Yasuda	New York, NY	98.5
10.	Blue Hill at Stone Barns	Pocantico Hills, NY	98.4
10.	Meadowood, Restaurant at	St. Helena, CA	98.4
12.	Guy Savoy	Las Vegas, NV	98.2
12.	Minibar	Washington DC	98.2
14.	Kuruma Zushi	New York, NY	98.0

An Important Destination

15.	Town House	Chilhowie, VA	97.6
16.	Momofuku Ko	New York, NY	97.4
17.	Cyrus	Healdsburg, CA	97.3
18.	Corton	New York, NY	97.2
18.	Eleven Madison Park	New York, NY	97.2
20.	McCrady's	Charleston, SC	96.8
20.	Schwa	Chicago, IL	96.8
22.	Coi	San Francisco, CA	96.7
22.	L'Atelier de Joël Robuchon	New York, NY	96.7
24.	Quince	San Francisco, CA	96.2
25.	Bouley	New York, NY	96.1
26.	Peter Luger	Brooklyn, NY	96.1
26.	Ubuntu	Napa, CA	96.1
28.	Providence	Los Angeles, CA	96.0
29.	Sushi Ran	Sausalito, CA	95.9
30.	Avenues	Chicago, IL	95.6
30.	Komi	Washington DC	95.6
32.	Daniel	New York, NY	95.5
32.	Spago	Beverly Hills, CA	95.5
32.	Sugiyama	New York, NY	95.5
35.	Commis	Oakland, CA	95.3
36.	Chez Panisse	Berkeley, CA	95.2
36.	North Fork Table & Inn	Southold, NY	95.2
38.	Marinus	Carmel, CA	95.1
39.	Sushi Taro	Washington DC	95.1
40.	Herbfarm, The	Woodinville, WA	95.0

Other Notable Restaurants

Highly Recommended

Aubergine	Carmel, CA	94.9
Miyake	Portland, ME	94.8
Volt	Fredericksburg, MD	94.8
Nishimura	West Hollywood, CA	94.7
Spiaggia	Chicago, IL	94.7
Sushi Seki	New York, NY	94.7
American Restaurant	Kansas City, MO	94.6
Charlie Trotter's	Chicago, IL	94.6
Blue Hill	New York, NY	94.5
Matsuhisa	West Hollywood, CA	94.4
O Ya	Boston, MA	94.4
Sanford	Milwaukee, WI	94.4
Soto	New York, NY	94.4
Elements	Princeton, NJ	94.3
L20	Chicago, IL	94.3
Citronelle	Washington DC	94.1
Craft	New York, NY	94.0
Cut	Beverly Hills, CA	94.0
Patina	Los Angeles, CA	94.0
Asanebo	Studio City, CA	93.8
Bern's Steak house	Tampa, FL	93.8
Café Boulud	New York, NY	93.8
Highland's Bar & Grill	Birmingham, AL	93.8
Momofuku Sääm Bar	New York, NY	93.8
Mori Sushi	Los Angeles, CA	93.8
Gary Danko	San Francisco, CA	93.7
Restaurant Eugene	Atlanta, GA	93.7
Saam - The Tasting Room	West Hollywood, CA	93.7
Sushi Zo	Los Angeles, CA	93.7
Everest	Chicago, IL	93.6
Gramercy Tavern	New York, NY	93.6
Momofuku Noodle Bar	New York, NY	93.6
Moto	Chicago, IL	93.6
No. 9 Park	Boston, MA	93.6
Nobu	New York, NY	93.6
Uchi	Austi, TX	93.6
Castagna	Portland, OR	93.5
Blackbird	Chicago, IL	93.4
Canlis	Seattle, WA	93.4
Mama's Fish House	Honolulu, HI	93.4
Raku	Las Vegas, NV	93.4
Sawa Sushi	Sunnyvale, CA	93.4
Totoraku (Secret Beef Place)	Los Angeles, CA	93.4
WD-50	New York, NY	93.4
Aquavit	New York, NY	93.3
Auberge de Soleil	Rutherford, CA	93.3
Hugo's	Portland, ME	93.3
Marea	New York, NY	93.3
Masa's	San Francisco, CA	93.2
Picasso	Las Vegas, NV	93.2
Ritz- Carlton Dining Room	San Francisco, CA	93.2
Topolobampo	Chicago, IL	93.2
Galatoire's	New Orleans, LA	93.1
Quinones at Bacchanalia	Atlanta, GA	93.1
Rover's	Seattle, WA	93.1
The Bazaar	West Hollywood, CA	93.1
Vetri	Philadelphia, PA	93.1
Il Grano	Los Angeles, CA	93.0
Michy's	Miami, FL	93.0
Osteria Mozza	Los Angeles, CA	93.0
Picholine	New York, NY	93.0
Pluckemin Inn	Bedminster, NJ	93.0
Chef Mavro	Honolulu, HI	92.9
Inn at Little Washington	Washington, VA	92.9
Locanda Verde	New York, NY	92.9
Suzuki's Sushi Bar	Rockland, ME	92.9
Tallula's Table	Kennett Square, PA	92.9
Bacchanalia	Atlanta, GA	92.8
Lucques	West Hollywood, CA	92.8
Swan Oyster Depot	San Francisco, CA	92.8
Uni	Boston, MA	92.8
Aldea	New York, NY	92.7
Niche	St. Louis, MO	92.7
Sushi Zen	New York, NY	92.7
Angelini Osteria	Los Angeles, CA	92.6
Fore Street	Portland, ME	92.6
Kiss Sushi	San Francisco, CA	92.6
Nobu Next Door	New York, NY	92.6
Annisa	New York, NY	92.5
Kyo Ya	New York, NY	92.5
La Folie	San Francisco, CA	92.5
LudoBites	Los Angeles, CA	92.5
Minetta Tavern	New York, NY	92.5
Sushi Ota	San Diego, CA	92.5
Charleston	Baltimore, MD	92.4
Frontera Grill	Chicago, IL	92.4
Hatsuhana	New York, NY	92.4
June	Peoria, IL	92.4
Sushi Nozawa	Studio City, CA	92.4

continued **19**

Benu	San Francisco, CA	92.3
Blackberry Farm	Walland, TN	92.3
Ame	San Francisco, CA	92.2
Bluestem	Kansas City, MO	92.2
Brigtsen's	New Orleans, LA	92.2
Chez Panisse Café	Berkeley, CA	92.2
Katsu-Ya	Studio City, CA	92.2
Lincoln	New York, NY	92.2
Modern, The	New York, NY	92.2
Neptune Oyster	Boston, MA	92.2
Sidney Street Café	St. Louis, MO	92.2
Boulevard	San Francisco, CA	92.1
Baumé	Palo Alto, CA	92.0
Binkley's	Cave Creek, CA	92.0
Crush	Seattle, WA	92.0
Esca	New York, NY	92.0
L'Etoile	Madison, WI	92.0
Mélisse	Santa Monica, CA	92.0
Morimoto	Philadelphia, PA	92.0
Revolver	Findlay, OH	92.0

Recommended

Jewel Bako	New York, NY	91.9
Morimoto	New York, NY	91.9
Tocqueville	New York, NY	91.9
ad hoc	Yountville, CA	91.8
Jardinière	San Francisco, CA	91.8
Kai	Chandler, AZ	91.8
Mizuna	Denver, CO	91.8
Alan Wong's	Honolulu, HI	91.7
Clancy's	New York, LA	91.7
Hot and Hot Fish Club	Birmingham, AL	91.7
Kajitsu	New York, NY	91.7
Saison	San Francisco, CA	91.7
Sierra Mar	Big Sur, CA	91.7
Bizen	Great Barrington, MA	91.6
Degustation	New York, NY	91.6
Jar	West Hollywood, CA	91.6
Le Pigeon	Portland, OR	91.6
Les Nomades	Chicago, IL	91.6
Nishino	Seattle, WA	91.6
Nougatine	New York, NY	91.6
Rialto	Cambridge, MA	91.6
Scalini Fedeli	Chatham, NJ	91.6
Scalini Fedeli	New York, NY	91.6
Ten Tables	Cambridge, MA	91.6
Adour	New York, NY	91.5
Chinois on Main	Santa Monica, CA	91.5
CityZen	Washington DC	91.5
George's Modern	La Jolla, CA	91.5
Kitchen at Brooklyn Fare, The	Brooklyn, NY	91.5
La Belle Vie	Minneapolis, MN	91.5

Matsuhisa Aspen	Aspen, CO	91.5
Michael Mina	Las Vegas, NV	91.5
Park Avenue Summer	New York, NY	91.5
SHO Shaun Hergatt	New York, NY	91.5
Stephan Pyles	Dallas, TX	91.5
Sushi of Gari	New York, NY	91.5
Trenton Bridge Lobster Pound	Trenton, ME	91.5
Victoria & Albert's	Orlando, FL	91.5
Amada	Philadelphia, PA	91.4
Birchrunville Store Café	Birchrunville, PA	91.4
Bouchon	Beverly Hills, CA	91.4
Bouchon	Yountville, CA	91.4
Justus Drugstore	Smithville, MO	91.4
Mansion on Turtle Creek	Dallas, TX	91.4
Nobu	Dallas, TX	91.4
NOCA	Scottsdale, AZ	91.4
Primo	Rockland, ME	91.4
Prune	New York, NY	91.4
Water Grill	Los Angeles, CA	91.4
Estiatorio Milos	New York, NY	91.3
Joël Robuchon at the Mansion	Las Vegas, NV	91.3
Lantern	Chapel Hill, NC	91.3
Spinasse	Seattle, WA	91.3
Sripraphai	Queens, NY	91.3
Gordon Ramsay at the London	West Hollywood, CA	91.2
Michael's Genuine Food & Drink	Miami, FL	91.2
North Pond	Chicago, IL	91.2
Tru	Chicago, IL	91.2
Union Square Café	New York, NY	91.2
Anneke Jans	Kittery, ME	91.1
Hatfield's	West Hollywood, CA	91.1
Prime Rib	Baltimore, MD	91.1
Terra	St. Helena, CA	91.1
Wallsé	New York, NY	91.1
Avec	Chicago, IL	91.0
Canteen	San Francisco, CA	91.0
Chez Fonfon	Birmingham, AL	91.0
Clio	Boston, MA	91.0
Craft	Dallas, TX	91.0
Craftsteak	Las Vegas, NV	91.0
Dressler	Brooklyn, NY	91.0
Erna's Elderberry House	Oakhurst, CA	91.0
Gordon Ramsay at the London	New York, NY	91.0
Hen of the Wood	Waterbury, VT	91.0
Joe's Stone Crab	Miami Beach, FL	91.0
Kihachi	Columbus, OH	91.0
Le Bec-Fin	Philadelphia, PA	91.0
Lotus of Siam	Las Vegas, NV	91.0
Palate Food & Wine	Glendale, CA	91.0
Redd	Yountville, CA	91.0

Shumi	Somerville, NJ	91.0
Stella!	New Orleans, LA	91.0
Sushi Ann	New York, NY	91.0
Al Di La	Brooklyn, NY	90.9
Aureole	New York, NY	90.
Beast	Portland, OR	90.9
Carlos	Chicago, IL	90.9
Deep Blue	Wilmington, DE	90.9
FIG	Charleston, SC	90.9
Lacroix at the Rittenhouse	Philadelphia, PA	90.9
Mas	New York, NY	90.9
Mastro's	Beverly Hills, CA	90.9
Mastro's	Scottsdale, AZ	90.9
Nobu Waikiki	Honolulu, HI	90.9
Petrossian	New York, NY	90.9
Rasika	Washington DC	90.9
ABC Kitchen	New York, NY	90.8
Dopo	Oakland, CA	90.8
Jack's Luxury Oyster Bar	New York, NY	90.8
Lark	Seattle, WA	90.8
Palena	Washington DC	90.8
Pok Pok	Portland, OR	90.8
Prime Meats	Brooklyn, NY	90.8
RM Seafood	Las Vegas, NV	90.8
Takashi	New York, NY	90.8
Tomo	Atlanta, GA	90.8
Troquet	Boston, MA	90.8
Woodfire Grill	Atlanta, GA	90.8
Acquerello	San Francisco, CA	90.7
AKA Bistro	Lincoln, MA	90.7
Bryant & Cooper Steakhouse	Roslyn, NY	90.7
Eve	Alexandria, VA	90.7
Felidia	New York, NY	90.7
Keen's Steakhouse	New York, NY	90.7
Palm, The	Beverly Hills, CA	90.7
Palm, The	New York, NY	90.7
Prospect	San Francisco, CA	90.7
Chauncey Creek Lobster Pier	Kittery, ME	90.6
Locke-Ober	Boston, MA	90.6
Maroni Cuisine	Northport, NY	90.6
Mia Dona	New York, NY	90.6
Nomi	Chicago, IL	90.6
Oceana	New York, NY	90.6
Rathbun's	Atlanta, GA	90.6
Roberta's	Brooklyn, NY	90.6
Roy's	Honolulu, HI	90.6
Yank Sing	San Francisco, CA	90.6
15 East	New York, NY	90.5
Abacus	Dallas, TX	90.5
Abbott's Lobster in the Rough	Noank, CT	90.5
Café Juanita	Kirkland, WA	90.5
Geronimo	Santa Fe, NM	90.5

Heartland	St. Paul, MN	90.5
Hog Island Oyster Co. & Bar	San Francisco, CA	90.5
L'Atelier de Robuchon	Las Vegas, NV	90.5
L'Espalier	Boston, MA	90.5
Mary's Fish Camp	New York, NY	90.5
Ninety Acres at Natirer	Peapack-Gladstone, NJ	90.5
Oga	Natick, MA	90.5
Seasonal	New York, NY	90.5
Spotted Pig	New York, NY	90.5
Sushiden	New York, NY	90.5
Telepan	New York, NY	90.5
Zuni Café	San Francisco, CA	90.5
Bar Crudo	San Francisco, CA	90.4
Café Boulud	Palm Beach, FL	90.4
Cochon	New Orleans, LA	90.4
Evvia	Palo Alto, CA	90.4
Georgian Room at the Cloisters	Sea Island, GA	90.4
Il Capriccio	Waltham, MA	90.4
Lilette	New Orleans, LA	90.4
Origami	Minneapolis, MN	90.4
Range	San Francisco, CA	90.4
Restaurant Martin	Santa Fe, NM	90.4
A.O.C.	West Hollywood, CA	90.3
Babbo	New York, NY	90.3
Bottega	Yountville, CA	90.3
Bouchon	Santa Barbara, CA	90.3
Casa Tua	Miami Beach, FL	90.3
Charleston Grill	Charleston, SC	90.3
Cosmos	Minneapolis, MN	90.3
Craigie on Main	Cambridge, MA	90.3
Frances	San Francisco, CA	90.3
Gilt	New York, NY	90.3
Joss Café & Sushi Bar	Annapolis, MD	90.3
Joss Café & Sushi Bar	Baltimore, MD	90.3
Mo-Chica	Los Angeles, CA	90.3
One Market	San Francisco, CA	90.3
Prime Steakhouse	Las Vegas, NV	90.3
Radius	Boston, MA	90.3
Spruce	San Francisco, CA	90.3
Gotham Bar & Grill	New York, NY	90.2
La Mer	Honolulu, HI	90.2
Aquagrill	New York, NY	90.2
Bar Boulud	New York, NY	90.2
Bonsoirée	Chicago, IL	90.2
Bresca	Portland, ME	90.2
Diner	Brooklyn, NY	90.2
Kokkari Estiatorio	San Francisco, CA	90.2
Má Pêche	New York, NY	90.2
Maialino	New York, NY	90.2
Okada	Las Vegas, NV	90.2
BLT Steak	New York, NY	90.1
Boucherie	New Orleans, LA	90.1
Fonda San Miguel	Austin, TX	90.1

Frasca Food & Wine	Boulder, CO	90.1	Fountain Restaurant	Philadelphia, PA	90.0
Graham Elliot	Chicago, IL	90.1	Hamersley's	Boston, MA	90.0
Kevin Rathbun Steak	Atlanta, GA	90.1	Harvest	Madison, WI	90.0
L'Absinthe	New York, NY	90.1	Hearth	New York, N	90.0
Nobu Miami Beach	Miami Beach, FL	90.1	Herbsaint	New Orleans, LA	90.0
RN74	San Francisco, CA	90.1	Higgins Restaurant & Bar	Portland, OR	90.0
Tony's	St. Louis, MO	90.1	Ippudo	New York, NY	90.0
Wildflower	Vail, CO	90.1	Joe's Steak & Stone Crab	Chicago, IL	90.0
Alma	Minneapolis, CO	90.0	Josie	Santa Monica, CA	90.0
Anton & Michel	Carmel, CA	90.0	Madrona Manor	Healdsburg, CA	90.0
Aria	Atlanta, GA	90.0	Mills Tavern	Providence, RI	90.0
Arun's	Chicago, IL	90.0	Montagna	Aspen, CO	90.0
B & B Ristorante	Las Vegas, NV	90.0	Naha	Chicago, IL	90.0
Bistro Jeanty	Yountville, CA	90.0	Nobhill Tavern	Las Vegas, NV	90.0
Biwa	Portland, OR	90.0	Oishii	Chestnut Hill, MA	90.0
Boqueria	New York, NY	90.0	Oishii	Sudbury, MA	90.0
Café Beaujolais	Mendocino, CA	90.0	Oishii Boston	Boston, MA	90.0
Campagne	Seattle, WA	90.0	Oyster Bar at Grand Central	New York, NY	90.0
City Grocery	Oxford, MS	90.0	Passionfish	Pacific Grove, CA	90.0
Cole's Chop House	Napa, CA	90.0	Pearl Oyster Bar	New York, NY	90.0
Commander's Palace	New Orleans, LA	90.0	Piccolo	Minneapolis, MN	90.0
Corduroy	Washington DC	90.0	Piperade	San Francisco, CA	90.0
Din Tai Fung	Arcadia, CA	90.0	R & G Lounge	San Francisco, CA	90.0
Dovetail	New York, NY	90.0	Sasabune	Los Angeles, CA	90.0
Elaine's on Franklin	Chapel Hill, NC	90.0	SD26	New York, NY	90.0
Emeril's	New Orleans, LA	90.0	Sfoglia	New York, NY	90.0
Fearing's	Dallas, TX	90.0	Tamarind	New York, NY	90.0
Fifth Floor	San Francisco, CA	90.0	Vie	Western Springs, IL	90.0
Five & Ten	Athens, GA	90.0	Vincent's on Camelback	Scottsdale, AZ	90.0
Five Islands Lobster Company	Georgetown, ME	90.0	Wheatleigh	Lenox, MA	90.0
Flagstaff House	Boulder, CO	90.0	Woodbury Kitchen	Baltimore, MD	90.0

Top Local Choice

(Restaurants that earn a rating below 90.0 are shown in increments of .5.)

2941	Falls Church, VA	89.5	Blackfish	Conshocken, PA	89.5
112 Eatery	Minneapolis, MN	89.5	Blaue Gans	New York, NY	89.5
1770 House	East Hampton, NY	89.5	Blu	Montclair, NJ	89.5
Al Forno	Providence, RI	89.5	Blue Ribbon	New York, NY	89.5
Animal	Los Angeles, CA	89.5	Blue Ribbon Sushi	New York, NY	89.5
Antoine's	New Orleans, LA	89.5	Blue Ribbon Sushi	Brooklyn, NY	89.5
Arizona Inn	Tuscon, AZ	89.5	Bob Chinn's Crab House	Wheeling, IL	89.5
Avra Estiatorio	New York, NY	89.5	Boka	Chicago, IL	89.5
Bar Bouchon	Beverly Hills, CA	89.5	Bond Street	New York, NY	89.5
Barbuto	New York, NY	89.5	Café Martorano	Ft. Lauderdale, FL	89.5
Beaker and Flask	Portland, OR	89.5	Campton Place	San Francisco	89.5
Ben & Jack's Steakhouse	New York, NY	89.5	Casa Mono	New York, NY	89.5
Bernards Inn, The	Bernardsville, NJ	89.5	Chifa	Philadelphia, PA	89.5
Bibou	Philadelphia, PA	89.5	Chops Lobster Bar	Atlanta, GA	89.5
Black Olive, The	Baltimore, MD	89.5	Cowboy Ciao	Scottsdale, AZ	89.5

David Burke Fromagerie	Rumson, NJ	89.5
db Bistro Moderne	New York, NY	89.5
Delfina	San Francisco, CA	89.5
Dévi	New York, NY	89.5
Drago	Santa Monica, CA	89.5
Dressing Room – A Homegrown Restaurant	Westport, NJ	89.5
EN Japanese Brasserie	New York, NY	89.5
Epic Roasthouse	San Francisco, CA	89.5
étoile	Yountville, CA	89.5
Fatty Crab	New York, NY	89.5
Frankies Spuntino	Brooklyn, NY	89.5
Friday Saturday Sunday	Philadelphia, PA	89.5
Grocery ,The	Brooklyn, NY	89.5
Il Casale	Belmont, MA	89.5
Irene's Cuisine	New Orleans, LA	89.5
Joshua's	Wells, ME	89.5
Kanoyama	New York, NY	89.5
Keens Steakhouse	New York, NY	89.5
La Toque	Napa, CA	89.5
Lao Sze Chuan	Chicago, IL	89.5
Latilla Room	Carefree, AZ	89.5
Laurelhurst Market	Portland, OR	89.5
Le Papillon	San Jose, CA	89.5
Lodge at Koele Dining Room, The	Lanai City, HI	89.5
Luce	San Francisco, CA	89.5
Magnolia Grill	Durham, NC	89.5
Marcel's	Washington, DC	89.5
Market Table	New York, NY	89.5
Marlow & Sons	Brooklyn, NY	89.5
Mercadito	New York, NY	89.5
Merriman's	Kamuela. HI	89.5
Middendorf's	Akers, LA	89.5
MiLa	New Orleans, LA	89.5
Mosca's	Avondale, LA	89.5
Musha	Santa Monica, CA	89.5
Nick & Toni's	East Hampton, NY	89.5
Nobu	Dallas, TX	89.5
Nobu 57	New York, NY	89.5
Nostrana	Portland, OR	89.5
Obelisk	Washington, DC	89.5
Oenotri	Napa, CA	89.5
Oliveto	San Francisco, CA	89.5
Park 75	Atlanta, GA	89.5
Pasta Nostra	Norwalk, CT	89.5
Peninsula Grille	Charleston, SC	89.5
Perbacco	New York, NY	89.5
Perry Street	New York, NY	89.5
Ping's Seafood	Brooklyn, NY	89.5
Primehouse New York	New York, NY	89.5
Rao's	New York, NY	89.5
Rat's	Hamilton, NJ	89.5
Restaurant Bonne Soiree	Chapel Hill, NC	89.5
Rivera	Los Angeles, CA	89.5
Rosemary's	Las Vegas, NV	89.5
Saul	Brooklyn, NY	89.5
Scalinatella	New York, NY	89.5
Shalimar	San Francisco, CA	89.5
Simpatica Dining Hall	Portland, OR	89.5
Slanted Door	San Francisco, CA	89.5
Spago	Las Vegas, NV	89.5
SPQR	San Francisco, CA	89.5
Strip House	New York, NY	89.5
Taka	Atlanta, GA	89.5
T-Bar Restaurant & Lounge	New York, NY	89.5
Tilth	Seattle, WA	89.5
Topper's	Nantucket, MA	89.5
Tria	Philadelphia, PA	89.5
Txikito	New York, NY	89.5
Union League Café	New Haven, CT	89.5
Urban Belly	Chicago, IL	89.5
Urban Farmer	Portland, OR	89.5
Vincenti	Brentwood, CA	89.5
Wildwood	Portland, OR	89.5
Xaviars at Piermont	Piermont, NY	89.5
Yoshi	San Francisco, CA	89.5
Yuet Lee	San Francisco, CA	89.5
Zahav	Philadelphia, PA	89.5
20.21	Minneapolis, MN	89.0
21 Federal	Nantucket, MA	89.0
98 Provence	Ogunquit, ME	89.0
À Côté	San Francisco, CA	89.0
Amber India	Mountain View, CA	89.0
Andina	Portland, OR	89.0
Artisan	Paso Robles, CA	89.0
Asian Jewels	Brooklyn, NY	89.0
Atlas Bistro	Scottsdale, AZ	89.0
August	New Orleans, LA	89.0
Aziza	San Francisco, CA	89.0
B&G Oysters	Boston, MA	89.0
Ballard Inn, The	Ballard, CA	89.0
Balsams	Dixville Notch, NH	89.0
Balthazar	New York, NY	89.0
Barclay Prime	Philadelphia, PA	89.0
Bayona	New Orleans, LA	89.0
Bistro 7	Philadelphia, PA	89.0
Blue Ridge Grill	Atlanta, GA	89.0
Bottega	Birmingham, AL	89.0
Bristol	Chicago, IL	89.0
Café Bizou	Sherman Oaks, CA	89.0
Café Castagna	Portland, OR	89.0
Café Lurcat	Minneapolis, MN	89.0
Café Sabarsky	New York, NY	89.0
Caffé Mingo	Portland, OR	89.0
Casanova	Carmel, CA	89.0
Cecconi's	West Hollywood, CA	89.0
Chillingsworth	Brewster, MA	89.0
Clyde Common	Portland, OR	89.0

continued **23**

Colicchio & Sons	New York, NY	89.0	Quality Meats	New York, NY	89.0
Comme Ça	West Hollywood, CA	89.0	Ray's Boathouse	Seattle, WA	89.0
Craftsman Restaurant & Bar	Minneapolis, MN	89.0	Redhead, The	New York, NY	89.0
			Restaurant Alba	Malvern, PA	89.0
Crossing, The	Clayton, MO	89.0	Resto	New York, NY	89.0
Custom House	Chicago, IL	89.0	River Café	Brooklyn, NY	89.0
Darrel & Oliver's Café Max	Pompano Beach, FL	89.0	Salts	Cambridge, MA	89.0
Del Posto	New York, NY	89.0	Sensing	Boston, MA	89.0
Doris & Ed's	Highlands, NJ	89.0	Sichuan Gourmet	Framingham	89.0
Erwin, An American Café & Bar	Chicago, IL	89.0	Sitka & Spruce	Seattle, WA	89.0
			Socarrat	New York, NY	89.0
Farmhouse Inn and Restaurant	Forestville, CA	89.0	Sotto Sotto	Atlanta, GA	89.0
Fearrington House	Pittsboro, NC	89.0	Standard Grill, The	New York, NY	89.0
Floataway Café	Atlanta, GA	89.0	St. Elmo's Steak House	Indianapolis, IN	89.0
Flour + Water	San Francisco, CA	89.0	Sushi Den	Denver, CO	89.0
Franco's	St. Louis, MO	89.0	Taylor Grocery	Oxford, MS	89.0
General Greene	Brooklyn, NY	89.0	Terroir Wine Bar	New York, NY	89.0
Gjelina	Venice, CA	89.0	Tía Pol	New York, NY	89.0
Globe	San Francisco, CA	89.0	Toro Bravo	Portland, OR	89.0
Great NY Noodletown	New York, NY	89.0	Trattoria Marcella	St. Louis, MO	89.0
Green Zebra	Chicago, IL	89.0	Victory 44	Minneapolis, MN	89.0
Havana Restaurant	Bar Harbor, ME	89.0	Wink	Austin, TX	89.0
High Cotton	Charleston, SC	89.0	Wu Liang Ye	New York, NY	89.0
Hiroshi	Portland, OR	89.0	Zealous	Chicago, IL	89.0
Hungry I	Boston, MA	89.0	4th & Swift	Atlanta, GA	88.5
Inn at Shelburne Farms	South Burlington, VT	89.0	A 16	San Francisco, CA	88.5
Jitlada	Los Angeles, CA	89.0	A Voce	New York, NY	88.5
Joe's	Venice, CA	89.0	Abattoir	Atlanta, GA	88.5
Kaygetsu	Palo Alto, CA	89.0	Abe & Louie's	Boston, MA	88.5
Koi Palace	San Francisco, CA	89.0	Abe & Louie's	Boca Raton, FL	88.5
Le Cirque	Las Vegas, NV	89.0	Absinthe	San Francisco, CA	88.5
Le Pichet	Seattle, WA	89.0	Anthony's	St. Louis, MO	88.5
Le Relais de Venise (L'Entrecote)	New York, NY	89.0	Applewood	Brooklyn, NY	88.5
			Asiate	New York, NY	88.5
Liluma	St. Louis, MO	89.0	Bar La Grassa	Minneapolis, MN	88.5
Little Giant	New York, NY	89.0	Bar Lola	Portland, ME	88.5
Locanda Vini e Olii	Brooklyn, NY	89.0	Bar Masa	New York, NY	88.5
Lon's at the Hermosa	Scottsdale, AZ	89.0	Black Trumpet Bistro	Portsmouth, NH	88.5
Marigold Kitchen	Philadelphia, PA	89.0	Brasserie by Niche	St. Louis, MO	88.5
Mark's American Cuisine	Houston, TX	89.0	Butcher Shop	Boston, MA	88.5
Maze	New York, NY	89.0	Café Poca Cosa	Tucson, AZ	88.5
Michael Mina	San Francisco, CA	89.0	Cakes and Ale	Atlanta, GA	88.5
MK	Chicago, IL	89.0	Campanile	Los Angeles, CA	88.5
Mustards Grill	St. Helena, CA	89.0	Canoe	Atlanta, GA	88.5
Nana's	Durham, NC	89.0	Capo	Santa Monica, CA	88.5
Nikolai's Roof	Atlanta, GA	89.0	Charlie Palmer Steak	Washington, DC	88.5
Noodle Pudding	Brooklyn, NY	89.0	Chestnut	Brooklyn, NY	88.5
Oriental Garden	New York, NY	89.0	Cindy's Backstreet Kitchen	St. Helena, CA	88.5
Orson	San Francisco, CA	89.0	Commerce	New York, NY	88.5
Ozumo	San Francisco, CA	89.0	Coppa	Boston, MA	88.5
Park Kitchen	Portland, OR	89.0	Coquette Café	Madison, WI	88.5
Pascal's Manale	New Orleans, LA	89.0	CulinAriane	Montclair, NJ	88.5
Perbacco	San Francisco, CA	89.0	Delmonico Steakhouse	Las Vegas, NV	88.5
Pesce Blue	Portsmouth, NH	89.0	Delmonico's	New York, NY	88.5
Purple Pig, The	Chicago, IL	89.0	Downey's	Santa Barbara, CA	88.5

Restaurant	Location	Score
East Coast Grill & Raw Bar	Cambridge, MA	88.5
Elio's	New York, NY	88.5
Foreign Cinema	San Francisco, CA	88.5
Four Seasons Pool Room	New York, NY	88.5
Fruition	Denver, CO	88.5
Grand Sichuan Eastern	New York, NY	88.5
Grill 23 & Bar	Boston, MA	88.5
Happy Chef Dim Sum House	Chicago, IL	88.5
Holeman & Finch	Atlanta, GA	88.5
Hungry Mother's	Cambridge, MA	88.5
Insieme	New York, NY	88.5
JCT Kitchen	Atlanta, GA	88.5
Jimmy Cantler's Riverside Inn	Annapolis, MD	88.5
JiRaffe	Santa Monica, CA	88.5
Johnny's Half Shell	Washington, DC	88.5
La Chaumière	Washington, DC	88.5
La Grotta	Atlanta, GA	88.5
La Mar	San Francisco, CA	88.5
Le Cirque	New York, NY	88.5
Local 188	Portland, ME	88.5
Lucia's	Minneapolis, MN	88.5
Lula	Chicago, IL	88.5
Magnolia	Charleston, SC	88.5
Mark's Duck House	Falls Church, VA	88.5
Meritage	St. Paul	88.5
New Wonjo	New York, NY	88.5
Oleana	Cambridge, MA	88.5
Petit Louis Bistro	Baltimore, MD	88.5
Pomme	St. Louis, MO	88.5
Porter House New York	New York, NY	88.5
Restaurant at the Setai	Miami Beach, FL	88.5
Rivoli	San Francisco, CA	88.5
Sepia	Chicago, IL	88.5
Spoon Thai	Chicago, IL	88.5
Stage Left	New Brunswick, NJ	88.5
Sushi Wabi	Chicago, IL	88.5
Syrah	Santa Rosa, CA	88.5
Ton Kiang	San Francisco, CA	88.5
Toro	Boston, MA	88.5
Upperline	New Orleans, LA	88.5
Vin de Set	St. Louis, MO	88.5
Willi's Wine Bar	Santa Rosa, CA	88.5
Zazu	Santa Rosa, CA	88.5
'ino	New York, NY	88.0
10 Arts	Philadelphia, PA	88.0
212 Market	Chattanooga, TN	88.0
231 Ellsworth	San Mateo, CA	88.0
A. R. Valentien	La Jolla, CA	88.0
Aburiya Kinnosuke	New York, NY	88.0
Antica Posta	Atlanta, GA	88.0
Arigato Sushi	Santa Barbara, CA	88.0
Atlas	St. Louis, MO	88.0
Bar Jules	San Francisco, CA	88.0
Beacon	New York, NY	88.0
Belvedere	Beverly Hills, CA	88.0
Bistro Bis	Washington, DC	88.0
Bistro Laurent	Paso Robles, CA	88.0
Bloom	Scottsdale, AZ	88.0
Blossom	Charleston, SC	88.0
Blue Bottle Café	Hopewell, NJ	88.0
Blue Door Fish	Miami Beach, FL	88.0
Blue Ribbon Bakery	New York, NY	88.0
Bocado	Atlanta, GA	88.0
Bradley Ogden	Las Vegas, NV	88.0
Breslin, The	New York, NY	88.0
Broders' Pasta Bar	Minneapolis, MN	88.0
Café Pasqual's	Santa Fe, NM	88.0
California Grill	Orlando, FL	88.0
Chef Vola's	Atlantic City, MJ	88.0
Chinatown Brasserie	New York, NY	88.0
Compound Restaurant, The	Santa Fe, NM	88.0
Congee Village Restaurant & Bar	New York, NY	88.0
Cookshop	New York, NY	88.0
Country Cat Dinner House and Bar	Portland, OR	88.0
Coyote Café	Santa Fe, NM	88.0
Craftbar	New York, NY	88.0
Dahlia Lounge	Seattle, WA	88.0
David Burke's Primehouse	Chicago, IL	88.0
Donovan's Steak & Chop House	San Diego, CA	88.0
Donovan's Steak & Chop House	Phoenix, AZ	88.0
Ebbitt Room	Cape May, NJ	88.0
Eddie V's Prime Seafood	Austin, TX	88.0
Elements at the Sanctuary on Camelback	Paradise Valley, AZ	88.0
Emilitsa	Portland, ME	88.0
Fairway Café & Steakhouse	New York, NY	88.0
Fandango	Pacific Grove, CA	88.0
Fleur de Lys	San Francisco, CA	88.0
Foundry on Melrose	Los Angeles, CA	88.0
Francine Bistro	Camden, ME	88.0
Franklin Café	Boston, MA	88.0
Fugakyu	Brookline, MA	88.0
Gautreau's	New Orleans, LA	88.0
Grill at the Ritz-Carlton	Clayton, MO	88.0
Harrison	New York, NY	88.0
Harvest Vine, The	Seattle, WA	88.0
Hashiguchi	Atlanta, GA	88.0
Hemingway's	Killington, VT	88.0
How to Cook a Wolf	Seattle, WA	88.0
Hungry Cat, The	Hollywood, CA	88.0
Hungry Cat, The	Santa Barbara, CA	88.0
Joe's Shanghai	New York, NY	88.0
Jordan Pond House	Mt. Desert Island, ME	88.0
Kinkead's	Washington, DC	88.0
La Petite Grocery	New Orleans, LA	88.0

continued **25**

Larkspur Restaurant & Bar	Vail, CO	88.0
Lawry's The Prime Rib	West Hollywood, CA	88.0
Le Coq au Vin	Orlando, FL	88.0
Le Vallauris	Palm Springs, CA	88.0
Lolita	Cleveland, OH	88.0
Lou	Los Angeles, CA	88.0
Market Restaurant and Bar	Del Mar, CA	88.0
McKendrick's Steakhouse	Atlanta, GA	88.0
Mercer Kitchen	New York, NY	88.0
MF Buckhead/ MF Sushi Bar	Atlanta, GA	88.0
Mirabelle	Austin, TX	88.0
Monarch	St. Louis, MO	88.0
Mr. K's	New York, NY	88.0
Musso & Frank's	Hollywood, CA	88.0
Nam	Atlanta, GA	88.0
Nan Thai Fine Dining	Atlanta, GA	88.0
NINE-TEN	La Jolla, CA	88.0
Nook	Los Angeles, CA	88.0
Nopa	San Francisco, CA	88.0
O Chamé	San Francisco, CA	88.0
Oceanique	Chicago, IL	88.0
Old Fashioned	Madison, WI	88.0
Osteria	Philadelphia, PA	88.0
Otto	New York, NY	88.0
Pacci Ristorante	Atlanta, GA	88.0
Paciarino	Portland, ME	88.0
Paley's Place	Portland, OR	88.0
Pamplemousse Grille	Solana Beach, CA	88.0
Peking Duck House	New York, NY	88.0
Ping	Portland, OR	88.0

Pinot Bistro	Studio City, CA	88.0
Proof	Washington, DC	88.0
Proof on Main	Louisville, KY	88.0
Public	New York, NY	88.0
Publican, The	Chicago, IL	88.0
Pulino's	New York, NY	88.0
Ramen Setagaya	New York, NY	88.0
Ritz-Carlton Atlanta Grill	Atlanta, GA	88.0
Sakagura	New York, NY	88.0
Sakura	Minneapolis, MN	88.0
Santacafé	Santa Fe, NM	88.0
Sapphire Grill	Savannah, GA	88.0
Savoy	New York, NY	88.0
Scarpetta	New York, NY	88.0
Sea Change	Minneapolis, MN	88.0
Solera	Minneapolis, MN	88.0
Spice Market	New York, NY	88.0
Suzanne's Cuisine	Ojai, CA	88.0
Sweet Basil	Vail, CO	88.0
Sweet Basil	Needham, MA	88.0
Szechuan Gourmet	New York, NY	88.0
Thurston's Lobster Pound	Bernard, ME	88.0
Tomoe Sushi	New York, NY	88.0
Valentino	Santa Monica, CA	88.0
Vidalia	Washington, DC	88.0
Wentworth-by-the-Sea	New Castle, NH	88.0
Wildfish	Scottsdale, AZ	88.0
Wish	Miami Beach, FL	88.0
Wolfgang's Steakhouse	New York, NY	88.0
Woo Lae Oak	New York, NY	88.0
Yakitori Totto	New York, NY	88.0

* While a rating of 100 is considered a perfect score, because a rating of Must Go is converted to a score of 105, it is possible for a restaurant to have an actual rating in excess of 100. For the purpose of creating the list of the Most Important Restaurants in the U.S., restaurants that are awarded a perfect score of 100 are listed in the order of their actual scores which follows; French Laundry 102.0; Per Se 101.5; Manresa 101.2; Masa 100.5; Alinea 100.2; Jean George 100.1.

Top Inexpensive Dining

Uniquely Delicious

Hot Doug's	Chicago, IL	9.7
Kreuz Market	Lockhart, TX	9.4
Provisions to Go	Atlanta, GA	9.0
Katz's Delicatessen	New York, NY	8.9
Una Pizzeria Napoletana	San Francisco, CA	8.9
Willie Mae's Scotch House	New Orleans, LA	8.9
Kopp's	Milwaukee, WI	8.8
DiFara's	Brooklyn, NY	8.7
Aurora Provisions	Portland, ME	8.6
Black Sheep Pizza	Minneapolis, MN	8.6
Humphrey Slocumbe	San Francisco, CA	8.6
Salumi Artisan Cured Meats	Seattle, WA	8.6

Dinosaur	Syracuse, NY	8.5
Oklahoma Joe's	Olathe, KS	8.5
Olympic Provisions	Portland, OR	8.5
Pizzeria Mozza	Los Angeles, CA	8.5
Alon's	Atlanta, GA	8.4
Bánh Mì Saigon Bakery	New York, NY	8.4
Central Grocery	New Orleans, LA	8.4
Tartine Bakery & Café	San Francisco, CA	8.4
Ted Drewes	St. Louis, MO	8.4
Camelia Grill	New Orleans, LA	8.3
Clam Box of Ipswich	Ipswich, MA	8.3
Cochon Butcher	New Orleans, LA	8.3
Duck Fat	Portland, ME	8.3
Dynamo Donut	San Francisco, CA	8.3

Ess-a-Bagel	New York, NY	8.3
Mama's on Washington Square	San Francisco, CA	8.3
Pizzeria Bianco	Phoenix, AZ	8.3
17th Street Bar & Grill	O'Fallon, IL	8.2
2 Amys	Washington DC	8.2
4505 Meats	San Francisco, CA	8.2
Flip Burger Boutique	Atlanta, GA	8.2
Flip Burger Boutique	Birmingham, AL	8.2
Frank Pepe's Napoletana	New Haven, CT	8.2
Jeni's Splendid Ice Cream	Columbus, OH	8.2
Sally's Apizza	New Haven, CT	8.2
Smitty's Market	Lockhart, TX	8.2
Brasa Rotisserie	Minneapolis, MN	8.1
Chase's Daily	Belfast, ME	8.1
John's Roast Pork	Philadelphia, PA	8.1
Pizzetta 211	San Francisco, CA	8.1
Roscoe's Chicken & Waffles	Hollywood, CA	8.1
8 Oz. Burger Bar	West Hollywood, CA	8.0
Blue Bottle	San Francisco, CA	8.0
Café du Monde	New Orleans, LA	8.0
Calumet Fisheries	Chicago, IL	8.0
Clinton Street Baking Company	New York, NY	8.0
Dooky Chase	New Orleans, LA	8.0
Keste Pizza & Vino	New York, NY	8.0
Macrina Bakery & Café	Seattle, WA	8.0
Mile End	Brooklyn, NY	8.0
Momofuku Milk Bar	New York, NY	8.0
Pizzeria Delfina	San Francisco, CA	8.0
White House Sub Shop	Atlantic City, NJ	8.0

Recommended

Egg	Brooklyn, NY	7.9
Hominy Grill	Charleston, SC	7.9
Joan's on Third	West Hollywood, CA	7.9
Johnnie's Beef	Chicago, IL	7.9
La Taqueria	San Francisco, CA	7.9
Saigon Sandwiches	San Francisco, CA	7.9
Ben Faremo, the Italian Ice King	Queens, NY	7.8
Bouchon Bakery	New York, NY	7.8
Bouchon Bakery	Yountville, CA	7.8
Fat Matt's Rib Shack	Atlanta, GA	7.8
J.T. Farnham's	Essex, MA	7.8
Jacques Torres Chocolate	Brooklyn, NY	7.8
Apple Pan	Los Angeles, Ca	7.7
Big Bob Gibson	Decatur, AL	7.7
Clam Shack	Kennebunkport, ME	7.7
Clementine	Westwood, CA	7.7
Franny's	Brooklyn, NY	7.7
Hampton Chutney Co.	Amagansett, NY	7.7
Hampton Chutney Co.	New York, NY	7.7
Huckleberry Café & Bakery	Santa Monica, CA	7.7
Kyotofu	New York, NY	7.7

Modern Apizza	New Haven, CT	7.7
Pho Grand	St. Louis, MO	7.7
Shake Shack	New York, NY	7.7
Tony Luke's	Philadelphia, PA	7.7
Tottono's	Brooklyn, NY	7.7
Vortex Bar & Grill	Atlanta, GA	7.7
Woodman's of Essex	Essex, MA	7.7
Big Wong	New York, NY	7.6
Chikalicious	New York, NY	7.6
Louis Lunch	New Haven, CT	7.6
Orange	Chicago, IL	7.6
Pho 75	Falls Church, VA	7.6
Pho 75	Philadelphia, PA	7.6
Pink's Famous Chili Dogs	Hollywood, CA	7.6
Bagaduce Lunch	Brooksville, ME	7.5
Barney Greengrass	Beverly Hills, CA	7.5
Bread Line	Washington DC	7.5
Bunk Sandwiches	Portland, OR	7.5
Cheese Board Pizza Collective	Berkeley, CA	7.5
City Market	Lulling, TX	7.5
Crabby Jack's	Jefferson, LA	7.5
Fritti	Atlanta, GA	7.5
Kuma's Corner	Chicago, IL	7.5
Lambert's Downtown BBQ	Austin, TX	7.5
Let's Be Frank	Culver City, CA	7.5
Paolo's Gelato Italiano	Atlanta, GA	7.5
Pizzeria Tra Vigne	St. Helena, CA	7.5
Stumptown Roasters	Portland, OR	7.5
Taqueria La Veracruzana	Philadelphia, PA	7.5
Trattoria Zero Otto Nove	New York, NY	7.5
Al's # 1 Italian Beef	Chicago, IL	7.4
Bette's Oceanview Diner	Berkeley, CA	7.4
burger joint	New York, NY	7.4
DeLorenzo's Tomato Pies	Trenton, NJ	7.4
Ferrara	New York, NY	7.4
L & B Spumoni Gardens	Brooklyn, NY	7.4
Mr. Bartley's Burger Cottage	Cambridge, MA	7.4
New Yorker Marketplace & Deli	Atlanta, GA	7.4
Philippe the Original	Los Angeles, CA	7.4
Porchetta	New York, NY	7.4
Zabar's Café	New York, NY	7.4
Punch Neapolitan Pizza	St. Paul, MN	7.4
A Salt & Battery	New York, NY	7.3
Amy's Bread	New York, NY	7.3
Barney Greengrass	New York, NY	7.3
Bobcat Bite	Santa Fe, NM	7.3
Casamento's	New Orleans, LA	7.3
City Bakery	New York, NY	7.3
Crown Candy Kitchen	St. Louis, MO	7.3
Elizabeth's	New Orleans, LA	7.3
Harry's Roadhouse	Santa Fe, NM	7.3
In-N-Out Burger	Los Angeles, CA	7.3
Manny's	Chicago, Il	7.3

continued **27**

Motorino	New York, NY	7.3	Adrienne's Pizzabar	New York, NY	7.0
Mr. Beef	Chicago, IL	7.3	Arthur Bryant's	Kansas City, MO	7.0
Original Pancake House	Chicago, IL	7.3	Beacon Drive-In	Spartenberg, SC	7.0
Pappy's Smokehouse	St. Louis, MO	7.3	Blue Ribbon BBQ	Newton,	7.0
Pat's King of Steaks	Philadelphia, PA	7.3	Bob Sykes BarB-Q	Bessemer, AL	7.0
Ray's Hell Burgers	Arlington, VA	7.3	"Co."	New York, NY	7.0
Super Duper Weenie	Fairfield, CT	7.3	Grimaldi's	Brooklyn, NY	7.0
Superdawg Drive-In	Chicago, IL	7.3	Hummus Place	New York, NY	7.0
Taim	New York, NY	7.3	Jack's Stack	Kansas City, MO	7.0
Uburger	Boston, MA	7.3	Jestine's Kitchen	Charleston, SC	7.0
V & T	New York, NY	7.3	Langer's Deli	Los Angeles, CA	7.0
Bintliff's	Portland, ME	7.2	Little T American Baker	Portland, OR	7.0
Burger Bar	Las Vegas, NV	7.2	Mamoun's Falafel Restaurant	New York, NY	7.0
Crif Dogs	New York, NY	7.2	OK Café	Atlanta, GA	7.0
Good Pie, The	St. Louis, MO	7.2	Screen Door	Portland, OR	7.0
Red's Eats	Wiscasset, ME	7.2	Shopsin's	New York, NY	7.0
'wichcraft	New York, NY	7.1	Smoque	Chicago, Il	7.0
Ben's Chili Bowl	Washington DC	7.1	Sun in My Belly	Atlanta, GA	7.0
Canter's	Los Angeles, CA	7.1	Voodoo Doughnut	Portland, OR	7.0
Ken's Artisan Pizza	Portland, OR	7.1	Walker Bros. Pancake House	Evanston, IL	7.0
Sears Fine Food	San Francisco, CA	7.1	Wurstküche	Los Angeles, CA	7.0
Stellina Pasta Café	St. Louis, MO	7.1			

Top Restaurants by Region

Boston & New England

1.	Miyake	Portland, ME	94.8
2.	O Ya	Boston, MA	94.4
3.	No. 9 Park	Boston, MA	93.6
4.	Hugo's	Portland, ME	93.3
5.	Suzuki's Sushi Bar	Rockland, ME	92.9
6.	Uni	Boston, MA	92.8
7.	Fore Street	Portland, ME	92.6
8.	Neptune Oyster	Boston, MA	92.2
9.	Bizen	Great Barrington, MA	91.6
9.	Rialto	Cambridge, MA	91.6
9.	Ten Tables	Cambridge, MA	91.6
12.	Trenton Bridge Lobster Pound	Trenton, ME	91.5
13.	Primo	Rockland, ME	91.4
14.	Anneke Jans	Kittery, ME	91.1
15.	Clio	Boston, MA	91.0
15.	Hen of the Wood	Waterbury, VT	91.0

New York Metropolitan & Upstate

1.	Jean Georges	New York, NY	100.0
1.	Masa	New York, NY	100.0
1.	Per Se	New York, NY	100.0
4.	Le Bernardin	New York, NY	98.6
5.	Sushi Yasuda	New York, NY	98.5
6.	Blue Hill at Stone Barns	Pocantico Hills, NY	98.4
7.	Kuruma Zushi	New York, NY	98.0
8.	Momofuku Ko	New York, NY	97.4
9.	Corton	New York, NY	97.2
9.	Eleven Madison Park	New York, NY	97.2
11.	L'Atelier de Joël Robuchon	New York, NY	96.7
12.	Bouley	New York, NY	96.1
12.	Peter Luger	Brooklyn, NY	96.1
14.	Daniel	New York, NY	95.5
14.	Sugiyama	New York, NY	95.5

Washington DC & the Mid-Atlantic

1.	Minibar	Washington DC	98.2
2.	Komi	Washington DC	95.6
3.	Sushi Taro	Washington DC	95.1
4.	Volt	Fredericksburg, MD	94.8
5.	Citronelle	Washington DC	94.1
6.	Vetri	Philadelphia, PA	93.1
7.	Inn at Little Washington	Washington, VA	92.9
7.	Talula's Table	Kennett Square, PA	92.9
9.	Charleston	Baltimore, MD	92.4
10.	Morimoto	Philadelphia, PA	92.0
11.	CityZen	Washington DC	91.5

12. Amada	Philadelphia, PA	91.4
12. Birchrunville Store Café	Birchrunville, PA	91.4
14. Prime Rib	Baltimore, MD	91.1
15. Deep Blue	Wilmington, DE	90.9

Atlanta & the South

1. Town House	Chilhowie, VA	97.6
2. McCrady's	Charleston, SC	96.8
3. Bern's Steak House	Tampa, FL	93.8
3. Highland's Bar & Grill	Birmingham, AL	93.8
5. Restaurant Eugene	Atlanta, GA	93.7
6. Galatoire's	New Orleans, LA	93.1
6. Quinones Room at Bacchanalia	Atlanta, GA	93.1
8. Michy's	Miami, FL	93.0
9. Bacchanalia	Atlanta, GA	92.8
10. Blackberry Farm	Walland, TN	92.3
11. Brigtsen's	New Orleans, LA	92.2
12. Clancy's	New Orleans, LA	91.7
12. Hot and Hot Fish Club	Birmingham, AL	91.7
14. Victoria & Albert's	Orlando, FL	91.5
15. Lantern	Chapel Hill, NC	91.3

Chicago & the Midwest

1. Alinea	Chicago, IL	100.0
2. Schwa	Chicago, IL	96.8
3. Avenues	Chicago, IL	95.6
4. Spiaggia	Chicago, IL	94.7
5. American Restaurant	Kansas City, MO	94.6
5. Charlie Trotter's	Chicago, IL	94.6
7. Sanford	Milwaukee, WI	94.4
8. L20	Chicago, IL	94.3
9. Everest	Chicago, IL	93.6
9. Moto	Chicago, IL	93.6
11. Blackbird	Chicago, IL	93.4
12. Topolobampo	Chicago, IL	93.2
13. Niche	St. Louis, MO	92.7
14. Frontera Grill	Chicago, Il	92.4
14. June	Peoria, IL	92.4

Las Vegas & the Southwest

1. Guy Savoy	Las Vegas, NV	98.2
2. Uchi	Austin, TX	93.6
3. Raku	Las Vegas, NV	93.4
4. Picasso	Las Vegas, NV	93.2
5. Binkley's	Cave Creek, AZ	92.0
6. Kai	Chandler, AZ	91.8
6. Mizuna	Denver, CO	91.8
8. Matsuhisa Aspen	Aspen, CO	91.5
8. Michael Mina	Las Vegas, NV	91.5
8. Stephen Pyle	Dallas, TX	91.5

11. Mansion on Turtle Creek	Dallas, TX	91.4
11. Nobu	Dallas, TX	91.4
11. NOCA	Scottsdale, AZ	91.4
14. Joël Robuchon at the Mansion	Las Vegas, NV	91.3
15. Craft	Dallas, TX	91.0
15. Craftsteak	Las Vegas, NV	91.0
15. Lotus of Siam	Las Vegas, NV	91.0

Los Angeles, Southern California & Hawaii

1. Urasawa	Beverly Hills, CA	99.3
2. Providence	Los Angeles, CA	96.0
3. Spago	Beverly Hills, CA	95.5
4. Nishimura	West Hollywood, CA	94.7
5. Matsuhisa	West Hollywood, CA	94.4
6. Cut	Beverly Hills, CA	94.0
6. Patina	Los Angeles, CA	94.0
8. Asanebo	Studio City, CA	93.8
9. Mori Sushi	Los Angeles, CA	93.8
10. Saam - The Tasting Room	West Hollywood, CA	93.7
10. Sushi Zo	Los Angeles, CA	93.7
12. Mama's Fish House	Honolulu, HI	93.4
12. Totoraku (Secret Beef Place)	Los Angeles, CA	93.4
14. The Bazaar	West Hollywood, CA	93.1
15. Il Grano	Los Angeles, CA	93.0
15. Osteria Mozza	Los Angeles, CA	93.0

San Francisco, Northern California, & the Pacific Northwest

1. French Laundry, The	Yountville, CA	100.0
2. Manresa	Los Gatos, CA	100.0
3. Meadowood, Restaurant at	St. Helena, CA	98.4
4. Cyrus	Healdsburg, CA	97.3
5. Coi	San Francisco, CA	96.7
6. Quince	San Francisco, CA	96.2
7. Ubuntu	Napa, CA	96.1
8. Sushi Ran	Sausalito, CA	95.9
9. Commis	Oakland, CA	95.3
10. Chez Panisse	Berkeley, CA	95.2
11. Marinus	Carmel, CA	95.1
12. Herbfarm, The	Woodinville, WA	95.0
13. Aubergine	Carmel, CA	94.9
14. Gary Danko	San Francisco, CA	93.7
15. Castagna	Portland, OR	93.5

continued

Top Restaurants by Cuisine

Ethnic Cuisine (Fine Dining)

1. O Ya (Asian)	Boston, MA	94.4
2. Momofuku Säam Bar (Korean)	New York, NY	93.8
3. Momofuku Noodle Bar (Mexican)	New York, NY	93.6
4. Topolobampo (Mexican)	Chicago, IL	93.2
5. Bazaar, The (Spanish)	West Hollywood, CA	93.1
6. Aldea (Portuguese)	New York, NY	92.7
7. Frontera Grill (Mexican)	Chicago, IL	92.4
8. Degustation (Spanish)	New York, NY	91.6
9. Chinois on Main (Asian)	Santa Monica, CA	91.5
9. SHO Shaun Hergatt (Asian)	New York, NY	91.5
11. Amada (Spanish)	Philadelphia, PA	91.4
12. Lantern (Asian)	Chapel Hill, NC	91.3
13. Sripraphai (Thai)	Queens, NY	91.3
14. Lotus of Siam (Thai)	Las Vegas, NV	91.0
15. Rasika (Indian)	Washington DC	90.9

French

1. French Laundry	Yountville, CA	100.0
1. Jean Georges	New York, NY	100.0
1. Per Se	New York, NY	100.0
4. Le Bernardin	New York, NY	98.6
5. Guy Savoy	Las Vegas, NV	98.2
6. Corton	New York, NY	97.2
6. Eleven Madison Park	New York, NY	97.2
8. L'Atelier de Joël Robuchon	New York, NY	96.7
9. Bouley	New York, NY	96.1
10. Daniel	New York, NY	95.5
11. Chez Panisse	Berkeley, CA	95.2
12. Aubergine	Carmel, CA	94.9
13. L20	Chicago, IL	94.3
14. Citronelle	Washington DC	94.1
15. Patina	Los Angeles, CA	94.0

Italian/Mediterranean/Greek

1. Quince	San Francisco, CA	96.2
2. Komi	Washington DC	95.6
3. Spiaggia	Chicago, IL	94.7
4. No. 9 Park	Boston, MA	93.6
5. Marea	New York, NY	93.3
6. Vetri	Philadelphia, PA	93.1
7. Il Grano	Los Angeles, CA	93.0
7. Osteria Mozza	Los Angeles, CA	93.0
10. Locanda Verde	New York, NY,	92.9
11. Angelini Osteria	Los Angeles, CA	92.6
12. Lincoln	New York, NY	92.2
13. Esca	New York, NY	92.0
14. Rialto	Cambridge, MA	91.6
15. Scalini Fedeli	New York, NY	91.6

Japanese

1. Masa	New York, NY	100.0
2. Urasawa	Beverly Hills, CA	99.3
3. Sushi Yasuda	New York, NY	98.5
4. Kuruma Zushi	New York, NY	98.0
5. Sushi Ran	Sausalito, CA	95.9
6. Sugiyama	New York, NY	95.5
7. Sushi Taro	Washington DC	95.1
8. Miyake	Portland, ME	94.8
9. Nishimura	West Hollywood, CA	94.7
10. Sushi Seki	New York, NY	94.7
11. Matsuhisa	West Hollywood, CA	94.4
11. O Ya	Boston, MA	94.4
11. Soto	New York, NY	94.4
14. Asanebo	Studio City, CA	93.8
14. Mori Sushi	Los Angeles, CA	93.8

New American

1. Manresa	Los Gatos, CA	100.0
2. Blue Hill at Stone Barns	Pocantico Hills, NY	98.4
3. Meadowood, Restaurant at	St. Helena, CA	98.4
4. Cyrus	Healdsburg, CA	97.3
5. Ubuntu	Napa, CA	96.1
6. Providence	Los Angeles, CA	96.0
7. Spago	Beverly Hills, CA	95.5
8. North Fork Table & Inn	Southold, NY	95.2
9. Marinus	Carmel, CA	95.1
9. Herbfarm, The	Woodinville, WA	95.0
11. Volt	Fredericksburg, MD	94.8
12. American Restaurant	Kansas City, MO	94.6
12. Charlie Trotter's	Chicago, IL	94.6
14. Blue Hill	New York, NY	94.5
15. Sanford	Milwaukee, WI	94.4

Progressive Cuisine

1.	Alinea	Chicago, IL	100.0
2.	Minibar	Washington DC	98.2
3.	Town House	Chilhowie, VA	97.6
4.	Momofuku Ko	New York, NY	97.4
5.	McCrady's	Charleston, SC	96.8
5.	Schwa	Chicago, IL	96.8
7.	Coi	San Francisco, CA	96.7
8.	Avenues	Chicago, IL	95.6
9.	Commis	Oakland, CA	95.3
10.	Saam - The Tasting Room	West Hollywood, CA	93.7
11.	Moto	Chicago, IL	93.6
12.	Castagna	Portland, OR	93.5
13.	WD-50	New York, NY	93.4
14.	Hugo's	Portland, ME	93.3
15.	Baumé	Palo Alto, CA	92.0

Steak & Seafood (Traditional)

1.	Peter Luger	Brooklyn, NY	96.1
2.	Cut	Beverly Hills, CA	94.0
3.	Bern's Steakhouse	Tampa, FL	93.8
4.	Swan Oyster Depot	San Francisco, CA	92.8
5.	Minetta Tavern	New York, NY	92.5
6.	Neptune Oyster	Boston, MA	92.2
7.	Trenton Bridge Lobster Pound	Trenton, ME	91.5
8.	Prime Rib	Baltimore, MD	91.1
9.	Craftsteak	Las Vegas, NV	91.0
9.	Joe's Stone Crab	Miami Beach, FL	91.0
11.	Mastro's	Scottsdale, AZ	90.9
12.	Prime Meats	Brooklyn, NY	90.8
13.	Bryant & Cooper Steakhouse	Roslyn, NY	90.7
13.	Keen's Steakhouse	New York, NY	90.7
13.	Palm, The	New York, NY	90.7

Top Moderately Priced Restaurants

1.	Momofuku Säam Bar	New York, NY	93.8
2.	Momofuku Noodle Bar	New York, NY	93.6
3.	Osteria Mozza	Los Angeles, CA	93.0
4.	Swan Oyster Depot	San Francisco, CA	92.8
5.	Chez Panisse Café	Berkeley, CA	92.2
5.	Neptune Oyster	Boston, MA	92.2
7.	ad hoc	Yountville, CA	91.8
8.	Ten Tables	Cambridge, MA	91.6
9.	Amada	Philadelphia, PA	91.4
9.	Prune	New York, NY	91.4
11.	Lantern	Chapel Hill, NC	91.3
12.	Spinasse	Seattle, WA	91.3
12.	Sripraphai	Queens, NY	91.3

14.	Michael's Genuine Food & Drink	Miami, FL	91.2
15.	Canteen	San Francisco, CA	91.0

Top Inexpensive Dining – Artisanal

1.	Hot Doug's	Chicago, IL	9.7
2.	Provisions to Go	Atlanta, GA	9.0
3.	Una Pizzeria Napoletana	San Francisco, CA	8.9
4.	DiFara's	Brooklyn, NY	8.7
5.	Aurora Provisions	Portland, ME	8.6
5.	Black Sheep Pizza	Minneapolis, MN	8.6
5.	Humphrey Slocombe	San Francisco, CA	8.6
5.	Salumi Artisan Cured Meats	Seattle, WA	8.6
9.	Olympic Provisions	Portland, OR	8.5
9.	Pizzeria Mozza	Los Angeles, CA	8.5
11.	Alon's	Atlanta, GA	8.4
11.	Tartine Bakery & Café	San Francisco, CA	8.4
13.	Cochon Butcher	New Orleans, LA	8.3
13.	Duck Fat	Portland, ME	8.3
15.	Dynamo Donut	San Francisco, CA	8.3
15.	Pizzeria Bianco	Phoenix, AZ	8.3

Top Inexpensive Dining – Non-Artisanal

1.	Kreuz Market	Lockhart, TX	9.4
2.	Katz's Delicatessen	New York, NY	8.9
2.	Willie Mae's Scotch House	New Orleans, LA	8.9
4.	Kopp's	Milwaukee, WI	8.8
5.	Dinosaur	Syracuse, NY	8.5
5.	Oklahoma Joe's	Olathe, KS	8.5
7.	Bánh Mì Saigon Bakery	New York, NY	8.4
7.	Central Grocery	New Orleans, LA	8.4
7.	Ted Drewes	St. Louis, MO	8.4
10.	Camelia Grill	New Orleans, LA	8.3
10.	Clam Box of Ipswich	Ipswich, MA	8.3
10.	Ess-a-Bagel	New York, NY	8.3
10.	Mama's on Washington Square	San Francisco, CA	8.3
14.	17th Street Bar & Grill	O'Fallon, IL	8.2
14.	Frank Pepe's Pizzeria Napoletana	New Haven, CT	8.2
14.	Sally's Apizza	New Haven, CT	8.2

Bakeries

1.	Provisions to Go	Atlanta, GA	9.0
2.	Aurora Provisions	Portland, ME	8.6
3.	Alon's	Atlanta, GA	8.4
4.	Tartine Bakery & Café	San Francisco, CA	8.4
5.	Chase's Daily	Belfast, ME	8.1
6.	Clinton Street Baking Company	New York, NY	8.0

continued

6.	Macrina Bakery & Café	Seattle, WA	8.0
8.	Joan's on Third	West Hollywood, CA	7.9
9.	Clementine	Westwood, CA	7.7
9.	Huckleberry Café & Bakery	Santa Monica, CA	7.7

Barbecue & Southern

1.	Kreuz Market	Lockhart, TX	9.4
2.	Willie Mae's Scotch House	New Orleans, LA	8.9
3.	Dinosaur	Syracuse, NY	8.5
3.	Oklahoma Joe's	Olathe, KS	8.5
5.	17th Street Bar & Grill	O'Fallon, IL	8.2
5.	Smitty's Market	Lockhart, TX	8.2
7.	Brasa Rotisserie	Minneapolis, MN	8.1
7.	Roscoe's Chicken & Waffles	Hollywood, CA	8.1
9.	Dooky Chase	New Orleans, LA	8.0
10.	Egg	Brooklyn, NY	7.9
10.	Hominy Grill	Charleston, SC	7.9

Coffee Shops & Diners

1.	Camelia Grill	New Orleans, LA	8.3
1.	Mama's on Washington Square	San Francisco, CA	8.3
3.	Orange	Chicago, IL	7.6
4.	Zabar's Café	New York, NY	7.4
4.	Bette's Oceanview Diner	Berkeley, CA	7.4
6.	Elizabeth's	New Orleans, LA	7.3
6.	Original Pancake House	Chicago, IL	7.3
6.	Harry's Roadhouse	Santa Fe, NM	7.3
9.	Bintliff's	Portland, ME	7.2
10.	Canter's	Los Angeles, CA	7.1

Dessert

1.	Kopp's	Milwaukee, WI	8.8
2.	Humphrey Slocumbe	San Francisco, CA	8.6
3.	Ted Drewes	St. Louis, MO	8.4
4.	Dynamo Donut	San Francisco, CA	8.3
5.	Jeni's Splendid Ice Cream	Columbus, OH	8.2
6.	Momofuku Milk Bar	New York, NY	8.0
7.	Café du Monde	New Orleans, LA	8.0
8.	Ben Faremo, the Italian Ice King	Queens, NY	7.8
9.	Jacques Torres Chocolate	Brooklyn, NY	7.8
10.	Kyotofu	New York, NY	7.7

Hot Dogs & Hamburgers

1.	Hot Doug's	Chicago, IL	9.7
2.	4505 Meats	San Francisco, CA	8.2
2.	Flip Burger Boutique	Atlanta, GA	8.2

4.	8 Oz. Burger Bar	West Hollywood, CA	8.0
5.	Vortex Bar & Grill	Atlanta, GA	7.7
5.	Apple Pan	Los Angeles, CA	7.7
5.	Shake Shack	New York, NY	7.7
8.	Louis Lunch	New Haven, CT	7.6
8.	Pink's Famous Chili Dogs	Hollywood, CA	7.6
10.	Kuma's Corner	Chicago, IL	7.5
10.	Let's Be Frank	Culver City, CA	7.5

Pizzerias

1.	Una Pizzeria Napoletana	San Francisco, CA	8.9
2.	DiFara's	Brooklyn, NY	8.7
3.	Black Sheep Pizza	Minneapolis, MN	8.6
4.	Pizzeria Mozza	Los Angeles, CA	8.5
5.	Pizzeria Bianco	Phoenix, AZ	8.3
6.	Frank Pepe's Pizzeria Napoletana	New Haven, CT	8.2
7.	Sally's Apizza	New Haven, CT	8.2
7.	2 Amys	Washington DC	8.2
9.	Pizzetta 211	San Francisco, CA	8.1
10.	Keste Pizza & Vino	New York, NY	8.0
10.	Pizzeria Delfina	San Francisco, CA	8.0

Sandwiches

1.	Katz's Delicatessen	New York, NY	8.9
2.	Salumi Artisan Cured Meats	Seattle, WA	8.6
3.	Olympic Provisions	Portland, OR	8.5
4.	Bánh Mì Saigon Bakery	New York, NY	8.4
4.	Central Grocery	New Orleans, LA	8.4
6.	Cochon Butcher	New Orleans. LA	8.3
6.	Duck Fat	Portland, ME	8.3
6.	Ess-a-Bagel	New York, NY	8.3
9.	John's Roast Pork	Philadelphia, PA	8.1
10.	Mile End	Brooklyn, NY	8.0
10.	White House Sub Shop	Atlantic City, NJ	8.0

Seafood

1.	Clam Box of Ipswich	Ipswich, MA	8.3
2.	Calumet Fisheries	Chicago, IL	8.0
3.	J.T. Farnham's	Essex, MA	7.8
4.	Clam Shack	Kennebunkport, ME	7.7
4.	Woodman's of Essex	Essex, MA	7.7
6.	Crabby Jack's	Jefferson, LA	7.5
6.	Bagaduce Lunch	Brooksville, ME	7.5
8.	Casamento's	New Orleans, LA	7.3
8.	A Salt & Battery	New York, NY	7.3
10.	Red's Eats	Wiscasset, ME	7.2

Guide to Artisanal Ingredients

The past 20 years have seen incredible advancements in the quality of American ingredients. So much so that we are confident in saying that many of our homegrown products can hold their own against the best of other countries. Local, artisanally raised ingredients have become so common that when we travel around the country sampling restaurants, we always come upon an advertisement for a weekly (and sometimes more than that) farmers market. And increasingly, the provenance of those ingredients – the name of the farmer who raised the tomatoes or the beef on your plate – is listed on restaurant menus. With some foods, diners are given several different varieties to choose from – three of the most common being oysters, cheese and beer. We thought it would be helpful to give you some guidance about these products. So we went out and asked a group of experts to furnish us with a concise guide to each, listing some of the best and most interesting varieties that you're likely to encounter on restaurant menus. Now get out there and slurp, sample, and chug away.

continued

Cheese   by Tia Keenan

American cheese culture has blossomed within the past decade, thanks to the pioneering work of artisanal cheese makers over the past 30 years. Many cheeses produced in the United States are now as complex, soulful, finely crafted and delicious as the celebrated curds of Europe. Every state in the union produces artisanal cheese, and the selection available to diners nowadays displays a rich diversity of milks, shapes, sizes and styles.

Following is a selection of high-quality cheeses from around the country that are available on a relatively wide scale, considering that they are, in fact, all hand-crafted products. After each name, in parentheses, is the type of milk used and the production style (see list below) – two of the key factors in determining a cheese's characteristics. While this roster is in no way definitive, we hope it will serve as an introduction that you can (and should) expand upon as you journey through the landscape of this growing (literally and figuratively) culture.

Fresh Rindless, young cheeses ideally eaten within days or weeks of production. Mild.

Bloomy & Soft-Ripened Younger, soft cheeses often with a white or ashed rind. Mild to Medium.

Washed Cheeses washed in liquid, usually a brine, beer or liqueur. Mild to Strong.

Natural Rind Hard cheeses with a rind that has developed naturally in the cave.

Blue Blue-veined cheeses. Medium to Strong.

Waxed Cheeses whose rinds are covered in wax to protect the cheese.

5-Spoke Creamery Browning Gold LANCASTER COUNTY, PENNSYLVANIA
(raw cow, natural rind) Pennsylvania may not be as famous for cheddar as Vermont or Wisconsin, but this cheese is an excellent example of the genre: rich and extra-aged with deep, nutty caramel flavors.

Andante Dairy Minuet PETALUMA, CALIFORNIA
(pasteurized goat, bloomy rind) Flaky texture and clean flavor characterize this goat cheese. Pay particular attention to the rind here, as it's a prime sample of Andante's finely tuned craftsmanship.

Beehive Cheese Co. Barely Buzzed UNTAH, UTAH
(raw cow, rubbed rind) Rubbed with coffee and lavender, this cheddar-style cheese is truly an American original. The rub produces notes of coffee and chocolate with a deftly dealt floral undertone and a hit of rich brown butter.

Bellwether Farms San Andreas PETALUMA, CALIFORNIA
(raw sheep, natural rind) A hard, aged cheese with a sweet, tangy paste redolent of citrus and pineapple. Inspired by the traditional sheep's-milk cheeses of Tuscany.

Bittersweet Plantation Dairy Fleur de Lys GONZALES, LOUISIANA
(pasteurized cow, bloomy rind) A triple-crème kiss of unctuous creamy goodness. Mild with a buttery, decadent paste.

Capriole Dairy Juliana GREENVILLE, INDIANA
(raw goat, bloomy rind) This creamy yet firm cheese is a textural dream: dense and light at the same time. The herbal tones and rich flavors are a testament to the true character of goat milk.

Consider Bardwell Farm Manchester WEST PAWLET, VERMONT
(raw goat, natural rind) Firm-textured and very dense, this fruity, nutty cheese tastes as bright as sunshine.

Cowgirl Creamery Red Hawk POINT REYES STATION, CALIFORNIA
(pasteurized cow, washed rind) An American classic: salty, sticky and just shy of aggressive. A good introduction to washed-rind, stinky cheeses.

Cypress Grove Truffle Tremor ARCATA, CALIFORNIA
(pasteurized goat, bloomy rind) A lesser-known and somewhat fancier sibling to the American stalwart Humboldt Fog, Truffle Tremor is a dense, creamy cheese with enough truffle flavor to please your palate without offending your wallet.

Jasper Hill Farm Winnemere GREENSBORO, VRMONT
(raw cow, washed rind) A seasonal winter cheese washed in Lambic-style ale and wrapped in spruce bark, resulting in an ultra-creamy, meaty, woodsy example of Vermont cheese-making prowess.

Lively Run Goat Dairy Cayuga Blue INTERLAKEN, NEW YORK
(pasteurized goat, blue) Chalky, mild and herbal, this is a singular style of blue cheese.

Locust Grove Farm La Mancha KNOXVILLE, TENNESSEE
(raw sheep, waxed) An American take on Manchego cheese, with all the sweet and salty notes of that Spanish variety. Rich and slightly piquant.

Meadow Creek Dairy Grayson GALAX, VIRGINIA
(raw cow, washed rind) A medium-bodied stinker with an edible orange-colored rind and pliable, deep-yellow paste, indicative of the cows' pasture-based diet. Eggy, grassy and addictive.

Mozzarella Co. Oja Santa DALLAS, TEXAS
(pasteurized goat, fresh) A fresh goat cheese of the highest order, wrapped in Oja Santa leaves, which lend a nice vegetal flair. Smooth and creamy, with an acidic zing.

Mouco Cheese Co. Colorouge FORT COLLINS, COLORADO
(pasteurized cow, bloomy rind) With a distinctive "red-smear" rind enveloping a gooey, complex paste, this mild, earthy cheese is a gem for the taste buds, and for the conscience: Mouco is at the forefront of environmentally conscious cheese making.

continued

Nettle Meadow Kunik WARRENSBURG, NEW YORK

(pasteurized cow and goat, bloomy rind) A heady combination of goat milk and Jersey cow cream, this cheese tastes like butter with a rind: a velvety, mild paste with a clean, grassy finish.

Pleasant Ridge Reserve Extra Aged DODGEVILLE, WISCONSIN

(raw cow, natural rind) An award-winning Alpine-style cheese, aged over a year, with a rich, dense paste and an occasional crystalline crunch. Made with milk from pastured cows, known for its complex, lush grass flavors.

Pt. Reyes Original Blue POINT REYES STATION, CALIFORNIA

(raw cow, blue) Smooth and creamy with a fine dose of minerality, this cheese is the standard bearer for Roquefort-style farmstead American blue. A good introductory blue.

Rivers Edge Chèvre Up in Smoke LOGSDEN, OREGON

(pasteurized goat, fresh) Bundled in smoked maple leaves and creamy beyond belief, this little dumpling of fresh goat cheese is like a comforting snack enjoyed beside a campfire.

Rogue Creamery Rogue River Blue CENTRAL POINT, OREGON

(raw cow, blue) Wrapped in grape leaves that have been soaked in a locally made pear brandy, this cheese has a flavor profile reflective of Oregonian bounty. Notes of pear, mushrooms and hazelnuts temper a healthy brininess.

Spring Brook Farm Tarentaise READING, VERMONT

(raw cow, natural rind) A terroir-driven, Alpine-style cheese, aged anywhere from 5 to 12 months. Its notes of grass, hay and mustard vary, based on the season and its maturity – but it's great at any age.

Sweet Grass Dairy Green Hill THOMASVILLE, GEORGIA

(pasteurized cow, bloomy rind) There's truth in advertising with this Camembert-style cheese: The flavors of fresh, sweet, green grasses are indeed prominent. A creamy bit of Southern hospitality.

Tumalo Farms Pondhopper BEND, OREGON

(raw goat, waxed) A semi-firm, Gouda-style cheese produced from a unique process of soaking the cheese curds in a locally brewed beer. The result is a tangy, hoppy, snackable cheese with nutty, floral notes.

Vermont Butter & Cheese Creamery Bonne Bouche WEBSTERVILLE, VERMONT

(pasteurized goat, bloomy rind) When eaten young, this ash-ripened cheese is tangy, earthy and creamy. As it ages it develops a spicy, red-pepper quality.

Tia Keenan (www.twitter.com/kasekaiserina) is a Chef Fromager, culinary consultant and teacher based in New York City.

Oysters by Rowan Jacobsen

The American oyster renaissance began about a decade ago and shows no signs of slowing down. Driving it are some breakthrough farming techniques that have allowed people to raise more perfect oysters than ever before, in more places than ever before.

Other than those harvested in the Gulf of Mexico, almost all oysters in North America are farmed, and that's a good thing: Because oysters are filter feeders, they actually clean the water while growing (one reason why oysters head the top of the sustainable seafood list). Filter feeding is also why different types of oysters can taste so different. Their flavor depends on where they grow: Pumping water across their gills as they eat plankton, they also absorb the minerals, salinity and other flavors of their bay. In general, oysters from the West Coast tend to be sweeter and those from the East Coast saltier. Also, most oysters are at their worst in summer, when they spawn, and at their plumpest and tastiest in late fall and early winter.

Following is a list of often-encountered varieties of North American bivalves – some of the most diverse and delicious oysters found anywhere.

Apalachicola APALACHICOLA BAY, FLORIDA
The last old-school oysters in America, Apalachicolas grow wild and are still harvested by hand the way they were in the 1800s, by a few hundred bay men plying tongs and small wooden skiffs in the shallow waters of this Florida panhandle gem of a bay. They tend to be large and gentle in flavor.

Beausoleil NEGUAC, NEW BRUNSWICK
Grown in floating trays in icy Canadian waters, Beausoleils stay small and light-flavored, with a pleasant, yeasty bread-dough flavor, making them the perfect starter oyster.

Bluepoint LONG ISLAND SOUND, CONNECTICUT AND NEW YORK
Dredged from the depths of Long Island Sound, Bluepoints have been the unofficial oyster of New York City for more than a century. Big, bold and balanced, with spiffy black-and-white shells, they fit right in with the city's ways.

Chesapeake CHESAPEAKE BAY, MARYLAND AND VIRGINIA
Once prodigious enough to supply an entire industry, Chesapeake oysters are down to less than 1% of their historical numbers, victims of over-farming. Today most are, frankly, a muddy mess. However, some varieties – specifically, Stingrays, Barcats, Rappahannocks and Lynnhavens – can still be very nice.

Chincoteague CHINCOTEAGUE BAY, VIRGINIA
Hailing from the same island as Misty the pony, Chincoteagues have none of the freshwater influence of the Chesapeake; instead they have a salty, almost bitter flavor. Small, thin-shelled, beer-friendly.

continued   **37**

Eagle Rock TOTTEN INLET, WASHINGTON
Grown in the same waters as Totten Inlet Virginicas (see below), these Pacific oysters have lovely fluted shells and a nice, balanced flavor – not too sweet, not too salty.

Effingham Inlet BARKLEY SOUND, BRITISH COLUMBIA
One of the few British Columbia oysters grown on the west coast of Vancouver Island, Effingham Inlets have an intense, Pacific-brine flavor that's very different from most West Coast oysters'. Grown in suspended nets, these babies never touch the ground and keep a lighter, pure taste because of it.

European Flat PROVENANCE VARIES
Any oyster that has "Flat" after its name is a European Flat, also known as Belon. The native oyster of Europe, it's difficult to grow in American waters. Famous (some would say notorious) for its intense metallic, iodine flavor, it's the ultimate love-it-or-leave-it oyster.

Fanny Bay DEEP BAY, BRITISH COLUMBIA
Oysters grown on the east coast of Vancouver Island, the Strait of Georgia, have a sweeter, less briny flavor than those from the Pacific side, thanks to the freshwater rivers pouring out of the mountains. Fanny Bays are tops, with their beautiful shells swirled with pink and purple.

Gulf GULF OF MEXICO, ALABAMA, LOUISIANA AND TEXAS
If you see a generic oyster in a restaurant or a supermarket, odds are it's from the Gulf of Mexico, whose bivalves cost less than half the price of other oysters. That's because the Mississippi Delta and other spots along the Gulf have the last bountiful wild oyster populations in the world. The oysters, harvested by dredge, are very large, thick-shelled and neutral in flavor.

Hama Hama HOOD CANAL, WASHINGTON
Big, natural-set oysters from the Hamma Hamma River Delta on Hood Canal, known for their full flavor and firm crunchiness, like a salted cucumber sandwich.

Hog Island Sweetwater TOMALES BAY, CALIFORNIA
Extraordinarily sweet oysters with a long, nori-flavored finish, these California beauties in purplish-black shells have a more refined flavor than most Pacific oysters and a rabid following. One of the best oysters with dry white wine.

Island Creek DUXBURY BAY, MASSACHUSETTS
Some of the briniest oysters you'll ever taste, Island Creeks are heaven with a cold beer. Coldwater currents in Duxbury Bay keep them firm and plump in summer, even when other Northeast oysters have started to soften.

Kachemak KENAI PENINSULA, ALASKA
Slow-grown oysters, suspended in the frigid waters of Alaska, Kachemaks delight with swirling flavors of green tea, salted honeydew and green apple candy. Hard to find, but well worth the hunt.

Kumamoto HUMBOLDT BAY, CALIFORNIA, AND PUGET SOUND, WASHINGTON
A smaller cousin of the common Pacific oyster, Kumamotos are always tiny, deep-cupped, pleasantly saccharine and full-bodied, with an alluring aroma of melon. A favorite of those with a sweet tooth.

Kusshi DEEP BAY, BRITISH COLUMBIA

The Canadian answer to the Kumamoto, Kusshis are raised in floating nets in the pristine waters of British Columbia, and tumbled in metal cylinders throughout their lives to break off their growing edge and force them to "cup up." The result is a bonsai oyster, small and delicate, with a watermelon-rind flavor.

Little Skookum PUGET SOUND, WASHINGTON

Rich and funky and not so salty, Little Skookums (sometimes called just Skookums) are some of the strongest-flavored oysters you'll find. Tucked into mudflats in an inlet in the far-southern tip of Puget Sound, they feed on a unique assemblage of plankton and have a more fishy quality.

Mystic NOANK RIVER, CONNECTICUT

Large, with stunning green-and-white shells and a robust flavor that's all brine, minerals and metal, these are graduate-level oysters raised on firm, sandy river bars.

Moonstone POINT JUDITH POND, RHODE ISLAND

Some of the biggest, boldest oysters on the market, from one of the most nutrient-rich bays, Moonstones are famed for their stony, flinty, coppery flavor, big body and firm texture.

Olympia PUGET SOUND, WASHINGTON

The only oyster native to the Pacific Northwest, Olympias are the size of half-dollars, with iridescent shells of orange, purple and green, coppery flesh and a distinctively tangy taste of celery salt. Stupendous with Bloody Marys for brunch.

Pemaquid DAMARISCOTTA RIVER, MAINE

Maine oysters are known for their white shells and ultra-clean taste, and those from the Damariscotta have the deepest, finest flavor. In addition to Pemaquids (named for Pemaquid Point, which juts into the Gulf of Maine where the Damariscotta ends), look for Glidden Points, Wawenauks and Wiley Points.

Totten Inlet Virginica PUGET SOUND, WASHINGTON

The East Coast oyster species *Crassostrea virginica* is raised in the sweet waters of Puget Sound, making for an untouched combination: fruity, briny, delicious.

Wellfleet WELLFLEET HARBOR, MASSACHUSETTS

Tucked into a sheltered harbor beside the classic New England town of Wellfleet, way out on Cape Cod, Wellfleets have long been famous for their North Atlantic flavor and a smell of childhood vacations by the seashore.

Widow's Hole GREENPOINT, NEW YORK

Several oyster farmers operate on the East End of Long Island, using submerged metal cages (to prevent predators from getting at the harvest). These oysters have burnt-orange-tinted shells, thanks to the local algae, and a rich cast-iron flavor. Varieties to look for: Widow's Holes, East Ends, Pipes Coves.

Willapa WILLAPA BAY, WASHINGTON

This pristine bay in southwest Washington state opens directly onto the Pacific, making its oysters more salty and savory than most from Hood Canal or Puget Sound. The big names include Oysterville Select, Hawks Bay, Shigoku.

Rowan Jacobsen is the author of the James Beard Award-winner A Geography of Oysters: The Connoisseur's Guide to Oyster Eating in North America *and of the website OysterGuide.com.*

Beer by Michael Sweeney

In 1983 there were only 80 breweries operating in the United States. Almost all of them brewed the same style of beer: the American pale lager. In the past 25 years, we've seen a true revolution in our national brewing scene. There are now more than 1,600 breweries in operation, producing a dazzling array of varieties – and the industry shows no sign of slowing down, as consumers become more sophisticated and chefs realize just how well a unique craft beer can be paired with their unique dishes.

One of the truly distinctive aspects of U.S. brewers is that, unlike their colleagues in Europe, they're not bound by history or tradition. So they work in styles from all around the globe, while also developing new ones – such as the California Common, the American Barleywine and the Black India Pale Ale. Of course, different areas of the country produce different beers, and the output of these artisanal breweries is by nature often limited. So it's important – not to mention fun – to check out the local talent's wares when visiting an area, since you probably won't find them at home.

Arranged by geographical region, the following list is a representative roster of craft beers being produced in the U.S. today, preceded by a glossary of terms often used in discussions of brew.

Malt Typically barley, but includes grains such as wheat, oats and rye. Provides the color, body and sweetness of the beer.

Hops A pungent flower used to help provide bitterness, flavor and aroma – the spice of beer.

Yeast A living fungus that helps to ferment the beer, changing the sugar from the malt into carbon dioxide and alcohol. Brewers use two main families of yeast that lend their names to types of beer: *ale yeast* (typically fermented between 60 and 75 degrees Fahrenheit) and *lager yeast* (typically fermented between 45 and 55 degrees Fahrenheit).

Imperial/Double Interchangeable terms, denoting a much bigger version of a beer's original style; usually this means they're higher in alcohol by volume (ABV), body and flavor.

Hefeweizen *Hefe* means "yeast" and *weizen* means "wheat" in German, two words that accurately sum up this traditional German ale. Brewed with a large (up to 50%) dose of wheat, it's light and slightly creamy, and authentic versions often have a note of banana or cloves as well.

India Pale Ale (IPA) A style of beer, dating back to the late 1700s, brewed with abundant malt and hops that historically ensured it aged properly during the nine-month sea voyage to India.

Pilsner A clean, crisp and clear lager style of beer that originated in the Czech Republic. The body is very light, but there is a decent amount of hop aroma and bitterness.

Saison A Belgian/French style of ale, originally brewed for farm workers during the harvest season.

Stout A member of the ale family, typically a black, roasty beer with plenty of body.

Tripel Belgian in origin, this golden ale can be kind of deceiving: It's typically very light and quaffable, but it's also typically a whopping 8–10% ABV.

Witbier A Belgian take on a wheat beer, featuring not only a creamy note from the wheat, but also spiciness from the ale yeast and from the addition of coriander.

Northeast

Allagash White PORTLAND, MAINE
This is a traditional witbier, brewed not only with a lot of wheat (creating a cloudy appearance), but also a "special blend of spices." A very stimulating beer.

Brooklyn Lager BROOKLYN, NEW YORK
This clean, crisp lager provides not only a smooth malty body, but also a bit of hop bitterness on the back end, which helps to balance the sweetness from the caramel malts.

Dogfish Head 90 Minute IPA MILTON, DELAWARE
Unlike West coast style IPAs with a big citrusy flavor and aroma, East coast style IPAs tend to be more earthy and grassy. 90 Minute IPA is no exception. Very malty, with a hop profile reminiscent of fresh tobacco.

Ommegang Hennepin COOPERSTOWN, NEW YORK
If you're ever at a loss for pairing beer with food, you can almost never go wrong with a Hennepin saison. It's wonderfully multifunctional: The spiciness that comes from the yeast works well with fish, poultry, pork and even greens.

Troegs Nugget Nectar HARRISBURG, PENNSYLVANIA
Not quite an IPA and not quite a red ale (darker in hue and sweeter in flavor), this beer is almost bursting with over-the-top hop flavor and aroma. As such, it packs a real punch: Tread carefully.

Victory Prima Pils DOWNINGTOWN, PENNSYLVANIA
With its grainy malt flavor and low bitterness, Victory Prima Pils is closely modeled on classic European-style pilsners. Its brown bottle also helps to minimize any skunkiness created by exposure to light.

South & Southwest

Abita Turbodog ABITA SPRINGS, LOUISIANA
This beer is styled after English brown ales, which have been brewed for hundreds of years. While brown in color, Abita's body remains relatively light. It definitely has plenty of notes of coffee and molasses, though.

Duck-Rabbit Milk Stout FARMVILLE, NORTH CAROLINA
When it's hot, you don't really think about drinking stouts. But being situated in the often-sultry South didn't keep Duck-Rabbit Brewery from brewing up some

dark beers. This one is augmented with lactose sugar to create a bit of creamy sweetness that helps balance the dark-roasted malts.

Real Ale Devil's Backbone BLANCO, TEXAS
A big problem with a lot of Belgian-style beers, especially tripels, is that they can often end up too sweet. Real Ale does a great job of not only providing a flavorful tripel, but of making sure it stays bone dry.

Terrapin Rye Pale Ale ATHENS, GEORGIA
Almost every craft brewery makes a pale ale, but this one really stands out. Blending noble herbal European hops with the citrusy American variety helps to create a depth of flavors that play pleasantly on alternating notes of grassiness and grapefruit.

Yazoo Hefeweizen NASHVILLE, TENNESSEE
There are few things quite like a true German-style hefeweizen – take a big whiff and you'll pick up unusual aromas such as banana and clove. The impressive part is that these aromas come from the same yeast that keeps this delicious beer cloudy.

Midwest & the Great Lakes

Boulevard Tank 7 KANSAS CITY, MISSOURI
A unique take on a Belgian saison, a traditional farmhouse ale, this beer combines a Belgian yeast strain with American hops, resulting in a taste that blends the Old World and the New.

Capital Brewing Supper Club MIDDLETON, WISCONSIN
A perfect gateway into the craft-beer world. Clean and crisp, which makes it very easy to drink; it harkens back to a time when lagers weren't all yellow and fizzy but had a big, bold flavor.

Founders Red's Rye GRAND RAPIDS, MICHIGAN
This play on an IPA includes a generous amount of rye malt that creates an underlying spiciness, helping to accentuate the hop character.

Goose Island Bourbon County Stout CHICAGO,ILLINOIS
Aged in bourbon barrels for 11 months, which gives the beer a complex flavor, redolent of oak and vanilla, that helps complement its dark, rich malts.

Schlafly Pumpkin ST. LOUIS, MISSOURI
It's pumpkin pie in a glass! While so many of its ilk end up too sweet or too cloying, the Schlafly Pumpkin ale perfectly balances the malt with the spice, making it one of the finest of its kind in the country.

Three Floyds Gumballhead MUNSTER, INDIANA
Packing a huge hop wallop of citrusy flavor and aroma, Gumballhead proves wheat beers don't have to be boring. Perfect for beating the summertime heat.

Mountain States

Avery Ellie's Brown Ale BOULDER, COLORADO
American brown ales can sometimes be middle of the road: not offensive, but also not extraordinary. Avery's version avoids this wishy-washy syndrome, providing plenty of character with a big chocolaty flavor.

Great Divide Espresso Oak-Aged Yeti DENVER, COLORADO
This luxurious imperial stout is aged in oak chips to provide a subtle oaky flavor. But it's the addition of espresso that makes this beer otherworldly.

New Belgium La Folie FORT COLLINS, COLORADO
A blend of different vintages, from the folks behind the popular Fat Tire amber ale. New Belgium's sour beer shouldn't stay under the radar, though: It has just enough malt sweetness to balance its tart, lactic sourness.

Odell 90 Shilling FORT COLLINS, COLORADO
A Scottish-style beer with a body that's lighter than your traditional Scottish ales, which helps to keep it easily quaffable, while still providing plenty of robust malty flavor.

Oskar Blues Little Yella Pils LYONS, COLORADO
What happens when Americans decide to tackle a traditional Czech-style pilsner? You get Little Yella Pils from Oskar Blues. While it has an assertive hop character and smooth, malty body, it ultimately stays clean and refreshing.

Ska Modus Hoperandi DURANGO, COLORADO
The ultimate enemy to almost any beer is light. Putting an IPA in an aluminum can is a stroke of genius, as it keeps this beer tasting like fresh hops straight from the Pacific Northwest.

West Coast

Alaskan Smoked Porter JUNEAU, ALASKA
It must be the long, cold winters that led Alaskans to create this mysterious beer. It's black and lush, but also has an in-your-face smokiness that helps complement its roasted malts.

Anchor Steam SAN FRANCISCO, CALIFORNIA
Fermented with a lager strain of yeast, but at a much warmer ale temperature, this original is probably America's first stylistic contribution to the beer world. Its grainy malt sweetness is backed up with a slight hop bitterness from Northern Brewer hops.

Firestone-Walker Union Jack IPA RASO ROBLES, CALIFORNIA
Probably the gold standard when it comes to West coast style IPAs, this beer provides not only plenty of bitterness for those looking for a bitter beer, but also a huge floral hop aroma. To get the most out of the hop flavor, drink it in as fresh a form as possible.

Lost Abbey Judgment Day SAN MARCOS, CALIFORNIA
When allowed to warm up a bit, this Belgian-style dark ale presents a big bouquet of dried fruit and a unique yeastiness. The flavor is equally complex, with rich caramel malt intertwining with a hint of chocolate.

North Coast Old Rasputin FORT BRAGG, CALIFORNIA
This hearty Russian Imperial Stout (the über-version of an imperial stout) provides not only plenty of decadent roasted malt, but also a luscious mouth feel. This beer is almost thick enough to be a blanket on a cold winter night.

Russian River Beatification SANTA ROSA, CALIFORNIA
One of the best examples of a sour beer produced in America. The aroma is funky and fruity, with a puckering tartness on the palate.

Michael Sweeney is the creator of STLHops.com, a craft-beer reference site, and has acted as beer consultant for a number of St. Louis-area restaurants.

Help Feed Others

We assume that if you are in a position to read this guide, life has treated you fairly well and you have no problem filling your belly. Unfortunately, that doesn't apply to everyone: There are people in our country who go hungry or who have trouble providing meals for themselves—and who could use your help. Well, here's an easy way to help them. Every time you go out to eat, take a dollar bill and put it aside. It might not seem like much, but if you're the sort of dining hobbyist we think you are, it will add up. At the end of the year, after it has developed into a small pile, send it to one of the organizations on the list below. (Of course you can always skip this exercise and just write a check today, too.) We aren't affiliated with any specific charity, but here are the names of some who are known for their good work in helping people who are hungry or who have trouble feeding themselves.

City Harvest Feeds 300,000 hungry New Yorkers every week through food drives and a combination of donations that include money, service, food products. Address: 575 8th Avenue, 4th Floor, New York, NY 10018, www.cityharvest.org

Feeding America Coordinates and supplies food to 37 million hungry Americans each year including 14 million children and 3 million seniors through 202 local member food banks. Address: 37 E. Wacker Drive #2000, Chicago, IL 60601, http://feedingamerica.org

God's Love We Deliver Prepares and delivers nutritious, high-quality meals to men, women and children living with HIV/AIDS, cancer and other serious illnesses who, because of their illness, are unable to provide or prepare meals for themselves. Address: 166 Avenue of the Americas, New York, NY 10013, www.glwd.org

Meals-on-Wheels Provides home-delivered meals services to people in need. The Meals On Wheels Association of America is the oldest and largest national organization composed of and representing local, community-based Senior Nutrition Programs in all 50 U.S. states, as well as the U.S. Territories. Address: 203 S. Union Street, Alexandia, VA 22314, www.mowaa.org

Share Our Strength Share Our Strength's highest priority is to make sure that every child in America gets the nutritious food he or she needs to learn, grow and thrive. They try to accomplish this by improving the access that families all across the country have to healthy, affordable food. Address: 1730 M Street NW, Washington, DC, 20036, http://strength.org

Maps of Notable Restaurants

Maps of Notable Restaurants

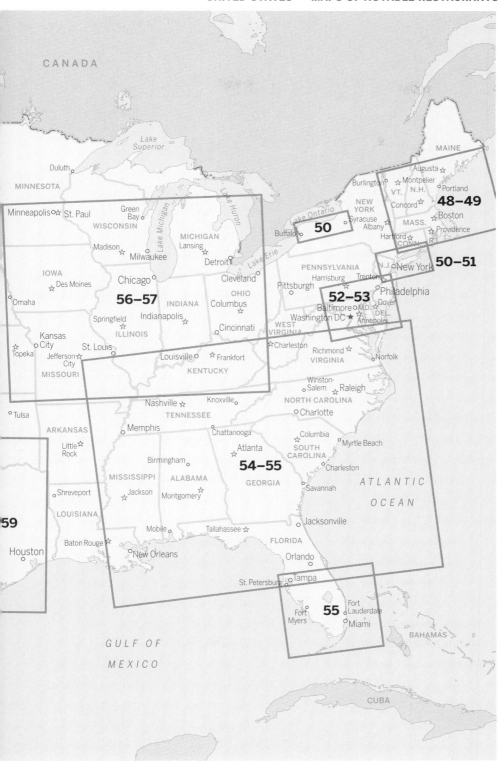

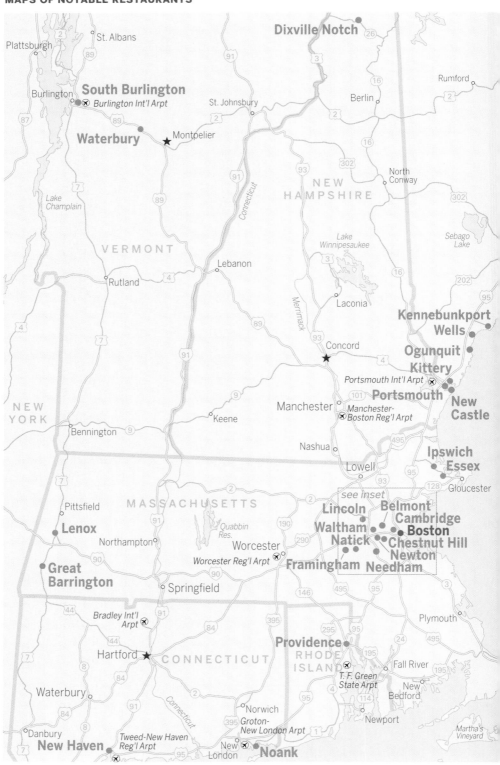

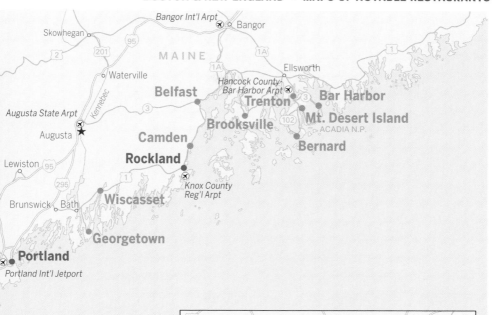

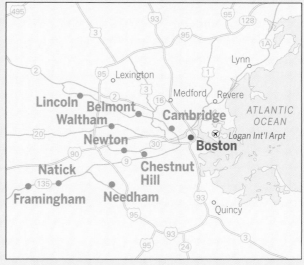

Boston & New England

Highly Recommended

BOSTON, MA		PORTLAND, ME	
Neptune Oyster	92.2	Fore Street	92.6
No. 9 Park	93.6	Hugo's	93.3
O Ya	94.4	Miyake	94.8
Uni	92.8		
		ROCKLAND, ME	
		Suzuki's Sushi Bar	92.9

Other locations with restaurants of note are indicated in gold. Please see chapters for more information.

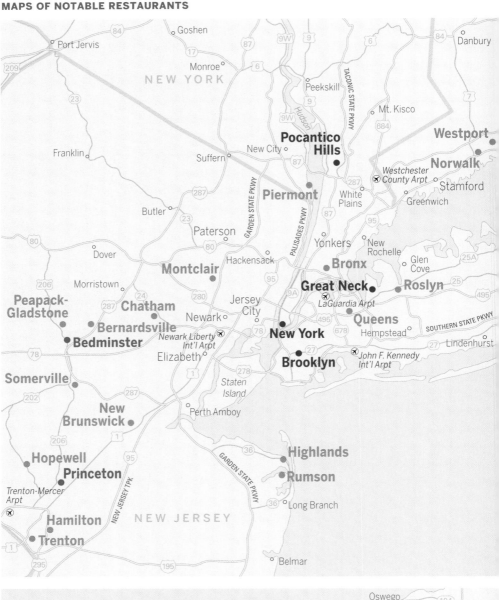

New York Metro, Long Island & Upstate

**♨ Most Important
Restaurants in the U.S.**

Highly Recommended

BROOKLYN, NY
Peter Luger 96.1

GREAT NECK, NY
Peter Luger 96.1

NEW YORK, NY
Bouley 96.1
Corton 97.2
Daniel 95.5
Eleven Madison Park 97.2
Jean Georges 100.0
Kuruma Zushi 98.0
L'Atelier de
    Joël Robuchon . . 96.7
Le Bernardin 98.6
Masa 100.0

Momofuku Ko 97.4
Per Se 100.0
Sugiyama 95.5
Sushi Yasuda 98.5

POCANTICO HILLS, NY
Blue Hill at
    Stone Barns 98.4

SOUTHOLD, NY
North Fork Table
    & Inn 95.2

BEDMINSTER, NJ
Pluckemin Inn 93.0

NEW YORK, NY
Aldea 92.7
Alto 92.9
Annisa 92.5
Aquavit 93.3
Blue Hill 94.5
Café Boulud 93.8
Convivio 92.6
Craft 94.0
Esca 92.0
Gramercy Tavern . . 93.6
Hatsuhana 92.4
Kyo Ya 92.5
Lincoln 92.2

Locanda Verde 92.9
Marea 93.3
Minetta Tavern 92.5
Modern, The 92.2
Momofuku
    Noodle Bar 93.6
Momofuku Ssam Bar 93.8
Nobu 93.6
Nobu Next Door . . . 92.6
Picholine 93.0
Soto 94.4
Sushi Seki 94.7
Sushi Zen 92.7
WD-50 . . . . 93.4

PRINCETON, NJ
Elements 94.3

Other locations with restaurants of note are indicated in gold. Please see chapters for more information.

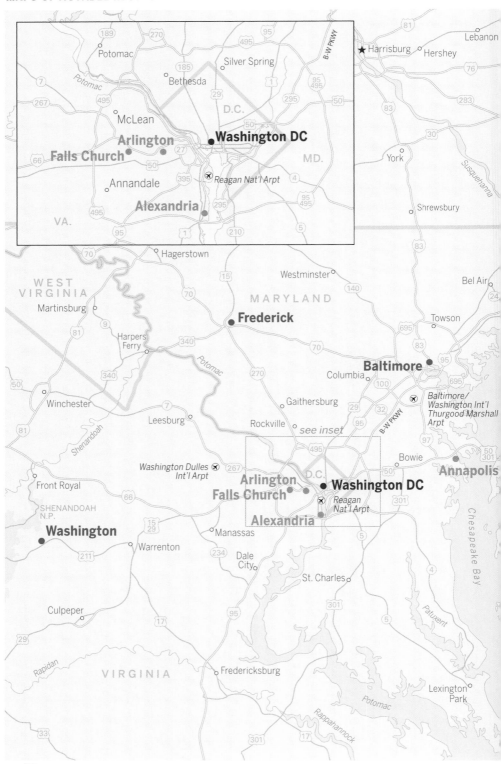

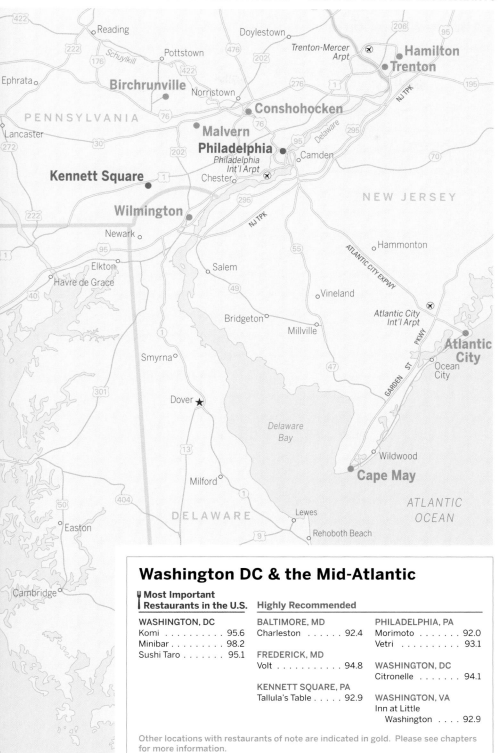

Washington DC & the Mid-Atlantic

Most Important Restaurants in the U.S.

Highly Recommended

WASHINGTON, DC
Komi	95.6
Minibar	98.2
Sushi Taro	95.1

BALTIMORE, MD
Charleston	92.4

FREDERICK, MD
Volt	94.8

KENNETT SQUARE, PA
Tallula's Table	92.9

PHILADELPHIA, PA
Morimoto	92.0
Vetri	93.1

WASHINGTON, DC
Citronelle	94.1

WASHINGTON, VA
Inn at Little Washington	92.9

Other locations with restaurants of note are indicated in gold. Please see chapters for more information.

Atlanta & the South

🍴 **Most Important Restaurants in the U.S.**

CHARLESTON, SC McCrady's 96.8	**BIRMINGHAM, AL** Highland's Bar & Grill 93.8
CHILHOWIE, VA Town House 97.6	**MIAMI, FL** Michy's 93.0

Highly Recommended

ATLANTA, GA Bacchanalia . . . . . . 92.8 Quinones at Bacchanalia . . . . 93.1 Restaurant Eugene . 93.7	**NEW ORLEANS, LA** Brigtsen's . . . . . . 92.2 Galatoire's . . . . . . 93.1 **TAMPA, FL** Bern's Steak house . 93.8 **WALLAND, TN** Blackberry Farm . . . 92.3

Other locations with restaurants of note are indicated in gold. Please see chapters for more information.

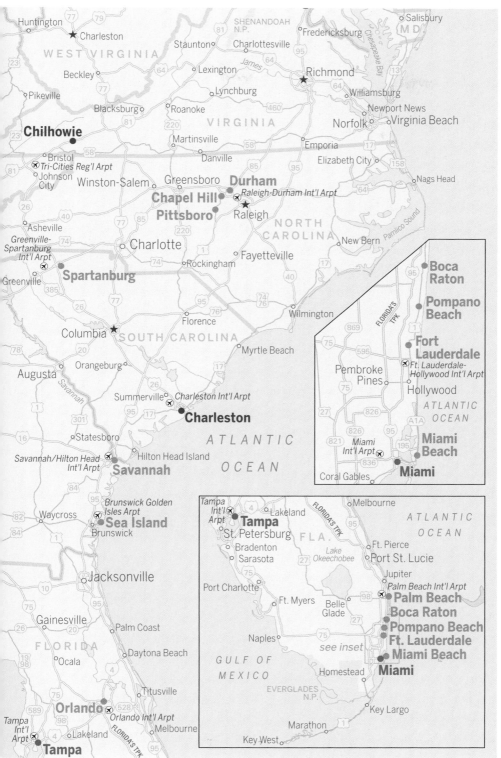

Chicago & the Midwest

🍴 Most Important
Restaurants in the U.S.

Highly Recommended

CHICAGO, IL
Alinea 100.0
Avenues 95.6
Schwa 96.8

Highly Recommended

CHICAGO, IL
Blackbird 93.4
Charlie Trotter's . . . 94.6
Everest 93.6
Frontera Grill 92.4

L20 . . . . 94.3
Moto 93.6
Spiaggia 94.7
Topolobampo 93.2

FINDLAY, OH
Revolver 92.0

KANSAS CITY, MO
American Restaurant 94.6
Bluestem 92.2

MADISON, WI
L'Etoile 92.0

MILWAUKEE, WI
Sanford 94.4

PEORIA, IL
June 92.4

ST. LOUIS, MO
Niche 92.7
Sidney Street Café . 92.2

Other locations with restaurants of note are indicated in gold. Please see chapters for more information.

57

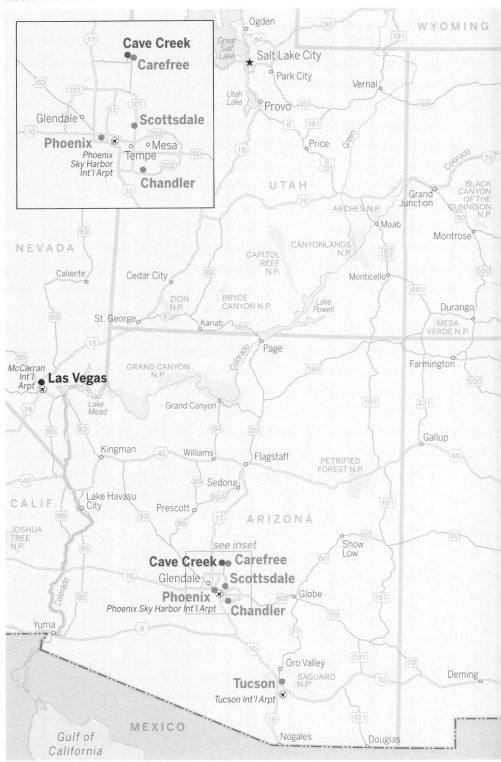

Las Vegas & the Southwest

Most Important Restaurants in the U.S.

LAS VEGAS, NV
Guy Savoy 98.2

Highly Recommended

AUSTIN, TX
Uchi 93.6

CAVE CREEK, AZ
Binkley's 92.0

LAS VEGAS, NV
Picasso 93.2
Raku 93.4

Other locations with restaurants of note are indicated in gold.
Please see chapters for more information.

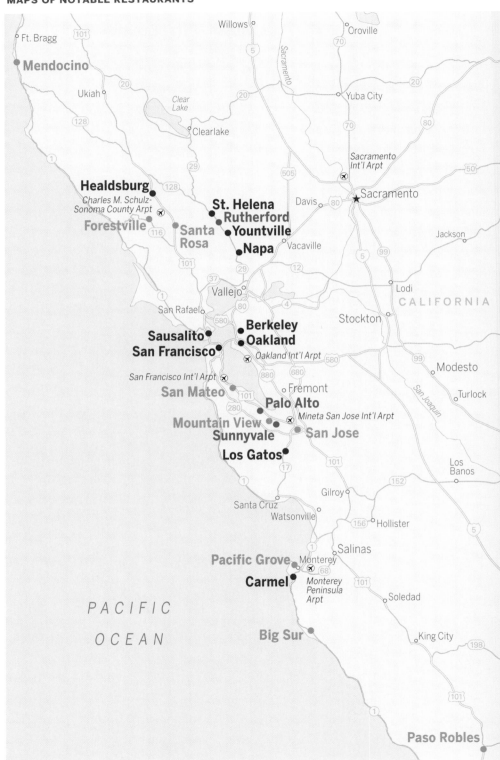

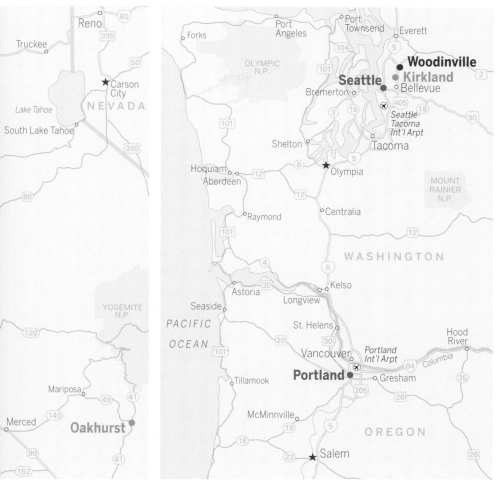

San Francisco, Northern California & Pacific Northwest

**Most Important
Restaurants in the U.S.**

BERKELEY, CA
Chez Panisse 95.2

CARMEL, CA
Marinus 95.1

HEALDSBURG, CA
Cyrus 97.3

LOS GATOS, CA
Manresa 100.0

NAPA, CA
Ubuntu 96.1

OAKLAND, CA
Commis 95.3

SAN FRANCISCO, CA
Coi 96.7
Quince 96.2

SAUSALITO, CA
Sushi Ran 95.9

ST. HELENA, CA
Meadowood,
     The Restaurant at 98.4

WOODINVILLE, WA
Herbfarm, The 95.0

YOUNTVILLE, CA
French Laundry, The 100.0

Highly Recommended

BERKELEY, CA
Chez Panisse Café . 92.2

CARMEL, CA
Aubergine 94.9

PALO ALTO, CA
Baumé 92.0

PORTLAND, OR
Castagna 93.5

RUTHERFORD, CA
Auberge de Soileil . . 93.3

SAN FRANCISCO, CA
Ame 92.2

Benu 92.3
Boulevard 92.1
Gary Danko 93.7
Kiss Sushi 92.6
La Folie 92.5
Masa's 93.2
Ritz-Carlton Dining
     Room 93.2
Swan Oyster Depot . 92.8

SEATTLE, WA
Canlis 93.4
Crush 92.0
Rover's 93.1

SUNNYVALE, CA
Sawa Sushi 93.4

Other locations with restaurants of note are indicated in gold. Please see chapters for more information.

Los Angeles, Southern California & Hawaii

🍴 **Most Important**
Restaurants in the U.S. | **Highly Recommended**

BEVERLY HILLS, CA
Spago 95.5
Urasawa 99.3

LOS ANGELES, CA
Providence 96.0

BEVERLY HILLS, CA
Cut 94.0

HONOLULU, HI
Chef Mavro 92.9
Mama's Fish House . 93.4

LOS ANGELES, CA
Angelini Osteria . . . 92.6
Il Grano 93.0
LudoBites 92.5
Mori Sushi 93.8

Osteria Mozza 93.0
Patina 94.0
Sushi Zo 93.7
Totoraku (Super
Secret Beef Place) 93.4

SAN DIEGO, CA
Sushi Ota 92.5

SANTA MONICA, CA
Mèlisse 92.0

STUDIO CITY, CA
Asanebo 93.8
Katsu-Ya 92.2
Sushi Nozawa 92.4

WEST HOLLYWOOD, CA
Lucques 92.8
Matsuhisa 94.4
Nishimura 94.7
Saam - The Chef's
Tasting Room . . . 93.7
The Bazaar 93.1

Other locations with restaurants of note are indicated in gold. Please see chapters for more information.

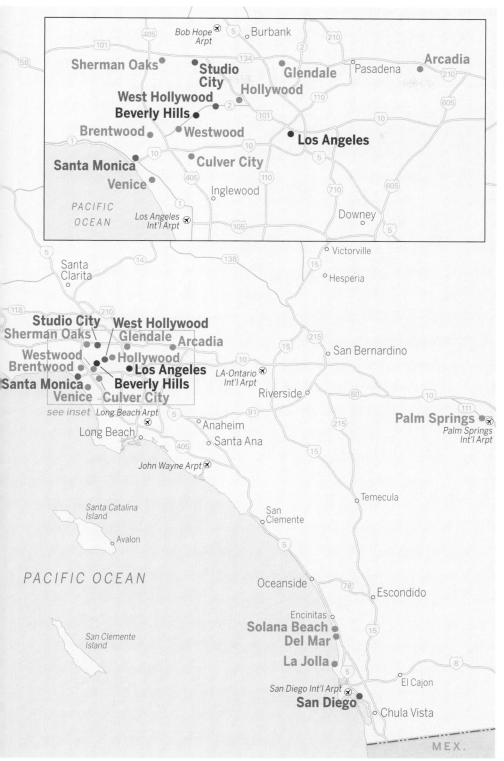

INSIDE THE GREATEST CHEFS'
KITCHENS AND OBSESSIONS

A SEASON IN THE KITCHEN
AT FERRAN ADRIÀ'S ELBULLI

THE SORCERER'S
APPRENTICES

LISA ABEND

"Abend gives an illuminating new look at the most influential chef of our time through the kaleidoscopic lens of his thirty-five stagiaires. An accomplished journalist and agile storyteller, Abend immerses herself in the heat, the anxiety, and the ingenuity of this pressurized world, bringing the characters—and the kitchen—to life."
—DAN BARBER, Executive Chef and Co-owner of Blue Hill Farm

"A unique, insider's vision... In the history of writing about restaurants, there have been few books displaying more sensitivity, insight, sympathy, and wisdom about the strange life of the modern cook."
—ADAM GOPNICK

AND AVAILABLE IN PAPERBACK:

"Riveting." —*THE WASHINGTON POST*

"[With a] nail-biting climax... fascinating glimpses of dynamic, press-friendly Boulud and perfectionist, introspective Keller."
—*NEW YORK POST*

"For all its sensuous detail . . . it's a book about the pursuit of excellence . . . a page turner that will make you think about food, and the creative process, in a different way." —*Dallas Morning News*

KNIVES AT DAWN

America's Quest for Culinary Glory at the Bocuse d'Or, the World's Most Prestigious Cooking Competition

ANDREW FRIEDMAN

Restaurant Reviews

Help Shape Opinion About the Hobby You Are Passionate About

- **Is Your Wine Cellar** overflowing with vintage bottles begging you to drink them?

- **Or Maybe** you're the type of golf nut who flies off to places like Pebble Beach or St. Andrews to play a few rounds?

- **How About Aspen and St. Moritz—** do you regularly visit the best ski resorts in order to spend dawn to dusk on your favorite slopes?

Atlanta
& the South

Athens 68 • Atlanta 68 • Birmingham 85 • Chattanooga 89 • Charleston 89 • Chilhowie 93 • Ft. Lauderdale 93 • Louisville 94 • Miami 94 • New Orleans 100 • Orlando 113 • Oxford 115 • Palm Beach & Boca Raton 115 • Raleigh-Durham 116 • Santa Rosa Beach 118 • Savannah 119 • Sea Island 120 • Tampa 120 • Walland 120

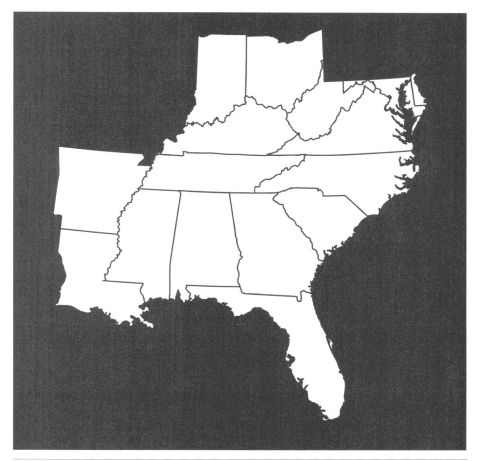

Athens GA

Five & Ten   90.0

Although Hugh Acheson was born and raised in Canada, the menu at his restaurant reads as if he's a Georgia native son. Doubters need only taste a few of Acheson's creations, like crisp veal sweetbreads with a custard of Red Mule grits and succotash or crispy catfish breaded in panko and served with a lemon emulsion, and they will be convinced faster than they can say Dixie. The vast preponderance of comments were favorable: "Chef Acheson makes imaginative use of local ingredients and puts together unexpected taste combinations," "a bit of culinary heaven stuck in the middle of a small town" and "worth the drive from Atlanta – and that says something."

Southern | Informal | Moderate | 1653 S. Lumpkin St. | 706-546-7300 | www.fiveandten.com | Dinner daily, Sun lunch

Atlanta GA

Restaurant Eugene   93.7

As President of the Board of Directors of the Southern Foodways Alliance, Linton Hopkins is naturally obsessed with the cuisine of the region. A stickler for ingredients (he was one of the founders of the local farmers' market), Hopkins creates dishes that are "a perfect representation of the New South – refined, regionally specific cuisine," like caviar harvested near Savannah, served atop buttermilk clouds, or a lightly smoked, locally raised pork belly served on a bed of Sea Island field peas. He's also a proponent of pickling – a traditional way of preserving the seasonal harvest – as revealed in a velvety soup of Vidalia onions studded with pickled onions or lamb rillettes served with mustard seeds and pickled vegetables. It's no wonder our reviewers said, "Hopkins' food shows simplicity, integrity and refinement," augmented by an "of-the-moment beverage program" and service that displays "Southern hospitality at its finest."

Southern | Casual | Expensive | BUCKHEAD | 2277 Peachtree Rd. | 404-355-0321 | www.restauranteugene.com | Dinner daily

Quinones Room at Bacchanalia   93.1

Anne Quatrano has always been a fan of the fine-dining genre (once represented in this city by the late Seeger's and JOËL Brasserie), and every Saturday night she sends the talented David A. Carson, who usually spends his time at Bacchanalia, downstairs to the Quinones Room, where he serves an eight-course tasting menu to 45 lucky diners. Using the excellent ingredients produced on Quatrano's farm, Carson crafts dishes like a terrine of foie gras served with Fuyu persimmons and spiced cocoa nibs or a duo of veal, crispy sweetbreads and braised cheek with truffled cabbage and Jerusalem artichoke. One reviewer said, "It reminds me of Chez Panisse," but there's a ramped-up ambience that's "very romantic . . . feels like your own private dining room." The result: "the best place in Atlanta to celebrate a special occasion."

New American | Casual | Expensive | MIDTOWN | 1198 Howell Mill Rd. | 404-365-0410 | www.starprovisions.com | Dinner Sat only

Bacchanalia   92.8

Located in a converted warehouse in an up-and-coming area of the city, Bacchanalia is the cornerstone of Anne Quatrano and Clifford Harrison's culinary empire, which includes four additional restaurants and a gourmet food shop. At the heart of Quatrano's cooking is the produce she raises on her farm, 30 miles north of Atlanta; it lays the foundation for her New American cuisine, which includes enough of a Southern twist to allow it to be associated with the area. It's not the flashiest cooking you'll ever experience – in fact, one reviewer called it "solid, accomplished and restrained" – but dishes like crispy veal sweetbreads with lentils, prunes and bacon and mortadella-stuffed Georgia quail served with farro risotto make this one of the best dining experiences in Atlanta.

New American | Casual | Expensive | MIDTOWN | 1198 Howell Mill Rd. | 404-365-0410 | www.starprovisions. com | Dinner Mon-Sat

RECOMMENDED

Tomo (12 miles north in Vinings)   90.8

While Atlanta has its fair share of Japanese restaurants, this nondescript storefront in Vinings is where you will find the city's top chefs eating sushi on their nights off. There are two reasons for the pilgrimage: Much of the fish that Tomohiro Naito serves is flown in from Tokyo, and Naito worked at Nobu's Las Vegas outpost before he opened this restaurant; Matsuhisa's influence can be seen in fusion dishes like Tomo Shrimp Stix (shrimp, asparagus and shiso wrapped in a spring roll skin and fried). "One of those extraordinary places" is how one reviewer described it, adding, "Thank goodness they are located in a suburban strip mall – otherwise I probably couldn't afford their excellent, fresh food."

Japanese | Informal | Expensive | VININGS | 3256 Cobb Pkwy. | 770-690-0555 | www.tomorestaurant.com | Lunch & Dinner Tue-Fri, Sat-Sun dinner only

Woodfire Grill   90.8

The comment "I love the smell that hits you as soon as you walk into this place" sums up the core appeal of Kevin Gillespie's restaurant, where nearly everything is cooked in a wood-burning oven or over a wood-burning grill. But what really sets Gillespie's efforts apart is that after "the terrifically sourced ingredients" are cooked over wood, "He plates them in a way you would expect to see in a more refined New American restaurant." Woodfire Grill has been hugely popular since Gillespie's appearance on a hit television program (some estimate business has increased tenfold), but the extra workload hasn't had a negative impact on the cooking or a "staff that is knowledgeable about the food" they are serving.

New American | Casual | Moderate | BUCKHEAD | 1782 Cheshire Bridge Rd. | 404-347-9055 | www.wood-firegrill.com | Dinner daily

Rathbun's   90.6

With a "sprawling menu" offering everything from an open-faced ravioli of chicken livers with aged balsamic to trofie pasta with baby eggplant and a basil fondue to sea scallop Benedict with country ham and grits, this is the type of upper middle restaurant that everyone loves. A few people did snipe, saying things like, "The overly large menu needs to be pared down to remove preps that were chic in 1989," but the majority agrees with those who called it, "one of the most innovative restaurants in Atlanta, with an eclectic menu and great service" served in a "hip converted-warehouse atmosphere."

New American | Casual | Expensive | INMAN PARK | 112 Krog St. | 404-524-8280 | www.rathbunsrestaurant. com | Dinner Mon-Sat

Kevin Rathbun Steak   90.1

It seems that every celebrity chef has opened a steakhouse these days. But while most efforts are less than noteworthy, this offering from Kevin Rathbun serves "the best steaks in Atlanta," offered amid "ultra-modern décor in a renovated warehouse" (a type of environment refreshingly different from the usual clubby steakhouse setting). You can begin your meal with a slew of different salads, and dishes like Maple Leaf Farms duck two ways or a grilled pork chop with cheddar cheese grits are available for the non-beef eaters in your party. One reviewer described it as "the perfect place for dinner when you want to plop down $100 for a prime-aged steak."

Steakhouse | Casual | Expensive | INMAN PARK | 154 Krog St. | 404-524-5600 | www.kevinrathbunsteak. com | Dinner Mon-Sat

Aria   90.0

Some restaurants succeed with creativity, others by offering an experience that's familiar. If you're not an adventurous diner and you happen to like places that fall into the latter category, head on over to this bustling dining room where Gerry Klaskala's menu features dishes like slow-braised pork shoulder and prime steak au poivre on a year-round basis. Given our preamble, you can imagine that opinions are split, with comments ranging from, "The décor is amazing, the servers charming, and the food fabulous" to "I have a copy of the very first menu, and it hasn't changed since the opening. Please consider more forward-thinking options."

New American | Casual | Moderate | BUCKHEAD | 490 E. Paces Ferry Rd. NE | 404-233-7673 | www.aria-atl.com | Dinner Mon-Sat

TOP LOCAL CHOICE

Chops Lobster Bar   89.5

Despite the mall location (which makes you feel you're at a chain restaurant), this steak-and-seafood specialist from the Buckhead Life Group serves what a number of reviewers claimed to be "the best steak in Atlanta." (We suspect an excellent "salt-and-pepper char crust" might have something to do with that.) The Lobster Bar has its fair share of fans, especially for the house special tempura-fried lobster tail. The "menu hasn't changed in years," nor has the "décor, which can use a bit of freshening up," but it's super-popular, so be ready to wait for a table even with a reservation.

Steakhouse | Casual | Expensive | BUCKHEAD | 70 W. Paces Ferry Rd. | 404-262-2675 | www.buckhead-restaurants.com | Dinner daily, Lunch Mon-Fri

Park 75   89.5

With a menu featuring Southern fare like Georgia white shrimp with creamy Anson Mill grits and tasso gravy, along with a full selection of steaks, this Four Seasons Hotel venue is the "perfect place for a sedate business lunch or dinner" (brunch and afternoon tea also come highly recommended). Furnishing "an excellent example of how a hotel restaurant can be elegant without being snobbish," it's also convenient after an event at the nearby Woodruff Arts Center or at Piedmont Park – not to mention being "one of the best spots in the city for celebrity spotting."

Southern/Steakhouse | Casual | Expensive | MIDTOWN | Four Seasons Hotel Atlanta | 75 14th St. | 404-253-3840 | www.fourseasons.com | Open daily except closed Sun dinner

Taka   89.5

Many reviewers say this is their favorite sushi restaurant in Atlanta – higher praise than it sounds. As one person explained, "For a landlocked town, Atlanta plays host to several sushi restaurants with exceptionally fresh fish. Taka is one, and the sushi is always a delight. The atmosphere is friendly without being overly trendy, and the sushi chefs are willing to chat and offer suggestions. Prices are reasonable for the quality and the area. The service is helpful and attentive." Another reviewer spoke of "standouts like the lobster salad, the Thai-style red snapper sashimi and the spicy scallop/ikaten rolls."

Japanese | Casual | Moderate | BUCKHEAD | 385 Pharr Rd. NE | 404-869-2802 | Lunch & Dinner Mon-Sat

Blue Ridge Grill   89.0

"Old-school steakhouse" is the best way to describe this restaurant from the same group that operates Bone's. But while the "cabin/lodge décor" pays homage to the Blue Ridge Mountains, the fare – dishes like mahi mahi in a Parmesan broth and a 22 oz. prime rib eye have little to do with Southern cuisine. There are always "lots of high rollers" enjoying a steak and the casual atmosphere, and comments like "good for corporate lunches" and "Your Mom and Dad will be proud if you take them here" signal that it attracts an older crowd.

Steakhouse | Casual | Expensive | BUCKHEAD | 1261 W. Paces Ferry Rd. | 404-233-5030 | www.blueridgegrill.com | Lunch & Dinner Sun-Fri, Sat dinner only

Floataway Café   89.0

Imagine an osteria in Italy where the cuisine focuses on regional fare. Now imagine they use ingredients grown in Georgia. That's what you will find at this "excellent neighborhood restaurant," where Anne Quatrano and Clifford Harrison's "varied menu" (now executed by Chris Martin and Matthew Adolfi) includes a salad of grilled Georgia peaches, Italian goat cheese and Marcona almonds, as well as local quail marinated in cherries before grilling. Located on the other side of town from most of the city's top restaurants, the dining room is full of Decatur families and professors from nearby Emory University enjoying "a deliciously casual night out."

Italian | Casual | Moderate | DECATUR | 1123 Zonolite Rd. | 404-892-1414 | www.starprovisions.com | Dinner Tue-Sat

Nikolai's Roof   89.0

Before the proliferation of luxury chains like the Ritz-Carlton and Four Seasons, the Hilton was one of the swankiest hotels in Atlanta. Part of its appeal was this restaurant, whose exotic combination of French and Russian cuisine was a sure bet to wow local palates. But the definition of fine dining has changed over the past three decades, and

"Nikolai's has lost the allure and sense of occasion it used to possess." But if fond memories count for anything, a slew of reviewers recounted celebrating everything from birthdays to marriage proposals here, with some still recommending it for those types of special occasions.

French | Formal | Expensive | DOWNTOWN | Hilton Atlanta | 255 Courtland St. NE | 404-221-6362 | www.nikolaisroof.com | Dinner Tue-Sat

Sotto Sotto   89.0

With 16 pasta dishes and mains like an oak-grilled veal chop served atop wild mush-rooms, this is where the vast majority of our Atlanta-based Italianistas like to get their culinary fix. "Inventive, well-prepared Italian in a cozy spot," "If you don't like risotto, it's because you haven't had it here" and "divine food and a chic New York–like atmo-sphere" are but some of the raves we collected. "A tremendous all-Italian wine list" and an "enthusiastic wait staff" round out the comments. Detractors say, "It's good but it's still Italian. Enough said."

Italian | Casual | Moderate | VIRGINIA HIGHLANDS | 313 N. Highland Ave. | 404-523-6678 | www.sottosottorestaurant.com | Dinner daily

4th & Swift   88.5

Though he's a Maryland native who cut his teeth working in Boston for Lydia Shire, Jay Swift offers a contemporary take on traditional Southern comfort food, like a carpaccio of local beets paired with chèvre from Sweetgrass Dairy and tangerine oil or a hazelnut-crusted Blue Ridge trout with a sweet-pea ragout and citrus-mint butter. "Everyone and his mother does farm-to-table, but 4th and Swift does it really well" is how one reviewer characterized Swift's cooking, while another described the place as "hip and busy, [with] an ever-changing menu that makes it conducive for return visits."

Southern | Informal | Moderate | OLD FOURTH WARD | 621 North Avenue NE | 678-904-0160 | http://4thandswift.com | Dinner daily

Abattoir   88.5

Take Fergus Henderson's offal-oriented St. John restaurant in London and combine it with the type of meat-intensive gastropub that is popping up all over the U.S. Tone it down a bit so that the food appeals to the more conservative Atlanta palate, and you've got this lively restaurant. Josh Hopkins offers up pickled Georgia ruby red shrimp and a charcuterie platter featuring ten different types of sausages, along with meaty fare like Berkshire pork belly served with a farm egg and BBQ brisket that is slow-braised in house. "A large and lively room" and "food and wine prices that are extremely reason-able" make this one of the Bacchanalia Group's most popular restaurants.

Gastropub | Informal | Moderate | MIDTOWN | 1170 Howell Mill Rd. | 404-892-3335 | www.starprovisions.com | Dinner Tue-Sat

Cakes and Ale   88.5

After spending two years at the Watershed Café, Billy Allin opened this restaurant that mixes Mediterranean and Southern fare, like a starter of arancini with citrus and fennel pollen, or quail served with eggplant, peppers, onion, soft polenta, figs and aged bal-samic. Comments were effusive: "my favorite restaurant in Atlanta," "worth the effort to snag a reservation," "We cannot recommend this place to enough people" and our favorite: "Local local local! Produce produce produce! This place stays out of the way of its ingredients like an air traffic controller landing creative food onto your palate."

Gastropub | Informal | Moderate | DECATUR | 254 W. Ponce de Leon Ave. | 404-377-7994 | www.cakesandalerestaurant.com | Dinner Tue-Sat

Canoe   88.5

Given that her family has been in Atlanta for seven generations, it's fitting that Carvel Grant Gould's menu reflects her local roots. "Think upscale country food": fried green tomatoes with smoked ham, local egg and chipotle celery root salad or slow-roasted Carolina rabbit with Swiss chard and sweet potato hash. Served by a "knowledgeable staff" in a "lovely setting" along the banks of the Chattahoochee River that is "worthy of a spread in *Southern Living* magazine," it's one of the few places in Atlanta where you can get a quality meal for lunch.

Southern | Casual | Moderate | VININGS | 4199 Paces Ferry Rd. NW | 770-432-2663 | www.canoeatl.com | Lunch & Dinner Sun-Fri, Sat dinner only

Holeman & Finch   88.5

Linton Hopkins continues his quest to create perfect Southern cuisine at this gastropub located next to Restaurant Eugene. There's a strong emphasis on a "terrific list of artisanal beers" and the "unique cocktails" that are served up by expert mixologist Greg Best, which diners can pair with small plates like locally raised pork belly with Anson Mill grits and chow chow or hand-cut pasta topped with pancetta and a farm egg. At 10:00 p.m. each evening, 24 lucky diners get to enjoy what is considered Atlanta's best hamburger, so carnivores are advised to "get there early so you can order a burger before they run out."

Gastropub | Informal | Moderate | BUCKHEAD | 2277 Peachtree Rd. | 404-948-1175 | www.holeman-finch.com | Lunch & Dinner daily

JCT Kitchen   88.5

"My favorite moderately priced restaurant in Atlanta" is how one reviewer described Ford Fry's place, which offers "modern interpretations of Southern classics," including dishes like Georgia white shrimp toast; Vidalia onion and potato soup; and Georgia rainbow trout wrapped in Benton's bacon and served with creamed corn and succotash. Also popular are the Sunday Night Suppers (you can order one fancy meat and three family-style sides). The only negative we could find was, "The crowd can be daunting and the dining room noisy."

Southern | Informal | Moderate | WESTSIDE | 1198 Howell Mill Rd. | 404-355-2252 | www.jctkitchen.com | Lunch & Dinner Mon-Sat, Sun dinner only

La Grotta   88.5

Since 1978 La Grotta has been the "special-occasion Italian restaurant of choice" for many of our Atlanta-based reviewers. It is well known that Chef Antonio Abizanda bends over backwards to make his customers happy, and if you can't find what you're looking for on the regular menu, he will be "happy to cook anything you want," provided the ingredients are in house. A "'70s nostalgic" atmosphere permeates a dining room that is filled with people who still dress up for dinner, which includes "lots of older men with plugs and their fifty-something wives enjoying their filet of beef topped with Gorgonzola sauce."

Italian | Casual | Expensive | BUCKHEAD | 2637 Peachtree Rd. | 404-231-1368 | www.lagrottaatlanta.com | Dinner Mon-Sat

Antica Posta   88.0

With a menu filled with classic dishes like fagioli Toscana, spaghetti ala pomodoro and lamb chops "scottadito", the Betti family provides what local diners say is "the most authentic Tuscan dining experience in Atlanta." The tasty food is complemented by "an excellent wine list offered at reasonable prices" and an atmosphere described as "rustic yet comfy." The owners are well known for going out of their way to please customers, and numerous reviewers say, "This is where you can find the best pizza in Atlanta."

Italian | Casual | Moderate | BUCKHEAD | 519 E. Paces Ferry Rd. | 404-262-7112 | www.anticaposta.com | Dinner daily

Bocado   88.0

While the owners describe their food as "a holistic approach to farm-to-table cuisine," dishes like poached farm egg with creamed chanterelles, pork schnitzel jus and chicken livers or pan-roasted chicken breast with local grits, collard greens and a white wine–Tabasco sauce make it fair to describe this lively restaurant as "a gastropub with a Southern flair." In addition to the "concise, well-executed menu" and "wonderful servers," there's a "reasonably priced wine and cocktail list" and a "crave-worthy" burger.

Southern | Informal | Moderate | WESTSIDE | 887 Howell Mill Rd. | 404-815-1399 | www.bocadoatlanta.com | Lunch & Dinner Mon-Fri, Sat dinner only

Hashiguchi   88.0

This middle-of-the-road sushi specialist located in Buckhead offers fish that is "fresh and satisfying" amid décor that is "understated and soothing." They also offer a broad menu of cooked food ranging from ramen to tempura, making it easy for those in your party who are fish-shy to find something to eat. Even the critical conceded that, "while not the best Japanese restaurant in the Atlanta area, Hashiguchi is worth a visit if you are looking for sushi and happen to be nearby."

Japanese | Informal | Moderate | BUCKHEAD | 3000 Windy Hill Rd. SE | 770-955-2337 | Lunch & Dinner Mon-Fri, Sat dinner only

McKendrick's Steak House (15 miles north in Dunwoody)   88.0

While dining customs in Atlanta have gotten more casual over the years, the informality hasn't yet reached this restaurant where "jacketed waiters dressed in black tie" are serving "huge slabs of beef." The "men's club feel" is not to everyone's taste, but "reasonably priced steaks" and "a well-stocked wine list" mean it's popular with the "I'll have some onion rings and creamed spinach with my steak" crowd, as well as local businessmen who like to throw down a few cocktails while discussing a business deal.

Steakhouse | Casual | Expensive | DUNWOODY | 4505 Ashford Dunwoody Rd. | 770-512-8888 | www.mckendricks.com | Dinner daily, Lunch Mon-Fri

MF Buckhead   88.0

With a sushi bar turning out exotic rolls, a robata grill serving Colorado lamb chops and an omakase room offering unusual creations like a hot pot with cod milt, the Kinjo brothers have every aspect of Japanese cuisine covered. MF is particularly popular with diners who enjoy large, party-style Asian restaurants and who offer comments like "deftly and precisely executed food," "top-notch sake list" and "a beautiful space." However, critics deride it for being "painfully trendy and filled with those wanting to see and be seen," while advising, "Look elsewhere if you're serious about sushi."

Japanese | Casual | Expensive | BUCKHEAD | 3280 Peachtree Rd., Suite 110 | 404-841-1192 | www.mfbuckhead.com | Dinner daily, Lunch Mon-Fri

Nam   88.0

This "upscale Vietnamese" from the Kinjo brothers (of MF Buckhead fame) benefits from the fact that Atlanta's traditional Vietnamese restaurants are located in Chamblee. Notwithstanding the convenience factor, comments include those we have come to expect about any upscale Asian eatery, ranging from "The cabbage soup and shaking beef and seafood spring rolls are among my favorite dishes" to "While an excellent option for those seeking a more luxurious and convenient alternative, head on out to the Buford Highway if you want real Vietnamese food."

Vietnamese | Casual | Expensive | MIDTOWN | 931 Monroe Dr. | 404-541-9997 | www.namrestaurant.com | Lunch & Dinner Tue-Fri, Mon, Sat dinner only

Nan Thai Fine Dining   88.0

If you're not in the mood to drive to the area the locals call Chambodia (a five-mile strip of ethnic restaurants just outside the city) or are looking to wear a nice pair of slacks to a Thai restaurant, visit this "stunning dining room" with "very authentic food and service." Though it's "not the most inventive cuisine," you will "feel like you're dining in an elegant hotel restaurant in Bangkok." Of course, the traditionalistas weighed in with their usual comment: "While the Thai food was delicious, you can get the same delicious food at more authentic places at cheaper prices."

Thai | Casual | Moderate | MIDTOWN | 1350 Spring St. NW | 404-870-9933 | www.nanfinedining.com | Dinner daily, Lunch Mon-Fri

Pacci Ristorante   88.0

From its perch on the top floor of the Hotel Palomar, Keira Moritz's Pacci offers a menu that features modern Italian dishes, like duck confit with polenta and blueberry marmalade and a pork chop served with fennel, roasted yam and a pomegranate-basil pesto. "Hip and new" while catering to a younger crowd, "it's a good place to show off your Rolex or your new Jimmy Choos." Another reviewer opined on the location, saying, "Hotel restaurants can be hit or miss, but Pacci is definitely a hit." AltoRex, the adjacent rooftop bar, is a lovely spot for a drink either before or after dinner.

Italian | Casual | Moderate | MIDTOWN | Hotel Palomar Atlanta | 866 W. Peachtree St. NW | 678-412-2402 | www.paccirestaurant.com | Open daily

Ritz-Carlton Atlanta Grill   88.0

It might be hotel food, but given the paucity of quality places to eat in downtown

Atlanta, this sedate room in the Ritz-Carlton fills a need for the local business community and visitors to the CNN Center. The menu combines what we will describe as "standard upscale hotel fare," like oxtail ravioli with black truffle butter, with a list of steaks and chops from the grill, as well as a Southern Selections category that includes offerings ranging from shrimp and grits to smoked chicken and baby back ribs.

American/Southern | Casual | Expensive | DOWNTOWN | 181 Peachtree St. NE | 404-659-0400 | www.ritzcarlton.com | Open daily

ACCEPTABLE

Agave   87.5

The consensus is this popular restaurant has served "the best Southwestern food in Atlanta" for close to ten years. Besides a list of favorites like blue corn chicken enchiladas and a chile-rubbed pork chop, the "affordable, consistent and creative" menu includes a few unusual preparations like a veal, chorizo and green chile meatloaf. An "excellent selection of tequilas" and a "lovely patio" make the experience all the more enjoyable.

Southwestern | Informal | Moderate | CABBAGETOWN | 242 Boulevard SE | 404-588-0006 | www.agaverestaurant.com | Dinner daily

Babette's Café   87.5

With dishes like a warm salad of roasted cauliflower with bacon, arugula and Gruyère and grilled beef tenderloin with Gorgonzola sauce and spicy onion rings, Marla Adams' menu reads like a culinary travelogue of the type of New American cooking that restaurants featured in the '90s. One reviewer recommended it as a place to take your in-laws, saying, "Mine loved it, and they are the pickiest of eaters." Another praised it for their attempts at recreating the meal from the *Babette's Feast*, calling such occasions "a must go."

New American | Informal | Moderate | PONCEYHIGHLAND | 573 N. Highland Ave. | 404-523-9121 | www.babettescafe.com | Dinner Tue-Sun, Sun lunch

French American   87.5
Brasserie

This reincarnation of the popular Brass-

erie Le Coze is one of the few quality restaurants located downtown. All the expected brasserie fare is here, along with a full selection of steaks, any of which, in what must be an attempt to promote Franco-American relations, can be topped with a slab of sautéed foie gras. Much of the décor was transported from the original Lenox Square location, and its authentic look caused one reviewer to tell us, "We recently moved back to the States from Paris, and this restaurant makes us feel like we are Parisians again."

French | Casual | Expensive | DOWNTOWN | 30 Ivan Allen Jr. Blvd. | 404-266-1440 | www.fabatlanta.com | Lunch & Dinner Mon-Sat

Georgia Grille   87.5

Karen Hilliard's restaurant draws its inspiration from the painter Georgia O'Keefe. Hilliard's menu includes a few dishes considered local favorites, like fried catfish, flatiron steak with poblano peppers and her award-winning lobster enchiladas (50% of our reviewers mentioned the enchiladas). It's "casual and fun," one reviewer suggested, but you need to call ahead as the small dining room is "full of suits who have dropped in for a margarita after work," making it "difficult to get a table."

Southwestern | Informal | Moderate | BUCKHEAD | 2290 Peachtree Rd. NE | 404-352-3517 | www.georgiagrille.com | Dinner daily

Haven   87.5

While Atlanta has a number of restaurants that draw people from across the city, there aren't many quality neighborhood places. Haven tries to fill that void, and the "clever" Southern menu, which includes dishes like a Low Country shrimp boil with corn, potatoes and andouille sausage or duck with red cabbage and brandied cherries, has reviewers calling chef Stephen Herman "a rising star." Others decry the fact that it's "unfairly overlooked in favor of the city's big guns" and say "the excellent food and service make it worth the drive, even if you don't live nearby."

Southern | Informal | Moderate | BROOKHAVEN | 1441 Dresden Dr. | 404-969-0700 | www.havenrestaurant.com | Dinner Tue-Sun, Sun brunch

Kyma   87.5

The Buckhead Life Group found yet another way to utilize the fresh seafood they source each day by opening this modern Greek restaurant, where elaborate mezze and salads are followed by all sorts of whole fish and crustaceans grilled over wood. Like the group's other properties, it offers a "wonderful atmosphere" with "delicious cocktails" and "good people watching," and one other plus: It's run by the son of the chef who ran Atlanta's legendary Pano's & Paul for many years. "Great Greek food without having to leave Atlanta" is how one reviewer described it.

Greek | Casual | Moderate | BUCKHEAD | 3085 Piedmont Rd. | 404-262-0702 | www.buckheadrestaurants.com | Dinner daily

Nuevo Laredo Cantina   87.5

A local magazine has named this simple roadhouse-style restaurant near the Georgia Tech campus the top Mexican restaurant in Atlanta for close to 20 years running. The menu is a bit more extensive than its compadres', including items like lobster tacos and the house specialty, Mexican brisket served with mashed potatoes and pico de gallo. Comments are mostly positive: "The wait staff is amazing and fast, and the food is

always wonderful" and "This is a destination spot." But beware: "It's small and crowded, and that means long lines most of the day."

Mexican | Informal | Moderate | MIDTOWN | 1495 Chattahoochee Ave. NW | 404-352-9009 | www.nuevolaredocantina.com | Lunch & Dinner Mon-Sat

Serpas True Food   87.5

What do you get when you take a chef who is born in rural Louisiana and move him to cosmopolitan Atlanta? You get "contemporary American cuisine with both a Southern and N'Awlins flair," and a menu on which dishes like trout stuffed with crab and mushrooms peacefully co-exist with a fried green tomato and crab salad stack. The large open dining room means "the noise level can be a bit overwhelming," but that won't matter after you order one or two of the "unusual cocktails" they've invented.

New American | Informal | Moderate | OLD FOURTH WARD | 659 Auburn Ave. | 404-688-0040 | www.serpasrestaurant.com | Dinner Tue-Sun,

Stoney River   87.5
Legendary Steaks

Their motto, "Comfort food in a sports jacket," signals that this restaurant, with branches as far away as Annapolis and St. Louis, is trying to appeal to an older crowd. Reviewers say, "The steaks compare to some of Atlanta's better steak restaurants, and you don't have to spend the same number of dollars"; the result is "an enjoyable meal despite the chain-restaurant atmosphere." P.S. Stoney River is a fictitious waterway.

Steakhouse | Casual | Moderate | COBB | 1640 Cumberland Mall | 678-305-9229 | www.stoneyriver.com | Lunch & Dinner daily

Tamarind Seed Bistro   87.5

"Fresh, spicy, relaxed and friendly" is how one reviewer described Nan's little sibling. A more enthusiastic admirer called it "truly the best Thai restaurant I have ever eaten in on the East Coast from NYC down to Miami," adding, "I lived in NYC for a time and I would compare every single Thai meal I had there with the ones I have had at Tamarind." One person spoke of "surprisingly high prices," but added "for correspondingly good food." The location makes it convenient for a pre-theater dinner or after a visit to one of the museums in the area.

Thai | Informal | Moderate | MIDTOWN | 1197 Peachtree St. NE | 404-873-4888 | www.tamarind-seed.com | Lunch & Dinner Sun-Fri, Sat dinner only

Watershed   87.5

Though Joe Truex has replaced Scott Peacock as chef, the kitchen at this restaurant owned by the Indigo Girls' Emily Saliers is still offering many of the same dishes that brought Watershed national attention, like creamy stone-ground shrimp grits with Pullman plank and a fried catfish platter with French fries and hush puppies. Given its focus on quality ingredients, execution and respect for tradition rather than reinvention, "it's a rarity among midrange Southern restaurants." The fried chicken, served on Tuesday nights until they run out, "is deserving of a special mention."

Southern | Informal | Moderate | DECATUR | 406 W. Ponce de Leon Ave. | 404-378-4900 | www.watershedrestaurant.com | Lunch & Dinner Mon-Sat, Sun brunch

Wisteria   87.5

One of the best neighborhood restaurants in Atlanta. Jason Hills' whimsical take on Southern comfort cuisine revolves around dishes like black-eyed peas hummus with homemade sweet potato chips, pimento cheese deviled eggs with pickled okra and spiced pecans and Southern-fried Tennessee catfish with green tomatoes and a spicy crawfish ragout. Other reasons to visit are the "good wine selections" and an "amazing

hamburger," which, when you combine them with a "comfortable atmosphere" and a "cozy environment," result in a "casual restaurant where the chef lets the food do the talking."

Southern | Informal | Moderate | INMAN PARK | 471 N. Highland Ave. | 404-525-3363 | www.wisteria-atlanta.com | Dinner daily

Bone's   87.0

With a décor reminiscent of the Palm restaurant in New York City, this classic Buckhead steakhouse has been catering to a business and moneyed crowd since 1979. Unfortunately, the great atmosphere can't overcome meat that "didn't seem like it was aged sufficiently" (though it claims to be) and a cooking method that results in "steaks lacking a char crust." However, a "great wine list," "cool environment" and "maybe the best service in Atlanta" argue in its favor.

Steakhouse | Casual | Expensive | BUCKHEAD | 3130 Piedmont Rd. NE | 404-237-2663 | www.bonesrestaurant.com | Lunch Mon-Fri, dinner daily

Hal's on Old Ivy   87.0

Proclamations that a restaurant serves Continental cuisine are rare in this day and age. But here is one place that does so and is proud of it – even if they do hedge their bets a bit by calling it "Creole Continental." The unusual combination results in a menu that mixes dishes like trout meunière, a 22 oz. bone-in rib eye and veal piccata. "People do love this place," said one reviewer, who added, however, "The beef's very good. Everything else, unless you like cigar smoke, is not worth the trouble."

Continental | Casual | Expensive | BUCKHEAD | 30 Old Ivy Rd. | 404-261-0025 | www.hals.net | Dinner Mon-Sat

Eurasia Bistro   86.5

In a city large enough to have at least one of every type of restaurant, Eurasia flies the fusion banner for the Atlanta area. The menu is full of dishes that sounded interesting 20 years ago – think rice-battered calamari with a jalapeño/cilantro salsa and spicy barbecue skate wing with marinated cucumbers – but that are standard fare in today's dining scene. The "warm brick walls are welcoming," and the "cozy ambience is an excellent accompaniment to the food."

Asian Fusion | Informal | Moderate | DECATUR | 129 E. Ponce De Leon Ave. | 404-687-8822 | www. northlakethai.com | Lunch Mon-Fri, dinner Mon-Sat

Nava 86.5

Smack-dab in the middle of the Acceptable range seems to be par for the course for a Buckhead Life Group restaurant. This Southwestern offering is no different, even though it has its share of fans who say things about it like "great food, great ambience, very romantic." But most reviewers counter with, "It's a tired concept" and "The food isn't close to being as good as when Kevin Rathbun was in charge of the kitchen."

Southwestern | Casual | Moderate | BUCKHEAD | 3060 Peachtree Rd. NW | 404-240-1984 | www. buckheadrestaurants.com | Dinner daily, Lunch Mon-Fri

Ritz Carlton 86.5
Buckhead Café

Mains are limited to grilled meats and seafood at this newly minted steakhouse, but there are a few contemporary touches offered as starters, like lobster flatbread with buffalo mozzarella, tomato fondue, arugula and tarragon pesto. It's popular with "people who want to enjoy the formality and ambience of the Ritz" at a lower price point than the more formal Dining Room's. Early birds find it "a good choice if you enjoy having breakfast in fancy surroundings."

New American | Casual | Expensive | BUCKHEAD | 3434 Peachtree Rd. NE | 404-237-2700 | www. ritzcarlton.com | Open daily

Alfredo's 86.0

"Outdated but charming" is one how reviewer described this old-school Italian restaurant, with another saying it's "what you imagine a restaurant owned by the Mafia looks like" (i.e., dark and clubby). It's "perfect when you need a fix of red sauce" as the menu is loaded with "gut-busting" southern Italian dishes like zuppa di clams, a rich lasagna al forno and nine preparations of veal. Don't be surprised if you have to wait for a table.

Italian | Casual | Moderate | CHESHIRE BRIDGE | 1989 Cheshire Bridge Rd. | 404-876-1380 | www. alfredositalianrestaurant.com | Dinner daily

Mosaic 86.0

One has to wonder when the banner on a restaurant's website advertises "the largest pet-friendly patio in Atlanta" rather than talk about their food. A glance at the menu offers insight into this marketing strategy: Dishes like smoked salmon/goat cheese bruschetta and grilled chicken with spinach pasta are not going to make anyone take special notice. One reviewer suggested people "visit for lunch when the same food as dinner is offered at more reasonable prices."

New American | Informal | Moderate | BUCKHEAD | 3097 Maple Dr. | 404-846-5722 | www.mosaicatl. com | Lunch & Dinner daily

Paces 88 86.0

Hotel food is always difficult to recommend and the cuisine at Paces 88 holds true to form. The menu is the standard amalgamation of dishes that won't offend anyone's palate, like smoked salmon flatbread with crème fraîche and chives, and grilled beef tenderloin with potato gratin and Béarnaise sauce. An "open and airy dining room, with creamy cool walls and dark wooden accents" makes it "a pleasant spot for breakfast, lunch and dinner."

New American | Casual | Expensive | BUCKHEAD | St. Regis Hotel | 88 W. Paces Ferry Rd. | 404-563-7910 | www.paces88.com | Open daily

Pricci   86.0

With comments like "good, but not quite worth the price" and "The entrées have a tendency to be overwrought," this entry from the Buckhead Life Group is not as well regarded as some of the other Italian restaurants in Atlanta. Those with a favorable view say, "Since Chef Piero Premoli arrived three years ago, he has lifted Pricci to new heights" and "There is some wonderful Italian cooking going on here these days," evidenced in the dish they call Crazy Lasagna, an amalgamation of veal Bolognese, béchamel and wild mushrooms, or more luxurious offerings like ravioli filled with Kobe beef.

Italian | Casual | Expensive | BUCKHEAD | 500 Pharr Rd. | 404-237-2941 | www.buckheadrestaurants.com | Lunch Mon-Fri, dinner daily

Prime   86.0

Located in the Lennox Square Mall, this restaurant operated by the Serve Group is yet one more Atlanta restaurant that complements a full steakhouse menu with a full sushi bar. While it's not the most highly recommended restaurant of its genre, one reviewer told us, "If you're in the Buckhead area and completely out of dining options you won't be disappointed if you book here." Athough most of our readers aren't the types who make use of Early Bird Specials, that didn't stop them from taking advantage of a 12 oz. strip for the bargain price of $15.50 served between 5:00 p.m.–6:30 p.m.

Steakhouse | Casual | Expensive | BUCKHEAD | 3393 Peachtree Rd. NE | 404-812-0555 | www.heretoserverestaurants.com | Lunch & Dinner daily

Vinings Inn   86.0

(12 miles north in Vinings)

Situated in a white clapboard house located near the Perimeter Road, the Vinings Inn is filled with families enjoying local, regional and international specialties ranging from grilled fish tacos, peach BBQ shrimp and grilled lamb chops

with a red-wine reduction and orzo. "An old-fashioned white-cloth restaurant in a charming old Vinings location" is the way people who enjoy the place describe it, while the less-enthused call the food "mostly decent, but unexceptional."

Eclectic | Casual | Moderate | VININGS | 3011 Paces Mill Rd. | 770-438-2282 | www.viningsinn.com | Lunch & Dinner Mon-Sat

Atmosphere   85.5

When the second-highest-rated French restaurant in a city gets this sort of score, we think it is fair to surmise that the natives haven't really cottoned to French cuisine. Still, our local reviewers say that when they have an urge for a bowl of moules frites or confit de canard, they happily utter, "C'est magnifique" about what is their go-to spot. The location, a "cute bungalow" that's been refurbished into a series of small dining rooms, offers an intimate dining experience.

French | Informal | Moderate | MIDTOWN | 1620 Piedmont Ave. | 678-702-1620 | www.atmospherebistro.com | Lunch & Dinner Tue-Sun

BluePointe   85.5

The focus here, at one of 11 Atlanta restaurants operated by the Buckhead Life Group, is on American seafood with an Asian influence, which includes offering guests a sushi bar. Comments about the food were surprisingly positive considering the rating, ranging from "consistently good and always the freshest fish" to "a great bar scene filled with beautiful people." Even critics managed to end on a positive note: "The tired space seems like a relic from the '80s. That said, the food is well executed and delicious."

Asian | Casual | Moderate | BUCKHEAD | 3455 Peachtree Rd. | 404-237-9070 | www.buckheadrestaurants.com | Dinner daily

ONE. midtown kitchen   85.5

To show you how far the club/restaurant

concept has come, Drew VanLeuven's hot spot features a half-dozen house-cured meats and six house-made pastas. But reviewers think it takes more than a list of artisanal cheeses to overcome an unfortunate environment: "Loud doesn't even begin to describe the noise level." One reviewer summed it up as "great if you like a nightclub-style restaurant; not so hot if your focus is on the food."

New American | Casual | Moderate | MIDTOWN | 559 Dutch Valley Rd. | 404-892-4111 | www.onemidtownkitchen.com | Dinner daily

Veni Vidi Vici   85.5

This is yet one more entry from the Buckhead Life Group, this time with the theme being a northern Italian rosticceria. There are 14 different pastas on offer, and the list of meats roasting on the spit includes Ashley Farms chicken, Maple Leaf Farm duck, Elysian Farm lamb and the house special, suckling pig. The comments run the gamut from "I've been eating here since elementary school" and "a good variety of meats, pastas and wine" to "How this place remains in business after all these years is a mystery."

Italian | Casual | Moderate | MIDTOWN | 41 14th St. | 404-875-8424 | www.buckheadrestaurants.com | Dinner daily, Lunch Mon-Fri

New York Prime   85.0

Given how easy it is to serve steaks that are on par with what the competition serves, it always surprises us to read comments like "probably my least favorite steakhouse in the city." New York Prime is run by the CentraArchy Group, which operates outposts in Boca Raton and Myrtle Beach. A number of reviewers mentioned the lobster service in a small red cart saying, "Seeing a single lobster fill up an entire red Radio Flyer wagon is an experience to remember!"

Steakhouse | Casual | Expensive | BUCKHEAD | 3424 Peachtree Rd. NE | 404-846-0644 | www.centraarchy.com | Dinner daily

Oscar's Villa Capri   85.0

While its name suggests Neapolitan cuisine, the restaurant's website pictures gondolas outside the Doge's Palace in Venice. Geographical confusion aside, Villa Capri offers "enormous shareable portions of a wide selection of dishes," ranging from classics like linguine with clam sauce to new creations such as veal and shrimp in a raspberry chipotle sauce served over cappellini. One reviewer sang the praises of the grouper Ana Capri, calling it "worth the entire visit."

Italian | Informal | Moderate | DUNWOODY | 2090 Dunwoody Club Dr. | 770-392-7940 | http://oscarsvillacapri.com | Dinner daily

Paul's   85.0

Fans of Paul Albrecht's cooking at Pano's & Paul's have followed him to this upscale restaurant in the Peachtree Hills, where the mishmash of food on offer ranges from sushi to fried green tomatoes to surf 'n' turf. Given the chef's background, we're not surprised to read comments like "boring food, anchored in the early 1990s," "mostly caters to old-time Atlantans who are loyal customers" and "popular with the let's stop in for a cocktail after work crowd."

Eclectic | Casual | Expensive | BUCKHEAD | 10 Kings Cir. | 404-231-4113 | www.thechefpaul.com | Lunch & Dinner Sun-Fri, Sat dinner only

OTHER RESTAURANTS MENTIONED

Hil, The (33 miles south in Serenbe) 84.5

A working arrangement between chef Hilary White and Farmer Paige (of the nearby Serenbe Organic Farm) means that ingredients like arugula, shallots, okra and braising greens end up as toppings on pizza or paired with ingredients like New York strip steak at this suburban spot with a lovely hilltop location. Some reviewers praised the "great seasonal food," but others felt "it lacked a bit of oomph. It's great having top-quality ingredients, but a chef has to do something special with them."

New American | Informal | Moderate | SERENBE | 9110 Selborne Lane | 770-463-6040 | www.the-hil. com | Dinner Tue-Sun, Fri-Sat lunch

Chopstix   84.0

Upscale Chinese food is a tough enough sell in a city like New York or Los Angeles, and it was hard to find an example in Atlanta that our reviewers could recommend. In that regard Chopstix lived up to expectations, with comments including the typical split of opinions regarding upscale ethnic food, including everything from "Have been going there for the wonderful Chinese food since I moved here 23 years ago" to "While it's a step above, it tastes just like takeout to me."

Chinese | Casual | Expensive | BUCKHEAD | 4279 Roswell Rd. | 404-255-4868 | www.chopstixatlanta. net | Dinner daily, Lunch Mon-Fri

Atlanta Fish Market   83.5

Though this Buckhead Life Group offering starts out with "some of the freshest fish in the city," a "lackluster kitchen" turns those fruits of the sea into run-of-the-mill restaurant food. "Loud and noisy," it has fans who applaud "the great vibe" while saying it's "one of the best places in the city to take out-of-town guests." But critics call it merely "a step above the nationally known seafood chains" and say "they should be able to do better considering the quality of the ingredients."

Seafood | Informal | Moderate | BUCKHEAD | 265 Pharr Rd. NE | 404-262-3165 | www.buckhead-restaurants.com | Lunch & Dinner daily

Cheap Eats

UNIQUELY DELICIOUS

Provisions to Go   9.0

Anne Quatrano and Clifford Harrison's

gourmet shop is sort of like Disneyland for foodies. Much of what they sell is made in-house: Besides the baked goods, various offerings of charcuterie (including a house-made frankfurter that reviewers swear by), and all of the cooked dishes, a portion of the organic produce on offer comes from the farm they live on. While comments like "I could spend all day here" and "the quality of the cheese shop alone is worth a visit" seem like reason enough to schedule a trip there, the comment that really caught our eye was this one: "Takeout seems like a ridiculous descriptor as you will both leave with, as well as eat at the counter, some amazing food!"

Bakery | Moderate | WESTSIDE | 1198 Howell Mill Rd. NW | 404-365-0410 ext. 134 | www.starprovisions.com | Open Mon-Sat

Alon's   8.4

"The best baguette in Atlanta" can be found at this venue that rivals Star Provisions for honors of top bakery/market in Atlanta. The "fresh and tasty fare" includes sandwiches like spicy Tunisian tuna salad and the "amazing garlic-roasted lamb," along with home-made soups and pre-made entrées like crab cakes and grilled salmon with basil oil. There's a nice selection of cheeses and "divine chocolates," and they even offer a concise selection of wine. Popular as a place to meet for lunch as well as for takeout, they have such a large following that the owners opened a second, larger location in Dunwoody.

Bakery | Inexpensive | VIRGINIA HIGHLANDS | 1394 N. Highland Ave | 404-872-6000 | www.alons.com | Lunch & Dinner, closed dinner Sun

Flip Burger Boutique   8.2

"Fine dining between two buns" is how Richard Blais (who in 2011 was the winner of Top Chef: All-Stars) describes his restaurant, and with comments like "fun, imaginative, flavorful and creative," it appears that reviewers agree. Burgers on offer include the Southern (country fried beef, pimento cheese, pickles and green tomato ketchup), the Philly (caramelized onions, green peppers and American cheese foam) and, for the high rollers, the A5 (A5-grade imported Japanese Kobe beef, foie gras torchon, truffle flavor, melted onions and red wine cheese foam). The non-beef burgers include turkey, spicy chicken and the aptly named chickpea-based faux-lafel. The best way to wash down your burger is with one of the "amazing milkshakes."

Hamburgers | Moderate | WESTSIDE | 1587 Howell Mill Rd NW | 404-343-1609 |www.flipburgerboutique.com | Lunch & Dinner daily

RECOMMENDED

Fat Matt's Rib Shack 7.8

Atlanta's most popular ribs spot generates a bit of controversy among our reviewers: Some deem it "a transcendent Southern barbecue experience," while others grouse, "Ribs that are boiled, not smoked, means if you are looking for good ribs, don't head here." It's a fun place, and the live blues music playing throughout the day adds to the funkiness of the experience. But as one reviewer told us, "It might do in a pinch, but there are better options."

Barbecue | MIDTOWN | 1811 Piedmont Ave. NE | 404-607-1622 | www.fatmattsribshack.com | Lunch & Dinner daily

Vortex Bar & Grill 7.7

This restaurant's website advertises "Cold Beer, Kick-Ass Burgers and Bad Habits," while featuring an extensive list of burgers that includes the Blue 'Shroom, the Black & Blue, the Big Blue Buffalo Burger and the Elvis – topped with peanut butter, bacon and fried bananas (do they really expect us to believe that Elvis ate his burgers that way?). As for the ambience, the only thing that rivals the list of burgers is the number of tattoos and piercings on your waiter's arms. As one reviewer put it, "Just leave the kids at home and go out for some adult fun."

Pub Food | Inexpensive | MIDTOWN | 878 Peachtree St. | 404-875-1667 | www.thevortexbarandgrill.com | Lunch & Dinner daily

Fritti 7.5

Reviewers "love the thin-crust, wood-fired pizza" at this restaurant, which is located next door to its popular sibling, Sotto Sotto. The two dozen types of pies are split into two categories: Seven classic styles, like Margherita, have been certified by the Verace Pizza Napoletana Association, and more adventurous creations, like one with pineapple, Gorgonzola and 12-year-old balsamic vinegar (described as "the best pizza you will ever taste") that are labeled Pizze Traditionale. On nice days you can enjoy your pizza on a lovely patio.

Pizzeria | Moderate | INMAN PARK | 309 North Highland Ave. | 404-880-9559 | www.sottosottorestaurant.com | Lunch & Dinner daily

Paolo's Gelato Italiano 7.5

"Mmmm, Nutella ice cream" is what one reviewer said about his favorite flavor at this "terrific little gelateria" in the Virginia Highlands area where the inventive flavors also include rose and passion fruit. Freshly made crepes and marzipan made in Italy have their share of fans, as does the gelato shooter (two mini-sized scoops served in a chocolate cone). "It's the perfect place to stop after dinner elsewhere, or in the middle of a typical Atlanta day when it's hot as hell."

Dessert | Informal | Inexpensive | VIRGINIA HIGHLANDS | 1025 Virginia Ave. NE | 404-607-0055 | www.paolosgelato.com | Lunch & Dinner daily

New Yorker 7.4
Marketplace & Deli

"It's not the Lower East Side of

Manhattan, but it will do in a pinch" is how one reviewer described what might be Atlanta's best Jewish-style delicatessen. While the location and appearance may leave something to be desired, "delights abound for those who are brave enough to cross the threshold." Given that comment, it's not surprising that another reviewer recommended, "It's better if you get your corned beef or pastrami sandwich to go."

Sandwiches | Inexpensive | BUCKHEAD | 322 Pharr Rd. | 404-240-0260 | Breakfast & Lunch Mon-Sat

OK Cafe   7.0

Every city needs a retro diner where the wait staff is dressed in '50s garb. The menu here is just what you'd expect, eggs and pancakes at breakfast and burgers, sandwiches and comfort food like chicken potpie and mac 'n' cheese at lunch and dinner. It's super-popular, so expect to wait in a line for food described as "fabulous, fattening and filling," including "casseroles like your mother made when you were a kid."

Diner | Inexpensive | BUCKHEAD | 1284 W Paces Ferry Rd NW | 404-233-2888 | www. okcafe. com | Open daily

Sun in My Belly   7.0

If you are looking for "the sort of place where you can while away an afternoon," check out this café in the Atlanta Botanical Gardens. The small menu is limited to a handful of starters, like cumin-spiked hummus, sandwiches like curried chicken and something called the Napoleon Complex – a hot pressed sandwich of prosciutto, Brie, fig jam and pickled red onion on a focaccia bun. There's a second location near Emory University that's described as "a great neighborhood place to meet a friend for breakfast or lunch."

Café | Inexpensive | MIDTOWN | 2161 College Ave. | 404-370-1088 | www.suninmybelly.com | Breakfast & Lunch daily

OTHER PLACES MENTIONED

Bread Garden   6.9

Looking to pick up a quick sandwich or a loaf of bread for dinner? Head over to this bakery in the Virginia Highlands where they offer a variety of breads and sandwiches, from baguettes to focaccia to Kalamata olive to country Italian. A few people spoke of "uneven service" – the counter staff has been known to be "missing in action" and "slow to respond to guests." If you can't make it to the shop, you can enjoy their breads in many of Atlanta's top restaurants.

Bakery | Inexpensive | VIRGINIA HIGHLANDS | 549 Amsterdam Ave. | 404-875-1166 | Breakfast & Lunch Mon-Sat

Mary Mac's Tea Room   6.8

Mary McKenzie opened this iconic restaurant in 1945. Sixty-five years later, the menu is still larded with fare like pot likker and fried chicken, served with an astonishing 37 side dishes, including the rarely seen (outside of these parts) Hoppin' John and Brunswick stew. Although it's "filled with more tourists than locals," it has maintained its status as a local institution and is "one of the few places still serving good old-fashioned Southern food."

Southern | Inexpensive | MIDTOWN | 224 Ponce de Leon Ave. NE | 404-876-1800 | www.marymacs. com | Lunch & Dinner daily

Taqueria del Sol   6.8

Even though the Taqueria del Sol team operates three branches around the city, you're likely to find a line of people waiting at each of their popular taquerias. While it's criticized for having a "college vibe" and "food that is less than memorable," there seem to be a few dishes reviewers love, with one person saying, "I need to remind myself to go when Green Hatch chiles are in season," while another admitted to being "addicted to the fish tacos," adding, "I am convinced they put crack in the cheese dip."

Mexican | Moderate | MIDTOWN | 1200-B Howell Mill Rd. | 404-352-5811 | www.taqueriadelsol.com | Lunch & Dinner Tue-Sat

Second Location: DECATUR | 3599 W. Ponce de Leon Ave. | 404-377-7668 | Lunch & Dinner Tue-Sat

Third Location: CHESIRE BRIDGE | 2165 Cheshire Bridge Rd. | 404-321-1118 | Lunch & Dinner Mon-Fri, Dinner only Sat

Busy Bee Café   6.4

Having opened its doors in 1947, the Busy Bee has been at the center of Atlanta's African American community for more than 60 years. The menu is a veritable tour of the best a soul food kitchen has to offer, like fried or smothered chicken, and more exotic fare like oxtails, chitlins and the infamous "Joe Lewis" ham hock. Its fans say, "It always satisfies my craving for Southern food."

Soul Food | Inexpensive | DOWNTOWN | 810 Martin Luther King Jr. Dr. SW | 404-525-9212 | www.the-busybeecafe.com | Lunch & Dinner Sun-Fri

Cameli's Gourmet Pizza   6.3

"Ya gotta' love a thin crust and lots of garlic," said one person about this contender for the best pizza in Atlanta,

while another added, "They are justifiably famous for their infamous Monster Slices." There is a wide selection of toppings, allowing "everyone from vegans, vegetarians and carnivores to find much to love." During the evening the "loud music" and "rowdy bar scene" make it feel more like a party than a pizzeria.

Pizzeria | Inexpensive | MIDTOWN | 699 Ponce de Leon Ave. | 404-249-9020 | www.camelispizza.com | Lunch & Dinner daily

Five Seasons Beer Company   6.0

It's unusual to find a microbrewery that employs a chef who claims to have a philosophy about the food he serves, but that's exactly what distinguishes this place from the competition. The "upscale pub food" includes house-made bratwurst, a sweet-onion turkey burger and an organically raised Georgia rib eye. While opinions about the quality range from "inconsistent" to "better than it should be," everyone is in agreement about the "excellent house-brewed beer."

Pub Food | Inexpensive | WESTSIDE | 1000 Marietta St. NW | 404-875-3232 | www.fiveseasonsbrewing.com | Lunch & Dinner daily

Second Location: SANDY SPRINGS | 5600 Roswell Rd. | 404-255-5911 | Lunch & Dinner Daily

Birmingham AL

HIGHLY RECOMMENDED

Highlands Bar & Grill   93.8

How does one calculate the extent of the impact that Frank Stitt has had on Southern dining? Not only is he single-handedly responsible for creating the thriving Birmingham dining scene, no other chef has done as much to promote the cooking of the South as Stitt. While he advertises his cuisine as French, evidenced in dishes like veal sweetbreads with a ragout of porcini and hedgehog mushrooms, other offerings like stone-ground baked grits with country ham, mushrooms, fresh thyme and Parmesan and a Fudge Farms pork porterhouse chop with local cabbage and a sorghum glaze have a distinctly Southern flair. Comments verge on the rapturous: "Frank Stitt still rocks the Birmingham dining scene at his flagship restaurant," "world-class cuisine where you would never expect to find it – worth a special trip from Atlanta" and, our favorite, "The citizens of Birmingham should collectively get on their knees and thank Frank Stitt for bringing fine dining to a city that didn't even know what it was missing."

Southern | Casual | Expensive | 2011 11th Avenue S | 205-939-1400 | www.highlandsbarandgrill.com |
Dinner Tue-Sat

Hot and Hot Fish Club   91.7

Think of Hot and Hot as the other side of the coin from the Highlands Bar & Grill. While
the latter's dining room has a calm and somewhat formal feel to it, making it a favorite
with the city's establishment, Hot & Hot is bustling with younger diners looking to make
a night out of its combination of good food and lively atmosphere. But a fun evening
isn't the only thing Chris and Idie Hasting offer: They and their crew will tantalize you
with dishes like an heirloom cauliflower gratin with Petals from the Past pecans and
bread crumbs or a roast venison chop with rutabaga, marjoram and persimmon juice. A
number of reviewers raved about an heirloom "tomato salad to die for," with one telling
us, "Nothing beats [it], except maybe their shrimp and grits, or maybe their donuts . . ."

Southern | Casual | Expensive | 2180 11th Court S. | 205-933-5474 | www.hotandhotfishclub.com | Dinner
Tue-Sat

Chez Fonfon   91.0

This bustling restaurant benefits from sharing a kitchen with Highlands Bar & Grill.
Frank Stitt's French menu features traditional brasserie fare like a croque madame as
well as the more exotic beef tongue Lyonnais, along with a host of dishes based on local
ingredients like a tartine with crabmeat, avocado and lemon or trout with brown butter,
capers and Brabant potatoes. One reviewer described it as "an excellent re-creation
of a brasserie adapted for the local market," and given that few quality restaurants are
open for the midday meal, it's not surprising that reviewers deem this "easily the best
lunch spot in town."

French Brasserie | Casual | Moderate | 2007 11th Ave. S. | 205-939-3221 |
Lunch & Dinner Tue-Fri, Sat dinner only

Bottega   89.0

With two popular French restaurants under his belt, Frank Stitt turned his attention to
the Italian table. Of course, when you put the word "Stitt" and "cuisine" into the same
sentence, it is guaranteed that Southern influences will find their way into the food. For
example, when's the last time you saw an Italian restaurant serve an egg salad in the
style of Lucca with fried oysters, or how about sweet potatoes in a dish of grilled pork
scaloppini with spinach, pine nuts and sultanas? No wonder reviewers described the
menu choices as "not just the usual suspects" and "exceptional northern Italian cuisine
with some well-considered regional inflections."

Italian | Casual | Moderate | 2240 Highland Ave. S. | 205-939-1000 | www.bottegarestaurant.com | Dinner
Mon-Sat

Ocean   87.5

While it might be low man on the totem
pole when it comes to the local dining
scene, reviewers claim Ocean is where
you can find "very fresh seafood" along
with "a touch of creativity in the kitchen."
But skeptics say "it's just the latest
iteration of a place that keeps chang-

ing names and formats," adding that "a sterile atmosphere" and "prices too high for the quality they serve" results in there being "better choices in town."

Seafood | Casual | Moderate | 1218 20th St. S. | 205-933-0999 | www.oceanbirmingham.com | Dinner Tue-Sat

OTHER RESTAURANTS MENTIONED

Wintzell's Oyster House   81.5

This famous oyster house with 11 locations around Alabama has its lovers as well as haters. Lovers say, "Been dining at Wintzell's for 30+ years, and the oysters Bienville, Monterey and Rockefeller are reliably good." But doubters warn, "Tread carefully if you're eating at a location that isn't the Mobile original." Non-bivalve fans can order a handful of local shrimp dishes, along with broiled and fried versions of flounder and catfish.

Seafood | Informal | Moderate | 605 Dauphin St. | 251-432-4605 | www.wintzellsoysterhouse.com | Lunch & Dinner daily

Cheap Eats

UNIQUELY DELICIOUS

Flip Burger Joint   8.2

"Fine dining between two buns" is how Richard Blais describes his burger restaurant, and with comments like "fun, imaginative, flavorful and creative," it appears our reviewers agree. The eclectic list of burgers on offer includes the Southern (country fried beef, pimento cheese, pickles and green tomato ketchup), the Philly (caramelized onions, green peppers and American cheese foam) and, for the high rollers, the A5 (A5-grade imported Japanese Kobe beef, foie gras torchon, truffle flavor, melted onions and red wine cheese foam). There are also a number of non-beef offerings, such as burgers based on turkey, spicy chicken and the aptly named chickpea-based faux-lafel. Don't forget to order one of the

"amazing milkshakes" with your burger.

Hamburgers | Inexpensive | 220 Summit Blvd. | 205-968-9200 | www.flipburgerboutique.com | Lunch & Dinner daily

RECOMMENDED

Big Bob Gibson   7.7
(80 miles north in Decatur)

Any foodie who is worth his weight in sauce will invariably veer off to stop at this barbecue pit while driving along I-65 between Birmingham and Nashville. While the nationally known Chris Lily is now stoking the logs (when he's not on the road promoting barbecue), the restaurant itself has been slicing up chickens and racks of ribs here since 1925. While reviewers "don't think it is as good as the hype would indicate," "it's a solid stop for BBQ lovers who are in the area."

Barbecue | Inexpensive | 1715 6th Avenue SE/US Highway 31 | 256-350-6969 | www.bigbobgibson.com | Open daily

Bob Sykes BarB-Q   7.0
(13 miles northeast in Bessemer)

Given the proximity to Birmingham (about a 20-minute drive from downtown), it's not surprising that locals are quick to jump into their cars and drive down to Bessemer when they're in the mood for "a good rack of barbecue ribs." Unfortunately, the rest of the 'cue isn't all that notable, despite the myriad of other meats available. It is a treat, however, to watch them smoke/grill the ribs on a large rack right in the dining room.

Barbecue | Inexpensive | 1724 9th Ave. N | 205-426-1400 | www.bobsykes.com| Lunch & Dinner Mon-Sat

"You're Wrong!!!"

Do You Disagree with the Reviews in this Guide?

Then we want to hear about it. But we don't want you to send one of those mealy-mouth negative comments to our inbox. We want you to take a stand and help shape opinions for our next guide. That's because people who disagree with us are just as important to us as the people who share our conclusions. And who knows—next year's results might be more to your liking. You might even see yourself being quoted.

www.opinionatedabout.com

Chattanooga TN

TOP LOCAL CHOICE

212 Market   88.0

While we wouldn't suggest that our readers travel from Nashville or Atlanta just to eat here, it would be difficult to do better if you happen to be in Chattanooga. The menu is a mix of Southern fare, like rock shrimp with grits, fried green tomatoes and local ham, and more internationally styled eats, like ginger-miso braised bison short ribs with wasabi mashed potatoes. An "extensive wine list" and "the mostly organic menu" cement it as "the best place to eat in a 100-mile radius."

New American | Informal | Moderate | CHATTANOOGA | 212 Market St. | 423-265-1212 | www.212market. com | Lunch & Dinner daily

Charleston SC

AN IMPORTANT DESTINATION

McCrady's   96.8

If one were to measure the correlation between the quality of a chef's cuisine and the extent of his reputation, Sean Brock might be the most underrated chef in the country. The restaurant's setting – a tavern-like building that dates from 1788 – works against Brock, whose molecular market cuisine is much more serious than the atmosphere suggests. Prepared by a kitchen staff of only six people, Brock's fare was described as "innovative without being stuffy"; "full of interesting ideas with a Southern twist" and "Low Country meets the Languedoc." Brock seems to be on such an upward trajectory that we concur with the reviewer who predicted, "in five years this could be the best restaurant in America."

At the heart of Brock's cuisine are original creations like foie gras cured as if it were bacon, along with dishes made with the terrific biodynamic ingredients that he grows on a two-and-a-half acre patch of land on Wadmalaw Island. The custom-raised produce turns up in dishes like handmade wild ramp pasta with stone crabs, chanterelles and nasturtium butter, along with a stupendous array of local fish and shellfish like smoked Carolina rainbow trout, which he serves with a salad of potato, parsley and egg. General Manager Clint Sloan supervises "one of the most extensive wine cellars" in the South, and the "knowledgeable servers are expert at explaining the cuisine." It adds up to an experience that one frequent visitor called "as consistent as it is sublime."

Progressive | Casual | Expensive | 2 Unity Alley | 843-577-0025 | www.mccradysrestaurant.com | Dinner daily

RECOMMENDED

FIG   90.9

With its emphasis on top ingredients prepared in a way that allows their flavors to shine, we weren't surprised when more than one reviewer referred to Mike Lata's restaurant as "the Blue Hill of the South." Lata's menu is loaded with the region's best products, like an appetizer of Crispy Creek Caw Caw pork trotters served with endive and a Sunnyside [up] Farm egg, or a main of Keegan-Filion Farm chicken "al mattone" (under a brick) served with Anson Mills farro, root vegetables and sautéed greens. Writing about this restaurant that's beloved by many, one reviewer told us, "The only problem with our meal was that we did not make another reservation before we left."

New American | Casual | Moderate | 232 Meeting St. | 843-805-5900 | www.eatatfig.com | Dinner Mon-Sat

Charleston Grill   90.3

In a city where casual dining dominates, the Charleston Place Hotel offers the most upscale culinary experience around. Michelle Weaver prepares four different menus: Pure, which might include dry-aged lamb chops, spring vegetables and rosemary/lemon jus; Lush, offering, for example, oxtail soup, bone marrow crostini, lemon and capers; Southern, including Okeechobee catfish and fried oysters with fried-ham gravy; and Cosmopolitan, featuring seared halibut and potato gnocchi with spring vegetable minestrone. The room is "beautiful" and the service "impeccable," and the 40-page wine list makes it "easy to find a bottle that goes with your food," regardless of which menu you order from.

New American | Casual | Expensive | Charleston Place Hotel | 224 King St. | 843-577-4522 | www.charlestongrill.com | Dinner daily

TOP LOCAL CHOICE

Peninsula Grille   89.5

When a local dining scene revolves around a combination of regional cooking and contemporary culinary technique, nuance is important. In this instance, Robert Carter puts more emphasis on the New American side of the menu, represented by dishes like pan-roasted Muscovy duck with a creamy spinach flan, than on the regional side, which features dishes like peach-glazed jumbo shrimp with sweet corn risotto, brandied peach butter and green-onion horseradish hush puppies. While the room is "a bit clubby," we got complaints about the noise level at the tables in the center. "Out of this world" is how someone described the wine list.

New American | Casual | Expensive | 112 N. Market St. | 843-723-0700 | www.peninsulagrill.com | Dinner daily

High Cotton   89.0

At this restaurant operated by the Maverick Group (they own the terrific Charleston Cooks cookware shop) "an excellent use of local and sustainable products" results in "well-crafted dishes" served by "a knowledgeable staff." The modernized version of Low Country cooking includes dishes like roast green tomato soup with avocado oil or an Eden Farms pork chop with field pea succotash, fried okra and smoked bacon hollandaise. They also offer a popular Sunday brunch where the more traditional cuisine includes old standbys like Carolina shrimp and grits and smoked chicken andouille sausage with okra, charred tomatoes and sweet corn-garlic broth.

Southern | Casual | Moderate | 199 E. Bay St. | 843-724-3815 | www.mavericksouthernkitchens.com | Dinner daily, Sat-Sun lunch

Magnolia   88.5

Put this restaurant in the category of solid upper middle dining, with enough of a regional bent to make it a top choice for a meal while you're in Charleston. What makes Donald Barickman's Low Country specialties different is that dishes like spicy shrimp and sausage, tasso gravy and cheddar cheese grits and what Barickman calls the Carolina Carpetbagger – twin filets of beef topped with fried oysters, Madeira and béarnaise sauce – are prepared by a kitchen of Culinary Institute graduates. The place is a bit large and noisy, though a wine list featuring "friendly pricing" allows you to drink well while enjoying what one reviewer described as "a terrific, casual, down-home meal."

Southern | Casual | Moderate | 185 E. Bay St. | 843-577-7771 | www.magnolias-blossom-cypress.com | Lunch & Dinner daily

Blossom   88.0

The focus is on seafood at this "Charleston staple." Opened in 1993, it is part of the group that operates Magnolia and Cypress. Adam Close took charge of the kitchen in 2007, and he pairs "the best of the Low-Country catch" with locally raised produce in dishes like buttermilk-fried shrimp with rosemary fries, slaw and cocktail sauce and pan-roasted black grouper with potato hash, rapini pesto and mustard butter. The "wonderful, casual setting" includes the type of open kitchen that was popular in restaurants that opened during the 1990s.

Seafood Casual | Moderate | 171 E. Bay St. |843-722-9200 | www.magnolias-blossom-cypress.com | Lunch & Dinner daily

ACCEPTABLE

Cypress   87.5

Of the three restaurants run by the HMGI Group (Magnolia and Blossom are the others), Cypress is the only place where the cooking style isn't focused on Southern cuisine. Craig Deihl's menu is split into two parts: locally inspired dishes like Keegan-Filion Farm chicken and dumplings and more classic American fare like a take-off on veal Oscar made with beef and topped with jumbo lump crab and asparagus. The short wine list is "surprisingly solid" when it comes to its top bottles, and a lively mezzanine bar allows you to watch the action in the kitchen while sipping your cocktail.

American | Casual | Expensive | 167 E. Bay St. | 843-727-0111 | www.magnolias-blossom-cypress. com | Dinner daily

Slightly North of   87.0
Broad (SNOB)

When you want a break from the New Southern cuisine that dominates the culinary scene in Charleston, go to this restaurant, where Frank Lee's French menu includes house-made pâtés and homey entrées like a rack of lamb with green beans, pearl onions and a Cabernet Sauvignon rosemary sauce. One reviewer couldn't resist a shot at the acronym, noting, "The name says it all" and calling it "somewhat pretentious," with "some of the food worth it, and some not."

French | Casual | Moderate | 192 E. Bay St. | 843-723-3424 | www.mavericksouthernkitchens.com | Dinner daily, Lunch Mon-Fri

Ocean Room   87.0
(27 miles southwest on Kiawah Island)

Converted from a contemporary Southern restaurant into a steakhouse, the Ocean Room also tempts non-red-meat eaters with farm-to-table dishes like Keegan-Filion Farm chicken with foraged mushrooms and wild arugula. While it looks good on paper, let's not forget it's a hotel restaurant, which shows in comments like "The food is fresh and good, but you won't find much imagination here." However, "the room is pleasant" and "It's a good choice if you don't want to make the drive into Charleston."

Steakhouse | Casual | Expensive | Kiawah Island Golf Resort | 1 Sanctuary Beach Dr. | 843-768-6000 | www.thesanctuary.com | Dinner Tue-Sat

Cru Cafe   87.0

Reviewers like this casual restaurant with its "interesting menu" featuring everything from a Caesar salad topped with grilled shrimp to more eclectic offerings like Thai seafood risotto or poblano and mozzarella fried chicken with potato gratin and honey chipotle salsa. The place is "small and quaint," and reviewers advise diners to "get a reservation if you can," but also say that "the food is good enough to warrant waiting in line for a table." If you can, try to reserve a seat at the kitchen counter, considered the most desirable location in the restaurant.

Eclectic | Informal | Moderate | 18 Pinckney St. | 843-534-2434 | http://crucafe.com | Lunch & Dinner Tue-Sat

Boathouse Restaurant   85.5

If you are looking for a simple, family-style restaurant where the food doesn't get fancier than crab cakes and broiled fish, all you have to do is travel 11 miles outside Charleston and you will find the type of waterfront restaurant that's popular up and down the Atlantic Coast. You'll get to enjoy your dinner with "great water views" and "beautiful sunsets."

Seafood | Informal | Moderate | 101 Palm Blvd. | 843-886-8000 | www.boathouserestaurants.com | Lunch & Dinner daily

Circa 1886   85.5

Located next to the Wentworth mansion and considered "the most romantic restaurant in Charleston," Marc Collins' place is where many locals go to celebrate special occasions. Unfortunately, the reviews are mixed: "Collins tries hard to update Southern cuisine – but not always successfully" and "solid but not spectacular." But it's still recommended

as a good choice for those who like dining in an environment that, as the name implies, "has the aura of days gone by."

Southern | Casual | Expensive | 149 Wentworth St. | 843-853-7828 | www.circa1886.com | Dinner Mon-Sat

OTHER RESTAURANTS MENTIONED

Hank's Seafood   83.5

Dishes like she-crab soup, oysters casino and shrimp and grits are in keeping with a place that advertises itself as a tribute to the seafood restaurants that sprang up in Charleston during the 1940s. The most famous was the now-shuttered Henry's – hence the current name. Reviews are split between people who say "It's the best seafood in Charleston" and others who call it "average at best."

Seafood | Moderate | 10 Hayne St. | 843-723-3474 | http://hanksseafoodrestaurant.com | Dinner daily

Cheap Eats

RECOMMENDED

Hominy Grill   7.9

With a breakfast menu featuring eggs, pancakes, homemade sausages, and the signature Big Nasty Biscuit (fried chicken breast, cheddar cheese and sausage gravy) and a lunch and dinner menu of Low Country specialties like shrimp and grits, fried chicken and purloo (a rice casserole with ham, sausage, shrimp and chicken wings), this is the type of Southern roadhouse that everyone dreams of finding. "It lives up to the press" is the consensus, though a few complained "it can get a little touristy."

Southern | Moderate | 207 Rutledge Ave. | 843-937-0930 | www.hominygrill.com | Open daily

Jestine's Kitchen   7.0

Every urban center needs a soul food restaurant, and Jestine's fills that spot in Charleston. The menu is filled with Low Country specialties, including po-boys, shrimp and grits, a pecan-crusted chicken breast and stuffed pork chops, along with the local color that one usually finds at these types of places. Comments range from "excellent, home-style cooking" to "bland food that's the same quality you find at a coffee shop."

Soul Food | Inexpensive | 251 Meeting St. | 843-722-7224 | Lunch & Dinner daily

OTHER PLACES MENTIONED

Sweatman's BBQ   6.7

(52 miles northwest in Holy Hill)

Many Charleston locals make a weekly trek to this "true temple of barbecue" an hour and a half outside the city. It's open only on Friday and Saturday, and whole hogs are butterflied and smoked over an open pit, after which diners line up to feast from a buffet where a series of chafing dishes hold different parts of the pig. For people who care about these things, the sauce is mustard-based, and reviewers say "getting there is half of the fun" as "it's on the way to nowhere."

Barbecue | Inexpensive | 1313 Gemini Dr./Highway 453 | 803-899-1500 | Lunch & Dinner Fri-Sat

Chilhowie VA

AN IMPORTANT DESTINATION

Town House Grill   97.6

Wedged between Kentucky, West Virginia, North Carolina and Tennessee, the town of Chilhowie, Virginia, might seem the least likely spot on earth to find a restaurant serving molecular cuisine. But that didn't stop John Shields and Karen Urie who, after answering an ad for a chef on Craigslist, decided to see whether the people of western Virginia would take to eating country ham served in the form of an inert gas. Fortunately, they did, and as with all good things, word quickly spread. It wasn't long before foodies from all over the country were making the trek to Chilhowie to try the food, including one reviewer who told us, "I recently had my sixth meal at the restaurant, and it gets better with each experience."

Shields, who worked at Alinea with Grant Achatz, has integrated a number of different styles into his cuisine. Michel Troigros' *cuisine acidulée* is apparent in a chilled vegetable "minestrone," the hyper-creative minimalism of Adoni Aduriz turns up in a tea-smoked loup de mer with charred skin served in a reduced fish broth, and a mousse of scrambled egg with peekytoe crab reveals Shields' own original hand. Karen Urie comes out of the Charlie Trotter kitchen, leading one to surmise that her pastries would be more traditional. But her "truffles" made of buttermilk, pistachio, peppermint and red wine are about as cutting-edge as dessert gets. What else can we tell you, other than it's worth the long drive (the nearest big city, Roanoke, is more than 100 miles away) for what one reviewer called "amazing food in the middle of nowhere."

Progressive | Casual | Expensive | 132 E. Main St. | 276.646.8787 | www.townhousegrill.com | Dinner Tue-Sat

Ft. Lauderdale FL

TOP LOCAL CHOICE

Café Martorano   89.5

By bringing the Southside of Philadelphia to his restaurant, Steve Martorano made this "one of the most unique dining experiences you will find in Broward County." Multiple reviewers mentioned the "must-have" Philly cheese steak sandwiches, "amazing" lobster Francese and "the best meatballs in the entire world." A major downside is a no-reservation policy that results in "a ridiculously long wait for a table." It's the perfect restaurant for people who like eating at larger-than-life places where the food is served at "larger-than-life prices."

Italian | Casual | Expensive | FT. LAUDERDALE | 3343 E. Oakland Park Blvd. | 954-561-2554 | www.cafemar-torano.com | Dinner daily

Second Location: HOLLYWOOD | Hard Rock Hotel | 5751 Seminole Way | 954-584-4450 | www.cafemar-torano.com | Dinner daily

Darrel & Oliver's Café Maxx 89.0

Opened during the Floribbean culinary craze of the '80s, Café Maxx is one of the last South Florida restaurants from that era (Chef Allen's is the other). However, Oliver Saucy's cuisine is more California-ish than Floribbean, evidenced by a number of dishes that have been on the menu for more than two decades, like a three-peppercorn filet mignon and lamb chops crusted with goat cheese and pine nuts. Reviewers who still enjoy it say, "I loved this place when I lived in the area in the '90s, and I still go there every time I'm in town."

New American | Casual | Expensive | POMPANO BEACH | 2601 E. Atlantic Blvd. | 954-782-0606 | www.cafemaxx.com | Dinner daily

Louisville KY

TOP LOCAL CHOICE

Proof on Main 88.0

"Reason enough to go to Louisville by itself" is what reviewers say about this restaurant located in a "hip little boutique hotel" on Main Street. Michael Paley's menu mixes traditional Italian fare, like bucatini carbonara with pancetta and pecorino with modern Southern creations like a country ham–wrapped pork chop paired with grain mustard crema and apple butter. The "cool décor" is an added attraction: The developers of the 21C hotel are notable art enthusiasts, and a rotating collection of contemporary sculpture and paintings is displayed throughout the hotel and restaurant.

Southern | Casual | Expensive | LOUISVILLE | 702 W. Main St. | 502-217-6360 | www.proofonmain.com | Dinner daily, Lunch Mon-Fri

Miami FL

HIGHLY RECOMMENDED

Michy's 93.0

After making her name at Azul, the "adorable" Michelle Bernstein opened this restaurant in 2008 in a still-developing area of Miami known as the Upper East Side, where she delivers a menu of Mediterranean-influenced comfort food via an assortment of carefully crafted small plates. Ask Bernstein to prepare a tasting menu of her best work and you will be bombarded with dishes like Kumamoto oysters wrapped in fatty tuna; crispy sweetbreads served with duck sausage and root vegetables; snapper française with mojo beurre blanc; and short ribs with creamy mashed potatoes and Moroccan carrots. There is something homey about Bernstein's cuisine; one reviewer described it as "what your mother would have liked to serve if she really knew how to cook." A third of reviewers said, in essence, "This is where you will find the best food in Miami."

Mediterranean | Casual | Expensive | UPPER EAST SIDE | 6927 Biscayne Blvd. | 305-759-2001 | http://michysmiami.com | Dinner Tue-Sun

RECOMMENDED

Joe's Stone Crab   91.0

One reviewer told the following story: "One Saturday evening a few years back, we asked the maitre d' how long it would take to get a table. He told us to go out and catch a movie and our table would be ready when we got back." That sums up the length of the wait at this iconic restaurant, where the Florida stone crab claws come three to five per order depending on their size (regulars are quick to order the jumbos when they're available). There's a host of classic side dishes, like garlic creamed spinach, Lyonnaise potatoes and cottage-fried sweet potatoes. Joe's is famous for offering priority seating to regulars, or to those who were gracious enough to "thank" the maitre d' on their last visit. Fortunately, anyone can avoid the brutal lines by going for lunch.

Seafood | Casual | Expensive | SOUTH BEACH | 11 Washington Ave. | 305-673-0365 | www.joesstonecrab.com | Lunch & Dinner Tue-Sat; Sun-Mon dinner only

Michael's Genuine Food & Drink   91.2

The focus is on the wood-burning oven at this trendy Design District restaurant from ex-Nemo chef/owner Michael Schwartz, where the plates come in Small (wood-roasted, double-yolk farm egg with cave-aged Gruyère and roasted tomato), Medium (crispy homemade pastrami with red cabbage slaw), Large (slow-roasted Berkshire pork shoulder with cheese grits) and Extra Large (wood-roasted Poulet Rouge chicken for two). What's unusual about the experience is that restaurants featuring high-quality market cuisine aren't often "cramped and crowded" while being "filled with a hip and trendy crowd." So think of this one as a sort of Chez Panisse lite with a Miami party vibe.

Mediterranean | Casual | Moderate | DESIGN DISTRICT | 130 N.E. 40th St. | 305-573-5550 | www.michaels-genuine.com | Lunch & Dinner Sun-Fri, Sat dinner only

Casa Tua   90.3

Hidden behind a high row of hedges, this chic hotel restaurant is always filled with well-dressed international diners enjoying well-made Italian fare – a combination you don't see very often in a place like South Beach. The cuisine comes with a contemporary edge – seared foie gras with a ginger and tomato marmalade; tagliatelle with crème fraîche and caviar; and seared lamb chops with grilled endive and pickled onions. Comments reflect the effort that has gone into the food: "One of my favorite places to eat on the Beach" and "It's refreshing to find a restaurant on the Beach that didn't lower standards to take advantage of the tourist trade."

Italian | Casual | Expensive | SOUTH BEACH | 1700 James Ave. | 305-673-1010 | www.casatualifestyle.com | Dinner daily

Nobu Miami Beach   90.1

Toro tartare with osetra caviar, spicy creamy crab, miso black cod . . . This outpost in the Shore Club maintains the quality in Nobu Matsuhisa's classic dishes. And as a bonus for those who like to eat local, the restaurant goes out of its way to source local fish that end up on the list of daily specials. Given its popularity, which in this instance is compounded by a shortage of quality restaurants in Miami Beach, a no-reservation policy means you are in for a substantial wait. One reviewer told us he "arrived at 11:00 p.m. only to be told there was a 45-minute wait for a table."

Japanese | Casual | Expensive | SOUTH BEACH | Shore Club | 1901 Collins Ave. | 305-695-3232 | www.noburestaurants.com | Dinner daily

TOP LOCAL CHOICE

Restaurant at the Setai   88.5

Given a menu that is jam-packed with Southeast Asian and Japanese dishes, served at prices high enough to finance hiring people to inspect every single grain of rice on your plate, one would think that reviewers would speak more highly of this "attractive and comfortable" venue in the Setai Hotel. But comments like "I don't think I would choose this restaurant unless I was staying in the hotel" are about as common as ones like "Every ingredient and spice tempts your palate." The setting is "as Zen as it gets," and "the service could not be any more attentive."

Asian | Casual | Expensive | SOUTH BEACH | The Setai | 2001 Collins Ave. | 305-520-6405 | www.setai.com | Open daily

Blue Door Fish   88.0

Claude Troisgros is still doing the cooking at this restaurant located in the Delano Hotel. Troisgros has been in charge since day one, which means that in a place like Miami Beach, where restaurants turn over their chefs on a regular basis, there must be something to his cuisine. His current menu focuses on fish, while offering a mix of new dishes, like Dover sole in almond caper brown butter, along with a list of "Classics" that he has been serving since the restaurant first opened, like roast Maine lobster with caramelized bananas.

Seafood | Casual | Expensive | SOUTH BEACH | Delano Hotel | 1685 Collins Ave. | 305-674-6400 | www.chinagrillmgt.com | Open daily

Wish   88.0

Ten years ago, when this place first opened – complete with an interior by designer Todd Oldham – it was considered one of the more serious restaurants on the Beach. But after a myriad of chef changes and a general decline in the South Beach dining scene over the decade, what used to be an interesting restaurant became, merely "perfect for the South Beach crowd – loud, expensive and ostentatious, while serving large portions of uninspired food" (as one reviewer put it, "I wish the old Wish was still around"). Now, however, Marco Ferraro has taken over the kitchen, and with dishes like heirloom tomato gazpacho with watermelon, avocado and spicy yuzu aioli along with garlic-ginger crusted cod with napa cabbage, rice noodles, shiitake mushrooms and macerated limes, the restaurant is on track to once again become one of the most desirable tables on South Beach.

New American | Casual | Expensive | SOUTH BEACH | The Hotel of South Beach | 801 Collins Ave. | 305-674-9474 | www.wishrestaurant.com | Lunch & Dinner Tue-Sun, Mon lunch only

Chef Allen's   87.5

Back in the late '90s, when chefs like Norman Van Aken, Douglas Rodriguez and Allen Susser ruled the Florida scene, the phrase "Floribbean Cuisine" meant something – specifically, a new and exciting fusion school of cooking. But today both the cuisine and Susser's version of it are considered old school, and his restaurant has fallen off the foodie radar as a result. But if you're someone who occasionally has a hankering for dishes like red snapper sautéed with mango and pistachios, you might agree with the reviewer who told us, "Susser's food has stood the test of time."

New American | Casual | Expensive | aventura | 19088 NE 29th Ave. | 305-935-2900 | www.chefallens.com | Dinner daily

Romeo's Café   87.0

There are three notable things about this restaurant: The décor is reminiscent of the tacky Italian restaurants that Hollywood depicted in the 1950s. There is no menu; rather, diners are paid a visit by the chef, who discusses the meal and then voilà! (or maybe we should say presto!), the food appears. And servers hype the food by asking things like, "Isn't the risotto delicious?" Reviewers who like this sort of thing described the experience as a "romantic interlude that happens to include fine dining."

Italian | Casual | Expensive | coral gables | 2257 SW 22nd St. | 305-859-2228 | www.romeoscafe.com | Lunch & Dinner Tue-Sat

Yuca   87.0

For those who ate at this restaurant when Douglas Rodriguez was pioneering the Nuevo Latino cuisine that became so popular over the next decade, it's sad to see that it has become just another tourist destination. Sure, they might still be serving foie gras with bananas and truffle-scented picadillo, but the fare "doesn't have the same level of vibrancy" that it had when it was in Coral Gables. Still, "the vibe is great" and "the people-watching on Lincoln Road" can't be beat.

Cuban | Casual | Moderate | south beach | 501 Lincoln Rd. | 305-532-9822 | www.yuca.com | Lunch & Dinner daily

Palme d'Or   86.0

With dishes like a soup of vine-ripened tomatoes, avocado mousse and micro basil or Dover sole, pumpkin and rosemary-infused chicken jus, offered at the bargain price of $42 for three small plates and $14 for each additional plate, Phillipe Ruiz's restaurant in the Biltmore Hotel looks like one of the best bargains in Miami. But comments like "uneven cooking" and "food that sounds better than it tastes" means this "attractive dining room" falls short with our reviewers.

French | Casual | Expensive | coral gables | Biltmore Hotel | 1200 Anastasia Ave. | 305-913-3201 | www.biltmorehotel.com | Dinner Tue-Sat

Perricone's Marketplace   85.5

Turn onto 10th Street from Brickell Avenue and you come upon this gourmet shop selling everything from salumi and cheese to prepared foods. But step through a door at the back of the shop and you will find a bustling café where a surprisingly large number of diners are enjoying an assortment of salads, pastas and hero sandwiches along with a handful of entrées. On weekdays it's filled with workers from the nearby offices, while the locals who live in the area enjoy quiet dinners during the evenings.

Italian | Informal | Moderate | brickell avenue | 15 10th St. SE | 305-374-9449 | www.perricones.com | Open daily

Smith & Wollensky   85.5

There was a time when reviewers enjoyed this restaurant, but it has become "the epitome of a B-level steakhouse." Others weren't as kind, saying, "I never understood what people saw in the place" and "There are too many good steak restaurants to bother with this one." We did find someone who offered positive words, saying, "It's better than most in the second tier, but it's definitely second tier."

Steakhouse | Casual | Expensive | south beach | 1 Washington Ave. | 305-673-2800 | www.smithandwollensky.com

OTHER RESTAURANTS MENTIONED

Blue Sea   84.5

Our reviewers are not in awe of this "other" restaurant in the Delano Hotel, a sushi bar off the lobby that consists of two long communal tables. The best description of the food was "mediocre," and the two most compelling reasons to go that were offered were "the Fellini-esque setting" and "if someone else is paying." Come breakfast-time, they switch from sushi and rolls to offerings like yogurt and granola.

Sushi | Informal | Expensive | south beach | Delano | 1685 Collins Ave. | 305-674-6400 | www. delano-hotel.com | Dinner Mon-Sat

China Grill   83.0

Given the name, you might think this is a Chinese restaurant, but it's actually a pan-Asian party place whose menu touches on every possible Eastern cuisine, from Kobe beef tartare to Thai shrimp cakes to Shanghai lobster. While it might not be the most discerning cuisine, "huge portions" and a space "filled with beautiful people" make this one of the Beach's most popular restaurants.

Pan-Asian | Casual | Expensive | south beach | 404 Washington Ave. | 305-534-2211 | www.chinagrillmgt.com | Lunch & Dinner daily

Barton G.   81.0

"All blow but little show" is the way this restaurant that earned one of the low-

est scores in our survey was described. Another compared the décor to "a banquet room at a synagogue." Not discouraged yet? How about, "horrid food, amateur service and head-splitting noise levels." At least they offer "great people-watching," but what do you expect from a restaurant that is "more about being a spectacle than a dining destination."

New American | Casual | Expensive | design district | 1427 West Ave. | 305-672-8881 | www.bartong.com | Dinner daily

Cheap Eats

UNIQUELY DELICIOUS

8 OZ. Burger Bar   8.0

Govind Armstrong decided there wasn't enough money in serving New American cuisine, so he converted his restaurant to a burger joint. But not just any burger joint: He focuses on sustainably raised meats – burgers are available in both corn- and grass-fed versions – and locally sourced ingredients. Other treats include Kobe beef corndogs, chicken potpie croquettes and a grilled-cheese/short rib sandwich. Reviewers say: "Great burgers and sides, and a small and tasty selection of cocktails and on-tap beers," and, "It's a perfect neighborhood hangout, and I keep going back."

Hamburgers | Inexpensive | south beach | 1080 Alton Rd. | 305-397-8246 | www.8ozburgerbarmiami.com | Open daily

RECOMMENDED

Shake Shack   7.7

The road to success in the food industry is traveled by restaurateurs who correctly calculated that people will pay more for an ordinary item if the quality is substantially improved. In this instance, Danny Meyer felt that he could charge a premium for a fast food–style hamburger if he used a higher-quality grind of meat. Well his gamble paid off, and a few short years later, you can now enjoy "juicy and beefy-tasting burgers." The Shack also offers hot dogs and bratwursts, plus beer, wine and frozen custard.

Hamburgers | Inexpensivel | south beach | 11 11 Lincoln Rd | 305-434-7787 | http://shakeshack. com | Open daily

OTHER PLACES MENTIONED

News Café   6.4

Your chef's salad comes with a side order of amazing people-watching at this South Beach coffee shop on steroids. While the menu pays tribute to as many nationalities and health food movements as possible, the quality of the food is "bleh." But "the experience is still enjoyable," if only for watching "the parade of amazing-looking passersby," which is as likely to include a supermodel or rap star

as a group of Iowa college students.

Coffee Shop | Moderate | south beach | 800 Ocean Dr. | 305-538-6397 | www.newscafe.com | Open daily

Versailles   5.4

This is the social and political center of Miami's Cuban community. But while the menu offers every Cuban dish imaginable, from ropa vieja to paella mariscada, "The quality of the food is no different than what you will find at dozens of diners all over the country." In spite of the mediocre chow, however, we must admit there is something about this amazingly popular place that is unique – and it's not just that it's open 24 hours a day, either.

Cuban | Informal | Inexpensive | calle ocho | 3555 SW Eighth St. | 305-444-0240 | Lunch & Dinner daily

New Orleans LA

Galatoire's   93.1

With its emphasis on seasonal ingredients, backed up by top-notch execution in the kitchen, Galatoire's is still the best of the old-line New Orleans dining rooms. The menu is loaded with classics, like oysters Rockefeller (invented here), soft-shell crabs smothered in étouffée, pompano meunière almondine (not one or the other, but both preparations together) and chicken bonne-femme, as well as eight or ten cuts of grilled meats and a half-dozen fresh fish of the day offerings. Reserving a table in the upstairs dining room "is strictly for tourists"; the multigenerational local clientele that remains devoted to the restaurant prefers to wait in line in order to sit in the downstairs dining room, especially at Friday lunch, when the cream of New Orleans society shows up to celebrate the end of the week.

Creole | Casual | Expensive | french quarter | 209 Bourbon St. | 504-525-2021 | www.galatoires.com | Lunch & Dinner Tue-Sun

Brigtsen's   92.2

Back in the 1980s, Frank Brigtsen was among the group of talented young chefs responsible for bringing Creole cuisine into the modern era. But while Frank's contemporaries were busy traipsing around the country with their publicists, Brigtsen stayed in New Orleans, where he kept his nose in his sauté pan. What makes his cuisine different? "Unlike other chefs who use local products to cook in a more international style, Frank never strayed from his roots, and you can still find the essence of New Orleans in his cuisine." That approach is evidenced in dishes like rabbit tenderloin with an andouille Parmesan grits cake or pan-roasted pork tenderloin with sweet potato dirty rice. This restaurant is easy to get to from downtown; one reviewer suggested taking the St. Charles Avenue trolley in order to enjoy this "real deal of modern Creole cooking."

Creole | Casual | Expensive | uptown | 723 Dante St. | 504-861-7610 | www.brigtsens.com | Dinner Tue-Sat

Clancy's   91.7

A fair number of tourists are willing to make the 20-minute trek from the French Quarter for the "solid food" and "pleasant, old school ambience" at this eatery tucked away in a quiet uptown neighborhood. Creole classics dominate the handwritten menu, like trout topped with crab meunière and grilled baby drumfish topped with salmon gravlax, while the meat dishes include the likes of chicken Clemenceau, lamb chops Webster or panéed veal smothered with lump crab meat and Béarnaise sauce. There's a decent wine list, and the butterscotch, dulce de leche and sea salt budino can give any dessert in NOLA a run for its money. With the tuxedo-clad waiters being some of the friendliest and most helpful in the city, and a short but thoughtful wine list that does its best to complement the food, it's not surprising to hear reviewers describe this veteran as "Galatoire's light."

Creole | Casual | Expensive | uptown | 6100 Annunciation St. | 504-895-1111 | Dinner Mon-Sat, Lunch Thu-Fri

Stella!   91.0

In a city where formality is rare, Scott Boswell's French Quarter restaurant offers perhaps the most refined dining experience in New Orleans. A menu described as "a product of, but not limited to, the local cuisine" features lobster, egg and truffles, Gulf shrimp and andouille risotto with melted Brie and mushrooms, and duck served five ways with a duck miso broth. Opinion splits over the lack of regional authenticity – fans love the "eclectic mix of global techniques," while critics would "like to see a greater focus on local ingredients and cuisine." But on the whole, "the unusual menu, the beautiful setting and the excellent service" make this "one of the top choices in the city."

New American | Casual | Expensive | french quarter | 1032 Chartres St. | 504-587-0091 | www.restaurantstella.com | Dinner daily

Cochon   90.4

Donald Link's ode to the pig is housed in a converted warehouse a few blocks from Lee Circle. Stephen Stryjewski's menu, made up of appetizers, small plates and a half-dozen large plates, offers pork in a variety of forms, from homemade charcuterie, boudin (removed from its casing and formed into a ball before being breaded and fried), crispy pig's ears, spicy grilled ribs and a fork-tender version of the namesake dish served with cabbage stewed in pork jus. It's stupendously popular, and diners are advised to book in advance as "attempting to go to without a reservation is an exercise in futility."

Cajun | Informal | Moderate | warehouse district | 930 Tchoupitoulas St. | 504-588-2123 | www.cochonrestaurant.com | Lunch & Dinner Mon-Fri Sat dinner only

Lilette   90.4

The best way to describe John Harris' cuisine is 90% New American, 10% Creole and 100% devoted to quality ingredients. Harris' bistro-style fare includes dishes like sweet and sticky fried beef short ribs or grilled redfish atop market vegetables with a Champagne beurre blanc, which one reviewer described as being "good enough to be served at a top bistro in Paris." A "small, quaint location" in a converted corner shop features large plate-glass windows that look out on Magazine Street, resulting in a "lively, well-lit dining room," especially on Saturdays, when you will find a combination of locals and visitors enjoying a leisurely lunch.

New American | Casual | Expensive | garden district | 3637 Magazine St. | 504-895-1636 | www.liletterestaurant.com | Lunch & Dinner Tue-Sat

Boucherie   90.1

Nathanial Zimet used to be known as "the guy who served delicious barbecue from a purple truck." But handing ribs through a window for the rest of his life didn't sound that appealing to Zimet, so he opened this restaurant in the space that housed Iris before its move to the French Quarter. Zimet's creations come in two sizes: small plates like boudin balls with aioli or a blackened shrimp and grit cake, and larger plates like a grilled Fudge Family Farms pork chop with fennel seed spaetzle. Reviewers call it "a gem" that serves "amazing food at affordable prices," which explains why the foyer always seems to be "filled with people who are waiting for a table."

Southern | Informal | Moderate | uptown | 8115 Jeannette St. | 504-862-5514 | www.boucherie-nola.com | Dinner Mon, Wed-Sat, Thu-Fri lunch

Commander's Palace   90.0

At one time, especially when Emeril Lagasse was the chef, this historic Garden District restaurant could stake a claim to being among the most important in the country. But those days are gone, and Ella Brennan's establishment has become more of a place that American presidents like to frequent when they come to town (Ronald Reagan was purportedly a fan), as well as a destination for the visiting country-club crowd, who are happy dining on tame, though well-made, étouffées and gumbos. A number of classic New Orleans cocktails, like the Sazerac and the Ramos Gin Fizz, provide liquid accompaniment. And the jazz brunch is popular, as is the option of dining on the terrace when the weather cooperates.

Creole | Casual | Expensive | garden district | 1403 Washington Ave. | 504-899-8221 | www.commanderspalace.com | Lunch & Dinner daily

Emeril's   90.0

If there was ever a restaurant where a chef's celebrity status might have a negative impact on the cuisine, this would be it. But put yourself in the hands of this kitchen and ask them to cook for you, and they will treat you like a knowledgeable diner rather than the ordinary tourist or someone visiting the city for a convention. A blend of Creole and New American cuisine, the menu features dishes like angel hair pasta with smoked mushrooms and a tasso cream sauce or flatiron steak with Gorgonzola-flavored potatoes and a tomato-balsamic vinaigrette. There's a terrific wine list that features bottles from all over the world including "a number of hard-to-find, reasonably priced Burgundies."

New Louisiana | Casual | Expensive | warehouse district | 800 Tchoupitoulas St. | 504-528-9393 | www.emerils.com | Dinner daily, Lunch Mon-Fri

Herbsaint   90.0

While it's the most formal of Donald Link's various restaurants, Herbsaint is more akin to an upscale bistro than a grand dining experience. Link made his name serving a refined version of Cajun fare, such as starters like Louisiana shrimp and grits with tasso and okra, while his mains trend more toward American and French fare, like grilled Green Field Farms chicken with turnip mashed potatoes or a Kurobuta pork belly cassoulet that is "so rich and unctuous that it brings new meaning to the phrase slow-cooked." Even the desserts attracted praise (they rarely do in New Orleans), with one person cautioning visitors "not to miss the exceptional banana cream pie."

Cajun | Casual | Expensive | 701 St. Charles Ave. | 504-524-4114 | www.herbsaint.com | Lunch & Dinner Mon-Sat

TOP LOCAL CHOICE

Antoine's   89.5

"One hundred years ago, Antoine's was Commander's Palace in its prime, but it has seen much better days," sums up the sentiment about this institution that dates back to the 1850s. But those in the mood for ancient dishes like oysters Bienville, trout Pontchartrain, poulet Rochambeau or a filet of beef, simply grilled and served with sides of Alciatore sauce and Brabant potatoes, accompanied by samples from the 25,000-bottle wine cellar, should consider booking a table. After all, even though "it has slipped a bit over the years," it remains "the perfect place to experience the taste and feel of classic New Orleans" throughout the eras – which are lovingly evoked in multiple dining rooms decorated in different period styles.

Creole | Casual | Expensive | french quarter | 713 St. Louis St. | 504-581-4422 | www.antoines.com | Lunch & Dinner Mon-Sat, Sun jazz brunch

Irene's Cuisine   89.5

A Southern Italian restaurant in the French Quarter that has managed not to succumb to the prevailing Creole influence is rare, though it does reflect the local heritage in dishes like soft-shell crab linguine in a crawfish sauce. "Behind the times in every way," it offers "the perfect meal for those who are in need of a rib-sticking garlic fix." Apparently their numbers are many, because the line of customers starts forming at 4:00 p.m. (of course, the limited reservation policy may have something to do with that).

Italian | Casual | Moderate | french quarter | 539 St. Philip St. | 504-529-8811 | Dinner Mon-Sat

MiLa   89.5

The road to Slade and Allison Vines-Rushing's restaurant runs through some of New York City's top kitchens. But now that these Mississippi and Louisiana (get the name now?) expats are back home, they are busy pleasing diners with their "Southern food with an elegant, modern twist," like oysters Rockefeller "deconstructed" and roasted rack of lamb with black-eyed pea purée, roasted okra and tomato jam. While comments like "the food is well-conceived and well-crafted" indicate that reviewers generally like the cooking, the experience is dragged down by an "unexceptional dining room."

New American | Casual | Moderate | business district | 817 Common St. | 504-412-2580 | www.milaneworleans.com | Lunch & Dinner Mon-Fri Sat dinner only

Middendorf's (42 miles northwest in Akers)   89.5

"I have a soft spot for Middendorf's as my uncle started taking me there by boat at age three. The food is fresh and wonderful, and the mix of people come from all walks of life." "My father turned me on to this place years ago, and I always stop there on our way to my parents' to buy the seafood gumbo or for a family meal." "For casual eating it's the top of its genre. Overlooking the lake, the setting is beautiful." These comments say it all about this veteran, whose specialty is thinly cut fried catfish.

Seafood | Informal | Moderate | akers | 30160 Highway 51 S. | 985-386-6666 | www.middendorfsrestaurant.com | Lunch & Dinner Wed-Sun

Mosca's (16 miles southwest in Avondale)   89.5

This roadhouse has its rabid fans, who have been enjoying its "weird mix of Italian and Creole cooking" for decades – even before Calvin Trillin immortalized the place in his seminal book for foodies, *American Fried* (1975). While Trillin discussed a number of dishes, like the Italian crab salad, spaghetti Bordelaise and chicken à la Grande, he was at his most poetic when writing about the oysters Mosca, a pie-like affair made with oysters, bread crumbs, Creole seasoning, olive oil and garlic, a concoction that could exist only within earshot of New Orleans.

Italian | Informal | Moderate | avondale | 4137 Hwy. 90 W. | 504-436-9942 | www.moscasrestaurant.com | Dinner Tue-Sat

August   89.0

Once the premier dining destination in the city, John Besh's first restaurant seems to have run into the speed bump of inconsistency, with comments like "I've had great meals as well as some ordinary ones" typifying our reviewers' reactions. It's a shame, because the room – an old tobacco warehouse built at the beginning of the 19th century – is always stunning, even if the cuisine, such as lacquered Berkshire pork belly with Louisiana crawfish, olives and blood orange, is often lacking. Overexpansion could well be the culprit: Besh now heads a seven-restaurant empire in the city.

New Louisiana | Casual | Expensive | warehouse district | 301 Tchoupitoulas St. | 504-299-9777 | www.restaurantaugust.com | Dinner daily, Lunch Mon-Fri

Bayona   89.0

The website for Susan Spicer's restaurant states: "Our restaurant gives you New Orleans, our menu gives you the world." There's a split of opinion about this concept – and a menu that ranges from a smoked salmon beignet to a Niman Ranch pork chop with crispy polenta and roasted red-pepper relish. Visitors feel "There isn't enough local flavor to the food." But residents who get to eat Creole and Cajun cooking on a daily basis find Spicer's cuisine "an inventive infusion of modern techniques and influence rooted in the classics." There's garden seating in nice weather, and the odds of celebrity-spotting here are among the highest in the city.

New American | Casual | Expensive | french quarter | 430 Dauphine St. | 504-525-4455 | www.bayona.com | Lunch & Dinner Wed-Sat, Mon-Tue dinner only

Pascal's Manale   89.0

Having opened its doors in 1913, this sedate spot in the Garden District beats Casamento's by six years for the distinction of the city's oldest Italian/Creole restaurant. Its second claim to fame is that this is where BBQ shrimp was invented and still reigns 78 years later as the specialty of the house. Other quirky dishes include a pan roast of local oysters, shrimp and crabmeat or veal Gambero, sautéed veal topped with shrimp. Comments were split between "You have not eaten until you have had the BBQ shrimp here" and "in many ways, of sentimental interest only."

Italian | Casual | Moderate | garden district | 1838 Napoleon Ave. | 504-895-4877 | www.neworleansrestaurants.com/pascalsmanale | Lunch & Dinner Mon-Fri Sat dinner only

Upperline   88.5

Set in a "cozy house near the Garden District," JoAnne Clevenger's restaurant is "as comfortable as an old shoe." Something of an insiders' secret, this dining room is typically filled with locals enjoying "Creole cuisine with a Southern flair," like fried green tomatoes with shrimp remoulade, crispy oysters St. Claude and veal grillades with mushrooms and cheddar grits. "Personal attention" from the staff makes for a "less touristy," "grown-up atmosphere." One reviewer attempted to describe the restaurant's place in the NOLA hierarchy by noting that "Along with Clancy's, they serve the best Creole cuisine outside of the Quarter."

Creole | Casual | Moderate | garden district | 1413 Upperline St. | 504-891-9822 | www.upperline.com | Dinner Wed-Sun

Gautreau's   88.0

A mix of smart-looking locals and well-heeled visitors can be found in this bustling uptown dining room with a classic New Orleans feel. But despite the authentic ambience, Sue Zemanick's cooking is not specific to the region, instead focusing on New American fare like seared sea scallops with cauliflower Polonaise and a bacon-wrapped pork tenderloin with Bloomsdale spinach, roasted peppers, corn and natural jus. Reviewers are pretty much split: One contingent says, "Great uptown restaurant with a wonderful atmosphere and amazing food," while others counter with, "It's missing a spark," adding, "You could eat this style of food anywhere in the country."

New American | Casual | Expensive | uptown | 1728 Soniat St. | 504-899-7397 | www.gautreausrestaurant.com | Dinner Mon-Sat

La Petite Grocery   88.0

"Romantic, with a menu that includes old favorites along with newer dishes" is how one reviewer described this restaurant – named in homage to the grocery store that stood on this site from the late 1800s to 1982. Justin Devillier's menu features starters like short ribs braised in Abita root beer with potato croquettes and house-made pickles, followed by mains of drum or grouper with a blue crab beignet and popcorn rice. It's not all that well-known, but those who have been there compliment the "impeccable food" and "a staff that will bend over backward" to please you. Near Napoleon Avenue, it's an ideal break after cruising the art galleries and antiques shops that line Magazine Street.

New Louisiana | Casual | Moderate | garden district | 4238 Magazine St. | 504-891-3377 | www.lapetitegrocery.com | Lunch & Dinner Tue-Sat

ACCEPTABLE

Bourbon House   87.5
Seafood & Oyster Bar

This Brennan-clan restaurant focuses on the local catch, presented in large towers of shellfish, oysters baked in one of four styles and mains like seafood au gratin. Reviewers call it "a reliable delivery of a fish and shellfish-centered menu," noting it offers "a more casual dining alternative to *les grandes dames*" of the city. It's one of the few quality restaurants located in the midst of the nonstop party that takes place on Bourbon Street every evening, making it "perfect for people-watching" while enjoying a drink or dinner.

Seafood | Casual | Moderate | french quarter | 144 Bourbon St. | 504-522-0111 | www.bourbon-house.com | Open daily

Drago's   87.5

There is only one reason anyone goes to this restaurant: oysters topped with minced garlic, butter, Parmesan cheese and ground pepper and placed on a hot grill. While the bivalves cook from underneath, the other ingredients melt until the oysters are coated with a "cheesy, garlicky, salty bit of heaven." They also serve a full seafood menu, but "nothing else is worth eating," save for a "fried soft-shell crab the size of a soccer ball" and the bread, which "you can dip into the cheesy butter" after you slurp down the oysters.

Seafood | Informal | Moderate | business district | Hilton | 2 Poydras St. | 504-584-3911 | www.dragosrestaurant.com | Lunch & Dinner Mon-Sat

Pelican Club   87.5

In an attempt to evoke a bygone style of dining, Richard and Jean-Stinnett Hughes converted a 19th-century townhouse in the heart of the French Quarter. There they offer a menu with one foot in the city (panéed Gulf shrimp with jumbo lump crabmeat) and the other firmly planted in America (roasted rack of Australian lamb with a rosemary pesto crust and truffled mashed potatoes). Not as well-known as some of the other restaurants in the Quarter, it's frequented by locals as well as visitors, one of whom called it "a standby when I visit the city."

New American | Casual | Expensive | french quarter | 312 Exchange Pl. | 504-523-1504 | www.pelicanclub.com | Dinner daily

Dante's Kitchen   87.0

A bit more obscure than other restaurants in the city (probably because it's located in the far-western reaches, 20 minutes from downtown), Dante's emphasizes locally grown ingredients in dishes like Cajun boudin rouge with sweet peppers and preserved peaches and the house specialty, redfish on the half shell (sautéed redfish topped with crabmeat and herbs). And with dishes like debris and poached eggs, a shrimp étouffée omelet and alligator sausage sliders, the Sunday brunch is one of the most popular meals of the week.

New Louisiana | Informal | Moderate | riverbend | 736 Dante St. | 504-861-3121 | www.danteskitchen.com | Dinner Wed-Mon, Lunch Sat-Sun

Deanie's Seafood   87.0

Reviewers say while it isn't as renown as other venues, "You will find the true New Orleans" at this seafood restaurant in the French Quarter. "The menu is a veritable roadmap of Creole treats, including barbecue shrimp, crawfish étouffée and crabmeat au gratin, along with "artery-clogging fried specialties" like oysters and soft-shell crabs. While some reviewers claim "It used to be better," "It's a good choice if you like to eat mountains of fried food."

Seafood | Informal | Moderate | french quarter | 841 Iberville St. | 504-581-1316 | www.deanies.com | Lunch & Dinner daily

Green Goddess   86.5

With dishes like Tumblin' Dice (cubes of seared tuna and watermelon), Shrimp Wearing a Grass Skirt (roasted shrimp with pineapple and coconut slaw) and Spooky Blue Corn Crepes (filled with a ragout of huitlacoche, wild mushrooms and brandy), it's easy to understand why local hipsters flock to this restaurant when they visit the Quarter. Reviewers call it "charming, exotic and intoxicating," while warning that it's so tiny that it's hard to get a seat when the weather isn't good enough to eat outside.

Eclectic | Informal | Moderate | french qtr | 307 Exchange Pl. | 504-301-3347 | www.greengoddessnola.com | Dinner Thu-Sun, Lunch daily

Iris   86.5

After making a name for themselves when they were located uptown, Ian Schnoebelen and Laurie Casebonne – who get our vote for local restaurant owners with the best names – moved their place to the heart of the French Quarter. (Boucherie now occupies their old premises.) Dishes like pork tenderloin from Fudge Farms wrapped in house-made bacon, with polenta, peperonata and baby greens, have reviewers calling Schnoebelen's cuisine "unique in a city that always tries to spin itself in the same Cajun and Creole direction."

New American | Informal | Moderate | french qtr | 321 N Peters | 504-299-3944 | www.irisneworleans.com | No dinner Tue, Lunch Thu-Fri

Jacques-Imo's   86.5

You're guaranteed to wait in the longest lines in the city for the privilege of eating Jacques Leonardi's cooking. The menu can make anyone's mouth water: shrimp and alligator sausage cheesecake, fried green tomatoes with shrimp remoulade, swordfish with Jack's voodoo mojo sauce, Carpet-Bagger steak with bleu cheese, onions oysters and hollandaise and panéed rabbit with oyster tasso pasta are just some of the tasty-sounding creations. "Guaranteed fun" say reviewers while warning, "Expect the dining room to be filled with students from nearby Tulane University eating dinner with their parents."

Cajun | Informal | Moderate | uptown | 8324 Oak St. | 504-861-0886 | www.jacquesimoscafe. com | Dinner Mon-Sat

Acme Oyster House   86.0

If you want to knock back some oysters and an ice-cold beer before rushing off to your next appointment, head on over to this Bourbon Street institution where they have been shucking them by the dozen since 1910. The cooked fare includes classics like étouffée, jambalaya and gumbo, as well all sorts of fried seafood dishes, which are served either on a platter or in a po-boy, with bread from Gambino's Bakery. While it's calm during the week, weekends means "lengthy lines that often reach around the block" of both tourists and locals alike.

Seafood | Informal | Inexpensive | french quarter | 724 Iberville St. | 504-522-5973 | www.acmeoyster.com | Lunch & Dinner daily

Bon Ton Café   86.0

"The best étouffée and bisque" are available year-round at this business district restaurant that opens its doors only on weekdays. A number of dishes based on longstanding recipes are unique: redfish Bon Ton, oysters Alvin and our favorite, fried catfish filet with Alzina's special sauce. If you want something simple, perhaps you'd prefer a piece of Gulf fish topped with grilled oysters, shrimp or sautéed crabmeat.

Creole | Casual | Moderate | business district | 401 Magazine St. | 504-524-3386 | www.thebontoncafe.com | Lunch & Dinner Mon-Fri

Brennan's   86.0

Despite a menu loaded with exotic-sounding Creole dishes like chicken Lazone and trout Kotwitz, the feeling is that this classic from the Brennan family "has seen better days." Still, despite the low rating, it's clear that people have a soft spot for it – especially at breakfast, when a dozen egg preparations sport names like Hussarde, Sardou and Lafourche.

Creole | Casual | Moderate | french quarter | 417 Royal St. | 504-525-9711 | www.brennansneworleans.com | Breakfast & Dinner daily

GW Fins   86.0

For years this was considered New Orleans' best straightforward seafood restaurant. Then Hurricane Katrina happened and "the spark went out of the cooking," though the "terrific variety of local and internationally caught fish" has remained the same. It still offers an "elegant atmosphere" and makes for a reasonable choice when one doesn't want to eat Creole-style cooking while in NOLA. Someone should consider changing the name as it sounds like a chain restaurant.

Seafood | Casual | Expensive | french quarter | 808 Bienville Ave. | 504-581-3467 | www.gwfins. com | Dinner daily

K-Paul's   86.0

It is not unusual for us to hear reviewers say, "Much better than the tourist trap I expected" when describing this iconic restaurant where Paul Prudhomme introduced blackened redfish – since copied at restaurants all over the country – back in 1979. Although the food isn't as unusual as it was in its heyday (and before Prudhomme became a brand), the kitchen is "still turning out decent versions" of his signature dishes like bronzed swordfish with hot Fanny sauce as well as his versions of local classics like étouffée, gumbo and jambalaya.

Cajun | Informal | Moderate | french quarter | 416 Chartres St. | 504-596-2530 | www.kpauls.com | Dinner Mon-Sat, Lunch Thu-Sat

Palace Café   85.5

All you need to know about this restaurant is that it's "Dickie Brennan's Palace Café." So, if you are the type of person who likes restaurants run by the Brennan family, we suspect you will like this one, too. Its particular theme is its support of local farmers and fisherman. The menu is fairly typical, but it does feature a few unusual appetizers, like a napoleon of pork and grits and something that goes by the name of crabmeat cheesecake.

New American | Casual | Expensive | french quarter | 605 Canal St. | 504-523-1661 | www.palacecafe.com | Lunch & Dinner daily

NOLA   85.0

Those who are drawn to Emeril Lagasse's cooking say, "I've always enjoyed this restaurant for its fresh ingredients and nice wine list." The contemporary Louisiana cuisine, like buttermilk fried chicken breast with bourbon mashed sweet potatoes and Smithfield ham cream gravy, makes it worthwhile to put up with what many consider the "slow" and "standoffish" service. The ambience of the dining room is relaxed in comparison to Emeril's namesake restaurant.

New Louisiana | Casual | Expensive | french quarter | 8115 Jeannette St. | 504-862-5514 | www.boucherie-nola.com | Dinner daily, Lunch Thu-Sun

OTHER RESTAURANTS MENTIONED

Dickie Brennan's   84.5
Steakhouse

When it comes to restaurants run by the Brennan family, you always know what you are getting: surprisingly good food for a place that caters to a crowd of tourists and conventioneers. The menu isexactly what you expected: starters featuring shrimp, oyster and crabs, followed by grilled steaks and different varieties of Gulf fish. "The Brennans always do a good job, and this is no exception" sums up reviewers' sentiments.

Steakhouse | Casual | Expensive | french quarter | 716 Iberville St. | 504-522-2467 | www.dickiebrennanssteakhouse.com | Dinner daily, Fri lunch

Mr. B's Bistro   83.5

Half of our reviewers – including one who claimed to have eaten here over 100 times – like this place, often referred to as "Brennan's lite" while the other half says, "The only reason to go is for the buzz in the room or for celebrity spotting." But one thing most people agree on is "terrific barbecue shrimp" which sets the standard in the city.

Creole | Casual | Moderate | french quarter | 201 Royal St. | 504-523-2078 | www.mrbsbistro.com | Lunch & Dinner daily

Red Fish Grill   82.5

Given how many local eateries are operated by branches of the Brennan family, perhaps the city should adopt this slogan for its restaurants: "If it's not one Brennan, then it's the other." In this instance it's Ralph, and his seafood restaurant was criticized for being "too busy" and "too touristy"; the food has "decent, but no spectacular flavors."

Creole | Casual | Moderate | french quarter | 115 Bourbon St. | 504-598-1200 | www.redfishgrill.com | Lunch & Dinner daily

Arnaud's   82.0

Of the city's three institutions (along with Antoine's and Galatoire's), Arnaud's hasn't bothered to maintain the same high standards, with one reviewer citing "faded glory that's as likely to disappoint as satisfy." While a few claim to still enjoy dishes like shrimp rémoulade and pommes soufflé, the consensus is, "it has been trading on its reputation" and "diners should do their best to avoid it."

Creole | Casual | Expensive | french quarter | 813 Bienville St. | 504-523-5433 | www.arnauds.com | Dinner daily

Court of Two Sisters   81.0

"It's an overpriced tourist place," "The food quality is very low," "a place solely for tourists – the buses stop right outside" and "I gave this an acceptable rating only because of the beautiful setting; you can get so much better food elsewhere in New Orleans" just about sum up how our reviewers feel about this restaurant. Okay, a few people claimed they enjoyed the Jazz Brunch on Sundays.

Creole | Casual | Expensive | french quarter | 613 Royal St. | 504-522-7261 | www.courtoftwosisters.com | Open daily

Emeril's Delmonico   80.5

Reviewers aren't wild about this effort from Emeril, saying it offers "the heaviest cooking of all haute Creole eateries, with black roux, demi-glace and foie gras wherever you turn." Another knock was directed at a kitchen that wouldn't accommodate a dietary restriction because "the chef will only let it leave the kitchen the way he likes to prepare it."

Creole | Casual | Expensive | garden district | 1300 St. Charles Ave. | 504-525-4937 | www.emerils.com | Dinner daily

Cheap Eats

UNIQUELY DELICIOUS

Willie Mae's Scotch House 8.9

Crisp on the outside and full of tender and steaming-hot meat on the inside: If anyone knows where you can find better fried chicken than what is served at this hole-in-the-wall located about a mile northwest of the French Quarter, do us a favor and let us know. Certainly our reviewers, who say things like "I can't imagine being in New Orleans without having at least one lunch here" and "an institution in the very best sense of the word," haven't been able to. The non-chicken eaters can opt for smothered veal or a fried pork chop that was

described as "not too shabby either," all of which which you can enjoy with sides like red beans and rice, potato salad or "a succulent plate of butter beans and greens." The modest lines mean you can expect a short wait for a table and, since the chicken is cooked to order in a frying pan, you can also expect a short wait for your food.

Southern | Inexpensive | seventh ward | 2401 Saint Ann St. | 504-822-9503 | Lunch Mon-Sat

Central Grocery   8.4

Given how many thousands of Italian cold-cut sandwiches are out there, finding one that stands apart from the competition is a significant achievement. But at this funny Italian grocery across from the French Market, you will be one of 50-odd people waiting in line to order the cherished muffuletta, a round, hard seeded roll that is filled with an assortment of Italian cold cuts and topped with giardiniera (marinated and pickled vegetables). You can eat your sandwich, which is the size of four normal-sized sandwiches, making it large enough to feed multiple people, while standing at one of a number of counters, or for a scenic lunch you can walk across the street and sit on a bench alongside the Mississippi River.

Sandwiches | Inexpensive | french quarter | 923 Decatur St. | 504-523-1620 | Lunch Tue-Sat

Camellia Grill   8.3

A local institution since 1946, the Camellia Grill is one of those places where the countermen greet regulars by pounding fists or with a "Yo, what up?" Despite the amusing sideshow, the food isn't any different from the standard greasy-spoon coffee shop fare that is available at diners all over the country, save for the omelets, which, because they are aerated in a malted mixer before the mixture is poured into the griddle, puff up while cooking. During the three years it was closed after Hurricane

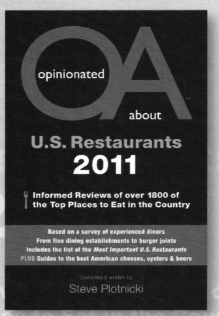

Katrina, fans covered the building with love notes, begging them to reopen.

Coffee Shop | Inexpensive | riverbend | 626 South Carrollton Ave. | 504- 309-2679 | www.camelliagrill.net | Open daily

Cochon Butcher   8.3

This "gem of a lunch counter" located around the corner from Donald Link's popular Cochon serves up the best sandwiches in New Orleans. The secret: its homemade, "show-stealing charcuterie," which Link features in sandwiches ranging from a Cuban made with cochon de lait, pastrami with sauerkraut on rye and the house version of the muffuletta. There's also a broad contingency that praises the boudin that Link makes in house, saying: "You have to make the two-hour trip to Cajun country to find one as good." A small butcher counter sells various cuts of meats to take home.

Sandwiches | warehouse district. | 930 Tchoupitoulas St. | 504-588-7675 | www.cochon-butcher.com | Open daily

Café du Monde   8.0

One wonders how many of those doughnut-like beignets they have served at this French Market classic, "a tourist trap that you absolutely have to visit," since it opened in 1862. Or maybe someone has kept count of the number of cups of chicory-flavored coffee (the other bestseller on the small menu) they've sold. At any event, being open 24 hours means you'll never have to go without a beignet, and if you arrive at 3:00 a.m. you will be surprised at how many people are sitting around sipping coffee while getting confectioners' sugar all over their clothing.

Dessert | Informal | Inexpensive | french quarter | French Market | 800 Decatur St. | 504-525-4544 | www.cafedumonde.com | Open daily

Dooky Chase   8.0

Much has been written about the Chases, who, after Hurricane Katrina struck, lived in a FEMA trailer across from their restaurant. Now in her 88th year, Leah Chase still works the stoves, turning out classics like shrimp Clemenceau as well as fried chicken that one reviewer described as "crisp, moist, plump, greaseless and entirely delicious," while Dooky sits in the restaurant's vestibule greeting their customers. Leah Chase is as passionate about art as she is about food, and the restaurant's elegant dining room – filled with beautiful contemporary African-American art – is worth a visit on its own.

Southern | Moderate | treme | 2301 Orleans Ave. | 504-821-0600 | Lunch Tue-Fri

RECOMMENDED

Crabby Jack's   7.5

When reviewers are willing to trek out to the edges of New Orleans just for a sandwich, you know that something special is going on. Indeed, Crabby Jack's, owned by the same people who own Jacques-Imo's, serves up "some of the most overstuffed and delicious po-boys" in the city. In addition to the standard fillings (oysters, shrimp), there are a number of sandwiches that step outside the box by including items like rabbit and duck. En route from the airport, one reviewer told us, "I always make it my first stop when I fly into town."

Sandwiches | Inexpensive | jefferson | 428 Jefferson Hwy. | 504-833-2722 | Lunch Mon-Sat

Casamento's   7.3

In business since 1919, Casamento's is the home of the oyster loaf (basically two thick slices of bread holding anywhere from a half dozen to a dozen fried oysters). It also offers a loaf with shrimp, fried trout or catfish. Other specialties include oysters on the half shell (some say they're the best in the city) or in a milk-based stew, along with a few Italian specialties like fried calamari or spaghetti and meatballs. The long lines can be oppressive, but once you get within eyeshot of the dining room, you will find yourself in front of the oyster shucker and you can pass the time by slurping up a few dozen.

Seafood | Inexpensive | uptown | 4330 Magazine St. | 504-895-9761 | www.casamentosrestaurant. com | Dinner Thu-Sat, Lunch Tue-Sat

Elizabeth's   7.3

It's worth traveling to the Bywater (the far eastern end of the city) for "the best brunch in New Orleans." The wide array of regional delights includes grit cakes with tasso gravy, cornbread waffles with a duck and sweet potato hash and the Cajun version of the British classic, bubble 'n' squeak (bacon, shrimp and cabbage topped with poached eggs and hollandaise). The savory dishes that are available at lunch and dinner include a BLT made with crisped hog jowls and sautéed boneless chicken with mushroom and tasso sauce. The ambience is as casual as it gets in this old tavern across from the Mississippi that has been converted into a roadhouse.

Eclectic | Inexpensive | bywater | 601 Gallier St. | 504-944-9272 | www.elizabeths-restaurant.com | Lunch & Dinner Tue-Sun

OTHER PLACES MENTIONED

Domilise's Po-Boys   6.5

It's surprising to find a long line of people waiting to place their order at this "hole in the wall of a restaurant" located in a quiet residential neighborhood about 20 minutes outside the French Quarter. The ordering procedure is as unusual as the venue: the employees multi-task, so your order-taker is also the one who builds your sandwich, and brings it to your table. You tell either of the two people manning the main counter what you want, then "watch [their] practiced hands make your sandwich using fresh

ingredients right before your eyes." In order to quench your thirst, a third worker serves drinks.

Sandwiches | Inexpensive | uptown | 5240 Annunciation St. | 504-899-9126 | Lunch Fri-Wed

Mother's   6.4

Everyone in the long line of people outside this "funky sandwich shop" located near the Superdome is waiting to order po-boys, which they've been serving on this site since 1938. The offerings range from the traditional (fried oysters) to the obscure (debris – a French loaf stuffed with roast beef drippings) to what they claim is "the world's best baked ham." The website boasts they serve 175,000 pounds of ham and roast beef a year. There is also classic Cajun fare, like rice, beans and sausages, and breakfast dishes like biscuits with blackened ham and chicory coffee. Whether it's worth the wait is highly debatable, though everyone agrees that décor-wise "it's a dump."

Sandwiches | Inexpensive | financial district | 401 Poydras St. | 504-523-9656 | www.mothersrestaurant.net | Open daily

Port of Call   6.4

New Orleans' most famous hamburger can be found at this high-energy tavern at the far edge of the French Quarter. "Massive and incredibly juicy" patties come with a steaming-hot baked potato "served with any fixings you desire." There is also steak on offer if you prefer your beef unground. Still, not everyone is a fan: "You wait in line for hours for what is just an ordinary burger," griped one reviewer. Blame the excessive wait on the"large portions"available at "affordable prices."

Hamburgers | Inexpensive | french quarter | 838 Esplanade Ave. | 504-523-0120 | www.portof- callneworleans.com | Lunch & Dinner daily

Orlando FL

RECOMMENDED

Victoria & Albert's   91.5

In a city where dining rooms are filled with children swarming around theme park characters, it wouldn't seem that many people would be willing to pay $125 a person for dinner. But the folks at Disney believed that such a market did in fact exist, and they created the V & A to cater to that clientele. From white truffles to Maine lobster to wild turbot to Kobe beef, you will have difficulty avoiding the luxury ingredients that abound on Scott Hunnel's menu (and why not at these prices?). Still, one reviewer who praised the food and wine pairings said, "It's hard to shake the fact that you're at Disney World," while another suggested leaving the kids with a sitter, saying, "At these prices Mickey and Minnie better be watching the kids."

New American | Formal | Very Expensive | Grand Floridian Resort & Spa | 4401 Floridian Way | 407-939-3463 | www.disneyworld.com | Dinner daily

TOP LOCAL CHOICE

California Grill   88.0

This is probably the most popular restaurant at Walt Disney World. And why not? With dishes like flatbread topped with mozzarella, heirloom tomatoes, balsamic onions and micro-basil; a short list of sushi rolls; and entrées like grilled pork tenderloin with goat cheese polenta, button mushrooms and a Zinfandel glaze, you would think you are dining in Yountville. Dinner includes "spectacular views" of the fireworks show that happens each evening. One person cautioned, "Make reservations in advance – on our last two visits to Orlando we couldn't get in!"

Californian | Informal | Expensive | Disney's Contemporary Resort | 4600 N. World Dr. | 407-939-3463 | www.disneyworld.com | Dinner daily

Le Coq au Vin   88.0

Contrary to popular belief, Orlando does not have a local ordinance mandating that people eat all of their meals in a theme park. So if you happen to be visiting the city without children in tow, consider checking out this "off-the-beaten path for tourists" French bistro "where you are likely to find local chefs dining on their night off." The menu is dominated by classics: onion tarte, steak tartare and cassoulet, though offerings like a chicken-and-sausage gumbo give the cuisine a decidedly Southern edge.

French Bistro | Casual | Expensive | 4800 S. Orange Ave. | 407-851-6980 | www.lecoqauvinrestaurant.com | Dinner Tue-Sun

ACCEPTABLE

Le Cellier Steakhouse   87.5

If you were the type of person who regularly drove a dog sled through the upper reaches of Québec, what would you want to eat after a long day of yelling "mush"? Why steak, *naturellement*. At least that's what the people at Epcot Center seem to think, having located this haven for meat eaters in the Canada Pavilion. It seems to be a good fit, as reviewers tell us, "This is one of the most difficult reservations to get in the entire complex." Besides the meat, you can also enjoy other unusual north-of-the-border treats, like cheddar cheese soup and chocolate "Moose."

Steakhouse | Casual | Expensive | Epcot Center/ Canada Pavilion | W. Seven Seas Dr. | 407-939-3463 | www.disneyworld.com | Lunch & Dinner daily

Flying Fish Café   85.5

Reviewers called this seafood specialist, with its nautical theme and location on Disney's Boardwalk, "a cute place for families," which seems a bit odd, given dishes like the potato-wrapped red snapper with a leek fondue that tips the scales at $36. Still, our panel seems willing to pay the fare, perhaps because the place "also works well for a romantic meal after you put the kids to bed." More than one reviewer even claimed, "It's my favorite restaurant in the Disney complex."

Seafood | Casual | Expensive | Disney BoardWalk Inn | 2101 N. Epcot Resort Blvd. | 407-939-3463 | www.disneyworld.com | Breakfast & Dinner daily

Artist Point   85.0

A "strict dress code" and a "higher price point" make this a different kind of dining experience for Disney World. They serve the cuisine of the Pacific Northwest, so the menu features items like Dungeness crab cakes and cedar-planked salmon, which are complemented by "an excellent list of wines from Oregon and Washington." Still, the dining room is full of kids (albeit ones that are behaved and well-dressed), causing one reviewer to say, "I'm always surprised when six children are sitting at the next table. Now, that's an expensive kid's meal!"

Pacific Northwest | Casual | Expensive | Wilderness Lodge Resort | 901 Timberline Dr. | 407-939-3463 | www.disneyworld.com | Dinner daily

Boma – Flavors of Africa   85.0

While every continent has animals, Walt Disney World has decided that their Animal Kingdom exhibit is the best fit for African cuisine. "Okay, it's a buffet – but what an interesting buffet," reviewers admit, with African flavors incorporated into dishes you and your children would recognize (corned beef boboti, anyone?). "After the banality of much of Disney's restaurants, this is a welcome change."

African | Informal | Moderate | Animal Kingdom Lodge | 2901 Osceola Pkwy. | 407-939-3463 | www.disneyworld.com | Breakfast & Dinner daily

Columbia   85.0

You don't find many restaurants that opened as a result of America's victory in the Spanish-American War. But this place, which began serving arroz con pollo in 1905 to waves of post-war Cuban immigrants, proudly fits that description. "I love Columbia for its old world charm, tableside service, and interesting food," runs a typical comment. More than 100 years later, it's developed eight locations around central and western Florida, and "Every one of the restaurants in the chain is consistently good."

Cuban | Casual | Moderate | 2117 E. Seventh Ave. | 813-248-4961 | www.columbiarestaurant.com | Lunch & Dinner daily

Emeril's   85.0

If you're tired of eating at the Walt Disney World complex, you can head on over to the Universal Orlando Resort and check out Emeril Lagasse's namesake restaurant, where he mixes Cajun fare like barbecue shrimp and pan-roasted redfish with such New American offerings as pork and clam Bolognese and sea scallops with butternut squash purée. Problem is, it leaves our reviewers a bit cold: "Emeril needs to get this place in shape," they say, adding it's "highly priced for the food you get and does not live up to Emeril's name."

New Louisiana | Casual | Expensive | Universal Resort | 6000 Universal Blvd. #702 | 407-224-2424 | www.emerils.com | Lunch & Dinner daily

Oxford MS

RECOMMENDED

City Grocery   90.0

As much historian as chef, John Currence is a virtual encyclopedia of the cooking of the South. While he preaches the gospel of the region's cuisine and is fanatical about the local ingredients, his menu is an unusual mix of Southern and Asian ideas, and includes dishes like grilled Caw Caw Creek pork chop with chili-stewed apples along with peanut-fried chicken confit with spicy Malaysian barbecue sauce and red pepper green beans. "Never had anything here that wasn't delicious," says one reviewer, though another felt "It's been hit or miss since Currence has opened additional restaurants."

Southern | Casual | Moderate | 152 Courthouse Sq. | 662-232-8080 | www.citygroceryonline.com | Lunch & Dinner Mon-Sat

TOP LOCAL CHOICE

Taylor Grocery   89.0

At this old, broken-down grocery store that looks like a set from the film *O Brother, Where Art Thou?* you will find "fried catfish that is as good as it gets." That and the "Mississippi gestalt" make it "a hell of a lot of fun" to eat here. They also serve all sorts of fried and barbecued food, and on game days you can order platters and set up a table along with the other home-team supporters on the Ole Miss campus.

Southern | Informal | Inexpensive | Old Taylor Rd. | 662-236-1716 | www.taylorgrocery.com | Dinner Thu-Sun

Palm Beach & Boca Raton FL

RECOMMENDED

Café Boulud   90.4

Once you leave the friendly confines of Miami, finding a good restaurant in South Florida can be difficult. That held true even in tony Palm Beach – until, that is, Daniel Boulud opened this outpost of his successful Manhattan bistro. Zach Bell's menu follows the same format as the New York location: There are four different styles of cuisine, ranging from a duo of beef with a potato gratin to octopus à la plancha served with chorizo, piquillo peppers and smoked-pepper aioli. There's a similarly good wine list, and you can enjoy "lovely patio seating" in the courtyard of the Brazilian Court Hotel.

French Bistro | Casual | Expensive | palm beach | Brazillian Court Hotel | 301 Australian Ave. | 561-655-6060 | www.danielnyc.com | Open daily

TOP LOCAL CHOICE

Abe & Louie's   88.5

The menu at this outpost of a popular Boston steakhouse offers a dozen cuts of dry-aged beef, various fish and seafood offerings (special mention: the popular swordfish chop) and daily specials that run the gamut from veal Oscar to lobster Fra Diavolo. The bar hosts a "lively singles scene," and you can supplement your meal with selections from "a well-stocked wine list." You're best off going on a weekday, as on weekends "the place is crawling with people who have flown in from cold-weather cities."

Steakhouse | Expensive | Moderate | boca raton | 2200 West Glades Rd. | (561) 447-0024 | www.abeand-louies.com | Lunch & Dinner Sun-Fri, Sat dinner only

Raleigh-Durham NC

RECOMMENDED

Lantern   91.3

If you were wondering what a pan-Asian restaurant that serves dishes like slow-cooked duck soup with mushrooms and noodles is doing in Chapel Hill, the answer is love. No, not just a chef's love of Asian cuisine. New Jersey native Andrea Reusing married a man from Chapel Hill, and so this charming city gained a chef who can turn out a top-notch version of Asian cuisine. Reusing is equally passionate about utilizing local ingredients, which turn up in dishes like North Carolina crabs prepared in a Vietnamese style; sake and tea-cured Cold Mountain pink trout; and barbecued Cane Creek Farm lemongrass pork. Reviewers praised the "very solid creative fusion cuisine," calling this "the best place to eat in the area," though a few criticized "a menu that hardly ever changes."

Asian | Informal | chapel hill | 423 W. Franklin St | 919-969-8846 | www.lanternrestaurant.com | Dinner Mon-Sat

Elaine's on Franklin   90.0

For those looking for contemporary Southern cuisine featuring regionally grown items, Bret Jenning's restaurant is a top choice in the Chapel Hill/Durham area. A "creative use of ingredients" turns up in dishes like a Labelle Farm foie gras BLT served with candied bacon, house-pickled tomatoes and arugula, and a pork tenderloin with sweet potato waffles and a warm bacon vinaigrette. Reviewers say it provides "occasional sparks of excellence in a modern take on Southern food," and "A perfectly executed version of upscale comfort food means I will return the next time I am visiting the area." Another plus is "one of the best wine lists in the Triangle."

Southern | Casual | Moderate | chapel hill | 454 W. Franklin St. | 919-960-2770 | www.elainesonfranklin.com | Dinner Tue-Sat

TOP LOCAL CHOICE

Magnolia Grill   89.5

When Ben and Karen Barker opened this restaurant in 1986, they were at the forefront of the New Southern cuisine movement. Twenty-five years later, reviewers are still calling their place "the defining restaurant of its genre," citing dishes like the soufflé of twice-baked grits topped with a ragout of mushrooms and shaved foie gras confit, or a grilled Eden Farm Berkshire pork chop served with a Creole mustard jus and apple-sauce. A "fair corkage fee" is another plus, but early closing hours are a huge minus. Still, "when it's at its best it can rival some of the top dining experiences in the world."

Southern | Casual | Moderate | durham | 185 E. Bay St. | 843-577-7771 | www.magnoliagrill.net | Dinner Tue-Sat

Restaurant Bonne Soirée   89.5

Francophiles looking for a well-cooked meal in the Research Triangle are likely to end up at this "lovely dining room reminiscent of a country inn." What they are after is Chip Smith's "solid French cooking," which features dishes like a leek, porcini and Gruyère tart or sweetbreads wrapped in veal, along with "a small but well-selected wine list" (with "excellent pairings") and a "knowledgeable staff" managed by Smith's wife, Tina Vaughn. While everyone agrees that Smith's cuisine is "perfectly executed," some reviewers faulted it as "lacking in inspiration."

french | Casual | Moderate | chapel hill | 431 W Franklin St. # 10 | 919-928-8388 | Dinner Tue-Sat

Fearrington House   89.0

One of the prestigious Relais & Châteaux properties in the States, Colin Bedford's kitchen is located in a European-style country inn in the heart of the Research Triangle. Unfortunately, while dishes like North Carolina white shrimp served with Perry Winkle Farm potato salad or seared foie gras with cornbread madeleines, port and pickled shallot sauce are well prepared, the food "doesn't have enough pizzazz to make it truly interesting." On the other hand, "a lovely atmosphere," "friendly service" and "a decent wine list" make it a pleasant experience, especially if you're spending the night there.

Southern | Casual | Expensive | pittsboro | 2000 Fearrington Village Ctr. | 919-542-2121 | www.fearrington.com | Dinner Tue-Sun

Nana's   89.0

Open since 1992, Scott Howell's eatery offers cuisine that's a bit more complex than some of the other restaurants in the region, with dishes like thick spaghetti with duck confit, shiitake and chanterelle mushrooms over a leek cream sauce and Kurobuta pork schnitzel with roasted Arkansas black apples and house-made sauerkraut. The feelings of reviewers are somewhat divided, with fans calling it "the most worldly and sophisticated restaurant in the Triangle," and the less-enthused finding "Solid cooking that won't disappoint nor impress, but there are better places to eat in the Triangle."

Southern | Casual | Moderate | durham | 2514 University Dr. | 919-493-8545 | www.nanasdurham.com | Dinner Mon-Sat

| ACCEPTABLE | OTHER PLACES MENTIONED |

Angus Barn   86.0

Opened in June of 1960, this "once-beloved" steakhouse was an institution until they lowered prices a few years back, and the quality of the food along with it. A large wine list is a draw, even though its prices have gone in the opposite direction of those of the food. Nevertheless, you can easily wait 30 minutes for a table, prompting one reviewer to joke, "If you're lucky, the line will be so long you'll leave."

Steakhouse | Casual | Moderate | 9401 Glenwood Ave. | 919-781-2444 | www.angusbarn.com | Dinner daily

Crook's Corner   84.5

Other than "the best shrimp 'n' grits" around, reviewers say the food at this restaurant is disappointing. The menu is straight out of the Southern cuisine handbook: chicken and country ham soup, jalapeño and cheddar hush puppies and Carolina barbecue. While it's a perfect fit for a college town, one reviewer told us, "I live in Chapel Hill, but only go about once a decade."

Southern | Informal | Moderate | chapel hill | 610 W. Franklin St. | 919-929-7643 | www.crookscorner.com | Dinner Tue-Sun, Brunch Sun

Four Square   84.0

Four Square is "one of the more civilized dining venues in town." Dishes like bisque of roasted pumpkin and salsify with a goat cheese marshmallow offer "a nice, contemporary take on Southern cuisine using top-notch local ingredients." However, while the comments about the food were fairly positive, a number of reviewers spoke of "management that made our visit unpleasant," causing them to vow, "We will never return."

Southern | Casual | Moderate | durham | 2701 Chapel Hill Rd. | 919-401-9877 | www.four-squarerestaurant.com | Dinner Mon-Sat

Revolution   82.5

With one reviewer telling us "the food is erratic" and "extremely variable – Revolution gave me one of the best and one of the worst dining experiences in the Triangle," it is fair to say that the food at this "big-city, modern in design and approach" restaurant is "hit or miss." But a "fairly good wine list" and a "very nice round bar area" make it a good choice for a cocktail, if not for dinner.

New American | Casual | Moderate | durham | 107 W. Main St. | 919-956-9999 | www.revolution-restaurant.com | Lunch & Dinner Mon-Sat

Weathervane   81.0

Considering that they operate one of the most successful gourmet and cookware shops in the country, we wonder why the owners of this shop can't run a better restaurant? It's "a lovely café that does not take advantage of the high-quality ingredients available in the retail shop," our reviewers say, though there's "a nice wine shop" on the premises; you can "buy a bottle and open it at the restaurant for a nominal corkage fee."

American | Informal | Moderate | chapel hill | University Mall/Hwy 15-501 at Estes Dr. | 919-929-9466 | www.southernseason.com | Open daily

Cheap Eats

OTHER PLACES MENTIONED

Mama Dip's Country Cooking   5.5

Because they often use ingredients one can purchase in the local grocery and serve dishes prepared by untrained cooks, places that offer regional American cuisine typically get low ratings with our reviewers. In this instance, comments like "It could be an okay local place, but nothing is executed well here" pretty much cover this local legend of a "soul food restaurant." A few did say, "I enjoyed the fried catfish and cornbread."

Southern | Inexpensive | chapel hill | 408 W. Rosemary St. | 919-942-5837 | www.mamadips.com | Open daily

Santa Rosa Beach FL

TOP LOCAL CHOICE

Fish Out of Water (73 miles east of Pensacola)   88.0

Given its location in a culinary wasteland, residents of the Water Color Inn & Resort should be thankful for this restaurant, whose menu features dishes like soup made from local chestnuts, oysters from Apalachicola Bay, Gulf tuna tartare, Florida hopper shrimp and local flounder and red snapper. An added bonus: "Children are welcomed, due to the vacation nature of the town," making this "one of the few places a where parents can enjoy a satisfying meal." A further plus: "stunning sunsets on the deck."

New American | Casual | Moderate | Water Color Inn & Resort | 34 Goldenrod Circle | 850-534-5050 | www.watercolorresort.com | Dinner daily (closed January)

Savannah GA

Sapphire Grill   88.0

While Paula Deen's place sucks up almost all of the culinary oxygen in Savannah, reviewers say, "Keep on walking past Lady & Sons to Chris Nason's cool, modern outpost." Nasan refers to his cooking as "coastal cuisine," exemplified by crab cakes with lobster cream and grilled Romaine lettuce, along with diver scallops, eggplant caviar and a fried quail egg. There's a "small-bistro atmosphere," and though the food was described as "pricey," the same person went on to say "I would return the next time I visited Savannah," a sound decision given the overall paucity of good places to eat in this quirky city.

New American | Casual | Moderate | 110 W. Congress St. | 912-443-9962 | www.sapphiregrill.com | Dinner daily

Elizabeth on 37th   86.5

With a menu filled with dishes based on local ingredients, like spicy Savannah red rice with Georgia shrimp and Half Moon River clams, Kelly Yambor continues to offer the type of New Southern cooking that was pioneered by the restaurant's founder Elizabeth Terry. But while the style of cooking might be the same, the level of enthusiasm isn't, with reviewers saying "The food is not as good as it used to be." But an "extensive and reasonably priced wine list" and a "beautiful, well-appointed dining room" cause even the most antagonistic to admit, "Though it doesn't have the magic it once had, it's still a lovely meal."

Southern | Casual | Expensive | 105 E. 37th St. | 912-236-5547 | www.elizabethon37th.net | Dinner daily

Lady & Sons   85.5

One expects to see Dr. Phil dining with Oprah and Regis Philbin at Paula Deen's restaurant. But rather than well-known celebrities, you are more likely to find a dining room filled with ordinary visitors (who have waited in two long lines) eating Southern dishes like peach BBQ grouper and chicken potpie. While a handful of reviewers called it "a comfortable and fun place to eat," the vast majority said it's a "total tourist trap," blasting the place as "way, way over-hyped." In fact, one weary reviewer claimed, "The only thing memorable about this restaurant was the long wait,"

Southern | Informal | Moderate | 102 W. Congress St. | 912-233-2600 | www.ladyandsons.com | Lunch daily, Dinner Mon-Sat

Cheap Eats

Mrs. Wilkes' Dining Room   6.9

Sema Wilkes began serving hungry boarders way back in 1943. Four generations of Wilkes have worked in the restaurant since that time, serving family-style platters of fried chicken, beef stew, meat loaf and sausage, along with 12 sides, to people seated at communal tables. Reviewers say "the authentic Savannah experience," described as "taking a page out of the 1950s," is something that "shouldn't be missed" – though one critic equated some of the food to "what you would find at a steam table."

Southern | Inexpensive | 107 W. Jones St. | 912-232-5997 | www.mrswilkes.com | Lunch Mon-Fri

Sea Island GA

Georgian Room at the Cloisters   90.4

You will have to drive more than 100 miles to find a formal dining experience on a par with the one at this luxurious Sea Island resort. Daniel Zeal's "refined Southern cuisine" includes chicken-fried pork belly with dates, Georgia pecan relish and maple barbecue sauce, and Maine lobster with tangerine butter, persimmons and sweet potato. "One of the best wine lists in the state" will help you wash down your food, and "a dining room that is the epitome of elegance," staffed with "servers who pamper you," does its best to reinforce the feeling that you are in the Old South. This is one of the few restaurants included in this guide where it's mandatory for men to wear a jacket to dinner.

New American | Formal | Expensive | The Cloisters | 100 Cloister Drive | 866-879-6238 | www.seaisland. com | Dinner Tue-Sat

Tampa FL

Bern's Steak House   93.8

The glowing comments about this venerable steakhouse include "If I get a choice, my last meal will be at Bern's," "It's not just the food, it's also about the atmosphere, attitude and service," "This is probably my second favorite restaurant in the U.S." and "For a place that is very high on the tourist food chain, the materials here are first-rate and the kitchen attentive." And that doesn't cover the wine list, described as "incredible," "divine," "extensive," "crazy," "huge" and "ginormous." Part of the experience is a separate dessert room, where you can top off your steak with a slice of German chocolate cake or a banana split while sipping a glass of aged Sauternes.

Steakhouse | Casual | Expensive | 1208 S. Howard Ave. | 813-251-2421 | www.bernssteakhouse.com | Dinner daily

Walland TN

Barn at Blackberry Farm, The   92.3

Reviewers wonder why the food at this luxurious resort, set in the foothills of the Smoky Mountains, doesn't match the spectacular setting. Some make the case that what the cuisine lacks in inventiveness, it makes up for in the combination of "spectacular ingredients," many of which (charcuterie, cheese and jams) have been grown or raised on the farm, "a helpful and caring staff" and "one of the best wine lists you will ever come across" (though the sommelier seems to hold back on the good stuff until you prove you know your varietals). But given the cost – it's "excruciatingly expensive (meals are included in the price of your room)" – more than one person commented that the place would benefit from hiring a world-class chef.

New American | Casual | Very Expensive | 1471 West Miller's Cove Rd. | 865-984-8166 | www.blackberry-farm.com | Dinner daily

Boston & New England

Bar Harbor ME

RECOMMENDED

Trenton Bridge Lobster Pound (5 miles east in Trenton)   **91.5**

Located just across the bridge from Bar Harbor, this is the favorite lobster pound of many a reviewer, with one going so far as to say, "It was the best lobster I've eaten in my life." There's a rumor that they have a permit to set traps in deeper, and colder, waters, resulting in a take of lobsters that offer "the most plump, moist and flavorful meat imaginable." And you can start the meal with "steamers that are as creamy as custard." One reviewer who downed a 3½ pound lobster with a bottle of vintage white Burgundy while sitting on a bench overlooking Thomas Bay described the entire experience as "sheer bliss."

Seafood | Informal | Moderate | trenton | 1237 Bar Harbor Rd. | 207-667-2977 | www.trentonbridgelobster.com | Lunch & Dinner daily in season

TOP LOCAL CHOICE

Havana   **89.0**

If you asked where we would expect to find a brash, Nuevo-Latino, party-style restaurant, Bar Harbor might be the last place we would guess. Yet here it is, and it is super-popular with both locals and visitors. Comments from fans were effusive: "So unbelievably fabulous that we ate there two nights in a row" and "still dreaming about the butter-poached lobster over the yam empanada with sweet corn drizzle." Also praised were "exemplary servers who do not quit trying to please their guests." A few spoil-sports snapped, "Latino-fusion cooking is a bit passé."

Pan-Latin | Informal | Moderate | 318 Main St. | 207-288-2822 | www.havanamaine.com | Dinner daily; closed in winter

Jordan Pond House   **88.0**

You need to book well in advance at this lovely spot in Acadia National Park that offers an "amazing setting overlooking Jordan Pond." Lunch is more popular than dinner, where the menu features simple American fare like baked scallops and lobster quiche. Popovers are the thing to order for dessert, as well as while having tea in the afternoon. "Just add some butter and strawberry jam and you'll be in heaven."

American | Informal | Moderate | Acadia National Park | 207-276-3316 | thejordanpondhouse.com | Lunch & Dinner daily May-Oct.

Thurston's Lobster Pound (18 miles west in Bernard)   **88.0**

Our reviewers have mixed feelings about this remote seafood restaurant located about 15 minutes outside of Bar Harbor. Despite its reputation among some diners as "the best lobster pound in the state," a fair share of our reviewers offered negative comments, like "no better than fair when compared to other pounds in the area" and "maybe I had an off lobster." Of course, the "lovely seaside setting" goes a long way in making it a pleasant experience.

Seafood | Informal | Moderate | bernard | Steamboat Wharf Rd. | 207-244-7600 | http://thurstonslobster.com | Lunch & Dinner daily in season

Cleonice Mediterranean Bistro   82.0
(21 miles northwest in Ellsworth)

Though dishes like dayboat cod cakes with herb aioli and Stone Cutter's osso buco with flageolet beans sound delicious, opinions about Cleonice and its menu of Mediterranean small plates, plus a raw bar, including local oysters and seafood tapas, are all over the map. Comments like "Rich Hanson serves fabulous food in a funky little restaurant" are countered with "It's clear that the kitchen has never tasted real Mediterranean cooking, or apparently their own."

Mediterranean | Informal | Moderate | ellsworth | 112 Main St. | 207-664-7554 | www.cleonice.com | Lunch & Dinner Mon-Sat, Sun dinner only

Cheap Eats

Bagaduce Lunch   7.5
(48 miles west in Brooksville)

"One of the better lobster rolls on the coast" is the big attraction at this takeaway shack by the side of Bagaduce Falls. It also offers fried seafood such as clams, scallops and haddock, and the onion rings are so good that they're serious contenders for "the best in the state." Add clean picnic tables to the mix, and no wonder some reviewers say, "This is where I take out-of-town guests for the true Maine experience."

Seafood | Inexpensive | brooksville | 145 Frank's Flat | Lunch & Dinner daily in season

Boston MA

HIGHLY RECOMMENDED

O Ya   94.4

Most chefs who open their own restaurants have résumés that include experience in famous kitchens. With the most notable name in his CV being that of Lettuce Entertain You Enterprises (where he was corporate chef), Tim Cushman's background is quiet by comparison; however, that hasn't curtailed his ability to create a popular restaurant. Rather than reflecting the mentorship of a Gagnaire or a Keller, Cushman draws his influence from Asia – specifically, from Japanese izakaya chefs. His Asian fusion menu is a delight to read and full of interesting-sounding creations like small plates of hamachi with spicy banana-pepper mousse and fried Kumamoto oyster with yuzu aioli and squid ink bubbles. Larger plates include five preparations of Wagyu beef and four of Poulet Rouge chicken, as well as eggs and truffles served four different ways. Wife Nancy Cushman handles the wines and cocktails and "would qualify for the title of master of sake if there were such a thing."

Japanese | Informal | Expensive | leather district | 9 East St. | 617-654-9900 | www.oyarestaurantboston.com | Dinner Tue-Sat

No. 9 Park   93.6

Perched atop Beacon Hill and facing the Massachusetts State House, this venue is the flagship of Barbara Lynch's six-restaurant empire, and the property that local ingredientistas typically name as their favorite dining spot in Boston. Lynch's varied menu combines the cuisines of the Italian and French countrysides, featuring dishes like her signature prune-stuffed gnocchi, a duo of Peking duck breast and confit leg with lentils and mustard greens or butter-poached lobster with Tuscan bread salad. Eating in the bar area is popular (you have the choice of ordering off either the dining room menu or the more casual bar menu) because of the expert mixologists, who shake, blend and stir up "a wide breadth of cocktails that span the decades, from pre-Prohibition classics to contemporary favorites." And Bostonians who occasionally play hooky during the workday recommended booking one of Lynch's "delicious multi-course lunch menus" that come with wine pairings.

Italian | Casual | Expensive | beacon hill | 9 Park St. | 617-742-9991 | www.no9park.com | Dinner Mon-Sat

Uni   92.8

Ken Oringer's sushi bar – a few steps down from his other eatery, Clio – is literally a restaurant within a restaurant. What sets it apart from the local competition is its fish, which one reviewer described as "knee-buckling good gems of the ocean." Sit back and let the chefs prepare an omakase that might include the house signature spoons – Japanese soup spoons filled with various delicacies, like the Uni Spoon (sea urchin, quail egg and osetra caviar), or fatty tuna minced with anchovy-caviar cream. Or try cooked dishes featuring luxury ingredients like a foie gras and barbecued eel sandwich served on sushi rice. A major benefit of sharing space with Clio is the dessert menu from Renae Herzog, who offers some of the most cutting-edge sweets in the country.

Japanese | Informal | Expensive | back bay | Eliot Hotel | 370 Commonwealth Ave. | 617-536-7200 | www.cliorestaurant.com | Dinner daily

Neptune Oyster   92.2

How can you go wrong with a restaurant that offers a raw bar with a dozen varieties of oysters as well as shrimp and sea urchin from Maine, along with crudos like hamachi tartare with pear-ginger vinaigrette and tuna ribbons with aioli? And if that isn't enough for you, how about one of the best lobster rolls in the country or entrées like lobster spaghettini or grilled swordfish with cherry tomato relish or cioppino? No wonder reviewers call this place "superb in every respect," even claiming "it's the best seafood restaurant of its kind in America." There's a carefully chosen wine list (owner Jeff Nace was once the beverage director at Olives), and the "service is as warm and friendly as the food is delicious."

Seafood/Raw Bar | Informal | Moderate | north end | 63 Salem St. | 617-742-3474 | www.neptuneoyster.com | Lunch & Dinner daily

RECOMMENDED

Rialto   91.6

Jody Adams made her mark serving Mediterranean cuisine. But after buying out her partners in 2007, she changed Rialto's format, and the focus is now on Italian regional cuisine, featuring the cooking from a different region each month. Recently, for example, her menu featured dishes from the Abruzzi/Mollise area: starters like a Maine lobster salad with avocado, fennel and vin santo, string pasta with fresh squid, capers, garlic and shaved bottarga, and slow-roasted duck with escarole, roasted fingerlings and Sicilian olives. While the restaurant has been around since 1994, "food that is subtle yet complex and flavorful," "a decent wine list" and "a handsome space" mean it's still "a top choice on the Cambridge side of the Charles River."

Italian | Casual | Expensive | harvard square | Charles Hotel | One Bennett St. | 617-661-5050 | www.rialto-restaurant.com | Dinner daily

Ten Tables   91.6

Krista Kranyak was hoping the Cambridge dining community would enjoy her cooking as much as the regulars who frequented her Jamaica Plain original. Well, she guessed right. Now diners can enjoy the same delicious food in two locations, each featuring its own discrete offerings. The menu here is a quirky mix of market cuisine and Mediterranean fare, like crispy bluefish cakes with marinated peppers and a sumac-yogurt sauce or Gianonne chicken à la mattone with smoked bacon and green garlic–vadouvan butter. Even simple dishes like a salad of Siena Farms baby red romaine with French feta, English peas, Breakfast radish, Persian cucumber and sherry vinaigrette are "bursting with flavor." One reviewer described the food as "moderately priced and delicious," while another praised Ten Tables for providing "the best service in Boston."

Mediterranean | Informal | Moderate | cambridge | 597 Centre St. | 617-524-8810 | www.tentables.net | Dinner daily

Clio   91.0

Though the menu had a French/Asian fusion slant to it when it first opened, these days Ken Oringer's cuisine is best described as "creative French with Asian influences." The menu features dishes like Nantucket Bay scallops with ginger salt, goat's-milk butter and argan oil, a cassoulet of lobster and sea urchin served with candied lemon or a Kobe rib eye with black fig chutney. Cutting-edge desserts are a specialty of the house (see review of Uni above); Renae Herzog turns out interesting creations, such as a milk chocolate croustillant with tangerine emulsion, cocoa crumble and black olive. Multiple reviewers called this their "favorite French restaurant in Boston."

French | Casual | Expensive | back bay | Eliot Hotel | 370 Commonwealth Ave. | 617-536-7200 | www.cliorestaurant.com | Dinner Mon-Sat

Troquet   90.8

It's easy to walk past this wine bar without realizing that its second-floor dining room is filled with diners who are enjoying a wine list "so good and so fairly priced" that "the food is almost an afterthought." Those who do manage to eat in-between sips of wine sup on starters like an English pea soup with peeky toe crab or a duo of foie gras with cherries and rhubarb agro dolce, along with entrées like slow-poached salmon with horseradish and Puy lentils or suckling pig with braised cabbage. The downstairs bar serves nearly 50 wines by the glass, each available in 2- or 4-oz. pours.

French Bistro | Casual | Expensive | theater district | 140 Boylston St. | 617-695-9463 | www.troquetboston.com | Dinner Tue-Sat

Locke-Ober   90.6

The merging of Lydia Shire's "Frenchified Yankee cuisine" and the amazing vintage Boston Brahmin–style dining room at this restaurant that goes back to the first half of the 19th century should add up to a venue that is buzzing with customers. But for some reason the combination has never really clicked, and as a result, Locke-Ober can feel old-fashioned and stodgy rather than retro and hip. It might help if they loosened things up a bit by dispensing with the silver serving platters and having the wait staff wear something more casual than tuxedos. When it comes to the food, however, Shire does a good job with longtime house classics like rum-and-tobacco-smoked salmon, JFK lobster stew, seasonal seafood, including soft-shell crabs and Nantucket Bay scallops and the rarely seen dessert Indian pudding.

American | Casual | Expensive | downtown | 3 Winter Pl. | 617-542-1340 | www.lockeober.com | Dinner Mon-Sat

L'Espalier   90.5

With opinions split between those who proclaimed, "This is the quintessential Boston dining experience" and others who snapped it's "an old-school restaurant with boring food," Frank McClelland's restaurant was an underachiever in our survey, given its reputation. The classic French cuisine features starters like a leek and potato soup with summer truffles and sautéed shrimp, along with entrées like smoked organic chicken or beef tenderloin that has been poached in port wine and is served with bone marrow. After years in an intimate town house, the restaurant recently moved to a new location on Boylston Street next to the Mandarin Oriental Hotel.

French | Formal | Expensive | back bay | 774 Boylston St. | 617-262-3023 | www.lespalier.com | Lunch & Dinner daily

Craigie on Main   90.3

After spending years on a quiet street off Harvard Square, Tony Maws moved his popular restaurant to the other side of Cambridge (one reviewer joked that Maws "swapped professors from Harvard Univerisity for those from nearby MIT"). While his new space is larger and "more bustling than the old one," his cuisine hasn't changed, and diners are still enjoying dishes like a soup of Long Island cheese squash with crispy matsutake mushrooms, a tempura of dayboat cod cheeks or organically raised lamb served three ways. The super-hungry can opt for either the six- or the ten-course tasting menus, while the more adventurous enjoy visiting the restaurant on Sunday evenings, when Maws offers his Chef's Whim Dinners. The wine list is ambitious and "based around Maws' commitment to serving small-producer, terroir-driven wines."

New American | Informal | Expensive | kendall square | 853 Main St. | 617-497-5511 | www.craigieonmain.com | Dinner Tue-Sun, Lunch Sun

Radius   90.3

There was a time when this showcase for chef Michael Schlow was considered the best contemporary restaurant in Boston. But after its management team opened Via Matta and the now-shuttered Great Bay, Radius slipped to the second tier. But reviewers are saying that "Schlow is back on track" now that he has bought out his partners. That he has been successful at it this quickly isn't all that surprising – even during the down times we would still collect the occasional comment lauding dishes like crunchy sweetbreads, beluga lentils, bacon, pear purée and walnuts or herb-basted chicken with molten potato cake, brussels sprouts and black truffle jus. You can also enjoy one of the city's best burgers, which is only available at lunch.

New American | Casual | Expensive | financial district | 8 High St. | 617-426-1234 | www.radiusrestaurant.com | Lunch & Dinner Mon-Fri. Sat dinner only

Hamersley's   90.0

Now that the neighborhood is filled with trendy restaurants, it's hard to imagine that

Gordon and Fiona Hamersley's restaurant helped pioneer fine dining in Boston's South End. Twenty-four years later, it is still populated with many of the regulars who have been dining there since the early days, along with young couples who live in what is a now-gentrified neighborhood. The menu combines country and contemporary French fare. The roast chicken with a broth "so delicious you want to eat it with a spoon" is a mainstay of the traditional side, while a grilled pork chop with a spicy mustard sauce and a watermelon and red onion salad is a good example of the menu's modern side. The bar area offers large plate glass windows, affording one the opportunity to enjoy dinner while watching the animated South End street scene.

French Bistro | Casual | Expensive | south end | 553 Tremont St. | 617-423-2700 | www.hamersleysbistro.com | Dinner daily, Sun brunch

Oishii Boston   90.0

Bostonians exhibit provincial pride when it comes to the fish at Ting San's establishments, claiming the "ethereal sushi" is world-class. But out-of-towners say that while the fish is of high quality, its local provenance would relegate Oishii to second-tier status in New York and Los Angeles, where the top sushi specialists fly much of their fish in from Japan. There is a long list of exotic rolls on offer – like the Maki Cover (spicy mayo, asparagus, cucumber and bonito flake) – which, depending on your point of view, are either "delicious" or "gimmicky."

Japanese | Casual | Expensive | south end | 1166 Washington St. | 617-482-8868 | http://oishiiboston.com | Lunch & Dinner daily

TOP LOCAL CHOICE

B&G Oysters   89.0

Oysters aren't the only focus of Barbara Lynch's casual South End seafood restaurant. Lynch places an equal emphasis on "simple but well-prepared" cooked fare, like chorizo- and risotto-stuffed calamari, ocean perch with spring onions and Yukon Gold potatoes or a lobster BLT that she serves with homemade bread and bread-and-butter pickles. And we can't overlook the "exceptional lobster rolls." A "smart" wine list complements the cuisine at this "fun spot," and if the wait is too long, you can go across the street to check out the Butcher Shop (see below). Outdoor dining is available in warm weather.

Seafood | Informal | Moderate | south end | 550 Tremont St. | 617-423-0550 | www.bandgoysters.com | Lunch & Dinner daily

Hungry I   89.0

Located on Beacon Hill's main thoroughfare, this "local institution" offers French/Continental cuisine – think loin of lamb pan-seared with shallots and deglazed with merlot and Stilton or veal sautéed with lobster, asparagus, Vermouth and cream – that fits the billing of this "eclectic, cozy dining room" as "the most romantic restaurant in Boston." Besides it being "the perfect reservation to snag for Valentine's Day," nearly every reviewer mentioned the "hard-to-beat Sunday brunch" that diners get to enjoy "in front of a roaring fire on cold winter mornings."

French | Formal | Expensive | beacon hill | 71 Charles St. | 617-227-3524 | www.hungryiboston.com | Dinner daily, Lunch Thu, Fri, Sun

Salts 89.0

While not considered the most exciting restaurant in town, Salts is a good choice for those who are looking for a romantic meal on the Cambridge side of the Charles River. Many of the featured ingredients come from the restaurant's own farm in New Hampshire, and dishes like monkfish with heirloom carrots, dried black olives, preserved lemon and mango led some reviewers to call this place a "hidden gem." But others suggest that after a change in ownership, the food doesn't reach the lofty heights that it once hit, and Salts should be downgraded to "a good neighborhood restaurant and nothing more."

New American | Casual | Moderate | kendall square | 798 Main St | 617-876-8444 | www.saltsrestaurant.com | Dinner Tue-Sat

Sensing 89.0

With Guy Martin of Le Grand Véfour in Paris as its consulting chef, everyone had high hopes for this contemporary French restaurant in the Fairmont Battery Wharf. But reviews have been mixed: a quince soup and a seared foie gras with banana bread, caramel and almond drew praise as "being on a level hard to find in Boston," but it was countered by "tasteless vegetable soup" and "steak cooked to the wrong temperature." Even the décor took a bit of a hit as being "reminiscent of a conference room in a suburban business restaurant."

French | Casual | Moderate | waterfront | 3 Battery Wharf | Three Battery Wharf | 617-994-9001 | www.sensingrestaurant.com | Open daily

Abe & Louie's 88.5

Busy Boylston Street, home of mass-market retailers like Crate & Barrel and the Apple Store, is the last place you would expect to find a bustling steakhouse with a clubby vibe. Yet Abe & Louie's has thrived in this location for over a decade. The menu presents you with a choice of a dozen cuts of prime dry-aged beef, various fish and seafood offerings, including a popular swordfish chop, and old-fashioned, time-tested daily specials that run the gamut from Veal Oscar to Lobster Fra Diavolo. The bar always features a "lively 30-plus singles scene," and the close proximity to Fenway Park makes it a popular spot before a Red Sox game.

Steakhouse | Casual | Expensive | back bay | 793 Boylston St. | 617-536-6300 | www.abeandlouies.com | Lunch & Dinner daily

Butcher Shop 88.5

Barbara Lynch does a complete 180° from her seafood-centric menu at her famed B&G Oysters, directly across the street (see above), and puts the emphasis on various cuts and preparations of meat at this casual bistro/trattoria. She makes her own terrines and sausages, and the rest of the menu features fare like farfalle Bolognese, Painted Hill bone-in rib eye or a Heritage pork chop served with spiced apples. The produce comes from her small greengrocer next door. The 100-plus-bottle wine list focuses on artisanal producers, and a butcher shop on the premises means you can take home the same charcuterie and meats they serve at the restaurant.

Italian | Informal | Moderate | south end | 552 Tremont St. | 617-423-4800 | www.thebutchershopboston.com | Lunch & Dinner daily

Coppa   88.5

Toro's Ken Oringer and Jamie Bissonnette decided they were ready to further expand their empire, and this time they branched out into Italian fare. As with their first effort, it didn't take long for local hipsters and young couples who live in the Southie neighborhood to begin enjoying small plates of "rustic Italian cuisine with flair," along with wood-burning-oven pizza and handmade pastas like calves' brain ravioli with chanterelle mushrooms. As the name implies ("coppa" is a type of cold cut), one can almost make a meal out of the "extensive list of delicious meats and salumi that are cured on the premises."

Italian | Informal | Moderate | south end | 253 Shawmut Ave. | 617-391-0902 | www.coppaboston.com | Lunch & Dinner Sun-Fri. Sat dinner only

East Coast Grill & Raw Bar   88.5

We dare you to find a more fun dining experience than Chris Schlesinger's Inman Square restaurant. Start off with a raw bar offering all sorts of local oysters, clams and New Bedford scallops, followed by ribs, pork and beef brisket that have been barbecued over an oak pit. Top things off with mains like Asian chile–blackened bluefish or a Cuban-style spit-roasted pork chop with mango mojo. There's a small but quirky wine list, or you can imbibe house-styled cocktails that include the Martini from Hell (vodka spiked with Scotch Bonnet peppers) and the Erupting Flaming Volcano (gin, brandy and five different types of rum). The place doesn't serve dessert, but fortunately, you can cool down from that 'cue with ice cream at Christina's just down the block.

New American | Informal | Moderate | inman square | 1271 Cambridge St. | 617-491-6568 | www.eastcoastgrill.net | Dinner daily, Brunch Sun

Grill 23 & Bar   88.5

One of the few independently owned steakhouses in Boston, Grill 23 vies with Abe & Louie's in the competition for the best steaks in town. It doesn't help that the meat is proffered by "old-school servers with gruff attitudes," though "a well-chosen wine list" goes a long way to make the experience better. The large and dramatic room can be super-noisy at times; one person recommended it as a "good place to go with someone you don't want to listen to."

Steakhouse | Casual | Expensive | back bay | 161 Berkeley St. | 617-542-2255 | www.grill23.com | Dinner daily

Hungry Mother   88.5

Though he cooked at a number of Boston-area kitchens after attending culinary school in Vermont, the first thing Barry Maiden did when given the opportunity to showcase his talents was to return to his Virginia roots. At Hungry Mother, he offers up a unique combination of flavors, what one reviewer called "modern Southern cuisine with French overtones." Maiden's daily menu features dishes like local scallops with Kentucky soy butter, pickled watermelon radishes and bacon or cornmeal catfish with dirty rice, mustard brown butter and chow chow, along with "various nibbles, bits and cool cocktails" that make for an all-around interesting evening.

Southern | Informal | Moderate | kendall square | 233 Cardinal Medeiros Ave. | 617-499-0090 | www. hungrymothercambridge.com | Dinner Tue-Sun

Oleana   88.5

Although she is of Scandinavian heritage, Ana Sortun has adopted the cuisine of the Eastern Mediterranean and executes it almost as expertly as if she'd been from that part of the world. Her extensive menu allows you to begin your meal with warm buttered hummus topped with thin slices of basturma, followed by dumplings made with lamb and eggplant; you can continue with entrées like a kibbeh of sockeye salmon with oyster mushrooms or a lamb steak with Turkish spices and a moussaka of fava beans. The "well-thought-out wine list" has "a particularly good selection of various varietals of white wine from Europe" that go well with the fare. The sizeable number of meat-free offerings makes it "highly recommended for vegetarians."

Mediterranean | Informal | Moderate | kenmore square | 134 Hampshire St. | 617-661-0505 | www.oleanarestaurant.com | Dinner daily

Toro   88.5

Few Boston restaurants have caught on with local diners as quickly as this South End tapas bar co-owned by Ken Oringer of Uni and Clio fame, and Jamie Bissonette. The Spanish-style fare that comes out of Bissonnette's kitchen ranges from small plates like dates stuffed with Serrano ham and blue cheese, cauliflower sautéed with chorizo or a bocadillo of uni to larger plates (served in the evenings) like paella or short ribs cooked with prunes. The "extensive list of tasty cocktails, wines and beers" makes the experience "loud, lively and fun."

Tapas | Informal | Moderate | south end | 1704 Washington St. | 617-536-4300 | www.toro-restaurant.com | Lunch & Dinner Sun-Fri. Sat dinner only

Franklin Café   88.0

With a menu full of creative comfort fare – like Hunter's sausage with warm sauerkraut and apple mustard, smoky skillet-roasted mussels or roast turkey meat loaf – we can understand why many reviewers say this is their go-to restaurant in Boston. The late hours are a plus: It's one of few local spots that serves after midnight, making it a popular stop for people who work in the restaurant industry. "Menu changes seasonally, chef-driven food" and "the best neighborhood place, with outrageously great food" were but some of the comments we collected. Of course, when so many people like a place it becomes "a pain to get a table."

New American | Informal | Moderate | south end | 278 Shawmut Ave. | 617-350-0010 | www.franklincafe.com | Dinner daily

Fugakyu   88.0

This elegant (for Coolidge Corner) restaurant is run by the same people who operate East Chinatown's East Ocean City Seafood, as well as other local Chinese and Japanese restaurants. While it might be "a notch below the top Japanese restaurants in Boston," the sushi and the cooked food are good enough to make it the first choice when people don't want to spend the sums commanded by Uni or Oishii. Extremely popular, it gets "jammed on both weekdays and weekends"; one reviewer wrote about "not being seated until 9:30 on a Wednesday night."

Japanese | Informal | Moderate | brookline | 1280 Beacon St. | 617-738-1268 | www.fugakyu.net | Lunch & Dinner daily

ACCPTABLE

EVOO   87.5

In a town that prides itself on having eateries that serve market cuisine at affordable prices, Peter and Colleen McCarthy's restaurant is Somerville's contribution to the genre. New England's delicious seafood turns up in dishes like seared New Bedford dayboat scallops with smoked bluefish risotto, which Peter McCarthy pairs with "the exceptional Duck, Duck, Goose" – a duck confit leg, seared Hudson Valley duck foie gras and slices of goose breast. Bargain hunters should visit Mondays through Thursdays, when McCarthy serves a seven-course Chef's Whim dinner for the bargain price of $60 or $90 with wine pairings.

New American | Informal | Moderate | somerville | 350 Third St. | 617-661-3866 | wwwevoorestaurant.com | Dinner daily, Lunch Mon-Fri

Gargoyles on the Square   87.5

You would have to travel far to find cuisine this progressive – think smoking cocktails to sous-vide veal cheeks with goat cheese and watermelon tartare. In fact, so many molecular techniques are utilized that one reviewer said, "If imitation is the sincerest form of flattery, then the chef here is flattering all of the molecular temples of North America and Europe." They also offer a number of popular theme dinners like Tokyo Tuesdays (a bento box and a trio of sakes) and Disco Sunday Brunch.

Progressive | Casual | Moderate | somerville | 219 Elm St. | 617-776-5300 | www.gargoylesrestaurant.com | Lunch & Dinner daily

Sorellina   87.5

This "smart-looking restaurant" is an attempt by the Mistral Group to create an Italian venue on par with Chicago's Spiaggia or NYC's Marea. But with "food that's merely adequate," they fall a bit short of their aspirations. Still, fans found the menu "sophisticated," with "interesting dishes" like a pasta of Kobe meatballs in a Barolo sauce or an osso buco of Colorado lamb with wild rice, faro risotto and eggplant agro dolce. The bar and the desserts also attracted praise.

Italian | Casual | Expensive | back bay | 1 Huntington Ave. | 617-412-4600 | www.sorellina-boston.com | Dinner daily

Taranta   87.5

Jose Duarte hails from Peru, and his nominally Italian cuisine contains enough Peruvian influences to categorize it as fusion. Some of the more interesting items include a salad of fresh crab meat with yellow Peruvian potatoes, avocado and botija olives and an espresso coffee–crusted filet mignon served over a parsnip purée with sautéed escarole in an algarrobina-vincotto sauce. A coalition of amigos and paisans swore the unusual combinations were "novel enough to be interesting" and "delicious enough to love," while critics wrote of "heavy sauces" and fusion cuisine "that didn't fuse."

Italian | Informal | Moderate | north end | 210 Hanover St. | 617-720-0052 | www.tarantarist.com | Dinner daily

T. W. Food   87.5

The cuisine at this "small, intimate restaurant" "well off the beaten path" focuses on purity of ingredients. Tim and Bronwyn Wiechmann do their best to source meat and produce that has been raised sustainably, resulting in dishes like smoked broccolini soup with marinated sibley squash, pastas house-made from whole local grains or Painted Hills Ranch flatiron steak with baby winter root vegetables. A "fair price point" and a series of organized theme dinners (like one featuring wild game) make it popular with the organic-minded foodie Cambridge crowd.

French | Informal | Moderate | cambridge | 377 Walden St. | 617-864-4745 | www.twfoodrestaurant.com | Dinner daily

Chez Henri   87.0

The half French/half New American menu at this Cambridge bistro, considered to be among the best of Boston's neighborhood restaurants, means you can opt for traditional dishes like steak au poivre or go for more eclectic fare like pan-roasted lobster with a spiced-corn broth and crispy coconut polenta. Nearly half of those who reviewed the place heaped praise on the "best Cuban sandwich you will ever have" (it's served only at the bar). An "intimate, charming" atmosphere and an "inexpensively priced" list of French wines accompanies the agreeable cuisine, which is "as close to Paris as one can get in Cambridge."

French | Casual | Moderate | cambridge | 1 Shepard St. | 617-354-8980 | www.chezhenri.com | Dinner daily

Eastern Standard   87.0

Open from breakfast until midnight, the menu at this Balthazar-style brasserie lists everything from eggs, salads and sandwiches to more substantial fare like salmon belly rillettes, rigatoni with lamb sausage and ricotta cheese and hanger steak frites. There's a serviceable wine list, and the late hours and Kenmore Square location make it popular with parents visiting their children at nearby Boston University. It's also one of the few quality places where you can eat after watching the Sox at Fenway, conveniently located around the corner.

French Brasserie | Informal | Moderate | kenmore square | Hotel Commonwealth | 528 Commonwealth Ave. | 617-532-9100 | www.easternstandardboston.com | Open daily

Carmen   87.0

Most of the Italian establishments in Boston's North End are happy catering to the less-than-knowledgeable tourist crowd rather than to hardcore foodies. But if you find yourself in the area and you happen to be hungry, some reviewers say that Carmen "might be the best Italian restaurant in Boston." A "good selection of small plates" like grilled asparagus with Parmesan cream is a major attraction, especially with those who aren't keen on eating starch. The "tiny space" means diners should watch out for "killer waits," especially on hot summer evenings.

Italian | Informal | Inexpensive | north end | 33 North Sq. | 617-742-6421 | www.carmenboston.com | Dinner Tue-Sun, Lunch Fri-Sat

Davio's   87.0

This Philadelphia transplant, half steakhouse, half northern Italian restaurant, means you can start your meal with bruschetta of La Quercia prosciutto and warm mozzarella, then follow it with pappardelle with slow-braised lamb and shaved pecorino, before moving on to a steak or a Niman Ranch double-cut pork chop with guanciale and pizzaiola sauce. Given this something-for-everyone menu, Davio's is quite popular with the business-meal crowd.

Steakhouse | Casual | Expensive | back bay | 75 Arlington St. | 617-357-4810 | www.davios.com | Dinner Tue-Sun, Lunch Fri-Sat

Harvest   87.0

Given its location in Harvard Square, it's not surprising that Harvest is popular with alums, professors and Harvard students enjoying dinner with visiting parents. Mary Dumont's contemporary New England fare adheres to a strict concept of seasonality, like Maine lobster soup spiked with Armagnac or leg of Jamison Farm lamb roasted in coffee and served with sumac-flavored yogurt and coffee lamb jus. There's an extensive wine list, and Sunday brunch is popular, especially when it's served on the outdoor terrace in nice weather.

American | Casual | Expensive | harvard square | 44 Brattle St. | 617-868-2255 | www.harvestcambridge.com | Lunch & Dinner daily

Via Matta — 87.0

Prior to becoming one of Boston's most successful chefs at Radius (see review above), Michael Schlow cooked with Pino Luongo and Mark Strausman at Coco Pazzo in New York City. So, it makes sense that he would expand his empire by opening a Tuscan-restaurant. There are few surprises on the menu, but solid versions of dishes like burrata with mushrooms and truffle oil or Meyer lemon–flavored chicken cooked under a brick can come in handy, especially at lunch when few quality restaurants in Boston are open.

Tuscan | Casual | Expensive | park square | 79 Park Plaza | 617-422-0008 | www.viamattarestaurant.com | Lunch & Dinner Mon-Fri. Sat dinner only

East Ocean City — 86.5

One of the top two choices for seafood-based cuisine in Chinatown, East Ocean is part of a restaurant group that operates both Chinese and Japanese venues in the Boston area. The setting is typical for a Hong Kong–style restaurant: Your selections are retrieved from fish tanks filled with various types of seafood before being thrown into the wok. Reviewers say, "Want authentic fare? Go here" and "Besides the tasty food, it's one of the cleanest places in Chinatown."

Chinese | Informal | Moderate | chinatown | 25 Beach St. | 617-542-2504 | www.eastoceancity.com | Lunch & Dinner daily

Lala Rokh — 86.5

One would expect Babak Binka's Persian restaurant to be located in Cambridge so that it, like so many other ethnic restaurants, could take advantage of the Harvard/MIT/Tufts axis. But it's situated on tony Beacon Hill, where an erudite and culturally diverse group of diners enjoys "beautiful presentations of tasty foods that are outside the everyday norm." The décor reflects the upscale environs and includes interesting Persian works of art from the owner's personal collection.

Persian | Casual | Moderate | beacon hill | 97 Mt. Vernon St. | 617-720-5511 | www.lalarokh.com | Dinner daily, Lunch Mon-Fri

Rendezvous — 86.5

Steve Johnson's 20-year-old bistro in Central Square is overshadowed by other restaurants in Cambridge. The market-based menu features dishes like wood-grilled pizza with oyster mushrooms, fontina and mozzarella, and skillet-roasted skate wing with baby brussels sprouts, cauliflower, pine nuts and Meyer lemon. Johnson also offers "a carefully chosen list of artisanal wines" that includes many selections from France and Italy. The three-course, $38 prix fixe menu served on Sunday evenings is a popular way for MIT professors to recharge before giving their Monday morning lectures.

Eclectic | Informal | Moderate | central square | 502 Massachusetts Ave. | 617-576-1900 | www.rendezvouscentralsquare.com | Dinner daily

Blu — 86.0

When Dante de Magistris was running the kitchen, Blu was able to overcome its unusual setting in the LA Sports health club. But opinions about the restaurant seem to have changed after he left, with reviewers likely to mention the "sterile, corporate environment" rather than the food. On the bright side (and it is bright, as the dining room is close to the gym), it's "perfect for an à la carte small-plates tasting of polenta fries, diver scallops and Asian-flavored duck wings" after a stint on the treadmill.

Mediterranean | Informal | Moderate | theater district | 4 Avery St. | 617-375-8550 | www.blurestaurant.com | Dinner Mon-Sat, Lunch Mon-Fri

Daily Catch — 86.0

Fans of this Italian seafood specialist call it "funky, fun and delicious." The key to its success are the "fresh seafood and pasta dishes," like linguine with clams or monkfish Marsala, "prepared simply and with an expert hand," avoiding the pitfalls of others in the North End that often specialize in overcooked noodles and heavy sauces. Diners are advised to stick to the Hanover Street branch; the Fan Pier location doesn't even have a bathroom.

Italian | Informal | Moderate | north end | 323 Hanover St. | 617-523-8567 | www.dailycatch.com | Lunch & Dinner daily

Oak Room   86.0

Back in the day, hotel dining meant formality. But now that dishes like Veal Marengo and Tournedos Rossini have gone the way of the cassette player, hotel restaurants serve simpler fare – in this case, steak. At the Oak Room, you find a combination: "Every sort of cocktail and cut of beef imaginable" is served with the type of "old school elegance" that one associates with an earlier era.

Steakhouse | Casual | Expensive | back bay | Fairmont Copley Plaza | 138 St. James Ave. | 617-267-5300 | www.theoakroom.com | Open daily

UpStairs on the Square   86.0

Reviews of this "fun and funky place" with a "festive atmosphere" were mixed, with comments on the half-New American/half-Italian menu ranging from "solid and creative" to "overpriced and uninspired." But everyone agrees it's great for drinks, especially with a big party. Our favorite review described it as "a drunkard's paradise where some of America's best writers and politicos have hidden in a glass of Scotch."

New American | Casual | Moderate | harvard square | 91 Winthrop St. | 617-864-1933 | www. upstairsonthesquare.com | Dinner daily

Restaurant Dante   86.0

Dante de Magistris hasn't managed to transfer the buzz that he generated when he was cooking at Blu over to his own restaurant. Of course, that doesn't mean that people don't like his modern Italian fare, like slow-roasted cod with salsa Genovese or a spiedino of lamb loin with balsamic vinegar and cocoa nibs. It's just that the "well-executed food" seems "a bit boring." The "cool space" makes it "a better place for taking in the scene while having a drink" than a dining venue.

Italian | Informal | Moderate | east cambridge | 40 Edwin H. Land Blvd. | 617-497-4200 | www.restaurantdante.com | Dinner daily, Lunch in summer

Les Zygomates   86.0

This restaurant, a sister to the Paris orig-original, is a favorite with the oenophiles in our survey, who enjoyed the "lengthy wine list," "solid bistro fare" and "brash atmosphere." The vast number of wines by the glass makes it popular with the after-work crowd, who drop in for a few pours while nibbling on selections from the raw bar or small plates ordered off the bar menu. A location close to South Station makes it "a good spot to grab a meal before or after catching a train."

French Bistro | Informal | Moderate | financial district | 129 South St. | 617-542-5108 | www.winebar.com | Dinner Mon-Sat, Lunch Mon-Fri

Mistral   86.0

Though this classic upper middle restaurant with a lively bar scene remains popular with local diners, reviewers are split about the cuisine: Some recommend it for "consistently good food" and a "nice wine list," while others claim "it's merely resting on its reputation." The diverse menu features everything from grilled pizzas to Dover sole to duck confit. However, with many entrées priced in the high $30s/low $40s, there is also a general feeling that the "quality of the food doesn't justify the prices," despite the large portion sizes.

Eclectic | Casual | Expensive | south end | 223 Columbus Ave. | 617-867-9300 | www.mistralbistro.com | Dinner daily, Sun brunch

Central Kitchen   86.0

If Gary Strack's restaurant (now in its 13th year) was located in a neighborhood like the South End, it would probably reflect the upscale clientele you find in a gentrified neighborhood. But given the site in Central Square, the dimly lit and minimally decorated room plays host to the local hipster crowd along with academics who have business at MIT. The food is a mishmash of bistro fare and includes starters like oysters, Swiss-style raclette and filet mignon tartare followed by mains like paella, cassoulet and what numerous people called the "best steak frites in Boston."

French | Informal | Moderate | central square | 567 Massachusetts Ave. | 617-491-5599 | www.enormous.tv/central | Dinner daily, Lunch Mon-Fri

75 Chestnut   85.5

The menu here, filled with comfort food dishes like seafood stew, sweet potato ravioli and a porterhouse pork chop with shallot mashed potatoes, straddles the line between pub grub and serious-restaurant fare – which sort of makes sense, as 75 Chestnut shares an owner with the Cheers bar (of TV show fame). Reviewers are quick to call it a "warm, reasonably priced neighborhood spot" where "lots of regular diners" order everything from "one of the best burgers in Boston" to the daily specials. It can get noisy when the decent-sized bar area fills up.

American | Informal | Moderate | beacon hill | 75 Chestnut St. | 617-227-2175 | www.75chestnut.com | Dinner daily, Sun brunch Oct-Apr

Blue Room   85.5

Not as well known as some other market-ingredient restaurants in the Boston area, Blue Room emphasizes dishes cooked over a wood-burning grill. Jorge Lopes' menu focuses on things like warm lamb's tongue with baby potatoes, skirt steak with cauliflower gratin and the vegetarian-friendly Three Little Gratins (made with quinoa, kasha and farro, which is served with spring baby vegetables). The wine list is both quirky and fairly priced, making it a perfect fit for the food, and a location in the heart of Kendall Square ensures its popularity with MIT academics along with the Cambridge hipster crowd.

New American | Informal | Moderate | central square | 1 Kendall Sq. | 617-494-9034 | www.theblueroom.net | Dinner daily, Sun brunch

Brasserie Jo   85.5

"If you stick to brasserie basics" like onion soup and steak tartare, you won't be disappointed at this offering from Chicago chef Jean Joho. The location, in the Colonnade Hotel, just across the street from the Prudential Center, means it's a popular spot with the business lunch crowd, especially for those who don't want to spring for the cost of a meal at nearby L'Espalier. However, a few people dismissed it as serving "nothing but hotel food." "Not worth a special trip, but okay if you're in the area" seems to be the consensus opinion.

French | Casual | Moderate | back bay | Colonnade Hotel | 120 Huntington Ave. | 617-425-3240 | www.brasseriejoboston.com | Lunch & Dinner daily

Helmand   85.5

One of the more popular ethnic spots in Cambridge features "massive portions" of "decent Afghan food" served in a "elegant atmosphere." Dishes like kakko (pan-fried pumpkin with yogurt and garlic), dwopiaza (lamb tenderloin with yellow split peas) and qoremay ma-he (sea bass sautéed with onion and tomatoes) are "tasty and fun," and the low price point makes the place affordable, especially for students and professors who need to entertain large groups of out-of-town visitors.

Afghan | Informal | Inexpensive | east cambridge | 143 First St. | 617-492-4646 | www.helmandrestaurantcambridge.com | Dinner daily

Jasper White's Summer Shack — 85.5

Up until 1995, Jasper White ran Jasper's, one of the top restaurants in Boston. After closing it, he did a stint as the executive chef for the Legal Sea Foods chain. Then he opened this place in 2000, sort of a mix between Legal and a New England clam bar. The simple fare includes clams and oysters on the half shell or dipped in batter and fried, and more ambitious entrées like monkfish scaloppini with tomatoes and rock shrimp. There are also buckets of steamers and boiled lobsters, plus ice-cold beers for washing it all down.

Seafood | Informal | Inexpensive | cambridge | 149 Alewife Brook Pkwy. | 617-520-9500 | www.summershackrestaurant.com | Lunch & Dinner daily

Mantra — 85.5

Despite the "awesome décor" and an "exceptionally attentive staff," Mantra has lost its identity, causing reviewers to ask, "Is it a French/Indian fusion restaurant or a nightclub?" A revolving door in the kitchen seems to have something to do with the identity crisis. Even its fans offer qualified compliments about dishes like goat cheese and potato tikki or a cumin-dusted Long Island duck breast, saying, "Although the food is good, it's become a bit dated."

Fusion | Casual | Moderate | downtown | 52 Temple Pl. | 617-542-8111 | www.mantrarestaurant.com | Lunch & Dinner Mon-Sat

Meritage — 85.5

Daniel Bruce has hit on a clever way to take advantage of the small plates craze – offer half- as well as full-sized portions of every dish. Bruce's New American menu is divided by the type of wine the dish goes with: For example, Island Creek oysters with caviar are listed under sparkling wine, and pan-roasted foie gras with a syrah cherry compote appears with fruity reds. The pairings are "painstakingly chosen," and the "spectacular views of Boston Harbor are hard to beat."

New American | Moderate | Casual | waterfront | 70 Rowes Wharf | 617-439-3995 | www.meritagetherestaurant.com | Dinner Tue-Sat

Dali Restaurant & Tapas Bar — 85.0

Many of our reviewers praised this "just plain funky and fun" tapas bar for Spanish food that "feels real, not contrived." The atmosphere is as lively as the cuisine, and the experience is enhanced by a terrific wine list that comes from the Wine & Cheese Cask across the street. If you're really hungry, there is paella and grilled lamb chops, but most people prefer to nibble on the small plates.

Spanish | Informal | Inexpensive | somerville | 415 Washington St. | 617-661-3254 | www.dalirestaurant.com | Dinner daily

Elephant Walk — 85.0

The de Monteiros say their half-Cambodian/half-French menu is the result of their being raised in a country that used to be part of the French Protectorate in the Far East. The unusual combination allows you to start your meal with a dish like nataing – ground pork simmered in coconut milk, garlic, crushed peanuts and chili pods – and follow it with roast chicken and potato gratin. They offer a special menu that addresses the needs of vegetarians, vegans and people on a gluten-free diet.

Cambodian | Informal | Inexpensive | porter square | 900 Beacon St. | 617-247-1500 | www.elephantwalk.com | Closed Sat lunch

Fireplace — 85.0

Considering Brookline's proximity to Boston (you can walk to it from Fenway Park), it is odd that its restaurants are more suburban than cosmopolitan. "Being a good restaurant there is like being the valedictorian of kindergarten," as one reviewer put it. "However, Fireplace does many things right." Jim Solomon's American menu includes dishes like a lobster mac 'n' cheese made with Asiago, mozzarella and Vermont Creamery blue, along with maple-glazed, spit-roasted chicken with mashed potatoes and sage brown butter.

American | Informal | Moderate | brookline | 1634 Beacon St. | 617-975-1900 | www.fireplace-rest.com | Lunch & Dinner daily

Giacomo's   85.0

Comments are mixed about this "classic red sauce restaurant," ranging from "the best of the North End southern Italian places" to "the quality of the food doesn't justify a place [being] this busy." But if you're in the mood for an old-fashioned plate of spaghetti, there's a reasonable chance you will enjoy the "freshly made pasta and sauces" as well as the "tasty specials listed on a chalkboard."

Italian | Informal | Inexpensive | north end | 355 Hanover St. | 617-523-9026 | http://giacomos-blog-boston.blogspot.com | Dinner daily

Grotto   85.0

"Aptly named" is what our reviewers say about this "casual, funky basement space" on Beacon Hill that describes itself as serving "decadent cuisine in a subterranean setting." This self-styled indulgent fare is Italian-based (think rich comfort food like gnocchi with braised short ribs and a Gorgonzola sauce) making it "perfect for cold nights." Another plus: It's one of the few restaurants in the neighborhood that is open for lunch.

Italian | Informal | Moderate | beacon hill | 37 Bowdoin St. | 617-227-3434 | www.grottorestaurant.com | Dinner daily, Lunch Mon-Fri

Legal Sea Foods   85.0

Before restaurants like Le Bernardin taught domestic diners how to appreciate high-quality fish, Legal was one of the country's go-to places for seafood. As the years went by and tastes became more sophisticated, diners lost interest in eating things like scrod or bluefish that were simply broiled. But Legal never changed its fish's stripes, and instead went mass-market (it's now a chain with over 30 locations). The original remains a perfectly harmless place, but "ultimately uninteresting" if you're looking for a unique fish-centric experience.

Seafood | Informal | Moderate | park square | 26 Park Plaza | 617-426-4444 | www.legalseafoods.com | Lunch & Dinner daily

Mamma Maria   85.0

"Very fancy-schmancy" compared to the other restaurants in Boston's North End – the prices are easily the highest in the neighborhood – Mama Maria offers a menu of classic Italian fare with a twist, like oven-braised spring chicken with baby brussels sprouts, Meyer lemon, green olives and Sicilian black rice pilaf. The setting is a town house across from where Paul Revere once lived. "You will be hard-pressed to find a place with a more romantic atmosphere."

Italian | Casual | Expensive | north end | 3 North Sq. | 617-523-0077 | www.mammamaria.com | Dinner daily

Metropolis Café   85.0

Another "small but fun" neighborhood restaurant where locals opt for dishes like salmon with lentils in a "cozy room" that offers "good service." They're open late, making it a useful spot after the Symphony or another event within earshot of the South End. There's a "decent Sunday brunch," although it's tough to get a seat. "Not exceptional, but I always enjoy it" is how one reviewer described it.

French | Casual | Moderate | south end | 584 Tremont St. | 617-247-2931 | www.metropolisboston.com | Dinner daily

Pigalle   85.0

Sort of half bistro/half brasserie, Marc Orfaly's quiet, dimly lit restaurant features sturdy French cuisine with a penchant for luxury ingredients. The menu offers classics like cassoulet along with more contemporary fare like shrimp poached in curried butter and lobster broth. There's an interesting bar menu influenced by Orfaly's travels to Indonesia, and because they don't have a full liquor license, they have crafted cocktails based on beer, wine and cordials.

French | Casual | Expensive | theater district | 75 Charles St. S. | 617-423-4944 | www.pigalleboston.com | Dinner Tue-Sat

Scampo   85.0

At this location in the Liberty Hotel (ironically, a former prison), Lydia Shire goes Italian and beyond with dishes like tandoori-fired sea scallops served on whipped white eggplant and chickpea flour pappardelle with crispy brussels sprout leaves and butternut squash. There are all sorts of handmade breads and pizzas, along with a mozzarella bar. While everyone seems to like the overall idea, we did get a few complaints about "bland sauces" and "an ambience that doesn't do the concept justice."

Italian | Casual | Moderate | beacon hill | Liberty Hotel | 215 Charles St. | 617-536-2100 | www.libertyhotel.com | Lunch & Dinner daily

Sportello   85.0

As if she doesn't have enough going on, Barbara Lynch, who operates No. 9 Park, The Butcher Shop and B & G Oysters, added this "haute lunch counter" to her stable of restaurants. Dishes like Roman gnocchi with a lamb ragú or local swordfish with prosciutto and olive oil mashed potatoes make this the best place to dine in "a neighborhood that's difficult to find a good meal in." There is also a bakery on the premises, allowing you to start your morning here with "all sorts of tasty breads and pastries" along with "the perfect cup of espresso."

Italian | Informal | Moderate | fort point | 348 Congress St. | 617-737-1234 | www.sportelloboston.com | Lunch & Dinner daily

OTHER PLACES MENTIONED

Beacon Hill Bistro   84.5

"Rustic bistro cuisine with a focus on local ingredients" is what you will find at this restaurant. Matt Molloy's résumé includes a stint at Lumière, and his training is evident in dishes like Gloucester monkfish with cider-braised cabbage and red-wine mustard sauce. "Prices are about 20% too high," reviewers complain, but what do you expect from a hotel eatery located in the most exclusive neighborhood in Boston?

French Bistro | Casual | Moderate | beacon hill | 25 Charles St. | 617-723-1133 | www.beaconhillbistro.com | Lunch & Dinner daily

Henrietta's Table   84.5

While the concept's terrific – a casual hotel restaurant serving cuisine that is based on local market ingredients – Peter Davis' food unfortunately doesn't come off tasting artisanal. Still, with its combination of New England and Southern specialties on the menu, it's a perfectly fine spot for casual meals like breakfast and lunch, and an appealing price point (entrées are around $15) makes it an especially good dinner choice for Harvard parents and their children. While the room is large, making it easy to get a table during the week, the Sunday brunch buffet is so popular that diners are advised to reserve in advance.

American | Informal | Inexpensive | harvard square | Charles Hotel | 1 Bennett St. | 617-661-5005 | www.henriettastable.com | Open daily

Peach Farm   84.5

Boston's foodies are wild about this establishment. The specialty is seafood, many specimens of which swim around in tanks in the back of the restaurant. It's praised for dishes like abalone with shredded duck, giant oysters in black bean sauce, salt and pepper squid or shrimp, and such seasonal fare as soft-shell crabs. There's not much atmosphere, but then again, this is Chinatown.

Chinese | Informal | Inexpensive | chinatown | 4 Tyler St. | 617-482-3332 | Lunch & Dinner daily

Petit Robert Bistro   84.5.

Few are enamored with this restaurant. Fans called it "Boston's best value-for-money bistro" and "the go-to bistro for my husband and me." But critics found "a number of missteps with the food: The French onion soup spent too much time under the salamander, and the pot-au-feu was way, way over-salted."

French Bistro | Casual | Moderate | kenmore square | 480 Columbus Ave. | 617-867-0600 | www.petitrobertbistro.com | Lunch & Dinner daily

Tamarind Bay   84.5

"Expertly done" curries and tandooris make this our reviewers' top choice for Indian food. While there is a plethora of such places in Cambridge, one person claimed it's his "favorite place to eat in Harvard Square," despite the "cramped quarters and crappy service."

Indian | Informal | Inexpensive | harvard square | 75 Winthrop St. | 617-491-4552 | www.tamarind-bay.com | Lunch & Dinner daily

Teatro   84.5

The combination of Italian staples – pastas, pizzas and larger plates like Chicken Milanese – make this "one of the best casual spots to dine at before the curtain goes up." While you might not make a special trip to eat here, it is certainly worth a visit if you have other business in the area. Aptly named for its location in the Theater District, the dining room has a similar feel to the South End's Mistral –

which is no surprise as, in fact, it's owned by the same people.

Italian | Casual | Moderate | theater district | 177 Tremont St. | 617-778-6841 | www.teatroboston.com | Dinner Tue-Sun

Durgin Park   84.0

They have been serving authentic New England fare on this site since 1827, offering a menu that runs the gamut from classic Yankee – chowder, Boston baked beans, broiled seafood, prime rib and Indian pudding (one of the few colonial desserts remaining) – to Italian specialties. The no-reservation policy means long waits for a table, and the "surly waitresses lend the experience an air of authenticity," say long-suffering reviewers. It's a shame the food isn't as appealing as the vintage surroundings.

American | Informal | Moderate | faneuil hall | 340 Faneuil Hall Market | 617-227-2038 | www. durgin-park.com | Lunch & Dinner daily

La Morra   84.0

At this reliable northern Italian eatery with "a decent collection of small plates," "fabulous pastas" and a "strong focus on seasonal specialties," they are known for paying attention to small details – expect to see the owners patrolling the multi-level, rustic dining room making sure their customers are happy. Working against the place is a menu described as "not terribly exciting" and an ambience described as "noisy."

Italian | Informal | Moderate | brookline | 48 Boylston St. | 617-739-0007 | www.lamorra.com | Dinner daily

OM   84.0

Put this in the category of a hip and trendy restaurant in an urban center where the action is at the bar and people pay little attention to the food. "Pretty terrible in every way" is how one person described the American fare, adding,

"They try to get over by making the food sound cool and interesting." Another reviewer told us that they rely on "fun drinks and a bar scene to make money," which makes him "happy to go there any time, providing someone else is paying for drinks and dinner."

New American | Casual | Moderate | harvard square | 92 Winthrop St. | 617-576-2800 | www.omrestaurant.com | Lunch & Dinner daily

Tapeo   84.0

Newbury Street – Boston's answer to New York's Madison Avenue – is not an obvious place to find a quality tapas bar. But while Tapeo might be "the low man on the Boston tapas totem pole," it nevertheless attracts an "upscale crowd" that enjoys sipping glasses of sherry while picking at a plate of ham or a racion of tortilla, often between stops at the local luxury boutiques. In the evenings, they're joined by a younger crowd of singles who fill the restaurant.

Tapas | Informal | Inexpensive | back bay | 266 Newbury St. | 617-267-4799 | www.tapeo.com | Dinner daily, Lunch Sat-Sun

Aquitaine   83.5

Comments about this restaurant that tries to approximate an authentic Parisian bistro run from "I have had several good meals there" and "a great romantic space" to "The food's a bit boring." The menu, with dishes like steak frites with truffle vinaigrette and a seafood cassoulet featuring monkfish and clams, is every bit as classic as the decor. "unexciting but good in a pinch" seems to sum it up best.

French Bistro | Informal | Moderate | south end | 569 Tremont St. | 617-424-8577 | www.aquitaineboston.com | Lunch & Dinner daily

Kingfish Hall   83.5.

While we realize that people who would ordinarily benefit from using this guide

typically avoid restaurants located in shopping malls or tourist destinations, you could do worse than this offering, described as "among the better options in Faneuil Hall." Another reviewer categorized it as "part of the overextended Todd English empire," adding, "It has an intriguing-sounding menu, but the food's not well executed."

Seafood | Informal | Moderate | faneuil hall | 188 Faneuil Hall Marketplace | 617-523-8862 | www.toddenglish.com | Lunch & Dinner daily

Sel de la Terre   83.5

The Provençal-influenced cooking at this more casual offering from Frank McClelland of L'Espalier fame includes starters like roasted white sweet potato soup with smoked maple syrup and mains like roast pork served with seasonal accompaniments. Erik Johnson, the wine director at L'Espalier, supervises a list that offers more than 100 wines to choose from.

French Bistro | Casual | Moderate | back bay | 255 State St. | 617-720-1300 | www.seldelaterre.com | Lunch & Dinner daily

Sibling Rivalry   83.5

Owned by restaurateur Robert Kinkead of Washington, D.C. fame and his brother David, this place's gimmick is that it features a dueling menu, with each brother having designed half of the Modern American dishes listed. Reviews were equally mixed, with one person describing the concept as a "foolish idea and not well-executed" and another saying the place is "inconsistent but still deserving of a recommendation."

New American | Informal | Moderate | south end | 525 Tremont St. | 617-338-5338 | www.siblingrivalryboston.com | Dinner daily

Vinny's at Night   83.5

Probably more famous for its unique location at the back of a convenience store than for its food, this simple red-sauce Italian restaurant in a "dodgy part of Somerville" features "massive portions of adequately cooked food," including homemade pastas and sausages, along with specials like eggplant parmigiana and lamb osso buco. While the food is nothing more than ordinary southern Italian fare, most reviewers seemed to believe "It's worth going there at least once for the cool experience."

Italian | Informal | Inexpensive | somerville | 76 Broadway | 617-628-1921 | www.vinnysonbroadway.com | Dinner daily, Lunch Tue-Fri

Atlantic Fish Co.   83.0

In a town where eating plainly broiled fish has long been a popular pastime, this restaurant aspires to fill the void created when Legal Sea Foods went mass market. On the plus side is a "wide and varied menu" that includes "an excellent cold seafood platter." But ultimately comments like "loud, busy and impersonal" and "It feels like an upscale Red Lobster" conspire against it, though some did say they enjoyed "a wine list with a few well-priced gems."

Seafood | Informal | Moderate | back bay | 761 Boylston St. | 617-267-4000 | www.atlanticfishrestaurant.com | Lunch & Dinner daily

No Name   83.0

This legendary restaurant has been serving fresh fish on this site since 1917. The formula is simple: a bare-bones building on a pier in the harbor offering large portions of Boston seafood specialties like chowders, scrod, swordfish, shrimp and scallops. Unfortunately, the eats have deteriorated, so much that one reviewer told us, "We sometimes joke that the reason it has no name is because of the poor quality of the food."

Seafood | Informal | Inexpensive | seaport district | 15 Fish Pier St. W. | 617-338-7539 | www.nonamerestaurant.com | Lunch & Dinner daily

Tangierino   83.0

This restaurant bills itself as "the first and only Moroccan chop house," and we have to admit we are not in a position to dispute that claim. The unusual menu which features a raw bar, appetizers like merguez and b'stilla, along with a full selection of steaks and chops, rivals New York City's Robert's Steakhouse at the Penthouse Executive Club for unusual places to consume a 20-oz. bone-in dry-aged rib eye. With "fabulous Casbah-style décor," it's super-popular, so expect a wait for a table.

Moroccan | Casual | Moderate | chelsea | 83 Main St. | 617-242-6009 | www.tangierino.com | Dinner daily

Avila   82.0

Our reviewing panel wasn't particularly impressed by this restaurant from the Davio's team that bills itself as serving modern Mediterranean cuisine. The eclectic menu ranges from halloumi cheese with dates and ouzo to black linguini tossed with shrimp and spicy Calabrese salami, and filet mignon served with Robuchon-style mashed potatoes. At least the location's convenient before the theater.

Mediterranean | Casual | Moderate | theater district | 1 Charles St. S. | 617-267-4810 | www.avilarestaurant.com | Lunch & Dinner daily

Parker's   81.5

This is where they invented Parker House rolls and Boston cream pie, and reviewers say they still do a good job with them both. Diners are advised to stick to these and other staples, like New England clam chowder and baked scrod; otherwise, the food at this institution "tastes institutionalized." Not surprisingly, "stodgy ambience" is part of the experience.

New England | Casual | Moderate | beacon hill | Parker House | 60 School St. | 617-227-8600 | www.omniparkerhouse.com | Open daily

Top of the Hub   81.5

This place in the Prudential Center does nothing to dispel the notion that the odds of getting a good meal atop a skyscraper are somewhere between slim and none. In fact, the food at the Hub was trashed so mercilessly that those who would like to admire the terrific view are advised to "consider having drinks in the bar before dining elsewhere."

New American | Casual | Expensive | back bay | Prudential Ctr | 800 Boylston St. | 617-536-1775 | www.selectrestaurants.com | Lunch & Dinner daily

Union Oyster House   81.5

This historic restaurant, established in 1826, has abandoned any pretense of offering quality dining. All the standard-issue New England seafood is on offer, including clams, oysters, chowders, broiled scrod and more exotic fare like lobster Newburg – and all of it is "mediocre in every way," making the colonial atmosphere the only reason to go.

Seafood | Informal | Moderate | faneuil hall | 41 Union St. | 617-227-2750 | www.unionoyster-house.com | Lunch & Dinner daily

Anthony's Pier 4   80.0

Is there anything else to say about this Boston institution other than it was one of Merv Griffin's favorites? Some people still like the place because of its status as a "Boston classic," saying you will be fine if you stick to simple fare like boiled lobster. But comments like "You can skip this overpriced tourist-trap" reflect the way most reviewers feel about it.

Seafood | Moderate | Casual | seaport district | 140 Northern Ave. | 617-482-6262 | www.pier4.com | Lunch & Dinner daily

Rustic Kitchen   80.0

Straddling New England and Italy, the menu features everything from baked stuffed haddock to pizzas. Nonetheless, "nothing memorable here" and "ordinary food for ordinary diners" is how reviewers describe this three-restaurant chain, with locations in the Back Bay, suburban Hingham and at the Mohegan Sun Resort in Connecticut. The saving grace seem to be their "freshly made pastas," but that isn't enough to prevent reviewers from calling it a "boring, trendy place without any substance to back it up."

Italian-American | Casual | Moderate | back bay | 1815 Massachusetts Ave. | 617-354-7766 | www.rustickitchen.biz/ | Lunch & Dinner daily

Cheap Eats

RECOMMENDED

Mr. Bartley's   7.4
Gourmet Burgers

There are 24 different types of hamburgers on the menu at this venerable Harvard Square coffee shop, along with other fare that is designed to appeal to hungry students, like franks and beans, macaroni and cheese and beef stew. The shtick is that the burgers are named after famous political figures and hometown heroes, like the Ted Kennedy – "a plump, liberal amount of beef" with cheddar cheese and mushrooms or the Dice K, accompanied with garlic, teriyaki, and a side of creamy cole slaw. "This unique place, which could only exist in a college town, has more character than 100 coffee shops put together."

Coffee Shop | Inexpensive | harvard square | 1246 Massachusetts Ave. | 617-354-6559 | www.bartleysburgers.com | Lunch & Dinner Mon-Sat

Uburger   7.3

This newish fast-food burger entry, located in the midst of Boston University student housing, tries to emulate the West Coast style of burger, à la In-N-Out. "Primal and just greasy enough" is how one reviewer described it, while a different set of comments spoke of a "dry, tasteless patty." But everyone agreed that they enjoy the "obscenely large shakes" and one reviewer described their fries as "the best in the Boston area."

Hamburgers | Inexpensive | kenmore square | 636 Beacon St. | 617-536-0448 | www.uburgerboston.com | Lunch & Dinner daily

OTHER PLACES MENTIONED

Friendly Toast   6.9

The formula at this "Portsmouth institution" proved so popular that its owners opened a branch in Cambridge. Sitting amid décor heavy on "flea-market and thrift-store kitsch," diners feast on dishes like Drunkard's French Toast (with a Grand Marnier sauce) and Le Petit Monstre (a chicken burrito with Tabasco cream cheese). Despite its popularity, our reviewers' comments were all over the map: "warm and comfortable spot for brunch/lunch with friends" was countered by "not much of an improvement over chain restaurants."

Coffee Shop | Inexpensive | kendall square | 1 Kendall Sq. | 617-621-1200 | http://thefriendlytoast.net | Open daily

Santarpio's   6.6

Since 1903, the Santarpio family has been entertaining diners at this old-school Italian bar and grill located within a stone's throw of the Sumner Tunnel. The main attraction is the thin-crust pizza, but there is also is a short menu of Italian-style barbecued meats, like sausage and lamb. The place is always packed – it isn't unusual to wait an hour for a table – with a combination of locals, college kids and those who are simply in the mood for a pie in a cool environment.

Pizzeria | Inexpensive | east boston | 111 Chelsea St. | 617-567-9871 | www.santarpiospizza.com | Lunch & Dinner daily

Charlie's Sandwich Shoppe 6.0

"The lines on the weekend are ridiculous, but the food is great and the coffee is hot" at this luncheonette that has been occupying the same location for more than 50 years. Breakfast is the big-ticket meal, with one reviewer proclaiming his undying love for their turkey hash. Just be forewarned from consuming too much of the celebrated java, as "the lack of a bathroom on the premises can make your morning a bit tricky."

Coffee Shop | Inexpensive | south end | 429 Columbus Ave. | 617-536-7669 | Breakfast & Lunch Mon-Sat

Emma's   5.9

You can order by the slice or by the pie at this Kendall Square pizzeria that's favored by thin-crust enthusiasts. "Fun toppings with lots of choices for vegetarians and great service" is how one reviewer described it, though another warned, "The toppings can get over complicated at times." The place is not universally loved; one reviewer called it "a local version of California Pizza Kitchen, inexplicably prized by Cambridge locals."

Pizzeria | Inexpensive | kendall square | 40 Hampshire St. | 617-864-8534 | www.emmaspizza.com | Lunch & Dinner daily

Finale   5.0

It's hard to imagine that a sweets specialist can fare this poorly in our survey. But with comments like "the desserts look pretty but taste like sugary cardboard" and "I have had better desserts at hundreds of places where they're an afterthought," to say that this isn't a favorite with our reviewers is an understatement.

Dessert | Inexpensive | park square | 30 Dunster St. | 617-441-9797 | www.finaledesserts.com | Lunch & Dinner daily

Boston Suburbs MA

RECOMMENDED

AKA Bistro   90.7

Chris Chung and Christian Touche each wanted a restaurant that reflected his particular background. Chung, who had trained as a sashimi chef, had become a local celebrity working at Uni, while the French-born Touche, who was the general manager at Clio, dreamed of owning a bistro. So how did they handle the conflict when they became partners? Simple: Rather than opening a fusion restaurant, they decided to create two restaurants in one. The result: Diners can choose to stick with one cuisine or the other, or they can start their meal with Chung's succulent creations, like Hawaiian poke with sweet onions and spicy and pickled mung beans, and finish it off with duck confit. "Who knew the combination could be so good?" is how one reacted to what might be the oddest pairing since Julia Roberts and Lyle Lovett.

Japanese/French | Casual | Expensive | lincoln | 145 Lincoln Rd. | 781-259-9920 | www.akabistrolincoln.com | Lunch & Dinner Mon-Sat, Lunch Sun only

Oga   90.5

Don't let the location in a strip mall fool you: This is one of the best Japanese restaurants in the Boston area, famous for serving high-quality fish at reasonable prices. Toru Oga delights his customers with everything from unusual rolls to an omakase worthy of being served in the center of the city. Oga's creative side comes out in dishes like Kobe beef with red mullet roe or sweet hamachi with escarole, diced tomatoes, chili threads and basil oil. Twice a year he organizes special dinners at which he pairs his creations with different styles of sake.

Japanese | Informal | Moderate | natick | 915 Worcester Rd./Rte. 9 | 508-653-4338 | www.ogasnatick.com | Lunch & Dinner daily

Il Capriccio   90.4

Ask someone who lives in Boston's western suburbs where you should go for dinner and the odds are they will send you to Richie Barron's restaurant in Waltham. Barron, who worked as a cook here before leaving to ply his trade at the Park Plaza Hotel in downtown Boston, returned in order to buy the place from its original owners. Barron's food is pretty much straight-down-the-line northern Italian fare, like a starter of snails with soft polenta, pastas like lasagna of scallop and leeks, and mains like pan-roasted veal tenderloin with wild mushrooms and parmesan potatoes. In addition to the tasty food, "fair prices" and "a killer wine list" explain why "they come from near and far to eat in this cozy restaurant."

Italian | Casual | Expensive | waltham | 888 Main St. | 781-894-2234 | www.bostonchefs.com/clients/IlCapriccio | Dinner Mon-Sat

Oishii   90.0

Locals exhibit provincial pride when it comes to the fish at Ting San's establishments, claiming the "ethereal sushi" is world-class. But out-of-towners say that while the fish is of high quality, its local provenance would relegate Oishii to second-tier status in New

York and Los Angeles, where top sushi specialists import much of their fish from Japan. There is a long list of exotic rolls on offer – like the Maki Cover (spicy mayo, asparagus, cucumber and bonito flake) – that, depending on your point of view, are either "delicious" or "gimmicky." Its popularity means you will wait for a table even on weeknights.

Japanese | Casual | Expensive| chestnut hill | 612 Hammond St..| 617-277-7888 | http://oishiisushi. chance365.net | Lunch & Dinner daily

Second Location: sudbury | 365 Boston Post Rd.| 978-440-8300 | http://oishiisushi.chance365.net | Lunch & Dinner daily

TOP LOCAL CHOICE

Il Casale   89.5

With comments like "the burrata appetizer is amazing," the "pastas are fresh and simple" and "the grappa cart is a terrific way to end your meal," it's not surprising that a number of reviewers call this suburbanite "my favorite Italian restaurant in the Boston area." In addition to the long list of small plates, they also offer a half dozen or so larger plates like a grilled pork rib-chop with Tuscan kale and pesto rosso. "Good for both a date as well as a large party," it sometimes suffers from its own popularity; one reviewer commented that "quality can slip on busy weekend nights."

Italian | Casual | Moderate| belmont | 50 Leonard St. | 617-209-4942 | http://ilcasalebelmont.com | Dinner Tue-Sun

Sichuan Gourmet   89.0

This restaurant dispels the notion that you can't find authentic Chinese cuisine in the suburbs. Dishes like double-smoked bacon, Chengdu-style scallops (the owners hail from that Sichuan-province city) and sliced beef with hot chili sauce are dubbed "authentic and tasty" by reviewers, with many of them calling it "my favorite Chinese restaurant." For years the devoted drove to Framingham to eat the tasty food, but management recently made things a bit more convenient for city dwellers by opening a location in Brookline.

Sichuan | Informal | Moderate | framingham | 271 Worcester Rd./Rte. 9 | 508-626-0248 | www.laosichuan.com | Lunch & Dinner daily

Fugakyu Cafe   88.0

This flashy restaurant, which is spread out over two floors, is run by the same people who operate Fugakyu in Brookline and East Ocean Seafood in Boston's Chinatown, among other Asian restaurants in the Boston area. While it might be "a notch below the top Japanese restaurants in Boston," the sushi and the cooked food are good enough to make it the first choice when people don't want to spend the sums commanded by other local sushi restaurants like Oga or Oishii.

Japanese | Informal | Moderate | sudbury | 621 Boston Post Rd. | 978-443-1998 | www.fugakyucafe.com | Lunch & Dinner daily

Sweet Basil   88.0

Suburbanites in the mood for southern Italian fare who don't want to put up with hassle of traveling into the North End can head on over to this BYO in Needham, where "fantastic classic Italian dishes" like linguine with clams and broccoli rabe, veal piccata and seafood Fra Diavolo are served in "large portions" and at "a low price point." Those who aren't in the mood for red sauce Italian can opt for a number of internationally styled dishes, like a Greek salad or skillet-seared steak over a curried vegetable samosa. It's one of the most popular places in the Boston suburbs, so expect to wait in long lines, especially on weekend nights.

Italian | Casual | Moderate | needham | 942 Great Plain Ave. | 781-444-9600 | www.sweetbasilneedham. com | Lunch & Dinner Mon-Sat, Sun dinner only

ACCEPTABLE

Blue Ginger   86.5

Diners who still enjoy a certain style of Asian fusion cuisine that was popular during the 1990s – like sake-miso marinated salmon or garlic and black pepper lobster with wasabi sauce – say "it's worth making the trip to suburban Wellesley" to sample Ming Tsai's cuisine. But those who tread less gingerly snap that the only reason for the restaurant's renown is the chef's Food Network and PBS cooking shows. A third point of view is expressed by oenophiles looking for a reason to enjoy a nice bottle of their favorite vino. In their view,"An excellent wine program tips the balance in the restaurant's favor."

Asian | Casual | Moderate | wellesley | 583 Washington St. | 781-283-5790 | www.ming.com | Lunch & Dinner Mon-Fri. Sat-Sun dinner only

Lumière   86.0

Finding a good restaurant outside a city's center is rarely easy, but you could do a lot worse than Michael Leviton's place if you happen to be in the near-western suburbs. Leviton is at the forefront of the local and sustainable movement, and his French-influenced menu features ingredients like Stonington, Maine "Diver Tim" sea scallops and hooked Gloucester "Damariscotta" cod, along with ingredients from purveyors like Gianne for chickens, Rain Crow Ranch for beef and Verrill Farms for produce.

French | Casual | Moderate | newton | 1293 Washington St. | 617-244-9199 | www.lumieresrestaurant.com | Dinner daily

OTHER PLACES MENTIONED

Not Your Average Joe's   76.5

Given that this chain operates 15 locations throughout the Boston metropolitan region, it won't surprise anyone to read that our reviewers called the pastas, salads and other casual eats here "average." Still, a special gluten-free menu makes it popular with people who suffer from celiac disease or wheat allergies.

American | Informal | Moderate | beverly | 45 Enon St. | 978-927-8950 | www.notyouraveragejoes.com | Lunch & Dinner daily

Hilltop Steak House   76.0

Famous for the giant plastic cactuses outside the restaurant, hovering over Route 1, this overblown version of Sizzler serves meat described as "absolutely poor" in quality. But that doesn't deter locals, who flock here in numbers so significant that the wait on weekends can be as long as two hours. Besides steak, it offers chicken, seafood lobster pie and a few Italian specialties, but frankly "you would be better off eating the cactuses," as one reviewer put it.

Steakhouse | Informal | Inexpensive | saugus | 855 Broadway/Rte. 1 | 781-233-7700 | www.hilltopsteakhouse.com | Open daily

Cheap Eats

UNIQUELY DELICIOUS

Clam Box of Ipswich   8.3

While they can't claim to have invented the fried clam, the owners of this iconic restaurant can brag about two things:

They've been in business in the same structure for more than 60 years, and, more important, many fried clam aficionados consider them "the best of the big-three fried clam shacks" located on Cape Ann. You can choose between regular or big bellies, as well as strips, which you can supplement with shrimp, scallops and haddock. It's a favorite among locals as well as tour-bus groups – expect a lengthy wait during the high season.

Seafood | Inexpensive | ipswich | 246 High St. | 978-356-9707 | www.ipswichma.com/clambox | Lunch & Dinner daily in season, call other times

RECOMMENDED

J.T. Farnham's   7.8

This is probably the least well known of the big-three fried clam restaurants located on Cape Ann, but what Farnham's lacks in renown and – according to some reviewers – quality, it makes up for with its location on an extension of Essex Bay. This setting means when the weather is good, you can eat your whole clam bellies and fried "scahlops" on a picnic bench overlooking the water. On days when it's too cold to eat in the open air, you can dine inside in a roadhouse-style dining room.

Seafood | Inexpensive | essex | 88 Eastern Ave. | 978-768-6643 | | Lunch & Dinner Mar-Nov

Woodman's of Essex   7.7

Legend has it that way back in 1914, this is where Chubby Woodman invented the fried clam. Nearly 100 years later, Woodman's remains the most popular of the various fried clam shacks that populate the Cape Ann peninsula. You can also order fried clam strips, lobster tails, scallops, shrimp and haddock, all available in platters or sandwiches. Those who are super-hungry can get a bucket of steamers followed by lobster. Everything on the menu is made with a gluten-free batter (they coat the shellfish in corn, not wheat flour), except for the

crab cakes and onion rings.

Seafood | Inexpensive | essex | 121 Main St./ Rte. 133 | 978-768-6057 | www.woodmans.com | Lunch & Dinner daily

Blue Ribbon BBQ   7.0

Blue Ribbon is widely heralded as the best barbecue for miles around. In fact, one reviewer told us, "Speaking as an ex-Texan, to me this tastes just like home." Especially recommended are the ribs and burnt brisket ends, supplemented by more esoteric offerings like Jamaican jerk chicken roll-ups and potato and kale soup. There are two locations, one on each side of the Charles River.

Barbecue | Inexpensive | newtown | 1375 Washington St. | 617-332-2583 | www.blueribbon-bbq.com | Lunch & Dinner daily

OTHER PLACES MENTIONED

Essex Seafood   6.0

This seafood stand is a "popular new-comer" to the Cape Ann fried clam competition. While some reviewers put it "in the top three on the Cape," others say they aren't yet willing to rate is as highly as its more famous neighbors. Being connected to a retail shop means it's "a good choice for those who want to down a few plates of shrimp and scallops and then buy some clams to fry them up at home."

Fried Clams | Inexpensive | essex | 143R Eastern Avenue | 978-768-7233 | www.essexseafood.com | Lunch & Dinner daily

Kelly's Roast Beef   5.3

They've been slicing roast beef since 1951. The quality is "slightly better" than at other fast-food restaurants, but that doesn't stop some reviewers from enjoying the occasional outing to this spot where they can look out over Revere Beach while eating their sandwiches.

Sandwiches | Inexpensive | revere beach | 410 Revere Beach Blvd. | 781-284-9129 | www.kellys-roastbeef. com | Open daily

Burlington VT

Hen of the Wood (27 miles southeast in Waterbury)   91.0

Back in 2005, Eric Warnstedt converted an 1830s grist mill into this award-winning restaurant. Since that time, no other local chef has demonstrated as strong a commitment to regional farmers and purveyors. Examples of the way Warnstedt utilizes the local larder can be found in dishes like a soup of spring-dug parsnips from Pete's Produce Farm, Rhode Island calamari sautéed with garlic, parsley, anchovies and chili flakes, and LaPlatte River Angus beef short ribs that Warnstedt braises in red wine. Reviewers call it "exceptional in every way" and "the most interesting food in the area" and caution diners not to miss "the incredible cheese board with a dozen or more selections" – most of them made in Vermont, naturally.

New American | Casual | Expensive | waterbury | 92 Stowe St. | 802-244-7300 | www.henofthewood.com | Dinner Tue-Sat

Inn at Shelburne Farms   89.0

While many restaurants increasingly grow their own fruits and vegetables, how many do their own butchering? Rib eyes and lamb chops from animals reared on the property are the focus at this dining room set in a stately 19th-century mansion on Lake Champlain. Unfortunately, despite all of the effort expended on the cuisine, the décor remains more memorable than the food, with many a reviewer sighing, "I wish the food was as spectacular as the setting" and "They do nothing to dissuade people of the notion that while the food in New England can be good, it typically lacks an edge."

American | Casual | Moderate | 1611 Harbor Rd. | 802-985-8498 | www.shelburnefarms.org | Open Breakfast & Dinner daily

A Single Pebble   87.5

Of all of the types of restaurants on the banks of Lake Champlain, who would expect one serving high-quality Szechuan cuisine? Yet Steve Bogart's place has been wokking it up since 2004. The menu includes dishes like steel-pot sha sha beef and tangerine chicken, plus daily specials based on market ingredients. One reviewer praised it as "the most authentic Chinese food I've had since I moved from Yunnan," saying that "the mock eel is to die for, and the Buddha beef will tempt any carnivore."

Chinese | Informal | Moderate | 133-35 Bank St. | 802-865-5200 | www.asinglepebble.com | Lunch & Dinner daily

Trattoria Delia   87.5

Every city has an Italian restaurant the locals love, and Delia is the one the denizens of Burlington have focused on, with comments like "Little Italy in Vermont." But critics call the food "ordinary," saying that dishes like saltimbocca and osso buco are "lacking in both creativity and execution." Fortunately, a "carefully chosen and well-priced wine list" goes a long way to improving the overall experience.

Italian | Informal | Moderate | 152 Saint Paul St. | 802-864-5253 | www.trattoriadelia.com | Dinner daily

Cape Cod MA

Chillingsworth   89.0

The dining room at this Cape Cod dowager, set on an estate built more than 300 years ago, attracted praise for being "relaxed while not serving bland beach food." The French menu has a few twists to it: black and white truffled mac 'n' cheese, snails in garlicky pesto cream with pistachios, tomato and grilled brioche and swordfish steak with roasted potatoes, tomato relish, fiddleheads and saffron mussel jus. "They've been at it for 30 years, which in the restaurant business is a true testament to perseverance. No gimmicks, just terrific food in the Francophile style."

French | Casual | Expensive | brewster | 2449 Main Street | 508-896-3640 | www.chillingsworth.com | Dinner daily May-Nov.

Brewster Fish House   87.0

Most fish restaurants on the Cape have been preparing the local catch the same way since the 1950s. But this seafood specialist clearly sets itself apart, doing its best to pair seasonality with a contemporary approach – like crispy calamari with an Asian black-bean aioli or grilled Atlantic swordfish with brussels sprouts, cranberries, and root-vegetable glace. It's "always fresh and lovely," and while "the no-reservation policy is a hassle," reviewers say "it's worth enduring the monumental wait for a table."

Seafood | Informal | Moderate | brewster | 2208 Main St./Rte. 6A | 508-896-7867 | www.brewsterfish.com | Lunch & Dinner Wed-Sun

Lobster Pot   87.0

While this "Provincetown tradition" serves all of the regional classics, it also manages to go a bit beyond the expected with dishes like Portuguese baked clams (with a topping of linguiça sausage, panko and Parmigiano) and a baked Southwestern-style halibut (tortilla crusted with salsa and cream). During the season there are long waits at dinner, and thus many of our reviewers preferred to go at lunch. "My favorite thing is to stop at the doorway raw bar and take my food up to the rooftop deck, where I can take in the views of P-Town Harbor," one regular confided.

Seafood | Informal | Moderate | provincetown | 321 Commercial St. | 508-487-0842 | www.ptown-lobsterpot.com | Lunch & Dinner daily in season

Wicked Oyster   87.0

Close to the Wellfleet inlet, Wicked Oyster offers up local oysters broiled with a tarragon glaze and the pan-roasted catch of the day served with Little Neck clams in a light cream broth: "A working knowledge of French technique means that this restaurant can do good things with what the ocean gives them." It also provides a host of landlubber dishes like grilled filet mignon with bourbon-caramel sauce and garlic smashed potatoes. A "nice atmosphere" and a "professional staff" round out the experience.

American | Informal | Moderate | wellfleet | 50 Main St. | 508-349-3455 | www.capecodchefs.com | Lunch & Dinner Thu-Tue, closed in winter

Dixville Notch NH

Balsams   89.0

"Step back to a kinder, gentler time" at this resort situated between the White Mountains and the Canadian border. The cuisine combines New England specialties, like chowder of smoked corn and scallops or a beef-barley soup made from roast beef, and New American offerings like pan-seared halibut with dumplings and caviar cream. The "better-than-expected food," "a wine list with more than 4,000 bottles" and "a lakeside setting worthy of the Swiss Alps" make it the best in a 50-mile radius.

American | Casual | Expensive | Route 26 | 603-255-0600 | www.thebalsams.com | Breakfast & Dinner daily; closed Apr & Nov

Great Barrington & the Berkshires MA

Bizen   91.6

Wearing a ponytail and bandana, Michael Marcus looks more like an aging hippie at a Grateful Dead concert than a sushi chef. Marcus started his career as a potter, specializing in Bizen-yaki style ceramics, and he used to sell his handmade tea cups to all of the top Japanese restaurants in Manhattan. Then he had to give up pottery for health reasons. It didn't take him long to notice the Berkshires were lacking high-quality sushi chefs, so he did what any nice Jewish boy from Queens would do when faced with that type of dilemma: He traded in his kiln for a set of Suisin knives. Now he offers "the best fish west of the Boston for 1,000 miles." The exquisite setting shows off his artisanal hand, especially in the omakase and tatami rooms which Marcus decorated himself.

Japanese | Informal | Expensive | great barrington | 17 Railroad St. | 413-528-4343 | Lunch & Dinner daily

Wheatleigh   90.0

Someone forgot to tell the people who summer in the Berkshires that formal dining has gone out of style. But that's not the case at this 1893 mansion turned luxury hotel, which is set in a 22-acre park designed by Frederick Olmstead. So if you know anyone who happens to be in the mood to don a jacket and tie the perfect Windsor knot, tell them to book a table here and step into an era when families like the Astors and Vanderbilts ruled the world. The food is French, evidenced by a menu running the gamut from escargots to foie gras to turbot to porcelet. "Impeccable service," a "stunning space" and "incredible views" make it ideal "when you need to be pampered."

French | Formal | Expensive | lenox | 11 Hawthorne Rd. | 413-637-0610 | www.wheatleigh.com | Lunch & Dinner daily

Mezze Bistro & Bar   85.5

Every college town needs at least one quality dining spot. Otherwise, how would they lure professors to the campus? And where would parents of students take their children to dinner when they visit? In the case of Mezze, which despite its Middle Eastern–sounding name specializes in farm-to-table cuisine, dishes like a soup of delicate squash with brown butter and sage are enjoyed by anyone who has a connection to Williams College, along with others who live or are visiting the northern Berkshires.

New American | Casual | Moderate | williamstown | 777 Cold Spring Rd. (Rte. 7) | 413-458-0123 | www.mezzerestaurant.com | Dinner daily

Red Lion Inn   84.0

If one were to imagine the perfect country inn, it would be the Red Lion. But don't get too excited: One taste of the "run-of-the mill, bland, American food"

will chase the pleasant thoughts from your mind. What's left is a restaurant that is useful for people attending cultural events like those at Tanglewood or Jacob's Pillow or for those who still enjoy eating dishes like Veal Oscar. Food aside, sitting on a wicker rocking chair on the Red Lion's regal veranda while having a cocktail is something everyone should do at least once.

American | Casual | Moderate | stockbridge | 30 Main St./Rte. 102 | 413-298-5545 | www. redlioninn.com | Open daily

Kennebunkport & Ogunquit ME

TOP LOCAL CHOICE

Joshua's (6 miles southwest in Wells)   89.5

Fresh, seasonal ingredients, many of which come from the Morther family farm, end up in dishes like Maine crab cakes with lemon-dill aioli or Atlantic haddock with a caramelized onion crust, chive oil and mushroom risotto. The "consistently delicious food" and an "approachable and affordable wine list" make this "one of the best places to eat in the state outside of Portland." One reviewer cautions "not to miss the delicious popovers." Another said he preferred eating the "just good, old-fashioned food" in the "warm and cozy bar" rather than the dining room.

New American | Casual | Moderate | wells | 1637 Post Rd. | 207-646-3355 | www.joshuas.biz | Dinner Mon-Sat

98 Provence   89.0

Most upscale resort areas offer a local version of the French bistro experience, and 98 Provence is the standard-bearer for the category on the southern Maine coast. Those who are enamored of the cuisine offer comments like "cassoulet to die for" and "you won't get any closer to France without getting on a plane." But others describe the cooking as "disjointed" – "every dish included one or two ingredients that weren't necessary." One reviewer did his best to play Solomon, criticizing the presentation as "a bit over the top" while decreeing, "The food is fabulous."

French Bistro | Casual | Expensive | ogunquit | 262 Shore Rd | 207 646-9898 | www.98provence.com | Dinner Wed-Mon; closed in winter

ACCEPTABLE

Ogunquit Lobster Pound   87.5

Conveniently located on Route 1 just north of the Ogunquit Village, this is one of the state's more southerly lobster

pounds. It offers outdoor seating in a park-like environment where, after you visit the ordering window, they attach your number to your lobster before throwing it into a large steamer near the back of the property. "It might not be the best pound in Maine, but it's fun just the same. BYOB a must.

Seafood | Informal | Moderate | ogunquit | Route 1 | 207-646-2516 | www.ogunquitlobster-pound.com | Lunch & Dinner daily May-Oct.

White Barn Inn   87.5

One would be hard-pressed to find as many good casual places to dine as in Maine. But formality still reigns at this European-style inn that caters to the crème de la crème of Kennebunkport society. Comments are split: Some enjoy the dishes like quail breast and foie gras on flaky pastry or cod and scallops with a ragout of chanterelles and a Champagne froth; others find the execution of the cuisine "a bit dull" and "fussy and self-conscious." Perhaps this reviewer nails it by saying, "If this restaurant wasn't located more than 50 miles from an urban area, we wouldn't even be talking about it."

French | Formal | Expensive | kennebunkport | 37 Beach Ave. | 207-967-2321 | www.whitebarninn. com | Dinner daily in season

Ramp Bar & Grill   87.0

Despite its proximity to Cape Porpoise, a location usually associated with seafood restaurants, Peter Morency's eclectic kitchen offers everything from wild cod with gnocchi and pesto to chicken and dumplings. One reviewer called it "great value for the price," while singling out the pulled pork and slaw as a favorite dish. Another commented on the "great food and unbeatable location" but admitted, "I hate talking it up, because this busy spot won't benefit from more exposure."

American | Informal | Moderate | kennebunkport | 77 Pier Rd.| 207-967-8500 | www.pier77restau-rant.com | Dinner daily in season, Wed-Sun other times

Arrows   86.5

We're aware that the rating appears to be too low considering this well-known restaurant's reputation, but a full third of our reviewing panel absolutely slammed the place; one dissatisfied customer claimed, "It was one of the worst meals I have had in years." The other two-thirds offer varying degrees of recommendation, especially for the dishes based on produce from the restaurant's own garden. But even their fans say that the place seems to have lost a step in recent years.

New American | Casual | Expensive | ogunquit | Berwick Rd. | 207-361-1100 | www.arrowsrestau-rant.com | Dinner Tue-Sun in season

Barnacle Billy's   85.5

This is your typical seasonal beach restaurant, offering steamers, chowders, lobster and every type of seafood imaginable – broiled, steamed or battered and fried – to the throngs who are starving after spending a day at the beach or out on their boat. Though it's "not a destination," it "will do if you're in the area," and reviewers prefer it to other restaurants offering a similar style of dining.

Seafood | Informal | Moderate | ogunquit | 50-70 Perkins Cove Rd. | 207-646-5575 | www. barnbilly.com | Lunch & Dinner daily in season

OTHER PLACES MENTIONED

Bandaloop   84.0

This is a favorite with many of our reviewers who own homes in the area. A "great bar scene" and a menu filled with casual fare like egg rolls, quesadillas, tofu baked with avocado/tomato salsa and a grilled pork chop with cumin Poblano peppers and Yukon Gold mashed potatoes (all made with local, organic ingredients) add up to "lots of fun." Year-round residents say they prefer it in the dead of winter "when things are less hectic."

Eclectic | Casual | Moderate | ogunquit | 2 Dock Square | 207-967-4994 | www.bandaloop.biz | Dinner daily in summer, Wed-Sun other times

Cheap Eats

Clam Shack   7.7

The first thing you notice about this simple roadside stand, nestled on the banks of the Kennebunk River by the side of the Taintown Bridge, is the long line of people waiting patiently to place their orders. Driven by the publicity from countless profiles in assorted food publications and television travel programs, the hungry diners come from all over the country to sample award-winning fried clams and what some reviewers describe as "the best lobster roll in Maine." But not everybody on our panel is a fan. When the subject of quality comes up, nonbelievers clam up – all they'll say is that the waits are just a reflection of large portions of "ordinary food" served at "cheap prices."

Seafood | Inexpensive | kennebunkport | Route 9 | 207-967-2560 | www.theclamshack.net | Lunch & Dinner daily May-Oct.

Maine Diner   5.8

Though it serves typical diner fare, like a tuna melt and a burger and fries, what makes this diner atypical is a menu that also features local favorites like a lobster roll, fried clam bellies and such daily specials as a New England boiled platter or a Yankee pot roast. Though it's not cheap (especially for the diner portion of the menu), the wait for a table can be lengthy during the tourist season.

Coffee Shop | Inexpensive | kennebunkport | 2265 Post Rd. | 207-646-4441 | www.mainediner.com | Open daily

Nantucket MA

Topper's   89.5

Based in the Wauwinett resort, chef Kyle Zachary offers what one reviewer called "fussy, over-the-top New American" cuisine – replete with dishes like creamy lobster soup, pickled ramps and corn foam and Kobe tenderloin Wellington with Cassia Madeira jus. The wine list is "big, interesting, but seriously overpriced," and despite the terrific service and beautiful setting, few of our reviewers think it's worth paying the tariff, which one person called "pricy, even for Nantucket." Which is why the $24 prix fixe lunch may be "the biggest bargain on the island."

New American | Moderate | Expensive | Wauwinet Resort | 120 Wauwinet Rd | 508-228-8768 | www.wauwinet.com | Open daily in season; call for off-season hours

21 Federal   89.0

21 Federal tries hard to overcome the stigma of being a seasonal restaurant in an exclusive summer resort town. Russell Jaehnig's "creative and well-executed" New American cuisine features dishes like a slow-roasted Portobello mushroom with Parmesan pudding and butter-basted lobster with potato gnocchi, chanterelles and English peas, which you get to enjoy amid a "classic Nantucket scene." A "lively bar" adds to the experience, and though diners are warned about a "hot dining room" and "amateurish service" during the high season, this place (one of the area's oldest) has "set the standard for dining on the island for years." As one reviewer said, "It's always a solid pick."

New American | Casual | Expensive | 21 Federal St. | 508-228-2121 | www.21federal.com | Dinner daily (May-Oct only)

New Haven CT

Abbott's Lobster in the Rough (54 miles east in Noank)   90.5

This is a Maine-style lobster pound, except it's located in a small town near the Connecticut–Rhode Island border. The crustaceans, which start at one and a quarter pounds and go up to seven, are prepared in a pressure cooker, resulting in "a steaming hot lobster" when you pick up your order. "I dare someone to find a better lobster outside of Maine" is how one reviewer put it. Expect a line on the weekends. A bonus: "You can enjoy your lobster while seated on benches that overlook a lovely marina."

Seafood | Informal | Moderate | noank | 117 Pearl St. | 860-536-7719 | www.abbotts-lobster.com | Lunch & Dinner daily May-Sept, weekends in October

Union League Cafe   89.5

Be they denizens of Yale or avid theatergoers, New Haven residents share a soft spot in their hearts for this "traditional French with a few contemporary pangs" that's a convenient spot for a meal before the curtain goes up at the Shubert Theater or the Yale Repertory Company. Jean Pierre Vuillermet has been in charge of the kitchen for 25 years, and reviewers say "You won't go wrong if you stick to simple fare like oysters, steaks and salads." A "comfortable dining room" and "a thoughtful wine list" argue for it being the best choice in the New Haven area.

French Bistro | Casual | Moderate | 1032 Chapel St. | 203-562-4299 | www.unionleaguecafe.com | Lunch & Dinner Mon-Fri. Sat dinner only

Griswold Inn   87.0

(54 miles east in Essex)

In Europe, it is not unusual to find centuries-old restaurants still operating at their original sites. But there are very few restaurants in the States that can make that claim. Happily, the Griswold Inn is an exception, having first opened its doors in this very building 235 years ago. The food, like lobster pot pie in a flaky crust, is the type of classic American cuisine one would expect to find in this setting. It's hardly cutting-edge, of course, but one reviewer wrote of his "fond memories of family meals complete with gracious service in the historic beamed dining room."

American | Casual | Moderate | essex | 36 Main St. | 860-767-1776 | www.griswoldinn.com | Lunch & Dinner Mon-Sat, Sun dinner only

Cheap Eats

Frank Pepe's Pizzeria Napoletana   8.2

They have been stretching out bundles of dough into pies – locally referred to as "apizz" – at this location since 1925. But it wasn't until the 1970s, when Calvin Trillin waxed poetic about the white-clam pizza, that Frank Pepe's became a mandatory stop for foodies. The result: "a waiting time that can be horrendous." One reviewer told of driving there from New York City, only to find a two-hour wait; when he was finally seated, they had run out of fresh clams, so he was forced to change his topping to sausage.

Pizzeria | Inexpensive | 157 Wooster St. | 203-865-5762 | www.pepespizzeria.com | Lunch & Dinner daily

Sally's Apizza   8.2

In 1938 Sally, the nephew of pizza master Frank Pepe (see above), decided he was going to go out on his own. He and his successors have been baking pies at this location ever since, still using the coal-fired oven they cooked in on their very first day. As to the ongoing debate as to who serves the best pizza, some swear by Pepe's ("a better crust"), others by Sally's ("better sauce"), and some just say, "Flip a coin – they're both great." There's only one Wooster Street location, so be prepared for "a hellacious wait."

Pizzeria | Inexpensive | 237 Wooster St. | 203-624-5271 | http://sallysapizza.com | Dinner Tue-Sun

RECOMMENDED

Modern Apizza   7.7

One reviewer told us when he's in the mood for a pizza topped with caramelized onions, he gets on line at Modern. But others beg to differ, arguing that "unless Pepe's and Sally's aren't open, or their lines are too long, why choose to eat pizza here?" (Of course, line size is no small thing, and Modern's is typically shorter than at the others.) One

philosophical soul shrugged, "People love to debate between Modern, Sally's and Pepe's. To me they're all great and all worth a visit."

Pizzeria | Inexpensive | 874 State St. | 203-776-5306 | www.modernapizza.com | Lunch & Dinner Tue-Sat, Sun dinner only

Louis' Lunch   7.6

Legend has it is that Louis Lassen invented the hamburger on this spot. Some 110 years later, the Lassen family still serves his invention, and still cooks them in the unusual gas broilers that Lassen designed – the patties are suspended on vertical racks, allowing the grease to drip down their sides while they cook. The ritual includes serving the burger with tomato, onion, cheese and toasted bread, which, one can argue, is evidence that the place predates the custom of using buns. Comments run from "tasty burger along with great history" to "weird but worth a visit" to "the quality has declined over the years." Condiment-lovers, note: Asking for ketchup is strictly taboo.

Hamburgers | Inexpensive | 261-263 Crown St. | 203-562-5507 | www.louislunch.com | Lunch & Dinner Thu-Sat, Tue-Wed lunch only

Portland ME

HIGHLY RECOMMENDED

Miyake   94.8

Given Portland's status as one of the country's premier commercial fishing centers— its wholesalers supply many of the top restaurants in the country – it's somewhat surprising that it wasn't until Masa Miyake moved here from New York City that the city could claim to have a top-flight sushi restaurant. Miyake's résumé includes slicing fish at Nobu and working in Oceana's kitchen, and he combines the best of the local catch with fish imported from Tokyo's Tsukiji Market. But "sushi is only part of what makes Miyake special": Masa's cooked dishes, like sea eel wrapped around a mixture of miso and brown butter or pork intestine slow-braised in sake and soya, make the omakase menu a unique experience. We suggest you reserve one of the six counter seats and go with the letting-the-chef-choose-your-dinner option. Miyake is located in a converted corner store at the edge of the West End. They don't have a liquor license, so make sure to bring your own.

Japanese | Informal | Expensive | 129 Spring St. | 207-871-9170 | Dinner Mon-Sat, Lunch Mon-Fri

Hugo's   93.3

Portland, Maine, is the last place one might expect to find progressive cooking. But that's what Rob Evans, a self-taught chef originally trained as an electrician, serves his customers, many of whom have traveled from out of state to eat here. Each day Evans' menu features 15 offerings, categorized as small, medium and larger plates, including creations like cornmeal-crusted soft-shell lobster with creamed corn gazpacho; foraged mushrooms, leeks and marjoram; confit of foie gras topped with salted and pickled cherries; and slow-cooked and honey-glazed Luce Farms pork belly with cabbage, apple, onion relish and charred rosemary. Even the desserts, like the house vanilla sundae with "usual and unusual toppings," get into the progressive act. More than 90% of our reviewers recommend the restaurant, offering comments like "everything I want in a restaurant – wildly creative yet unpretentious" and "the food was full of creativity and honesty, and the ingredient combinations were original."

Progressive | Informal | Exoensive | 88 Middle St. | 207-774-8538 | www.hugos.net | Dinner Tue-Sat

Fore Street   92.6

It's an oft-used – and oft-misapplied – term, but Sam Hayward's restaurant really does seem to be "the Chez Panisse of New England." A vegetable crisper greets you in the entrance, and the aroma of meats that are grilling over wood or roasting in a wood-burning oven wafts through the dining room. The locally raised ingredients on Sam Hayward's menu, almost too voluminous to list, include chicken and beef, as well as seafood off of the dayboats in the country's number-one commercial fishing port. In summer you can enjoy seasonal fare like a signature goat cheese and heirloom tomato tart or anything made with Maine blueberries. But some prefer it in the dead of winter, when crowds are thinner, the waters colder and the local seafood absolutely perfect.

Market American | Informal | Expensive | 288 Fore St. | 207 775-2717 | www.forestreet.biz | Dinner daily

RECOMMENDED

Bresca   90.2

After toiling at pastry stations for the likes of Guy Savoy and Charlie Trotter, Krista Kern wanted to add having a child to her list of achievements. She settled in Portland and opened this intimate 16-seat dining room, where her Italian fare often features dishes rarely seen on these shores, like the Friulian Toc (sautéed endive topped with smoked mozzarella and lardo in a pool of creamy polenta) and a sea urchin pasta so rich and delicious one reviewer called it "among the most hedonistic pasta dishes I ever ate." One could also argue that Bresca is worth visiting just for the luscious desserts, like a vanilla panna cotta with orange-flower water and white pepper sorbet. An intelligent and well-chosen wine list caps off the experience.

Italian | Informal | Moderate | 111 Middle St. | 207-772-1004 | www.bresca.org | Dinner Tue-Sat

Five Islands Lobster Company (44 miles north in Georgetown)   90.0

This is where you will find "the best lobsters in Maine," served steamed in the shell or served in "one of the most sought-after lobster rolls in the state," along with an assortment of fried seafood that includes their award-winning fried clams. You can also opt for a lighter meal of grilled haddock or salmon. Unfortunately, the combination of "delicious food" and "terrific views" on Sheepscot Bay means that it's extremely popular, and you can expect to find long lines of people waiting for the privilege of eating here.

Seafood | Informal | Moderate | georgetown | 1447 Five Islands Rd. | 207-371-2990 | www.fiveislandslobster.com | Lunch & Dinner daily May-Oct.

TOP LOCAL CHOICE

Bar Lola   88.5

With a "big nod to the best ingredients that Maine has to offer," Guy and Stella Hernandez offer small plates like Cavendish Farms quail with wilted greens and a pine nut purée or homemade brioche with crispy mortadella and a fried egg, and larger plates like a seared duck breast with heirloom cabbage and a cider glaze. Beers and wines that are "well matched" and a "beautiful and tranquil" dining room moved one reviewer to hail Bar Lola as "the best of Portland's neighborhood restaurants."

New American | Informal | Moderate | 100 Congress St. | 207-775-5652 | www.barlola.net | Dinner Wed-Sun

Local 188   88.5

The menu at this small plates specialist, described as "the best hang-out lounge in Portland," features Mediterranean fare based on local ingredients, like a pâté of chicken liver, egg and olive or lamb keftedes with whipped feta cheese and dill. The cocktails are "creative" and the dining room "artful," and an enthusiastic following of hipsters make it "loud, fun and noisy." It's' a favorite with the after-work crowd, as well as the local art community (the art museum and the Maine College of Art are down the street).

Mediterranean | Informal | Moderate | 685 Congress St. | 207-761-7909 | www.local188.com | Dinner daily, Lunch Sat-Sun

Emilitsa   88.0

While most U.S. cities have a least one Greek restaurant, it's surprisingly difficult to find one that serves farm-to-table cuisine. But in a state where the concept of local and sustainable is a way of life, this restaurant, located in the heart of the city's arts district, has adopted that format. All of the staples are on hand, beginning with "mouth-watering salads" and followed by classics like moussaka and local fish roasted over herbs. Given the generally low standard of Greek cooking in the U.S., "the delicious and authentic food" here is a breath of fresh air.

Greek | Informal | Moderate | 547 Congress St. | 207-221-0245 | www.emilitsa.com | Dinner Mon-Sat

Paciarino   88.0

Everyone seems to love this pasta specialist, where the spaghetti, ravioli, maccheroni and sheets of lasagna are fabricated daily before being served with a variety of sauces ranging from pomodoro and Bolognese to a tuna ragú. The greeting is warm and the atmosphere cozy, and with most dishes priced under $15, the food is "a relative bargain for the quality." One knock is the lack of non-pasta choices; those who are on a gluten-free diet will have a hard time finding something to eat.

Italian | Informal | Moderate | 468 Fore St. | 207-774-3500 | www.paciarino.com | Lunch & Dinner Tue-Sat

Five fifty-five   87.5

With an energy level more likely to be found in Boston than in Portland, Steve Corry's restaurant is the liveliest spot on the local dining scene. Corry's quirky New American creations include truffled lobster mac 'n' cheese, the Not so Boaring Risotto (made with boar sausage) and the Sticky Pig, a pork chop glazed with Blossom Meadow honey served with sautéed apples. There is also a buzzing bar room with its own menu and Michelle Corry's warm greeting, which is "every bit as welcoming as her husband's menu is whimsical."

New American | Informal | Moderate | 555 Congress St. | 207-761-0555 | www.fivefifty-five.com | Dinner daily, Lunch Sun

Ribollita   87.5

Those who are looking for a change of pace from the typical local fare should head for this "intimate and quiet restaurant" where chef/owner Kevin Quiet has been serving his "well-made" zuppas, pastas and other examples of traditional Italian cucina for more than 10 years. With offerings like a caramelized-onion tart with black olives and goat cheese, as well as pan-seared gnocchi with pea tendrils and crispy prosciutto, Quiet's menu goes well beyond the regional cooking that one might associate with a restaurant named after a Tuscan soup.

Italian | Informal | Moderate | 41 Middle St. | 207-774-2972 | www.ribollitamaine.com | Dinner Mon-Sat

Street and Co.   87.5

For a town that supplies much of the country with seafood, Portland is oddly lacking in high-end fish specialists – that is, save for Street and Co., where the delights of the ocean turn up in appetizers like local squid with calamari, chorizo, garlic and hot peppers and mains

like sole Francese or scallops in Pernod and cream ("two of my favorite seafood dishes in the country," as one reviewer put it). The more critical recommend that you "stick to the basics," adding that the cuisine is "less successful when they try to emulate some of the more ambitious restaurants in town."

Seafood | Casual | Moderate | 33 Wharf St. | 207-772-8833 | www.streetandco.com | Dinner Tue-Sun

Back Bay Grill   87.0

Linen tablecloths and "an incredibly professional front of the house" make BBG a standout in a city known for casual dining. It's a favorite with the over-50, blue-blazer crowd, which is not surprising given its style of cuisine and somewhat formal atmosphere. Larry Matthews Jr.'s New American fare comes with a twist, like Maine crab cakes with harissa aioli and an onion-and-melon salad or duck two ways (sautéed breast and confit leg served with Parmesan risotto). Not to be missed is the tasty truffled popcorn served at the bar; one person remarked, "I could eat it all night."

New American | Casual | Moderate | 65 Portland St. | 207-772-8833 | www.backbaygrill.com | Dinner Tue-Sun

Blue Spoon   86.5

Put this under the category of solid neighborhood restaurant. Though it has a smallish menu, a partnership with two local farmers and a penchant for doing something unique with what would otherwise be simple fare (like "first-rate" franks and beans or chicken roasted under a brick) mean you will likely end up waiting for one of the 10 tables. "Comfortable, unpretentious but upscale enough to feel special," it tempts one reviewer to call this friendly place his "home away from home."

New American | Informal | Moderate | 89 Congress St. | 207-773-1116 | Lunch & Dinner Mon-Sat

Caiola's Restaurant   86.5

Caiola's turns six this year. The quirky menu mixes New American fare, like a starter of lobster pudding served with a corn salad, with Mediterranean-inspired dishes like chile-and-orange–marinated swordfish alongside chorizo, chickpeas and spinach. The restaurant's stated goal is to be one of Portland's top neighborhood places, and one person described it as "having a little something for everyone," from vegetarian options to a juicy steak. They also offer one of the most popular Sunday brunches in the city.

New American | Informal | Moderate | 58 Pine Street | 207-772-1110 | http://caiolas.com | Dinner Tue-Sun, Lunch Sun

David's 388   86.5

When residents of the well-heeled towns south of the city don't want to drive into Portland for dinner, this is their first choice. With only six tables, plus another four seats at the chef's counter, diners are able to watch David Turin prepare small plates like brûléed-pear salad with aged cheddar and sun-dried cherry vinaigrette or ginger-and-scallion–crusted salmon with wasabi mashed potatoes. A planned expansion caused one fan to say, "I hope the intimate atmosphere doesn't suffer."

New American | Informal | Moderate | 388 Cottage Rd. | 207-347-7388 | www.davids388.com | Dinner daily

J's Oyster   86.5

Considering that the town is centered around its working waterfront, Portland is pretty much devoid of touristy restaurants. This one, located on Portland Pier, is one of the rare exceptions. A popular place to sit back and down a cold beer (or two) while savoring a platter of bivalves, this joint was once a favorite with many of our reviewers. But they seem to have changed their minds in recent years, including one who questioned "whether the oysters have been actually shucked on the premises."

Seafood | Informal | Moderate | 5 Portland Pier | 207-772-4828 | www.jsoyster.com | Lunch & Dinner daily

Sonny's   86.5

The people who brought you Local 188 (see above) have opened this pan-Latin restaurant where dishes like Jamaican salt-fish cakes and a Cuban-style Palomillo steak, with Meyer Farms meat, happily co-exist on the menu. It's only natural that "a good bar scene" comes with the territory, and the dressy but casual ambience means you are "suitably dressed in a suit as well as jeans and a t-shirt." It's one of the few restaurants in town that is open for lunch.

Pan-Latin | Casual | Moderate | 83 Exchange St. | 207-772-7774 | http://sonnysportland.com | Lunch & Dinner daily

Robinhood Free Meeting House   86.0
(44 miles north in Georgetown)

While this restaurant is not as well-known as some of the others that opened during Maine's food revolution back in the 1990s, Michael Gagnés cooking has enjoyed a considerable local following for the past 17 years. The menu, which includes dishes ranging from Thai rocket calamari to butter-poached Maine lobster, reflects Gagnés experience of working in kitchens all over the world. Fans say, "You should not miss the 72-layer cream cheese biscuits," which are distributed nationally (you might have seen them in the frozen section in your local supermarket).

Eclectic | Informal | Moderate | georgetown | 210 Robinhood Rd. | 207-371-2188 | www.robinhood-meetinghouse.com | Dinner daily

Harraseeket Lunch & Lobster   85.5
(15 miles north in S. Freeport)

Its close proximity to L.L. Bean and

Freeport's other outlet shops has made this waterfront spot one of the few lobster pounds in Maine to attract nationwide attention. Its devotees describe it as serving lobsters, steamers and other "well-prepared food using local ingredients," which they can enjoy on a sunny terrace overlooking the bay. But crabs slam the place as a "tourist trap with not much bang for the price tag."

Seafood | Informal | Moderate | south freeport | 36 Main St. | 207-865-3535 | www.harraseeketlunchandlobster.com | Lunch & Dinner daily May-Oct.

Cinque Terre   85.0

Despite word-of-mouth claiming this as one of Portland's best places to eat, the reviews we collected about Lee Skawinski's tribute to the Italian table were mixed. One comment – "it didn't meet expectations over two visits" – pretty much sums up reviewer sentiment. On the plus side, "the warm, rich dining room" and open hearth of the kitchen make for a cozy room in which to enjoy dishes like a tartare of Kobe beef shoulder with salsa rosa or pan-roasted cod with a tomato fondue.

Italian | Casual | Moderate | 36 Wharf St. | 207-347-6154 | www.cinqueterremaine.com | Dinner daily

OTHER PLACES MENTIONED

Front Room   84.0

Despite significant local acclaim, our reviewers are less than enamored of chef/owner Harding Lee Smith's restaurant, with its mix of Italian- and New England–style comfort fare. We received numerous complaints of "mediocre food" which, to add insult to injury, is served in a "loud, smoky environment," along with comments like "I know it's one of the most popular places in town, but it doesn't work for me."

New American | Casual | Moderate | 73 Congress St. | 207-773-3366 | www.thefrontroomrestaurant.com | Open daily

Corner Room   83.5

It's hard to recommend this restaurant (the sister to Harding Lee Smith's Front Room) when it attracts comments like "Have dinner here only if you like eating in a trendy, loud atmosphere and enjoy being treated rudely by the wait staff." On the other hand, a few reviewers praised the lunch service. One reported that "My brother, a fellow foodie, and I stopped in here for lunch on a Tuesday, and we felt we had escaped to Italy for a few hours."

Italian | Casual | Moderate | 110 Exchange St. | 207-879-4747 | www.thefrontroomrestaurant.com | Lunch & Dinner Mon-Fri. Sat-Sun dinner only

Salt Exchange   82.5

With a location on Commercial Street facing the waterfront, the Salt Exchange competes with J's Oyster House for the title of most touristy restaurant in Portland. Unfortunately, like many restaurants catering to that trade, they take advantage of the situation. "Small portions," "slow service" and food described as "marginal" puts this on the "no reason to go there" list.

American | Casual | Moderate | 245 Commercial St. | 207-347-5687 | www.thesaltexchange.net | Lunch & Dinner Tue-Sat

Black Point Inn   81.5
(12 miles south in Prouts Neck)

An exquisite setting on a bluff reveals a classic New England inn, complete with views of Saco Bay and the Atlantic Ocean. Pity that it's marred by "sub-par food" that includes "fish that was overcooked," "lobster that was raw in places" and "oysters on the half shell served at room temperature." We hear it's better at lunch if you stick to sandwiches and other simple fare.

American | Casual | Expensive | prouts neck | 510 Black Point Rd. | 207-883-2500 | www.blackpointinn.com | Lunch & Dinner in season

Cheap Eats

UNIQUELY DELICIOUS

Aurora Provisions   8.6

While you can start your day with one of their delicious homemade pastries and "what might be Portland's best cup of coffee," this "café/sandwich bar with panache" really shines at lunchtime. Given the lack of quality places to eat at midday, this is where you will find the town's food elite enjoying soups like a house-made fish chowder, along with sandwiches like smoked turkey with Horlick's cheddar and peach salsa. A few people complained about "high prices," but most say it's fairly priced considering "the high quality of the food."

Bakery | Inexpensive | 64 Pine St. | 207-871-9060 | www.auroraprovisions.com | Breakfast & Lunch Mon-Sat

Duck Fat   8.3

When he isn't behind the stoves employing molecular culinary techniques, you can find Rob Evans frying up some of the best French fries you have ever tasted at this small sandwich shop just a block away from his highly ranked Hugo's (see above). The delicious frites are complemented by "an eclectic mix of soups, paninis and salads," but true diehards order the poutine, a large bowl of fries topped with cheese curds and duck gravy. There is beer and wine for the adults, while children can order from a list of beverages that range from a local brand of root beer on tap to a variety of exotic milk shakes, like chai latte.

Sandwiches | Inexpensive | 43 Middle St. | 207-774-8080 | www.duckfat.com | Lunch & Dinner daily

RECOMMENDED

Bintliff's American Cafe   7.2

Located in a converted private house in the Back Bay, this breakfast and lunch specialist serves "the best eggs Benedict in Portland (they offer eight different variations)," along with other brunch fare like a vegetable frittata and apple/cinnamon French toast. You can enjoy your meal while sitting on a stool at the "cozy bar" in the upstairs dining room, and when the weather permits you can enjoy the "generous portions" from a table on the outdoor deck.

Coffee Shop | Inexpensive | 98 Portland St. | 207-774-0005 | www.bintliffscafe.com | Breakfast & Dinner daily

OTHER PLACES MENTIONED

Becky's   6.4

When's the last time a diner mixed local blueberries into the oatmeal or featured fresh Maine shrimp on the menu? Or how about a platter of broiled local seafood featuring scallops, haddock and clams? The setting, along Portland's commercial wharf amid fish wholesalers and the like, means you're likely to be eating next to a fisherman who brought in the morning's catch or a chef or an assortment of locals looking to grab a hearty New England–style breakfast.

Coffee Shop | Inexpensive | 390 Commercial St. | 207-773-7070 | www.beckysdiner.com | Breakfast, Lunch & Dinner daily

Hot Suppa!   6.4

They used to serve only breakfast and lunch here (in local parlance, "suppa" refers to a midday meal – perhaps because that's when the early-rising local fisherman would eat dinner). But the confusion didn't last very long, as so many people were enjoying their "famous corn beef hash" and a "memorable Cubano sandwich" that they decided to open for supper – er, at night.

Coffee Shop | Inexpensive | 703 Congress St. | 207-871-5005 | http://hotsuppa.com | Breakfast & Lunch daily, Dinner Tue-Sat

Portsmouth NH / Kittery ME

Anneke Jans   91.1

Just across the bridge from New Hampshire, this restaurant caters to the year-round community that lives in the Portsmouth area as well as the summertime tourist trade. Charlie Cicero's menu is filled with treats, like grilled Littleneck clams served in a spicy tomato broth or a boneless pork chop with balsamic-braised cipollini onions. Though one reviewer found it to be nothing more than a "great neighborhood restaurant," others said the "Quality of the food is on par with many more expensive restaurants" in the state. "A lively bar scene," and service from a "fun yet mature staff" makes this a strong contender for the best all-around dining experience between Boston and Portland.

New American | Casual | Moderate | kittery | 60 Wallingford Sq. | 207-439-0001 | www.annekejans.net | Dinner daily

Chauncey Creek Lobster Pier   90.6

If you're in Boston and in the mood for the classic lobster pound experience, Maine's southernmost pound is a mere 60 miles away. You can start with selections from a raw bar or the "chowdah" of the day before moving on to lobsters in all sizes. The ambience – you eat on a floating pier, so you might be able to watch a lobsterman pull up and unload his catch – is as authentic as it is lovely. And you can BYOB – anything from a six-pack to that special Chardonnay you've been saving for the right occasion.

Seafood | Informal | Moderate | kittery | 16 Chauncey Creek Rd. | 207-439-1030 | www.chaunceycreek. com | Lunch & Dinner daily in season

Pesce Blue   89.0

Though it looks sleek and cosmopolitan, Cliffe Arrand's restaurant doesn't seem out of place in otherwise quaint Portsmouth. Chef James Walter is committed to sourcing the highest-quality seafood, which turns up simply grilled or in dishes like pan-roasted bass served with brussels sprouts, caramelized onion and prosciutto ragout. If you visit at lunch, look for the Zuppa di Mare, otherwise known as New England clam chowder; made from scratch and topped with a hunk of haddock, it was described by one reviewer as "bound to make you forget any other chowder you've ever had."

Seafood | Casual | Moderate | portsmouth | 103 Congress St. | 603-430-7766 | www.pesceblue.com | Lunch & Dinner daily in season, call other times

Black Trumpet Bistro   88.5

From the "Old World atmosphere" of a nearly 200-year-old shipping warehouse, "Evan Mallet works hard to offer the best local products and to cook them honestly and creatively." The "beautiful plates" of Mediterranean-inspired fare, like pan-seared potato dumplings with sautéed snails in a sage brown butter or roasted monkfish with spaghetti squash and a lobster nage, are "worth a trip" on some nights and merely "superb on others." The upstairs wine bar offers a view of tugboats doing their thing.

New American | Casual | Moderate | portsmouth | 29 Ceres St. | 603-431-0887 | www.blacktrumpetbistro.com | Dinner daily

Wentworth by the Sea   88.0

Okay, it's a Marriott. But it's also a 137-year-old island resort, and the hotel giant's "stunning renovation has created a beautiful oasis." Daniel Dumont's kitchen plays it on the safe side, but his New American cuisine, featuring dishes like a pan-roasted foie gras with pea and vanilla fleur de sel or a pork T-bone steak with apple-cheddar-bacon bread pudding, was "surprisingly good for a hotel chain." Diners also get to enjoy the "lovely views of the harbor" at breakfast and lunch and at dinner on summer evenings.

New American | Casual | Expensive | new castle | 588 Wentworth Rd. | 603-422-7322 | www.wentworth.com | Open daily

OTHER PLACES MENTIONED

Oar House, The   83.0

The menu at this popular Portsmouth restaurant ranges from advanced pub food like chipotle barbecue chicken pizza to ambitious mains like haddock with a seafood stuffing or a rack of lamb with roasted garlic. The food isn't cheap, causing one reviewer to say, "For the price I'd go elsewhere." Another agreed, saying the "mediocre food in relation to the other restaurants in the area" makes it "more of a place for tourists."

American | Informal | Moderate | portsmouth | 55 Ceres St. | 603-436-4025 | www.portsmouthoarhouse.com | Lunch & Dinner daily

Cheap Eats

OTHER PLACES MENTIONED

Friendly Toast   6.9

This "legendary Portsmouth institution" has always catered to local hipsters. Sitting amid décor filled with "flea market and thrift store kitsch," diners feast on dishes like Drunkard's French toast (with a Grand Marnier sauce) at breakfast or Le Petit Monstre (a chicken burrito with Tabasco cream cheese) at lunch. Comments are all over the map: "A warm and comfortable spot for brunch/lunch with friends" is countered by "not a real improvement over chain restaurants."

Coffee Shop | Inexpensive | portsmouth | 113 Congress St. | 603-430-2154 | http://thefriendly-toast.net | Open daily

Providence RI

RECOMMENDED

Mill's Tavern   90.0

Every city should have a restaurant like Mill's Tavern. As with its predecessors, Olives and Fore Street, local ingredients are handled with care and served in a fun environment. Whether cooked in the wood-burning oven or over the wood-burning grill or in an everyday sauté pan, Jaime D'Oliveira's dishes are some of the tastiest in New England. Relying on local ingredients whenever possible, they include Point Judith calamari dredged in chickpea flour, coastal sturgeon marinated in black beans and roasted in the wood-burning oven and a veal porterhouse grilled over a blend of woods and served with fava beans and lardons. Large and lively, Mill's Tavern is also known for "a bustling bar scene" in addition to its tasty food.

New American | Casual | Expensive | 101 North Main St. | 401-272-3331 | www.millstavernrestaurant.com | Dinner daily

Al Forno   89.5

To say that Johanne Killeen and George Germon simply serve Italian food doesn't begin to give them their due. Rather, the two chefs have expanded the boundaries of Italian cucina, not by combining unusual elements but by making the dishes decadent – loaded with rich ingredients and sauces: think baked pasta with tomato, cream and five cheeses or wood-roasted, honey-glazed leg and breast of duck with prune-stuffed bread gnocchi and kumquat jam. And of course grilled pizza – the dish that the duo created and built their reputation on – is on the menu as well. True to the cuisine's roots, portions are generous, making Al Forno "perfect for family-style dining."

Italian | Casual | Expensive | 577 South Main St. | 401-273-9760 | www.alforno.com | Dinner Tue-Sat

ACCEPTABLE

OTHER PLACES MENTIONED

Rue de L'Espoir Creative Cooking   85.0

Deborah Norman's restaurant "has been around forever," and her American bistro cuisine makes it easy for Brown University parents and their children to enjoy a night away from the books. Norman's menu offers small plates like fried calamari with a Thai dipping sauce, a fig and pistachio salad or what she terms "serious eats" like roast sea bass with shrimp and potato hash. Comments range from "one of the best restaurants in Providence" to "not worth the money."

New American | Casual | Moderate | 99 Hope St. | 401-751-8890 | www.therue.com | Open daily

Hemenway's Seafood Restaurant   83.5

Given the quality of the local catch, one would think that the fare at this seafood house would be more adventurous than baked scrod and "any fish Oscar style." But this is New England, where traditions (even bad ones) reign supreme, and in typical fashion, the plain fare is "overcooked and over-buttered." There's a "casual, bar-like atmosphere" and "friendly service" from a staff formally dressed in vests and ties.

Seafood | Casual | Moderate | 121 South Main St. | 401-351-8570 | www.hemenwaysrestaurant.com | Dinner Mon-Fri. Lunch Mon-Sat

Rockland ME

HIGHLY RECOMMENDED

Suzuki's Sushi Bar   92.9

Given that sushi counters have long been the domain of male chefs, "it's a pleasure to see a woman" wielding the knives at this restaurant in the heart of downtown Rockland. Beyond broadening perceptions about who can properly remove the sinew from a piece of toro, Keiko Suzuki turns daily specials like tuna, shrimp, sea urchin, oysters and crab – all from nearby waters – into "refined plates" that manage to "uphold the Japanese tradition of culinary craftsmanship." Keiko's kitchen also turns out delicious cooked fare, like Maine crab cakes with bonito dashi silver sauce or homemade udon with Maine shrimp, shiitake mushrooms and wakame in a kelp dashi broth. The place is beloved by the locals, who say an establishment of this quality was "long needed in the Rockland area."

Japanese | Casual | Expensive | 419 Main St. | 207-596-7447 | www.suzukisushi.com | Dinner Tue-Sat

Primo   91.4

After making her name in the Berkshires at the Old Chatham Sheepherding Company Inn, Melissa Kelly and partner Price Kushner decided to move to Maine. Set in a late-19th-century Victorian house, the restaurant features numerous dishes made with produce raised on its own farm, like pot-bellied ravioli stuffed with herbs, kale, pancetta and ricotta, and items that are locally sourced, like grilled pumpkin swordfish served in a San Marzano tomato sauce. Even the charcuterie comes from pigs raised a short walk from the kitchen. The place is "surprisingly well-staffed" with "professional servers" who have worked there for years, something that is unusual for a restaurant in a resort community. We suggest you arrive early so you can "tour the farm before your meal."

Italian | Casual | Expensive | 2 S. Main St. | 207-596-0770 | www.primorestaurant.com | Dinner daily, May-Dec.

Francine Bistro (5 miles north in Camden)   88.0

In a "lovely setting" a short walk from Camden Harbor, Brian Hill does his best to show-case Maine's organic farmers. His menu might include a sweet corn and chanterelle soup or crispy dayboat halibut with leeks, chilies and crab. Some reviewers claim that the "cooking hasn't been the same" since Hill opened a second venue (a comfort-food spot named Shepherd's Pie). Still, many maintain, diners would be "hard pressed not to leave with a warm glow." An "esoteric wine list" caps off the experience.

New American | Casual | Moderate | camden | 55 Chestnut St. | 207-230-0083 | www.francinebistro.com | Dinner Tue-Sat

Cafe Miranda   84.0

Considering it offers dishes like sea scallops with black bean sauce, four-cheese chili and fire-roasted apples with blue cheese, not to mention a burger menu with 25 versions, calling Kerry Altiero's menu "eclectic" is an understatement. The wine list is nearly as long as the menu, and the bread from the wood-fired brick oven is nothing short of "addictive."

Eclectic | Informal | 15 Oak St. | 207 594 2034 | www.cafemiranda.com | Dinner daily

Cheap Eats

Chase's Daily   8.1

(26 miles north in Belfast)

The Chase family was at the forefront of the restaurants-operating-their-own-farms trend when they opened this vegetarian place in 2000 . Each morning, a truck pulls up behind the brick building, which dates from 1888, and the second generation of Chases turns the daily harvest into breakfast fare like an omelet with wilted escarole and feta cheese, and lunch fare like fried jasmine rice topped with tofu and seasonal vegetables like pumpkin. The "delicious breads and pastries" are "worth a visit on their own," and if we had a croissant for every person who said, "We were halfway through our meal before we realized it was all vegetarian" we could afford to open our own bakery. There's dinner on Friday, and also a market selling whatever ingredients they can't use in the kitchen.

Bakery | Inexpensive | belfast | 96 Main St. | 207-338-0555 | Breakfast & Lunch Tue-Sun, Dinner Fri.

Red's Eats   7.2

(33 miles south in Wiscasset)

The shtick at this shack located at the foot of the bridge crossing the Sheepscot River in Wiscasset is that they somehow manage to stuff an entire one-pound lobster into a hot-dog roll. As you can imagine, the lines on a nice summer day can be quite long. Comments are split between "best lobster roll in the world" and "It's not worth waiting 30 minutes for a lobster roll that is no better or worse than at other places in the area."

Seafood | Inexpensive | Moderate | wiscasset | Route 1 | 207-882-6128 | Lunch & Dinner daily in season

Woodstock VT

Hemingway's (18 miles west in Killington)   88.0

Shortly after it opened 25 years ago, Hemingway's was a contender for the best restaurant in the state. But like many middle-aged types, it's now tending to rest on its laurels, resulting in one reviewer calling it "overrated in a field of fresh new choices – they aren't really trying anymore." Still, it's "one of the nicest meals in the area," and dishes like a wood-roasted loin of pork with a cheddar corn cake are still "popular with the Killington après-ski crowd" in the dead of winter and the "hiking and climbing crowd" in summer.

New American | Casual | Expensive | killington | 4988 US Route 4 | 802-422-3886 | www.hemingways-restaurant.com | Dinner Tue-Sun

Simon Pearce   86.0

(5 miles east in Quechee)

It's not that you will eat badly at this picturesque spot. It's just that reviewers feel "this restaurant exists for the sole purpose of selling the heavy blown glass" that manufacturer Simon Pearce is known for. Fortunately, the American fare, like horseradish-crusted cod with mashed potatoes, is lighter than the glass but still not a compelling enough reason to go out of your way to eat here.

American | Casual | Moderate | quechee | 1760 Main St. | 802-295-1470 | www.simonpearce.com | Lunch & Dinner daily

Red Rooster at the   84.0
Woodstock Inn

While this inn resembles something out of a Norman Rockwell painting, its cuisine is more like painting by numbers. Despite management's efforts to update the menu, simple, stick-to-the-ribs American fare, like New England clam chowder and herb-crusted salmon with an English pea velouté, rules. One reviewer called it "a good choice after a long day of skiing."

American | Casual | Moderate | Woodstock Inn & Resort | 14 The Green | 802-457-1100 | www.woodstockinn.com | Lunch & Dinner daily

Chicago & the Midwest

These are some of the things our reviewers do to kill time *in-between* meals

....

Accountant, Movie Producer,
Political Scientist, Studio Musician,
Law School Professor, Zen Buddhist Sensei,
Anthropologist, Cookbook Author,
High Tech Entrepreneur, Fashion Model,
Psychologist, Wine Educator, Tax Attorney,
Physicist, Mortgage Broker,
Gastroenterologist, Professor of Finance,
Actuary, Housewife, Wine Dealer,
Auctioneer, Physician, Computer Programmer,
Chef, Veterinary Cardiologist, Pizzaiolo,
Food Writer, Copywriter, Geologist,
Nuclear Arms Expert, English Professor,
Marketing Consultant, College Student

....

Join their ranks by signing up to participate
in our 2012 Dining Survey. Who knows, maybe the
thing you do to kill time in-between meals
will show up on next year's list.

www.opinionatedabout.com

Chicago IL

Alinea   100.0

When he isn't out at the forge having his personally designed utensils made, Grant Achatz is busy bombarding diners with foams, herb gelées, dehydrated Pop-Rock-like chips and puddings, powders and smoke made tableside. But the fact that a chef might vaporize an ingredient or two doesn't mean his cuisine is merely smoke and mirrors. Achatz plied his trade in Thomas Keller's French Laundry, and his cooking is firmly rooted in the market-based fare his mentor is known for. The result is a cuisine unlike some other modern restaurants', where technique is postured for technique's sake. Instead Achatz applies science to the best ingredients money can buy, and the result is a meal that is a "once-in-a-lifetime experience in molecular gastronomy." If anyone needs proof of how his little experiments turn out, all they have to do is look at the stats: 97% of our reviewers rated Alinea in the two highest categories, with three-quarters of them saying it was a Must Go.

There are two different menu options – the 12-course Tasting and the 24-course Tour de Force – each featuring dishes like truffle explosion; mustard ice cream (adhered to one of those quirky serving utensils); hot potato, cold potato; Wagyu beef with powdered A-1; and lamb three ways cooked on a hot stone. Of course, when you're talking about such a highly stylized dining experience, some people are bound not to like it, and Achatz was criticized for "a cuisine and presentation that was too precious," with one frequent visitor complaining that "conceptually, nothing has changed from when the restaurant first opened." But those are the exceptions, and the vast majority of comments are in line with the following sentiment: "Words cannot express the experience – culinary bliss is as close as I can get."

Progressive | Casual | Very Expensive | lincoln park | 1723 N. Halsted St. | 312-867-0110 | www.alinea-restaurant.com | Dinner Wed-Sun

Schwa   96.8

Sometimes when we try to craft a thesis about a restaurant, our summary of the various opinions doesn't have the same impact as allowing readers to simply see the comments themselves. In the case of Schwa, to say they were glowing is an understatement: "creativity on steroids"; "If there was only one restaurant I could go to in Chicago, it would be Schwa"; "phenomenal in every way, with taste, texture and presentation nearly perfect"; "Along with the inspirational food, the exuberance of the chef and his staff is truly refreshing"; "my favorite restaurant in a city blessed with many great restaurants" and "Small, loud, cool and innovative, Schwa was more fun than ought to be legal" are but a few of the raves we collected.

What everyone is gushing about is Michael Carlson's quirky Progressive American cuisine and his unique creations – like a spring salad of strawberry, fava, fennel and goat cheese; quail egg ravioli with ricotta and brown butter that is "to die for"; and a surf 'n' turf dish of veal cheeks and branzino with brussels sprouts and mushrooms. Amazingly, it all happens in a cramped, small kitchen, where Carlson and a second chef do everything from cooking the food to serving it to the 26 lucky individuals seated in the small space. The only negative part of the experience is attempting to get a reservation; one person complained that it took three weeks to have his phone call returned. But, he quickly added, "It was worth whatever effort it took for the privilege of being able to eat the cool food." As a wise old diner we know put it: "In these days of the celebrity chef, how often does one find someone this brilliant who is actually behind the stoves cooking the food himself?"

Progressive | Informal | Expensive | wicker park | 1466 N. Ashland Ave. | 773-252-1466 | www.schwarestaurant.com | Dinner Tue-Sat

Avenues   95.6

When chef Graham Elliot Bowles was at the helm, Avenues was the darling of foodies. After Bowles left to open his own restaurant, he was replaced by the very capable Curtis Duffy. Expectations were high: Duffy was a former second to Grant Achatz at Alinea, and everyone hoped to see the same type of magic. But it didn't happen right away, and in the months following the change of command, enthusiasm for the restaurant waned. That didn't deter Duffy, who wanted to prove that he could play in the top chefs' league. So he kept at it, tweaking his dishes here, adjusting them there, quietly improving all aspects of his cuisine. For close to two years, we didn't see many reviews of this place. But one day Duffy seemed to make a breakthrough, and when word got out, the raves started to trickle in.

Duffy has modified the cuisine he learned under Achatz, shifting the balance between ingredients and technique by placing a greater emphasis on market-fresh fare. This adjustment is best evidenced in dishes like a spring pea soup that Duffy pours over a frozen dome of ginger juice and coconut milk, which a number of reviewers called "the single best dish I ate all year." Another raved, "The guy can cook vegetables as well as anyone in the U.S.," which becomes obvious when you taste the whole roasted cauliflower with braised carrots, maitake mushrooms, black cardamom marshmallow and Swiss chard. Dragging the experience down is the venue, a typical hotel dining room that doesn't do the innovative cuisine justice.

Progressive | Casual | Very Expensive | river north | Peninsula Hotel | 108 E. Superior St. | 312-573-6695 | www.peninsula.com | Dinner Tue-Sat

HIGHLY RECOMMENDED

Spiaggia   94.7

There was a time when Spiaggia could stake a claim to being the best Italian restaurant in the country. But after Paul Bartolatta left, it went through a period when it seemed to be drifting in Lake Michigan with no one steering the ship. Tony Mantuano was brought in to set the place back on course, and it wasn't long until the kitchen was once again stirring the organic risotto properly. Mantuano also lent the northern Italian fare his personal touch, apparent in dishes like a terrine of rainbow trout with tawny port and bay leaf gelée; agnolotti with fennel pollen and crispy veal breast; and Santa Barbara spot prawns with polenta, sea urchin and Italian osetra caviar. The experience is enhanced by a voluminous wine list, and the dining room offers beautiful views of the lake. Criticism was directed at the prices for both food and wine, which were described as "unacceptably high."

Italian | Formal | Expensive | gold coast | 980 N. Michigan Ave. | 312-280-2750 | www.spiaggiarestaurant.com | Dinner daily

Charlie Trotter's   94.6

Back in the late '80s, at a time when fine dining in the Midwest was dominated by classic French restaurants like Le Français and La Maisonette, Charlie Trotter brought his personal brand of New American cuisine to Chicago, revolutionizing fine dining in the region in the process. Other chefs followed his lead, and it didn't take long for the Windy City to have one of the most vibrant dining scenes in the country. Twenty-two years later, Trotter is still turning out dishes like Maine diver scallops with crispy sweetbreads and petite celery and South Dakota bison tenderloin with candied espresso and salsify. But despite widespread agreement about Trotter's role in establishing Chicago as an important dining destination, opinions are split about how much of an effort one should still make to eat here. While about half of our reviewers continue to be fans, saying that "The meals remain well-cooked and the food is still high quality," those in tune with more current trends in fine dining call it "passé," muttering that "Trotter's penchant for finishing dishes tableside harkens back to the '90s."

New American | Formal | Expensive | lincoln park | 816 W. Armitage Ave | 773-248-6228 | www.charlietrotters.com | Dinner Tue-Sat

L20   94.3

This restaurant from the Lettuce Entertain You group has become the central focus of one of those debates that lines natives up against visitors. One Chicagoan after another showers praise on the "meticulously prepared seafood using well-sourced ingredients," while those who have traveled specifically to eat at L20 are much less effusive, describing the cuisine as "very good but not remarkable." Arguments aside, there are a few standout dishes, including butter-poached arctic char, olive-oil-poached halibut and a "delicious" cod with fingerling potatoes and caviar that one reviewer raved about, despite his lack of enthusiasm for the rest of his meal. Unfortunately, when it comes to convincing people who are sitting on the fence, the high food and wine prices certainly don't help the restaurant's cause. *Note: Since we collected these comments, chef Laurent Gras has departed.*

French | Formal | Expensive | lincoln park | 2300 N. lincoln park W. | 773-868-0002 | www.l2orestaurant.com | Dinner Wed-Mon

Everest   93.6

Diners are given the opportunity to sample Jean Joho's Alsatian-influenced French cuisine at this Lettuce Entertain You group offering on the 40th floor of the Chicago Stock Exchange building. Joho's cooking is often compared to the late Marc Haeberlin's at the Auberge de L'Ill in Illhaeusern, and for good reason, as Joho spent the early years of his career working in that restaurant's kitchen. The cuisine is the type of hearty French fare you don't see very much in the U.S., with one diner describing his dinner of oysters with horseradish and a cucumber Riesling fleurette, crusted Berkshire pork cheeks and poached veal tongue with a choucroute salad and a filet of venison with wild huckleberries, braised pear and Alsatian knepfla as "a meal that can brace you for the cold Chicago winter." David Johnston's wine list complements the edibles, with more than 1,600 offerings, and the combination of the food, wine and the "high in the sky" location makes this one of the most romantic restaurants in the city.

French | Formal | Expensive | loop | Chicago Stock Exchange | 440 S. La Salle St., 40th floor | 312-663-8920 | www.everestrestaurant.com | Dinner Tue-Sat

Moto   93.6

With a quarter of our reviewers placing this restaurant in the two highest categories and another third saying they couldn't recommend it, to say that opinions are split about Homaro Cantu's Moto would be an understatement. Diners can choose between a 10- or a 20-course menu, both filled with dishes that offer some of the most unusual preparations you have ever seen, ranging from an edible menu (vegetable and fruit "ink" on soybean and potato starch "paper") to carbonated Champagne grapes to a fish filet that cooks at the edge of your table in a box filled with steaming hot tomatillo sauce – in eight minutes flat. As one of our more cerebral reviewers put it, it's "the perfect restaurant for those who want to be philosophical about what they eat," while another told us, "The food was so interesting that I actually preferred it to restaurants where the food tasted better." We suggest that fainthearted diners do their best to avoid the place.

Progressive | Casual | Very Expensive | loop | 945 W. Fulton Mkt. | 312-491-0058 | www.motorestaurant.com | Dinner Tue-Sat

Blackbird   93.4

Among savvy locals, owner Paul Kahan's farm-centric restaurant is one of the most beloved in Chicago. But being the number four or five restaurant in a city where many foodies visit for only a three-day weekend means that Blackbird is not as well-known to outsiders as it could be. Chef Mike Sheerin's typical daily menu might feature crispy veal sweetbreads with Meyer lemon and Chioggia beets, wood-grilled California sturgeon with bacon and bourbon caramel and Cantonese pork belly with crispy shrimp and preserved green tomato. A few people commented that "The concept isn't as unique as it used to be," while complaining that the room is "small, crowded and noisy." But the majority of reviews were more in line with the person who called it "the perfect marriage of cuisine as craft and dining as an art."

New American | Casual | Expensive | loop | 619 W. Randolph St. | 312-715-0708 | www.blackbirdrestaurant.com | Lunch & Dinner Mon-Fri Sat dinner only

Topolobampo   93.2

Purists typically don't like fancy versions of ethnic cuisine, but they seem to have made an exception for Rick Bayless' restaurant. Though he's a top celebrity chef who is often away filming his TV show or doing a book tour, to his credit we didn't receive a single complaint about him not being in his kitchen. The restaurant's success is built on the following principles: Craft a Mexican cuisine that adheres to tradition but is prepared by chefs with formal culinary training. Result: The snapper in a Oaxacan mole sauce and the puerco pipian verde are more refined than they would be at your typical Mexican restaurant. Of course, when it comes to ethnic food, there is always one rotten poblano in the bunch – in this instance, a reviewer who wrote, "The ingredients and execution are nice enough, but it's not as tasty as real Mexican food."

Mexican | Casual | Expensive | river north | 445 N. Clark St. | 312-661-1434 | www.fronterakitchens.com | Lunch & Dinner Tue-Fri, Sat dinner only

Frontera Grill   92.4

Many U.S. diners first cut their teeth on serious Mexican fare at Rick Bayless' informal sibling to his more upscale Topolobampo. You can start your meal with selections from a raw bar featuring sustainable seafood, like oysters on the half shell served with various homemade Mexican salsas, or assorted ceviches of salmon, shrimp and tuna. There are also sopas, tamales and enchiladas, and mains that might include grilled shrimp in an atole of corn and poblano pepper or duck breast in red-peanut mole. Since the place is ridiculously popular, we recommend going for lunch if possible, as reviewers reported "waits for a table that can be up to two hours long."

Mexican | Casual | Moderate | river north | 445 N. Clark St. | 312-661-1434 | www.fronterakitchens.com | Lunch & Dinner Tue-Sat

RECOMMENDED

Les Nomades   91.6

Thirty years ago, going out for a romantic meal meant putting on a coat and tie or a lovely dress and journeying to an intimate town house. While speaking in hushed tones in a candlelit room, you dined on what were, at the time, exotic dishes like consommé of duck with a quenelle of cèpes and organic root vegetables or loin and sweetbread of veal with pearl onions, forest mushrooms and sauce Périgueux. And though the decades have passed, the ritual is alive and well at this establishment known for "attentive service from a highly professional staff" who happily serve you a "refined French meal." One thing that has changed is the wine list, which has been "picked over."

French | Casual | Expensive | streeterville | 222 E. Ontario St. | 312-649-9010 | www.lesnomades.net | Dinner Tue-Sat

North Pond   91.2

A renovated Craftsman-style house – formerly part of a skating rink complex – makes a perfect match for the American cuisine with a modern edge at North Pond. Bruce Sherman's menu emphasizes organic ingredients, with entrées like sweetbreads paired with sweet onions, polenta and a red pepper coulis that are prepared in a simple but careful manner. And while he is prone to adding a modern component to almost every dish, the result is the type of "comfortable and reliable food" that won't offend those who are not the most discerning of diners. The setting in the middle of Lincoln Park "couldn't be more gorgeous," especially if you're able to snag a table on the patio, which offers a lovely view of the Chicago skyline.

New American | Casual | Expensive | lincoln park | 2610 N. Cannon Dr. | 773-477-5845 | www.northpond-restaurant.com | Lunch & Dinner Tue-FriSun; Sat dinner only

Tru   91.2

"Of the major Chicago restaurants, Tru is the one that leaves me cold," summarizes the consensus about this establishment. While it offers all the trappings of an important dining experience, a full third of our reviewers rated Tru Acceptable or lower. The signature caviar dish – a mini plexiglass staircase with a different variety on each step – is indicative of the style-over-substance approach that plagues the restaurant. One reviewer said that Gale Gand's wonderful desserts "were worth a visit by themselves, but unfortunately man can't live on dessert alone." Note: Anthony Martin has replaced Rick Tramonto as executive chef, which may outdate the rating and comments.

French | Formal | Expensive | streeterville | 676 N. St. Clair St. | 312-202-0001 | www.trurestaurant.com | Dinner Mon-Sat

Avec   91.0

Featuring dining at communal tables, this long, narrow wine bar (from Blackbird's Paul Kahan) is among the most popular of Chicago restaurants with our reviewers. The food is a mix of French and New American small plates, like chorizo-stuffed Medjool dates with smoked bacon and piquillo pepper–tomato sauce; house-made boudin with braised pork and poblanos; and wood-fired flatbread with beets, olives, arugula and Manchego cheese. It "falls just short of the level of cuisine Kahan is serving at Blackbird" is how one reviewer praised the fare; however, the combination of a tiny space and large portions of "tasty but uncomplicated food" means a "horrendous wait" unless you get there early.

French | Casual | Moderate | loop | 615 W. Randolph St. | 312-377-2002 | www.avecrestaurant.com | Dinner daily

Carlos   90.9

People often tire of restaurants that have been in business as long as Carlos and Debbie Nieto's place. But multiple reviewers told us it was "still worth the trip to the suburbs" to eat here. Opinions vary as to what sets the restaurant apart. Some say it's chef Ramiro Velasquez's command of culinary technique, with one reviewer noting that "everything, from his soups to his terrines to the way he handles simple red meat dishes, was prepared perfectly." But another line of thinking says it's Velasquez's willingness to include modern components in his cuisine – like adding chocolate to parsnip soup or sweet popcorn to a vegetable terrine – that makes the difference. If you are someone who likes traditional dining, there's a good chance you will find this "the best food in the city."

French | Formal | Expensive | north shore | 429 Temple Ave. | 847-432-0770 | www.carlos-restaurant.com | Dinner Wed-Mon

NoMI   90.6

Well, what do you know – a restaurant in a hotel located on a high floor that our reviewers actually recommend. The pretty dining room and terrific view are part of the appeal, as is the garden terrace, which comes to life when the weather gets warmer. But the main draw is the contemporary French cuisine, which emphasizes seasonal ingredients and careful preparations. Throw in a sushi bar and "a dynamic wine program" and you have a good choice for Michigan Avenue shoppers looking for good but uncomplicated food for lunch or dinner (supplemented by attractive views of the Chicago skyline at night).

French | Casual | Expensive | gold coast | Park Hyatt Chicago | 800 N. Michigan Ave., 7th floor | 312-239-4030 | www.nomirestaurant.com | Open daily

Bonsoirée   90.2

This small venue supports the proposition that Chicago is the hottest bed of progressive cooking in the country. Shin Thompson and Luke Creagan's Japanese-inflected menu features creations like smoked pork shoulder with a hominy-coriander tostone and soy sauce flakes and miniature uni grilled cheese with French onion soup "dust." The "super-casual environment" makes it a good choice for diners who are looking for progressive cuisine but don't want to bother with the formalities of a place like Avenues or Alinea. They don't have a liquor license, so you have to BYO, making it the most cost-effective of the city's modern dining experiences.

Progressive | Informal | Expensive | logan square | 2728 Armitage Ave. | 773-486-7511 | www.bon-soiree.com | Dinner Tue-Sun

Graham Elliot   90.1

When Graham Elliot Bowles was cooking at Avenues, a few of the more savvy diners we know preferred his cuisine to Grant Achatz's food at Alinea. But with his own restaurant, Bowles decided to try to make molecular cuisine accessible to diners at a lower price point. At first the reviews were all over the map, ranging from "fantastic food in a casual atmosphere" to "This is the sort of restaurant that traditionalists point to as an example of modernism gone wrong." But lately the comments are more like, "Go once and you will count the days until you can go back." We hope the trend continues as Bowles was always one of our favorite chefs.

Progressive | Casual | Moderate | river north | 217 W. Huron St. | 312-624-9975 | www.grahamelliot.com | Dinner Mon-Sat

Arun's   90.0

When Thai food first hit these shores, and dishes like pad Thai seemed exotic, it made sense to create a fine dining experience that revolved around the cuisine. But with Thai restaurants now pervasive, and diners finding out that they can get the same, or better, versions of dishes for less, Arun has lost much of its cachet. What's left is a debate in which one side says, "Fantastic since the day it opened," countered by, "There are better choices at one-fifth the cost." One thing everyone will agree on is that Arun's is still the best place to eat a bowl of Mossaman curry while wearing a sport coat.

Thai | Casual | Expensive | northwest | 4156 N. Kedzie Ave. | 773-539-1909 | www.arunsthai.com | Dinner Tue-Sun

Joe's Seafood, Prime Steak & Stone Crab   90.0

Sometimes restaurant chains come up with a good idea, as was the case when the Lettuce Entertain You group convinced the owners of the iconic Joe's Stone Crab in Miami Beach to allow them to open this offshoot. While comments like "where stone crabs reign supreme" and "a place for those who want a feel of the past" are to be expected, when they are combined with sentiments like "the steaks were as good as the claws," "a great wine list" and superior service," the reviews make us want to book a table. It's a popular hangout for local chefs, too.

Seafood | Casual | Expensive | river north | 60 E. Grand Ave. | 312-379-5637 | www.joes.net | Lunch & Dinner daily

Naha   90.0

Ask a native to recommend a restaurant that offers no-nonsense fare, and Carrie Nahabedian's restaurant is usually first or second on the list. After years in California, Nahabedian returned to her native Chicago and crafted a cuisine that blends California sensibilities with the cooking of her Armenian heritage. The result is a menu featuring dishes like lightly fried Lake Ontario smelts with lemon and pimenton or roast squab with foie gras and a crisp potato cake scented with Armenian rose petal marmalade.

Along with "clean-tasting food made with thoughtfully sourced ingredients," our reviewers enjoyed a "nice, comfortable atmosphere" and "a well-thought-out wine list."

New American | Casual | Expensive | river north | 500 N. Clark St. | 312-321-6242 | www.naha-chicago.com | Lunch & Dinner Mon-Fri Sat dinner only

Vie   90.0

Vie is named after its chef Paul Virant, and this graduate of Paul Kahan's kitchen at Blackbird graces suburbia with a cosmopolitan dedication to local and seasonal fare. His devotion shows up in dishes like marinated Wisconsin summer squashes with lemon, Vidalia onions and burrata or fried and wood-grilled Gunthorp Farm chicken with Tuscan kale. "One of the most innovative, full-flavored restaurants I've ever had the pleasure to dine in" is how one reviewer described it, while another said, "currently one of the most admired restaurants in the Chicago area." Sounds to us like it's worth a trip to the 'burbs.

New American | Casual | Moderate | western suburbs | 4471 Lawn Ave. | 708-246-2082 | www.vierestaurant.com | Dinner Mon-Sat

TOP LOCAL CHOICE

Bob Chinn's Crab House   89.5

We counted five different crab entrées and eight shrimp preparations at this old-school North Shore seafood house, which has Chinese overtones due to its owner's ethnicity. They also offer broiled fish and a host of fried seafood dishes and steamed lobsters, including three variations of surf 'n' turf. While the style of cooking is from an earlier era in our nation's culinary history, it's a "fun experience" and "The food can still hit the spot"; as one reviewer told us, it's "never inspired but usually tasty."

Seafood | Informal | Moderate | wheeling | 393 S. Milwaukee Ave. | 847-520-3633 | http://bobchinns.com | Lunch & Dinner daily

Boka   89.5

The reviews of this Lincoln Park small plates restaurant have improved since Giuseppe Tentori took over the kitchen. Tentori's eclectic fare includes mac 'n' cheese with edamame; crispy veal sweetbreads with chanterelles and Moroccan barbecue sauce; and a rack of lamb with shiitake mushrooms, Savoy cabbage and mustard jus. Given the quality of the food, the restaurant is often so busy that Tentori can't offer his guests a tasting menu. Reviewers summed it up as "fantastic, hip dining on Halstead featuring innovative dishes and a chic atmosphere," while cautioning about a two-bottle limit on BYO wines.

New American | Casual | Moderate | lincoln park | 1729 N. Halstead St. | 312-337-6070 | www.bokachicago.com | Dinner daily

Lao Sze Chuan   89.5

Chicago's most popular Szechuan restaurant offers happy diners a series of signature dishes – like shrimp in mayonnaise sauce, beef maw, Chengdu dumplings and Tony's three-chili chicken – that have risen to near-cult status. Some say "the huge menu can be daunting," but one reviewer offered advice for those who might be lacking expertise in this regional Chinese cuisine: "Don't let the scary-looking peppers fool you. Just tell them you want your food not that hot, and then dig into delicacies like Szechuan-style rabbit or the exotic-sounding LaLaLa Extremely Spicy Diced Fish LeShan style."

Chinese | Informal | Inexpensive | chinatown | 2172 S. Archer Ave. | 312-326-5040 | www.laoszechuan. com | Lunch & Dinner daily

Urban Belly   89.5

While a trendsetter in terms of progressive cuisine, Chicago is following a movement started in another city with Urban Belly. Described as "a cross between New York City's Momofuku Noodle Bar and Republic Noodles," the menu of Bill Kim, an alumnus of Bouley, offers three categories: dumplings (with duck and pho spices); noodles (udon with shrimp, coriander and sweet chili lime broth) and rice (with pork belly and pineapple). Some reviewers raved, "It's so good, I can't wait to go back," but others limited their enthusiasm to "a solid modern Asian restaurant that's nice when you're in the neighborhood, but not worth a detour."

Asian | Informal | Moderate | logan square | 3053 N. California Ave. | 773-583-0500 | www.urbanbelly-chicago.com | Lunch & Dinner Tue-Sun

Bristol   89.0

It's "all meat all of the time" at this gastropub that bases its cuisine on that of Fergus Henderson's London restaurant St. John. Chef/owner Chris Pandel's menu features dishes like a charcuterie board of chicken liver mousse, black pudding and smoked brisket served with horseradish mustard, which you can follow with a goat liver sausage served with rhubarb mustard, zucchini and almonds. There are raves for the tasty roast chicken, as well as for the wine list and cocktails. It's hugely popular with the local BYO crowd, who love the "tasty food," "low prices" and "fair corkage fees."

Gastropub | Informal | Moderate | bucktown | 2152 N. Damen Ave. | 773-862-5555 | www.thebristolchicago.com | Lunch & Dinner daily

Custom House   89.0

With seafood and vegetarian restaurants under his belt, Shawn McClain couldn't resist opening a restaurant focused on meat. The menu is "reminiscent of Tom Colicchio's Craft," and true to the form, McClain braises or roasts artisanally raised meats and poultry that diners can pair with more than a dozen side dishes. It's a hearty cuisine, ideal for adding a few pounds of natural insulation to guard against the cold Chicago winter. They also serve one of the most sought-after hamburgers in the city. Multiple comments expressed surprise at "how clean the meat-based cuisine tasted, proof that culinary training makes a difference."

New American | Casual | Expensive | printer's row | 500 S. Dearborn St. | 312-523-0200 | www.customhouse.cc | Lunch & Dinner daily

Erwin, An American Café & Bar   89.0

There is no shortage of neighborhood restaurants ambitious enough to serve dishes like a caramelized onion tart with Danish blue cheese and walnuts or cornmeal-crusted whitefish with sweet potatoes and cranberry-ginger compote. But few of them evoke comments like "I love everything about Erwin; brunch is just as good as dinner, and there is something for everyone," and "A gem and something of a relic, Erwin was one of the first to do locally sourced food." Erwin Drechsler has been serving his take on modern American comfort food at this location since 1994.

New American | Casual | Moderate | lakeview | 2925 N. Halsted St. | 773-528-7200 | www.erwincafe.com | Dinner Tue-Sun, Sunday brunch

Green Zebra   89.0

While we expected to hear vegetarians and locavores say positive things about Shawn McClain's restaurant, we didn't expect to hear reviewers call dishes like fresh fettuccine with basil, pistachio, giardiniera, garlic and Parmesan and a smoked sweet potato croquette, brown butter, cauliflower and petite Syrah reduction "so good that even devoted meat-eaters will enjoy themselves." Adding to the positive experience is a "tranquil dining room" and "service that is polished and professional," qualities that set the restaurant apart from typical vegetarian options.

Vegetarian | Casual | Moderate | noble square | 1460 West Chicago Ave. | 312-243-7100 | www.greenzebrachicago.com | Dinner daily, Lunch Sun

MK   89.0

MK stands for Michael Kornick, whose menus for the last 12 years have featured dishes like seared diver scallops with ramps and minted pea purée and a combo that pairs Lake Erie whitefish with Maine lobster. While the restaurant's success was built on a strong local following, some people feel it's now "living on past laurels," reflected by the fact that the dining room is "filled with weekend suburban diners and the concierge-referral crowd" rather than city-dwellers.

New American | Casual | Expensive | near north | 868 N. Franklin St. | 312-482-9179 | www.mkchicago.com | Dinner daily

The Purple Pig   89.0

There's an Italian slant to the offal-based cuisine at this gastropub where house-made charcuterie resides alongside dishes like lardo crostini; pig's ear with crispy kale and a fried egg; and milk-braised pork shoulder with mashed potatoes. It's super-popular, with a no-reservation policy that means you can expect a wait. One astute reviewer, who commented on how unusual it is for a gastropub to thrive in the heart of the Michigan Avenue shopping district, said, "I get a kick out of seeing a middle-aged woman eating marrow bones with her Ralph Lauren shopping bags at her side."

Gastropub | Informal | Moderate | river north | 500 N. Michigan Ave. | 312-464-1744 | http://thepurplepigchicago.com | Lunch & Dinner daily

Zealous   89.0

Everyone seems to have positive things to say about the food at Michael Taus' restaurant, where the New American fare with an Italian tinge includes dishes like braised pork shoulder with sweet chili glaze and a turnip-scallion cake. But despite the plethora of favorable comments, the restaurant hasn't caught on. One reviewer said, "I live down the street, and the place is always empty. I've had some good meals there, but I don't know how they stay in business."

New American | Casual | Expensive | river north | 419 W. Superior St. | 312-475-9112 | www.zealousrestaurant.com | Dinner Tue-Sat

Happy Chef Dim Sum House   88.5

Chicago has a small but vibrant Chinese food scene, and Happy Chef is where a number of our reviewers enjoy eating dim sum and other Cantonese dishes like shrimp and lobster in a black bean or ginger and scallion sauce, along with what are purportedly "the best salt-and-pepper squid and shrimps in the city." Located in a strip mall in the city's small Chinatown, the venue is a bare-bones affair, lacking in creature comforts and so casual that one reviewer wrote of his BYOB meal, except the "B" in this case wasn't a bottle of wine but beer.

Chinese | Informal | Inexpensive | chinatown | 2164 S. Archer Ave. | 312-808-3689 | http://happychefdimsumhouse.com | Lunch & Dinner daily

Lula   88.5

"Our favorite restaurant in Chicago – I've lost track of the number of times we visited" and "Over the years my appreciation of it has grown" are among the kudos collected by this popular place in Logan Square. The eclectic menu offers dishes like house-made lardo with chilled octopus confit; melon with sumac and basil; and pork spare ribs with escargot, romesco, pine nuts and mint. Even breakfast was praised for its "excellent ingredients and preparations." It's a bit far from downtown, but convenient as a neighborhood restaurant or when visiting the Logan Theatre.

Eclectic | Informal | Moderate | logan square | 2537 N. Kedzie Blvd. | 773-489-9554 | www.lulacafe.com | Open Wed-Mon

Sepia   88.5

In contrast to this restaurant's setting, a converted print shop that dates from 1890, the colorful New American menu is quite up to date: white gazpacho, olive oil jam, toasted almonds, verjus gelée and flatiron steak with potato confit and maitake in a coffee-béarnaise sauce. The South Loop location means it's "full of people who work in the nearby financial district" enjoying food that is "simple, but well done." No wonder our reviewers tell us it's one of their "favorite places in Chicago for a business lunch."

New American | Casual | Moderate | south loop | 123 N. Jefferson St. | 312-441-1920 | www.sepiachicago.com | Dinner daily, Lunch Mon-Fri

Spoon Thai   88.5

Management's decision to translate the menus that were written only in Thai into English means that now everyone can enjoy the same food as Thai natives (and speakers). The move catapulted this restaurant to cult status with Chicagoland's Cheap Eats community, and if you ask them about it they are quick to tell you that this is the only place in the city where you can find "the real flavors of Thailand." The "reasonable prices" make it easy to include lots of people in your party so you can "order as many things as possible." Make sure to tell them to "make the food Thai style" in order to get the most authentic experience.

Thai | Informal | Inexpensive | logan square | 4608 N. Western Ave. | 773-769-1173 | www.spoonthai.com | Lunch & Dinner daily

Sushi Wabi   88.5

"If only sushi culture revolved around freshwater and lake fish," sighed one reviewer about Chicago, which lacks the sort of high-quality sushi restaurants that you can now find in almost any major American city. That said, Wabi is "among the best of its kind" in the Windy City, attracting comments like, "It always exceeds my expectations" and "This dark and dingy space makes for a cool place to eat sushi." But others complained about "high prices" and said they reserve eating here for occasions when they "absolutely must have sushi."

Japanese | Informal | Moderate | west loop | 842 W. Randolph St. | 312-563-1224 | www.sushiwabi.com | Lunch & Dinner Mon-Fri Sat-Sun dinner only

David Burke's Primehouse   88.0

Despite its reputation as a first-class meat-and-potatoes town, Chicago wants for top-class steakhouses. With that caveat, a number of our reviewers say that "the best steaks in the city" can be found in this modern James Hotel venue. Sourcing beef from Creekstone Farms in Kansas, it offers cuts that are aged between 28 and 75 days. As to be expected when David Burke is in charge, many of the sides accompanying the tasty steaks "have interesting twists, or they're just excellent renditions of the classics."

Steakhouse | Casual | Moderate | river north | James Chicago Hotel | 616 N. Rush St. | 312-660-6000 | www.davidburke.com | Open daily

Oceanique   88.0

"You wouldn't expect such a fine seafood restaurant in Evanston, but here it is." Filled with suburbanites and Northwestern professors, this French fish house has been serving "pristine seafood" executed in a "classy and classic" fashion for more than 20 years. There were a few complaints about "erratic service," but those were offset by praise for the "huge wine list." The comments can be summed up by this one: "not a luxe restaurant, but a comfortable one, with fish dishes that stretch beyond the fried and grilled."

French | Casual | Moderate | evanston | 505 Main St. | 847-864-3435 | www.oceanique.com | Dinner Mon-Sat

The Publican   88.0

Super-popular as a place to drop in for a drink and a few small plates, this lively gastropub from the Blackbird team serves the type of hearty dinner fare one expects to see in London rather than Chicago. You can start with oysters, fried steamer clams with sweet potatoes, lemon and olive oil, or spicy pork rinds that are "absolutely addictive," then follow with entrées of boudin blanc, sweetbreads, calves' brains and a ham chop that is cooked in hay and served with wild rice and chestnut-bacon jam. The tempting array of dishes causes reviewers to say, "make sure you go hungry."

Gastropub | Informal | Moderate | loop | 837 W. Fulton Market | 312-733-9555 | www.thepublicanrestaurant.com | Dinner daily, Lunch Sun

ACCEPTABLE

Chicago Chop House   87.5

Since it's criticized for being "tourist-centric" and "treating everyone like a conventioneer," we were surprised see a number of comments claiming "the steaks are a rank above what they serve at the other steakhouses." "Reasonable prices" and "an authentic Chicago feel" mean "it can be jammed to the point of feeling uncomfortable," one visitor complained, especially during the holiday season. A number of reviewers mentioned the charred rib eye as their favorite dish.

Steakhouse | Casual | Expensive | river north | 60 W. Ontario St. | 312-787-7100 | www.chicagochophouse.com | Dinner daily

one sixtyblue   87.5

Put this on the list of ingredient-driven, casual restaurants in Chicago that most people seem to enjoy. Michael McDonald's New American menu offers starters like smoked pork belly with Asian pear and jicama coleslaw, and such mains as a Sonoma duck breast with baby bok choy and Thai barbecue sauce. It's anything but formal dining, and they seemd to have gone through a bit of a soft period when changing chefs, but recent reviews describe it as "bustling and fun, with terrific food."

New American | Casual | Expensive | loop | 1400 W. Randolph St | 312-850-0303 | www.onesixtyblue.com | Dinner Mon-Sat

Atwood Café   87.0

With comments like "nice place off State Street to stop for lunch while shopping" and "good for a pre-opera or theater meal," the Atwood Café might be the most useful restaurant in the Loop. The New American menu offers dishes like bison short ribs braised in red wine and served with whipped potatoes, braised greens and a Dijon glaze. "Well-prepared" at "reasonable prices" sums up the cuisine, while "classic" describes the setting in the Reliance Building, built in 1895.

New American | Casual | Moderate | loop | 1 W. Washington St. | 312-368-1900 | www.atwoodcafe.com | Lunch & Dinner daily

Francesca's on Taylor   87.0

Mussels with spicy tomato sauce; pizza with arugula, cherry tomatoes and Parmesan; linguine with seafood; and pork chops with peppers in a white wine sauce make this offering from Scott Harris the

"number-1 fun old-school Italian restaurant" in Chicago. With a list that offers a number of "fairly priced wines that are well matched to the food" and the "solid, classic" cucina, it's "a good choice for large parties looking for a fun night out."

Italian | Informal | Moderate | university village | 1400 W. Taylor St. | 312-829-2828 | www.miafrancesca.com | Dinner daily, Lunch Mon-Fri

Japonais   87.0

Chicago's answer to the large, party-style Japanese restaurants that have been turning up in major U.S. cities ever since Nobu popularized the genre. While the food has its moments, the experience is as much about the ambience as the menu, and the "fun and lively atmosphere" makes it a perfect choice for those who are looking to spend their evening sipping Champagne while blowing wads of cash on platters of seared toro, Kobe beef and lobster.

Japanese | Casual | Expensive | river north | 600 W. Chicago Ave. | 312-822-9600 | www.japonaischicago.com | Dinner daily, Lunch Mon-Fri

Le Colonial   87.0

Perfect if you're the type who enjoys eating upscale Vietnamese food in an environment reminiscent of the era when the country was a French colony (which means you care about the environment more than the food). Word from our reviewers is that the restaurant went through a down phase and lost its buzz for a while, but management brought in a new chef, and now "the flavors are more interesting and vibrant." Still, most people go for the "quaint atmosphere" in a "classic row-house setting."

Vietnamese | Casual | Moderate | gold coast | 937 N. Rush St. | 312-255-0088 | www.lecolonialchicago.com | Lunch & Dinner daily

Rosebud   87.0

This veteran of the Chicago steakhouse wars keeps on churning out "good enough food" that is "similar to other steak restaurants." In addition to the usual cuts of steaks and chops, there are a host of classic dishes, ranging from salads like Crab Louie to an entrée of American whitefish from Lake Superior. Now in its 31st year, it's considered "a classic," and some reviewers say it "rivals the best steakhouses in the city."

Steakhouse | Casual | Moderate | streeterville | 192 E. Walton St. | 312-397-1000 | www.rosebud-restaurants.com | Dinner daily, Lunch Mon-Fri

Morton's   87.0

One would think that if there was a chance that any city could have a Morton's that stands out from the others, it would be Chicago. After all, this is the place where it all started. But based on reviewers' reports about the chain's eight local branches, you might as well be eating at the location in Denver. As for how it stacks up against other national beef chains, "above average but overpriced" and "a bit stuffy and more formal" express the consensus.

Steakhouse | Casual | Expensive | loop | 1050 N. State St. #1A | 312-266-4820 | www.mortons.com | Dinner daily

Vermilion   87.0

While a blend of Indian and French cuisine is fairly typical, a merger of Indian and Latino cuisine is anything but. Overall, "they handle the fusion well" at Vermilion. True, "the combination seems alternatively precious and clashing, but a number of dishes are worthy of recommendation," including blue-corn-crusted scallops with a kali mirch, Latin calabasa and goat cheese purée and Indian marinated churrasco steak with chorizo and plantain chips. A "lovely atmosphere" and "unusual cocktails" might make it worth your while to visit.

French | Casual | Expensive | river north | 10 W. Hubbard St. | 312-527-4060 | www.thevermilion-restaurant.com | Dinner daily, Lunch Mon-Fri

Yoshi's Café   87.0

Now in its 28th year, Yoshi and Nobuko Katsumura's restaurant has managed to outlast the Asian-fusion cuisine era. Maybe that's because Yoshi displays a delicate hand in preparing dishes like hamachi carpaccio with a daikon salad and a grapefruit ponzu sauce and a grilled duck breast with a three-mushroom salad. Reviewers say while the "dependable food" will never set the world on fire, when you add "a good wine list" and "good service," you end up with "a safe haven for Lincoln Park residents."

Asian | Casual | Moderate | lincoln park | 3257 N. Halstead St. | 773-248-6160 | www.yoshiscafe.com | Dinner Tue-Sun, Lunch Sun

Café Ba-Ba-Reeba   86.5

This tapas bar from the Lettuce Entertain You group, helmed by chef Gabriel Sotelino has both friends and foes. Friends said it's "one of the best tapas spots in Chicago," offering "tons of choices, reasonable prices, a fun atmosphere, great location and great drinks." But foes disparaged the "overpriced, Americanized tapas," and insisted, "While the ambience nails Barcelona, the food here is Mall of America." Those occupying the middle ground advised, "Skip the larger dishes like paella", and "You will do better if you stick to simple fare, like jamon and grilled shrimp."

Tapas | Informal | Moderate | lincoln park | 2024 N. Halsted St. | 773-935-5000 | www.cafe-babareeba.com | Dinner daily, Lunch Mon-Fri

Crofton on Wells   86.5

The upside of this dining room, which is oddly lacking in ambience for a restaurant located downtown, is that it's a good place to eat when you want to have a conversation. Suzy Crofton's New American fare isn't overly creative, but dishes like her signature crab cake served with yellow pepper butter and lovage oil and heirloom pork tenderloin with cornbread pudding and smoked-apple chutney seem to keep our reviewers happy. One said Crofton's food "reminded me of the fare at Gramercy Tavern during its early years."

New American | Casual | Moderate | river north | 535 N. Wells St. | 312-755-1790 | www.croftonon-wells.com | Dinner Mon-Sat

La Petite Folie   86.5

Given a menu offering "a number of well-done classics," like puff pastry with a fricassee of escargots and wild mushrooms, and a status as "an oasis in what is otherwise a culinary desert," it's no wonder that this "hidden little French gem in Hyde Park" is consistently filled with the local intelligentsia. Revewers recommended it as a good place to catch a meal before a performance at the Court Theater, "but not worth the drive from downtown."

French | Casual | Moderate | hyde park | 1504 E. 55th St. | 773-493-1394 | www.lapetitefolie.com | Lunch & Dinner Tue-Fri, Sat-Sun dinner only

Mon Ami Gabi   86.5

Given comments like "faux French" and "Disney-esque but edible – good place to take kids or adults who have never been outside the U.S.," it isn't surprising that this bistro with outposts in Oak Brook, Las Vegas, Bethesda and northern Virginia is part of the Lettuce Entertain You group corporate empire. The fare is the typical slate of onion soup, chicken frites and beef bourguignon, which diners enjoy in a "warm and cozy" dining room in winter or on "a lovely patio with views of Lincoln Park" in warm weather.

French Bistro | Casual | Moderate | lincoln park | 2300 N. Lincoln Park W. | 773-348-8886 | www.monamigabi.com | Dinner daily

Nacional 27   86.5

This formula restaurant from the Lettuce Entertain You group features "good ceviches," a "great drinks menu" and a host of Latin fusion dishes ranging from tacos to paellas, plus both Argentine and Brazilian barbecue. As is usually the case with restaurants with a reputation for being "fun with large groups," the "go-there-to-be-seen" crowd that frequents the place is more interested in the party than the food. The "upscale atmosphere" means "prices that are considerably higher than your local taqueria's."

Latin | Informal | Moderate | river north | 325 W. Huron St. | 312-664-2727 | www.leye.com | Dinner Mon-Sat

Salpicón   86.5

"Colorful, attractive, with attentive service and real Mexican food that is both well-presented and well-prepared" is how one reviewer described Priscilla and Vincent Satkoff's establishment. Since the place opened back in 1995, Priscilla has done her best to refine the cuisine of her native Mexico by tucking the high-quality ingredients that she sources from artisanal producers, like Miller Farms and Brookfield Farms, beneath her salsas and moles. Along with running a tight dining room, Vincent Satkoff has organized one of the city's best wine lists, which is quite unusual for a Mexican restaurant. The attractive setting, complete with frescoes and a location on a lovely Old Town street, caps off the experience.

Mexican | Casual | Moderate | old town | 1252 N. Wells St. | 312-988-7811 | www.salpicon.com | Dinner daily, Lunch Sun

Gene & Georgetti   86.0

When this restaurant opened in 1941, Al Capone had been in jail for ten years; otherwise, we are sure he would have been a regular at this "slice of Chicago" located under the El in the River North area. Unfortunately, while the atmosphere remains "as cool today as it was when Sinatra used to eat there," at best the steaks rate a B+, and better-quality meat can be found at a number of the other top steakhouses in the city.

Steakhouse | Informal | Expensive | river north | 500 N. Franklin St. | 312-527-3718 | www.gene-and-georgetti.com | Lunch & Dinner Mon-Fri

Gibsons Bar & Steakhouse 86.0

Given comments like "I don't like the steaks, though I like some of the other fare," "fun, but don't expect the highest-quality ingredients" and "pedestrian steaks in a businessmen-only atmosphere," it isn't surprising that this restaurant couldn't muster a higher rating. It's a popular watering hole for pro athletes who like to order a big steak and a bottle from the "decent list" while their agents are picking up the tab.

Steakhouse | Casual | Expensive | gold coast | 1028 N. Rush St. | 312-266-8999 | www.gibsons-steakhouse.com | Lunch & Dinner daily

Mirai Sushi 86.0

Not surprisingly, given its location far from either ocean, Chicago doesn't have a particularly strong sushi culture. But if you find yourself in the Windy City and you are desperate for toro, Mirai is arguably the best of what Chicago does offer. It's a "popular and trendy spot," always filled with local diners who enjoy creative rolls and "cooked fare prepared with a deft touch." There's a "good sake selection," although reviewers complained that "the service can be mixed."

Japanese | Informal | Moderate | wicker park | 2020 W. Division St. | 773-862-8500 | www.miraisushi.com | Dinner daily

Fogo de Chão 85.5

This is probably the best of the Brazilian churrascarias that have recently opened in the Chicago area, despite the fact that it operates in more than a dozen locations around the U.S. Not for the most discerning diner, but if you are in the mood to pig out on a "massive salad bar" and "a plentiful assortment" of meats, you can eat as much as you want until they have to carry you out of the place.

Brazilian | Casual | Moderate | river north | 661 N. LaSalle St. | 312-932-9330 | www.fogodechao.com | Lunch & Dinner Mon-Fri Sat-Sun dinner only

Pane Caldo 85.5

If the prices at Spiaggia make you wince after you've spent the day shopping at the luxury boutiques on Rush Street, this slightly lower-key but still luxurious northern Italian restaurant will be happy to welcome you. At times the cuisine can get a bit fussy – think ravioli of avocado or lobster in a saffron fennel sauce – but a "great location" and a "decent wine list" do a good job of capping off the day. Of course, with the money you save by skipping Spiaggia, you might be enticed to stop at the nearby Prada boutique. . . .

Italian | Casual | Expensive | gold coast | 72 E. Walton St. | 312-649-0055 | www.pane-caldo.com | Lunch & Dinner daily

Pump Room 85.5

The good news is that it's "classic and timeless" with a setting that's "unique and formal," making it a "perfect place for cocktails and appetizers after a busy afternoon of shopping." The bad news comes in comments like, "I really can't believe this place can survive with the quality of food they deliver," and "It's not worth eating average food just to eavesdrop on low-level political operatives." But there's one line of thought that says, "You have to go to experience a little slice of Chicago both past and present."

American | Formal | Expensive | gold coast | Ambassor East Hotel | 1301 N. State Pkwy. | 312-787-7200 | www.pumproom.com | Breakfast & Dinner daily

Shaw's Crab House 85.5

This old-school seafood restaurant pleases with checkerboard floors, chrome bar stools and a sign that points to the Oyster Bar written in a typeface that was popular when Ike was president. In an attempt to appear modern, it also offers a full menu of sushi and a daily selection of a half-dozen types of oysters on the half shell, along with crabs and lobsters, plus regional classics like the rarely seen sautéed Lake Superior whitefish à la Grenobloise. It's "pricey, but worth it," which means it's "hard to come by a table on weekends."

Seafood | Casual | Expensive | river north | 21 E. Hubbard St. | 312-527-2722 | www.shawscrab-house.com | Dinner daily, Lunch Sun-Fri

Signature Room   85.0

If you were wondering whose signature they had in mind when they named this restaurant, here's a hint: It's located at the top of the Hancock Tower. Unfortunately, while John had a lovely Hancock, the food here is not a thing of beauty, and poor John's restaurant is typically described as "overpriced, overrated and full of tourists" who don't know the first thing about food. Even the setting, with its wonderful view, is not without its downside: One reviewer told us, "The last time I was there, seeing three different people making marriage proposals made me nauseous!"

New American | Formal | Expensive | streeter-ville | John Hancock Tower | 875 N. Michigan Ave., 95th fl. | 312-787-9596 | www.signatureroom.com | Lunch & Dinner daily, closed Sat lunch

Café Spiaggia   85.0

We were surprised to see a lack of a consensus about this casual sister of the famous northern Italian restaurant. What could be bad about simple fare like pizzas, pastas, salads and a half-dozen entrées, including olive-oil-poached tuna with a white bean aioli from the Spiaggia kitchen? Yet while some reviewers raved, "You get to eat some of the same food

that they serve next door while wearing jeans," others dismissed it as a "poor, down-market version of the original with a pompous staff."

Italian | Casual | Moderate | river north | 980 N. Michigan Ave. | 312-280-2750 | www.spiaggia-restaurant.com | Dinner daily

Mercat a la Planxa   85.0

Jose Garces' attempt to recreate his success at Amada in Philadelphia falls short. "Good grill work" featuring "high-quality ingredients" is compromised by "rushed service" and a sense this is "yet one more restaurant from an absentee chef." The Catalan menu includes the standard assortment of hams, cheeses and salads, but it's the cooked dishes, such as slow-braised short ribs, paired with diver scallops or Serrano-wrapped tuna paired with foie gras, that set the kitchen apart.

Catalan | Informal | Moderate | south loop | Blackstone Hotel | 638 S. Michigan Ave. | 312-765-0524 | www.mercatchicago.com | Dinner daily

Rhapsody   85.0

What with Rhapsody's proximity to the Chicago Symphony Orchestra, half the comments we collected mentioned visiting it before a performance, with one reviewer going so far as to say, "The valet parking at the restaurant is the cheapest parking you will find if you also happen to be going to a concert." Dean Zanella's "Italian-ish menu" features veal meatballs with ricotta salata, pappardelle with a boar ragú and swordfish with pep-eronata, Sicilian olives and parsley oil. It's also useful for a lunch before or after visiting the Art Institute.

Italian | Casual | Expensive | loop | 65 E. Adams St. | 312-786-9911 | www.rhapsodychicago.com | Lunch & Dinner Tue-Fri, Sat-Sun dinner only

OTHER PLACES MENTIONED

Bin 36   84.5

It's all about wine, cheese and light bar

food at this wine bar cum restaurant, where they do their best to educate neophyte oenophiles as well as keep more savvy wine drinkers happy. They provide a short menu of bistro-style fare that ranges from a sautéed Alaskan halibut to a lamb sirloin, and while the food is solid enough to stand on its own, at the end of the day, reviewers say, the experience is mostly about "the interesting wine flights" and the way the food is "carefully chosen" to go with them.

New American | Casual | Moderate | river north | 339 N. Dearborn St. | 312-755-9463 | www.bin36.com | Open daily

Bistro Campagne   84.5

Reviewers say that "with all of the new places popping up, it's easy to overlook tried-and-true places like Bistro Campagne." Don't expect the moon: it's primarily a neighborhood restaurant, offering up dishes like a macaroni gratin, a roast chicken with a mushroom ragout and a daube of boeuf served with celery root purée. There's "an inexpensive wine list," complemented by an ambience that is "as warm and comfortable" as the food is "consistent."

French Bistro | Informal | Moderate | lincoln square | 4518 N. Lincoln Ave. | 773-271-6100 | www.bistrocampagne.com | Lunch & Dinner daily

Red Light   84.0

Because of the blaring music and lively atmosphere, Jackie Shen's venue gives the impression that it is as much club as restaurant. Shen's pan-Asian cuisine takes you on a tour of the continent with dishes like Japanese ahi tuna, Vietnamese spring rolls, Thai pork chops and Peking duck. Even those who give it a sideways thumb say the "appetizers are fine, with good heat," while describing the mains as "lackluster."

Pan-Asian | Casual | Moderate | loop | 820 W. Randolph St. | 312-733-8880 | www.redlight-chicago.com | Dinner daily, Lunch Mon-Fri

Shanghai Terrace   82.5

"Meh" is the best way to describe this upscale venue. While it provides an opportunity to enjoy classics like Kung Pao chicken or wok-seared Wagyu beef and chili prawns, the cynical shrug off the offerings as "the Walt Disney version of Chinese food." At least the elegant, spacious setting in the tony Peninsula Hotel won kudos; as one reviewer put it, "There was enough room between my table and the next one over to cram in an entire Chinatown-sized restaurant."

Chinese | Casual | Expensive | river north | Peninsula Hotel | 108 E. Superior St., 4th floor | 312-573-6695 | www.chicago.peninsula.com | Lunch & Dinner Mon-Sat

SushiSamba   82.5

The local branch of a chain operating in New York, Miami, Las Vegas and Tel Aviv features "gorgeous patrons and an energetic vibe" along with a rooftop patio full of people "chilling out with an exotic cocktail in hand." While everyone would agree that the restaurant "was never about the food," reviewers did mention the occasional standout, such as the flash-fried crabs.

Japanese | Casual | Moderate | river north | 504 N. Wells St. | 312-595-2300 | www.sushisamba.com | Lunch & Dinner daily

Wildfire   81.0

Until we started to read the comments, we thought this was a Southwestern restaurant. Silly us; it seems the name refers to the thing that they cook steaks over. But given comments like, "My steak had to be redone twice before they got it perfectly medium rare," it seems the chefs were just as confused as we were. Another person told us, "All I can recommend this place for is that it smells nice, but I never eat well there."

Steakhouse | Casual | Expensive | river north | 159 W. Erie St. | 312-787-9000 | www.wildfirerestaurant.com | Dinner daily

Cheap Eats

UNIQUELY DELICIOUS

Hot Doug's 9.7

The recommendation rate is running at 100% for Doug Sohn's hot dog emporium, called "a hotbed for some of the most innovative culinary ideas in the city, only wrapped in a casing." While traditionalists can order a basic dog topped with mustard and sauerkraut, Sohn puts his formal culinary training to good use in the list of daily specials, with creations like Catalonian pork sausage with saffron rouille and Manchego cheese, cherry pork sausage with cherry-blackberry cream sauce and Sartori raspberry cheese, and the world-renowned foie gras and Sauternes duck sausage with truffle aioli, foie gras mousse and sel gris. If these "mouth-watering creations" aren't enough, on Saturdays Sohn cooks his fries in duck fat, creating "the perfect side dish for what are easily the haute-est hot dogs in the country." Given all these kudos, it's no wonder that this unusual spot ranks as the highest-rated Cheap Eats restaurant in our guide.

Hot Dogs | Inexpensive | northwest | 3324 N. California Ave. | 773-279-9550 | www.hotdougs. com | Lunch Mon-Sat

Calumet Fisheries 8.0

The Kotlick family has been frying and smoking fish at this odd little shack on the South Side for the past 62 years. Those who prefer their seafood fried can choose among shrimps, catfish, scallops, oysters and smelts, while chubs, salmon, shrimp and trout are all smoked on the premises. The unusual location in a deserted industrial area makes it a hassle to get to, but one reviewer who made the effort called it "a real gem, especially for the hot smoked shrimps."

Seafood | Inexpensive | south deering | 3259 E. 95th St. | 773-933-9855 | www.calumetfisheries. com | Open daily

RECOMMENDED

Johnnie's Beef 7.9

Chicagoans say, "If you want the best Italian beef sandwich in town, Johnnie's is a must go," and "For the prices they charge you can eat two sandwiches." In fact, one reviewer who must have superior olfactory skills claimed, "It's the best smelling restaurant in the six-county area." But another found the appeal limited: "One needs to try it once, but that should be enough." Others picked the sandwich apart by talking about "delicious beef, but not the best giardinera."

Sandwiches | Inexpensive | elmwood park | 1935 S Arlington Heights Rd. | 847-357-8100 | Lunch & Dinner daily

Orange 7.6

You'll have a difficult time finding a quirkier breakfast spot than this local mini-chain. There's an extensive juice bar, as well as "fruishi" (three different types of fruit draped over sushi rice), omelets and scrambles like green eggs and ham (made with basil pesto) and various types of exotic pancakes (i.e., cinnamon roll or jelly doughnut) and French toast (orange rosemary or chai). Reviewers found that "the super-creative food is worth the wait," and be prepared for an "insane wait time on weekends."

Breakfast | Inexpensive | roscoe village | 2011 W. Roscoe Ave. | 773-248-0999 | www.orangeres-taurantchicago.com | Open daily

Kuma's Corner 7.5

This "unabashed heavy-metal bar" serves some of the best hamburgers in Chicago. The burgers are named after different metal bands, like the Iron Maiden (avocado, cherry peppers, pepper Jack and chipotle mayo), the Judas Priest (bacon, apples walnuts and dried cranberries with blue cheese dressing) and the Led Zeppelin (goat cheese, oregano, Kalamata olives, tzatziki and onion).

Super-crowded, it's so loud that "the noise level can be maddening" at times.

Hamburgers | Inexpensive | logan square | 2900 W. Belmont Ave. | 773-604-8769 | www.kumas-corner.com | Lunch & Dinner daily

Al's # 1 Italian Beef   7.4

There is a strong geographic split regarding Al's. Two-thirds of reviewers (who happen to live in Chicago) recommend the place, saying things like "It sets all standards for Italian beef." But the other third, who, coincidentally, live outside of the city, say things like "possibly the worst beef sandwich in existence." If we could add our two cents to the debate, we wonder why the beef has to be sitting in gravy all day. Can't they simply get a pair of tongs and dunk it before slapping it into the roll?

Sandwiches | Inexpensive | river north | 1079 W. Taylor St. | 312-226-4017 | www.alsbeef.com | Open Mon-Sat

Manny's   7.3

Each city has an old-school New York–style deli: Katz's in NYC, Famous Fourth Street Deli in Philly, Attman's in Baltimore, Langer's in L.A. and Shapiro's in Indianapolis. In Chicago the place of choice is Manny's, where the corned beef sandwiches are "huge" and the potato pancakes are "to die for." Like the other delis mentioned, it always seems to be full of the unusual mix of characters that frequent this type of place, which in this instance includes "everyone from the mayor to truck drivers on their lunch break grabbing a fat sandwich."

Delicatessen | Inexpensive | loop | 5700 S. Cicero Ave. | 773-948-6300 | www.mannysdeli.com | Open daily

Mr. Beef   7.3

What's funny about the different Chicago beef sandwich specialists is that each manages to attract at least one person who claims that "This is the best example of the genre," while someone else says, "It's not as good as the competition." A third point of view expressed about Mr. Beef came from a reviewer who declared, "The restaurant is riding on past glory," although on "some days you can get a glimpse of what once made them great."

Sandwiches | Inexpensive | near north | 666 N. Orleans St. | 312-337-8500 | Open Mon-Sat

Original Pancake House   7.3

At this place – the higher rated of the two major pancake chains in the Chicago area – the house specialty is the Dutch Baby pancakes, which are baked in an oven (like a soufflé). There are a dozen other types of pancakes, plus waffles, omelets, crepes and sandwiches. With nine locations, including one located off Rush Street, it is one of the most convenient breakfast spots in the city.

Coffee Shop | Inexpensive | gold coast | 22 E. Bellevue Pl. | 312-642-7917 | www.originalpancakehouse.com | Breakfast & Lunch Daily

Superdawg Drive-In   7.3

This popular hot dog stand has "super fries" and "super burgers" to go along with "nice dogs" served at an actual old-time drive-in. Even those who aren't big fans of Chicago-style dogs say, "The fries are really good, and the place is cute." The rest of the menu is what you expect at a fast-food place: Polish sausage and chicken breast sandwiches, fried shrimp and grilled cheese, along with "super shakes." "The cool drive-in décor" (straight out of the '60s, including two large hot dogs dancing on the roof) is an integral part of the experience.

Hot Dogs | Inexpensive | northwest | 6363 N. Milwaukee Ave. | 773-763-0660 | www.superdawg.com | Lunch & Dinner daily

Smoque BBQ   7.0

Comments like "clean and spiffy," "not

particularly authentic," and "benefiting from a location near the lily-white 'burbs" don't really suggest a good BBQ venue. But the lack of a down-home atmosphere aside, this is a popular spot with our reviewers, who claim it serves some of the "best barbecue in the metropolitan area." A key to understanding its appeal is the "very impressive brisket," which does its best to emulate the version they serve at places like Kreuz Market or Smitty's in Lockhart, Texas.

Barbecue | Inexpensive | northwest | 3800 N. Pulaski Rd. | 773-545-7427 | www.smoquebbq.com | Lunch & Dinner Tue-Sun

Walker Bros. The Original Pancake House   7.0

Although the similarly named Original Pancake House chain (see above) gets a slightly higher rating, many reviewers tell us that this is where local families in the know come to devour "one of the best traditional breakfasts in the U.S.," feasting on large plates of pancake specialties like Dutch Baby, apple, German and the Danish Garden, all of which are doing their best to impersonate a soufflé. They also have more classically styled pancakes, including a number filled with fruit or nuts, as well as nine different oven-baked omelets, Belgian waffles, French toast, crepes, salads and sandwiches.

Coffee Shop | Inexpensive | evanston | 825 W. Dundee Rd. | 847-392-6600 | www.walkerbros.net | Open daily

OTHER PLACES MENTIONED

Honey 1 BBQ   6.6

How can you not like the barbecue from a restaurant whose slogan is "Where the Smoke Is No Joke"? While it's considered the best barbecue in the city, a few reviewers spoke of inconsistency, but they all agreed that "when it's on, it's terrific." The barbecue is southern-style, meaning that it's an adventure in smoked pork ranging from ribs to tips to hot links. There's chicken and fish, too, but don't forget that you're there for the ribs.

Barbecue | Inexpensive | bucktown | 2241 N. Western Ave. | 773-227-5130 | www.honey1bbq. com | Lunch & Dinner Tue-Sun

Lou Mitchell's   6.0

This legendary coffee shop in the Loop features the unusual gimmick of serving eggs with double yolks. That's right: Order a pair of eggs sunny side up and your waiter will bring a frying pan to your table with four yolks staring you in the eyes. Otherwise the rest of the food is standard coffee-shop fare, save for the bonus box of Milk Duds they hand you on your way out.

Coffee Shop | Inexpensive | loop | 565 W. Jackson Blvd. | 312-939-3111 | www.loumitchell-srestaurant.com | Breakfast & Lunch daily

Big Star   5.8

With Blackbird, Avec and the Publican already under his belt, Paul Kahan decided he wasn't busy enough, so he opened this "hip taco joint." Add trendy cocktails and "cheap beer" to the mix, plus "a soundtrack that fits the hipster vibe," and you can understand why Big Star's "a favorite with the tattooed and pierced crowd." Small, constantly crowded and loaded with energy, it's a popular stop for people in the restaurant industry after they get off work.

Taqueria | Inexpensive | wicker park | 1531 N. Damen Ave. | 773-235-4039 | www.bigstarchicago. com | Lunch & Dinner daily

Cleveland OH

Lolita   88.0

Michael Symon looks to Adriatic environs for his culinary inspiration at this location that formerly housed Lola, his first venture. Lolita is more casual than its predecessor, with a menu that harks back to Symon's Greek heritage, like hanger steak served with chickpeas and skordalia, and also draws on the cuisine of Italy, like crispy chicken livers with bacon and soft polenta. The "good, casual fare" is complemented by a "good wine list" and a "fun atmosphere" in an area of the city that one reviewer described as "an emerging neighborhood."

Mediterranean | Informal | Moderate | tremont | 900 Literary Rd. | 216-771-5652 | www.lolabistro.com | Dinner Tue-Sun

Columbus OH

Kihachi   91.0

Columbus' first stroke of luck came when Honda built a factory 30 miles northwest of the city. The second was when Ryuji Kimura, who had worked in a number of notable Japanese restaurants in New York, decided to move to Columbus and open a restaurant that catered to the plant's executives. And while the strip-mall location means that it looks no different from a half dozen other Asian eateries in the area, step inside and you will find what one reviewer called "a real Japanese restaurant." There's a printed menu, but hardly anyone orders from it; most diners take a seat at the counter and tell chef Kimura to do his thing. "Don't be surprised if you're the only non-Japanese person in the restaurant."

Japanese | Informal | Expensive | 2667 Federated Blvd. | 614-764-9040 | Dinner Mon-Sat

Alana's Food & Wine   86.5

Ask any self-proclaimed foodie based in Columbus where to have dinner and odds are he will tell you to go to "this fun little place." It's a favorite with the locavore crowd, part of the allure being "the deliberately amateurish nature of the cooking and presentation." This impacts the main courses more than the starters, so, if you're the type who prefers professionalism, the best way to deal is to "eat a progression of appetizers before moving on to dessert."

New American | Informal | Moderate | 2333 N. High St. | 614-294-6783 | www.alanas.com | Dinner Tue-Sat

The Refectory   85.5

The comments about this "old school French restaurant" are split. The ayes declare it's "the best fine dining in Columbus," while the nays say, "I hear Chef Blondin knows how to cook, I guess he just doesn't want to." We note that Richard Blondin worked with Paul Bocuse and Pierre Orsi before he abandoned the banks of the Rhône for those of the Scioto. One reviewer said wine offerings that include "listings and prices from years ago" make it worth a visit.

French | Formal | Expensive | 1092 Bethel Rd. | 614-451-9774 | www.therefectoryrestaurant.com | Dinner Mon-Sat

Cheap Eats

UNIQUELY DELICIOUS

Jeni's Splendid Ice Cream   8.2

Jeni Britton Bauer has established a reputation for making some of the best artisanal ice cream in the U.S (though it's still not as well-known outside of the Columbus area as it should be). She makes a true ice cream, not a French-style custard, so the flavors are clearer. Many of her flavors are seasonal, and many are derived from local products. The signature is salty caramel; the others range from good versions of the classics to innovations like mango lassi and sweet corn. One reviewer declared, "A must go not only for the people of Columbus, but for everyone in the country."

Ice Cream | Inexpensive | short north | 714 N. High St. | 614-294-5364 | www. jenisicecreams. com | Open daily

Second Location: dublin | 1 W. Bridge St. | 614-792-5364 | Open daily

Third Location: grandview | 1281 Grandview Ave. | 614-488-2680 | Open daily

Fourth Location: bexley | 2156 E. Main St. | 614-231-5364 | Open daily

See website for additional locations

Findlay OH

HIGHLY RECOMMENDED

Revolver   92.0

After spending 10 years working at places like Emeril's, Trio, Spring and Green Zebra, Michael Bulkowski and his wife, Debi, returned to their hometown and opened this delightful restaurant. Bulkowski drew inspiration from the food he ate while growing up – specifically, his Polish grandmother's cooking – to craft what he terms Modern Midwestern cuisine. The result? Dishes (local rutabaga soup with cranberry-cashew pesto, cinnamon-spiced duck meatballs with tempura squash and goat cheese and Lake Erie walleye with roasted cauliflower and farm-egg vinaigrette) that "single-handedly disprove the notion that you can't eat well in the Midwest." The interior is exceptional: Bulkowski and his wife have adorned it with mid-century-modern tiles, glass and fixtures, making it one of the few restaurants where "the décor is as hip as the food."

New American | Casual | Moderate | 110 East Sandusky Street | 419-424-4020 | www.revolverrestaurant. net | Dinner Mon-Sat

Indianapolis IN

TOP LOCAL CHOICE

St. Elmo's Steak House   89.0

This is the kind of "classic steakhouse" one hopes to find in towns that don't offer many dining options: chilled martinis, shrimp cocktails served with a "zesty," "horseradish-overloaded sauce" and big steaks served by waiters wearing bowties and slightly worn tuxedos. And we can't forget the "classy steakhouse vibe" and a wine list containing some "hidden gems at good prices." There were few complaints – one was about a limited choice of sides – but a typical comment was "a must stop when I'm in Indy."

Steakhouse | Casual | Expensive | 127 S. Illinois St. | 317-635-0636 | www.stelmos.com | Dinner daily

Kansas City MO

American Restaurant   94.6

After starting her career here as the executive chef, Debbie Gold has now returned to the place where she first made a name for herself. Gold's cooking, best described as a "luxurious version of New American cuisine," revolves around a "superb and original command of ingredients"; it includes dishes like Campo Lindo 63-degree egg with porcini, summer truffle and rice pudding and duck breast with turnips, pickled blueberries and pumpernickel jus. No review of the American Restaurant would be complete without mentioning its history. It was constructed in 1971 by the Hallmark Corporation, across from their corporate offices, as a tribute to American cuisine. James Beard developed the opening menu. The dining room was designed by Warren Platner, the architect of New York's World Trade Center, and is evocative of Windows on the World, the restaurant at that now-demolished complex.

New American | Informal | Expensive | crown center | 200 E. 25th St. | 816-545-8001 | www.theamericanrestaurantkc.com | Dinner Mon-Sat; Lunch first Fri of the month

Bluestem   92.2

Colby and Megan Garrelt's restaurant in Westport is Kansas City's best example of the type of contemporary urban dining that is typical of New York and Los Angeles. Offering "finesse without the fussy," Colby Garrelt's cuisine relies on careful pairing of ingredients, like Wagyu beef tartare with a chimuchurri cloud, creamy potatoes and a crispy salad and Campo Lindo hen served piccata style with capers, lemon, greens and roasted garlic gnocchi. "The best serious restaurant in town" is how one reviewer described it, while another upped the ante to "the best restaurant in the state," adding, "I wish I lived in Kansas City so I could visit more often."

New American | Casual | Expensive | 900 Westport Rd. | 816-561-1101 | www.bluestemkc.com | Dinner Tue-Sat,, Lunch Sun

Justus Drugstore (21 miles north in Smithville)   91.4

Destination diners looking for an exemplary use of local ingredients prepared with modern culinary technique should visit this restaurant located in the former Justus family drugstore. John Justus loves Berkshire pork, which he prepares as starters (a pork terrine with brioche and a poached egg and a pork-tail fritter served with wild arugula vinaigrette) and mains (Newman Farm pork served two ways: as a brined rib eye and as a house-made sausage served with soft polenta, onion, mint, lemon and elderflower white wine). Reviewers call it "farm-to-table cooking at its finest" and "worth the 30-minute drive from downtown." However, a few complained about the "excruciatingly slow pace of the meal."

New American | Informal | Moderate | smithville | 106 West Main St. | 816-532-2300 | www.drugstorerestaurant.com | Dinner Tue-Sun

Starker's Reserve   87.5

Since it opened in 1972, this has been one of Kansas City's more formal dining experiences. Purchased in 2006 by its chef, John McClure, it now offers a menu that's a mix of New American fare like grilled La Belle Farms foie gras with Creole beignet and a strawberry and pistachio salad, and classic house dishes like filet mignon with Alaskan King crab meat asparagus and béarnaise sauce. The "simple, well-prepared food" and "award-winning wine list" add up to "an old-school dining experience" at a "quaint restaurant that is worth the wait."

New American | Casual | Expensive | 201 W. 47th St. | 816-753-3565 | www.starkersreserve.com | Dinner Mon-Sat, Lunch Mon-Fri

Le Fou Frog   84.0

Depending on the reviewer, the Frog has "great atmosphere and authentic bistro fare" or it serves "overpriced food in a run-down, cranky dining room." You judge for yourself. The menu offers a combination of classics like onion soup and steak au poivre and contemporary creations like ostrich tenderloin in a sauce of lingonberries and coffee extract.

French Bistro | Informal | Moderate | river-market | 400 E. Fifth St. | 816-474-6060 | www.kansascitymenus.com/lefoufrog | Dinner Tue-Sun, Lunch Thu

Cheap Eats

Oklahoma Joe's   8.4

Just over the border in Kansas and located inside a converted gas station is one of the few barbecue restaurants that our panel was able to reach a consensus on – namely, that it "is the best BBQ I have ever had." Expect to find a long line of people waiting their turn to order "barbecue chicken that was so moist and tender I thought it was cooked sous vide" and pork ribs that were "good enough to make even a Hasidic Jew convert."

Barbecue | Inexpensive | 3002 W. 47th St. | 913-722-3366 | www.oklahomajoesbbq.com | Lunch & Dinner Mon-Sat

Arthur Bryant's   7.0

Propelled onto the national dining scene when Calvin Trillin made the brash claim that it was "the best restaurant in the country," this restaurant lost its founder in 1982. The current owners who carry on his tradition do a good enough job to attract comments like "It's still the best barbecue I've tasted in the country." Brisket is the thing here, especially an order of burnt ends that are doused with the house's famous vinegar-based sauce.

Barbecue | Inexpensive | 1727 Brooklyn Ave. | 816-231-1123 | www.arthurbryantsbbq.com | Lunch & Dinner daily

Jack Stack Barbeque   7.0

Some barbecue restaurants are nothing but shacks, but Jack's feels more like a micro-brewery. In keeping with the more upscale atmosphere, it's not surprising that the menu here goes deeper than your typical BBQ outlet, including items like grilled salmon and blackened prime rib as well as sides like cheesy cream corn and baked beans, which one reviewer called "two of the best sides I've ever had in a barbecue joint."

Barbecue | Inexpensive | 101 W. 22nd St. | 816-472-7427 | www.jackstackbbq.com | Lunch & Dinner daily

Gates Bar-B-Q   6.3

Gates & Sons manages to operate six successful locations in a crowded 'cue market. Their reputation was built on their sauce, and the menu offers the standard K.C. barbecue fare, with the addition of mutton, something you don't often find. As to be expected when it comes to an issue as personal as barbecue quality, some people say it's "the best 'cue in Kansas City," while others counter with "not up to the competition."

Barbecue | Inexpensive | 1221 Brooklyn Ave. | 816-483-3880 | www.gatesbbq.com | Open daily

Stroud's   6.1

The menu at Stroud's offers every part of the chicken, including gizzards, livers,

legs, thighs, wings and breasts. Your bird is fried to order in a pan, which means you'll be waiting around for 40 minutes while the outside is getting nice and crispy. Add some biscuits, gravy and mashed potatoes to the mix and you end up with "large portions of Southern-style comfort food" that is "served family-style." Another claim to fame: Stroud's has been choking their own chickens since 1933, causing one reviewer to comment on the "hands-on approach."

Chicken | Inexpensive | 5410 NE Oak Ridge Dr. | 816-454-9600 | www.stroudsrestaurant.com | Dinner daily, open 2 PM Fri & Sun

Madison WI

HIGHLY RECOMMENDED

L'Etoile   92.0

While market-to-table cuisine might be typical these days, it wasn't the case when L'Etoile opened in 1976. Odette Piper was one of the chefs that made it so. In 2005, Piper sold her interest to Tori (executive chef) and Traci Miller, and they have done a good job of continuing her mission; one reviewer said, "The restaurant has never lost focus of what it stands for." It's kept the faith so well, that in 2010 it and its "amazing wine list" moved down the street into a larger and more comfortable space. But there's a divergent strain among the comments; one reviewer said that despite "great ingredients," a "cuisine that might have been unique 20 years ago seems generic today."

New American | Casual | Expensive | 1 S. Pinckney St. | 608-251-0500 | www.letoile-restaurant.com | Dinner Mon-Sat

RECOMMENDED

Harvest   90.0

Tami Lax and Derek Rowe's restaurant has always been overshadowed by its better-known neighbor and alma mater, L'Etoile. Derek Rowe's farm-to-table menu includes dishes like seared sea scallops with carrot purée and Wisconsin grass-fed skirt steak with chickpea fries, pickled red onions and harissa; the result is "an honest version of market-to-table cuisine" and food that is "well executed but not too fussy." Now that their competitor has moved to the next block, one of our reviewers who is given to puns predicted that "Harvest should reap the benefit" by getting more attention from diners.

New American | Casual | Moderate | 21 N. Pinckney St. | 608-255-6075 | www.harvest-restaurant.com | Dinner Mon-Sat

TOP LOCAL CHOICE

Old Fashioned   88.0

This tribute to the taverns and supper clubs that were popular with an earlier generation of diners is where you will find "all the gooey, fatty foods of Wisconsin." The menu, which ranges from brats to wursts and from beer-battered walleye served with shredded cabbage and tartar sauce to large platters of locally made cheese, adds up to "a delicious evening of fun," especially once you add a "great list of local beers." But not everyone is enamored, with some reviewers saying that "retro mid-American food sounds better than it tastes" and "no matter how you slice it, it's still bologna."

American | Informal | Moderate | 23 N. Pinckney St. | 608-310-4545 | www.theoldfashioned.com | Open daily

Milwaukee WI

HIGHLY RECOMMENDED

Sanford   94.4

On its face, Sanford looks like the local installment of the upper middle restaurant that you find all over the country. But with "many dishes influenced by Milwaukee's local ethnic groups," Sandy D'Amato's cuisine is "imaginatively conceived, carefully prepared, and artfully presented." The menu features dishes like lamb coppa with pickled fennel and golden raisins; duck breast glazed with lekvar (prune butter) and roasted apricots; and veal cooked for 17 hours, topped with a paprika and caraway seed crust and served with a leek and poppy-seed slaw. It's uniformly recommended by our reviewers; comments included "a marriage of Midwestern pride and culinary genius"; "While L'Etoile might get the press, Sanford is the best restaurant in Wisconsin" and "a must if you live in Milwaukee; worth the drive for people who live in Chicago."

New American | Informal | Moderate | 1547 N. Jackson St. | 414-276-9608 | www.sanfordrestaurant.com | Dinner Mon-Sat

TOP LOCAL CHOICE

Coquette Café   88.5

Nick Burki and Chris Hatleli do such a good job with the French fare at this restaurant in Milwaukee's historic Third Ward that we didn't find a single reviewer who complained that Sandy D'Amato had sold his interest in the restaurant. The fare includes flatbreads with various toppings, like fennel sausage with roasted mushrooms and Asiago cheese, as well as larger plates like trout à la Grenobloise with watercress and glazed radishes and roast chicken. "A nice Wisconsin version of a French brasserie," it's one of the few quality restaurants in town that is open for lunch.

French | Casual | Moderate | 316 N. Milwaukee St. | 414-291-2655 | www.coquettecafe.com | Lunch & Dinner Mon-Fri, Sat dinner only

ACCEPTABLE

Karl Ratzsch   87.0

We never cease to be amazed by restaurants that have not taken advantage of the improved ingredients that have come onto the market over the past 30 years. Of course, that doesn't stop certain reviewers from praising Karl Ratzsch for "the wonderful, old-world feel," claiming that the "number of places where you can enjoy a traditional German meal of crackling pork shank or bratwurst from Usinger's are dwindling." But others say expeditions to this landmark should be strictly for "anthro-pological reasons" and recommend going "only if you need to shake the dust off your lederhosen."

German | Informal | Moderate | 320 E. Mason St. | 414-276-2720 | www.karlratzsch.com | Dinner Mon-Sat, Lunch Wed-Sat

Cheap Eats

UNIQUELY DELICIOUS

Kopp's Frozen Custard   8.8

While reviewers are willing to travel long distances for a meal, it is rare to read comments like "I drive from Madison (80 miles away) just to eat here" when

the topic is dessert. But this local institution makes the case that "there is no better way to showcase Wisconsin's terrific dairy products" than with frozen custard. Besides chocolate and "their signature vanilla," each day Kopp's offers two custom custards, ranging from the exotic red velvet cake to the more traditional butter pecan. Always crowded, the "unique modern architecture" makes the experience all the more unusual. They also serve a full menu of fast food.

Ice Cream | Inexpensive | 7631 W. Layton Ave. | 414-282-4312 | www.kopps.com | Open daily

Minneapolis/St. Paul MN

RECOMMENDED

La Belle Vie   91.5

The city's top dining experience is located at the back of a smart apartment building that dates from 1927. Tim McKee's delicate, French-inspired cuisine includes creations like a starter of poached lobster with goat cheese agnolotti, harissa and hen of the woods mushrooms, as well as mains like a grilled lamb rib eye with eggplant, cauliflower and anchovies. Multiple reviewers say, "It's my favorite high-end dining spot in town," and the dining room is always filled with people celebrating birthdays, engagements, anniversaries and other special occasions – or even those capping off a day visiting the Walker Art Museum across the street. The "beautiful, formal atmosphere" is enhanced by "impeccable service," and while some described the experience as "pricy," the consensus was that "the delicious and beautiful-looking food" was worth it.

French | Casual | Expensive | loring park | 510 Groveland Ave. | 612-874-6440 | www.labellevie.us | Dinner daily

Heartland   90.5

Lenny Russo, a native of Hoboken, New Jersey, looks like he should own the top Italian restaurant in town. Instead, Russo became a student of the ethnic cooking of his adopted region, and his menu contains dishes like a smoked freshwater fishcake with dilled crème fraîche and a golden chanterelle mushroom conserve; braunschweiger with garlic aioli, sauerkraut and walnut croustades; and a casserole of white beans, wild boar, smoked pork and pheasant confit marketed under the moniker "Midwestern Cassoulet." Among the numerous glowing comments for this "absolute gem," this one says it all: "If the Twin Cities restaurant scene is distinctive by virtue of its use of local farms, then Heartland is the superlative among the distinctive."

New American | Informal | Expensive | downtown | 289 E. Fifth St. | 651-699-3536 | www.heartland-restaurant.com | Dinner Tue-Sun

Origami   90.4

Due to the wonders of FedEx, UPS and other international shipping services, most major cities in the U.S. have at least one Japanese restaurant that sources fish from Tokyo's Tsukiji Market. At Origami "60% of the tasty pieces that are served make the journey across the Pacific" before ending up between your chopsticks. Like other more serious sushi parlors, the focus here is not on special rolls or flashy preparations, just simple cuts of "superbly fresh and expertly crafted" morsels of fish and high-quality rice; the best are doled out one piece at a time to diners who make the "wise decision to sit at the counter and allow the chefs to do their thing."

Japanese | Informal | Expensive | warehouse district | 30 N. First St. | 612-333-8430 | www.origamirestaurant.com | Lunch & Dinner Mon-Fri Sat-Sun dinner only

Cosmos   90.3

Dishes like Wild Acres chicken breast with dark meat risotto, fresh corn and English pea purée, and grilled bone-in pork loin with chorizo beans, tomatillo mole and corn salsa led a number of reviewers to mention the "inventive cuisine" and "creative combinations" on Håkan Lundberg's menu. Even the desserts drew praise: "They looked so beautiful I wanted to take a photo rather than eat them," said one reviewer. The "chic and modern setting" appeals to a "swanky crowd with lots of attractive couples out on dates," but the cuisine-focused know that "the real action is at the Kitchen Table," where Lundberg serves multi-course meals that can cost as much as $200 a person.

New American | Casual | Expensive | downtown | Graves 601 Hotel | 601 First Ave. N. | 612-312-1168 | www.cosmosrestaurant.com | Open daily

Alma   90.0

Of the top dining spots in the Twin Cities, Alex Roberts' restaurant serves the most straightforward version of farm-to-table cuisine. Roberts learned his trade working with David Bouley, and his cuisine is based on the "hyper-fresh and hyper-local produce" theory of cooking. Not surprisingly, dishes like a crispy soft-cooked egg with smoked mushrooms, arugula and fontina cheese fondue, and local trout with lemon orzo, mascarpone, sweet peas and crispy artichoke were described as "a can't-miss for anyone who enjoys innovative food prepared by one of the best chefs in the country." One reviewer waxed poetic about the legumes: "I'm not a vegetarian, but I usually eat vegetarian here because the dishes are so delicious."

New American | Informal | Expensive | northeast | 528 University Ave. SE | 612-379-4909 | www.restaurantalma.com | Dinner daily

Piccolo   90.0

We asked a number of Twin Cities chefs where they liked to eat, and every one of them mentioned Doug Flicker's restaurant. Labeled a "small plates extravaganza," Flicker's menu – dishes like smoked eel with magnalista lardo and cauliflower pickles; scrambled brown eggs with pickled pigs' feet, truffle butter and Parmigiano; and Callister Farms chicken with pistachios, prunes, artichokes and rosemary olive oil – is as interesting to read as it is to eat. The comments border on the delirious: "By far the best meal I've had in the Twin Cities," "Every bite is bursting with delicious flavor" and "Piccolo is the type of restaurant that will put the Twin Cities on the map."

Italian | Casual | Moderate | southwest | 4300 Bryant Ave. S. | 612-827-8111 | www.piccolompls.com | Dinner Wed-Mon

20.21   89.0

When your senses of sight and sound grow tired of experiencing the exhibits and per-
formances at the Walker Art Center, this Wolfgang Puck restaurant will tantalize your
senses of taste and smell. The pan-Asian cuisine features Chinese chicken salad with
crispy wontons, candied cashews and hot-and-sweet mustard dressing and a Thai seafood curry with shiitake mushrooms and Thai basil. There are "stunning views of downtown Minneapolis," along with "patio seating in warm weather," and many recommend
"walking through the sculpture garden before enjoying dinner."

Pan-Asian | Informal | Expensive | loring park | Walker Art Center | 1750 Hennepin Ave. | 612-253-3410 |
www.wolfgangpuck.com | Lunch & Dinner Tue-Sat

112 Eatery   89.5

Restaurants with "interesting food at won't-break-the-bank prices," served in a "fun
environment with a downtown vibe" always attract a huge following. Calling Isaac
Becker's menu "eclectic" would be an understatement: It's jam-packed with quirky
dishes like burrata with poached Maine lobster, tagliatelle with foie gras meatballs and
ahi tuna with a peanut Bolognese and shell peas. Even the 112 Burger was called "fantastic," with its "reasonably sized patty, perfect bun, and delicious melted Brie."

Gastropub | Informal | Moderate | downtown | 112 N. Third St. | 612-343-7696 | www.112eatery.com |
Dinner daily

Café Lurcat   89.0

After Richard D'Amico refurbished this popular venue overlooking Loring Park, it earned
a Top Local Choice distinction – surprising for a place that's part of a 20-restaurant
chain. In a "sleek, modern dining room," diners can enjoy dishes like crispy ahi and basil
spring rolls with ginger and soy or a Berkshire pork tenderloin with fig compote, roasted
onions and St. Pete's Select blue cheese. You can eat more casually at the bar, where
the menu focuses on servings of finger food like chipotle and garlic chicken wings, tuna
pizza and "one of the best burgers in town."

New American | Casual | Moderate | loring park | 1624 Harmon Pl. | 612-486-5500 | www.cafelurcat.com
| Dinner daily

Craftsman Restaurant & Bar   89.0

It would be disappointing if a restaurant with this name didn't have an Arts and Crafts
décor. But not to worry – the Dooleys haven't let us down, and if you're in the mood to
sit on chairs that look like they were designed by Stickley and enjoy dishes like grilled
venison leg with delicata squash, barley risotto and dried-cherry balsamic made from
organic ingredients, this is the perfect choice for you. Unfortunately, word has it that
the food has been up and down since Mike Phillips left the kitchen.

New American | Informal | Moderate | south minneapolis | 4300 E. Lake St. | 612-722-0175 | www.crafts-
manrestaurant.com | Dinner daily, Lunch Sun

Victory 44   89.0

"The best foodie spot in North Minneapolis" is what reviewers say about this restaurant where "artistic presentations of local foods" are served at "absurdly affordable prices." The blackboard menu offers 18 different types of small plates like bacon frites, kabocha squash lasagna and steak and potatoes, which goes for the rock-bottom price of $7. Big spenders can enjoy the chef's five-course tasting menu for the ridiculously low price of $30. As you might expect, the combination of high quality and low prices means you will likely wait in line for the privilege of eating here.

Gastropub | Informal | Inexpensive | north minneapolis | 2203 44th Ave. North | 612-588-2228 | www. victory-44.com | Lunch & Dinner daily

Bar La Grassa   88.5

After his huge success at 112 Eatery (see above), Isaac Becker decided to spread his wings with a "bustling and upbeat" Italian small plates restaurant. Its "stunning menu" is filled with dishes that have quickly become local favorites (ricotta pizzette and bruschetta topped with soft eggs and lobster, to name two), along with pastas like farfalle with smoked sweetbreads and Berkshire pork tenderloin with peperone salsa. Reviewers "love, love, love this place," so it's "a good idea to make reservations way in advance."

Italian | Informal | Moderate | north loop | 800 N. Washington Ave. | 612-333-3837 | www.barlagrassa. com | Dinner daily

Lucia's   88.5

Every city needs its "local version of Chez Panisse," and Lucia Watson's restaurant has been accorded that honor in the Twin Cities. Each day diners are offered a choice of four starters, like mixed greens with Bent River camembert on cherry-hazelnut bread and honey-thyme vinaigrette, along with a quartet of mains like roasted Callister chicken breast with sage-golden raisin butter and brussels sprouts, all for prices that barely break $20. And there is always an entrée geared toward vegetarians. "Nice organic cooking" and "tasty ingredients" sum up the comments.

New American | Informal | Moderate | uptown | 1432 W. 31st St. | 612-825-1572 | www.lucias.com | Lunch & Dinner Tue-Sun

Meritage   88.5

Of all the places one would expect to find French brasserie cuisine that is "as delicious as it is correct," we doubt anyone would guess St. Paul, Minnesota. If you don't believe us, take a look at this comment: "Man, these people understand French cooking. The onion soup was rich, sweet, well-made. The beet salad was simple but well-balanced. And an order of short ribs was rich but not too heavy." There's an oyster bar, and in a nod to chef Russell Klein's heritage, they also offer Jewish soul food classics like matzoh ball soup. It adds up to "a true feel and taste of Paris in the heart of this Midwestern city."

French | Casual | Moderate | downtown | 410 St. Peter St. | 651-222-5670 | www.meritage-stpaul.com | Lunch & Dinner Tue-Sun

Broders' Pasta Bar   88.0

After working your way through a dozen appetizers and salads at this "South Minneapolis staple," you can choose from a list of 21 "wonderful pastas" that range from simple preparations like spaghetti with Calabrian meatballs to the more exotic stringozzi with lobster, squash and truffle cream. Made using "the best ingredients" and served at "affordable prices," the cucina has reviewers saying, "I could eat here every night" – which it seems some folk perhaps literally do, given the constantly "long line of people waiting to get into the place."

Italian | Informal | Moderate | south minneapolis | 5000 Penn Ave. S. | 612-925-9202 | www.broders.com | Dinner daily

Sakura   88.0

Those looking for a less cerebral sushi experience than Origami should head out to St. Paul, where they can enjoy platters of "fun rolls," many of which are named after players on the Minnesota Wild hockey team (who conveniently happen to play nearby and whose players have been known to frequent the restaurant), along with cooked dishes like "light-as-air tempuras" and shabu shabu. Comments range from "super-fresh and reasonably priced" to "good before or after a Wild game but not worth the drive from Minneapolis by itself."

Japanese | Informal | Moderate | downtown | Carriage Hill Plaza | 350 St. Peter St. | 651-224-0185 | www.sakurastpaul.com | Lunch & Dinner daily

Sea Change   88.0

With a successful French restaurant and a tapas bar under his belt, Tim McKee decided to conquer the best the ocean has to offer at this handsome restaurant in the Guthrie Theater. Sustainable seafood's the thing. There's a raw bar with selections like diver scallops with crispy bone marrow and gremolata; starters like smoked tuna tartare with Calabrian peppers, quail egg, and black olives; and mains like sable fish with morcilla, burnt bread and clams. Reviewers say this food is "incredibly fresh and exquisitely prepared. This was one of the best seafood dining experiences I have had in a long time."

Seafood | Casual | Moderate | downtown | 818 S. Second St. | 612-225-6499 | www.seachangempls.com | Lunch & Dinner Tue-Sun, Mon dinner only

Solera   88.0

This popular tapas bar from La Belle Vie's Tim McKee and Bill Somerville mixes traditional Spanish small plates like shrimp à la plancha and patatas bravas with "creative tapas that are a joy to eat," like a dish of monkfish with white asparagus in chorizo broth or grilled short ribs with sunchokes and baby carrot. And for those who have a grand appétit, there are a number of interesting paellas on offer, like one with braised lamb, garbanzo beans and piquillo peppers. A "good list of Spanish wines" and "an amazing collection of sherries" complement the diverse menu.

Spanish | Informal | Moderate | downtown | 900 Hennepin Ave. | 612-338-0062 | www.solera-restaurant.com | Dinner daily

ACCEPTABLE

Barrio Tequila Bar   87.5

While the menu at this restaurant features 14 types of Mexican small plates along with nine tacos, it's fair to say that the experience is "more about the 100 different types of tequila that are on offer than the food," which is "not always authentic." Still, it's "always prepared with care and precision." The really hungry can chose from a half dozen larger plates like grilled skirt steak. But "the drinks are why you go."

Mexican | Informal | Moderate | downtown | 925 Nicollet Ave. | 612-333-9953 | http://barriotequila. com | Lunch & Dinner daily

Al Vento   87.0

Minneapolis may not have a large Italian population, but it still needs a place where locals can go for a tasty bowl of spaghetti and meatballs. Al Vento is their number one choice, and Jonathan Hunt, a graduate of the Johnson and Wales College of Culinary Arts, keeps them happy with a menu that features both red sauce classics and more refined fare like a grilled duck breast with root vegetables and apple agro dolce. Located away from downtown, Al Vento has the "romantic atmosphere," "well-chosen wine list" and "friendly price point" that make it "the ultimate date-night restaurant."

Italian | Casual | Moderate | south minneapolis | 5001 34th Ave. S. | 612-724-3009 | http://alventorestaurant.com | Dinner daily, Lunch Sun

Fuji Ya   87.0

"They started the sushi trend in Minneapolis" is what reviewers say about this place, which has now become "the most popular Japanese restaurant in town." Specialty rolls include the aptly named Dynamite (yellowtail with Thai chili pepper and spicy chili bean sauce rolled with lettuce, kaiware sprouts and cucumber) along with the cooler (and vegetarian) Futo (spinach, cucumber, oshinko, tamago, kampyo squash, and inari). "Though it's not known for serving the best fish," reviewers say "you can't beat the fun atmosphere."

Japanese | Informal | Moderate | uptown | 600 W. Lake St. | 612-871-4055 | www.fujiyasushi.com | Dinner Tue-Sun

Manny's   87.0

From the masculine atmosphere to the triple-tiered seafood platters to the rolling meat carts displaying "big, big portions" of "excellent steaks," all the indicia of a top-notch steakhouse are present at what is easily the most popular cow palace in the city. Numerous reviewers commented on the new digs in the Foshay Building (now the W Hotel), saying that the new location makes it "a good choice for a business lunch" as well as "a nice night out."

Steakhouse | Casual | Expensive | downtown | W Hotel | 825 Marquette Ave. S. | 612-339-9900 | www.mannyssteakhouse.com | Open daily

I Nonni   86.0

"If you're in downtown Minneapolis and looking for an upscale Italian restaurant – tough." You're going to have to get in your car and drive out to West St. Paul, where you will find Nonni. The cooking features "generous portions of delicious pasta dishes" and "an osso buco that has been a talking point among local foodies for years." And you can have the privilege of washing it all down with what was described as "the best list of Italian wines in the Midwest after Spiaggia in Chicago."

Italian | Casual | Moderate | west st. paul | 981 Sibley Memorial Hwy. | 651-905-1081 | www.inonnirestaurant.com | Dinner Mon-Sat

Bradstreet Crafthouse   85.5

The craft they are talking about at this Graves 601 Hotel venue is the ancient craft of mixology. The menu is limited to beef sliders, a quesadilla stuffed with duck confit, a toast/cheese plate and a handful of additional dishes included in various set menus. But "the mixed drinks are where it's at." The "encyclopedic list" of "elegant cocktails" includes numerous Prohibition Era concoctions like the Aviation, the Dark & Stormy, and our favorite, Corpse Reviver # 2.

Bar Food | Informal | Moderate | downtown | 601 First Ave. | 612-312-1821 | http://bradstreet-crafthouse.com | Dinner Tue-Sat

Luci Ancora   85.5

Locals are happy to frequent this "wonderful little neighborhood restaurant" featuring "great, simple Italian food" along with "exceptional service." Both the pastas and the mozzarella are freshly made in-house, and the more adventurous can order dishes like grilled Berkshire pork loin with honey truffle glaze, sautéed greens and roasted apples. "Friendly owners" cap things off. It might not be a destination, but it makes for a good option when you're in or near Highland Park.

Italian | Informal | Moderate | highland park | 2060 Randolph Ave. | 651-698-6889 | www.ristoranteluci.com | Dinner Tue-Sun, Lunch Tue-Fri

Barbette   85.0

This "great little bistro" is the place to fill up on large portions of homey classics like coq au vin or a braised veal breast with spaetzle and red cabbage. You can spend the entire day here – nursing a cappuccino in the morning, moving to a quiche for lunch, indulging in the aforementioned veal breast for supper, and for a late-night bite (until 1:00 a.m.) knocking back a platter of oysters. "Friendly and casual" with "a great wine selection," it "hits on all cylinders, morning, noon and night."

French Bistro | Informal | Moderate | uptown | 1600 W. Lake St. | 612-827-5710 | www.barbette.com | Open daily

Gardens of Salonica   85.0

"When I want Greek this is where I go" typifies the comments we collected about the Gardens of Salonica. Even less-enraptured reviewers offered a little praise ("not special, but certainly adequate, given the other options for Greek food in Minneapolis"). In addition to the restaurant, there is also a small Hellenic market, where you can stock up on the delicious feta, babaganoush, hummus, marinated artichoke hearts, gyros and

almost everything else they offer, to eat at home.

Greek | Informal | Moderate | northeast | 19 Fifth St. NE | 612-378-0611 | www.gardensofsalonica.com | Lunch & Dinner Tue-Sat

OTHER PLACES MENTIONED

128 Café   84.5

This is where local families go to chow down on simple fare like a well-made Caesar salad, barbecue baby-back ribs and grilled beef tenderloin with blue cheese herb butter and mashed potatoes. The cozy ambience – it's located in a converted corner snack shop that dates from the 1950s – causes reviewers to sum it up as "a delightful little restaurant with good food, reasonable prices and lovely atmosphere."

American | Informal | Moderate | merriam park | 128 Cleveland Ave. N. | 651-645-4128 | www.128cafe.net | Dinner daily

The Butcher Block   84.5

Though the name seems to signify a steakhouse, this restaurant offers an all-Italian menu that features dishes like bucatini all' amatriciana and short ribs cacciatore (The Italian Butcher Block would have been a better moniker). A "strange location" and a "so-so décor" don't help, either. Those quibbles aside, "the food is delicious."

Italian | Informal | Moderate | northeast | 308 East Hennepin Ave. | 612-455-1080 | http://thebutcherblockrestaurant.com | Dinner Tue-Sun

Kincaid's   84.0

Part of a steakhouse chain that operates nine different locations from Norfolk, Virginia to Honolulu, this branch is "popular with the power-lunch crowd," whose members enjoy feasting on "the best porterhouse in the city," "juicy hunks of salmon" and "an amazing lobster mac 'n' cheese." It also offers "one of the best patios" in town – "you shouldn't be surprised if you see Garrison Keillor" and other local celebrities or sports stars lunching here. Critics pan it for being "overpriced" and "pretentious," with fare that in terms of quality is one step up from "bar food."

Steakhouse | Casual | Expensive | downtown | 380 St. Peter St. | 651-602-9000 | http://kincaids. com/page/home | Dinner daily, Lunch Mon-Fri

Vincent   84.0

Vincent Francoual's crowded restaurant features a traditionally styled menu that offers a few rarely seen dishes, like tripe braised in cider, as well as bistro stalwarts like cassoulet. At lunch, it's famous for the Vincent Burger, a takeoff on New York's famous DB Bistro Moderne's burger that's made from ground beef, braised short ribs and smoked gouda. The atmosphere is "great for either a date or dinner with close friends," reviewers say, adding that the location near Symphony Hall makes it ideal for a pre-concert meal.

French Bistro | Casual | Expensive | downtown | 1100 Nicollet Mall | 612-630-1189 | www.vincentarestaurant.com | Dinner Mon-Sat, Lunch Mon-Fri

The Corner Table   83.5

The Corner Table might be considered "Minneapolis' answer to St. Paul's Heartland" (see review above). Scott Pampuch's "über-green menu" features classic Midwestern fare like poached baby carrots with arugula, crispy shallots and a dill and lemon vinaigrette and pork loin with summer beans, maple syrup, potato purée, chanterelle mushrooms and onions. Reviewers suggest that "The best way to experience the restaurant is to reserve the Kitchen Table, with its never-ending parade of dishes that Pampuch keeps serving until you say uncle."

New American | Informal | Moderate | southwest | 4257 Nicollet Ave. | 612-823-0011 | www.cornertablerestaurant.com | Dinner Tue-Sat

Sanctuary   83.5

It's fortunate that this venue is close to the Guthrie Theater; reviewers say, "It's okay before a performance, but I wouldn't go there outside of a pre-theater meal." For one thing, "The tables are too close together" (not surprising, since they aim to accommodate as many theatergoers as possible pre-curtain). Kinder critics call it "a charming little restaurant with good food and a friendly staff" as well as "bargain fixed-price menus" on weekdays.

New American | Casual | Moderate | downtown | 903 Washington Ave. S. | 612-339-5058 | http:// sanctuaryminneapolis.com | Dinner daily

St. Paul Grill   83.5

This "elegant restaurant" with a "clubby and comfortable" atmosphere is a perfect fit for Minnesota's state capital. The food is nothing you haven't seen before: decent offerings of grilled meats and fish, consumed along with martinis and other stiff drinks concocted from their "incomparable spirits list." Reviewers are split on the place: Some say it's a must go when visiting the Twin Cities, while others say, "It fails to live up to its billing."

Chophouse | Casual | Expensive | downtown | 350 Market St. | 651-224-7455 | www.stpaulgrill. com | Lunch & Dinner daily

B.A.N.K.   83.0

It would be hard to find more beautiful environs: Converted from an Art Deco–era bank, with 40-foot ceilings and private booths for quiet conversation, "The room screams power." Unfortunately, reviewers describe it as "a space in search of a restaurant." Not surprisingly, it's frequented by the after-work happy-hour crowd, people willing to put up with "mediocre food" for the "great atmosphere and cocktails."

New American | Casual | Moderate | downtown | Westin Minneapolis | 88 S. Sixth St. | 612-656-3255 | www.bankmpls.com | Open daily

D'Amico Kitchen   83.0

This is the old Jean-Georges space in the Chambers Hotel, owned by the chain that brought you Café Lurcat. Alas, unlike its illustrious sibling, D'Amico has a rating that's much more typical for a link in a 20-restaurant chain. People like the service and the ambience, but when it comes to the predominantly Italian menu, comments like "I didn't have such a great dinner" reflect reviewer sentiments. Maybe it will improve with time.

Italian | Casual | Moderate | downtown | 901 Hennepin Ave. | 612-767-6960 | www.damico-kitchen.com | Open daily

Levain   82.5

Levain was once an ambitious restaurant that closed and reopened with a bistro format. There is little agreement as to whether the revamp made it better or worse. Fans praise it as a "cozy restaurant" serving "fabulous food" in a "lovely atmosphere" and with "consistently good service." But critics complain that "the food has been dumbed down," saying the "uninspired bistro fare" is "super-heavy and over-seasoned."

French | Casual | Moderate | downtown | 4762 Chicago Ave. S | 612-823-7111 | www.cafelevain.com | Dinner Tue-Sun

Hell's Kitchen   81.5

This unusual restaurant, "beloved in its original hole in the wall location," has all the indicia of a theme restaurant now that it has moved into an office building. Breakfast is the thing: lemon ricotta pancakes, large portions of huevos rancheros and eggs served with foie gras, delivered to your table by servers wearing pajamas. Reviewers say, "It lost something when it changed locations." They offer live music during Sunday brunch.

American | Informal | Moderate | downtown | 80 S. Ninth St. | 612-332-4700 | www.hellskitcheninc.com | Open daily

Nicollet Island Inn   79.5

Despite "an ideal location on St. Anthony Main/Nicollet Island," this has "never been a serious food place." Still, people report enjoying it for romantic occasions and other special celebrations. One meal they seem to do well is Sunday brunch – which makes sense: How badly can you screw up eggs and pancakes?

American | Casual | Expensive | nicollet island | 95 Merriam St. | 612-331-1800 | www.nicolletis-landinn.com | Dinner Mon-Sat, Lunch daily,

OM   77.0

Few people like this Indian restaurant with "poor food quality, mediocre service even though place was empty, and a $150 bill for two." Part of the problem may be that OM's founder, chef Raghavan Iyer, is no longer associated with it. Even the space was criticized as "too loud and dark." No wonder reviewers say, "Really overrated – skip it."

Indian | Casual | Expensive | downtown | 401 First Ave. N. | 612-338-1510 | www.omminneapolis.com | Dinner Mon-Sat

Cheap Eats

UNIQUELY DELICIOUS

Black Sheep Pizza   8.6

Reviewers tell us "the best pizza in the Twin Cities" emerges from Jordan Smith's coal-fired oven. Among the pies on offer are hot salami and chili peppers; chicken and pickled peppers; and meatball, ricotta and garlic – and, of course, you can build your own using 23 different toppings. "My God, is this good pizza," says one reviewer, who goes on to add, "You will have to wait for a long time, but the piping hot, perfectly charred pizzas are worth the wait." You can wash 'em down with a "quality selection of beers."

Pizzeria | Inexpensive | warehouse district | 600 Washington Ave. N. | 612-342-2625 | www.black-sheeppizza.com | Lunch & Dinner daily

Brasa   8.1

Brasa means "rotisserie" in Spanish. But Alma's Alex Roberts has co-opted the term for this 'cue shack specializing in "great interpretations of Southern fare." In addition to rotisserie chicken, Roberts offers such entrées as slow-roasted pork and fried catfish, along with "tasty sides" like cheese grits and cornbread. Meats are "tender and flavorful," and the use of locally raised, organic ingredients means "you can definitely taste the higher level of quality" over other barbecue restaurants. The result is "an absolutely delicious family-style restaurant" that is "as enjoyable for young children as it is for their parents."

Southern | Inexpensive | summit hill | 600 Hennepin Ave. E. | 612-379-3030 | www.brasa.us | Lunch & Dinner daily

RECOMMENDED

Punch Neapolitan Pizza   7.3

Due to the magic of an 800-degree oven, it takes just a bit more than a minute for your pie to be ready at this "the pizza version of the film *Gone in 60 Seconds*." Popular as it is quick, it garnered reviewer raves like "The wood fire taste provides amazing flavor no matter which pizza you choose"; "The pizza is delicious, intriguing, authentic and healthy"; and "The buffalo mozzarella pizza is not just a pizza, it is a Cirque du Soleil ride for your mouth." With seven locations, it's super-convenient for everything from a quick lunch to a family meal.

Pizzeria | Inexpensive | highland park | Calhoun Village Shopping Center | 3226 W. Lake St. | 612-929-0006 | www.punchpizza.com | Lunch & Dinner daily

OTHER PLACES MENTIONED

Blue Door Pub   5.8

The gimmick at this "neighborhood pub" is a selection of Juicy Blucys – cheese stuffed inside of the burger patty.

Variations on the theme include blue cheese and finely chopped garlic, Swiss cheese and caramelized onions, and pepper jack cheese with diced jalapeños. While some understandably find the Blucys overrated, many more call them "possibly the best burgers in the Twin Cities." Certainly, BDP transcends the pub-grub genre with carefully considered ingredients and competent execution, and it's clear that reviewers take this place seriously.

Hamburgers | Inexpensive | merriam park | 1811 Selby Ave. | 651-493-1865 | www.thebluedoorpubmn.com | Lunch & Dinner daily

Al's Breakfast   5.4

This is one of those old places where legend and history outweigh the food. Located in a converted tool shed in Dinkytown (appropriate, since the place is sort of dinky), it has been a hangout for musicians and students from the nearby University of Minnesota since the '50s. Day after day, long lines of people wait to sample the "generic, greasy-spoon fare" from one of the 14 stools. It's also famous for being the narrowest restaurant in the city.

Diner | Inexpensive | dinkytown | 413 14th Ave. SE | 612-331-9991 | Breakfast & Lunch daily

Quang   5.9

While the Twin Cities offers successful versions of many different cuisines, Vietnamese doesn't seem to be one of them. That doesn't mean Quang is without its fans, who insist "the only thing wrong with the place is that they don't offer sea bass pho seven days a week" (it is available only on weekends). But others say, "While they've taught a generation of local residents how to eat pho, the food is no better than decent."

Vietnamese | Inexpensive | uptown | 2719 Nicollet Ave. S. | 612-870-4739 | www.quangrestaurant.com | Lunch & Dinner Wed-Mon

Peoria IL

June   92.4

To most people, the idea of a fine dining establishment in Peoria sounds like the punch line of a joke. But if anyone out there is searching for evidence that the heartland has evolved beyond roasts and stews, look no further than this restaurant. Josh Adams spent years commuting from his native Peoria to Chicago to work at such establishments as Green Zebra and Vie. When he and his wife decided to start a family, he opened this place. Now the people in his hometown delight in Adams' "farm-to-table cuisine with a molecular edge," which includes dishes like a Green Gold Acres farm-fresh egg with house-made guanciale and coffee-smoked shiitake mushrooms or 72-hour sous vide Wagyu short ribs. A full 100% of reviewers recommended it, offering comments like "They take pride in what they bring to the table" and "as good, and arguably better, than similar restaurants in Chicago."

Progressive American | Casual | Expensive | 4450 North Prospect Rd. | 877-682-5863 | www.junerestaurant.com | Dinner Tue-Sat

St. Louis MO

Niche   92.7

With plaudits encompassing everything from "fresh ingredients" to "inventive preparations" to "knowledgeable servers" to "yummy wine and cocktails," this offering from Gerard Craft is the hands-down winner for best restaurant in St. Louis. Featuring what was described as "hearty and soul-satisfying farm-to-table cooking," Craft's menu tantalizes diners with offerings like a foie-gras banh mi with carrots, radishes, cilantro and jalapeño; lasagna stuffed with truffled béchamel, wild mushrooms, fontina cheese, a farm egg and sage brown butter; and a crispy pig trotter stuffed with a mixture of leg meat and vegetables. Reviewers rave, "Amazing things are done with unexpected ingredients," "went four times over the past year and I have yet to be disappointed" and "When you walk through the door you have entered into a place that makes you feel you are in another city." Diners are also advised to "look out for the special theme dinners" that Craft likes to prepare, many of which revolve around pork.

New American | Casual | Expensive | benton park | 1831 Sidney St. | 314-773-7755 | www.nichestlouis.com | Dinner Tue-Sun

Sidney Street Café   92.2

There was a time when St. Louis residents looking for sophisticated dining had to travel out of town. But that changed when Kevin Nashan opened this restaurant, and 12 years later, this is where you can find the city's establishment having dinner. But despite his success, Nashan refused to rest on his laurels. In recent years he has started a charcuterie program and has built a garden using the space that rings the restaurant's parking lot. The result is dishes like a crab corn cake with peppers, onions and jalapeño cream sauce or pecan-encrusted rabbit with basil sausage and roasted root vegetables. It's common to read comments like "In the decade plus that we have been customers, the food has been consistently excellent. The old favorites mixed with the new items make it hard to decide what to choose."

New American | Casual | Expensive | benton park | 2000 Sidney St. | 314-771-5777 | www.sidneystreet-cafe.com | Dinner Tue-Sat

RECOMMENDED

Tony's   90.1

When the Mobil Guide awarded Vince Bommarito's establishment its highest rating, it catapulted the place to national recognition. But that was back in the day, and now, while some reviewers maintain that it still deserves similar kudos, most feel Tony's is "locked in the ways of the past," adding, "If you like that old-fashioned, heavily sauced, over-composed, Continental-style Italian food, you might like Tony's because they are still doing it this way." Even the vaunted service couldn't muster consensus, with some calling it "magical" and others decrying it as "overbearing." One reviewer took the middle ground, saying, "While the food is from several culinary movements past, it's well done, making it worth a visit if you like that style of cuisine."

Italian | Casual | Expensive | downtown | 410 Market St. | 314-231-7007 | www.tonysstlouis.com | Dinner Mon-Sat

TOP LOCAL CHOICE

The Crossing (8.5 miles west in Clayton)   89.0

Jim Fiala's first venture attracts comments like "my favorite restaurant in St. Louis" and "The food has that something special about it that makes coming here a treat." The New American menu is fairly simple: local beets paired with goat cheese, shallots and sherry vinegar or braised Missouri lamb served with crushed potatoes and radish sprouts. A "small, intimate dining room" and "the ability to conduct a conversation" make it a popular spot for business lunches. Numerous reviewers heaped praise on the $32, four-course tasting menu.

New American | Casual | Expensive | clayton | 7823 Forsyth Blvd. | 314-721-7375 | Dinner daily, Lunch Mon-Fri

Franco's   89.0

The city's top French bistro has reviewers saying things like "What a blessing to the neighborhood this place is." The mostly traditional menu offers fare like pan-roasted sweetbreads and duck confit, along with a few local specialties like country-fried frogs' legs with grits or grilled Missouri rainbow trout with a crawfish-cognac cream sauce. An "owner who is full of personality" and a "terrific location in a carriage house built in 1899" (adjacent to Soulard Farmer's Market) evoke comments like "While Franco's isn't the best restaurant in St. Louis, it's always good."

French Bistro | Informal | Moderate | benton park | 1535 S. Eighth St. | 314-436-2500 | www.eatatfranco.com | Dinner daily, Lunch Mon-Fr

Liluma   89.0

If you operate one of the top dining locations (The Crossing) and you want to offer customers your style of hospitality at a lower price point, you open a restaurant like Liluma, where diners can enjoy everything from "one of the city's top burgers" to a rib eye of Mangalitsa pork served with applewood smoked bacon and white balsamic vinegar. As an added benefit, Jim Fiala's "simple but elegant" restaurant is "located on a busy corner in a trendy part of town," and the outdoor patio offers "some of the best people-watching in the city."

New American | Casual | Expensive | central west end | 236 N. Euclid Ave. | 314-361-7771 | www.fiala-food.com | Lunch & Dinner Mon-Sat

Trattoria Marcella   89.0

Opened in 1995 with a commitment to serving local ingredients, Steve Komorek's restaurant is still serving up favorite dishes like the "addictive flash-fried spinach," the "fabulous calamari" and (our favorite) "Can you say roasted wild mushrooms with polenta fries?" Adding to the appeal are a "good wine list" and "a cozy room," though a number of people found the latter "noisy and overcrowded." But even the negative comments mostly ended on a positive note: "A bit expensive, but the food makes it all worthwhile," and "While not as popular as it once was, the food is still very good."

Italian | Casual | Moderate | lindenwood park | 3600 Watson Rd. | 314-352-7706 | www.trattoriamarcella.com | Dinner Tue-Sat

Anthony's   88.5

This scaled-down version of Tony's offers more casual fare like pastas with ricotta and sausage or a polenta-encrusted pork chop, or even a burger, in a bar area that is "straight out of the '60s." Given that the food is prepared in the same kitchen as its big brother, only at lower prices, it's a popular spot on the business lunch circuit. Given its proximity to Busch Stadium (a mere block away), it's also a hit with both fans and players for a pre- or post-game meal.

Italian | Casual | Moderate | downtown | 10 S. Broadway | 314-231-7007 | www.tonysstlouis.com | Dinner Tues-Sat

Brasserie by Niche   88.5

Gerard Craft decided to capitalize on his success at Niche by opening this lively brasserie in the city's Central West End, where diners enjoy "simple French fare done right" in an atmosphere that has "great energy" and "absolutely captures the feel of a busy Parisian brasserie." Whether it be a frisée salad, vichyssoise, mussels with frites or braised short ribs with mashed potatoes, the "authentic food" led a number of reviewers to say, "We have had many delicious meals here." There is outdoor dining in good weather and what many call "the best brunch menu in the city."

French Brasserie | Informal | Moderate | central west end | 4580 Laclede Ave. | 314-454-0600 | www.brasseriebyniche.com | Dinner Tue-Sun, Lunch Sun

Pomme   88.5

Bryan Carr runs the kitchen at this "small, elegant restaurant" where the menu features dishes like pea ravioli with prosciutto, mint and Parmesan cheese or boneless short ribs with a mustard-parsley crust that's described as "dark, rich and succulent." A few people commented about the "high-end prices" (a number of entrées cost more than $30), though most reviewers were focused on things like the "wonderfully prepared food, perfect portion sizes and delightful atmosphere." A "nice but expensive wine list" (limited to French bottles) rounds out the experience.

French | Casual | Expensive | clayton | 40 N. Central Ave. | 314-727-4141 | http://pommerestaurants.com | Dinner Tue-Sat

Vin de Set   88.5

The bistro menu mixes French dishes, like a tarte flambé with applewood-smoked bacon and Gruyère, along with American fare like lobster potpie. But while the food had its share of fans, many reviewers focused on the building – the historic Centennial Malt House – which offers high ceilings, arched doorways and a cathedral skylight. When the weather is warm, the star of the show becomes the rooftop patio, offering its "beautiful view of the city," although a few diners dared to call the interior "just as charming."

French | Casual | Moderate | lafayette square | 2017 Chouteau Ave. | 314-241-8989 | www.vindeset.com | Lunch & Dinner Tue-Fri

Atlas Restaurant   88.0

Taken over by Pomme's Bryan Carr in 2010, Atlas has maintained its level of quality. The contemporary bistro fare – think filets of trout with preserved lemon sauce, zucchini crepe and carrot flan – is complemented by a handful of Italian-influenced dishes like rigatoni with savory herb meatballs in a rustic tomato sauce. Reviewers put it in the category of "cute neighborhood restaurant," where a "quiet dining room" makes it ideal for "a simple dinner with good food" in an "environment that lacks pretension."

French | Casual | Moderate | central west end | 5513 Pershing Ave. | 314-367-6800 | www.atlasrestaurantstl.com | Dinner Tue-Sat

Grill at the Ritz-Carlton   88.0

While they bill themselves as offering classic American beef and seafood, which sounds like a typical surf 'n' turf experience, the reality is that the Ritz's menu is filled with New American dishes like a tempura-fried and chilled adobo spiced shrimp duo and a pastrami-spiced flatiron steak. In keeping with its location, the dining room is likely to be filled with hotel guests or locals celebrating special occasions. And true to hotel dining room form, they offer one of those massive Sunday brunches that includes unlimited food from "the best seafood bar in St. Louis."

New American | Casual | Expensive | clayton | Ritz-Carlton St. Louis | 100 Carondelet Plaza | 314-863-6300 | www.ritzcarlton.com | Dinner Tue-Sat

Monarch   88.0

After an extensive remodeling, Josh Galliano's venue now offers diners two different menus. Those after a casual meal can dine in the Southern Bistro on the likes of smothered chicken and sweet-potato-wrapped catfish. But the main dining room offers a more formal experience, featuring dishes like cedar-planked salmon and Mediterranean-style lamb. "One of the best wine lists in St. Louis" and "great drinks" (they employ three full-time mixologists) complement the two menus. Reviewers say, "wonderful food and an exciting new interior" and "This place is made for foodies."

New American | Casual | Expensive | maplewood | 7401 Manchester Rd. | 314-644-3995 | www.monarchrestaurant.com | Dinner Mon-Sat

Al's Restaurant   87.5

Given how many Italian restaurants are located in St. Louis, we were happy to see this steakhouse, and a non-chain place to boot. Frequently described as "the most old-school restaurant in town" ("hasn't changed in 35 years"), it's considered "the perfect choice for people who like to eat lots of meat" served by "old, stern waiters" in a "classy environment." No wonder reviewers called it "the perfect place to take your grandparents."

Steakhouse | Casual | Expensive | downtown | 1200 N. First St. | 314-421-6399 | www.alsrestaurant.net | Dinner Tue-Sat

Dominic's   87.5

While The Hill is well known for its old-school dining experiences, Dominic Galati's restaurant takes the concept to another level. It's more upscale than its neighbors, and in the wood-paneled room diners enjoy dishes like gnocchi Bolognese and veal piccata with mushrooms – many finished tableside. Candlelight is a nice touch that makes it "a good place to enjoy a romantic dinner" and to observe old Italian men out for an evening with their mistresses.

Italian | Casual | Expensive | the hill | 5101 Wilson Ave. | 314-771-1632 | www.dominicsrestaurant.com | Dinner Mon-Sat

Kemoll's   87.5

Although it's now located on the 40th floor of the Metropolitan Square building, Kemoll's has been hosting celebrations since 1927. Unlike other high-rise eateries, where the cuisine is likely to be French or New American, the food here leans toward the Italian, with a few dishes cast in a Continental style. The views are beautiful, with the tables facing Eero Saarinen's Arch the most popular. Reviewers seem to have a soft spot for this local institution, saying it's still "a

great place for that special night."

Italian | Casual | Expensive | downtown | 1 Metropolitan Sq. | 314-421-0555 | www.kemolls.com | Dinner Mon-Sat

Mike Shannon's   87.5

Mike Shannon turned a successful baseball career (he played with the Cardinals when they won the 1964 and 1967 World Series) into dual roles as a broadcaster for the club and the owner of this popular downtown steakhouse (the proximity to Busch Stadium makes it a favorite for a pre-game meal). There's a full menu of steaks, seafood and chops, and the walls are full of "one-of-a-kind" Cardinal memorabilia. Reviews seem to split between "a typical steakhouse experience" and "low-quality food in a tacky atmosphere."

Steakhouse | Casual | Expensive | downtown | 620 Market St. | 314-421-1540 | www.shannonsteak.com | Dinner daily, Lunch Mon-Fri

Roberto's Trattoria   87.5

In a city where the competition among Italian restaurants is fierce, comments like "the best Italian restaurant in the South County area" and "If you want the best Italian in St. Louis, you must go to Roberto's" made us take notice. The classic menu features "pricy versions" of "excellently executed dishes" like shrimp scampi, linguine primavera and veal saltimbocca. It's located in a mall, with all that implies appearance-wise ("You would never expect a quality dining experience by looking at it from the outside").

Italian | Casual | Moderate | south st. louis | 145 Concord Plaza | 314-842-9998 | www.robertos-trattoriastl.com | Lunch & Dinner Tue-Fri

Giovanni's on the Hill   87.0

Where do visiting celebrities and politicians dine when visiting St. Louis? They go to Giovanni's, where since 1975 the eponymous owner has been cranking out dishes like pappardelle alla Bella Oprah (yes, that Oprah); farfalle with salmon in a cream sauce (created for President Reagan); and involtini di pollo alla Presidente Bush (we haven't ascertained which one). "Incredible, decadent, rich and yummy food," say Giovanni's fans. But the opposition party claims, "The pasta dish he made for Reagan was the last creative thing he did."

Italian | Casual | Expensive | the hill | 5201 Shaw Ave. | 314-772-5958 | www.giovannisonthe-hill.com | Dinner Mon-Sat

Herbie's Vintage 72   87.0

After Herbie Balaban passed away in 2000, a number of restaurateurs tried to make a go of this legendary place, but it took the Monarch management team, who took over in 2009, to find the right formula. The menu mixes Continental classics from the old regime, like pasta with morel mushrooms and French onion soup, with additions like shrimp and grits. There's a "popular bar" featuring "three expert mixologists" to go along with the "quirky, retro" atmosphere.

Eclectic | Casual | Moderate | central west end | 405 North Euclid Ave. | 314-769-9595 | www.her-bies.com | Lunch & Dinner Sun-Fri, Sat dinner only

Terrene   87.0

"This is a sophisticated restaurant with one of the prettiest gardens to dine in" say the supporters of what was one of the town's first restaurants to feature local and sustainable ingredients. "It's great that they emphasize being a green restaurant, but I think they focus on that aspect to the detriment of the cooking," critics carp. The focus on organic ingredients means there are "lots of vegetarian dishes on offer," but that doesn't stop meat eaters from enjoying dishes like a small plate of sweetbreads with bacon and poached egg.

New American | Casual | Moderate | central west end | 33 N. Sarah St. | 314-535-5100 | www.terrene-stlouis.com | Dinner Tue-Sat

Frazer's   86.5

A "well-worn glove that fits," Frazer Cameron's restaurant has been a Benton Park institution since 1992. Cameron travels the world to seek out dishes, and the result is a "quirky and sometimes downright strange hodgepodge of comfort food" and the most eclectic menu in the city, ranging from Thai lettuce wraps to Moroccan spiced tilapia to porcini chicken. The menu changes daily, and there are "always more specials than dishes listed on the menu."

Eclectic | Informal | Moderate | benton park | 1811 Pestalozzi St. | 314-773-8646 | www.frazer-goodeats.com | Dinner Mon-Sat, Lunch Mon-Fri

Lorenzo's Trattoria   86.5

Ask our average reviewer about dining on The Hill and he'll tell you not to bother, as most of the places there are geared toward tourists. But if you insist on eating dishes like linguine with a shellfish sauce and veal piccata in the heart of St. Louis' Little Italy, Larry Fuse's restaurant is a step up from most of the mundane places." While the "warm and homey atmosphere makes you feel like you live in the neighborhood," one reviewer complained, "The food was better when Fuse was doing the cooking himself."

Italian | Informal | Moderate | the hill | 1933 Edwards St. | 314-773-2223 | www.lorenzostratto-ria.com | Dinner Tue-Sun, Lunch Tue-Fri

Modesto   86.5

A perennial winner of the Best Tapas Bar in St. Louis designation awarded by various members of the local food media, Modesto offers a traditional menu that lists everything from hams, cheeses and flatbreads to a broad selection of fish and meats cooked a la plancha. And if you're really hungry, there are four different paellas on offer. "A fine Spanish wine list" and food that's "reasonably priced" mean it's "a good choice for a large group of people" who want to graze on small plates while downing pitcher after pitcher of sangria.

Spanish | Informal | Moderate | the hill | 5257 Shaw Ave. | 314-772-8272 | www.saucemagazine. com/modesto | Dinner Mon-Sat

1111 Mississippi   86.0

Paul and Wendy Hamilton decided the Cal-Ital format was suited for the middle of the country. The menu mixes California cuisine – slow braised Duroc pork belly with crispy shallots and Marsala jus – along with Italianesque creations like fettuccine and shellfish in a spicy cream sauce. A "reasonably priced wine list" and "great outdoor seating" are pluses, but they don't make up for only "slightly above average" food. One reviewer called it "a good introduction to better dining for those who typically go to chain restaurants."

Cal-Ital | Casual | Moderate | lafayette square | 1111 Mississippi Ave. | 314-241-9999 | www.1111-m. com | Lunch & Dinner Mon-Fri Sat dinner only

Cardwell's at the Plaza   86.0

Bill Cardwell's New American menu features creations like grilled, house-smoked shrimp with a three-mustard balsamic glaze and a seafood stew in a truffled fish broth. One reviewer called it "Our home away from home – there's something for everyone to eat," noting that many dishes are made from "well-sourced local produce." It has a strong following among the Clayton business community, which populates the place at midday; in fact, a number of reviewers told us they prefer it for lunch rather than for dinner.

New American | Casual | Expensive | clayton | 94 Plaza Frontenac | 314-997-8885 | www. cardwellsattheplaza.com | Lunch & Dinner daily

King and I Thai   86.0

This institution in the South Grand area, the most popular Thai restaurant in

St. Louis, has reviewers saying, "I am addicted to the papaya salad and the green curry with shrimp." While the food is available in various degrees of hotness (you can specify a scale of 1–5, with 5 being the hottest), the staff will dare you to try it as hot as possible. One reviewer suggests you "request a sunken table in the back and bring a lot of friends, so you can try everything."

Thai | Informal | Moderate | south grand | 3157 S. Grand Blvd. | 314-771-1777 | www.thaispicy.com | Lunch & Dinner Tue-Sun

Mai Lee   86.0

Locals are engaged in a debate about the oldest Vietnamese restaurant in the St. Louis area. Fans applaud the "incredibly high quality and authentic Vietnamese food," including "excellent pho and interesting daily specials revolving around whole fish." But naysayers reply, "For all the great Vietnamese restaurants that we have in St. Louis, this one doesn't cut it for me." An "odd location at the bottom of a parking garage" adds fuel to the negatives' fire.

Vietnamese | Informal | Moderate | brentwood | 8396 Musick Memorial Dr. | 314-645-2835 | www. maileerestaurant.com | Lunch & Dinner Tue-Sun

Mosaic   86.0

What is the definition of tapas fusion food? Perhaps it's Ben Lester's "incredibly inventive" menu, which combines various types of small plates like mozzarella caprese, maple-glazed sherry scallops and pulled Korean BBQ pork. We saw numerous comments like "it's my favorite small plates place in town" and collected almost as many about "the terrific lounge." It's a particularly good place for a party of six to have a night out while sharing a dozen or more plates of food.

New American | Casual | Moderate | downtown | 1001 Washington Ave. | 314-621-6001 | www. mosaictapas.com | Dinner daily, Lunch Sun-Fri

Pueblo Solis   86.0

Whether you're among those who believe "this is easily the best Mexican restaurant in St. Louis" or those who say "they serve nothing more than standard Mexican fare," you will find it is "difficult to get a table" at this popular place where the chips come with three types of salsa and the reservations usually come with a waiting time. The fare includes the typical queso fundido, chile rellenos, enchiladas, etc., along with a few more substantial dishes like filet steak with russet potatoes in a mole sauce.

Mexican | Informal | Moderate | south city | 5127 Hampton Ave. | 314-351-9000 | www.pueblosolisstl.com | Dinner daily

Duff's   85.5

It's open for dinner. But when a restaurant advertises that they serve lunch until 5:00 p.m., we think it's fair to say that's where they focus their efforts. A quick look at Duff's menu confirms this feeling: It lists a slew of salads and sandwiches along with lighter entrées like spinach-feta strudel. Reviewers say "the food is fine, nothing amazing" and recommend it "in good weather when you can sit outside, as the people-watching is the best thing about this place."

Eclectic | Informal | Moderate | central west end | 392 N. Euclid Ave. | 314-361-0522 | www.dineatduffs.com | Lunch & Dinner Tue-Sun

Charlie Gitto's on The Hill 83.5

While everyone knows that St. Louis is the home of toasted ravioli, there is disagreement about who actually invented the dish. But ask the owners of this restaurant and they will tell you that this is where, in 1947, Gina Oldani accidentally dropped a ravioli into a pot of boiling oil instead of water. Presto! Toasted ravioli was born. Comments ranged from "old-school Italian done right" and "highly recommended for a classic St. Louis Italian Hill experience" to "fine for St. Louis util-ity Italian" and "It's much too dated."

Italian | Casual | Expensive | the hill | 5226 Shaw Ave. | 314-772-8898 | www.charliegittos.com | Dinner daily

LoRusso's Cucina   82.0

Looking for an Italian restaurant that doesn't focus on artisanal ingredients, but where dishes like ziti con vodka and osso buco are prepared by a robust and gregarious chef who looks like he was hired by central casting? Head on over to Rich and Terri LoRusso's, where the red and cream sauces are complemented by an "extensive wine list" and an atmosphere" that "matches the ideal of the Italian family restaurant." One of the few upscale Italians not located on The Hill.

Italian | Informal | Moderate | lindenwood park | 3121 Watson Rd. | 314-647-6222 | www.lorussos.com | Lunch & Dinner Wed-FriTue, Sun dinner only

Top of the Riverfront   81.5

What are the odds that we would be able to recommend a restaurant that rotates while you eat? Well, not very good, and this restaurant in the Millennium Hotel offering "stunning views of the St. Louis skyline" is not much of an exception. Still, it makes for "a romantic dinner" or "a good place to enjoy cocktails before eating dinner elsewhere. "My daughter still remembers visiting when she was three years old" is typical of the positive comments we collected.

American | Casual | Expensive | downtown | Millennium Hotel St. Louis | 200 S. Fourth St. | 314-241-3191 | www.millennium-hotels.com | Dinner Tue-Sat, Lunch Sun

Cheap Eats

UNIQUELY DELICIOUS

Ted Drewes   8.4

Until its rebirth a few years ago, frozen custard was passé. But don't tell that to the legions who have been enjoying the 28 different flavors this beloved local institution has been serving since 1931. The house specialty is the Concrete, a milk shake "so thick it won't spill out of the cup even if you turn it upside down." In the summer months the St. Louis police force directs traffic in their two lots, while "the size of the line in the winter months is not to be believed."

Dessert | Inexpensive | st. louis hills | 4224 S. Grand Blvd. | 314-352-7376 | www.teddrewes.com | Open daily

17th Street Bar & Grill   8.1

(19 miles east in Fallon)

More than one reviewer told us, "I didn't like barbecue until I had it at 17th Street Bar & Grill," which isn't all that surprising given that "the legendary Mike Mills" has won just about every barbecue award in the country. Although Mills is famous for his ribs, the menu offers a variety of smoked meats, ranging from brisket to links to a pork steak. The sides garnered less enthusiasm, save for the "excellent deep-fried pickles," and the banana pudding served in a mason jar was described by one reviewer as "a standout."

Barbecue | Inexpensive | fallon | 1711 W. Highway 50 | 618-622-1717 | http://17thstreetbarbecue.com | Lunch & Dinner daily

Pho Grand   7.7

This contemporary-looking Vietnamese restaurant has been the stalwart of St. Louis's Grand Avenue ethnic food corridor for more than 20 years. Its long-term fans say that dishes like the spring rolls, vermicelli with shrimp and garlic sauce and "deliciously clean-tasting bowls of steaming hot pho" are weekly staples. One reviewer went so far as to say "The prices are so low, there simply is no better food value in St. Louis, which might explain why they go out of their way to turn the tables as quickly as they can."

Vietnamese | Inexpensive | south grand | 3195 S. Grand Blvd. | 314-664-7435 | www.phogrand.com | Lunch & Dinner Wed-Mon

Crown Candy Kitchen   7.3

Words fail to describe Crown Candy Kitchen. Opened in 1913 by two friends from Greece, it remains a mint-condition version of a corner candy store of that era. The menu is standard luncheonette fare: grilled cheese, burgers and sandwiches like the Heart-Stopping BLT (one reviewer swore there must be a pound of bacon on it), along with "awesome shakes" and an assortment of sundaes. The one major downside is the "excruciatingly long line of people" waiting for a booth at this "throwback to an era when calories didn't count."

Dessert | Inexpensive | old north st. louis | 1401 Saint Louis Ave. | 314-621-9650 | www.crowncandykitchen.net | Lunch & Dinner daily

Pappy's Smokehouse   7.3

Mike Emerson (Pappy) serves ribs so succulent and juicy that, in order to keep up with the demand, he keeps two mobile smokers parked outside his restaurant, cranking out hundreds of slabs a day. Sporting a beard that would make any hillbilly proud, he's usually schmoozing with the people waiting on the long line to be seated. Diners are advised to "get there early before they run out of food," especially on Sundays, when hordes literally descend on the place.

Barbecue | Inexpensive | midtown | 3106 Olive Street | 314-535-4340 | http://pappyssmokehouse.com | Dinner daily, Lunch Mon-Sat

The Good Pie   7.2

Many a reviewer says here is where you can find "the best wood-fired oven pizza in St. Louis," featuring an "excellent crust and simple toppings." It's a Neapolitan-style pie, meaning that it's crispy on the outside and soft in the center and the toppings are sparse, allowing the high-quality ingredients of the dough to shine through. There are also "delicious salads," a "great house wine" and "great beers on tap." No wonder reviewers say they "love, love, love this place."

Pizzeria | Inexpensive | midtown | 3137 Olive St. | 314-289-9391 | www.thegoodpie.com | Lunch & Dinner Mon-Sat

Stellina Pasta Café   7.1

"Pasta creativity rules" at this "adorable little café." The name is a bit of a misnomer: Although three organic, homemade pasta specials (lasagna, stuffed and long cut) are featured each day, they offer sandwiches and salads, too, which collected just as many positive comments, with the South Side Smoke (pulled pork, caramelized onions and smoked gouda on a sea salt ciabatta) being a favorite. And let's not forget "the delicious cupcakes for dessert." Unfortunately, be prepared to wait for a table, as "this little gem is no longer a secret."

Italian | Inexpensive | midtown | 3342 Watson Rd. | 314-256-1600 | www.stellinapasta.com | Lunch & Dinner Tue-Sat

Onesto   6.3

One of the most popular pizzerias in the St. Louis area allows diners to choose from all the classic pies or to customize with toppings that include jalapeños, andouille sausage, free-range smoked chicken and Gulf shrimp. There are also sandwiches, like the Mile High roast beef and a grilled cheese described as "the best you ever had." It's small and friendly, and one reviewer told us, "We love sitting on the patio on a nice day watching the world go by."

Pizza | Inexpensive | princeton hts. | 5401 Finkman | 314-802-8883 | www.onestopizza.com | Lunch & Dinner Mon, Wed-Sat, Sun dinner only

These are some of the things our reviewers do to kill time *in-between* meals

....

Accountant, Movie Producer,
Political Scientist, Studio Musician,
Law School Professor, Zen Buddhist Sensei,
Anthropologist, Cookbook Author,
High Tech Entrepreneur, Fashion Model,
Psychologist, Wine Educator, Tax Attorney,
Physicist, Mortgage Broker,
Gastroenterologist, Professor of Finance,
Actuary, Housewife, Wine Dealer,
Auctioneer, Physician, Computer Programmer,
Chef, Veterinary Cardiologist, Pizzaiolo,
Food Writer, Copywriter, Geologist,
Nuclear Arms Expert, English Professor,
Marketing Consultant, College Student

....

Join their ranks by signing up to participate
in our 2012 Dining Survey. Who knows, maybe the
thing you do to kill time in-between meals
will show up on next year's list.

www.opinionatedabout.com

Las Vegas & the Rockies

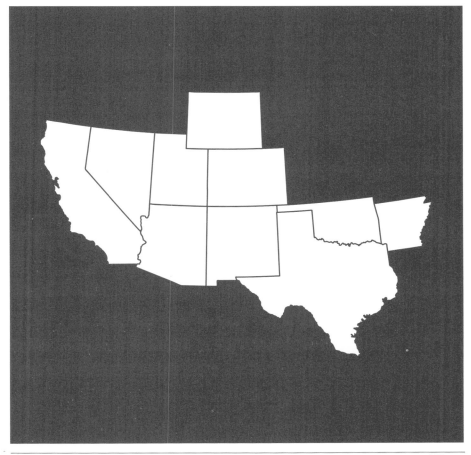

Aspen CO

Matsuhisa Aspen   91.5

We don't know how Nobu Matsuhisa does it. He operates 27 restaurants around the world, and we have yet to find one that we can't recommend. His Aspen outpost is no different, and due to the miracle of overnight shipping, all of his signature treats, like ankimo pâté with caviar, popcorn rock shrimp and lobster with wasabi pepper, are on hand. "Shockingly good in a town full of inedible food" was a typical comment, although we did get a few complaints about "less than stellar service," which is to be expected during high season in a ski resort.

Japanese | Casual | Expensive | 303 E. Main St. | 970-544-6628 | www.nobumatsuhisa.com | Dinner daily in winter; check hours other times of year

Montagna   90.0

"This was by far the most comfortable place we ate at in Aspen" is what our reviewers said about this restaurant in the Little Nell hotel. Ryan Hardy's farm-to-table menu keeps the "ski and be seen crowd" happy with dishes like Dungeness crab risotto with heirloom melon and purple basil and Columbia River wild sturgeon with black summer truffles and celeriac purée. "Great service," an "excellent wine list" and "a lovely outdoor seating area" came together to produce this overall comment: "I was surprised to find this level of dining in a place like Aspen."

New American | Casual | Expensive | Little Nell | 675 E. Durant St. | 970-920-6330 | www.thelittlenell.com | Dinner Wed-Sun, Lunch daily

Piñons   85.5

Most restaurants in resort areas have trouble staying in business for more than a season, yet Piñons has been an Aspen institution for more than 20 years. You won't find anything too exotic on Rob Mobilian's menu, which features large hunks of grilled proteins like elk and lamb. All that meat, along with the terrific wine list, is intended to restore the calories burned off during an arduous day on the slopes. It's "an authentic Aspen experience without being over the top."

New American | Casual | Expensive | 105 S. Mill St. | 970-920-2021 | www.pinons.net | Dinner daily

Austin TX

Uchi   93.6

Evidence of Austin's cultural superiority among Texas cities is on display at Cole Tyson's restaurant. One of the few non-Japanese chefs operating at this level, Tyson made his mark by serving progressive fusion fare like baby yellowtail sashimi with crispy koshi hikari rice, a Ringger Family Farm egg and sweet soy broth, or what he calls Bacon Steakie – Niman Ranch pork belly that is "melt in your mouth tender" after being cooked sous vide for 24 hours before being flash-fried to a crispy crust. Meanwhile, sushi purists can order pristine cuts of top-quality fish, much of it sourced from Tokyo's

Tsukiji Market. Fans talk about the "innovative, risky combinations that deliver," adding, "This is the best restaurant in Austin by a wide margin." Even critics ended on a positive note saying, "slightly pretentious, slightly more expensive, but still absolutely delicious."

Japanese | Casual | Expensive | south lamar | 801 S. Lamar Blvd. | 512-916-4808 | www.uchiaustin.com | Dinner daily

RECOMMENDED

Fonda San Miguel   90.1

More than a decade before chefs like Rick Bayless and Bobby Flay put Mexican cooking on the map, Tom Gilliland opened this restaurant serving the cuisine of all seven regions of Mexico. Thirty-six years later, after a few remodels and the addition of a collection of artwork featuring some of Mexico's best-known artists, Gilliand's restaurant is still turning out excellent versions of classics like enchiladas de pato, pollo pibil and pescado a la Veracruzana. What sets the cuisine apart are the "excellent homemade salsas," "amazing tortillas" and "a thoughtful use of spicing," which gives diners the opportunity to appreciate "ingredients that are higher in quality" than you are used to seeing in most Mexican restaurants.

Mexican | Casual | Moderate | allandale | 2330 W. North Loop Blvd. | 512-459-4121 | www.fondasanmiguel.com | Dinner Mon-Sun, Lunch Sun

TOP LOCAL CHOICE

Wink   89.0

This "tiny, tiny restaurant" located in a nondescript strip mall focuses on "locally sourced ingredients prepared in fun and creative ways." Mark Paul and Stewart Scruggs man the kitchen, and a typical menu might include a seared lobster cake with arugula and sorrel aioli or Sika venison with Romanesco cauliflower, oyster mushrooms and a Riesling gastrique. Chef Mark is also lauded for being "the best host in the state." And there's a "considerable wine list," offering "many bottles that are fairly priced by local standards." The result: a venue that reviewers call, "the best of the upper middle places in Austin."

New American | Moderate | clarksville | 1014 N. Lamar Ave. | 512-482-8868 | www.winkrestaurant.com | Dinner Mon-Sat

Eddie V's Prime Seafood   88.0

With entrées like Gulf snapper with fresh Jonah crab costing less than $30 and prime-aged 16-oz. New York strip steaks priced under $40, many reviewers find this a "slightly cheaper version of a top fish or steakhouse." One reviewer, who reminded us we're talking about inland Texas, marveled at "fresh fish in a town that isn't known for its seafood joints." While there's "nothing on the menu you haven't seen elsewhere," they do a good-enough job with a format that other local restaurants seem to have trouble with.

Seafood | Casual | Expensive | downtown | 9400 Arboretum Blvd. | 512-342-2642 | www.eddiev.com | Dinner daily

Mirabelle   88.0

The draw at this restaurant, now in its 13th year, is its effort to make everyone happy.

The menu includes everything from crab cakes with basil oil to duck spring rolls with a papaya dipping sauce to pork tenderloin with tropical fruit and watermelon jus. One reviewer called it "a safe choice for your mother from Nebraska, as well as for your friends from Boise and your mistress from Austin." The wine list plays it equally safe, but instead of aping the menu's diversity, the choices have been narrowed to bottles from either Napa or Sonoma.

New American | Casual | Moderate | spicewood springs | 8127 Mesa Dr. | 512-346-7900 | www.mira-bellerestaurant.com | Lunch & Dinner Mon-Fri Sat dinner only

ACCEPTABLE

Jeffrey's   86.5

Opened in 1975, Ron & Peggy Weiss' restaurant is the Grande Dame of the Austin dining scene. Deegan McClung is in charge of the kitchen these days, and he has updated the restaurant's menu with dishes like pressed quail on golden raisin purée with sautéed Boggy Creek farm greens and grilled foie gras. Reviewers say, "As far as fine dining in Texas goes, this is about as good as it gets," though the nostalgic demur, "It's not quite as refined as it was back in the old days."

New American | Casual | Expensive | clarksville | 1204 W. Lynn St. | 512-477-5584 | www.jeffreysofaustin.com | Dinner daily

Roaring Fork   85.0

This is one of four Roaring Fork locations that are operated by the Eddie V's restaurant group. It's best described as an "upscale chain restaurant" where everybody seems to start their meal with a kettle of green chili which they follow with dishes like panfried trout with brown butter or a bacon-wrapped pork tenderloin with Mexican street corn and cheese grits. The moderate prices make it perfect for families (it's always full of University of Texas students with their parents in tow), who seem to like the "fun atmosphere" and the "great downtown location."

Southwestern | Casual | Moderate | downtown | 701 S. Congress St. | 512-583-0000 | www.roaring-fork.com | Dinner daily, Lunch Mon-Fri

OTHER RESTAURANTS MENTIONED

South Congress Café   82.0

On the simple side is warm goat cheese salad with shaved prosciutto, while lamb loin dusted with cocoa and fresh blackberries is an example of the complex. It adds up to "perfectly, safe, acceptable food," "slightly retro and slightly hip." As one reviewer put it, "In New York this place would be gone in 60 seconds, but in Austin it's one of the few places with both a good vibe and decent cooking."

New American | Casual | Moderate | |s. austin | 1600 S. Congress Ave. | 512-447-3905 | www.southcongresscafe.com | Lunch & Dinner daily

Cheap Eats

UNIQUELY DELICIOUS

Kreuz Market   9.4
(29 miles south in Lockhart)

Among the restaurants on the rarified list of Cheap Eats places with a rating over 9.0 is this temple of barbecue serving what one seasoned reviewer called "the world's best brisket." They also smoke ribs, turkey, ham, sausages and prime rib, but it's the brisket that's as "as complex as a bottle of single-vineyard wine," that drives the rating. No wonder pit masters from all over say "It's worth the pilgrimage" to this "large, cavernous space" to figure out what makes the brisket tick. Meanwhile reviewers applaud the "spectacular Texas barbecue."

Barbecue | Moderate | lockhart | 619 N. Colorado St. | 512-398-2361 | www.kreuzmarket.com | Lunch & Dinner Mon-Sat

Smitty's (29 miles south in Lockhart) 8.2

The owners of Smitty's and Kreuz Market used to be partners. When they decided to split, Kreuz moved and Smitty's remained in this historic space where they have been slowly smoking cuts of meat since the turn of the century. As with any divorce, friends of the former duo often side with one or the other. In this case, Smitty's supporters prefer the "good and fatty brisket" to the competition's more famous version, declaring, "For history, atmosphere and barbecue that delivers, Smitty's is arguably the best barbecue joint in Texas."

Barbecue | Moderate | lockhart | 208 S. Commerce St. | 512-398-9344 | www.smittys-market.com | Breakfast & Lunch daily

RECOMMENDED

City Market (43 miles so. in Luling) 7.5

Lockhart-area residents are swimming in barbecue sauce; around this small town south of Austin three top-quality smoke-houses turn out high-quality versions of an assortment of meats ranging from brisket to ribs to sausages. Opened in 1958, City Market is the newcomer on the block, but that doesn't mean it doesn't have its fair share of fans, who claim it's "on the short list for serious barbecue aficionados" and "reliably in the running with the Lockhart legends and – on some days – surpassing them."

Barbecue | Moderate | luling | 4726 Richmond Ave. | 877-526-2271 | www.lulingcitymarket.com | Lunch & Dinner daily

Lamberts Downtown Barbecue 7.5

In a crowded barbecue environment, Louis Lambert and partners decided to open an upscale restaurant featuring live music. While the combination is usually a recipe for disaster, Lambert has done it correctly, causing reviewers to say; "What do you know, fancy BBQ does

work. The meats are tasty in their own way, and there are good sides and desserts." Others commend it as "a true new Austin original where food and service are always great."

Barbecue | Moderate | downtown | 401 W. Second St. | 512-494-1500 | www.lambertsaustin.com | Lunch & Dinner daily

OTHER PLACES MENTIONED

Salt Lick 6.6

The national reputation developed by this Austin institution seems to have worked against it, with reviewers now calling the place "touristy and overrated" and saying, "Growth over the years has caused the Salt Lick to lose its edge." Of course, the dip in quality doesn't prevent it from having a fervent group of supporters who say things like, "One of my favorite BBQ places in Texas" and "It lives up to the reputation for delicious meats." They allow BYOB, so come with a cooler of your favorite drinks.

Barbecue | driftwood | 18300 Farm Rd. 1826 | 512-858-4959 | www.saltlickbbq.com | Lunch & Dinner daily

Hoover's 6.5

Those looking for a break from barbecue while still enjoying an inexpensive meal should consider this restaurant where the "down-home Southern specialties are served with a smile." The food ranges from burgers to sandwiches to salads, and the truly adventurous can order dishes like a ham steak with Jezebel sauce. And if you insist on 'cue, they offer numerous smokehouse selections, the most notable being sausage from the Southside Market in Elgin, Texas.

Southern | n. austin | 13376 Research Blvd. | 512-335-0300 | www.hooverscooking.com | Lunch & Dinner daily

Stubb's 6.0

The general feeling about this iconic

location that is a full-time barbecue joint as well as a part-time music venue (on weekends only) is that it was better when founder C. B. Stubblefield was alive (he passed away in 1995, but you can still see his face on jars of his famous barbecue sauce that is sold all over the country). What's left in his wake is barbecue that reviewers say "will make do when I can't get down to Lockhart or Luling." Those who are less picky say, "Good 'cue and good music – what's not to love?"

Barbecue | Inexpensive | downtown | 801 Red River St. | 512-480-8341 | www.stubbsaustin.com | Lunch & Dinner daily

County Line   5.8

The low man on the barbecue totem pole attracted comments like "overpriced and just not that good," "overrated barbecue" and "barbecue for out-of-state college students." Of course, even an ugly duckling has its admirers, and those on

the pro side deem it "a good example of Texas BBQ" and an "Austin classic that serves the best sides in town."

Barbecue | west lake hills | 6500 W. Bee Caves Rd. | 512-327-1742 | www.countyline.com | Lunch & Dinner daily

Hut's   5.8

Our reviewers are split about this "Austin classic." Fans call burgers like the Fats Domino (jalapeños, onions, cheddar and New Orleans spices) and the Boodieburger (sour cream, mushrooms and Swiss cheese) "not quite perfect but pretty darn close." But detractors deride it as "average," saying the "greasy and bland burgers" are "overhyped." You wouldn't know that a controversy exists from looking at the long lines of people waiting for a table.

Hamburgers | Inexpensive | downtown | 807 W. Sixth St. | 512-472-0693 | www.hutsfrankandangies.com | Lunch & Dinner Mon-Sat

Boulder CO

RECOMMENDED

Frasca Food & Wine   90.1

Lachlan Mackinnon-Patterson and Bobby Stuckey's restaurant is an oasis in the Denver/Boulder corridor. A French Laundry alumnus, Lachlan combines his classical training with his fanaticism for the cuisine of Italy's Friuli region, and the result is refined versions of dishes like a minestra of sweet corn with Montasio cheese and basil or hand-cut pasta alla chitarra with chanterelles. Meanwhile, in the process of featuring the wines of Friuli, Stuckey has assembled one of the most interesting lists in the country. "Terrific food and wine from a region that is traditionally unrepresented" results in what some say is "the best food in the state," with a few claiming "It would hold its own in any city in the country." They recently expanded into the store next door.

Italian | Casual | Moderate | 1738 Pearl St. | 303-442-6966 | www.frascafoodandwine.com | Dinner Mon-Sat

Flagstaff House   90.0

"The cuisine is better than you might expect" at this former summer cabin built in 1929. A member of the second generation of the Monette family is now in charge of the kitchen, and he has updated the cuisine with French/American dishes like pancetta-wrapped quail with tree oyster mushrooms and Kurobuta pork cheeks braised in Marsala wine and served with goat cheese agnolotti. But the food isn't the only reason to go: Other strong draws are the setting – the restaurant is built into the side of a cliff at an altitude of 6,000 feet – and a 12,000-bottle, fairly priced wine cellar, which long-term customers love to peruse, especially during wild game season.

New American | Casual | Expensive | 1138 Flagstaff Rd. | 303-442-4640 | www.flagstaffhouse.com | Dinner daily

Dallas TX

RECOMMENDED

Stephan Pyles Restaurant   91.5

One of the founders of the Southwestern cuisine movement, Stephan Pyles opened his first restaurant, Routh Street Café, in 1983. Twenty-two years later, he developed this beautiful space in Dallas' Art District. Ceviches and tiraditos, along with a variety of flatbreads from a wood-burning oven that Pyles serves at lunch, complement scrumptious-sounding starters that include halibut cheeks with spicy orange and ginger and lenguado with smoked corn and sweet potato. The contemporary Southwestern theme continues with mains like a slow-smoked natural pork chop with green chile hominy and what Pyles calls Contemporary Arroz con Pato, a sous-vide smoked duck leg with achiote rice and shellfish. "Worth a visit," say reviewers, who add that it's "a good choice in a town that isn't overflowing with good restaurants."

Southwestern | Casual | Expensive | downtown | 1807 Ross Ave. | 214-580-7000 | www.stephanpyles.com | Lunch & Dinner Mon-Fri, Sat dinner only

Mansion on Turtle Creek   91.4

The Mansion has gone through some changes over the past few years. Dean Fearing, who oversaw the kitchen for two decades, decided it was time to move on four years ago. Enter Bruno Davaillon (formerly of Mix in Las Vegas), who tilted the menu in the direction of Europe with dishes like a sweet corn ravioli with a shrimp Bolognese sauce or confit and breast of duck with foie gras and a potato mousseline. Of course, Davaillon didn't completely discard tradition, and he still serves the signature tortilla soup. It all happens in a setting described as "the epitome of North Dallas elegance," which makes it "a popular stop with the ladies-who-lunch crowd."

New American | Casual | Expensive | turtle creek | 2821 Turtle Creek Blvd. | 214-443-4747 | www.mansiononturtlecreek.com | Open daily

Nobu   91.4

What can we say about Nobu Matsuhisa that hasn't already been said? Given the number of restaurants he runs, we keep expecting we will come upon a location our reviewers can't recommend. But that never turns out to be the case, including at this outpost in the Rosewood Crescent Hotel, where you are likely to find "cowboys and debutantes enjoying the house classic dishes" like toro tartar and spicy creamy shrimp. Given how difficult it is to find high-quality fish in the city, reviewers say "this is your best bet if you have a craving for sushi. True, there were some complaints about a "static menu," but the same reviewer chalked it up to "being a chain, albeit a good one."

Japanese | Casual | Expensive | downtown | 400 Crescent Ct. | 214-252-7000 | www.noburestaurants.com | Dinner daily

Craft   91.0

While one reviewer praised this Craft location in the trendy W Hotel for cooking that features "able preparations that are in keeping with Tom Colicchio's now-famous concept" of a mix-and-match menu, he added, "The limited range of top-quality local produce puts it a notch below the New York original." The menu offers a similar combination of high-quality, seasonally inspired roasts, sautés and braises of meats, fish and fowl, which diners can pair with careful preparations of market vegetables. The reviewers who complain about the "high prices" should keep in mind that part of what you pay for is the ability to enjoy your roast chicken in an "especially lively setting."

New American | Casual | Expensive | victory park | W Hotel | 2440 Victory Park Ln. | 214-397-4111 | www.craftrestaurant.com | Open daily

Abacus   90.5

Kent Rathbun's restaurant is the perfect choice for those who like the style of big-city, upper middle dining that allows "a crowd with an air of entitlement" to dig into dishes like lobster-scallion shooters with red chile-coconut sake or cocoa nib–crusted venison with butter-poached salsify, roasted brussels sprouts and huckleberry-port sauce. Those who like the style talk about the "inventive cuisine in a high-energy atmosphere." But those who dislike dining in this manner say, "The best dishes were the simplest ones," while complaining about items with "too many ingredients" and "a chef who has to justify high prices by pouring a luxury ingredient on each dish."

New American | Casual | Expensive | uptown | 4511 McKinney Ave. | 214-559-3111 | www.abacus-restaurant.com | Dinner Mon-Sat

Fearing's   90.0

For more than two decades, Dean Fearing, the most iconic chef in all of Texas, plied his craft at the Mansion at Turtle Creek. But every show finishes its run, and in 2007 Fearing moved his pots and pans to the Ritz-Carlton, where he continues to serve his personal take on Southwestern fare in dishes like barbecue shrimp tacos and a Southwestern surf 'n' turf of a pan-roasted spiced filet paired with chicken-fried Maine lobster. While the ratings fell on the positive side of the recommended line, reviews were mixed, with those in favor saying, "Fearing has been creating masterpieces for years" and critics speaking of "a parade of wealthy people who are enjoying food that is slightly better than hotel quality."

Southwestern | Casual | Expensive | uptown | Ritz-Carlton Hotel | 2121 McKinney Ave. | 214-922-4848 | www.ritzcarlton.com | Lunch & Dinner daily

Denver CO

RECOMMENDED

Mizuna   91.8

Reviewers say that Frank Bonanno's restaurant has "raised its game," obviously so much so that its rating hovers on the edge of Highly Recommended. Chef Tony Clement and "a kitchen that is paying greater attention to local ingredients and the way they are prepared" might have something to do with the improvement. While their lobster mac 'n' cheese (made with mascarpone and beurre blanc) is rightly famous, diners say that dishes like sea bass with celeriac risotto or a grilled veal rib eye with crispy olive oil–poached potatoes and sauce vierge "now rise to the same level." One diner who has eaten here for a year said "it was always as good as it gets in Denver," and then added "and in fact it just got better."

New American | Casual | Expensive | southwest | 225 E. Seventh Ave. | 303-832-4778 | www.mizunadenver.com | Dinner Tue-Sat

TOP LOCAL CHOICE

Sushi Den   89.0

Run by three brothers, one of whom lives in Tokyo and who scours the Tsukiji Fish Market every morning, Sushi Den stands for the proposition that being able to serve high-quality fish has less to do with a restaurant's proximity to the sea than to the wonders of FedEx. "Absolutely the best sushi in Denver" and "the freshness is apparent in the texture and flavor of the fish" sum up the comments. Every night "The joint is jammed," and it's "as much a place to be seen" as it is a place to dine.

Japanese | Moderate | platt park | 1487 S. Pearl St. | 303-777-0826 | www.sushiden.net | Lunch & Dinner Mon-Fri Sat-Sun dinner only

Fruition   88.5

Alex Seidel and Paul Attardi are so committed to serving a local and sustainable cuisine they purchased a farm where they can grow ingredients for their restaurant. The result is the type of fare diners have come to expect from a farm-to-table restaurant: pasta carbonara with house-cured pork belly, a six-minute egg and Parmesan broth or braised pork cheeks with toasted farro, citrus-braised endive and a quince glaze. Reviewers say the "upscale comfort food" is "well cooked and beautifully served," making this a "solid neighborhood" venue that's "worth a trip."

New American | Casual | Moderate | southeast | 1313 E. Sixth Ave. | 303-831-1962 | www.fruitionrestaurant.com | Dinner daily

ACCEPTABLE

Rioja   86.5

Given the name, one would think this is some sort of Spanish restaurant, or at least a tapas bar. But alas, the closest this establishment gets to Spain is a saffron Manchego risotto served with a seared Muscovy duck breast; rather, our reviewers called the cooking "unfussy yet creative" American fare that can be "uneven but capable of generating excitement at its best." Some like it for its "well-selected wine list," which is "reasonably priced for the quality on offer."

New American | Casual | Moderate | lodo | 1431 Larimer St. | 303-820-2282 | www.riojadenver.com | Dinner daily, Lunch Wed-Sun

Domo   86.0

Denver isn't the most obvious choice for an Asian restaurant but "Domo serves surprisingly good Japanese food for this part of the country." While the menu features udon, soba and donburi, the house specialty is nabe, various stews with meat or fish. Those who are critical complain about "overcooked food," "inattentive service" and "a setting reminiscent of an attraction at Epcot Center." It's as much about being a tourist attraction as it is a dining venue, with Japanese-style gardens as well as a Japanese country museum on the premises.

Japanese | Moderate | southwest | 1365 Osage St. | 303-595-3666 | www.domorestaurant.com | Lunch & Dinner Mon-Sat

Jax Fish House 86.0

The menu at this "boisterous and crowded" restaurant seems better suited to New England than to Colorado. Among the draws are a raw bar, making it "one of the few go-to spots for bivalves" in the city, and an eclectic list of prepared dishes like chicken and crawfish gumbo or pan-seared New England scallops with whipped Yukon Gold potatoes. A "thin wine list" and a no-BYO policy means that local oenophiles who enjoy slurping oysters while sipping on a vintage bottle from their own cellar don't visit as often as they might.

Seafood | Casual | Moderate | downtown | 1539 17th St. | 303-292-5767 | www.jaxfishhousedenver.com | Dinner daily

Kevin Taylor's at the Opera 85.5

There are restaurants in what we call the upper middle category that, in spite of their inherent flaws, still manage to serve food that our reviewers find appealing. Then there are ones like Kevin Taylor's that attract comments like "The food was beyond safe," "nothing there to keep my interest" and "a nice pre-theater option, but definitely not for the discerning food lover." If you do go, expect to find a "beautiful room," "excellent service" and "knowledgeable sommeliers" who offer diners "well-thought-out wine pairings."

New American | Casual | Moderate | northwest | Hotel Teatro | 1106 14th St. | 303-820-2600 | www.coloradoeats.com | Dinner Mon-Sat

Barolo Grill 85.0

Given that Denver's population isn't long on Italian heritage, owner Blair Taylor and staff do their best to deliver a quality northern Italian experience. "They care about what they're doing and the food reflects it," says one reviewer. "Each summer they send the staff to Italy so they can brush up on their culinary tech-

nique." But a New Yorker who spends a lot of time in Denver feels "the food is merely adequate," while citing "a terrific Italian wine list" and "Blair Taylor's ebullient personality" as the reasons to go.

Italian | Casual | Expensive | cherry creek | 3030 E. Sixth Ave. | 303-393-1040 | www.barologrilldenver.com | Dinner Tue-Sat

OTHER PLACES MENTIONED

Elway's 80.5

As to be expected when a restaurant is fronted by a local sports legend (in this instance, former Denver Broncos quarterback John Elway), "mediocre food, a terrible wine list and a dining room with a corporate feel" dominate the experience. One reviewer told us, "The only reason to dine at this noisy, football field–sized place is to have the opportunity to pose with or ask for an autograph from the amiable owner."

Steakhouse | Casual | Moderate | cherry creek | 2500 E. First Ave. | 303-399-5353 | www.elways.com | Lunch & Dinner daily

Tamayo 80.0

We know Richard Sandoval knows how to cook – once upon a time his signature restaurant, Maya, was admired by foodies. But since he opened restaurants around the country, the quality has diminished proportionately to the number of new locations. Still, this venue does attract some comments like, "It tries to do something different and executes at a higher level than chain Mexican joints." But a more typical reviewer talks about "food that serves as proof that people will eat anything."

Mexican | Casual | Moderate | lodo | 1400 Larimer St. | 720-946-1433 | www.modernmexican.com | Lunch & Dinner Mon-Fri Sat-Sun dinner only

Houston TX

TOP LOCAL CHOICE

Mark's American Cuisine   89.0

The saying "Everything's big in Texas" is proved true by this restaurant's large portions of dishes like grilled Panama shrimp with a ragout of jumbo lump crabmeat served atop a South Carolina shrimp and grit cake with a chili-spiked lime sauce, roasted green chiles and cilantro coulis. Otherwise, reviewers say that Mark Cox's restaurant seems to be "frozen in time," with food that is "reasonably well-executed but terminally boring." Still, it's the best place to eat in a town that wants for good restaurants, making it "the number-one special-occasion restaurant in the city."

New American | Casual | Expensive | montrose | 1658 Westheimer Rd. | 713-523-3800 | www.marks1658.com | Lunch & Dinner Mon-Fri Sat-Sun dinner only

Las Vegas NV

WORTH PLANNING A TRIP AROUND

Guy Savoy   98.2

In the pantheon of top Parisian chefs, Guy Savoy was never considered as important as some of his peers. He lacked the innovation of a Passard or a Gagnaire, and he wasn't a master technician like Pacaud or Ducasse. Still, he has been around long enough to be an important part of the nouvelle-cuisine movement, and his cooking at his Paris restaurant was good enough to be awarded the highest honors in dining. But here in the States it's a different story; as far as our reviewers are concerned, when it comes to a French chef transporting his cuisine to a different location, Savoy, whose cooking is described as having "flair and soul," has been more successful than anyone else, and that includes Messrs. Ducasse and Robuchon.

Along with Savoy's signature dishes – like artichoke and truffle soup and crispy sea bass with delicate spices – domestic ingredients show up in dishes like a carpaccio of Santa Barbara spot prawns with tomato tartare and a crustacean granité, and luxury ingredients turn up in butter-poached sweetbreads with a potato and truffle sandwich or roasted foie gras en cocotte with a cardamom-infused duck bouillon. Warm and attentive service and a pricey wine list are part of what one person called "a hugely expensive evening." But as an astute reviewer pointed out, "serving a limited number of diners each evening makes this level of fine dining possible."

French | Formal | Very Expensive | strip | Caesars Palace | 3570 Las Vegas Blvd. S. | 702-731-7731 | www.harrahs.com | Dinner Wed-Sun

HIGHLY RECOMMENDED

Raku   93.4

Whenever someone recommends a Vegas restaurant that isn't on the Strip we immediately take notice – especially when it makes our list of the top 100 restaurants in the country. In this instance, the focus is on the "superb aburiya cooking" in an "off the beaten track location." While a number of people dismiss the raw fish preparations, calling them "pedestrian," they rave about offerings like aged dashi (house-made tofu),

which they say "serves as a reference point" for the dish, and offerings cooked over the robata grill, ranging from tsukune (chicken meatballs) to foie gras. Reviewers call Raku "a very special and soulful restaurant," adding, "It's better than many izakaya restaurants I've been to in Japan." No wonder it's the number-one spot to see local chefs having dinner on their nights off or after they've finished service in their own kitchens.

Japanese | Casual | west side | 5030 W. Spring Mountain Rd. | 702-367-3511 | www.raku-grill.com | Dinner Mon-Sat

Picasso   93.0

Only in Las Vegas could you find a restaurant decorated with actual Picassos worth millions of dollars. (One reviewer asked, "I wonder how many of the patrons have seen a Picasso before?") Julian Serrano's food is not quite as majestic as the Cubist paintings adorning his walls, but his French cuisine, featuring dishes like pan-seared U-10 dayboat scallops with potato mousseline and veal jus and sautéed medallions of fallow deer with caramelized green apples and zinfandel sauce, is artful enough to make this the third-highest-rated restaurant in town. A few reviewers criticized "a small menu that hardly ever changes," while others point out that Serrano is actually in the kitchen cooking, "a rarity for this city." In addition to the beautiful art and solid food, the dining room offers an exceptional view of the dancing fountains at the Bellagio.

French | Formal | Expensive | strip | Bellagio Hotel | 3600 Las Vegas Blvd. S. | 702-693-7223 | www.bellagio.com | Dinner Wed-Mon

RECOMMENDED

Michael Mina   91.5

Not only do our reviewers say this is Michael Mina's best restaurant – the rating here bested his San Francisco location by 2.5 points – it also offers better people-watching and a wine list that's described as "terrific, even by Las Vegas standards." A number of Mina's signature seafood dishes are on hand, including his black mussel soufflé, miso-glazed black cod and lobster potpie, while meat eaters can enjoy a whole roasted lobe of foie gras with apricot chutney and vincotto. One reviewer advised diners to "stay away from the signature trio dishes," while another commented that his meal was surprisingly delicious and "It didn't seem mass-produced," which is amazing when you consider how many restaurants Mina operates these days.

New American | Casual | Expensive | strip | Bellagio Hotel | 3600 Las Vegas Blvd. S. | 702-693-7223 | www.michaelmina.net | Dinner Thu-Tue

Bouchon   91.4

While Thomas Keller's attention to detail and commitment to excellence are clearly in evidence at this French bistro, diners expecting something like "French Laundry light" are barking up the wrong tree. Instead, you will find an excellent raw bar and user-friendly bistro cuisine, like pan-seared tuna with ratatouille and roast chicken with red rice and lardons, served by a friendly staff in a lively enviroment. "Solid food with excellent ingredients; they stick to the middle road, but execution is flawless" is the comment that describes it best. One of the few good places for a casual meal on the Strip.

French | Casual | Moderate | strip | Venetian | 3355 Las Vegas Blvd. S. | 702-414-6200 | www.bouchon-bistro.com | Open daily

Joël Robuchon at the Mansion   91.3

This is one of those strange situations where opinions are so polarized that 40% of our reviewers rated this restaurant as a must go, while nearly 30% said it was merely acceptable or worse. Let's take people who have positive things to say first: "Virtually flawless in every respect" and "The 16-course menu is a master's thesis in flavor pairings and attention to detail" are comments from the restaurant's fans. But those less enamored with the experience said, "It's hard to believe this shockingly ordinary restaurant has anything to do with Robuchon" and "proof that in Las Vegas the house always beats the suckers." In this instance, the difference in opinion is cause to give one pause, especially given the $385 price tag for the tasting menu.

French | Formal | Very Expensive | strip | MGM Grand | 3799 Las Vegas Blvd. S. | 702-891-7925 | www.mgmgrand.com | Dinner daily

Craftsteak   91.0

While many celebrity chefs have opened steakhouses – it's a quick way to generate extra income – Tom Colicchio was the first chef who actually tried to improve the experience. Colicchio's menu is awash with beef sourced from producers like Snake River Farms, Harris Ranch and Brandt Beef, while offering nine cuts of domestic and Australian Wagyu beef. Reviewers say, "It's accessible to anyone – I ordered veal breast, but you can easily prove your manhood by dropping well over a $100 on a piece of meat." As at Colicchio's other venues, "they treat vegetables with great respect."

Steakhouse | Casual | Expensive | strip | MGM Grand Hotel | 3799 Las Vegas Blvd. S. | 702-891-7318 | www.mgmgrand.com | Dinner daily

Lotus of Siam   91.0

This restaurant transcends its category, with half our reviewers anointing it as "the best Thai in the U.S." Chef/owner Saipin Chutima dials up the heat in dishes like a fiery-hot papaya salad, shrimps in bacon blankets, sea bass in drunken noodles, and sautéed lobster and crispy duck in cognac sauce. Along with the amazing food, there's a superb wine list, with an especially good selection of Rieslings "to help calm the fire in your mouth." The restaurant is located in an off-the-Strip shopping mall, and there's no décor or even service to speak of, but those are small details when it comes to this unusual restaurant that is "actually better than the hype."

Thai | Casual | Moderate | east side | 953 E. Sahara Ave. | 702-735-3033 | www.saipinchutima.com | Lunch & Dinner Mon-Thu, Fri lunch only

RM Seafood   90.8

Back in 2005, Rick Moonen closed his restaurant in New York City and moved to Las Vegas. Soon after, he opened this venue with a focus on sustainable seafood. Moonen offers two dining formats: The upstairs dining room offers a chef's tasting menu featuring dishes like wild striped bass with variations of cauliflower; the more casual downstairs room has simpler fare like crab cakes with chipotle aioli and shrimp corn dogs. A "great raw bar" and a "wide variety of different fish on offer" make it "the perfect choice for even the pickiest of pescatarians."

Seafood | Casual | Expensive | strip | Mandalay Bay Resort | 3930 Las Vegas Blvd. S. | 702-632-9300 | www.rmseafood.com | Dinner Tue-Sat

L'Atelier de Robuchon   90.5

With comments like "go here instead of the Mansion" and "Robuchon's less-formal restaurant doesn't suffer by comparison," we think it's fair to say that a number of our reviewers prefer this restaurant over its bigger brother. The menu contains Robuchon's greatest hits, like the langoustine croustillant with basil sauce and foie gras–stuffed free-range quail, accompanied by his infamous pommes purée. Most reviewers were positive, offering comments like, "It's a great way to experience Robuchon's cooking in a more casual and affordable setting." But a large contingent of contrarians dismiss it as a "high-end chain restaurant," complaining about "food that is formulaic."

French | Casual | Expensive | strip | MGM Grand | 3799 Las Vegas Blvd. S. | 702-891-7358 | www.mgmgrand.com | Dinner daily

Prime Steakhouse   90.3

This steakhouse from Jean-Georges Vongerichten was one of the first restaurants to open after Las Vegas decided it would benefit from an association with celebrity chefs. Thirteen years later, Prime is still vying for the honor of the town's top meat palace. Of course, this is Vegas and it's hard to get consensus on anything, so we found it remarkable when multiple reviewers called this "the steakhouse in town I'd first return to." And since it's Vegas, diners are advised to "bring a big bankroll" and "be prepared for "a wine list priced for suckers."

Steakhouse | Casual | Expensive | strip | Bellagio Hotel | 3600 Las Vegas Blvd. S. | 702-693-8255 | www.bellagio.com | Dinner daily

Okada   90.2

One of the better choices for sushi in Vegas, Okada can be enjoyable, provided you realize that the fish isn't at the level you would find at the very top sushi restaurants in the country. (It's the curse of serving sushi, or any other sea creature, in the middle of the desert.) But if you are looking for lots of different specialty rolls, Kobe beef by the ounce and assorted Japanese fusion dishes, it is more than satisfactory. The place is a bit quieter and more tranquil than some of the other restaurants in town, and the beauty of the room – one reviewer suggests "you should reserve a table near the lagoon if you're looking for a romantic evening" – can be as much of a draw as the food on your plate.

Japanese | Casual | Expensive | strip | Wynn Las Vegas | 3131 Las Vegas Blvd. S. | 702-248-3463 | www.wynnlasvegas.com | Dinner daily

B & B Ristorante   90.0

With its Batali-esque menu, which even goes so far as to offer a pasta-tasting section, along with a list of Italian wines that runs incredibly deep, it isn't surprising that this offering from Mario Batali and Joe Bastianich attracted comments like, "What's on the plate is similar to Babbo" and "the food's almost as good as Babbo's" and "a sort of Babbo West." (In fact, so many people made the comparison that it made us wonder why they left the extra letters out of the name.) Also attracting commentary – of a less flattering sort – is the noise level, driven by artists like R.E.M. and Hendrix blaring on the restaurant's sound system while you're trying to get a mouthful of pasta onto your fork.

Italian | Casual | Expensive | strip | Venetian Hotel | 3355 Las Vegas Blvd. S. | 702-266-9977 | www.bandbristorante.com | Dinner daily

Nobhill Tavern   90.0

The focus at this offering from the Michael Mina Group is on Bay Area comfort food. The menu features dishes like Bay Shrimp Louie and cioppino, along with other homey classics like Maine lobster pie and osso buco. Reviewers described the "high level of care that is taken in executing some high-quality ingredients," as well as a "low-key atmosphere," thanks to a location set away from the casino floor. Add "a well-thought-out wine list" and interesting cocktails like the Cable Car, and you have "one of the better places to eat on the Strip."

American | Casual | Expensive | strip | MGM Grand | 3799 Las Vegas Blvd. S. | 702-891-7337 | www.mgmgrand.com | Dinner daily

TOP LOCAL CHOICE

Nobu   89.5

While this restaurant in the Hard Rock is "indistinguishable from other Nobus," we agree with the reviewer who said, "It's impressive how Nobu maintains a high standard at his restaurants as he expands his empire." The menu is world-famous by now, and the quality of the fish here is usually good enough for most diners, except for the pickiest sushi eaters. But while the restaurant excels at prepared dishes, like spicy creamy crab and miso-marinated black cod, a major downside is the "horrendously loud atmosphere" and the less-than-knowledgeable servers who "didn't know the food from the rocks that make up the sushi wall."

Japanese | Casual | Expensive | strip | Hard Rock Hotel & Casino | 4455 Paradise Rd. | 702-693-5090 | www.nobumatsuhisa.com | Dinner daily

Rosemary's   89.5

Michael and Wendy Jordan's restaurant has three things going for it: It's not on the Strip, the $55 prix-fixe menu is a contrast to typical Vegas pricing, and everyone enjoys their American bistro cuisine. Having spent time working in New Orleans for chefs like Lagasse and Spicer, the Jordans display their culinary lineage in dishes like risotto with homemade tasso ham, crawfish and smoked-tomato jus or a grilled pork chop with Hoppin' John and a Creole-mustard reduction sauce. It's one of the few better restaurants that serves lunch (Fridays only), and "The $28 prix fixe menu is a huge bargain."

New American | Casual | Moderate | north las vegas | 8125 W. Sahara Ave. | 702-869-2251 | www.rosemarysrestaurant.com | Dinner daily, Fri lunch

Spago   89.5

Back in the day when the only places to eat in town were buffets, steakhouses and Continental restaurants, someone had the brilliant idea to bring big-name chefs to Las Vegas, and asked Wolfgang Puck to open a branch of Spago. That was nearly 20 years ago and the town has been overrun with celebrity-chef restaurants since that time, yet Spago is still going strong, with Eric Klein serving a number of Puck's classics as well as dishes like Wiener schnitzel made with Snake River Farms Kurobuta pork. The location in the Forum Shops at Caesars means you can "expect a very large check" at the end of your meal to go along with the hefty credit card bills for your pre-dinner purchases.

Californian | Casual | Expensive | strip | Forum Shops at Caesars | 3500 Las Vegas Blvd. S. | 702-369-6300 | www.wolfgangpuck.com | Dinner daily

Le Cirque 89.0

One of the smallest dining rooms in a Las Vegas hotel features a beautiful anteroom that shields the restaurant from the casino noise. One person described the cooking and service, which is reminiscent of the New York location, as "solid French cuisine" (featuring dishes like roast chicken with black truffles and foie gras macaroni or Burgundy snails in garlic-herb butter) "that unfortunately comes with a French attitude." One of its best features is that it's easy to book a table, making it "a great last-minute option" when Picasso doesn't have an opening. If you're looking for a romantic evening, ask for a spot by the window.

French | Formal | Very Expensive | strip | Bellagio Hotel | 3600 Las Vegas Blvd. S. | 702-693-7223 | www.bellagio.com | Dinner Tue-Sun

Delmonico Steakhouse 88.5

An easy way for a celebrity chef to earn extra cash is to open a steakhouse. He slaps his name on the door and tosses a few signature dishes on the menu, but for the most part, you might as well be eating at some no-name eatery. This entry is from Emeril Lagasse, and it comes with the typical ups and downs. Mainly, your steak can be great, or not. But while quality can vary, the one constant you can be sure of is a "crowded and noisy" dining room that is "always packed with conventioneers."

Steakhouse | Casual | Expensive | strip | Venetian | 3355 Las Vegas Blvd. S. | 702-414-3737 | www.emerils.com | Lunch & Dinner daily

Bradley Ogden 88.0

For the past 22 years, Bradley Ogden has been turning out an honest version of New American cuisine based on "painstakingly selected artisanal ingredients" prepared in a respectful way. However, while the style of cooking he employs was once novel, it's become a little plain for some of our reviewers; one described it as "quality food if you're happy with solid cuisine with no imagination." There's an "excellent wine list" along with great service even by Las Vegas standards, though the "middlebrow setting" off the casino floor at Caesars is disappointing for a meal that costs this much.

New American | Casual | Expensive | strip | Caesars Palace | 3570 Las Vegas Blvd. S. | 702-731-7731 | www.harrahs.com | Dinner Wed-Sun

ACCEPTABLE

Bartolotta Ristorante di Mare 87.5

Paul Bartolotta made his name as the chef at Spiaggia in Chicago. And while he hasn't attained the same level of success at his Las Vegas restaurant, we have seen steady improvement in the reviews over the past two years. The shtick here is the "fabulously expensive fish," flown in daily from Italy and paraded around the dining room on big silver platters before being brought to your table. Service issues have hindered the rating: One diner wrote of "excellent langoustines by the piece," but also of a $70 turbot that was "torn apart" by the waiter.

Italian | Formal | Expensive | strip | Wynn Las Vegas | 3131 Las Vegas Blvd. S. | 702-770-9966 | www.wynnlasvegas | Dinner daily

Carnevino 87.5

If you have an extra $150 to drop on a dry-aged steak, check out this Italian offering from Mario Batali and Joe Bastianich, which serves a New York strip steak that has been sleeping in their meat locker for nine months. Otherwise, "The food is nothing special" and "The markups on wine are in keeping with the rest of Las Vegas – terrible." A dining room that opens onto the casino floor is another mark against it. On the plus side, more than one person raved about "the best hamburger in Vegas."

Italian | Casual | Expensive | strip | Palazzo Hotel | 3325 Las Vegas Blvd. S. | 702-789-4141 | http://carnevino.com | Lunch & Dinner daily

Aureole   87.0

Some chefs are able to successfully expand their businesses, while others flounder. Our reviewers put this offshoot of Charlie Palmer's signature restaurant in the middle, saying the experience is plagued by "inconsistent execution" and "average food at high prices." One thing that everyone comments on is the "wine angels": The restaurant's sommeliers are attached to wire cords, allowing them to leap all over the wall of wine. But even here, there's disagreement: Some call them "a major attraction," others, "a huge distraction."

New American | Casual | Expensive | strip | Mandalay Bay | 3950 Las Vegas Bld. S. | 702-632-7401 | www.charliepalmer.com | Dinner daily

Fleur de Lys   87.0

When a chef opens a bad clone of his main restaurant, the comments from our reviewers can be brutal. As in: "Sadly, one of the worst dining experiences I've had in a restaurant of this caliber. Will not be going back" and "Hubert Keller gone wild in Vegas. Avoid." Still, if you're a fan of the San Francisco original, all of Keller's classic dishes are here. Additional pluses: a "dramatic room" that centers on an "incredible bubble sculpture" and a "well-defined list featuring numerous Alsatian wines."

French | Formal | Expensive | strip | Mandalay Bay | 3950 Las Vegas Bvd. S. | 702-632-7777 | www.mandalaybay.com | Lunch & Dinner daily

Mix   87.0

Alain Ducasse's over-the-top Las Vegas venture is a "trendy, see-and-be-seen restaurant" that is "not recommended for serious food connoisseurs." A few dishes attracted praise, like the mac 'n' cheese, but the general consensus is that it's "not worth the hype nor the extravagant expense." Noise is another problem; one reviewer who enjoyed his meal complained that "everyone in the room was yelling." Mix is located on the top floor of the Mandalay Bay, and one thing that can't be ruined are the beautiful views.

French | Casual | Expensive | strip | Mandalay Bay | 3950 Las Vegas Bld. S. | 702-632-9500 | www.mandalaybay.com | Dinner daily

N9NE Steakhouse   86.0

To some people this place offers a "mouthwatering, butter-cutting, cooked-to-perfection-steak." But to others it's nothing more than "a factory with all the pejorative connotations," including "okay steak" and a "wine list that is way marked up." Even the clientele came under scrutiny, with some reviewers calling their fellow diners "jet-setters" and others deeming them "B-level celebrities." One reviewer took it all in stride: "It's a steakhouse in Vegas, so you know exactly what you're getting into."

Steakhouse | Casual | Expensive | strip | Palms Casino & Resort | 4321 W. Flamingo Rd. | 702-933-9900 | www.n9negroup.com | Dinner daily

Sushi Roku   86.0

Reading comments like "it blends terrific people-watching with quality Japanese food" and "I'm happy to groove to the music with some deliciously fresh fish placed before me," we were surprised at the degree of positive feedback on this chain of contemporary Japanese restaurants owned and operated by the people behind Boa Steakhouse. Complaints often focused on value for money: "I had an omakase at the sushi bar, and while there was some decent fish, it should have been better at the price."

Japanese | Casual | Expensive | strip | 3500 Las Vegas Blvd. S. | 702-733-7373 | www.sushiroku.com | Lunch & Dinner daily

OTHER PLACES MENTIONED

Buffet Bellagio   84.0

With a myriad of choices from sushi to lobster ravioli to carving stations to chicken Parmesan, "This was easily the best of the buffets I tried in Vegas." As with any buffet, not everything is worth eating, and "the space is tired and could use refurbishing." But if you like trying a variety of different styles of cuisine in bulk, it makes for a good choice, as "Where else could you eat an unlimited amount of duck confit?"

Eclectic | Moderate | strip | Bellagio Hotel | 3600 Las Vegas Blvd. S. | 702-693-8255 | www. bellagio.com | Open daily

Emeril's New Orleans   84.0
Fishhouse

For people who think they would benefit from our guide, this restaurant (to which a celebrity chef has lent his name for a dining format he operates only in gambling resorts) is the antithesis of the dining experience they are seeking. But while, true to form, it was described by one reviewer as "embodying everything I hate about Vegas," more than one person was surprised by the "thoughtfully prepared seafood."

Seafood | Casual | Moderate | strip | MGM Grand | 3799 Las Vegas Blvd. S. | 702-891-7374 | www.emerils.com | Lunch & Dinner daily

Valentino Las Vegas   84.0

Given that our reviewers aren't wild about the Santa Monica original, what are the odds they will like this clone in the Venetian? Not very good – in fact they called it even "worse than the flagship." And the "crazy high" markups on wine

don't help. Those who do enjoy it recommend that you ask for a table on the patio overlooking the casino, where you can still eat well while "ordering off the less-expensive grill menu."

Italian | Casual | Expensive | strip | Venetian | 3355 Las Vegas Blvd. S. | 702-414-3000 | www.welovewine.com | Dinner daily

BOA   83.5

The gimmick here is the pairing of a steakhouse menu that is competitive with the top chains' with "a nice view of the nightlife" at the restaurant's bar. "Everything about it is mouthwatering, from the food to the clientele," sighed one reviewer, and several opined that along with the eye candy, "The tableside preparation of the Caesar salad makes this a cut above."

Steakhouse | Casual | Expensive | strip | Caesar's | 3500 Las Vegas Blvd. S. | 702-733-7373 | www.boasteak.com | Lunch & Dinner daily

Tao Restaurant   81.5
& Nightclub

In order to appreciate this "big, loud and hip" restaurant, you have to quash any notion of a quality dining experience. But those in the mood for a "fun, high-energy evening" think of it as "a solid place to grab a bite before clubbing." Those who've managed the attitude adjustment say, "I go for the atmosphere, but I've been pleasantly surprised by the decent food." Those who haven't snap, "Awful food in a pretentious atmosphere."

Pan-Asian | Moderate | strip | Venetian | 3355 Las Vegas Blvd. S. | 702-388-8588 | www.taolasvegas.com | Dinner daily

Cheap Eats

RECOMMENDED

Burger Bar   7.2

When celebrity chefs started branching out into beef, Hubert Keller followed suit

– only he opted for the ground form. The range of burgers runs the gamut from *au naturel* to the usual list of toppings to the "Hey, it's Vegas, baby, can you slap a slab of foie gras on?" Reviewers say, "It's just the right thing after a night in the casino" – especially if luck was against you and a burger and beer now suits the budget.

Hamburgers | Inexpensive | strip | Mandalay | 3930 Las Vegas Blvd. S. | 702-632-9364 | www.burgerbar.com | Lunch & Dinner Daily

Phoenix/Scottsdale AZ

HIGHLY RECOMMENDED

Binkley's (35 miles north in Cave Creek)   92.0

Conventional wisdom says you won't be able to find progressive cooking in fly-over country. But Kevin Binkley is doing his best to change that at this restaurant our reviewers deem "one of the only true gourmet dining spots in the Phoenix area." Binkley's background includes a stint at the French Laundry, which overlapped with the time Grant Achatz was there, and his clientele is now benefiting from the contemporary culinary techniques on display in dishes like crispy seared foie gras served with quince, butternut squash, peanuts, cranberries, radish, spicy kaffir lime marshmallows and coconut or root beer–braised short ribs with pumpkin and patty pan squash. Locals waxed poetic: "Fantastic, inventive cuisine" and "classy, elegant, upscale and, most important, wonderful" were among the comments we collected. Though happy overall, one reviewer "wished [Binkley] took more chances with his menu."

New American | Casual | Expensive | cave creek | 6920 E. Cave Creek Rd. | 480-437-1072 | www.binkleysrestaurant.com | Dinner Tue-Sat

RECOMMENDED

Kai (19 miles south in Chandler)   91.8

Those looking to eat local, out-of-the-ordinary ingredients should drive down to the Wild Horse Pass Resort, where Michael O'Dowd serves dishes like a composition of peekytoe crab and sweet leaves with compressed saguaro blossom watermelon; a goat's-meat torta with a chia-seed popover and locally grown Medjool dates; and a grilled tenderloin of buffalo raised by the Cheyenne River Tribe paired with smoked-corn purée and cholla buds. Even the breads are made with grains harvested from a nearby reservation, and the olive oil they use comes from olives raised in groves on the banks of the Gila River. "As delicious as it is unusual," say our reviewers, making it "worth the schlep from the Phoenix/Scottsdale area" just to eat here. Clearly this is "one of the most interesting restaurants in the country."

Southwestern | Casual | Expensive | chandler | Wildhorse Pass Resort | 5594 W. Wildhorse Pass Blvd. | 602-225-0100 | www.wildhorsepassresort.com | Dinner daily

NOCA   91.4

What's a nice Jewish boy from Chicago to do when he tires of the cold weather as well as his job as a stock trader? The answer is obvious; even though he has never been in the food business, he moves to sunny Scottsdale and opens a restaurant based on high-quality ingredients prepared in ways that local diners haven't seen before. That describes Eliot Wexler's establishment, where you can start your meal with a wild fluke crudo with a Champagne gastrique and smoked sea salt, follow it with linguine with crab, crème fraîche and basil, and cap it off with lamb "T-Bones" served with melted leeks, haricots verts and a carrot nage. Reviewers laud the "fantastic food combined with wonderful service" which Wexler offers to diners at a "very reasonable price point" in a "casual atmosphere," making this expatriate's place "a breath of culinary fresh air" for the Phoenix/Scottsdale area.

Modern American | Casual | Moderate | scottsdale | 3118 East Camelback | 602-956-6622 | www.restaurantnoca.com | Dinner daily in season; closed Mon in summer

Mastro's   90.9

Though this nine-restaurant mini-chain of steakhouses is based in the Phoenix area, it attracts its share of national attention due to its Beverly Hills branch one block from Rodeo Drive. This location caters to the same type of glitzy clientele: Expect a dining room filled with women sporting flashy jewelry and toting designer handbags and a parking lot where Bentleys are not a rarity. Note: Non-steak eaters won't find anything inventive here, as the menu is "limited to the standard alternative steakhouse fare like salmon or roast chicken."

Steakhouse | Casual | Expensive | scottsdale | 8852 E.Pinnacle Rd. | 480-941-9700 | www.mastrosrestaurants.com | Dinner daily

Vincent's on Camelback   90.0

Still thought of as a "Valley institution," Vincent Guerithault's restaurant was considered the best in the area once upon a time. Unfortunately, as with most restaurants coming up on a quarter-century in operation, "the menu is a little old school" and "the room can use some updating." But neither of those seems to deter reviewers from enjoying the unique mix of Southwestern and French cuisine found in dishes like a lobster chimichanga with basil beurre blanc and avocado corn salsa or a rack of lamb with spiced pepper jelly. An "exquisite wine list" and "terrific service" add up to "a "quaint and superb" experience.

Southwestern | Casual | Expensive | scottsdale | 3930 E. Camelback Rd. | 602-224-0225 | www.vincentsoncamelback.com | Dinner Mon-Sat

Cowboy Ciao   89.5

The combination of Southwestern and International cuisines that the name of this "Valley standby" references results in dishes like Dungeness crab enchiladas with toasted pepitas and avocado salsa; short rib risotto with asparagus, pecorino Romano and truffle oil; and grilled swordfish with citrus-roasted turnips and beets and a sesame-mint beurre blanc. An "amazing wine list" and "superb service for a casual restaurant" make this an especially good choice for families who are vacationing and for whom a successful evening depends on choosing a restaurant where the menu is "diverse enough to make everyone happy."

Southwestern | Casual | Expensive | scottsdale | 7133 E. Stetson Dr. | 480-946-3111 | www.cowboyciao.com | Lunch & Dinner daily

Latilla Room (34 miles north in Carefree)   89.5

While you can't beat the atmosphere at this elegant resort, the owners of the Boulders haven't had similar success with this "restaurant that keeps trying to reinvent itself." Even with that proviso, reviewers deem it a "high-quality experience" and "a perfect place for a quiet and romantic dinner." Stephen Jones is the latest chef, and on his New American menu you can expect dishes like asparagus soup with tempura squash blossoms and Calico bass with a Nopales black bean fricassee with broiled corn, wild baby arugula and a piquillo pepper purée.

New American | Casual | Expensive | carefree | The Boulders | 34631 N. Tom Darlington Dr. | 480-488-7316 | www.theboulders.com | Dinner daily

Atlas Bistro   89.0

Scottsdale residents looking for a neighborhood restaurant are quick to reserve at this restaurant where $55 gets you a three-course dinner of lobster ravioli with caviar, Caesar salad with a quail egg and an Australian rack of lamb with merguez couscous. The ability to BYO is not only "a major plus," it's made even easier by the fact that the restaurant shares space with the AZ Wine Company, affording those who forgot to bring a bottle a chance to run next door and pick one up before dinner.

New American | Casual | Expensive | scottsdale | 2515 N. scottsdale Rd. | 480-990-2433 | www.azeats.com/atlasbistro | Dinner Tue-Sat

Lon's at the Hermosa   89.0

One reviewer said that this restaurant in the Hermosa Inn "exemplifies everything you'd want people to understand about the Southwest: a mellow setting, rustic beauty and food that is elegant without being overstated or pretentious." But one person's elegance is another person's "safe," evidenced in dishes like roast Jidori chicken with basil mashed potatoes. As a result, reviewers deem this "a great spot for a celebration, but because of the setting, not the food." It's more highly recommended in the spring or fall, when you can dine on the lovely patio.

New American | Casual | Expensive | paradise valley | Hermosa Inn | 5532 N. Palo Cristi Rd. | 602-955-7878 | www.lons.com | Open daily

Donovan's Steak & Chop House   88.0

"One of the best in the Phoenix area" is what reviewers say about this "New York-style steakhouse" that also operates branches in the San Diego area. The list of cuts runs the gamut from filets to rib eyes to strips to porterhouses, while the chops side of the menu includes pork and veal; other options include tuna steak and a rack of lamb. Despite the plethora of beef palaces in the U.S., the good ones always seem to elicit superlatives from their admirers, as in: "Donovan's gets my nod as the best place in the county for this type of meal."

Steakhouse | Casual | Expensive | phoenix | 3101 E. Camelback Rd. | 602-955-3666 | www.donovans-steakhouse.com | Dinner Mon-Sat

Bloom   88.0

One of 13 restaurants operated by Fox Restaurant Concepts, Bloom chooses to focus on contemporary American cuisine: items like raw bigeye tuna with sesame, avocado, citrus and chiles or grilled flank steak with roasted potato, caramelized onion and a blue cheese fondue. They also offer "one of Scottsdale's better upmarket bar scenes," along with a "large, if pricy selection of wines by the glass." Reviewers profess a fondness for the "hip location and décor," adding, "While the cuisine might be predictable, they manage to do a nice job with it."

American | Casual | Moderate | scottsdale | 8877 N. Scottsdale Rd. | 480-922-5666 | www.foxrestaurantconcepts.com | Lunch & Dinner daily

Elements at the Sanctuary on Camelback   88.0

Although it's super-crowded, due to Beau MacMillan's appearance on a popular television cooking show, reviewers are split about the food at this "gorgeous location" with "spectacular views overlooking Paradise Valley." Some of the divide in opinions results from McMillan's approach: Rather than cook the food of the region, he offers the type of upper middle, new American cuisine that can be found throughout the country, like foie gras pudding with vanilla quince compote or pan-roasted chicken with roasted garlic mash and sweet onion pancetta jus. Still, reviewers say, it's worth going to enjoy the "ultra-romantic setting," especially at sunset.

New American | Casual | Expensive | paradise valley | 5700 East McDonald Drive | 480-607-2300 | www.sanctuaryoncamelback.com/content/food.html | Open daily

Wildfish Seafood Grille   88.0

Part of the Eddie V's group, which operates the Roaring Fork restaurants as well as a series of Texas steakhouses, Wildfish is characterized as "a slightly cheaper version of a top fish restaurant." Entrées like swordfish steak frites with grilled mushrooms and truffled French fries and jumbo Georges Bank scallops sautéed with citrus fruit, macadamia nuts and brown butter go for under $30. One reviewer, who reminded us that we are talking about the middle of the desert, praised the "fresh fish in a town that isn't known for great seafood joints."

Seafood | Casual | Expensive | scottsdale | 7135 E. Camelback Rd. #130 | 480-994-4040 | www.eddiev. com | Dinner daily

TOP LOCAL CHOICE

Christopher's   87.5
Restaurant/Crush Lounge

One benefit of moving to a larger space is an expanded menu: Christopher Gross' signature dishes, like red pepper soup and truffle-infused filet mignon, are now joined with creations like a goat cheese and roasted-garlic pizza and a sous vide lobe of foie gras that tilts the scales at a whopping $110. Wider choices aside, however, the quote that's most on point said, "Great on a great night, less so on a bad one. Better when you're more focused on the party than the food."

French | Casual | Expensive | phoenix | 2502 E. Camelback Rd. | 602-522-2344 | http://christophersaz.com | Lunch & Dinner daily

Coup des Tartes   87.5

"Romantic and quaint" and "charming and intimate" are about what we expected to hear about this "cute little restaurant." The menu is filled with French comfort food classics like a three-onion tarte, a Roquefort salad and the house version of chicken Cordon Bleu, coated with panko bread crumbs after being stuffed with ham and Gruyère cheese. You end the meal with "some of "the best desserts in the city." All this, plus "the ability to bring your own wine," caused a reviewer to describe it as "one of the best insider restaurants in Phoenix."

French | Casual | Moderate | phoenix | 4626 N. 16th St. | 602-212-1082 | www.nicetartes. com | Lunch & Dinner Tue-Fri, Sat dinner only

Marcellino 87.5

While the "sophisticated" Italian restaurant prospers in upscale suburbs all over the country, a distinct shortage oddly exists in an area that gives the impression of being one gigantic upscale suburb. Luckily, there's this "elegant" example of the genre (with high prices to match), reviewed as "the perfect place for a romantic evening." Everyone raves about the "delicious pastas," and on weekends you can enjoy your filet con tartufo in a Barolo sauce while being serenaded by live opera singers.

Italian | Casual | Expensive | scottsdale | 7114 E. Stetson Dr. | 480-990-9500 | http://marcellinoristorante.com | Lunch & Dinner daily

Razz's Restaurant & Bar 87.5

The best way to understand Erasmo (Razz) Kamnitzer's cooking is to look at how he categorizes his creations. Dishes like a duck cake with a nopalito cactus sauce and veal sweetbreads en croûte with truffle red wine sauce and rhubarb compote are on something he calls his "Light Meals" menu. It's no wonder reviewers say things like "we sometimes find his sauces too rich!" Razz's fans prefer to spend the evening "sitting at the bar and ordering a chef's tasting menu while watching him do his thing."

Continental | Casual | Moderate | scottsdale | 10315 N. Scottsdale Rd. | 480-905-1308 | www.razzsrestaurant.com | Dinner Tue-Sat

T. Cook's 87.5

The upside: a restaurant called "the most beautiful in the Valley" featuring "upscale food," "fine service" and "a romantic dining room" that makes you feel like you're at a resort on the Mediterranean. The flipside: a generic menu that has little to do with Southwestern cuisine and on which "Neither the ingredients nor the way they're prepared are really outstanding." One thing they excel at is brunch, with one reviewer calling the experience "two hours of heaven."

Southwestern | Casual | Expensive | phoenix | Royal Palms | 5200 E. Camelback Rd. | 602-808-0766 | www.royalpalmshotel.com | Open daily

Tarbell's 87.5

Back in 1994, well before it became fashionable, Mark Tarbell opened this restaurant to serve organic vegetables and sustainable fish. Seventeen years later, Tarbell is still turning out staples like tempura calamari with chili sauce and grilled organic Irish salmon with a molasses-lime glaze and a crispy potato cake. Problem is, reviewers say "The menu is getting boring" and "The upscale comfort food is a bit long in the tooth." Criticisms aside, it's still "one of the busiest restaurants in the Scottsdale area."

New American | Casual | Moderate | scottsdale | 3213 E. Camelback Rd. | 602-955-8100 | www.tarbells.com | Dinner daily

Deseo 87.0

Where else but in Scottsdale could you find a restaurant that offers a dish called Millionaire Tacos, a yuca taco filled with hamachi, ahi tuna and lobster? That, along with dishes like arepas with caviar, is the kind of food Douglas Rodriguez is offering at this Latin-inspired restaurant in the Westin. Unfortunately, reviewers are split on it, some calling it "a very good Spanish restaurant in your typical hotel setting" and others, conversely, saying it's "typical hotel food in a lovely setting."

Latin | Casual | Expensive | scottsdale | Westin Kierland | 6902 E. Greenway Pkwy. | 480-624-1030 | www.kierlandresort.com | Dinner Wed-Sun

Prado 86.5

Another hotel restaurant in the area that attracts mixed reviews (see Deseo, above). In this instance, a change in cuisine from Spanish to Italian (think a pork chop with Tuscan beans and orange-ginger jam) further complicates the situation. "The menu leaves something to be desired" and "small portions for such hefty prices" sum up the comments.

Italian | Casual | Expensive | scottsdale | 4949 E. Lincoln Dr. | 480-627-3004 | www.pradolife.com | Open daily

Rancho Pinot   86.0

Opened in 1993 and a "Valley mainstay" ever since, Rancho Pinot benefits from the time chef Chrysa Robertson has spent working for Nancy Silverton and Mark Peel at Campanile and Terra. Her pedigree shows in rustic dishes like handmade pasta with duck confit, black lentils, leeks and toasted crumbs and a Berkshire pork osso buco braised "posole style" with hominy, cotija cheese and slaw. Reviewers say they like the "simple, well-prepared food" and the "fairly priced wine list," adding that the cuisine's "not super-creative but everything on the menu is good."

Italian | Casual | Expensive | scottsdale | 6208 N. Scottsdale Rd. | 480-367-8030 | www.ranchopinot.com | Lunch & Dinner Mon-Sat

J & G Steakhouse   85.5

Jean-Georges Vongerichten's steakhouse atop the Phoenician Hotel seems to possess a number of problems that typically plague restaurants run by absentee chefs. "The staff is clueless," "food unworthy of Jean-Georges' name" and "fantastic views but the food doesn't hold up – there are better in Phoenix" are typical of the comments we collected. In its favor are a setting so lovely it remains "one of the top places in town to celebrate a special event."

Steakhouse | Casual | Expensive | scottsdale | 6000 E. Camelback Rd. | 480-214-8000 | www. jgseakhousescottsdale.com | Dinner daily

Los Sombreros   85.0

Upscale Mexican restaurants in upscale suburban neighborhoods are always problematic. Some reviewers love them ("The marinated pork is to die for, as are the margaritas. We drive up from Tucson just to eat here"), while others hate them, usually on authenticity grounds ("The guacamole and margaritas are good, but the rest of the food is sub-par"). The lack of consensus doesn't hinder the popularity of this place, however, and a no-reservation policy means you should "expect to wait for a table."

Mexican | Casual | Moderate | scottsdale | 2534 N. Scottsdale Rd. | 480-994-1799 | www.lossombreros.com | Dinner daily

Roaring Fork   85.0

This is one of four Roaring Forks operated by the Eddie V group. It's best described as an "upscale chain" where everybody seems to start their meals with a kettle of Hatch green chili and follow with dishes like panfried trout with brown butter or a bacon-wrapped pork tenderloin with Mexican street corn and cheese grits. Perfect for families on vacation who like to take advantage of the "fun atmosphere" and a "great location in the heart of Scottsdale."

Southwestern | Casual | Moderate | scottsdale | 4800 N. Scottsdale Rd. | 480-947-0795 | www. roaringfork.com | Dinner daily

OTHER RESTAURANTS MENTIONED

Different Pointe of View   82.0

While one would hope that the name refers to the restaurant's perspective about cuisine, the extra e at the end of the word "pointe" means that they are talking about the panorama, not the food. Not surprisingly, reviewers say things like, "The view is great, but the food is touristy and I don't plan on returning," although a few feel "it's worth going just for the view and wine list." Hey, it's in a Hilton, so what do you expect?

New American | Casual | Expensive | phoenix | Tapatio Cliffs | 11111 North 7th St. | 602-866-6350 | www.differentpointeofview.com | Dinner Tue-Sat

Cheap Eats

Pizzeria Bianco   8.3

Ask any of the top pizza makers around the country whose pies they admire the most, and odds are they will put Pizzeria Bianco near the top of their list. The back story is simple: Bronx native Chris Bianco and his girlfriend, Susan Pool, opened this restaurant in 1994, based on the principle of using only the highest-quality ingredients: Sicilian oregano, San Marzano tomatoes, organic flour, purified water and mozzarella. The results are "flawlessly executed" versions of "some of the best Neapolitan-style pizza any-where," topped with "incredible organic ingredients," many of which are made in-house. Unfortunately, an excess of quality can lead to excessive popular-ity, especially when a place seats only 42. Fortunately, they just extended their hours (they now serve continuously from 11 a.m. to 10 p.m.), which should ease the waiting times considerably.

Pizzeria | Moderate | phoenix | 623 E. Adams St. | 602-258-8300 | www.pizzeriabianco.com | Lunch & Dinner Tue-Sat

Santa Fe NM

Geronimo   90.5

The dichotomy between what natives prefer and what visitors expect from the Santa Fe dining scene can be found at this restaurant set in an adobe home built in 1756 and wedged between the art galleries that populate Canyon Road. Locals are happy having a New American eatery that approximates the type of dining experience you can find in other cities, while travelers say they're disappointed that the cooking isn't representa-tive of the Southwest. The comments that result range from "Here is the best of Santa Fe, creative cooking with a good variety of dishes" to "While I really wanted to like the food at what is the most comfortable spot in Santa Fe, it was just boring."

New American | Casual | Expensive | 724 Canyon Rd. | 505-982-1500 | www.geronimorestaurant.com | Dinner daily

Restaurant Martín   90.4

Before he opened this restaurant, Mexican-born Martín Rios built his reputation as Santa Fe's best chef during stints at the Inn at Anasazi and Geronimo. At lunch Rios gives a nod to Southwestern cuisine with an apple-smoked beef tenderloin enchilada served with house-made green and guajillo chiles, while the evening menu is dominated by New American dishes like Maple Leaf Farm duck breast in an almond golden-raisin purée with turnips, fingerlings and Venezuelan chocolate-pepper jus. Rios's fans rave: "I think this is the best restaurant in Santa Fe. The food is always well presented and deli-cious, the service is great, and they offer wonderful patio seating in the summer."

New American | Casual | Moderate | 526 Galisteo St. | 505-820-0919 | www.restaurantmartinsantafe.com | Lunch & Dinner Sun-Fri, Sat dinner only

Café Pasqual's   88.0

No other restaurant signifies the Santa Fe dining experience as well as this simple corn-er café in the heart of downtown. The menu has everything you ever dreamed of eating in this city: Breakfast brings dishes like chile relleno con huevos topped with Anaheim chiles and jack cheese, while you might enjoy chicken mole enchiladas at lunch, or a fat burrito filled with pork loin adovada, guajillo chile and cilantro rice for dinner. Fame does have its price: "It's horribly crowded" and "always jammed with tourists," resulting in "cooking that can get sloppy at times." Still, Pasqual's is such an institution that many reviewers say, "I can't imagine visiting Santa Fe without having at least one meal there."

Southwestern | Moderate | 121 Don Gaspar Ave. | 505-983-9340 | www.pasquals.com | Open daily

Compound Restaurant   88.0

There was a time when this restaurant was considered "the undisputed leader in the city," but reviewers say those days are gone and they are now "coasting on vapors." Mark Kiffin is yet one more local chef who shuns the cuisine of the region in favor of New American fare, like potato latkes with house-cured salmon gravlax or buttermilk roast chicken with creamed spinach and foie gras pan gravy. Of course, it has its fair share of fans, who say things like, "When Kiffen is on it's still one of the top three restaurants in Santa Fe."

New American | Casual | Expensive | 653 Canyon Rd. | 505-982-4353 | www.compoundrestaurant.com | Lunch & Dinner Mon-Sat, Sun dinner only

Coyote Café   88.0

This local institution rose to national attention when Mark Miller was doing the cooking. It's now run by Eric DeStefano and the Geronimo (see above) team, who increased the restaurant's capacity by adding an upper deck to the space. The menu leans a bit more a toward contempoary American style than it did during Miller's tenure; dishes like New Mexican sweet corn soup with black truffles and fresh thyme or Tellicherry pepper elk tenderloin with roasted-garlic smashed potatoes are typical. "Not quite as good as it was in its heyday, but still very good," sums up our reviewers' sentiment.

Southwestern | Casual | Expensive | 132 W. Water St. | 505-983-1615 | www.coyotecafe.com | Dinner daily

Santacafé   88.0

With a menu split between dishes like a roasted poblano relleno with three-mushroom quinoa and chipotle cream or grilled New Zealand rack of lamb with rosemary risotto, this restaurant, "popular with an older crowd of diners," has one foot in the Southwest and the other in the rest of America. Reviewers describe the food as "solid, with a few misses," while praising "a fairly priced wine list" and "one of the nicest patios" in the city. It's set in a building that dates back to the 19th century.

New American | Casual | Expensive | 231 Washington Ave. | 505-984-1788 | www.santacafe.com | Lunch & Dinner daily

ACCEPTABLE

The Shed   87.0

While they advertise themselves as serving "creative cuisine," this "Santa Fe institution" dating from 1953 (in a building that dates from 1692) serves a standard list of Southwestern dishes like quesadillas, enchiladas, and green chile stew. Problem is, the place is so large and popular (you will likely wait 45 minutes for a table) that "the kitchen is turning out too many orders to put any thought into the food." That, and a dining room filled with gringos who can't hack spices, means the kitchen uses "a light hand on the seasoning."

Southwestern | Moderate |
113 1/2 E. Palace Ave. | 505-982-9030 |
www.sfshed.com | Lunch & Dinner Mon-Sat

Inn of the Anasazi   86.0

Heralded when Martín Rios was at the helm, this dining room at "one of the loveliest locations in Santa Fe" seems to have encountered a speed bump. Oliver Ridgeway has been trying to get things back on track with dishes like wine and chile-braised short ribs with pepper jack grits. But with comments like "The food is unevenly prepared" and "The service can be amateurish," it seems the restaurant has a ways to go before returning to prior levels of excellence.

Southwestern | Casual | Expensive | Inn of the Anasazi | 113 Washington Ave. | 505-988-3236 |
www.innoftheanasazi.com | Open daily

OTHER RESTAURANTS MENTIONED

La Casa Sena   83.0

The "best wine list in town" and a "patio that is lovely in summer" can't overcome food described as "either dull or ridiculous." A few moderates said, "I have had some good meals here, and I have had some badly cooked dishes here. You take your chances." But the comment that sums up the prevailing sentiment was "In short, it's pleasant for the clueless, but gastronomes need not apply."

Southwestern | Casual | Moderate |
Sena Plaza, 125 E. Palace Ave. | 505-988-9232 |
www.lacasasena.com | Lunch & Dinner daily

Cheap Eats

RECOMMENDED

Bobcat Bite   7.3

You will find a long line of people waiting for a table at what some would argue is "the best lunch spot in Santa Fe." What they're after are hamburgers that weigh in at a whopping 10 ounces and that are often topped with Jack cheese and green chiles. There are a handful of other items – grilled cheese, chicken or ham sandwiches – but the reason everyone is willing to "drive out to the middle of nowhere" (technically, five miles out of town) is the "big and juicy" hamburgers.

Hamburgers | Inexpensive | 418 Old Las Vegas Hwy. | 505-983-5319 | www.bobcatbite.com |
Lunch & Dinner Tue-Sun

Harry's Roadhouse   7.3

While Café Pasqual gets all the press, many reviewers say this is where you'll find the top breakfast in Santa Fe. You start with "possibly the best cinnamon rolls ever" and continue with offerings like mushroom tacos (eggs scrambled with oyster, chanterelle and shiitake mushrooms, with Oaxacan cheese and a tomatillo-chipotle salsa). Lunch brings burgers and a slew of sandwiches, while dinnertime might mean turkey meatloaf or a New York strip steak. Reviewers described it as a "delicious, crowded, upscale café" with "desserts worth bringing a new belt for."

Southwestern | Moderate | 96 B Old Las Vegas Hwy. | 505-989-4629 | Open daily

Tucson AZ

RECOMMENDED

Primo   91.4

While they spend May through December at their restaurant in Rockland, Maine, during the winter months, chef/partners Melissa Kelly and Price Kushner offer Tucson residents their bounty at this J.W. Marriott resort. Having originally made their name in the

Berkshires at the now-defunct Chatham Sheepherding Company, Kelly and Kushner turned their back on the New American cuisine that brought them fame, and direct their efforts towards the Italian table instead. A stickler when it comes to using local produce, Kelly will serve you pansotti, pot-bellied ravioli stuffed with herbs, kale, pancetta, ricotta and egg yolk or a pork saltimbocca on a bed of roast garlic mashed potatoes with a mushroom Madeira jus.

Italian | Casual | Expensive | JW Marriott Resort | 3800 W. Starr Pass Blvd.. | 520-791-6071 | http://primo.jwmarriottstarpass.com | Dinner Tues-Sun

TOP LOCAL CHOICE

Arizona Inn   89.5

Step into 1930s Tucson at this "charming resort" that the Greenway family has been running since the beginning. While "The menu plays it safe," reviewers say the kitchen does a good job with things like a quesadilla of duck confit and poblano cream or Colorado lamb chops with garlic mashed potatoes and a morel mushroom sauce. Reviewers were just as enthusiastic about breakfast and brunch, when you can tour the "gorgeous grounds" before your meal. "Good food with service to match" in a "one-of-a-kind atmosphere" sum up the scene.

American | Formal | Expensive | 2200 E. Elm St. | 520-325-1541 | www.arizonainn.com | Open daily

Café Poca Cosa   88.5

Kudos to Suzana Davila. Her upscale Mexican cuisine didn't attract a single comment about inauthenticity. Whether it's chicken in a chile, chocolate and wine sauce, the tamale pie of the day, or mesquite carne asada with a tomato-chipotle sauce, reviewers were quick to applaud Davila's "terrific, inventive" dishes. One reviewer offered the ultimate in praise: "In a region where you can throw a stone in any direction and hit a Mexican restaurant, it's hard to find ones that stand out. Yet Café Poca Cosa does."

Mexican | Casual | Moderate | 110 East Pennington St. | 520-622-6400 | www.cafepocacosatucson.com | Lunch & Dinner Tue-Sat

Vail CO

RECOMMENDED

Wildflower   90.1

Paul Wade's menu at this "lovely space" in the Lodge at Vail comes in two parts. First, there's what he calls Cuisine in Balance (no gluten, no lactose, no hormones), featuring dishes like thyme-basted sea trout with fennel pollen, Niçoise vegetables and tomato jam. Then there's what he calls American Alpine Cuisine (heritage, local, authentic, inspired), which features hearty dishes like roast Berkshire pork shoulder with sourgum-plum mustard, winter greens and whole wheat gnocchi. Wildflower is "relaxed and elegant," reviewers say, citing "ambitious cuisine for a ski resort." "An amazing wine list" results in a meal that's "expensive but worth it."

New American | Casual | Expensive | 174 E. Gore Creek Dr. | 970-476-5011 | http://lodgeatvail.rockresorts. com | Dinner Tue-Sat during season

TOP LOCAL CHOICE

Larkspur Restaurant & Bar   88.0

Looking for some golden osetra or a 20-oz. Wagyu steak? You can find them both at this "wonderful ski country restaurant" where "awesome views" accompany the "rustic cuisine." Those not in the mood for luxury ingredients can dig into creations like spot prawns with Anson Mills grits, Walla Walla onions, porcini mushrooms, Spanish chorizo and a shellfish broth or a grilled pork chop with apple purée, spaetzle, chanterelles and mustard jus. Since it gets jammed in the evening, a few reviewers prefer it during the day, calling it "the best option for a slope-side lunch."

New American | Casual | Expensive | 458 Vail Valley Dr. | 970-754-8050 | www.larkspurvail.com | Dinner daily

Sweet Basil   88.0

The cuisine – crispy pork and pistachio terrine with apple and plum mostarda, and seared yellowfin tuna with a chili-glazed lobster spring roll and honshimeji mushrooms – is what you expect to find in an upscale resort town: "good but not distinguished." Still, it's "highly worthwhile in the context of Vail dining," and we have reviewers who say "I've gone here every year for the past 20 years and always enjoyed myself." One fan even went so far as to declare, "When I die and go to heaven I'd like this to be my local restaurant."

New American | Casual | Expensive | 193 E. Gore Creek Dr. | 970-476-0125 | www.sweetbasil-vail.com | Lunch & Dinner daily

Los Angeles, Southern California & Hawaii

Honolulu & the Other Islands HI

Mama's Fish House (MAUI)   93.4

With 100% of reviewer comments mentioning either the "spectacular views," the "casual island atmosphere" or the "exquisite setting right on the water," we suspect that the non-culinary aspects of this iconic Maui seafood house, dating from 1973, play a big role in its high rating. Yet surprisingly, given the touristy location, the cooking comes in for its share of praise, including "the best and freshest fish on the island," "the epitome of island cuisine" and "preparations that are old school but surprisingly well-done" (cases in point: the papaya and watercress bisque and the macadamia nut-crusted mahi mahi with a tropical fruit salad). The experience also includes "fast and efficient service" when compared to the area's usual standard. Even so, the island context weighed heavily with most reviewers. Maybe this person, who gave the restaurant a very strong recommendation, summed it up best: "On Maui, it is certainly an important destination. On the mainland . . . not so much."

Seafood | Casual | Expensive | paia | Mama's Fish House Restaurant & Inn | 799 Poho Place | 808-579-8488 | www.mamasfishhouse.com | Lunch & Dinner daily

Chef Mavro   92.9

If you're looking to eat luxurious ingredients – say, truffles in season or a half dozen types of caviar or Wagyu beef prepared by a chef with good French chops after you ride that last wave of the day on Waikiki, George Mavrothalassitis' restaurant is the place for you. Every reviewer gave it a rating of Recommended or higher. The experience was described as "food executed to perfection . . . everything is fresh and local whenever possible," and one reviewer said, "Chef Mavro understands what makes Franco-Hawaiian haute fusion fare tick." The only real criticism focused on the "the limited food and wine choices" (the menu is arranged in three-, four- and six-course prix fixes). Diners are "strongly encouraged to select the wine pairings that have been selected for each menu."

French | Casual | Expensive | honolulu | 1969 S. King St. | 808-944-4714 | www.chefmavro.com | Dinner Tue-Sat

Alan Wong's   91.7

With its focus on the flavors of the Pacific Rim and a reliance on local ingredients, Alan Wong's cooking is a perfect fit for Honolulu's population with its multicultural heritage. Wong serves a number of signature dishes, and for most of the restaurant's 15 years, offerings like Poki-Pines (crispy wonton ahi poke balls on avocado with wasabi sauce) and Da Bag (clams, Kalua pig and shiitake mushrooms steamed in a foil bag) have resulted in reviews that described the "wonderfully inventive fare" at a restaurant that is "upscale yet down to earth." But the latest comments from our panelists were mixed, maybe reflecting Wong's recent surge in popularity: Critics cite "average food for a high-end restaurant" and a "dining room staff that doesn't have the polish it once had."

Hawaiin | Casual | Expensive | honolulu | 1857 S. King St. | 808-949-2526 | www.alanwongs.com | Dinner daily

Nobu Waikiki   90.9

We are so tired of singing Nobu's praises that we thought we would let this reviewer do it for us instead: "Yes, there are Nobu locations across the world. But this is what happens when a restaurant with the faculty to deliver top-notch Japanese cuisine meets a world-class seafood delivery system (aka the Pacific) head-on. This is one of the best meals you can find (on the island). From cold appetizers (the new-style sashimi) to hot entrées to the sushi itself, it's all delicious and beautifully prepared." If that wasn't good enough for you, how about "Great use of local products with Nobu style. Seasonal ingredients are featured in both the hot kitchen as well as sushi bar."

Japanese | Casual | Expensive | honolulu | Waikiki Parc Hotel | 2233 Helumoa Rd | 808-237-6999 | http://noburestaurants.com | Dinner daily

Roy's   90.6

While the franchised versions of his restaurants are not well thought of, Roy Yamaguchi's original Hawaii Kai location attracts comments like "a classic that sets the standard for all Hawaiian restaurants." Known as one of the first chefs to serve Hawaiian-fusion cuisine, Yamaguchi made his name with dishes like the Canoe for Two appetizer, which, depending on the day, can include shrimp sticks, Szechuan baby-back ribs, island ahi poke, pork and shrimp lumpia, edamame and crisped seafood pot stickers. Mains include roasted macadamia nut mahi mahi with a lobster butter sauce. The room gets "crowded and noisy," however, and some reviewers complained about the scene being "touristy."

Hawaiian | Casual | Expensive | honolulu | 6600 Kalanianaole Hwy. | 808-396-7697 | www.roysrestaurant.com | Dinner daily

La Mer   90.2

Looking to show off your tan after spending a long day on the beach? Put on a crisp white shirt and grab a sport coat and you will fit in perfectly at this elegant restaurant. The French seafood cuisine includes medallions of Big Island lobster with a carpaccio of yellow beets and a warm lobster soup, and Chilean sea bass and Kurobuta pork belly atop Alsatian choucroute. The "formal service" is a signature aspect of the experience, and diners are advised to "get there early" in order to secure a table on the terrace, which offers "lovely views of Waikiki."

French | Casual | Expensive | honolulu | Halekulani Hotel | 2199 Kalia Rd. | 808-923-2311 | www.halekulani.com | Dinner daily

TOP LOCAL CHOICE

The Lodge at Koele Dining Room (LANAI)   89.5

Hidden beneath this resort's rustic name is a Four Seasons hotel, which means the quality of the food here is similar to what you typically find at an upscale hotel chain. With one difference: "This is the island of Lanai, and since you are a captive audience, they don't seem compelled to try very hard." The result is that "good service and ambience" accompanies "well-done but typical Hawaiian resort hotel fare." But with only a handful of choices at your disposal, it's easily "the best you can do in Lanai City."

New American | Casual | Expensive | lanai city | Four Seasons Resort Lanai | 1 Keomoku Highway | 808-565-4580 | www.fourseasons.com/koele | Dinner Fri-Tue

Merriman's (BIG ISLAND) 89.5

With cattle grazing on its lush slopes, produce nourished on rich volcanic soil and the Pacific's catch only a rod and reel away, Peter Merriman provides much for locavores to revel in. The best that Hawaii has to offer turns up in dishes like gnocchi made with Hirabara Swiss chard, Hamakua mushrooms, macadamia nut pesto and Big Island goat cheese or butter-poached Kona lobster stuffed with kabocha pumpkin and sweet corn. Given Merriman's commitment to local and sustainable cuisine, it's fitting that someone described his restaurant as "the Chez Panisse of the Big Island, and perhaps Hawaii."

New American | Casual | Expensive | kamuela | 65-1227 Opelo Road | 808-885-6822 | www.merrimansha-waii.com | Lunch & Dinner daily

ACCEPTABLE

Lahaina Grill (MAUI) 87.5

Looking to escape what passes for island cuisine at most Maui restaurants, characterized by one reviewer as "fruit salsa over fish"? Then head to this 17-year veteran that offers pumpkin seed-crusted blue crab cake and Kona coffee-roasted Mountain Meadows rack of lamb in a coffee-cabernet demi-glace. The food provoked comments ranging from "one of the three best restaurants on the island" to "ruined by over-saucing and a heavy hand in the kitchen."

New American | Casual | Expensive | lahaina | 127 Lahainaluna Road | 808-667-5117 | www.lahainagrill.com | Dinner daily

Hoku's 86.0

Built in the 1960s, the Kahala is a classic resort/luxury destination. Which means that it's not surprising that the featured restaurant offers "acceptable hotel fare tarted up a bit." The cuisine is in the island tradition: sushi and sashimi based on local fish, foie gras with Asian pear and Kurobuta pork loin with apple miso and kabocha risotto. Your meal comes with a "nice wine list" and the obligatory "spectacular views."

Hawaiian | Casual | Expensive | honolulu | Kahala Hotel & Resort | 5000 Kahala Ave. | 808-739-8760 | www.kahalaresort.com | Dinner daily

Los Angeles CA

WORTH PLANNING A TRIP AROUND

Urasawa 99.3

This restaurant has a long and distinguished heritage. Eight years ago it was known as Ginza Sushi-ko, and aficionados considered this the best example of Japanese cuisine in America. Then Thomas Keller convinced its chef-owner, Masa Takayama, to follow him to New York (today the restaurant Masa sits next door to Keller's Per Se in the Time Warner Center), creating an opportunity for a long-term Ginza Sushi-ko sous-chef, the "Zen-like" Hiroyuki Urasawa, to assume command in L.A. After purchasing the unassuming restaurant on the second floor of a Rodeo Drive office building from his former employer and changing the name, Urasawa turned what many of our reviewers feel what was once the best Japanese restaurant in the country into the best restaurant in the country, period.

Reserving a stool at the nine-seat counter is the best way to watch Hiro work his magic, which begins with eight or nine Kyoto-style specialties, including delicacies like toro tartaree with caviar, a ball of homemade tofu topped with gold leaf, foie gras cooked shabu-shabu style and Kobe beef that you cook on a small hibachi grill. It's at that point in the meal that Hiro really gets to work, serving 15 different cuts of sushi before the grand finale, in which live langoustines flop around the chef's counter until he turns them into your dinner (talk about fresh!). Eating with this gracious host is an intimate experience, and you will end up spending most of your evening, and the better part of your paycheck, enjoying what one reviewer called "the ultimate omakase at the ultimate price."

Japanese | Casual | Very Expensive | beverly hills | 218 N. Rodeo Dr. | 310-247-8939 | Dinner Tue-Sat

AN IMPORTANT DESTINATION

Providence   96.0

When he was cooking at the Water Grill in downtown Los Angeles, Michael Ciramusti conquered his first challenge – creating a seafood restaurant worthy of national recognition. But he moved on to bigger fish when he decided to open his own place in the space vacated by Patina in its transfer to the Disney Center. A fanatic about high-quality ingredients, Ciramusti installed a special cold room in his kitchen so that his fish can be butchered at a perfect temperature. The attention to detail appears to have paid off, as many of our reviewers feel that Ciramusti serves the best New American seafood in the country.

Some of the creations are truly inspired: his Dungeness crab with sweet peas, crispy soba and sriracha mayonnaise; his signature Santa Barbara sea urchin served in a farm egg filled with a Champagne beurre blanc; his dayboat halibut from Sitka, Alaska, served with burdock, shiso and lemon. Non-fish eaters will find that Ciramusti handles dishes like foie gras ravioli or roast tenderloin of veal with chanterelles and shimeji mushrooms with the same level of skill and aplomb. Partner Donato Poto, a veteran of numerous top L.A. restaurants (including Bastide in its heyday), does an equally good job of managing the front of the house.

Seafood | Casual | Expensive | hollywood | 5955 Melrose Ave. | 323-460-4170 | www.providencela.com | Lunch & Dinner Mon-Fri Sat-Sun dinner only

Spago   95.5

When this restaurant first opened, dishes like the signature smoked salmon pizza and pepper-crusted flash-seared tuna caused a sensation. That era is long over (though the pizza is still available at lunch), but Lee Hefter deserves credit for maintaining food at a high level of quality at what is still Wolfgang Puck's flagship – in fact, on many days you will find Puck working the room. And though the restaurant is set up to cater to "season ticket holders" like Julia Roberts and Diana Ross, comments such as "Wolfgang visited our table, and he was more than happy to engage in a lengthy conversation about the food" were typical.

The menu is a mix of classic New American fare, like a layer cake of roast Chino Farms beets with goat cheese and hazelnuts or agnelotti with peas and mascarpone, along with Asian-inspired creations such as "Hong Kong"–style Virginia striped bass and contemporary takes on European classics like spicy beef goulash. The wine list is "over-the-top loaded" with some of the greatest bottles ever, and it's still the best restaurant in the country for celebrity spotting. As with other places that cater to VIPs, we got a number of complaints that "mere mortals don't eat as well as the famous people do."

Californian | Formal | Very Expensive | beverly hills | 176 N. Cañon Dr. | 310-385-0880 | www.wolfgang-puck.com | Lunch & Dinner Mon-Sat, Sun dinner only

Nishimura   94.7

Firmly ensconced near the top of the second tier of Los Angeles Japanese restaurants, Hiro Nishimura's venue offers fish lovers the opportunity to experience a level of quality that is somewhere between what you will find at a temple like Urasawa and some of the city's other better-known sushi haunts. Frequented by a steady stream of Angelenos and Japanese expats, Nishimura maintains a focus on pristine fish, especially mounds of glistening sashimi, some of which is dressed in a light sauce. Modern flourishes turn up as well, like a popular starter of oysters topped with uni or grilled eggplant stuffed with shrimp and avocado. The spare decor is part of the experience and, along with the pricey fare, led one of our reviewers to say, "Everything is minimalist except the bill."

Japanese | Casual | Expensive | beverly hills | 8684 Melrose Ave. | 310-659-4770 | Lunch & Dinner Mon-Fri Sat dinner only

Matsuhisa   94.4

Nobu Matsuhisa has moved what was his very first restaurant into the space that used to house L'Orangerie. But while the new dining room is larger and the setting more luxurious, the famous cuisine hasn't changed, and all of his renowned dishes are on hand, from yellowtail with jalapeño, crab in a spicy, creamy sauce and squid that is cut to make it look like pasta and served with a garlic sauce. Mains might be donburi or udon, or you can opt for a more ambitious offering like halibut cheeks teriyaki or lobster sautéed with black pepper sauce. As with most of the top Japanese restaurants in our guide, "the real action is in the omakase room," where one luxury ingredient after another is doled out in an attempt to eat away at the bank accounts of compliant Hollywood types and Japanese businessmen who occupy the stools at the counter.

Japanese | Casual | Expensive | beverly hills | 129 N. La Cienega Blvd. | 310-659-9639 | www.nobumat-suhisa.com | Lunch & Dinner Mon-Sat, Sun dinner only

Cut   94.0

It's "all Kobe all the time" at this steakhouse in the Beverly Wilshire Hotel run by none other than Wolfgang Puck. There is Wagyu raised in Australia, or you can stick with domestic Wagyu from Snake River Farms in Idaho. Not in the mood to splurge? Well, you can ask them to grill up some ordinary, corn-fed, domestically raised prime beef, which comes in 21- or 35-day aged versions. Non-steak lovers can opt for Kurobuta pork chops, Kobe short ribs or a turbot flown in from the North Sea. There are a myriad of sides and sauces to go with the meats, and "the beautiful Richard Meier–designed dining room" provides the backdrop for a scene that could exist only in Beverly Hills.

Steakhouse | Casual | Expensive | beverly hills | Beverly Wilshire Hotel | 9500 Wilshire Blvd. | 310-275-5200 | www. wolfgangpuck.com | Dinner Mon-Sat

Patina   94.0

There was a time when Patina was a destination for serious foodies. It was located in a simple, whitewashed dining room on Melrose Avenue, and Joachim Splichal's Modern European cuisine captured imaginations. Enter corporate investors who purchased everything that Splichal had his name on and moved the restaurant to the Frank Gehry–designed Walt Disney Concert Hall. In its new location, Patina still attracts a number of

L.A. residents who have a long-term relationship with the restaurant, but now it's "more about catering to symphony-goers, businessmen and tourists" looking for a high-quality meal downtown. Executive chef Tony Esnault 's menu stays on the classic side of contemporary French cuisine, with offerings like bone-in turbot with leeks and a roast loin of Colorado lamb with a chive and goat cheese flan.

French | Formal | Expensive | downtown | Walt Disney Concert Hall | 141 S. Grand Ave. | 213-972-3331 | www.patinagroup.com | Dinner daily

Asanebo   93.8

While some of the best-known Japanese restaurants in the city are found on the stretch of Ventura Boulevard from Studio City to Sherman Oaks (affectionately known as "the sushi trail"), Asanebo is the one our reviewers claim is the best along that strip. The cuisine reflects both the classic style, with pristine cuts of fish covering compact mounds of highly polished rice, and more progressive preparations like chopped eel molded with rice and topped with sweet anago sauce or cooked dishes like steamed skate wings. In addition to the delicious food, they are known for "making you feel at home," an extra benefit given the reputation for gruffness that others on the sushi trail have earned.

Japanese | Casual | Expensive | studio city | 11941 Ventura Blvd. | 818-760-3348 | Lunch & Dinner Tue-Fri, Sat-Sun dinner only

Mori Sushi   93.8

Few chefs are as dedicated to their craft as Morihiro Onodera. Not only does he visit the Japanese market each morning to obtain the highest-quality fish, he grows and mills his own rice and even fabricates the ceramic plates and bowls he uses at the restaurant. With a pleasant personality and a good command of the English language, Mori opened this restaurant 10 years ago, after working for masters like Nobu and Yasuda in New York City. Take a seat at his counter and your feast will begin with freshly made tofu that's nearly as creamy as ice cream, followed by an array of the best of the Japanese fish market. The mostly glowing comments included "creative treatments and an excellent staff," "sublime, authentic experience" and "This is where many of the city's top chefs like to eat sushi on their days off."

Japanese | Casual | Expensive | west l.a. | 11500 W. Pico Blvd. | 310-479-3939 | www.morisushi.org | Lunch & Dinner Mon-Fri Sat dinner only

Saam – The Chef's Tasting Room   93.7

What do you do after opening two tapas restaurants, a patisserie and one of L.A.'s liveliest bars, and still have a chunk of interior space left over in one of the most attractive spots in the city? Well, if you're José Andrés, you reach across the country into your bag of tricks and open a variation of your popular Minibar in Washington, D.C., the restaurant that drives your brand. Thursday through Saturday, Andrés serves diners a 22-course, prix-fixe extravaganza that includes dishes like olive oil bon bon, bagel and lox steam bun, hot-and-cold foie soup with corn and Not Your Everyday Caprese. The avalanche of inventive fare, which costs a surprisingly low $120, inspires comments like "an adventure in small plates molecular cooking" and "the most innovative and playful cuisine in L.A.; out of 22 courses, maybe two weren't exciting."

Progressive | Casual | Expensive | west hollywood | SLS Hotel | 465 S. La Cienega Blvd. | 310-246-5545 | www.thebazaar.com | Dinner Thu-Sun

Sushi Zo   93.7

Take a seat at the counter of this nondescript storefront in a strip mall wedged between Beverly Hills and Culver City, and Keizo Seki will dazzle you with 24 different cuts of fish, including a number of varieties that you probably have never seen before. Seki is a purist, and if you dare to ask him for a specialty roll or some other type of concoction served at more Americanized sushi restaurants, he will respond by barking, "We don't serve junk here." Our reviewers clearly seem to agree with Seki's boast, telling us that "This tiny omakase-only restaurant serves some of the best and freshest fish I ever tasted." But there are downsides. Besides the lackluster ambience (one reviewer compared it to eating in a Subway), the beer list is limited, and there's a no-BYO policy.

Japanese | Informal | Expensive | palms | 9824 National Blvd. | 310-842-3977 | Lunch & Dinner Mon-Fri Sat dinner only

Totoraku (Super Secret Beef Place)   93.4

Though the sign outside says nothing more than Teriyaki House, teriyaki is the last thing you will find here, and we are confident that this is "one of the most unusual restaurants you will ever visit." The phone number is unlisted, and Kaz, the owner, won't give you a reservation without an introduction from an existing customer. There is only one thing on the menu: beef omakase (not Kobe, but the highest level of domestic prime), which includes various servings of raw beef, including carpaccio and tartare and an unusual carpaccio of liver, followed by an assortment of cuts that you grill over a hibachi. A committed wine-lover, Kaz has decorated the shelves of what is one of L.A.'s most unique BYOBs with empty bottles of some of the greatest wines ever made.

Japanese | Informal | Expensive | west l.a. | 310-838-9881 | Dinner Wed-Sat

The Bazaar   93.1

Imagine a restaurant that serves a myriad of types of small plates, ranging from traditional tapas to molecular gastronomic creations, located in a trendy hotel where hundreds of people are creating a scene. That's the best way we know to describe this unusual restaurant in the SLS Hotel, where the combination of "the food, the space, the people is unlike anything you've seen in L.A. or likely anywhere else." What's amazing is that in spite of the scene, nearly everyone likes the food, especially the more unusual takes on tapas, like foie gras cotton candy or miso linguini with smoked trout roe, tomato, lemon and chervil. José Andrés also operates a patisserie on the premises that offers a similar, unusual mix of traditional and modern confections and pastries.

Spanish | Casual | Expensive | beverly hills | SLS Hotel | 465 S. La Cienega Blvd. | 310-246-5555 | www.thebazaar.com | Dinner daily

Il Grano   93.0

It's fitting that in sushi-crazed Los Angeles, the top Italian restaurant specializes in crudo. Each morning chef/owner Sal Marino visits the Japanese market, where he competes with the city's top sushi chefs for slabs of fish that end up in preparations like sea scallops with a citrus glaze, hamachi in a tonno sauce or fluke wrapped around pickled asparagus. Marino is also an avid student of contemporary Italian culinary technique, and "a modern edge to the cuisine" shows up in creations like squid ink spaghetti with a creamy sea urchin sauce or risotto with shrimp from Santa Barbara and English pea foam. The restaurant is at its peak in late summer, as Sal grows more than 40 different types of heirloom tomatoes that he turns into an all-tomato tasting menu.

Italian | Casual | Expensive | west l.a. | 11359 Santa Monica Blvd | 310-477-7886 | www.ilgrano.com | Lunch & Dinner Mon-Fri Sat dinner only

Osteria Mozza   93.0

How can you go wrong with a restaurant where Nancy Silverton prepares your food behind something called a Mozzarella Bar? The concept is such a no-brainer that we're surprised no one thought of it before. Besides cheesy preparations that are one more delicious than the next, there are antipasti like grilled octopus with potato or crispy pig trotters with cicoria, pastas like a classic orecchiette with Swiss chard and sausage, and more ambitious presentations like calf's brain ravioli. Given that Mario Batali and Joe Bastianich are partners in the restaurant, it makes sense that "the mains bear a slight resemblance to the fare at Lupa in New York City" and that the wine list is "chock-full of the types of unusual bottles" Bastianich specializes in importing from Italy.

Italian | Casual | Moderate | hollywood | 6602 Melrose Ave. | 323-297-0100 | www.mozza-la.com | Dinner daily

Lucques   92.8

Every major U.S. city seems to have a restaurant that is compared to Chez Panisse, and our reviewers have nominated Lucques for that honor in Los Angeles. Opinions of Suzanne Goin's market-based cuisine vary. Some reviewers rave about dishes like carrot soup with yogurt and green harissa or braised beef short ribs with sautéed greens, cipollinis and horseradish cream, while there were a few who left disappointed, given the national reputation that Goin enjoys. But then, there is a third contingent that says the best way to enjoy Lucques is to see it as a "high-quality neighborhood place" with "top-flight, ingredient-based cooking." A number of our reviewers told us they enjoy the set-menu Sunday Night Suppers, which often are supervised by Goin herself.

Mediterranean | Casual | Expensive | west hollywood | 8474 Melrose Ave. | 323-655-6277 | www. lucques.com | Lunch & Dinner Tue-Sat, Sun-Mon dinner only

Angelini Osteria   92.6

In a city overrun with run-of-the-mill Italian eateries, a "Tuscan-influenced menu with a touch more imagination" allows Gino Angelini's restaurant to stand above the pack. It's hardly a temple of cuisine; the room is small and cramped, and the atmosphere casual yet buzzy: The table next to you is as likely to be filled with movie stars, business diners discussing a deal and an entire family digging into pastas like green lasagna with a veal ragù or a leg of pork roasted in a wood-burning oven. A well-crafted wine list is a plus, although it is fair to describe it as pricey. A few people commented that the restaurant has slipped a bit since Angelini opened a second location, but most still appreciate what has been described as "real food at a fair price."

Italian | Casual | Expensive | fairfax/melrose | 7313 Beverly Blvd. | 323-297-0070 | www.angeliniosteria. com | Lunch & Dinner Tue-Fri, Sat-Sun dinner only

LudoBites   92.5

Until Bastide closed its doors, some argued that Ludovic Lefebvre served the best contemporary French cuisine in the U.S. there. He thought of opening his own restaurant, but dealing with investors and a 24-hour-a-day job didn't sound that appealing. Ludo and his wife, Krissy, found the best of both worlds when they opened LudoBites, a pop-up restaurant that operates in a succession of temporary locations around the city. Each iteration features a unique menu that mixes new creations, like foie gras dynamite with lychee and tuna, and "crazy good" dishes from the Bastide days, like crème fraîche panna cotta with caviar caramel. The concept's been incredibly popular with the local food cognoscenti – so much so that, when Version 6.0 was announced, so many people tried to book tables that the OpenTable servers crashed.

French | Informal | Expensive | various | www.ludolefebvre.com | Check website for opening times

Sushi Nozawa   92.4

Called the "sushi Nazi" by a number of reviewers, chef Nozawa is known for his propensity to tell customers what they are going to have for dinner. While he does leave some room for negotiation, expecting true flexibility on his part can mean finding yourself on the wrong side of the chef, something we don't recommend if you want to eat well. There's a split of opinion about the fish: Some say that Nozawa gets "first pick at the Japanese market each morning," while others say it is "far from the best in the country." It helps if you sit at the counter and Nozawa takes a liking to you, which isn't that difficult if you can demonstrate that you're a true sushi lover.

Japanese | Informal | Expensive | studio city | 11288 Ventura Blvd. | 818-508-7017 | www.sushinozawa. com | Lunch & Dinner Mon-Fri

Katsu-Ya   92.2

Katsuya Uechi has accomplished a not-so-easy task: operating Japanese restaurants that are trendy and fun, without sacrificing quality in the process. Granted, sushi purists might not prefer Americanized creations like crispy rice cakes topped with spicy tuna or halibut carpaccio topped with sliced tomato, but fans go wild for the place, saying things like, "I almost hate to rate it so high. It's too crowed already." An "elegant and high-class environment," which includes the occasional celeb downing a Kobe/foie gras combo, doesn't hurt either. The original Studio City location is considered better than the satellites that have opened in Brentwood and the L.A. Live entertainment and shopping complex over the past few years.

Japanese | Informal | Moderate | studio city | 11680 Ventura Blvd. | 818-985-6976 | www.katsu-yagroup. com | Dinner daily, Lunch Mon-Fri

Second Location: brentwood | 11777 San Vicente Blvd. | 310-207-8744 | www.sbe.com/katsuya | Dinner daily, Lunch Mon-Fri

Third Location: downtown | 800 W. Olympic Blvd. #220 | 213-763-5483 | www.sbe.com/katsuya | Dinner daily

Mélisse   92.0

With the demise of L'Orangerie, finding a quality contemporary French meal in L.A. can be difficult. But reviewers say Josiah Citrin's restaurant is the best in the category, declaring, "You have to go France to experience similar culinary expertise." Chef Ken Takayama's menu is loaded with luxury ingredients, with dishes like a lobster Bolognese with cappellini, black truffles and basil; a rotisserie chicken stuffed with summer truffles and a side of potatoes Parmentier; and a potato purée atop a mixture of braised short ribs and foie gras. Comments alternate between "always tasty, with interesting menu items, good wine selection and reasonable corkage" and "Recent honors for the restaurant mean that prices have skyrocketed, while the food has stayed the same. Still delicious, but overpriced."

French | Casual | Expensive | santa monica | 1104 Wilshire Blvd. | 310-395-0881 | www.melisse.com | Dinner Tue-Sun

RECOMMENDED

Jar   91.6

With a stint in Mark Peel's kitchen at Campanile on her resumé, it's not surprising that Suzanne Tracht has a thing for cooking meat. While some reviewers refer to her restaurant as an "upscale steakhouse" (she calls it a "modern chophouse"), the braising in Tracht's background shows in carefully prepared comfort fare like a coq au vin with applewood-smoked bacon or her signature pot roast, which someone said "takes the dish to a whole new level." You can top your grilled meats with original sauces like a lobster béarnaise, as well as order from a long list of sides that include exotic offerings like a purée of kabocha squash, leeks, sage and medjool dates.

New American | Casual | Expensive | west hollywood | 8225 Beverly Blvd. | 323-655-6566 | www.thejar.com | Lunch & Dinner daily

Chinois on Main   91.5

Of all the comments we get to read, few were as amusing as the ones we collected about Wolfgang Puck's Santa Monica restaurant. One reviewer compared the noise level to "being on the tarmac at LAX," yet said he keeps returning for the delicious cuisine, telling us, "I can't get enough of the curried lobster and deep-fried whole catfish." They also offer a "wonderful wine list that won't kill your wallet." Of course, if you're a traditionalist, you should stay away from Asian-fusion food that one diner called "an imitation at insulting prices."

Asian | Casual | Expensive | santa monica | 2709 Main St. | 310-392-9025 | www.wolfgangpuck.com | Dinner daily, Lunch Wed-Fri

Bouchon   91.4

While Thomas Keller's attention to detail and commitment to excellence are clearly in evidence at this French bistro, diners expecting something like "French Laundry light" are barking up the wrong tree. Instead, you will find an excellent raw bar and user-friendly bistro cuisine, like pan-seared tuna with ratatouille and roast chicken with red rice and lardons, served by a friendly staff in a lively environment. "Solid food with excellent ingredients; they stick to the middle road, but execution is flawless" is the comment that describes it best. The Rodeo Drive location makes it handy for refueling during, or after, a day of power-shopping.

French Bistro | Casual | Moderate | beverly hills | 235 N. Cañon Dr. | 310-271-9910 | www.bouchonbistro.com | Lunch & Dinner daily

Water Grill   91.4

Downtown Los Angeles was a dining desert until Michael Cimarusti put this restaurant on the map. When he left to open Providence, the talented David LeFevre took the reins in the kitchen. But in February he passed the baton to Amanda Baumgarten, who continues to serve the delicious seafood-based cuisine the restaurant had become famous for. Baumgarten offers what many consider to be the best raw bar in the city, plus starters like bigeye tuna tartare with green papaya and Thai chiles and mains like Scottish king salmon sautéed with trumpet mushrooms and black garlic purée. A "creatively assembled" wine list and "a location in a beautiful Art Deco building" cap off what is arguably downtown's best dining experience.

Seafood | Casual | Expensive | downtown | 544 S. Grand Ave. | 213-891-0900 | www.watergrill.com | Lunch & Dinner Mon-Sat, Sun dinner only

Gordon Ramsay at the London   91.2

The comments we collected about this downscale version of the London restaurant that made Gordon Ramsay famous (a tasting menu in West Hollywood costs approximately half as much as one in London) indicate it's suffering from an acute case of absentee chef-itis. "I like this place very much, although it seems to often be empty and lacks personality" and "It lost its charm due to too many chef shuffles since its opening" are typical. The contemporary British menu features a number of dishes based on ingredients from the U.K., like Scottish lobster tails, scallops from the Isle of Skye, beef from Cambridgeshire and pork from Gloucester.

European | Casual | Expensive | west hollywood | London Hotel | 1020 N. San Vicente Blvd | 310-358-7788 | www.gordonramsay.com | Dinner daily

Hatfield's   91.1

When their restaurant became so popular they had to turn customers away, Quinn and Karen Hatfield moved it into the old Citrus space, more than doubling the capacity. It was the payoff of a long journey. After training with a myriad of notable mentors, Quinn Hatfield decided to focus his attention on his own seasonal menus, which include dishes like hamachi Croque Madame – hamachi, prosciutto, brioche and a fried quail egg – and date- and mint-crusted rack of lamb. Karen Hatfield helps you finish your meal, turning out desserts like sugar and spice beignets, which she serves with chocolate fondue and a vanilla milkshake.

New American | Casual | Expensive | fairfax/melrose | 6703 Melrose Ave. | 323-935-2977 | www.hatfieldsrestaurant.com | Lunch & Dinner Mon-Fri Sat-Sun dinner only

Mastro's   91.1

Though this 10-restaurant mini-chain is based in Phoenix, it attracts its share of national attention because its owners were smart enough to open in the heart of Rodeo Drive. The location makes it convenient for shoppers or for those who are staying in the area and don't want to pay a premium to have the name Puck branded onto their steak. Non-carnivores won't find anything inventive here as the "non-steak offerings menu are limited to the standard alternative steakhouse fare like salmon or roast chicken."

Steakhouse | Casual | Expensive | beverly hills | 633 Anton Blvd. | 714-546-7405 | www.mastrosrestaurants.com | Dinner daily

Palate Food & Wine   91.0

Octavio Becerra's small plates menu allows you to attack your meal from a number of directions: homemade charcuterie, in the form of both sliced meats and terrines, assorted vegetables that are pickled in-house, and larger plates like yellowtail poached in olive oil with a picholine tapenade and a sauce vierge. Any can be followed up with a selection of 15 different cheeses. But while the food offers some great opportunities for people who like to nibble, the real draw is a wine list on which "the selections are terrific" and the "markups are modest." We suspect it would be even more popular if it were in a more central location, rather than Glendale.

Wine Bar | Informal | Moderate | valley | 933 S. Brand Blvd. | 818-662-9463 | www.palatefoodwine.com | Dinner daily, Fri-Sat lunch

The Palm   90.7

While the New York original has historically been a clubhouse for people in industries like advertising and insurance, the Beverly Hills branch is "deal central" – the clientele is heavy with talent agents, record company executives and other assorted L.A. types. The food is the same as back East – steaks, gigantic lobsters and a few Italian specialties. However, unlike the New York mother ship (whose interior is divided into a series of little rooms), the L.A. location is all one room, allowing you a full view of the deal-making in action.

Steakhouse | Casual | Expensive | beverly hills | 9001 Santa Monica Blvd. | 310-550-8811 | www.thepalm.com | Dinner daily, Lunch Mon-Fri

A.O.C.   90.3

Most locals love this Mediterranean small plates restaurant from Suzanne Goin, serving up comments like, "Top-notch food and a good wine list earns it five stars in my book." Along with the usual list of suspects on the tapas menu, like platters of charcuterie and a variety of salads, there are a few ambitious offerings like skirt steak with Roquefort butter and arroz negro with squid and saffron aioli. But before you get too excited, consider a much less-enthusiastic contingent of reviewers, who argue, "While the food is fine, what is on the plate is underwhelming, considering who's in charge of the kitchen."

Mediterranean | Informal | Moderate | west hollywood | 8022 W. Third St. | 323-653-6359 | www.aoc-winebar.com | Dinner daily

Mo-Chica   90.3

If we said you could find a modern Peruvian restaurant run by a Gordon Ramsay–trained chef in a food court in South Central, would you believe us? Well, if you don't, check out Ricardo Zarate's restaurant, where the mushroom risotto is made with quinoa instead of rice and the arroz con pollo is deconstructed before being assembled on the plate. Filled with "amazing, well executed, nourishing, mind-blowing food," Mo-Chica provides an experience that is "as delicious as it is unique." While prices are more in keeping with the setting than the quality (it's one of the most cost-efficient meals in town), Zarate serves a five-course tasting menu for $35 one Thursday each month.

Peruvian | Casual | Moderate | south central | 3655 S. Grand Ave. | 213-747-2141 | wwww.mo-chica.com | Lunch & Dinner Mon-Sat

Din Tai Fung   90.0

The Chinese population in the San Gabriel Valley is so extensive that this dumpling specialist, which operates seven locations in Asia, decided to open a branch in Arcadia. Locals rave about "the most outstanding Shanghai soup dumplings outside of Asia," saying they "have traveled for an hour in L.A. traffic for the privilege of eating them." Such cultlike devotion ensures that, more often than not, you'll find yourself taking a number from the hostess and waiting 30 minutes for a table.

Chinese | Informal | Inexpensive | arcadia | 1108 S. Baldwin Ave. | 626-574-7068 | www.dintaifungusa.com | Lunch & Dinner daily

Josie   90.0

Back in 2001, after working in a number of the city's top restaurants (including two stints serving hearty game dishes as the executive chef at the Saddle Peak Lodge), Josie Le Balch and her husband, Frank Delzio, opened what has become a Santa Monica mainstay. Dishes like frogs' legs with garlic brown butter, preserved Meyer lemon and roasted tomato or pan-roasted venison with black barley risotto and oyster mushrooms are evidence of Le Balch's culinary lineage. The combination of "robust food" and "low-key atmosphere" causes reviewers to declare: "Few L.A. restaurants are able to combine high-quality cooking with a dining room that offers a casual, neighborhood feel."

French | Casual | Expensive | santa monica | 2424 Pico Blvd. | 310-581-9888 | www.josierestaurant.com | Dinner daily

TOP LOCAL CHOICE

Drago   89.5

Celestino Drago built one of the most popular restaurants in the Los Angeles area by offering diners a menu of expertly prepared Italian fare, including a soup of spelt and borlotti beans; rigatoni with Kobe meatballs and Romano cheese; and Coho salmon in a broth of white wine, baby spinach and thyme. The formula was so successful that he opened Downtown and Beverly Hills locations. As is typical for an L.A Italian restaurant, the paeans ranged from "delicious pasta courses" to "good for celeb-spotting."

Italian | Casual | Moderate | santa monica | 525 S. Flower St., Ste. 120 | 213-228-8998 | www.celestinodrago.com | Lunch & Dinner Mon-Fri Sat-Sun dinner only

Second Location: beverly hills | 410 N. Cañon Dr. | 310-786-8236 | www.celestinodrago.com | Lunch & Dinner Mon-Sat-Sun

Third Location: downtown | 525 S. Flower St., Suite # 120 | 213-228-8998 | www.dragocentro.com | Dinner daily, Lunch Mon-Fri

Vincenti   89.5

Diners at this venue owned by Maureen Vincenti (what are the odds that someone with that name would own a restaurant on San Vicente Blvd.?) dig into staples like potato gnocchi with a ragú of shrimp, lobster, seppia and asparagus or oven-roasted quail with couscous, mushrooms and crispy homemade guanciale – food that one reviewer called "fairly authentic, considering how popular it is with Hollywood types." Though the servers were deemed "friendly and knowledgeable," diners are warned that "special treatment is reserved for celebs, even if you become a regular."

Italian | Casual | Expensive | brentwood | 11930 San Vicente Blvd. | 310-207-0127 | www.vincentiristorante.com | Dinner Mon-Sat, Fri lunch

Animal   89.5

If you like eating gastropub grub while surrounded by hipsters enjoying interesting-sounding (and often tasting) creations like a hamachi tostada with fish-sauce vinaigrette; veal brains with vadouvan; and foie gras moco loco – a burger topped with grilled Spam and sautéed foie gras – run, don't walk to Animal. However, be prepared for "a meal prepared by chefs who have acquired a level of celebrity that is in excess of their abilities." The disparity also turns up in service that some find less than desirable: The kitchen refuses to make any changes. One reviewer asked for the blue cheese fondue that came with his ribeye to be served on the side; another asked for bread crumbs to be left off his broccoli (due to an allergy). Both requests were refused.

Gastropub | Informal | Moderate | west hollywood | 435 N. Fairfax Ave. | 323-782-9225 | www.animalrestaurant.com | Dinner daily

Bar Bouchon   89.5

The downside of this more casual offshoot of Bouchon, Thomas Keller's popular bistro, is that it offers a limited menu. The upside is that hungry diners can enjoy lighter fare like oysters, steak tartare and paninis from morning well into the night. Being able to knock back a dozen icy bivalves and a glass of Champagne at any point in the day makes it a perfect stop for shoppers who need to recharge at 4:00 p.m. or who are looking to tide themselves over before dinner. A "lovely setting looking out on what must be the only lawn in the Rodeo Drive shopping area" makes for a relaxing meal.

French Bistro | Informal | Moderate | beverly hills | 235 N. Cañon Dr. | 310-271-9910 | www.bouchonbistro.com | Lunch & Dinner daily

Musha   89.5

"It's a good sign that this restaurant is brimming with Japanese customers," reviewers said about this Torrance-based izakaya – so many, in fact, that it opened a branch in Santa Monica. As is typical for this style of dining, there are dozens of small plates on offer, ranging from sashimi to casseroles to all sorts of meat, fish and vegetables cooked over a robata grill, as well as a few more exotic items like a mackerel filet seared tableside by a butane torch. "Loud and lively," it's filled with "servers who seem genuinely happy to be working here."

Japanese | Informal | Moderate | santa monica | 424 Wilshire Blvd. | 310-576-6330 | http://musha.us | Dinner daily

Rivera   89.5

New Mexico native John Sedlar is credited as the chef who introduced Southwestern cuisine to Los Angeles. But after forming a partnership with industry veteran Bill Chait, he has branched into other styles of Latin cooking. The result is a "creative pan-Asian restaurant" where diners are offered three different types of cuisine – Mexican/Southwestern, Spanish and Portuguese, each served in its own dining room decorated in a regionally appropriate style. Long respected as one of the city's top chefs, "Sedlar finally has a showcase befitting his talents," and his "genuine love for Latin cuisine comes through in his food."

Pan-Latin | Casual | Expensive | downtown | 1050 S. Flower St. | 213-749-1460 | www.riverarestaurant.com | Lunch & Dinner Mon-Fri Sat dinner only

Cecconi's 89.0

The CV of Cecconi's goes as follows: Begun in London in 1978 by Enzo Cecconi; developed immediately into a popular watering hole for celebrities and London's elite; fell into disrepair in the late '90s; purchased by the group that operates a number of sought-after restaurants and private clubs, like The Ivy and Soho House, and that likes to expand its brand names. This offering, located across from the Pacific Design Center, is the group's first foray into the Los Angeles dining scene, and the "buzzy dining room" is the "perfect place to have someone shave truffles on your risotto" after you buy a new Christian Liagre sofa.

Italian | Casual | Expensive | west hollywood | 8764 Melrose Ave. | 310-432-2000 | www.cecconiswesthollywood.com | Open daily

Café Bizou 89.0

A $2.00 corkage fee makes this "well-priced" three-restaurant chain (they also operate locations in Pasadena and Santa Monica) a favorite with the BYOB crowd. But people who aren't in the habit of bringing a bottle to a restaurant seem to be less enthusiastic, calling the food "just average" and saying that the major attraction is the "low prices." But if wine is going to be the major focus of your evening, you will probably enjoy sipping your bottles while tucking into dishes like sweetbreads with potato pancakes and roast chicken and frites.

French Bistro | Casual | Moderate | sherman oaks | 14016 Ventura Blvd. | 818-788-3536 | www.cafebizou.com | Lunch & Dinner daily

Comme Ça 89.0

While Sona, the restaurant where he made his name, is shuttered, David Myers is still making local diners happy at his lively bistro in the heart of the Melrose Avenue luxury shopping district. The brasserie menu features all of the expected classics, like escargots persillade and a free-range chicken breast diable with flageolet beans and cipollini onions. By day the dining room is filled with business diners, shoppers and visitors to the city; during the evenings, it becomes "a sexy hideaway" frequented by a "chic West Hollywood crowd" where you "dine on the hearty French fare by candlelight."

French Bistro | Casual | Moderate | west hollywood | 8479 Melrose Ave. | 323-782-1104 | www.commecarestaurant.com | Lunch & Dinner daily

Gjelina 89.0

The number of Los Angelenos in the film and TV industries who go through long periods of downtime between jobs makes the city's restaurants unusually lively at lunchtime. This Mediterranean affair is among the liveliest, and some of the best-looking people in the city come here to stuff themselves with interesting salads, sandwiches and pizzas, along with small plates like grilled Monterey Bay squid with lentils, roasted peppers and salsa verde or a Niman Ranch lamb burger with harissa aioli. In the evening the fare's a bit more substantial – think Dungeness crab risotto with arugula, mascarpone and parmesan. "Sexy ambience and wonderful food to go with it" does a good job of summing up the experience.

Mediterranean | Informal | Moderate | venice | 1429 Abbott Kinney Blvd.. | 310-450-1429 | www.gjelina.com | Lunch & Dinner daily

Jitlada   89.0

This is one of this those ethnic restaurants with a cult following that swears, "It lives up to its hype." The list of must-eat dishes is long: coconut, lotus and red snapper soup; crispy Morning Glory salad; soft-shell crabs with mangoes; green curry with frogs' legs; and Crying Tiger pork are but some of the dishes that seem to be on every single table in the restaurant. One reviewer said it "tastes like Thai food in Thailand that was cooked by Thai people with Thai ingredients." Diners are advised to discuss spicing with their servers as "levels can range from timid to injurious." It's one of the few ethnic restaurants in the city where you stand a good chance to spot celebs, though in this instance rockers instead of movie stars.

Thai | Informal | Moderate | silverlake | 5233 W. Sunset Blvd. | 323-663-3104 | www.jitlada.com | Dinner daily, Lunch Tues-Sun,

Joe's   89.0

What do you get when you combine the quintessential neighborhood restaurant with food good enough to make people want to travel? You get Joe Miller's "iconic" venue, with its "relaxed, but serious food." The California/French menu features dishes like porcini ravioli in a broth of parmesan and wild mushrooms and grilled Ahi tuna paired with pan-seared foie gras and potato rosti. One reviewer suggests going for lunch, when you can enjoy "the beautiful patio and welcoming service." As an extra benefit, the "Lunch specials are particularly good value," while "The $39 prix fixe on Sunday evenings is a steal."

Californian | Informal | Moderate | venice | 1023 Abbot Kinney Blvd. | 310-399-5811 | www.joesrestaurant. com | Lunch & Dinner Tue-Sun

Campanile   88.5

Once one of the most beloved restaurants in the city, Campanile hasn't been the same since Mark Peel and Nancy Silverton divorced, people say. Now comments like "It's a shell of what it once was" and "The place is full of families with kids running riot" are typical. Yet others still enjoy Mark Peel's unusual mishmash of trattoria and brasserie fare, telling us, "The food is great if you stick to the house classics like pappardelle with boar and braised short ribs." The simple comfort food makes the restaurant a favorite with the BYOB crowd.

Mediterranean | Casual | Moderate | la brea | 624 S. La Brea Ave. | 323-938-1447 | www.campanileres-taurant.com | Lunch & Dinner Mon-Sat, Lunch Sun only

Capo   88.5

Fifty percent of the comments we collected about Bruce Marder's Santa Monica Italian eatery mentioned the cost of the meal. Sure, there was praise for some of the food, especially the burrata, the crab torta, even the steaks, but more typical were comments like "Everything is great here but the bill," "They must be testing out how high they can make the prices before people object," and "Good food, but for the same money you could feed 24 people and have leftovers." As to be expected in L.A., there's a positive correlation between high prices and good celeb-spotting.

Italian | Casual | Expensive | santa monica | 1810 Ocean Ave. | 310-394-5550 | www.caporestaurant.com | Dinner Tue-Sat

JiRaffe 88.5

Fifteen years is a long time for a restaurant to be in business in trend-conscious Los Angeles. But Raphael Lunetta has kept this "longstanding Santa Monica institution" on track for a decade and a half. Specializing in "Californian French, as we like to call it," the menu offers tomato tart with burrata cheese, caramelized balsamic onions and basil pesto and almond-crusted rainbow trout with corn, peppers, capers and lemon-brown butter. The wine list includes some "plum cherries from the Napa Valley" at reasonable prices.

French | Casual | Expensive | santa monica | 502 Santa Monica Blvd. | 310-917-6671 | www.jirafferestau-rant.com | Dinner Mon-Sat

Belvedere 88.0

The main dining room in the Peninsula Hotel is recommended mostly for the "amazing breakfast and lunch scenes," when Beverly Hills power brokers and their clients occupy the tables, and for the Sunday brunch, when it's full of local families who are there to chow down on the astonishing buffet. Just remember that it's hotel food, and while it is good and dependable, it is nothing more than "straight down the middle cuisine that will never set the world on fire."

New American | Casual | Expensive | beverly hills | 9882 S. Santa Monica Blvd. | 310-788-2306 | www.peninsula.com | Open daily

Foundry on Melrose 88.0

Eric Greenspan's reputation as "the big, loud chef who competed on *Iron Chef*" precedes him. The cuisine has as much personality as its creator, and among the dishes on offer are whimsical creations like tater tots with a cheese fondue and violet mustard; or a grilled cheese sandwich with taleggio, raisin bread and an apricot-caper purée, along with hearty mains like mustard-glazed short ribs with spaetzle, green grapes and golden beets. Reviewers say, "The menu has both hits and misses," but a "fun atmosphere" and "good service" make it "a nice spot for a special night out."

New American | Casual | Expensive | mid-city west | 7465 Melrose Ave. | 323-651-0915 | www.thefoundry-onmelrose.com | Dinner daily

The Hungry Cat 88.0

Suzanne Goin and David Lentz have brought the casual fish restaurant (think Boston's Neptune Oysters or Mary's Fish Camp in NYC) to Hollywood. The raw bar features clams, oysters, shrimps and a variety of crabs including king, stone and snow, which you can follow with small plates like oyster and pork belly beignets or larger ones like pan-roasted grouper. Getting to slurp your oysters in a "hip, happening scene" is a plus, as is the ability to just drop by and grab a quick casual meal, which makes it "a good choice for pre/post-theater or movie eats."

Seafood | Informal | Moderate | hollywood | 1535 N. Vine St. | 323-462-2155 | www.thehungrycat.com | Lunch & Dinner daily

Lawry's The Prime Rib 88.0

If you are desperate to eat a two-inch-thick slab of prime rib that has been paraded around the dining room in a silver cart, sliced by someone wearing a foot-high toque and served by waitresses dressed as if they are the staff at a Beverly Hills mansion, Lawry's is for you. It's a chain these days, with four other locations, but this is the original, where "real men" have ordered the Diamond Jim Brady cut (a bone-in, extra-thick serving) since 1938.

Steakhouse | Casual | Expensive | west hollywood | 100 N. La Cienega Blvd. | 310-652-2827 | www.lawrysonline.com | Dinner daily

Lou   88.0

"One of L.A.'s most interesting restaurants" is how one reviewer described this wine bar featuring "creative cuisine that works seamlessly with the eclectic selection of wines." The concept is brought to you by Lou Amdur, and each day he chooses 30 different wines to be paired with dishes from D. J. Olsen's kitchen, like a frittata made with baby potatoes, piquillo peppers and avocado or lamb Bolognese with maitake mushrooms. It's a perfect choice for those who are squeamish about ordering unfamiliar wines, as "the staff is adept at talking wary patrons through bouts of oeno-insecurity."

Wine Bar | Informal | Moderate | hollywood | 724 Vine St. | 323-962-6369 | www.louonvine.com | Dinner Mon-Sat

Musso & Frank's   88.0

Claiming everyone from Charlie Chaplin to Humphrey Bogart among its past clientele, and Johnny Depp and Nicolas Cage among its current, this is the last remaining bastion of old Hollywood. The atmosphere is classic – leather booths and waiters dressed in short red jackets – and the menu offers everything from grilled meats to what they call Prepared Entrées (i.e., macaroni with mushroom gravy and beef Stroganoff). Eating at the bar is popular with solo diners who stop by on their way home from the studio for a martini and "one of the last, best Caesar salads" (made from scratch by the bartender), along with classics like lamb chops with mint jelly.

American | Casual | Moderate | hollywood | 6667 Hollywood Blvd. | 323-467-7788 | http://mussoandfrank.com | Lunch & Dinner Tue-Sat

Nook   88.0

James Richardson's restaurant offers our locally based reviewers a reasonable place to grab a low-key meal. "Nice wines and a knowledgeable staff," along with dishes like horseradish-crusted local halibut and maple mustard–glazed rib eye, make it a reliable pick almost any day of the week – which explains why "there is almost always a wait for a table." One reviewer suggests visiting for a late lunch or after 8:00, "when things quiet down a bit."

New American | Casual | Moderate | west l.a. | 11628 Santa Monica Blvd. #9 | 310-207-5160 | www.nookbistro.com | Lunch & Dinner Mon-Fri Sat dinner only

Pinot Bistro   88.0

Considering how difficult it is to find a high-quality non-sushi meal in the Valley, Pinot seems like an oasis in the dessert. Chef Octavio Bercerra has left to open Palate Food & Wine, but his departure doesn't seem to have affected our reviewers, who are still enjoying "updated French classics" like a napoleon made with burrata, heirloom tomatoes and tapenade or a spring lamb gratin with garlic mashed potatoes and ratatouille.

Diners can choose to eat in the fireplace room, with its traditional décor, or in the Man Ray room, which features a more modern design.

French Bistro | Informal | Moderate | sherman oaks | 12969 Ventura Blvd. | 818-990-0500 | www.patina-group.com | Lunch & Dinner Mon-Fri Sat-Sun dinner only

Valentino   88.0

It might be an old war-horse, but if you are happy eating simple but properly prepared pastas, fish and meats, you could do worse than to book a table at Piero Selvaggio's restaurant. The wine list is one of the best in the country, and the restaurant excels with a special menu during white truffle season. But even long-term customers see Valentino for what it is: a place for a reliable, but unexciting dinner. Comments like "I eat there regularly, and while I've had the occasional good dish, I never had a meal that wowed me" are typical.

Italian | Casual | Expensive | santa monica | 3115 Pico Blvd. | 310-829-4313 | www.valentinorestaurant.com | Dinner Tue-Sat, Fri lunch

ACCEPTABLE

Crustacean   87.5

More about a big night out than a distinguished meal – think of the Blue Elephant restaurants in major European cities – Crustacean features a cuisine with a pan-Asian emphasis. "Better for a group or a large party" than for a couple seeking a fine dining experience, it's gimmicky and there's a huge scene. But that didn't stop one of our reviewers from raving about the "heavenly garlic noodles" that accompany almost every dish.

Asian | Casual | Expensive | beverly hills | 9646 Little Santa Monica Blvd. | 310-205-8990 | www.houseofan.com | Dinner daily, Lunch Mon-Fri

Empress Pavilion   87.5

While the prevailing local wisdom is that the best Chinese food resides in the San Gabriel Valley, those who live on Los Angeles' West Side and don't want to drive an additional 15 miles happily cram into this downtown restaurant for delights like steamed siu liung bao, slippery shrimp and seafood hot pot with satay sauce and vermicelli. Opinions are split between those advocates who say that "it's rightly popular," so arrive early, as "many items sell out by 1:00 p.m." and others who claim it's "no better than any of the other restaurants in Chinatown."

Chinese | Informal | Moderate | chinatown | 988 N Hill St. | 213-617-9898 | www.empresspavilion.com | Lunch & Dinner daily, Sat-Sun brunch

Simon L.A.   87.5

If you want to feel like you're eating in Las Vegas without having to make the six-hour drive from Los Angeles, book a table at this lively venue in the Sofitel, where Kerry Simon (known as the rock 'n' roll chef) serves "updated comfort food" like tomato soup with a grilled cheese sandwich and a lamb chop with sunchoke purée, asparagus and morel sauce. Unfortunately, upper middle cuisine in a hotel is a style that our reviewers usually don't warm up to, resulting in comments like "My meal was perfectly fine, but I see no reason to go back there."

New American | Casual | Expensive | west hollywood | Sofitel LA | 8555 Beverly Blvd. | 310-358-3979 | www.sofitella.com | Open daily

Sushi Sasabune   87.5

For many years this restaurant was located in a warehouse in the Little Tokyo section of West L.A., but after the sushi craze took the country by storm, investors came on board and moved it to shiny new headquarters in an office building on Wilshire Blvd, while opening other branches in New York and Honolulu. The concept hasn't changed – it's still an omakase-only affair – and while the place has its fair share of fans, opinion seems to have shifted for the worse – one comment was "not at all what it once was; still okay, but I miss the original location."

Japanese | Informal | Moderate | west l.a. | 12400 Wilshire Blvd. | 310-268-8380 | Lunch & Dinner Mon-Fri Sat dinner only

Chaya Brasserie   87.0

Chaya was all the rage back in the day. And while fare like a Cobb salad with yuzu dressing and pappardelle with Kobe beef Bolognese and truffle oil is still popular with a few of our reviewers, most of them have moved on to some of the more extravagant versions of the Asian party restaurant that have opened over the years. Still, some reviewers tell us things like, "Every time I go, I'm surprised by how much I like the place," while others counter with comments like, "It's perfect if you enjoy eating amid a bunch of suits having drinks after work."

Asian | Informal | Moderate | west hollywood | 110 Navy St. | 310-396-1179 | www.thechaya.com | Dinner daily, Lunch Mon-Fri

The Ivy   87.0

The Ivy is eternal. They are still happily (and profitably) serving the same exact California cuisine that they've been featuring since they opened in the 1980s (think mesquite-grilled Columbia River king salmon), and it remains an A-list celebrity hangout to this day. Reviews of the food are mixed – "great lunchtime spot with delicious salads" to "the food is old-fashioned and overpriced" pretty much cover the cuisine, although one astute reviewer may have sized it up correctly when he asked, "Where else can you pay $40 for a salad while watching Verne Troyer [the actor who played Mini-Me in the Austin Powers movies] being

hounded by the paparazzi?"

Californian | Casual | Expensive | west hollywood | 113 N. Robertson Blvd. | 310-274-8303 | Open daily

Pacific Dining Car   87.0

While L.A. has a number of cheap-eats places that can be described as "vintage," few full-service restaurants remain from the Golden Age of Train Travel. Opened in 1921, PDC is a remnant of that era, and proof of its provenance is the Great Combinations section on the menu – various steaks paired with an assortment of seafood, a style that once upon a time signified luxury. It's open from breakfast through dinner, and reviewers say "the perfect steak and eggs" served among "beautiful table settings" offers "a wonderful way to start your day."

Steakhouse | Casual | Expensive | downtown | 2700 Wilshire Blvd. | 310-453-4000 | www.pacific-diningcar.com | Open daily

Stefan's at L.A. Farm   87.0

With two restaurants, a catering business and a steakhouse on the way, Stefan Richter is living proof that a chef can leverage an appearance as a finalist on *Top Chef* into a thriving business. While a nutmeg-crusted halibut in lobster broth is a good example of his larger plates, most reviewers were enamored with the "great small-bites menu," a list of 15 dishes that cost between $3 and $5 and include everything from sliders to Kumamoto oysters to a bite-size portion of foie gras.

New American | Casual | Moderate | santa monica | 3000 W. Olympic Blvd. | 310-449-4000 | http://stefansatlafarm.com | Lunch & Dinner Mon-Fri Sat-Sun dinner only

Border Grill   86.5

Susan Feniger and Mary Sue Milliken, who made their name of the television program *Too Hot Tamales*, are still holding court at this modern Mexican cantina where the fare includes dishes like grilled chicken chilaquiles and a sofrito-marinated rack of lamb. A long-standing favorite in the heart of downtown Santa Monica, Border Grill is still packing them in, though one reviewer noted that it's starting to show its age, saying, "Though it's always crowded, it's not the powerhouse of a restaurant it once was."

Mexican | Informal | Moderate | santa monica | 1445 4th St | 310-451-1655 | www.bordergrill.com | Lunch & Dinner daily

Hamasaku   86.5

Naming dishes after celebrities used to be a specialty of Jewish delicatessens. But Michael Ovitz and his partners have brought the concept to sushi rolls, with preparations named after customers ranging from Charlize Theron to Angie Harmon. While most reviewers preferred the cooked food (the sushi isn't recommended for serious fish fanatics), if you're the type who likes jazzed-up rolls – "five different-colored sauces covering the rice, inside out, deep fried, and standing up on stilts, etc." – this place is for you.

Japanese | Casual | Expensive | santa monica | 11043 Santa Monica Blvd. | 310-479-7636 | www.hamasakula.com | Lunch & Dinner Mon-Fri Sat dinner only

Michael's   86.5

During the California cuisine craze of the 1980s, this was one of the country's most important dining destinations. But Michael McCarty's restaurant is now over 30 years old, and though current chef Michael Stern's cuisine – butter-poached monkfish with creamy risotto, spinach, bacon lardons and shellfish essence – remains popular with the loyal clientele that has been eating there since they opened their doors, those less-nostalgic critics contend the overall experience is "a far cry from the days when the likes

of Ken Frank, Mark Peel and Jonathan Waxman tended to the stoves."

New American | Casual | Expensive | santa monica | 1147 Third St. | 310-451-0843 | www.michaelssantamonica.com | Lunch & Dinner Mon-Fri Sat dinner only

Angeli Café   86.0

Evan Kleiman (author of *Cucina Fresca* and host of *Good Food* on KCRW) opened this restaurant during the culinary revolution of the 1980s, While it is little-known to people outside of the city, regulars still pack the place to enjoy "simple, well-prepared, rustic Italian food," like a platter of deep-fried vegetables and calamari or a Ligurian fish soup. "It's the perfect place for picky eaters," as there are enough salads, pastas, pizzas and mains to make everyone happy.

Italian | Informal | Moderate | fairfax/melrose | 7274 Melrose Ave. | 323-936-9086 | www.angeli-caffe.com | Dinner daily, Lunch Tue-Fri

Father's Office   86.0

Although they offer "one of the best burgers in L.A." along with other tasty gastropub fare like a duck confit salad and sweet potato fries, a lack of flexibility – they won't serve ketchup or extra salad dressing or make adjustments for people with food allergies – led a number of people to say they can't recommend the place. One reviewer called it "the home of the burger Nazi: Eat it their way or don't eat it at all."

Gastropub | Informal | Moderate | santa monica | 1018 Montana Ave. | 310-736-2224 | www.fathersoffice.com | Dinner daily, Lunch Mon-Fri

Sushi Roku   86.0

From "blends Hollywood people-watching with quality Japanese food" to "I'm happy to groove to the music with some deliciously fresh fish placed before me," we were surprised at the number of positive comments about this link in a chain of contemporary Japanese restaurants owned and operated by the Innovative Dining Group. Complaints often focused on the final tabs: "I had an omakase at the sushi bar, and while there was some decent fish, it should have been better at the price."

Japanese | Casual | Expensive | hollywood | 8445 W. Third St. | 323-655-6767 | www.sushiroku.com | Lunch & Dinner Mon-Fri Sat-Sun dinner only

Yamashiro   86.0

Built in 1914 by a pair of brothers as a mansion to house their vast collection of Asian art, this scenic spot (complete with an imported, 600-year-old pagoda) was converted into a restaurant in the '80s. As with so many places in stunning settings, however, the vista upstages the cuisine. Comments ranged from "decent sushi and service, but it's really the view that draws most guests" to "The best thing about this place is the amazing view from atop the Hollywood Hills. Actually, that's the only good thing."

Japanese | Casual | Expensive | Hollywood Hills | 1999 N. Sycamore Ave. | 323-466-5125 | www.yamashirorestaurant.com | Dinner daily

Napa Rose   85.5
(27 miles southeast in Anaheim)

"Filled with families who are tired after a busy day visiting the attractions at Disneyland," this restaurant garnered reviews that were better than we expected. The favorable comments included: "Disney's version of an upscale Cal-Ital restaurant with a focus on wine does not disappoint"; "very acceptable cuisine despite young kids running through the restaurant"; "If you are at Disneyland and can pay the price tag, you might as well eat here every night as there are no other choices at this level"; and our very favorite: "Despite the location, the food here ain't Mickey Mouse."

Californian | Casual | Moderate | anaheim | 1600 S. Disneyland Dr. | 714-300-7170 | disneyland.disney.go.com | Dinner daily

Polo Lounge   85.5

While nobody goes here to actually eat, we think it's fair to say that every single movie star (both real and aspiring), agent, director, producer and mogul in town has enjoyed at least one meal in this historic dining room dating from 1912. What they come for: power breakfasts and lunches featuring "a lavish setting," "solicitous service" and "food that is good enough" to keep the L.A. celebrity crowd returning. It's such a scene that a number of reviewers who recommended it also admitted, "I couldn't remember anything that I ate."

American | Casual | Expensive | beverly hills | Beverly Hills Hotel | 9641 Sunset Blvd. | 310-887-2777 | www.beverlyhillshotel.com | Open daily

The Hobbit   85.0
(34 miles southeast in Orange)

"It's a bit old school" is an understatement when describing "this restaurant that exists in a '80s time warp." They are still using the format from that bygone era – a single seating during which you are served a seven-course meal featuring entrées like veal saltimbocca and rack of lamb. Even the wine list, once a major drawing card, was described as "somewhat tired and without depth." It seems to fall into the category of "worth going once for the experience."

Continental | Formal | Very Expensive | orange | 2932 E. Chapman Ave. | 714-997-1972 | www.hobbitrestaurant.com | Dinner daily, Lunch Tue-Fri y

OTHER PLACES MENTIONED

Mr. Chow   84.5

We never understood restaurants that were full of diners who were there for reasons other than eating the food. Elaine's in New York City is a classic example, and Mr. Chow is another. Why the society crowd tolerates food at this level is beyond our scope of comprehension. I mean, how much would it cost them to hire a chef who would raise this restaurant's ratings into the Acceptable category? "Go if you're interested in who's eating there, rather than what they are wearing, we mean are eating."

Chinese | Casual | Expensive | beverly hills | 344 N. Camden Dr. | 310-278-9911 | www.mrchow.com | Lunch & Dinner Mon-Sat, Sun dinner only

XIV   84.5

Any restaurant that has a menu offering dishes like a $65 lobster potpie makes us wonder if the price point is truly a function of their food costs, or a sign that investors are trying to accelerate the amortization of a Philippe Starck–designed dining room? Since we're not privy to their profit-and-loss statements, we'll never know. But what we can tell you from the low rating is, "it appears that Michael Mina might have overextended himself" by opening too many restaurants.

New American | Casual | Expensive | west hollywood | 8117 Sunset Blvd. | 323-656-1414 | www.sbe.com/xiv | Dinner Tue-Sat

Geisha House   84.0

When a restaurant's website boasts that celebrities like Ashton Kutcher are among its investors, comments like, "If you want to get wasted on horrible sake-tinis or douse Americanized sushi rolls in tubs of thickened wasabi soy sauce, then this is your place," don't surprise us. Some reviewers take a different view, saying that "good-enough sushi" and a "trendy Hollywood crowd," which includes "spotting the occasional low-caliber celebrity," make it "worth spending an evening here."

Japanese | Casual | Expensive | hollywood | 6633 Hollywood Blvd. | 323-460-6300 | www.dolcegroup.com | Dinner daily

Nick & Stef's Steakhouse 84.0

This corporate steakhouse run by the

Patina Group is "a good choice for a business dinner downtown" or a "meal before an event at the Staples Center." A BYO policy offering free corkage, "service that is always spot-on" and a neighborhood with "plenty of convenient parking options" work in its favor. And going there for lunch means "you are likely to bump into some of L.A.'s top movers and shakers," who are downing cocktails while discussing the high-rise they are building on the next block.

Steakhouse | Casual | Expensive | downtown | 330 S. Hope St. | 213-680-0330 | www.patina-group.com | Dinner daily, Lunch Mon-Fri

Boa Steakhouse   83.5

The gimmick here is the pairing of a steakhouse that is competitive with the top chains in the country with "a nice view of the nightlife" at the restaurant's bar. While the steaks might be no different from those you can order elsewhere, a number of reviewers said the "tableside preparation of the Caesar salad makes this a cut above." One reviewer who is a fan told us, "Everything about it is mouth-watering, from the food to the clientele."

Steakhouse | Casual | Expensive | west hollywood | 9200 W. Sunset Blvd. | 310-278-2050 | www.boasteak.com | Dinner daily, Lunch Mon-Fri

Dan Tana's   83.5

This old-school Italian in West Hollywood specializes in the "I used to be a celebrity" crowd. From the hushed atmosphere to the oversized bills, it has all the indicia of a place that was important to a prior generation of diners. The fare's what you'd expect – pastas, veal chops and steaks, served in a room full of people who range from families celebrating Grandma's birthday to tourists who want to gawk at easy-to-spot (former) celebs.

Italian | Casual | Moderate | west hollywood | 9071 Santa Monica Blvd. | 310-275-9444 | www.dantanasrestaurant.com | Dinner daily

Village Idiot   83.0

This gastropub with "a great bar scene" allows British expats to feel at home, with specialties like a steak-and-potato pie or an oak-grilled pork sausage served with caramelized onion, Yukon mash and a port wine sauce. "Always packed to the brim with Melrose stragglers who are happy to talk beer, sports or Hollywood" during football season (that would be soccer to you Yanks), it's full of expatriate fans watching Premiership (the British soccer league) matches on weekend mornings.

Gastropub | Informal | Moderate | west hollywood | 7383 Melrose Ave. | 323-655-3331 | www.villageidiotla.com | Dinner daily

Arroyo Chop House   83.0

The only thing that sets this Smith brothers–run restaurant apart from some of the better-known chains is the Pasadena location, which makes it convenient for those who find themselves east of the city and who don't want to drive downtown for a big juicy steak. Otherwise, all of the "standard steakhouse fare" can be found here, along with the type of "clubby and comfortable atmosphere" associated with the genre.

Steakhouse | Casual | Expensive | pasadena | 536 S. Arroyo Pkwy. | 626-577-7463 | www.arroyochophouse.com | Dinner daily

Pace   83.0

An unusual mix of celebrities in the hippie vein, organic ingredients, art-laden walls and live musicians makes this Laurel Canyon Italian "a fun space with good food and interesting people-watching." One person suggested you "check out the unusual pizzas, like the Aphrodite pie – basil pesto, thinly sliced potatoes, chopped green beans and fresh mozzarella," but another dismissed the "average food," describing the place's allure as "a return to the hanging ferns of the

'60s." Maybe you'll get lucky and sit next to Joni Mitchell while having dinner.

Italian | Casual | Moderate | hollywood | 2100 Laurel Canyon Blvd. | 323-654-8583 | www.peaceinthecanyon.com | Dinner daily

Yujean Kang's   83.0

Back in 1992, a "cleaned-up version of Chinese cuisine" was a novel concept, and Yujean Kang was the darling of the day. But 20 years later, the novelty of healthy Asian eats has worn off, and "Boy, has this place gone downhill," sighed several reviewers. But "a superb list of wines" goes a long way toward calming those skeptics, who prefer "a more authentic" version of dishes like a braised pork chop with garlic – namely, with a bit more grease in it. And to be fair, the place has its loyalists, who insist it remains "one of the finest Chinese restaurants in the country."

Chinese | Casual | Moderate | pasadena | 67 N. Raymond Ave. | 626-585-0855 | www.yujeankangs.com | Lunch & Dinner daily

Giorgio Baldi   82.5

The low rating for this celebrity-laden restaurant is reflected in comments like "full of celebs and bad food," "tables too close together," "They never honor your reservation," "The waiter kept banging into my wife's chair" and "overpriced and arrogant – they push you out the door as soon as you set your fork down." We did make note of the outlier who said it serves "the best Italian cuisine in Los Angeles County."

Italian | Casual | Expensive | santa monica | 114 W. Channel Rd. | 310-573-1660 | www.giorgiobaldi.us | Dinner Tue-Sun

Koi   81.0

Pop quiz: Why is it that celebrities like Keith Richards and Beyoncé always seem to frequent restaurants that our reviewers don't think much of? Answer: Have you ever seen a gossip columnist write about a celebrity's good taste in cuisine? That should tell you all you need to know about Koi, and who is eating there and why. If all this isn't warning enough, we can also tell you about "sub-par wait staff and the snobbish welcome"?

Japanese | Casual | Expensive | west hollywood | 730 N. La Cienega Blvd. | 310-659-9449 | www.koirestaurant.com | Dinner daily

Cheap Eats

UNIQUELY DELICIOUS

Pizzeria Mozza   8.5

Nancy Silverton's restaurant (which shares a space with Osteria Mozza, although there are two distinct entrances) is among the elite pizzerias in the country. While "the pizza dough is worth eating on its own," there are a number of exotic toppings on offer, like Ipswich clams, goat cheese, egg, Yukon Gold potato and Bermuda onions, along with classic pies like a Margherita. The menu also features a number of the same items served at Osteria (no mozzarella dishes, though), along with an abbreviated version of their wine list. "Dare I say our best meal in L.A.," "ingredients are impeccably fresh, and the crust is perfect" and "the pizza with fried squash blossoms and the butterscotch budino desert are cravings I deal with everyday" sum up reviewer comments.

Pizzeria | Moderate | hollywood | 641 N. Highland Ave. | 323-297-0101 | www.mozza-la.com | Lunch & Dinner daily

Roscoe's House of   8.1
Chicken & Waffles

Every part of the chicken comes either fried or smothered in gravy at this Hollywood soul food classic, along with an order of sweet-and-spicy waffles. Sides include grits, fries, biscuits and yams, and the late hours on weekends (they are open until 4:00 a.m.) means

"there's a good chance your chicken will come with a side order of local color." Among the celebrity sightings reported have been players on the Lakers or Clippers, and Snoop Dog took Larry King to dinner here too. Poultry prevails even at breakfast, when you can get your waffles with an order of chicken sausage.

Southern | Inexpensive | hollywood | 1514 N. Gower St. | 323-466-7453 | www.roscoeschickenandwaffles.com | Open daily

8 Oz. Burger Bar   8.0

A few years back, Govind Armstrong decided there wasn't enough money in serving New American cuisine, so he converted his restaurant (known as Table 8) to a burger joint. The focus is on sustainably raised meats – burgers are available in both corn- and grass-fed versions – and locally sourced ingredients. Other treats include Kobe beef corndogs, chicken potpie croquettes and a short-rib grilled cheese sandwich. Reviewers say, "great burgers and sides, and a small but tasty selection of cocktails and on-tap beers," and "It's a perfect neighborhood hangout, and I keep going back."

Hamburgers | Inexpensive | west hollywood | 7661 Melrose Ave. | 323-852-0008 | www.8ozburgerbar.com | Lunch & Dinner daily

RECOMMENDED

Joan's on Third   7.9

With some of the best baked goods in the city, a full selection of charcuterie and cheeses and sandwiches and prepared foods that range from an apricot-glazed ham and Brie sandwich to turkey meatloaf to quiche Lorraine, we dare anyone to find a more diverse menu than the one featured at this "bustling gourmet marketplace in West Hollywood." And making your Korean short ribs taste even better is "some of the best people-watching in the city." One downside of the experience, unfortunately, is having to endure standing in long lines to order the food (after you do so, however, you can sit down; runners bring your selections to the table).

Sandwiches | Inexpensive | west hollywood | 8350 W. Third St. | 323-655-2285 | www.joanson-third.com | Breakfast & Lunch Mon-Sat

Apple Pan   7.7

This unusual coffee shop, which exclusively offers seating at a U-shaped counter, is as close to classic Americana as it gets. The steak burger has been on the menu since 1927, and the hickory burger has been in service since 1945. The only other items available are sandwiches featuring Southern baked ham, tuna and egg salad, and you can end your meal with a slice of "delicious" apple, cream or pecan pie. The place is very popular, so you can "expect to wait" 10 or so minutes for a stool.

Hamburgers | Inexpensive | west l.a. | 10801 W. Pico Blvd. | 310-475-3585 | Lunch & Dinner Tue-Sun

Clementine   7.7

Reviewers tell us that this little shop in Westwood featuring "delicious sandwiches, baked goods and salads" is "one of L.A.'s secret gems." The reason: A former Campanile chef is in charge of the kitchen, and his pedigree shows in dishes like a soup of chicken, green chiles and pinto beans and mains like Thai steak salad or cheesy meatloaf. While it's predominantly a takeout shop, they offer café seating either inside or at a one of a half dozen alfresco tables.

Café | Inexpensive | westwood | 1751 Ensley Ave. | 310-552-1080 | www.clementineonline.com | Open daily

Huckleberry Café & Bakery 7.7

Zoe Nathan delivers "satisfying comfort food" and "amazing pastries and breads" at one of the most popular breakfast and lunch spots in the city. There is also a full menu of "interesting prepared dishes" like green eggs and ham (La Quercia prosciutto with pesto) for breakfast or a warm Niman Ranch burger served later in the day. While it's "not inexpensive," reviewers say "the excruciatingly long lines" prove it's "worth every penny for the amount of love and care put into the vast array of foods."

Café | Moderate | santa monica | 1014 Wilshire Blvd | 310-451-2311 | http://huckleberrycafe.com | Breakfast & Lunch Tue-Sun

Pink's Famous Hot Dogs   7.6

"Be prepared for a 20-minute wait" for the honor of being able to place your order at this Hollywood legend where the hot dogs have come in two sizes since 1939. There's an assortment of toppings, but pros know to order the 10-inch stretch dog with chili and mustard. For a more involved experience, you can order one of the specials, like the Rosie O'Donnell Long Island Dog (mustard, onions, chili and sauerkraut) and the Three Dog Night (three hot dogs wrapped in a burrito).

Hot Dogs | Inexpensive | la brea | 709 N. La Brea Ave. | 323-931-4223 | www.pinkshollywood.com | Open daily

Barney Greengrass   7.5

While the West Coast outpost of one of New York's iconic Jewish appetizing shops is not quite up to the original, it's still one of the best places to grab a bagel and lox in Los Angeles. Along with a full slate of smoked fish, there are eggs, omelets and French toast for breakfast, while sandwiches filled with pastrami and other meats appear at lunch. Given the location on the top floor of Barneys in Beverly Hills, it's no wonder this is "a popular lunch spot for both power shoppers and powerful agents."

Delicatessen | Moderate | beverly hills | Barneys | 9570 Wilshire Blvd., 5th fl. | 310-777-5877 | www.barneygreengrass.com | Breakfast & Lunch daily

Let's Be Frank   7.5

Commercially fabricated frankfurters are so pervasive that one would hardly recognize the grass-fed, artisanal version of the genre as a hot dog. This particular purveyor of such tasty franks generates comments that fall into two categories: Gourmets call it a "damn good hot dog" and "the single best hot dog I've ever had," while the nutritionally orientated call it "the best clean hot dog in the world" and "a healthy hot dog stand." Lest this all sound too high-falutin' for a frank, bear in mind eating here is an "alfresco dining experience," as the franks are served out of a truck parked at the Helms Bakery complex.

Hot Dogs | Inexpensive | culver city | Helms Bakery Complex | Helms Ave. | www.letsbefrankdogs.com | Lunch Wed-Sun

Philippe the Original   7.4

Legend has it that in 1918, Philippe Mathieu accidentally dropped a French roll into a gravy pan and the French Dip sandwich was born. Beef is the most famous of the dips, although they also serve pork, lamb, ham or turkey, which you can top with Swiss, Monterey Jack, blue or American cheese before slathering your sandwich with homemade mustard. There are two soups that change daily, and they also serve breakfast, but let's face it, you're there for a dip.

Sandwiches | Inexpensive | downtown | 1001 N. Alameda St. | 213-628-3781 | www.philippes.com | Open daily

In-N-Out Burger   7.3

In-N-Out has a cult following, which is not so easy for a chain with close to 200 locations. Part of the mystique has to do with what used to be an secret menu, which is now available to everyone on the Internet. Feast on creations like the 2 x 4 (two patties and four pieces of cheese), the 3 x 3 or the monstrous 4 x 4. They even serve a burger for the gluten-intolerant, in which the bun is replaced with a lettuce wrap. The rest of the fare – fries, sodas, shakes – is more conventional.

Hamburger | Inexpensive | westwood | 3640 Cahuenga Blvd. | 800-786-1000 | www.in-n-out.com | Lunch & Dinner daily

Canter's   7.1

Attention, all aficionados of *Curb Your Enthusiasm*: If you were wondering where Larry David took the head of the kidney clinic when he was trying to avoid giving Richard Lewis his own *rognon* – Canter's is your place. Located in the old Jewish neighborhood, it's been "a bit of New York in Los Angeles" since 1931. Open 24 hours, seven days a week, it caters to a combination of expats, old-timers, locals and tourists who enjoy noshing on everything from bagels and lox to bowls of matzoh ball soup.

Coffee Shop | Inexpensive | hollywood | 419 N. Fairfax Ave. | 323-651-2030 | www.cantersdeli.com | Open daily

Langer's Deli   7.0

Ever since food writer Jonathan Gold declared that the pastrami at Langer's was superior to the pastrami at Katz's in New York City, a controversy has hovered over this restaurant. Truth is, we never heard anyone who wasn't a resident of Los Angeles make that claim. Friendly competition aside, this is "the best pastrami in town," served in a classic Jewish deli atmosphere. Note the limited hours below.

Delicatessen | Inexpensive | downtown | 704 S. Alvarado St. | 213-483-8050 | www.langersdeli.com | Breakfast & Lunch Mon-Sat

Wurstküche   7.0

Are you into weird brats? Joseph Pitruzzelli's sausage emporium serves 21 different types of them, beginning with German (bratwursts and bocks), Italian (hot with pork and vegetarian), gourmet (smoked chicken and turkey with sun-dried tomato and mozzarella) and exotic (rattlesnake and rabbit with jalapeño peppers). You eat your sausages at large communal tables in a warehouse setting with sides like truffle fries. As a bonus, the "large quantity of brews encourages conversation and new encounters," say sociable reviewers.

Hot Dogs | Inexpensive | japantown | 800 E. 3rd Street | 213-687-4444 | www.wurstkucherestaurant.com | Lunch & Dinner daily

OTHER PLACES MENTIONED

Griddle Café   6.6

If you enjoy eating pancakes the size of pizzas or eggs prepared in more ways than you can imagine, against a backdrop of blasting blues music and fellow diners who look like they just came from the late show at some rock venue – run, don't walk to this funky Hollywood coffee shop. Prices that are "astonishingly low," considering that "an order of pancakes can serve an entire third-world nation," means you're in for a considerable wait if you don't get there early.

Coffee Shop | Inexpensive | hollywood | 7916 Sunset Blvd. | 323-874-0377 | www.thegriddlecafe.com | Breakfast & Dinner daily

Umami Burger   6.6

One doesn't normally associate umami, the Asian concept of savory, with fast food. But in multicultural L.A., the concept has been applied to the hamburger, resulting in toppings, like green chilies with malt liquor or a turkey miso burger with baba ganoush. Fans say it "lives up to the hype," adding, "Port and Stilton on a flavorful burger is nothing to shake a stick at." You can enjoy "some of the best fries in L.A." with your burgers, too.

Hamburgers | Inexpensive | midtown | 850 S. La Brea Ave. | 323-931-3000 | www.umamiburger.com | Lunch & Dinner daily

Du-Par's   6.4

How you feel about a diner that has been cranking out fresh fruit and cream pies since 1938 depends on how you feel about diner culture. If you're the type who thinks that "classic surroundings" and "time-worn techniques and effort" outweigh humble ingredients, you should slide into a booth at the very next opportunity. But if your definition of fresh fruit means fresh that day rather than once fresh and now preserved, you will find nothing noteworthy here.

Coffee Shop | Inexpensive | west hollywood | 6333 W. Third St. | 323-933-8446 | www.du-pars.com | Open daily

Cora's Coffee Shop   6.2

Bruce Marder's attempt to capitalize on his success at Capo features standard breakfast fare, save for Wagyu beef and eggs, and offerings like polenta and sausage and Chinese chicken salad. at lunch and dinner. There's a lovely patio, but it can't overcome food described as "not much better than what they serve at your neighborhood coffee shop."

Coffee Shop | Inexpensive | santa monica | 1802 Ocean Ave. | 310-451-9562 | www.corascoffee.com | Breakfast & Lunch Tue-Sun

Nate 'n Al   5.5

This is where Hollywood agents, with their television- and movie-star clients in tow, wolf down fat sandwiches. All the requisite elements of a New York–style kosher deli are on hand, including surly waitresses who have been working here for more than 40 years. Note that it's "kosher-style," which means that those who eat "treif" can order a ham sandwich or add Swiss cheese to their pastrami sandwich if they're in the mood.

Delicatessen | Inexpensive | beverly hills | 414 N. Beverly Dr. | 310-274-0101 | www.natenal.com | Open daily

Malibu CA

Nobu Malibu   92.5

This comment sums up the sentiment that many of our reviewers expressed about Nobu Matsuhisa's restaurants: "I resent that it's basically a chain, but because the food is amazing. I never get sick of eating here." The menu at this location is pretty much the same as what you find at Nobus around the country (tuna tartare with osetra caviar, spicy creamy crab, miso black cod etc.), with one exception: the daily specials board, which is always filled with "exotic dishes offered at exotic prices." Otherwise, this is your "typical Malibu place – very busy and with service that is very inattentive unless you're a movie or television star" (many of whom are in attendance, often with their children in tow).

Japanese | Casual | Expensive | 3835 Cross Creek Rd. | 310-317-9140 | www.nobumatsuhisa.com | Dinner daily

Saddle Peak Lodge   90.9

A number of our reviewers make an annual pilgrimage to this rustic yet elegant restaurant for "the most exotic menu of game dishes in the country." Even during the off-season you will find elk, bison and ostrich on the menu. But diners beware: The cuisine during the hunting season is praised to a far greater extent than it is during the rest of the year, when the New American/Continental cuisine served on a year-round basis is a bit safe for our survey participants, with one person saying, "In summer this is a must go only if you love eating things like elk that time of year." Sunday brunch is popular when diners can enjoy "the lovely views over Malibu Canyon."

Continental | Casual | Expensive | 419 Cold Canyon Rd. | 818-222-3888 | www.saddlepeaklodge.com | Dinner Wed-Sun, Lunch Sun

Palm Springs CA

LG's Prime Steakhouse   90.0

While LG's contends for the honor of serving the best quality steaks south of Los Angeles, the rest of the menu at this three restaurant mini-chain doesn't attract the same quality of comments as the prime beef – with one exception: The Caesar salad, made tableside, might just be "the best in the country." A lengthy and pricey wine list and ice creams from McConnell's in Santa Barbara cap off what some say is "the best place to eat while driving on the I-10 between L.A. and Phoenix."

Steakhouse | Casual | Expensive | 255 S. Palm Canyon Dr. | 760-416-1779 | www.lgsprimesteakhouse.com | Dinner daily

Second location: la quinta | 78525 Highway 111, Suite 100 | 760-771-9911 | www.lgsprimesteakhouse.com | Dinner daily

Third location: palm desert | 74-225 Highway 111. | 760-779-9799 | www.lgsprimesteakhouse.com | Dinner daily

TOP LOCAL CHOICE

Le Vallauris   88.0

Le Vallauris is the number-one choice for people who still enjoy eating dishes like rack of lamb in a dining room featuring Flemish tapestries and Louis XV furniture. The rest of the menu – sea urchin custard with blue crab, beef cassis-Bordelaise and duck with honey and black pepper – neither offends nor tantalizes. Reviewers say, "My favorite in the desert. Make sure you eat in the magnificent outdoor courtyard." It's very old Palm Springs, and "anyone who is/was anyone, has dined here."

French | Casual | Expensive | 385 W. Tahquitz Canyon Way | 760-325-5059 | www.levallauris.com | Lunch & Dinner daily

ACCEPTABLE   OTHER RESTAURANTS MENTIONED

Cuistot   85.0

Of the three major upscale Palm Springs area restaurants, Cuistot, with a menu featuring dishes like a fresh beet and cream cheese Napoleon with smoked salmon and a duo of duck breast and leg confit with a foie gras truffle sauce, is probably the most French. It's also the most casual: The Palm Springs clientele likes getting dressed up, but Cuistot has "a mixture of people; some are dressed nicely, while others look like they came straight from the swimming pool."

French | Casual | Expensive | palm desert |72-595 El Paseo | 760-340-1000 | www.cuistotrestaurant.com | Lunch & Dinner Tue-Sat, Sun dinner only

Wally's Desert Turtle   83.5

While the city's Mid-Century Modern architecture may be back in vogue, that era's funny combination of French and northern Italian cooking (also known as Continental cuisine) has gone the way of the typewriter. But it's alive and well at Wally's, where a well-heeled crowd, many of whom pre-date the Mid-Century Modern era by a number of decades, are patrons. "It's a good place to go if you want to reminisce about the good old Rat Pack days," said one reviewer.

Continental | Casual | Expensive | rancho mirage | 71-775 Highway 111 | 760-568-9321 | www.wallys-desert-turtle.com | Dinner daily, Fri lunch

San Diego-La Jolla CA

HIGHLY RECOMMENDED

Sushi Ota   92.5

All the key indicia that you are within the confines of one of California's top sushi places are present here. The first is the location in a dreary strip mall, directly across the street from gas stations and taco stands. The second – "super-fresh, high-quality fish, including tuna, sea urchin and a number of other varieties that come from local waters," doled out in "preparations that range from classic to contemporary" – is responsible for the third: a line of people waiting for a table that usually extends out the door. Reviewers weren't as enamored with the service (one complained that they put a one-hour time limit on his meal), but if you "sit at the counter and put yourself in the chef's hands," you will enjoy what one reviewer described as "easily the best sushi between Los Angeles and the Mexican border."

Seafood | Casual | Expensive | san diego | 4529 Mission Bay Dr. | 858-270-5670 | www.sushiota.com | Dinner daily, Lunch Tue-Fri

RECOMMENDED

George's California Modern   91.5

In business since 1984 and known as George's by the Cove for more than 20 years, ever since Trey Foshee became its chef, and they changed the name to George's Modern, there has been an uptick in the ratings for this La Jolla mainstay. Foshee's New American menu is stocked with produce sourced from the legendary Chino Farms (they supply produce to Chez Panisse and Spago, among others), which turn up in dishes like a peach, prosciutto and burrata salad or an ancho chile–grilled pork chop with creamed corn and peppers. Located in the heart of La Jolla Village, California Modern offers a combination of "solid food" and "an exceptional view" that make it "the perfect location for guests from out of town."There's also a more casual rooftop bistro upstairs.

New American | Casual | Expensive | la jolla | 1250 Prospect St. | 858-454-4244 | www.georgesatthe-cove.com | Dinner daily

TOP LOCAL CHOICE

A. R. Valentien   88.0

Put the cooking at this luxury resort in the category of "well-done but standard upscale hotel food." Bocuse d'Or winner Jeff Jackson's menu, featuring dishes like a house-made charcuterie platter and roasted organic chicken with a mushroom, bacon and green garlic flan, plays second fiddle to the "interesting Mission architecture" and "a view of the Torrey Pines golf course that can't be beat." Reviewers say, "It's a good choice if you are staying at the hotel, but not worth making a special trip for."

New American | Casual | Expensive | la jolla | The Lodge at Torrey Pines | 11480 North Torrey Pines Rd. | 858-777-6635 | www.arvalentien.com | Lunch & Dinner daily, Sat-Sun brunch

Donovan's Steak & Chop House   88.0

"The best in the San Diego area," claim reviewers about this "New York–style steak-house." The list runs the gamut from filets, rib eyes, strips and porterhouses, while the chops side of the menu begins with pork and veal varieties and continues with tuna steak and a rack of lamb. In a country brimming with steakhouses, the good ones always seem to manufacture fans who say things like, "Donovan's gets my nod as the best place in the country for this type of meal."

Steakhouse | Casual | Expensive | la jolla | 4340 La Jolla Village Dr. | 858-450-6666 | www.donovans-steakhouse.com | Dinner Mon-Sat

Market Restaurant and Bar   88.0

Given its proximity to Chino Farms, it's not surprising that every reviewer mentioned the "terrific ingredients" that Carl Schroeder sources. But that's where the agreement ended: Reviewers split over the cooking itself, with some praising the "beautiful presen-tations" and "sophisticated" style, while others called the dishes "oversauced and over-wrought, preventing the underlying ingredients from being enjoyed to their full extent." There's a full menu of sushi, but it's available only in the lounge, causing one reviewer to say, "I was looking to throw down $100 on a platter of toro before ordering my $30 steak, but I settled for a salad instead."

New American | Casual | Expensive | del mar | 3702 Via de la Valle | 858-523-0007 | www.marketdelmar.com | Dinner daily

NINE-TEN   88.0

Many people are familiar with La Jolla's Grande Colonial Hotel, built in 1913. But few of them are familiar with Jason Knibb's cuisine, which features dishes like local swordfish with Chino Farm fingerling potatoes, fennel, shallots, Castelvetrano olives and Romesco sauce. The combination of traditional venue and contemporary cuisine means that "a mixed crowd of young diners and establishment elders" enjoy "sophisticated food" based on "excellent ingredients and a deft kitchen." Other items that act in the restaurant's favor are a "thoughtful wine list" and "splendid views of the Pacific."

New American | Casual | Expensive | la jolla | Grande Colonial | 910 Prospect St. | 858-964-5400 | www.nine-ten.com | Open daily

Pamplemousse Grille   88.0

When it comes to choosing a special-occasion restaurant in the North San Diego suburbs, Jeffrey Strauss' restaurant often edges out the competition. The innovative menu features starters like a kimchee seafood martini, as well as entrées like a mixed grill of game: venison chop au poivre, quail marinated in lemon thyme and a smoked duck breast. Strauss' wine expertise rivals his knowledge of food, and he offers a series of "fantastic though expensive" wine dinners. A number of reviewers complained about a dining room with a "high level of noise."

New American | Casual | Expensive | solano beach | 514 Via de la Valle | 858-792-9090 | www.pgrille.com | Dinner daily, Fri lunch

ACCEPTABLE

Pacifica Del Mar   86.5

Despite a mall location, "reliable seafood," an "excellent wine selection" and "great ocean views" more than compensate. Tommy DiMella dishes show an Asian influence, like lemongrass-kaffir lime mahi mahi in a shiitake broth with a green papaya crab salad. Comments ranged from "consistently good food at reasonable prices for the quality" to "the food was good, but the service was hurried so they could turn our table."

Seafood | Casual | Moderate | del mar | 1555 Camino Del Mar | 858-792-0476 | www.pacificadel-mar.com | Lunch & Dinner daily

Arterra   86.0

This restaurant caused a stir when it was announced that its menu would be designed by Bradley Ogden and executed by Jason Maitland. All went well, until Maitland moved on. Now, while it's commended for serving "local ingredient-based food with a bit of a twist," like flatbread pizza topped with duck confit and goat cheese or roasted Jidori chicken breast paired with beef short ribs and Thumbelina carrots, reviewers say, "It was better when Maitland was running the kitchen." It can't seem to overcome its location in the Marriott Del Mar, either.

New American | Casual | Expensive | del mar | 11966 El Camino Real | 858-369-6032 | www.arterrarestaurant.com | Lunch & Dinner Mon-Fri Sat dinner only

Bertrand at Mr. A's   85.0

Given how restaurants atop skyscrapers are derided, we were pleasantly surprised when we read the comments about this "spectacular location," operated by the group that runs Mille Fleurs. For maximum enjoyment, try to "grab a seat on the terrace" and "watch the planes land while enjoying your truffled mac 'n' cheese." Complaints came in two varieties: prices – the view is factored into the cost – and a lingering nostalgia for the original Mr. A's, which reviewers hinted was "a favorite with local mobsters."

New American | Casual | Expensive | san diego | 2550 Fifth Ave., 12th fl. | 619-239-1377 | www.bertrandatmisteras.com | Dinner daily, Lunch Mon-Fri

Tapenade   85.0

After attracting raves at New York City's Park Bistro, Jean-Michel Diot moved his family to La Jolla and opened this restaurant. That was 14 years ago, and San Diego diners are still enjoying his cuisine. Diot trained in Paul Bocuse's kitchen in Lyon, and his restaurant is "a bit more formal" than what you typically find in an area where casual dining reigns. Reviews of the cuisine are mixed – fans call it "their favorite French dining in San Diego," while critics say, "The food is boring, predictable and unremarkable."

French | Casual | Expensive | la jolla | 7612 Fay Ave. | 858-551-7500 | www.tapenaderestaurant.com | Lunch & Dinner Tue-Fri, Sat-Sun dinner only

WineSellar & Brasserie   84.0

Reviewers say the food is "good enough" to warrant a trip to this wine store/brasserie where a big part of the attraction is being able to buy any bottle in the shop and take it up to dinner. The menu is "standard French fare with a California twist," like Niçoise salad, wild Pacific halibut with pommes purée and pepper-crusted venison, but "the real attraction is a store full of those hard-to-get cult wines and a nominal corkage fee."

French | Casual | Moderate | mira mesa | 9550 Waples St. | 858-450-9557 | www.winesellar.com | Lunch & Dinner Thu-Sat, Tue-Wed dinner only

El Bizcocho   84.0

When Gavin Kaysen used to run this kitchen at this resort, diners were as interested in the tasting menu as in their golf scores. But now that he's moved to New York's Café Boulud, this has become yet one more restaurant that

proves the proposition that it's difficult to find a high-quality meal in the tony suburbs. Or as one reviewer put it, "They can't seem to find a chef to fill Kaysen's shoes, but it's still a great lunch place after golf."

New American | Casual | Expensive | rancho bernardo | 17550 Bernardo Oaks Dr. | 858-675-8550 | www.ranchobernardoinn.com | Dinner Tue-Sat

OTHER PLACES MENTIONED

Mille Fleurs   83.0

Consistently winning "best French restaurant" awards, this venue remains "one of the most popular special-occasion restaurants in San Diego." But reviewers say it's coasting on its reputation; "way stiff, way overpriced and nothing is innovative," antagonists argue. More moderate souls say it was "once very good – and is still tasty on occasion, [but] the décor and cuisine sorely need an update."

French | Casual | Expensive | rancho santa fe | 6009 Paseo Delicias | 858-756-3085 | www.millefleurs.com | Dinner daily, Lunch Tue-Fri

Marine Room   81.0

Located on the strip in La Jolla Village, this restaurant has "one of the most spectacular views on the California coast" and "a handsome interior" that are wasted on "food that leaves a lot to be desired." While it might be "worth visiting for the unforgettable after-dinner drinks," some ask, "Why eat here when George's is right down the street?"

French | Casual | Expensive | la jolla | 2000 Spindrift Dr. | 858-459-7222 | www.marineroom.com | Dinner daily

Roppongi   78.0

It seems this pan-Asian small plates restaurant featuring a sushi bar has become "a bit tired over the years." There was a time when "The concept was unique," but now it's just "one of many restaurants serving this style of cuisine." It's considered "expensive," but prices drop by 50% if you dine before 6:00 p.m.

Pan-Asian | Casual | Expensive | la jolla | 875 Prospect St. | 858-551-5252 | www.roppongiusa.com | Lunch & Dinner daily

Cheap Eats

OTHER PLACES MENTIONED

Hodad's   6.4

This Ocean Beach classic is like something out of a '60s movie. Think of a hamburger joint filled with a combination of hipsters, surfers, rock 'n' roll musicians, bikers, students and the occasional family eating single, double and even triple "loosely packed, messy and juicy" burgers along with "amazing onion rings" and "delicious shakes" to an ear-shattering sound track. It's the classic place to refuel after a perfect day on the beach, conveniently located down the block.

Hamburgers | Inexpensive | ocean beach | 5010 Newport Ave. | 619-224-4623 | www.hodadies.com | Lunch & Dinner daily

Santa Barbara CA

RECOMMENDED

Bouchon   90.3

This country French restaurant, opened by veterans of the old Wine Cask, has served solid Gallic classics for the past dozen years. Diners enjoy dishes like a French-style four-onion soup with a Gruyère-sourdough gratin, local halibut with red creamer potatoes and a braised Kurobuta pork shank with yams and applesauce. There's an "interesting selection of regional wines" that includes "a superb list by the glass," as well as a "pleasant Mediterranean décor" and "friendly service." Reviewers say "It's the best restaurant in Santa Barbara," while acknowledging that "It might not be the most exciting food" in the area.

French | Casual | Expensive | 235 N. Cañon Dr. | 310-271-9910 | www.bouchonbistro.com | Lunch & Dinner daily

TOP LOCAL CHOICE

The Ballard Inn (32 miles northwest in Ballard)   89.0

When it comes to finding a cuisine that's atypical for its region, few venues are more surprising than this "elegant inn." Stints with Ming Tsai and Gary Danko are important entries on chef Budi Kazali's résumé; his lineage shows in dishes like Thai-style coconut kabocha squash soup with Kaffir lime crème and rack of lamb with red miso–eggplant caviar and red pepper coulis. "One of the best spots in the Central Coast wine country: romantic with fabulous food and a great wine list – especially from local winemakers."

Asian-Fusion | Casual | Expensive | ballard | 2436 Baseline Ave. | 800-638-2466 | www.ballardinn.com | Dinner daily

Downey's   88.5

Thirty years is a long time for a restaurant to be in business. But that's the mark John and Liz Downey's establishment is going to hit next year. The "genre is mid-1980s California cuisine," like local sea bass with citrus-basil sauce, leafy greens and parsley potatoes. But as is typical when discussing old-timers, reviewers are split. Some praise the "most consistent food in Santa Barbara," while to others, the "food seemed a little dated." One critic added, "I'm never impressed when all entrées have the same sides."

Californian | Casual | Expensive | santa barbara | 1305 State St. | 805-966-5006 | www.downeyssb.com | Dinner daily

Arigato Sushi   88.0

Given that Santa Barbara is responsible for providing high-quality seafood to some of the top Japanese restaurants in the state (and the country) – not to mention the significant amount of wealth in the area – it's somewhat surprising that this city doesn't have a top-notch sushi restaurant of its own. But with reviewers saying "The vast and interesting menu has improved and the quality of the fish is excellent," it appears that Arigato Sushi is on an upward trajectory.

Japanese | Casual | Expensive | 1225 State St. | 805-965-6074 | www.arigatosushi.com | Dinner daily

The Hungry Cat   88.0

Suzanne Goin and David Lentz have brought an offshoot of their Hollywood fish restaurant to Santa Barbara. The raw bar features clams, oysters, shrimps and a variety of crabs, including king, stone and snow, which you can follow with small plates like oyster and pork belly beignets or larger ones like pan-roasted grouper. Getting to slurp your oysters in a "hip, happening scene" is a plus, as is the ability to just drop by and grab a quick casual meal, which makes it "a good choice for pre/post-theater or movie eats."

Seafood | Informal | Moderate | santa barbara | 1535 N. Vine St. | 323-462-2155 | www.thehungrycat.com | Lunch & Dinner daily

Suzanne's Cuisine (32 miles northwest in Ojai)   88.0

After getting an MBA from the U. of Chicago, Suzanne Roll decided she would rather spend her time visiting farmers' markets than reading spreadsheets, so she deciced to open a restaurant. One reviewer identified the key to successfully enjoying this place: "Don't set your expectations to the level of fine dining, and you'll do all right." Almost every reviewer mentioned the "excellent and fairly priced wine list," with one adding, "Where else can you find Sine Qua Non at below-auction prices?"

Californian | Casual | Moderate | ojai | 502 W. Ojai Ave. | 805-640-1961 | www.suzannescuisine.com | Lunch & Dinner Wed-Mon

ACCEPTABLE

Olio e Limone   87.5

Every affluent city needs the type of Italian restaurant where you can enjoy the food without concentrating too much. That best describes Alberto and Elaine Morello's restaurant, where everyone from seniors to people on dates enjoy "strong entrées" like duck ravioli with porcini cream sauce or a veal chop with roast potatoes and rosemary jus. Reviewers described the food as "not inventive but reliably prepared" and accompanied by "the type of killer wine list you'd expect in a wealthy town."

Italian | Casual | Expensive | santa barbara | 11 W. Victoria St. | 805-899-2699 | www.olioelimone.com | Lunch & Dinner Mon-Sat, Sun dinner only

Hitching Post   86.0
(43 miles northwest in Buellton)

Made famous in the film *Sideways*, the Hitching Post offers a classic example of Santa Maria–style barbecue – slabs of beef slowly cooked over red oak logs. Unfortunately, while it's a fun place, complete with a great little list of local wines that emphasizes pinot noir, the quality of the meat is "sub-par" compared to that of a top steakhouse. But it's good enough as a stopover for hungry travelers driving along the north-south axis on the California coast.

Steakhouse | Informal | Moderate | buellton | 3325 Point Sal Rd. | 805-937-6151 | www.hitchingpost1.com | Dinner daily

Brothers at Mattei's Tavern   85.5

(33 miles north in Los Olivos)

How cool is it to eat in a tavern that dates from 1886 with the Santa Barbara wine country a stone's throw away? Matt and Jeff Nichols opened their restaurant in 1996, moving it into this historic tavern in 2002, and they have been serving dishes like grilled pork rib chop with brandy glaze, honey butter, applewood-smoked bacon and mashed potatoes here ever since. The combination of "credible cook-ing and a historic dining room make for a relaxed wine country dinner."

New American | Casual | Expensive | los olivos | 2350 Railway Ave. | 805-688-4820 | www.matteistavern.com | Dinner daily

Cheap Eats

OTHER PLACES MENTIONED

La Super-Rica Taqueria   6.8

This otherwise nondescript taco stand attracted national recognition during the 1970s, when Julia Child said it was one of her favorite places to eat. The first thing you notice upon entering is the "pat-pat-pat sound of fresh tortillas being made to order." Tacos are often available with unusual fillings like cactus paddles or Petrale sole. It's a very popular place, and the lines can be excruciatingly long, so we suggest that you arrive close to opening time.

Mexican | Inexpensive | 622 Milpas St. | 805-963-4940 | Lunch & Dinner Thu-Tue

Is your belly overflowing with information about the restaurants you have been visiting?

Well, then, we would like you to tell us about your experience. Just go to the web address below and sign up for our 2012 dining survey.

It will be going live this summer. Sign up now and we'll send you an email notifying you when the survey's up.

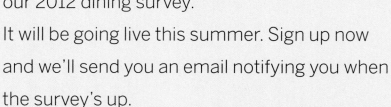

www.opinionatedabout.com/2012

New York Metropolitan Area, including Long Island, Northern New Jersey & Upstate New York

Hamptons &
the East End of Long Island NY

AN IMPORTANT DESTINATION

North Fork Table & Inn   95.2

After toiling in a number of Manhattan kitchens, including Gramercy Tavern and Aureole, Gerry Hayden and Claudia Fleming decided it was time to escape the rat race. Fortunately, Mike and Mary Mraz, also veterans of Gramercy Tavern, wanted to do the same. They formed a partnership and set out to find a place to call their own. Fleming located a run-down, white clapboard inn on the North Fork, and after a careful restoration (Fleming actually decorated the place herself), they opened what is easily the best restaurant on Long Island.

Almost all of the produce on Hayden's menu comes from local farms just down the road. And if you have an early dinner reservation, don't be surprised to see a local fisherman delivering his daily catch, which might turn up in dishes like a crudo of Block Island fluke with melon, poached ginger, sunflower seeds and micro cilantro, or a paella of Shinnecock monkfish, Gulf shrimp and house-made chorizo. Fleming's desserts are as delightful as they were during her Gramercy Tavern days, and the Mrazes offer the type of professional service you don't usually see on the East End of Long Island.

New American | Casual | Expensive | southold | 57225 Main Rd. | 631-765-0177 | www.northforktablean-dinn.com | Lunch daily, Dinner Thu-Mon

RECOMMENDED

The Palm   90.7

Having served steaks in this 300-year-old building since 1980, this Hamptons offshoot of The Palm allows you to enjoy a true New York City steakhouse experience at the beach. During the season, it's filled every night with people chomping on what they feel are the best steaks in the country, especially "the jaw-dropping double-cut New York strip." Lobsters range from three to six pounds, and there are also a few Italian entrées. It all comes with classic sides and a classic atmosphere that's reminiscent of the original. Popular with everyone from homeowners to celebs, it's not unusual to find the likes of Calvin Klein hosting a dinner for 12.

Steakhouse | Casual | Expensive | east hampton | Hunting Inn | 94 Main St. | 631-324-0411 | www.thepalm.com | Dinner Daily

TOP LOCAL CHOICE

1770 House   89.5

If it were in Manhattan it would be one of dozens of places, but "in the Hamptons it's just below the top tier" – that's what reviewers say about this restaurant located in a house that actually dates from 1663. Up until 2002, when Kevin Penner took over the kitchen, it was a place where people wore jackets to dinner. But Penner replaced the duck à l'orange with butter-poached lobster with sweet corn risotto, mascarpone and basil. The dress code got more modern – i.e., casual – too.

New American | Casual | Expensive | east hampton | 143 Main St. | 631-324-1770 | 1770house.com | Dinner daily

Nick & Toni's   89.5

Because it's often filled with movie stars, rappers, media executives and flush weekend homeowners, this can be the toughest reservation in the Hamptons. The cuisine is simple Mediterranean fare, with some dishes cooked in a wood-burning oven, and there are enough local ingredients in play to make the food interesting, like a salad of grilled local peaches served with runny gorgonzola. As with many other local restaurants, "The quality suffers during the high season" due to the sheer volume of people flooding its gates.

Mediterranean | Casual | Expensive | east hampton | 136 N. Main St. | 631-324-3550 | www.nickandtonis.com | Dinner Wed-Sun

ACCEPTABLE

Rowdy Hall   87.5

This casual bar and grill in an alley in the heart of East Hampton serves the best hamburger in town, along with advanced pub food like local flounder meunière or pork Milanese with bitter greens and red onions. There's a nice list of beers and ales and a better than average wine list for a casual restaurant of this type. The wait for a table is never too long, making it "the perfect place to grab a quick meal after seeing a movie down the block."

American | Informal | Moderate | east hampton | 10 Main St. | 631-324-8555 | www.rowdyhall.com | Lunch & Dinner daily

Duryea's Lobster Deck   87.0

The Duryea family has been in the lobster business for decades, so it's a bit of a surprise that they can't scrounge together a better operation than this one. But since the Hamptons aren't flush with restaurants where you can enjoy a steamed lobster while looking out over a large body of water (even though it looks out on Lake Montauk rather than the ocean), "this BYOB will do," especially when the days are long and you can crack a claw while watching a beautiful sunset.

Seafood | Informal | Moderate | montauk | 65 Tuthill Rd. | 631-668-2410 | www.duryealobsters.com | Lunch & Dinner during season

Citta Nuova   86.0

A location in the heart of the town means this Italian small plates restaurant from Kevin Penner is jammed every meal of the day. The varied menu includes platters of salumi and cheese, various pastas and a handful of mains, which you can enjoy in a lively environment – largely the result of a bar dominated by large-screen TVs showing whatever New York sports team happens to be playing. "Good for large parties."

Italian | Informal | Moderate | east hampton | 29 Newtown Ln. | 631-324-6300 | www.cittanuova.com | Open daily

Babette's   85.5

Keep walking past the Coach and James Perse shops and you will come upon this "quasi-health food restaurant." The diverse menu includes everything from pan-seared local fluke to pecan-crusted tempeh. In summer, it's super-popular for breakfast, with long lines of young people with rental shares enjoying their French toast while watching the crowds parade up and down Newtown Lane.

Eclectic | Informal | Moderate | east hampton | 66 Newtown Ln. | 631-329-5377 | Open daily during summer; call other times

American Hotel   85.0

Unlike most Hamptons restaurants that feature large, lively dining rooms, the American Hotel, which dates back to 1876, is reminiscent of the type of inn you would expect to find in a small town in New England. Unfortunately, along with the retro vibe comes retro food that is "in desperate need of updating." For many years, it offered one of the country's best wine lists, but unfortunately it's been picked over and re-priced.

American | Casual | Expensive | sag harbor | 49 Main St. | 631-725-3535 | www.theamericanhotel. com | Open daily

OTHER PLACES MENTIONED

Bobby Van's Steakhouse   83.0

If you were fortunate enough to visit this restaurant back when the Hamptons weren't overrun by investment bankers, you would probably find more than one famous artist or writer nursing a stiff drink at the bar. These days the place is part of the family of restaurants operated by the people who brought us Smith & Wollensky, and the artists and writers have been replaced by hungry tourists, most visiting for the weekend.

Steakhouse | Casual | Expensive | bridgehampton | Montauk Hwy. | 631-537-0590 | www.bobbyvans. com | Lunch & Dinner daily

Cheap Eats

RECOMMENDED

Hamtpton Chutney   7.7
Company

The menu at this sandwich shop revolves around an Indian rice and lentil crepe known as the dosa. Some of the fillings are traditional, like curried potatoes and peas, while others are decidedly less so, like smoked turkey, arugula and roasted

tomatoes. There's also a soup of the day, as well as a number of subcontinental-inspired beverages like cardamom iced coffee and orange blossom lemonade.

Indian | Inexpensive | amagansett | Main St. | 631-267-3131 | www.hamptonchutney.com | Lunch during summer; call other times

OTHER PLACES MENTIONED

Lobster Roll (Lunch)   5.9

Even though it's only 75 miles away as the crow flies, Napeague doesn't have the type of high-quality seafood special-ists that you find on Cape Cod."Lunch," as it is lovingly known to the throngs who keep it packed throughout the season, is as good as it gets. Even so, cynics snap, "This could be the most overrated sea-food restaurant in the world."

Seafood | Inexpensive | napeague | 1980 Montauk Hwy. | 631-267-3740 | www.lobsterroll. com | Lunch & Dinner daily in season

World Pie   5.2

One would think that making accept-able pizza wouldn't be that difficult. But that doesn't hold true of this "Hamptons stalwart," whose pies were described as "slightly better than what you can find in the frozen foods section of your super-market." A few people recommended it as a "good choice when there are a lot of kids in your party."

Pizzeria | Moderate | bridgehampton | 2402 Montauk Hwy. | 631-537-7999 | Lunch & Dinner daily

Nassau & Western Suffolk Counties NY

AN IMPORTANT DESTINATION

Peter Luger Steak House   96.1

When it comes to places to eat corn-fed beef, anyone who tells you they know a res-taurant that serves better steak than Peter Luger doesn't know what they are talking about. Whenever a shipment of prime short loins arrives at any of the top meat whole-salers in New York City, Luger is given "first pick," meaning that their buyer is allowed to walk through the wholesaler's cold box and choose the ones that look the best. Of course, that doesn't mean every steak at the restaurant is perfect, but the exceptionally high rating for a steakhouse is a good indication of how often the system works.

In addition to the "ethereal porterhouse steaks," the menu offers quirky starters and side dishes, from hot-house tomatoes that one slathers with a sickly sweet steak sauce and horseradish to hash brown potatoes, that round out what is a uniquely American regional dining experience. It's rumored that this suburban location doesn't measure up to the Brooklyn original. But tell that to the hordes who ensure that reservations are tough to come by any day of the week. Lunch is a good alternative; that's also when they serve one of the area's best hamburgers, made from the trimmings of 28-day-aged steaks and priced at an über-bargain $5.95.

Steakhouse | Informal | Expensive | great neck | 255 Northern Blvd. | 516-487-8800 | www.peterluger.com | Lunch & Dinner daily

RECOMMENDED

Bryant & Cooper Steakhouse   90.7

While a number of notable steakhouses have opened on Northern Boulevard between Great Neck and Roslyn over the past 15 years, the one that has made the biggest im-pact on our reviewers is the easternmost one. You can order a slew of cuts, including a porterhouse reminiscent of the one served at the great Peter Luger, though our review-ers favor the prime sirloin, calling it "a cut above" all other items on the menu. Loud, crowded and noisy, the dining room is always filled with a veritable Who's Who of the North Shore.

Steakhouse | Casual | Expensive | roslyn | 2 Middle Neck Rd. | 516-627-7270 | www.bryantandcooper.com | Lunch & Dinner daily

Maroni Cuisine   90.6

Mike Maroni has brought the tasting menu to everyday dining. Each night his kitchen turns out a mixture of Italian dishes and whatever else he is in the mood to cook. A typical meal might include meatballs in marinara sauce, Memphis-style barbecue ribs, a Maine lobster roll and cheese ravioli in a cream sauce topped with shaved truffles. During the week you can order à la carte, but on weekends it's strictly the tasting menu. Opinions range from "I love this crazy place" to "I don't get it. It's just an endless stream of average food." Whichever camp you're in, don't expect to linger as you get only around 90 minutes to take it all in before they turn over your table.

Italian | Informal | Expensive | northport | 18 Woodbine Ave. | 631-757-4500 | www.maronicuisine.com | Lunch & Dinner Tue-Sat

ACCEPTABLE

Morton's, The Steakhouse 87.0

The show is great at this link in one of the country's biggest steakhouse chains – your waiter brings a cart to your table that acts as a visual menu, displaying every cut of steak and side dish, including potatoes the size of softballs. Unfortunately, the quality is "merely average," but ultimately it's a better choice than many of the other chains out there. A pro-BYOB policy gives it another advantage, as most of the top steakhouses make you buy wine from their lists.

Steakhouse | Casual | Expensive | great neck | 777 Northern Blvd. | 516-498-2950 | www.mortons.com | Dinner daily

Coolfish 86.0

This type of restaurant annoys our reviewers no end. It starts out with good enough ingredients, but the level of culinary ambition is so low that the result is no better than acceptable. That doesn't stop the restaurant from attracting hordes of hungry diners looking for food that imparts a sense of dining in Manhattan, but priced in a way that suits the Long Island market. The comment that sums it up best seems to be "This place lost its buzz years ago."

Seafood | Casual | Moderate | syosset | 6800 Jericho Tpke. | 516-921-3250 | www.tomschaudel.com | Dinner daily, Lunch Mon-Fri

"You're Wrong!!!"

Do You Disagree with the reviews in this guide?

Then we want to hear about it. But we don't want you to send one of those mealy-mouth negative comments to our inbox. We want you to take a stand and help shape opinions for our next guide. That's because people who disagree with us are just as important to us as the people who share our conclusions. And who knows—next year's results might be more to your liking. You might even see yourself being quoted.

www.opinionatedabout.com

New York City: Manhattan NY

WORTH PLANNING A TRIP AROUND

Per Se   100.0

Most celebrity chefs who open additional locations take the easy way out. They find a hotel that wants to be associated with a top toque and, in exchange for a cut of the profits, license their names and enter into consulting agreements whereby they visit a few days a month to supervise the key personnel. Meanwhile, all of the other employees actually work for the hotel, and the overall experience just doesn't live up to the standard of quality found at the chef's flagship restaurant. Thomas Keller rejected that approach, building a $12 million restaurant in the Time Warner Center, where he supervises all of the employees as well as every aspect of the meal. And while the experience might fall a hair short of the French Laundry, the restaurant where Keller built his reputation, one reviewer told us, "My meal there still haunts me – all the tastes, the feel of the place – it's a must go."

All of Keller's classic dishes are on hand, and executive chef Eli Kaimeh does such a good job that you might think their creator is back in the kitchen preparing them. The kitchen also excels at seasonal offerings like soft scrambled eggs served with crispy sweetbreads, herb-roasted sturgeon in an onion beurre blanc and a roast cap of beef served with crispy bone marrow and trumpet mushrooms. But where Keller's investment really pays off is in the staff, which looks after diners with the proficiency of a well-oiled team at a top restaurant in France. Of course, the experience isn't without potential pitfalls: "perfect but uninspired" and a wine list "jam-packed with cherries but priced in a way that will make some people spit cherry pits" were among the few critical comments. The location (in a mall) doesn't help either, although the view from the fourth-floor dining room, overlooking Central Park and the East Side skyline, is "one of the loveliest in the city," especially during one of the three weekly lunch services.

French | Formal | Very Expensive | upper west side | Time-Warner Center | 10 columbus circle, 4th fl. | 212-823-9335 | www.perseny.com | Dinner daily, Lunch Fri-Sun

Jean Georges   100.0

Flagship restaurants always seem to suffer when their founding celebrity chef starts cashing in on his or her name. But that doesn't apply to Jean-Georges Vongerichten who, despite opening restaurants all over the world, has taken steps to ensure that his namesake is as good now as it was on the day it opened. How does he do it? It's simple: Besides constantly updating his cuisine, Vongerichten often stands at the pass of the kitchen, inspecting each plate before it enters the dining room. This unyielding commitment to maintaining high standards has resulted in Jean Georges being one of only 14 restaurants in the country that reviewers say is Worth Planning a Trip Around.

Vongerichten's unique approach to French cooking revolves around a clever use of acids, combined with innovative spicing and flavor combinations,yielding a "bold and highly assertive" cuisine. The approach means that even simple preparations, like tuna ribbons with avocado and soy or a tartare of Japanese snapper with champagne grape gelée, are "bursting with flavor." There are numerous signature dishes on the menu, including the caviar egg, scallops with a raisin and caper emulsion and an "absolutely sublime" wild turbot in a sauce vin jaune. Lunch is unusually popular, not only because the large-windowed dining room offers views over Central Park, but also because diners can take advantage of a 20-item prix-fixe menu that offers two courses for the low cost of $32, plus $16 for each additional course. All in all, the experience is best described by a reviewer who marveled, "In spite of the restaurant being nearly 15 years old, it still serves one of the most vibrant and original cuisines you will find anywhere."

French | Formal | Very Expensive | upper west side | Trump International Hotel & Tower | 1 Central Park W. | 212-299-3900 | www.Jean-Georges.com | Dinner Mon-Sat, Lunch Mon-Fri

Masa   100.0

For many years Masa Takayama ran a restaurant in Beverly Hills called Ginza Sushiko. Among his fans was Thomas Keller of French Laundry fame, who was so enamored with Masa's food that when Keller was planning to open Per Se, he convinced Masa to close up shop in Beverly Hills and follow him to New York. At first, opinions about Masa were all over the map, with the price of a meal at the heart of the discussion: Dinner cost an eye-popping $350, quickly rising to $500 if you added luxury ingredients like fugu and truffles, causing many to question whether raw fish could ever be worth that price. But there was a second group of diners – ones who possessed extensive experience with Japanese cuisine – who said things like, "It's the only restaurant in the country on par with the top restaurants in Japan." Some diners find the quality of the fish dazzling; in fact, a pastry chef of Japanese descent told us she gave up eating sushi on a weekly basis so she could afford to eat at Masa once a month.

We guess persistence pays off, because 18 months ago we began seeing an upward arc in the reviews, so much so that the restaurant has been promoted into the category of worth planning a trip around, a distinction held by only three other Japanese restaurants in the country. We can't tell if the more favorable ratings are a function of the food getting better or whether American diners now know more about sushi than they used to, an assumption with some credence as three years ago, when we first began collecting comments about the restaurant, one of the very first reviewers warned, "You won't appreciate it unless you have experience eating sushi in Japan." The only way to find out is to try it yourself, providing you are flush enough to cover the cost of the meal.

Japanese | Casual | Very Expensive | upper west side | Time Warner Center | 10 columbus circle, 4th fl. | 212-823-9800 | www.masanyc.com | Dinner Mon-Sat, Lunch Tue-Fri

Le Bernardin   98.6

Before the sushi craze began, Gilbert and Maguy Le Coze had taken it upon themselves to teach American diners how to eat fish. It wasn't an easy task. Most of us were used to seafood that had been frozen or that had been sitting on trawlers at sea for a few weeks. Now, in large part due to the Le Cozes' efforts, you will find fresh fish at restaurants all over the country. But that wasn't the only difficulty the two restaurateurs faced. Inherent in being a successful seafood specialist is the ability to compete with other top restaurants that may offer more varied menus, a task made more arduous when it must be sustained over an extended period of time. Things became even more tenuous when Gilbert Le Coze passed away in 1994; Eric Ripert took charge of the kitchen, and by continuing the policy of sourcing the best fish and seafood that money can buy and preparing them in a way that is creative yet respectful, he has been able to maintain this restaurant's high ranking for more than 17 years.

Ripert's creations include a progressive tasting of Kumamoto oysters en gelée, sea urchin risotto with toasted nori and a citrus emulsion and a surf 'n' turf of escolar and

Kobe beef with eggplant fries, pesto and anchovy sauce. Michael Laiskonis' terrific desserts, like dark Amedei chocolate with sweet potato pearls, are among the best in the country, and oenophiles could spend an hour or two poring over award-winning wine director Aldo Sohm's list. Having said all that, the restaurant is at a bit of a crossroads these days as seafood prepared with French culinary technique is not as unusual as it once was, and the proliferation of superior sushi restaurants has lessened the demand for cooked fish. Some reviewers dared to wonder "Has Le Bernardin lost a step?" But traditionalists who want a serious, contemporary French meal based on high-quality ingredients and top-notch cooking insisted, "Hands down, it's the finest, most exquisite seafood this side of the Atlantic."

French | Formal | Very Expensive | midtown west | 155 W. 51st St | 212-554-1515 | www.le-bernardin.com | Dinner Mon-Sat, Lunch Mon-Fri

Sushi Yasuda   98.5

Editor's Note: Since we collected the ratings for this review, chef Yasuda has returned to his native Japan. In his place stands Mitsuru Tamura, his protegé. We have decided to leave the review as is, as a lasting tribute to chef Yasuda, who has provided us and our reviewers with numerous enjoyable meals. We wish him well, and we hope to share a meal with him at his new Tokyo venture.

The most popular Japanese restaurant in our survey (it was rated 50% more often than Nobu) is where you can find Yasuda, the Yoda of New York City sushi chefs. With a minimalist dining room as his backdrop, Yasuda stands behind his corner of the counter, arms folded, cutting an imposing figure as he greets everyone who enters the restaurant. Several features make a meal here stand out. The first is the ability to sample flights of fish, like multiple grades of fatty tuna or different varieties of salmon. Another is the amazing rice. In fact, the master will tell you it's as important as the fish, a statement supported by one reviewer who said, "It's worth eating there for the rice alone."

Regulars will tell you the experience is significantly enhanced if you sit at the counter and allow Yasuda to serve you himself. Not only does he orchestrate your omakase as if conducting a symphony, but his tutelage on the rituals and customs of sushi etiquette adds significant value to the experience. The place is beloved by so many of our reviewers that the only way we can communicate the way they feel about it is to allow you to read a sampling of their comments: "Yasuda's love for his art translates into something special for you"; "This is one of, if not my favorite restaurant in the world"; "I'm not sure that life gets much better than sitting at Yasuda's end of the sushi bar and having him serve you whatever he desires"; "I could eat this every day for the rest of my life."

Japanese | Casual | Very Expensive | midtown east | 204 E. 43rd St. | 212-972-1001 | www.sushiyasuda. com | Dinner Mon-Sat, Lunch Mon-Fri

Kuruma Zushi   98.0

Diners used to eating in Japan, where the top sushi restaurants often resemble cheap lunch counters, will feel right at home at this simple restaurant on the second floor of a small office building in Midtown East. Fortunately, the minimal décor and small space – it has a 12-seat counter and a dining room of six tables – isn't all that Toshihiro Uezu's restaurant has in common with its Japanese counterparts. What they also share are a number of ingredients that were last seen swimming in the Sea of Japan before making their way to Uezu's display counter courtesy of Tokyo's Tsukiji fish market.

Better known for his man-sized cuts of sashimi than for his sushi, Uezu combines his imported fare with the best of the North American catch to create an array of flavors and textures so dazzling that more than one person claimed "you won't find a restaurant with better fish in the entire U.S." Of course, quality at this level comes at a hefty price: A full-blown omakase costs between $200 and $400 per person (plus beverages, tip and tax). Fortunately, you don't have to go whole hog, and one person wrote about the amazing quality of the fish on the $50 set menu, which he described as "so good I can't imagine what the better stuff is like."

Japanese | Informal | Very Expensive | midtown east | 7 E. 47th St., 2nd fl. | 212-317-2802 | www.kurumazushi.com | Lunch & Dinner Mon-Sat

AN IMPORTANT DESTINATION

Momofuku Ko   97.4

David Chang is one of the great American success stories. The son of immigrant parents, after attending Trinity College he decided to become a chef (unlike his friends who were on track to become bankers and lawyers). Following stints with Tom Colicchio at Craft and Andrew Carmellini at Café Boulud, David decided it was time to go out on his own. But instead of immediately opening a restaurant, he took a trip to Japan and Korea in order to better understand his roots. When he returned to the U.S. he opened Momofuku Noodle Bar, which might be the most famous such eatery on the planet. Eventually he upped the ante by opening Ssäm Bar, and after moving Noodle Bar to a larger space, David filled the vacated space with Ko, his first fine-dining concept.

There are only 12 counter seats available over three seatings a day (one at lunch and two at dinner,) and diners from all over the world compete for a seat at the Ko counter. Though the menu is constantly changing, some of the dishes mentioned in the comments were a smoked egg, scallop with uni, yuzu and burnt apples, grilled and steamed sea bass, the now-famous frozen foie gras served over pine nut brittle, deep fried short ribs and sous vide lamb belly served with a daikon and potato soup. Virtually every reviewer loved the "unforgettable and innovative flavor combinations"; criticism was mostly directed at "mediocre wine pairings" and a computer-run reservation system that makes securing a reservation "infuriatingly difficult." But all is forgiven because of the food. As one panelist put it: "I would love to rate this restaurant lower, but every dish of my meal was spot on."

Progressive | Informal | Very Expensive | east village | 163 First Ave. | 212-254-3500 | www.momofuku. com | Dinner daily, Lunch Fri-Sun

Corton   97.2

Paul Liebrandt has finally found a home. After a number of illustrious attempts at creating an important restaurant based on the principles of molecular gastronomy, he struck up a partnership with Drew Nieporent who, while revamping the old Montrachet space, agreed to build Liebrandt a brand-new kitchen. Liebrandt was so pleased with the result that he decided to put his gas masks on the shelf, and now he's applying some of the most contemporary culinary techniques to some of the best ingredients in the city. The result: A cuisine that appears conservative on its face, but that is actually one of the most modern and progressive in the country.

Liebrandt's new focus on turning out perfectly cooked food is evident in seasonal dishes like squash soup with a tempura crab; hand-rolled, smoked pasta in a black truffle sauce; squab wrapped in pancetta, which more than one reviewer described as "sublime"; and Maine Lobster Royale, with Parmesan crumble and lemon verbena. Truth is, we were a bit surprised at how quickly the restaurant rose in the ranks of our survey, but after reading comments like "Liebrandt's thoughtful menu is without flaws" and "He understands how to make food flavorful while keeping it interesting," it's not that difficult to see why it happened.

French | Casual | Expensive | tribeca | 239 W. Broadway | 212-219-2777 | www.cortonnyc.com | Dinner Mon-Sat

Eleven Madison Park   97.2

Now that 34-year-old Daniel Humm has successfully turned "Eleven Mad" around from being just another upper middle restaurant serving New American cuisine to a place where diners can enjoy a refined French meal prepared by a highly trained chef, he faces his next challenge: How to fill 140 seats each night while keeping the cuisine at a level usually achieved only when serving half that number? First, a bit about Daniel's background: Swiss-born, tall and thin as a string bean (rumor has it he used to ride with the junior national bike team in Switzerland), he spent his formative years in the kitchen of Gerard Rabaey at Le Pont de Brent in Montreux. Eventually he became the executive chef at San Francisco's Campton Place Hotel, where the attention he garnered caused him to be noticed by Danny Meyer, who hired him to revitalize the kitchen at this beautiful restaurant.

A good way to describe Humm's cooking is "subtle yet full flavored," and while many dishes rely on unusual ingredient combinations – like a salad of heirloom tomatoes and watermelon or poached lobster served with Chantenay carrots – they work because Humm's kitchen takes the time and effort to balance sweetness, acidity and textures perfectly. First-time visitors should not miss Humm's signature dish: roast Muscovy duck scented with lavender, honey and spices. "Excellent service and a stunning dining room" complement the cuisine, and wine director John Ragan is so good at his job that one reviewer told us, "If I ever open a restaurant, I'd like him to be my sommelier." Which brings us back to Mr. Humm's challenge, which has been fairly daunting given the recent economic environment. All we can say is he should keep at it so more people can find out what one person already knows: "My 11-course tasting menu was sensational and well worth a visit."

French | Casual | Very Expensive | flatiron | 11 Madison Ave. | 212-889-0905 | www.elevenmadisonpark. com | Dinner Mon-Sat, Lunch Mon-Fri

L'Atelier de Joël Robuchon   96.7

In 2003, after seven years away from the spotlight, Joël Robuchon returned to the dining stage with a new concept. Having spent a good amount of time in both Spain and Japan, Robuchon felt that if he combined the counter-seating formats of the Spanish tapas bar and the Japanese sushi restaurant, while installing highly trained chefs who were able to prepare a cuisine that relied on top-notch ingredients, the result would be a more casual, yet still high-quality version of the fine-dining experience that was the specialty of the French.

As a result of this unique merger of East-West dining styles and techniques, you can sample small-plate versions of a number of Robuchon's famous dishes, like crispy langoustine en papillote or sea urchin in lobster gelée with cauliflower cream, or the very hungry can opt for larger plates like steak tartare with hand-cut French fries or quail stuffed with foie gras, potato purée and black truffle. Fans of this restaurant tend to agree with the reviewer who described Robuchon's menu offerings as "pinnacles of perfection." But others, while acknowledging the high standard of cooking, see it as "an example of French cuisine having been turned into a commodity."

French | Casual | Very Expensive | midtown east | Four Seasons Hotel | 57 E. 57th St. | 212-829-3844 | www.fourseasons.com | Dinner daily

Bouley   96.1

David Bouley is a restless soul. After 25 years of success, he decided to reinvent himself by building a new restaurant a block away from his old one (making this the third incarnation of Bouley). And while he was at it, he decided to revamp his style of cooking. He's in a somewhat Zen phase these days, and the Japanese influence on his cuisine has resulted in his cooking becoming somewhat more minimalist than it was when the restaurant was located on West Broadway.

The mix of French, Japanese and Spanish influences in Bouley's cuisine is readily apparent in dishes like a sashimi of scallops wrapped over a Kumamoto oyster in a seaweed sauce with caviar, Dungeness crab and egg whites in a truffle dashi or black cod topped with a sweet onion foam and truffle dust. The experience isn't for everyone, and people who don't care for it say things like "the meal can be unexciting almost to the point of tedium." Then there are those who have eaten his cooking since he first came onto the scene and who will tell you "if you catch him when he's on, David is one of the best chefs in the country."

French | Casual | Very Expensive | tribeca | 163 Duane St. | 212-964-2525 | www.davidbouley.com | Lunch & Dinner daily

Daniel   95.5

After Daniel Boulud's flagship received only a "highly recommended" in our first survey, one of our reviewers wrote us to complain about the unjustly low score. So for his benefit, as well as for the benefit of anyone else who thinks Daniel is still underrated, we would like to explain. Each evening, Daniel serves more than 200 people, resulting in food that many reviewers say "isn't prepared with the same level of care as at some of the other top restaurants in the city" that serve between 75 and 90 people per night. A quick look at our collected data demonstrates this dynamic: Though 93% of reviewers recommended Daniel, only 15% rated it as Must Go, a very low percentage given a restaurant of this stature.

With that on the table, reviewers also say you can eat very well here if you hit it on the right night. And while the cuisine has the reputation of being traditional French, Boulud's cuisine is far more modern than people realize. Dishes like Louisiana shrimp with Ibérico ham and a tasting of melons or halibut baked on Himalayan rock salt with curried yogurt and Thai basil are as good as what you would find at top contemporary restaurants in Paris today. Unfortunately, while the dishes can be innovative, the overall scene isn't really tailored to foodies, but contains the sort of fussy, fawning service that is geared towards a combination of socialites, visiting dignitaries, Upper East Side families commemorating special occasions, a celebrity or three and out-of-towners who want to dress up for a fancy night out. The impressive wine list comes with impressive prices, making the no-BYO policy the final straw for a number of our reviewers.

French | Formal | Very Expensive | upper east side | 60 E. 65th St. | 212-288-0033 | www.danielnyc.com | Dinner Mon-Sat

Sugiyama   95.5

In an environment where Nobu- and Morimoto-style restaurants monopolize the Japanese landscape, chef Nao Sugiyama continues to quietly offer his brand of classical omakase at this small but elegantly designed Midtown restaurant, which he operates with his wife, Kaori. Serving a seasonal cuisine based on market ingredients, including many sourced from Japan, his restaurant was described as "the best non-sushi-intensive Japanese restaurant in the U.S.," although the same reviewer added that "The quality of the fish in the sashimi platter can compete with the best Japanese restaurants in the city."

In addition to the delicious fish and interesting appetizers, ranging from the house version of ankimo (monkfish liver) to a melée of mushrooms served in a smoky fish broth, you can delight in soft-shell crabs prepared in a light tempura batter, lobster grilled and topped with a garlic sauce, silky black cod marinated in miso and wagyu beef cooked on heated stones. Chef Nao and his wife are among the warmest hosts you can find, and while table seating is available, diners are advised to sit at the counter, where Nao will serve you directly and happily explain the ingredients in each dish.

Japanese | Casual | Expensive | midtown west | 251 W. 55th St. | 212-956-0670 | www.sugiyama-nyc.com | Dinner Tue-Sat

HIGHLY RECOMMENDED

Sushi Seki   94.7

This otherwise nondescript sushi specialist is the subject of two debates. The first is over the merits of their post-modern style of sushi, which basically means cuts of high-quality fish with unusual toppings. The second revolves around who serves the best version of post-modern sushi, Seki or Sushi of Gari (an argument further complicated by the fact that Seki used to slice fish at Gari before he went out on his own). Debate aside, if you're the type of person who likes preparations like tuna topped with tofu paste, fluke topped with a mesclun and pine nut salad and salmon topped with a sautéed tomato, you will absolutely love this restaurant. It's popular with night owls (they serve until 2:30 a.m.), which gives you the opportunity to munch on a tasty uni hand roll while sitting next to a famous chef who has popped in after the dinner service.

Japanese | Informal | Expensive | upper east side | 1143 First Ave. | 212-371-0238 | Dinner Mon-Sat

Blue Hill   94.5

While Dan Barber's restaurant gives the appearance of a luxury bistro, nearly 60% of our reviewers rated it in the two highest categories, and a whopping 88% placed it in the top three. The success stems from the use of "farm-fresh ingredients," which Barber "gently filters through the prism of the latest cooking techniques." Barber's tasting menu tantalizes with seasonal dishes based around mushrooms, various preparations of Berkshire pig or the amazing Stone Barns chickens, which a number of reviewers say are "the best you will find outside of France." Be warned: the food is gently seasoned, causing one reviewer to comment, "You won't enjoy yourself unless you like subtle cuisine." But the comment that best highlighted the experience suggests that diners should "arrive late to see them carrying in tomorrow's dinner, hooves and all."

New American | Casual | Expensive | greenwich village | 75 Washington Pl. | 212-539-1776 | www.blue-hillfarm.com | Dinner daily

Soto   94.4

After year's of running Atlanta's top Japanese restaurant, Sotohiro Kosugi packed up his Suisin knives and shipped them to Manhattan. Hiring the architect who designed the Momofuku restaurants, he now slices fish in a sleek-looking space in the heart of Greenwich Village. Kosugi's cuisine is focused on creative sashimi preparations, like thinly sliced fluke flavored with yuzu or long fin squid wrapped around a quail egg and uni, a dish Tom Colicchio told us was "one of the best things I ever ate." Mrs. Kosugi prepares the cooked food, like light-as-air tempura or a broiled langoustine stuffed with mushrooms and uni that rivals her husband's fish dishes for deliciousness. Complaints are directed at the "extremely slow pace of the meal" and servers prone to making the occasional mistake, aspects that prevent the restaurant from achieving a higher rating.

Japanese | Casual | Expensive | greenwich village | 357 Sixth Ave. | 212-414-3088 | www.sotonyc.com | Dinner Mon-Sat

Craft   94.0

What originally made Tom Colicchio's eatery a standout was a kitchen that demonstrated a command of culinary technique that was a step or two beyond other restaurants featuring market cuisine. Add the dose of creativity that executive chef Damon Wise brought to the mix, and the restaurant consistently earned a rating of "an important destination" in past surveys. But then *Top Chef* came along, and with it the opportunity to open additional locations. Wise was promoted to the position of executive chef for the entire restaurant group. All of a sudden the reviews switched from delirious to disappointed, and they stayed that way – until James Tracey was hired as the chef de cuisine. Now Craft is back to reliably offering one of the most enjoyable meals in the city, especially if you tell the kitchen to cook for you, allowing Tracey to bombard you with "sophisticated preparations of the best ingredients the daily market has to offer."

New American | Casual | Expensive | gramercy | 43 E. 19th St. | 212-780-0880 | www.craftrestaurant.com | Dinner daily

Café Boulud   93.8

Some of the best French cooking in the country can be found at this luxury bistro that many call "the best restaurant in the Daniel Boulud empire." Each evening Gavin Kaysen's menu features four different styles of cuisine: traditional, international, contemporary and market, and it isn't surprising to see the kitchen offering cassoulet, porchetta and Vietnamese pho all at the same time. The large variety of well-prepared dishes, highly professional service and a "wonderfully chosen selection of wines" make the place a top-notch dining experience. The downsides: pricing that is a bit steep for bistro fare, a "cramped dining room" and a clientele that is on the older side (one reviewer wrote, "I felt out of place being under 70 the last time I was there").

French | Casual | Expensive | upper east side | 20 E. 76th St. | 212-772-2600 | www.danielnyc.com | Open daily

Momofuku Ssäm Bar   93.8

After revolutionizing contemporary dining at his Momofuku Noodle Bar, David Chang took things to an even higher level at this restaurant, described by one of our reviewers as "the beginning of a new paradigm in dining." Oysters with Kimchi sauce, hamachi with horseradish edamame and an assortment of hams with red-eye gravy: These are but some of the tasty and original dishes Chang offers. But his true showstopper is the Bo Ssäm, a marinated pork shoulder slow-cooked for eight hours that can feed at least 10 people (one reviewer described as "possibly the greatest casual restaurant dish of all time"). The environment is loud and fun, and while we could easily fill a few pages with raves about the food, the one that summed it up best was, "Would this be my choice for my last meal? It's certainly in the running."

Asian | Informal | Moderate | east village | 207 2nd Ave. | 212-254-3500 | www.momofuku.com | Lunch & Dinner daily

Gramercy Tavern   93.6

After owner Danny Meyer and chef Tom Colicchio parted ways, this beloved eatery traveled through a rocky patch. Mike Anthony was given the task of returning the restaurant to its glory days, and though he had long been considered among the best chefs in the country when he cooked with Dan Barber at Stone Barns, it took a while for him to adapt his subtle ways to the more full-flavored style of cooking Gramercy Tavern was known for. But now it seems the Tavern is back on track, and reviewers say that dishes like grilled sturgeon with broccoli, beans, leeks and oysters "are on a par with what they serve at any of the top restaurants in the city." The same terrific Danny Meyer service team remains in place, a well-stocked wine list complements the food and the menu in the front-room tavern is still "one of the best bargains in the city."

New American | Casual | Expensive | gramercy | 42 E. 20th St. | 212-477-0777 | www.gramercytavern. com | Dinner daily, Lunch Mon-Fri

Momofuku Noodle Bar   93.6

This is where David Chang revolutionized the contemporary dining experience. Having designed a restaurant featuring a counter seating format, Chang took the money he saved on servers and went out and hired cooks talented enough to be working for chefs with names like Boulud and Vongerichten. Using the same artisanal ingredients found at the city's best restaurants as a starting point, Chang created a cuisine that's as "inspirational as it is delicious." Dishes range from smaller plates like greenmarket brussels sprouts with kimchi purée and cubes of Benton's bacon and pink shrimp from Maine served atop a puddle of dashi-simmered Anson Mill grits to the classic Momo – ramen soup laden with Berkshire pork and finished with a shower of chopped market vegetables. It's an amazing success story, one that has already spawned three other successful restaurants and a bakery, with more on the way.

Korean | Informal | Moderate | east village | 171 Firstt Ave. | 212-254-3500 | www.momofuku.com | Lunch & Dinner daily

Nobu   93.6

Nobu Matsuhisa's New York flagship still churns out delicious versions of his globally famous cuisine. Despite complaints that the menu never changes, the kitchen is applauded for the way it "faithfully produces superb renditions of Nobu classics" like rock shrimp tempura, spicy and creamy crab and a version of black cod marinated in miso and sake that has inspired copies the world over. There is less enthusiasm for the sushi than for the cooked food, though that's expressed mainly by the type of sushi fanatic who spends outlandish sums on fish flown in from Japan. There's a good wine list, and for those spur-of-the-moment types, Nobu Next Door (see below) has a strictly drop-in policy (no reservations accepted) – plus the bonus of the same menu.

Japanese | Casual | Expensive | tribeca | 105 Hudson St. | 212-219-0500 | www.myriadrestaurantgroup. com | Dinner Mon-Sat, Lunch Mon-Fri

WD-50   93.4

While there's a case to be made that Wylie Dufresne is the most talented chef in America, reviewers aren't always enthusiastic about his cuisine. Take his foie gras knots – a torchon of liver mixed with a stabilizer, then formed into ribbons and tied into knots. While the ingenuity is admirable, some see the end result as a gimmick; as one reviewer put it: "Why foie? What was wrong with red licorice?" In contrast are comments that take an effusive tone, like "a must for anyone with an interest in contemporary cooking"; "He elevates molecular gastronomy from being about kitschy food science to a truly transcendental dining experience"; and "I believe that his work will help shape the face of gastronomy in the future." The only way to decide if it's for you is to try it for yourself. But be forewarned: Like the contemporary composer Milton Babbitt, who wrote a famous article called "Who Cares If You Listen?", Wylie "cooks for himself and cares not what we think."

Progressive | Informal | Expensive | lower east side | 50 Clinton St. | 212-477-2900 | www.wd-50.com | Dinner Wed-Sun

Aquavit   93.3

There was a time, especially during chef Marcus Samuelsson's reign, when Aquavit would have earned a rating that was a couple of points higher. But when you don't take the appropriate steps to update your cuisine, it atrophies, drawing comments like "it needs an infusion of creativity" to become topical. Ironically, the one thing about Aquavit that has changed – its move to modernist digs a few years back – is unpopular. Many reviewers longed for the original space, with its serene ambience created by a peaceful waterfall. Still, some loyalists prefer restaurants that remain the same, and many reviewers still "die for" the" modern Scandinavian cuisine" (now overseen by Marcus Jernmark, who was Samuelsson's number two). One exception: the reviewer (obviously a comedian in his spare time) who dismissed the restaurant by warning that "eating too much dill can shorten your life span."

Swedish | Casual | Expensive | midtown east | 65 E. 55th St. | 212-307-7311 | www.aquavit.org | Dinner daily, Lunch Sun-Fri

Marea   93.3

In our book, you can call a restaurant successful when people who are normally lukewarm about its type of cuisine give it a strong recommendation. Such is the case with Marea. After his success at the Alto and Convivio (both recently shuttered after he split with his partners), Michael White renovated the old San Domenico space and turned his hand to a menu of Italian seafood. A typical meal might begin with crudos that rely on "fish that can match up against what they serve at some of the top sushi restaurants in town," followed by "pastas that are as good as the ones served at Babbo during its prime"; numerous reviewers singled out White's fusili with octopus and bone marrow. If anything is holding the rating back, it is the "mains that don't live up to the quality of the other courses." Hopefully White will adjust, and when he does we expect to see an additional point or two on the rating.

Italian | Expensive | Casual | midtown west | 240 Central Park South | 212-582-5100 | www.marea-nyc.com | Dinner daily, Lunch Mon-Fri

Picholine   93.0

There was a time when Picholine was a go-to restaurant for many of our reviewers. It fell out of favor for a number of years, but now a renovated dining room and a revamped menu have given this Terrance Brennan establishment a second life. Starters might include sea urchin panna cotta or foie gras cooked shabu shabu style, while mains might venture into rabbit with snails served on tagliatelle or heirloom chicken Kiev with a liquid foie gras center. The restaurant was ahead of the curve when it came to serving cheese, and the legendary Max McCalman's "cheese cart remains a wonder to behold." Dinner is served until 11:30 p.m., which means that Picholine "is still the best place to dine near Lincoln Center" after a show.

French | Casual | Expensive | upper west side | 35 W. 64th St. | 212-724-8585 | www.picholinenyc.com | Dinner daily, Lunch Wed-Sun

Locanda Verde   92.9

After wowing them night after night when he was in charge at Café Boulud, which he followed with a stint putting A Voce on the map, chef Andrew Carmellini is now packing them in at Robert DeNiro's Greenwich Hotel in TriBeCa. A master at giving rustic Italian fare a sophisticated spin, Carmellini features dishes like a light-as-air fritto misto of rock shrimp and Ipswich clams or a wood-fired pork chop topped with a light purée of peperoncini. The result is "a cuisine that is far more interesting than it would be in the hands of a less talented chef." And the desserts prepared by Karen DeMasco of Craft fame, like La Fantasia – chocolate and marsala gelatos, caramel tartufo and cacao croccante – are among the richest and most delicious in the city.

Italian | Informal | Moderate | tribeca | 377 Greenwich St. | 212-925-3797 | http://locandaverdenyc.com | Open daily

Aldea   92.7

After working for chefs David Bouley, Alain Ducasse and Kurt Gutenbrunner, followed by a three-and-a half-year stint with Marco Morerira as the executive chef at Tocqueville, George Mendes decided he wanted his own restaurant. Now you can find him at Aldea, serving a cuisine based on his Portuguese heritage, with dishes like shrimp with garlic, coriander, pimenton and pressed shrimp jus; Hampshire pork loin and shoulder with onion soubise; honey-crisp apples and Savoy cabbage; and what he calls arroz con pato – paella-style rice laced with chunks of duck confit and chorizo. Mendes is routinely labeled "a chef to watch," one who executes "brilliant Iberian cooking served in a lovely setting, at an even lovelier price point."

Portuguese | Casual | Expensive | flatiron | 31 W. 17th St. | 212-675-7223 | www.aldearestaurant.com | Dinner Mon-Sat, Lunch Mon-Fri

Sushi Zen   92.7

One reviewer told us this "quiet, contemporary restaurant" on the edge of the Theater District was the site of his best meal this year, adding that "The fish rivaled what I ate when I visited Japan." That makes sense to us, since the restaurant sources the vast majority of its fish from Tokyo's Tsukiji Market. At the heart of the operation is a mentor to many of the top toques in Manhattan, chef Suzuki, whose classic style of omakase is "understated and underrated." The experience isn't limited to raw fish. There is always an interesting list of daily specials, like dark miso soup cooked with a lobster head or delicate dishes like one of grilled Japanese vegetables that both tastes and looks like a course at one of the city's top French restaurants.

Japanese | Casual | Expensive | midtown west | 108 W. 44th St. | 212-302-0707 | www.sushizen-ny.com | Dinner Mon-Sat, Lunch Mon-Fri

Nobu Next Door   92.6

As the name implies, this is a no-reservation version of the famous restaurant adjacent (see review above). The menu is virtually the same, save for a few unique daily specials, and the atmosphere is a bit less formal and thus more inviting. Reviewers summed it up by saying it makes for "a great choice if you've just gotten out of the movies or a concert, have left your dinner options open, and realize you have a hankering for some squid pasta in garlic sauce."

Japanese | Casual | Expensive | tribeca | 105 Hudson St. | 212-334-4445 | www.myriadrestaurantgroup. com | Dinner daily

Annisa   92.5

For years, Anita Lo's mix of French, Asian and Mediterranean cuisines kept this intimate dining room filled. But in 2009, it was destroyed in a fire. Undeterred, Lo rebuilt her beloved restaurant, and now it's back to one of the best spots to dine in the city. Lo's menu still offers her signature dish, Shanghai soup dumplings stuffed with seared foie gras, along with entrées that include skate with Korean flavors or filet of beef with a mustard seed crust. A unique wine list assembled by Roger Dagorn, exclusively featuring the labels of female winemakers, complements the cuisine. The dining room is small and intimate; one reviewer told us, "I always recommend Annisa to out-of-town guests who are looking for a calm and civilized dining experience."

Asian | Informal | Expensive | west village | 13 Barrow St. | 212-741-6699 | www.annisarestaurant.com | Dinner daily

Kyo Ya   92.5

It's easy to walk past this basement restaurant located on an East Village side street without noticing that "one of the most authentic, Kyoto-style kaiseki experiences in the country" happens to be inside. But venture down the stairs and they might offer you thin slices of yuba stuffed with sea urchin or a bowl of Japanese white turnip potage with tsukune-style minced chicken. And if you're lucky, you can celebrate the start of the hamachi season with a few slices taken from a hunk of fish delivered from Tokyo's Tsukiji Market earlier that day. They allow BYO, if you don't wish to choose from their list of rare sakes.

Japanese | Casual | Expensive | east village | 94 E. 7th St. | 212-982-4140 | Dinner daily

Minetta Tavern   92.5

For decades, Minetta Tavern lingered as a southern Italian warhorse that no one cared about. Enter Keith McNally, who freshened up the dining room with its vintage 1937 decor, and changed the cuisine to French bistro fare, including an entire steak frites menu. Featuring dry-aged, grain-fed Creekstone Farms beef, these steaks made Minetta Tavern an overnight sensation, and nowadays, it's virtually impossible to get a table. But those lucky enough to snag one can dig in to a heavily charred New York strip steak along with frites or aligot potatoes. Another option: what many reviewers swear is "the best hamburger in the country." However, watch out for a dining room called "noisy beyond description."

French Bistro | Informal | Expensive | greenwich village | 113 MacDougal St. | 212-475-3850 | www.minettatavernny.com | Dinner daily, Lunch Mon-Fri

Hatsuhana   92.4

When Yasuda was in charge of the counter, many people considered this the best sushi restaurant in the city. But when he left, the management failed to replace him with someone of similar stature. So these days Hatsuhana heads up the second tier of New York sushi restaurants, frequented by those who still find it "dependable for a business lunch." It's not as pricy as some of the other top sushi places, and diners looking to save even more should check out a "set menu that's a bargain." Those who are looking to luxuriate should check out the list of daily specials, though they can quickly run up the price of your meal.

Japanese | Casual | Expensive | midtown east | 17 E. 48th St. | 212-355-3345 | www.hatsuhana.com | Dinner Mon-Sat, Lunch Mon-Fri

Lincoln   92.2

What's a chef to do after running the kitchen at one of the top French restaurants in the country? Why, return to his native Italian roots, of course. After spending six years as Thomas Keller's right-hand man at Per Se, Jonathan Benno did just that when he joined with the Patina Group to helm this handsome new Italian restaurant, part of the ongoing renovation of Lincoln Center. Now diners can precede a performance of *Tosca* with a feast that includes a terrine of oxtail, foie gras and beef tongue served with giardiniera and a mustard seed agro-dolce; spaghetti with bottarga, capers, Taggiasca olives and bread crumbs; or Hampshire pork loin with black kale, farro and a sage sauce. While the rating reflects the initial reactions to the restaurant, the consensus was that Benno "still has the brakes on," and most reviewers are looking forward to the time when he gets more comfortable in the kitchen.

Italian | Casual | Expensive | lincoln center | 142 W. 65th St. | 212-359-6500 | www.lincolnristorante.com | Lunch & Dinner daily

The Modern   92.2

When he first burst onto the scene, Alsatian-born Gabriel Kreuther seemed to have a huge future ahead of him. When it was announced he had been hired to run this kitchen, expectations grew higher. Kreuther started slowly – comments like "I preferred his cooking at Atelier" were typical – but now there's been an uptick in the ratings, with comments like "It's not often that a highly reviewed restaurant exceeds my expectations." The fare is influenced by Kreuther's native province: foie gras poached in Gewürztraminer with turnips or Vermont suckling pig with parsnip purée and roasted pineapple. "Top-notch service, even for a Danny Meyer restaurant," and a dining room that overlooks the MOMA sculpture garden enhance the experience. Some prefer the more casual fare in the no-reservations tavern area.

French | Casual | Expensive | midtown west | Museum of Modern Art | 9 W. 53rd St. | 212-333-1220 | www.themodernnyc.com | Dinner Mon-Sat, Lunch Mon-Fri

Esca   92.0

Dave Pasternack is so obsessed with fish that when he's not behind the stoves he's likely to be out on a boat on the high seas, commandeering a rod and reel. His dedication to serving the finest fruits of the sea (both his own catch and those sourced from top suppliers) shows up in a crudo of tilefish with blood oranges or an appetizer of baccalà stewed with porcini mushrooms and Yukon gold potatoes. Pasta is Pasternack's strong suit, and our reviewers rave about dishes like rigatoni with blue fin tuna meatballs or maccheroni alla chitarra with crab and sea urchin. Entrées range from traditional dishes like monkfish sautéed with broccoli rabe and raisins to a more adventurous frito misto that includes skate and scrod in the assortment of delights. Add a terrific list of Italian wines to the mix, and the result, many claim, is "the best restaurant in the Batali/Bastianich empire."

Italian | Casual | Expensive | theater district | 402 W. 43rd St. | 212-564-7272 | www.esca-nyc.com | Dinner daily, Lunch Mon-Sat

RECOMMENDED

Jewel Bako   91.9

Dressed more like an eccentric investment banker than a restaurateur, Jack Lamb (who began his culinary career at Bouley Bakery) runs what is arguably the hippest sushi restaurant on the planet. Fortunately, he cares about the quality of the fish he serves, and if you follow his suggestions, he will personally deliver a few dishes to your table, while bragging that his is only one of two or three Japanese restaurants in the country serving that particular specimen. While our rating doesn't place it in the top New York City sushi echelon, a surprising number of reviewers say it's their favorite place to eat sushi in the city. A good wine program, a benefit of sharing a space with Degustation, is another huge plus, though oenophiles are also offered the option of bringing their own.

Japanese | Informal | Expensive | east village | 239 E. 5th St. | 212-979-1012 | Dinner Mon-Sat

Morimoto   91.9

"Nobu light" is how some people describe the Japanese fusion fare served at this second offering from Iron Chef Masaharu Morimoto (the original is in Philadelphia), where the menu in the main dining room features dishes like Kumamoto oysters with foie gras, uni and teriyaki sauce and a surf 'n' turf of Kobe beef and hamachi ribbons. But if you want a more refined dining experience and are willing to spend a significant amount of money to get it, consider dining at the omakase bar, where the chefs, including Morimoto himself on some nights, dole out tasting menus based on luxury ingredients that start at $250 a person and quickly spiral upward.

Japanese | Casual | Expensive | chelsea | 88 Tenth Ave. | 212-989-8883 | www.morimotonyc.com | Dinner Mon-Sat, Lunch Mon-Fri

Tocqueville   91.9

Marco Moreira and Jo-Ann Makovitzky's restaurant was so popular that they moved down the block to a much larger venue, which is somewhat more formal than the old one. Moreira's cuisine, a mix of French, New American and International styles, includes dishes like sea urchin with angel hair pasta carbonara and a schmaltz-roasted country chicken with baby carrots and potato mousseline. The duo seems to have been rewarded for their efforts, as we have noticed an uptick in the reviews since the move. It's a go-to place for many of our reviewers, who say things like, "I thought it couldn't get better, but they outdid themselves in the new space."

New American | Casual | Expensive | flatiron | 1 E. 15th St. | 212-647-1515 | www.tocquevillerestaurant.com | Lunch & Dinner Mon-Sat

Kajitsu   91.7

Centuries before being a vegetarian or vegan was in fashion, the Zen Buddhists in Japan invented a cuisine based on the principle of not taking life, called shojin. Some astute cook figured out that the best way to jazz up a cuisine that didn't feature luscious cuts of toro or slabs of Kobe beef was to use vegetables, herbs, legumes and seeds at a point in their growing season when they would yield the most flavor. Shojin is on full display at Kajitsu, a restaurant that has captivated the imaginations, as well as the taste buds, of the city's dining community. It would be an understatement to describe the dishes from Masato Nishihara's kitchen as "precious," but the eight-course Hana menu might include jewel-like treats like simmered daikon radish with red miso or crispy phyllo dough with nama-fu and potato. Reviewers are "amazed at the subtle flavors" as well as the incredibly sedate atmosphere, with one person saying, "There's zen and then there's Zen."

Japanese | Informal | Expensive | east village | 414 E. 9th St. | 212-228-4873 | www.kajitsunyc.com | Dinner Tue-Sun

Degustation   91.6

Take one bite of Wesley Genovart's cooking and you will feel you've been transported to a hip tapas bar in Barcelona. That's because Genovart, who grew up in Mallorca until moving to Fresno for high school, cooks such an authentic version of modern Spanish cuisine that it wouldn't surprise us if his mother used to sneak transglutaminase into his baby food! Genovart has created a number of terrific signature small plates, like squid stuffed with short ribs or a deliciously gamey lamb belly that he cooks sous vide before crisping it à la plancha. His is one of the most wine-friendly cuisines in the city, and a favorite with the BYOB crowd. And how can we not mention owner Jack Lamb, who always seems to be scurrying around making sure everyone is happy?

Spanish | Informal | Expensive | east village | 239 E. 5th St. | 212-979-1012 | www.degustationnyc.com | Dinner daily

Nougatine   91.6

Given that the food is prepared by the same kitchen as his namesake eatery, it's no surprise that this is everybody's favorite "other" restaurant from Jean-Georges. Additional attractions are the lively dining room (it's actually the extended bar area of the main restaurant), an attractive price point (many entrées are below $30) and an ability to order dishes from the Jean Georges menu. Plus, on occasion "the kitchen has been known to throw an oldie-but-goodie (a classic dish that dates from Vongerichten's days at JoJo)" onto the menu, a treat for those who have been following him since he began his New York City career.

French | Casual | Expensive | upper west side | Trump International Hotel & Tower | 1 Central Park West | 212-299-3900 | www.Jean-Georges.com | Open daily

Scalini Fedeli   91.6

If you favor New York–style northern Italian dining, Michael Cetrulo's restaurant does its best to bring the standards of top European restaurants to a cuisine that, too often in the U.S., is prepared by chefs without formal culinary training. Cetrulo presents inventive offerings like pappardelle in a sauce of venison and hare finished with Barolo wine and bitter chocolate, or a juniper and black pepper crusted venison chop with a port and balsamic vinegar sauce. The dining room is "ornate and showy," which explains the well-dressed clientele and the large number of limos waiting outside.

Italian | Casual | Expensive | tribeca | 165 Duane St. | 212-528-0400 | www.scalinifedeli.com | Dinner Mon-Sat

Adour   91.5

After determining that his personal style of haute cuisine wasn't a good fit for the New York market, Alain Ducasse closed his restaurant in the Essex House and opened a (slightly) less formal one in the space that once housed Lespinasse in the St. Regis Hotel. The result – somewhere between a grand restaurant and an upper middle spot like Gotham Bar and Grill – gets mixed reviews. Some diners praise the "wonderfully precise cooking" with its "perfectly balanced flavors," while others find the food good but "not up to par with some of the other top places in town." An attractive room and a helpful staff are both pluses, though an expensive wine list is not.

French | Casual | Expensive | midtown east | St. Regis Hotel | 2 E. 55th St. | 212-710-2277 | www.adour-stregis.com | Dinner daily

Park Avenue Summer   91.5

We're used to restaurants changing menus based on the season, but the Stillman family (Smith & Wollensky, Bobby Van's, Quality Meats, etc.) has created a dining concept in which even the name and décor of the restaurant change along with the cuisine. It might sound hokey, but Craig Koketsu manages to pull it off, which means you get to enjoy dishes like halibut and summer truffles with a brioche-crusted poached egg while dining amid golden-hued décor during summer and venison chops with pomegranate and pumpkin seeds surrounded by a burnt-orange color scheme in the fall. There are always a large number of seasonal vegetables on offer, which led one reviewer to describe the place as a "poor man's Blue Hill." The well-heeled clientele makes for great people-watching.

New American | Casual | Expensive | upper east side | 100 E. 63rd St. | 212-644-1900 | www.parkavenuesummer.com | Lunch & Dinner daily

SHO Shaun Hergatt   91.5

There's one thing that New York doesn't have a lot of: restaurants that serve upscale hotel food. This offering, from a chef with stints at the Ritz-Carlton in Sydney and the

Setai in Miami Beach, is as close as it gets. That doesn't render the cuisine without merit; guests can enjoy starters like a slow-poached farm egg with caviar and cauliflower purée and mains like sous vide lamb belly served with fermented garlic and riberry jus. Working against the place are a "gloomy financial district location" and an uneven kitchen whose "outstanding dishes" alternate with "ones of enormous indifference."

Asian | Casual | Expensive | financial district | The Setai | 40 Broad St. | 212-809-3993 | www.shoshaunhergatt.com | Dinner daily, Lunch Sun-Fri

Sushi of Gari | Gari | Sushi of Gari 46   91.5

We laughed when we saw that these restaurants sparked an authenticity debate. The controversy arises from Masatoshi "Gari" Sugio having pioneered a post-modern style of sushi in which the fish comes with various toppings, like fresh salmon with sautéed tomato or fluke topped with a green salad and pine nuts. While the style clearly has its fans, one reviewer notes that "Sushi purists should consider eating elsewhere." But those with an open mind should just sit back and let the chef serve an omakase, a tasting menu in which the unusual pieces are served one at a time, or order the Tuna of Gari: eight unique preparations, ranging from minced to seared to diced, along with a small spicy tuna roll.

Japanese | Informal | Expensive | upper east side | 402 E. 78th St. | 212-517-5340 | www.sushiofgari.com | Dinner daily

Upper West Side | 370 Columbus Ave. | 212-362-4816 | www.sushiofgari.com | Lunch & Dinner daily

Midtown West | 347 W. 46th St. | 212-957-0046 | www.sushiofgari.com | Dinner daily, Lunch Mon-Fri

Prune   91.4

Few restaurants in New York have as much character as this matchbox described as "noisy, cramped, terrific and unique." Gabrielle Hamilton's menu focuses on offal-oriented dishes that one doesn't normally associate with an American chef, like marrow bones with a parsley salad, grilled marinated veal heart or sweetbreads sautéed with bacon and capers. A few non-meat items win raves too, like twice-cooked chestnuts with fresh ricotta that's "one of the best vegetarian dishes in the city." Given all the different parts of the animal that Hamilton uses, it isn't surprising that she also grinds up one of the city's best burgers for lunch. There's a popular Sunday brunch featuring a dozen different types of Bloody Marys.

Gastropub | Informal | Moderate | east village | 54 E. 1st St. | 212-677-6221 | www.prunerestaurant.com | Lunch & Dinner daily

Estiatorio Milos   91.3

This branch of a popular Montreal Greek restaurant offers a bright, lively dining room along with an atmosphere that's buzzy but not too loud. The imported fish is proudly displayed on ice on a table at the back of the dining room, allowing ambitious diners to choose their own meals while also learning how to say "red snapper" in Greek. The fish is priced by the pound, and this level of quality doesn't come cheap, so the meal can get a bit dear. As for the cooking, don't expect cutting-edge cuisine. In fact, it wouldn't hurt the kitchen to show some ambition instead of just throwing everything onto the grill.

Greek | Casual | Expensive | midtown west | 125 W. 55th St. | 212-245-7400 | http://milos.ca/newyork | Dinner daily, Lunch Mon-Fri

Union Square Cafe 91.2

Now in its 26th year, USC is such a fixture on the New York dining scene that it seems it's been around for at least twice as long (lest we forget, this is where Danny Meyer made his name offering his distinct brand of service and hospitality). Michael Romano, with help from Carmen Quagliata, still tends the restaurant's stoves, and their menu continues to offer the unique mix of New American cuisine (like the signature filet mignon of tuna or pan-roasted Giannone chicken with Anson Mills polenta) and homey Italian fare (like the Wednesday special of roast porchetta) that has captured the imagination of diners since the restaurant opened.

New American/Italian | Casual | Expensive | gramercy | 21 E. 16th St. | 212-243-4020 | www.unionsquarecafe.com | Lunch & Dinner daily

Wallsé 91.1

With comments like "This is a cozy restaurant with a delightful staff and a unique menu," "Authentic Austrian cooking is something of a rarity in New York City, and this is its pinnacle" and "I felt like I was having a meal cooked by my Hungarian mother," we had a difficult time finding reviewers who didn't like the Kurt Gutenbrunner's flagship. And with a menu filled with tasty dishes – like chestnut soup with Armagnac prunes and a Viennese mélange; steamed halibut with cucumbers, dill and mushrooms; and venison goulash with spatzle – it's easy to understand why so many people like the place.

Austrian | Casual | Expensive | west village | 344 W. 11th St. | 212-352-2300 | http://kg-ny.com | Lunch & Dinner daily

Gordon Ramsay at the London 91.0

Acting like a raving lunatic on TV might put some tushies into seats, but it doesn't fool some reviewers, who approach this restaurant as if it's part of a chain that's trying to take advantage of its celebrity chef's popularity. "The food was well executed but boring," jeers one of our more jaded reviewers, while another calls it, "One of the most sterile, unimaginative, lackluster restaurants it has ever been my uncomfortable displeasure to visit." But, of course, there are others who rave about Ramsay's style of nouvelle cuisine: "I've been three times and have never been disappointed," says one, while another describes the chef's table lunch as "one of the best meals I have had in New York City."

French | Formal | Very Expensive | midtown west | London Hotel | 151 W. 54th St. | 212-468-8888 | http://gordonramsay.com | Dinner Tue-Sat

Sushi Ann 91.0

This was once the New York outpost of a century-old Tokyo restaurant called Sushisay; its owners severed their ties with their Japanese partners a few years back, however, changing the restaurant's name in the process. It was once considered among the top two or three sushi places in the city, too. But New Yorkers know a lot more about the rituals of eating raw fish these days and now consider this "among the top second-tier sushi restaurants." In its favor are a "friendly staff" and a "convenient Midtown East location," while "small portions and large prices" cut the other way.

Japanese | Casual | Expensive | midtown east | 38 E. 51st St. | 212-755-1780 | www.sushiann.com | Dinner Mon-Sat, Lunch Mon-Fri

Aureole   90.9

A new location and a new chef have helped Aureole improve its rating to the extent that we can now recommend it. The New American fare features starters like a ceviche of Nantucket Bay scallops with watermelon radish, spicy coconut, fresh Yuzu zest and ginger tamarind sauce, along with mains like Columbia River sturgeon with smoked potato purée, leeks, Hon-shumeji mushrooms and a caviar crème fraîche sauce. Despite the improvement, it still attracts an older clientele, inspiring one reviewer to comment that it's a" good place to take your in-laws for a swanky dinner."

New American | Casual | Expensive | midtown west | 135 W. 42nd St. | 212-319-1660 | www.charliepalmer.com | Dinner daily, Lunch Mon-Sat

Mas   90.9

Though the French farmhouse menu corroborates the restaurant's name, "a light hand" combined with the modern culinary technique that chef Galen Zamarra picked up in David Bouley's kitchen makes this the most delicate rustic cuisine you're likely to experience. Favorite dishes include the signature tuna flash-seared in a beurre noisette, Maine lobster gently poached in a carrot consommé and heartier fare like slowly braised short ribs with polenta or vegetarian-stuffed cabbage. It's one of the most user-friendly restaurants you will ever visit: Diners are encouraged to mix and match from the à la carte and tasting menus. The staff is among the kindest in the city, and the farmhouse-chic décor is unique for an urban establishment.

French | Casual | Moderate | greenwich village | 39 Downing St. | 212-255-1790 | www.masfarmhouse.com | Dinner daily

Petrossian   90.9

Given that the name above the door is synonymous with caviar, you will have to search long and hard to find better fish eggs than those at this import from Paris. Add an exquisite dining room in a building that dates from 1909, along with the close proximity to Carnegie Hall, and plenty of people find this a useful restaurant. Unfortunately, an "outdated menu" means there's not much worth visiting for besides the fish eggs or smoked fish. Put another way, "This place is great if caviar is on the diet, and you also happen to be a billionaire."

French | Casual | Very Expensive | midtown west | 182 W. 58th St. | 212-245-2214 | www.petrossian.com | Lunch & Dinner daily

ABC Kitchen   90.8

Considering that Jean-Georges opens new restaurants faster than you can say Vongerichten, we didn't expect much of this place when it was announced. Our bad, as the talented "Dan Kluger's culinary pedigree shines through here." The cuisine is as eclectic as it gets. Pretzel-crusted calamari with marinara and mustard aioli, kasha and bowtie pasta with veal meatballs and crunchy roasted Chatham cod with glazed mushrooms with chili and mint are but some of the mouthwatering dishes. One reviewer counted "eight visits and not a disappointing meal yet," while another waxed poetic about "one of the best burgers in the city" made with akaushi beef.

New American | Casual | Moderate | flatiron | ABC Carpet | 35 E. 18th St. | 212-475-5829 | www.abckitchennyc.com | Lunch & Dinner daily

Jack's Luxury Oyster Bar   90.8

The following comment seems the ideal summary: "Calling Jack's Luxury Oyster Bar 'quirky' doesn't quite capture it. The cooking is inventive without being precious, and the quality of the food is even more remarkable for having been prepared in a kitchen reminiscent of a railway dining car. With two dozen seats, it's a wonder that such a place can exist at all. But the small size ultimately adds to the quirkiness. Even more unusual is that in spite of its name, Jack's is not principally a seafood restaurant. It's a contemporary American restaurant that happens to specialize in seafood. In fact, my sense is that the whimsical name narrows its appeal to the public because the presumption is, it's largely a seafood/shellfish restaurant."

New American | Informal | Expensive | east village | 101 Second Ave. | 212-253-7848 | Dinner Mon-Sat

Takashi   90.8

With ingredients sourced from purveyors like Dickson's Farmstand Meats in Chelsea Market and Kansas' Creekstone Farms, reviewers say this Tokyo-style restaurant answers the age-old question, "Where's the beef?" It seems like every part of the carcass is on offer, ranging from tame cuts like short ribs, skirt steak and rib eye to "the best offal I ever had," which includes heart, tongue, liver and the scrumptious-sounding fourth stomach. Ordering is only half the fun: You cook the delicate slices of beef over a personal hibachi and eat them with tasty side dishes like the grilled vegetables of the day and bakudan, a mixture of rice and seaweed wrapped in a sesame leaf.

Japanese | Informal | Expensive | west village | 456 Hudson St. | 212-414-2929 | www.takashinyc.com | Dinner daily

Felidia   90.7

This is the restaurant that made the Bastianich family name. Though she is often away, taping her television program or appearing at a food-related event, Lidia Bastianich has entrusted her kitchen to the talented Fortunato Nicotra, who sneaks the occasional modern touch into the northern Italian cuisine, like borage tagliatelle with Hudson Valley Moulard duck or blue fin tuna grilled only on one side and served with a salad of beets, peaches, Humboldt Fog goat cheese and balsamic vinaigrette. Some people feel the restaurant has seen better days, but fans say, "You'll find yourself liking it more than you expected."

Italian | Casual | Expensive | upper east side | 243 E. 58th St. | 212-758-1479 | www.lidiasitaly.com | Dinner daily, Lunch Mon-Fri

The Palm   90.7

Having served steaks at this address since Prohibition, The Palm encapsulates the New York steakhouse experience. Some 85 years later, you can still find what many feel are the best steaks in the city, especially "the jaw-dropping double-cut New York strip." Lobsters range from three to six pounds, and there are also a few Italian entrées. It all comes with classic sides and a classic New York atmosphere, complete with cartoons of famous customers on the walls. Palm Too, its first offshoot directly across the street, serves the same fare, but many of our reviewers have a soft spot for the original.

Steakhouse | Informal | Expensive | midtown east | 837 Second Ave. | 212-687-2953 | www.thepalm.com | Dinner Mon-Sat, Lunch Mon-Fri

Second Location: midtown east | 840 Second Ave. | 212-697-5198 | www.thepalm.com | Dinner daily, Lunch Mon-Fri

Third Location: midtown west | 250 W. 50th St. | 212-333-7256 | www.thepalm.com | Dinner daily, Lunch Mon-Sat

Fourth Location: tribeca | 206 West St. | 646-395-6393 | www.thepalm.com | Dinner daily, Lunch Mon-Fri

Mia Dona   90.6

After Donatella Arpaia and Michael Psilakis split, we thought this restaurant was toast. But Arpaia reached deep into her Italian roots, reinventing the place to such an extent that reviewers note a definite improvement. The menu is more straightforward Italian these days, like her mother Maria's polpette con salsa pomodoro (meatballs braised in tomato sauce), which caused a mini-sensation when they first appeared on the scene. Meanwhile entrées, like roasted baby chicken with roasted peppers and sweet and sour cipollini onions, are all priced below $20. It can get a bit noisy at times, but given the combination of good food and low price point, its popularity is easy to understand. At lunchtime, you can swing by and grab some meatballs pressed in a focaccia sandwich from a cart parked out front on the sidewalk,

Italian | Casual | Moderate | upper east side | 206 E. 58th St. | 212-750-8170 | www.miadona.com | Dinner daily, Lunch Mon-Fri

Oceana   90.6

While a move to attractive new quarters off Sixth Avenue was a vast improvement over their old townhouse location, they didn't do enough to improve the food at this New American seafooder, which has "never been the same since Cornelius Gallagher left his position as the executive chef," reviewers claim. On the plus side, the fish is super-fresh, and they offer one of the best raw bars in the city. But this is now more of a casual restaurant geared to business diners, pre-theater diners and the tourist crowd, rather than a serious fish restaurant.

Seafood | Casual | Expensive | midtown west | 120 W. 49th St. | 212-759-5941 | www.oceanarestaurant. com | Dinner daily, Lunch Sun-Fri

15 East   90.5

After moving their highly successful Tocqueville into larger premises down the block, Marco Moreira and Jo-Ann Makovitzky opened this Japanese restaurant. The first wave of reviews were lackluster: "unexceptional fish" and "I can get better sushi at my local take-out place," typified the comments. But there's been an uptick over the past year, especially if you ask to sit with chef Masa, who built a reputation as one of the best sushi chefs in the city at Jewel Bako. If you're lucky, he will be flush with various types of fish when you visit, like the night he offered an uni tasting, featuring samples from Hokkaido, Maine and Santa Barbara.

Japanese | Casual | Expensive | flatiron | 15 E. 15th St. | 212-647-0015 | www.15eastrestaurant.com | Dinner Mon-Sat, Lunch Mon-Fri

Mary's Fish Camp   90.5

The ongoing debate that revolves around this slice of New England in Greenwich Village is over who makes the best lobster roll – Mary's Fish Camp or its rival, Pearl Oyster Bar (run by a former partner of Mary's, both in life and in lobsters). Judging by its higher rating, reviewers give the edge to Mary's, which also serves steamers, fried clams, broiled fish and other seafood far. But the most unique thing on the menu is a bowl of lobster knuckles, which, despite the hassle in cracking them open, yield a good amount of sweet meat. Just as in Maine, the best way to end your meal is with ice cream – the hot fudge sundae is especially terrific.

Seafood | Informal | Moderate | greenwich village | 64 Charles St. | 646-486-2185 | www.marysfishcamp. com | Lunch & Dinner Mon-Sat

Seäsonal   90.5

Despite its small Austrian population, Manhattan has always managed to have a contemporary Austrian restaurant that the dining community finds relevant. First, there was the heralded Vienna 79 back in the 1970s, followed in subsequent decades by Danube and then Wallsé. Wolfgang Ban and Eduard F's place is the latest entry. Whether referring to traditional fare like potato soup with taleggio and speck or Wiener schnitzel, or more contemporary offerings like duck with bacon, squash and black trumpet mushrooms, almost every reviewer told us that this is a restaurant to watch. In fact, although the downtown foodie population is notorious for its refusal to dine north of 23rd Street, one Greenwich Village-based reviewer was impressed enough to tell us, "It's worth the trip uptown!"

Austrian | Casual | Expensive | midtown west | 132 W. 58th St. | 212-957-5550 | www.seasonalnyc.com | Dinner daily, Lunch Mon-Sat

The Spotted Pig   90.5

Be sure to take your cholesterol medication before you pay a visit to April Bloomfield's homage to the British gastropub, where "every dish seems to be based on cream, butter or fat." After the "stupendous waits" (they don't take reservations), your pre-bypass meal might include chicken liver on toast, poached duck egg with lamb tongue and grilled skirt steak with summer beets and horseradish cream. The scene at lunch is much calmer, when the cuisine includes more casual fare: a bruschetta of mozzarella with summer squash or a Cubano sandwich. Bloomfield also serves "one of the most talked-about burgers in the city."

Gastropub | Informal | Moderate | west village | 314 W. 11th St. | 212-620-0393 | www.thespottedpig.com | Lunch & Dinner daily

Sushiden   90.5

This duo of Midtown sushi restaurants comes in handy for business lunches or dinners as well as for pre-theater dining. It's been around for ages, causing one reviewer to pay tribute to its dedication to quality, saying, "Many have come and gone, but the 'Den has endured." While not close to the city's best, it's solidly established in the second tier of Japanese restaurants, making for a good alternative when you're not in the mood to spend exorbitant sums of money for fish flown in from Japan.

Japanese | Informal | Expensive | midtown west | 123 W. 49th St. | 212-398-2800 | www.sushiden.com | Lunch & Dinner Mon-Sat

Second Location: midtown east | 19 E. 49th St. | 212-758-2700 | www.sushiden.com | Lunch & Dinner Mon-Sat

Telepan   90.5

We used to hear a lot more about Bill Telepan when he was cooking at the now-defunct Judson Grill. But since he opened his own restaurant, his name doesn't seem to be mentioned as often. Among those who are familiar with Telepan's cooking, though, his restaurant is as popular as ever, and dishes like lobster Bolognese and roast trout with artichokes, faro, shell beans and arugula inspired comments like "This is a classy, tasty spot that doesn't get the press and attention it deserves." If you like drinking New World wines, you might find it worth going just so you can take advantage of the "huge list of California cult offerings."

New American | Casual | Expensive | upper west side | 72 W. 69th St. | 212-580-4300 | www.telepan-ny. com | Lunch & Dinner daily

Babbo   90.3

Fame can be a double-edged sword. While his renown causes throngs to flock to his flagship, there are those who say that Mario Batali's kitchen has a hard time keeping up with the crowds, resulting in food that doesn't always live up to expectations. Fortunately, when the kitchen is on, it's capable of turning out delicious versions of Batali's classic dishes, like lamb's tongue salad or the signature mint love letters with spicy lamb sausage. There is less unanimity regarding the entrées: A sizable contingent of reviewers recommends "forgoing the mains entirely" and sticking exclusively to the starters and pastas. Joe Bastianich's wine list is loaded with cherries and treasures, although the pricing is not really consumer-friendly.

Italian | Casual | Expensive | greenwich village | 110 Waverly Pl. | 212-777-0303 | www.babbonyc.com | Dinner daily

Gilt   90.3

No review of Gilt can begin without mentioning the sumptuous décor: The room occupies part of the Villard Houses, built by a railroad financier in 1882, and fully reflects the splendor of that gilded era. Given that backdrop, Justin Bogle's menu, which includes dishes like Matsutake mushroom with roasted chicken consommé, smoked egg, pine and huckleberry and monkfish loin with charred eggplant, cauliflower and harissa, seems restrained by comparison. Though the restaurant earned its highest press accolades after Bogle was hired, it was actually more popular with our reviewers when Paul Liebrandt and Christopher Lee were in charge of the kitchen.

New American | Formal | Expensive | midtown east | New York Palace Hotel | 455 Madison Ave. | 212-891-8100 | www.giltnewyork.com | Dinner Tue-Sat

Aquagrill   90.2

Although you rarely hear foodies talking about it, you never see empty tables at Jeremy and Jennifer Marshall's narrow SoHo dining room. What draws the crowds is the exquisite fish and shellfish, which includes "the best selection of oysters in the city," along with entrées like Jeremy's signature falafel-crusted salmon with hummus and preserved lemons and a bouillabaisse described a "easily the best version I've had outside of the South of France." There are also seasonal specialties, like stone crab claws or shad roe or pink shrimp from Maine. If the preparations are a bit too fussy for your taste, you can always order any fish simply grilled or pan-sautéed. Working against the restaurant is a wine list that doesn't match up to the terrific cuisine, compounded by the no-BYOB policy.

Seafood | Casual | Expensive | soho | 210 Spring St. | 212-274-0505 | www.aquagrill.com | Lunch & Dinner daily

Bar Boulud   90.2

"At last, some edible fare in what historically has been the food-free Lincoln Center zone" sums up the reviewer response to Daniel Boulud's latest offering. At the heart of its success is the house-made charcuterie, fabricated by a *traiteur* imported from Lyon "who lives up to his pedigree," along with classic brasserie fare, such as a velouté of leek and potatoes or a simple roast chicken with apples, braised endives, parsnips and cider jus. The location makes it perfect before, after, or even during the theater, opera or ballet. It's also "great for a business lunch," being situated somewhat outside the Midtown maelstrom.

French | Casual | Moderate | lincoln center | 1900 Broadway | 212-595-0303 | www.danielnyc.com | Lunch & Dinner daily

Gotham Bar and Grill   90.2

In opening this restaurant, chef Alfred Portale helped to define a category of dining that some reviewers describe as the "upper middle," yet few restaurants in our survey engendered opinions that were so radically opposed. Proponents say ,"It's still going strong after 25 years," while the 25% of reviewers who rated it Acceptable or lower countered with "cuisine stuck in the past." Avatars of New American cuisine, the dishes include a sweet corn soup with lobster and a shellfish emulsion and curry-spiced Muscovy duck breast with foie gras, toasted cashews and apricot chutney. Portale's famous plating style, with ingredients mounted in vertical stacks, makes a dish look like a supplication to the food gods.

New American | Casual | Expensive | greenwich village | 12 E. 12th St. | 212-620-4020 | www.gothambarandgrill.com | Dinner daily, Lunch Mon-Fri

Má Pêche   90.2

While reviewers recommend this Midtown offering from David Chang, it hasn't attracted the same sort of raves as his other restaurants (the various Momofukus) have. It's a little surprising, since the super-talented Tien Ho runs the kitchen, and his modern spin on Vietnamese cuisine results in offerings like Niman Ranch beef tartare with soy, scallion and mint or Eden Brook trout served with sunchoke, cashews and fish sauce. While reviewers described the food as "simple, with dishes that are well-balanced and tasty," they also said, "David who? There's little evidence here of the excitement that Chang elicits at his downtown places."

Vietnamese | Casual | Moderate | midtown west | Chambers Hotel | 15 W. 56th St. | 212-254-3500 | www.momofuku.com | Dinner daily, Lunch Mon-Sat

Maialino   90.2

Unlike other restaurateurs who bastardize their original restaurant with branches, Danny Meyer only opens places that have a unique concept. This Roman trattoria is his latest, and its debut took place with such ease that "one would never know this is

Meyer's first Italian restaurant." Nick Anderer is in charge of the kitchen, and he offers a menu of "simple, but excellently prepared pastas," like spaghetti alla carbonara and bucatini all'Amatriciana, along with "rustic mains" like cod in spicy tomato sauce and a suckling pig for two. Reviewers say the "really well-done Roman fare," along with an "easy feeling," means that" Danny Meyer has done it again."

Italian | Casual | Expensive | gramercy | 2 Lexington Ave. | 212-777-2410 | www.maialinonyc.com | Lunch & Dinner daily

BLT Steak   90.1

Though he has severed his relationship with the restaurant, Laurent Tourendel's spirit lingers on at this part steakhouse/part luxury bistro that, despite its rating, inspired some strongly negative feelings from our reviewers. Part of the problem is the garishly dressed Upper East Side crowd that has turned this restaurant into "more of a side-show than a steakhouse." Still, reviewers say the food, featuring the traditional setup of shareable sides and huge steaks, is "competitive with other top steak restaurants in town." During the day the room is full of "expensive suits enjoying their power lunches."

Steakhouse | Casual | Expensive | midtown east | 106 E. 57th St. | 212-752-7470 | www.bltsteak.com | Dinner daily, Lunch Mon-Sat

DBGB Kitchen & Bar   90.1

With the opening of this restaurant, Daniel Boulud has successfully expanded his brand in a way that appeals to a younger clientele. While some might like it for the people-watching, it's the numerous varieties of sausages, from Thai to Tunisian to a classic boudin noir, and burgers that come with toppings ranging from traditional to exotic, that makes this East Village spot tick. And the bistro dishes, like roasted bone marrow or a simple steak frites, aren't bad either. Unfortunately, the "ambience is horrid," with a noise level that is "excruciating even when it's at its lowest level."

French | Informal | Moderate | east village | 299 Bowery | 212-933-5300 | www.danielnyc.com | Lunch & Dinner daily

L'Absinthe   90.1

What is arguably the best brasserie food in the city can be found at this "very grown-up" restaurant on the Upper East Side. Whether it be cassoulet, choucroute or a simply roasted rack of lamb, Jean-Michel Bergougnoux's cooking comes as close to casual Parisian fare as you will find in the States. Problem is, the restaurant's clientele tends to be older, well-heeled and on the conservative side, resulting in an ambience that lacks the usual lively brasserie flair. A "lackluster wine list" and a no-BYOB policy mean that Franco-Oenophiles don't visit quite as often as they might like to.

French | Casual | Expensive | upper east side | 227 E. 67th St. | 212-794-4950 | www.labsinthe.com | Lunch & Dinner daily

Boqueria   90.0

The menu at Boqueria focuses on traditional tapas, with a few more adventurous dishes thrown into the mix. Start out with platters of ham and cheese and cooked fare like gar-lic shrimp or fried chorizo, and follow them with dishes like seared diver scallops with English peas, lemon confit and bacon vinaigrette. There are also a few larger plates, like paellas and fideos. One reviewer thought the quality had declined since a second location opened, saying the food "lacks the culinary imagination it has shown in the past."

Tapas | Informal | Moderate | chelsea | 53 W. 19th St | 212-255-4160 | www.boquerianyc.com | Lunch & Dinner daily

Second Location: soho | 171 Spring St. | 212-255-4160 | www.boquerianyc.com | Lunch & Dinner daily

Dovetail   90.0

While it's been lauded by the local media, our reviewing panel is somewhat mixed on John Fraser's New American eatery. Fraser first came to the attention of New York diners when he was cooking at Compass. But while the reactions to his cooking there were nearly all positive, it doesn't engender the same level of consensus here, with comments ranging from "first-class culinary technique, with a contemporary sensibility that is well-grounded in traditional approaches" to "high-end ingredients but overwrought preparations." But it seems that Fraser's fans have won the argument, as the restaurant has recently doubled the size of the dining room.

New American | Casual | Moderate | upper west side | 103 West 77th St. | 212-362-3330 | www.dovetailnyc.com | Dinner daily, Lunch Fri-Sun

Hearth   90.0

While the cuisine might appear to be country Italian at first glance – hearty fare like a stuffed cabbage of veal and sweetbreads or hand-cut pappardelle topped with slow-cooked duck ragù – the years Marco Canora spent in Tom Colicchio's kitchen have polished his technique to an unusually refined extent for a rustic cucina. A fun way to dine is to wait for a seat at the kitchen pass, where the chefs serve you directly. There are also popular special-event dinners like a summer pig roast. Paul Grieco has put together a good wine list, but his no-BYOB policy rubs some people the wrong way. "A great neighborhood restaurant that borders on being a destination."

Italian | Informal | Expensive | east village | 403 E. 12th St. | 646-602-1300 | www.restauranthearth.com | Dinner daily

Ippudo   90.0

One of the more recent entries into the East Village ramen sweepstakes, Ippudo had one reviewer raving about broth he claimed was "liquid pork." In addition to the half-dozen variations on ramen, arguably Japan's national dish, there are small plates like fried oysters with wasabi mayo, a spring roll that's a takeoff on a Philly cheese steak and a casserole of spicy tofu, minced pork and crunchy noodles. A "lively atmosphere" and "prices that won't break the bank" can mean waits as long as an hour and a half. The good news is that, while you wait, you can enjoy a few orders of the "outstanding barbecue pork buns" that are offered on the bar menu.

Japanese | Informal | Moderate | east village | 65 4th Ave. | 212-388-0088 | www.ippudo.com | Lunch & Dinner daily

Oyster Bar at Grand Central Terminal   90.0

While there are raves for the selection of oysters and other shellfish, as well as for the delicious chowders, stews and pan roasts, there is less enthusiasm for the cooked dishes on the menu, with one person going as far as to say,"If it isn't raw or served in a soup bowl, don't eat it." There is an eclectic list of wines, many available by the glass, and the vintage setting in the vaulted basement of Grand Central Terminal is as retro as it gets and a cherished remnant of old New York.

Seafood | Informal | Moderate | midtown east | Grand Central Terminal | 212-490-6650 | www.oyster-barny.com | Lunch & Dinner Mon-Sat

Pearl Oyster Bar   90.0

The owner of Pearl and the owner of Mary's Fish Camp used to be partners in business as well as life, and their split resulted in joint custody of their famous lobster roll. While our reviewers lean toward Mary's version, a few claim they prefer Pearl's. Similarities aside, there is a greater emphasis on cooked food here, and the room has a cozy, neigh-borhood feel that led one person to comment,"I always feel like a Cornelia Street insider when I bring someone here for dinner."

Seafood | Informal | Moderate | west village | 18 Cornelia St. | 212-691-8211 | www.pearloysterbar.com | Dinner Mon-Sat, Lunch Mon-Fri

SD26   90.0

For 20 years, from a spot on Central Park South, the legendary Tony May catered to an older, monied and sophisticated crowd of diners at his elegant San Domenico. But with a move to Madison Square Park and with May's daughter Marisa taking on a greater role, and Matteo Bergamini replacing Odette Fada behind the stoves, the restaurant has reinvented itself, as a younger, looser place (as suggested by the symbolic name change). Now you are more likely to see the place filled with fresh-faced lawyers and bankers with attractive women in tow, enjoying dishes like wild bass aquapazza with zucchini and tomato sarda fregola. Reviewers talk about food that is "better than one would imagine," considering that the front room has become one of the hottest pickup scenes in the city.

Italian | Casual | Expensive | flatiron | 19 E. 26th St. | 212-265-5959 | www.sd26ny.com | Dinner daily, Lunch Mon-Fri

Sasabune   90.0

At this New York City branch of a well-known Los Angeles restaurant, the routine is the same as on the West Coast: It's all omakase all the time, and a meal includes a dozen different types of fish prepared in the house style, which typically means dressing the fish with a light soy or some type of flavored sauce. However, it hasn't managed to catch on here the way it did in L.A., as reflected in comments like "It's excellent as a neighborhood restaurant, but probably not worth an excursion."

Japanese | Informal | Expensive | upper east side | 401 E. 73rd St | 212-249-8583 | Dinner Tue-Sat, Lunch Tue-Fri

Sfoglia   90.0

Who would imagine that an Italian restaurant transplanted from Nantucket could cap-ture the imagination of Manhattan's Upper East Side? The decor recreates the ambi-ence of an Italian countryside inn, and the rustic fare includes a few modern touches, like English pea soup with crisp duck prosciutto and ricotta gnocchi with rock shrimp, broccoli rabe, raisins and lemon cream. When it first opened, it was so popular you needed to book a month in advance, but happily, an expansion into the brownstone next door has made obtaining a reservation easier, at least on weeknights – though tables before and after events at the 92nd Street Y (catty-corner from the restaurant) are still hard to come by.

Italian | Informal | Moderate | upper east side | 135 E. 92nd St. | 212-831-1402 | www.sfogliarestaurant. com | Dinner daily, Lunch Mon-Sat

Tamarind   90.0

Now that Tabla has closed its doors and the culinary team at Devi has split, Tamarind has become the city's top Indian restaurant. Always more traditional than its two competitors, Tabla offers a menu of all the classic moghul dishes, many are cooked in a tandoor in the glassed-in kitchen that separates the bar area from the dining room. There's a $25 lunch menu available on weekdays, making it a great choice for a business meal, and those in search of lighter fare can opt for the next-door tearoom, which offers a series of sandwiches and desserts as well as a variety of exotic teas.

Indian | Casual | Moderate | gramercy | 41-43 E. 22nd St. | 212-674-7400 | www.tamarinde22.com | Lunch & Dinner daily

Avra Estiatorio   89.5

A number of restaurants have followed in the footsteps of the successful Estiatorio Milos. Avra is one, proffering fish that's more reasonably priced than the competition's, and the strategy works: Every evening the place is filled with people enjoying salads, spreads and a slew of fish sold by the pound. Reviewers say it's "loud, crowded and noisy," adding, "The food is exactly the same as when they opened eleven years ago."

Greek | Casual | Expensive | midtown east | 141 E. 48th St. | 212-759-8550 | www.avrany.com | Lunch & Dinner daily

Barbuto   89.5

After a heralded career that included cooking at Michael's in Santa Monica and Jams in New York, Jonathan Waxman bought himself a wood-burning oven and decided to serve market Italian fare, like a fitto misti of vegetables with pimenton aioli or a Hampshire pork chop with red cabbage and golden raisins. Though Waxman's food can be delicious at times, causing one *Top Chef* host who lives nearby to tell us," It's my favorite place to eat in the neighborhood," inconsistency in the kitchen and an acoustical nightmare (it's located in a converted garage) had a negative impact on the rating. Pray for good weather and a seat on the outdoor patio.

Italian | Informal | Moderate | west village | 775 Washington St. | 212-924-9700 | www.barbutonyc.com | Lunch & Dinner daily

Ben & Jack's Steakhouse   89.5

This might be the best of the various Peter Luger copies (i.e., places proffering prime porterhouse steak that's broiled, sliced and served in a sizzling butter sauce), which have become so popular over the past decade. The secret of its success, our reviewers say, is "better quality meat" that is "perfectly aged and charred" and sides that are even "more plentiful" than the ones offered by the competition. The Midtown East location makes for a convenient alternative to The Palm when you happen to be in a porterhouse rather than a New York strip state of mind. A "steadily improving wine list" further enhances the experience.

Steakhouse | Casual | Expensive | midtown east | 219 E. 44th St. | 212-682-5678 | www.benandjacksssteakhouse.com | Dinner daily, Lunch Mon-Sat

Blaue Gans   89.5

With dishes like pork goulash and the rarely seen kavalierspitz on the menu, this bras-serie from Kurt Gutenbrunner is one of the few places in the country offering tradi-tional Austrian cooking. It isn't particularly well-known, a situation that one reviewer blamed on the quiet location as well as the internal ambience. But others enjoy eating in a venue where they can hear their dinner companions, and they praise it for being a "lovely, grown-up place" with good-quality Mittel European cooking brought to the table by "charming and knowledgeable servers."

Austrian | Informal | Moderate | tribeca | 139 Duane St. | 212-571-8880 | http://kg-ny.com | Lunch & Dinner daily

Blue Ribbon   89.5

The Bromberg brothers have been serving their unique mishmash of comfort cuisines at this location since 1992. The menu is so varied that a large party can start with the delights of a raw bar, move on to matzo ball soup, enjoy a pu pu platter and then dig into entrées like seafood paella or a steak with mushroom gravy. It all comes with an atmosphere described as "kinetic," especially after midnight, when the place fills up with diners taking advantage of the 4:00 a.m. closing time.

American | Informal | Moderate | tribeca | 97 Sullivan St. | 212-274-0404 | www.blueribbonrestaurants.com | Open daily

Blue Ribbon Sushi   89.5

There's a split of opinion about this sushi duo (the second's in Park Slope) from the Bromberg brothers. One fan called the SoHo location "one of my favorite downtown restaurants," while another countered with, "It's difficult to recommend B-quality sushi." Many frequenters favor the more gimmicky fare, like rolls of yellowtail with straw mushrooms or lobster, shiso and caviar. Still, even if it's not a serious sushi expe-rience, it's handy if you're in the neighborhood. *Note: See Outer Boroughs section for the Brooklyn location.*

Japanese | Informal | Moderate | soho | 119 Sullivan St. | 212-343-0404 | www.blueribbonrestaurants.com | Lunch & Dinner daily

Bond Street   89.5

Given its reputation as a party place and not a serious restaurant, we were surprised to see how many people said favorable things about this restaurant. Of course, that doesn't mean the ambience isn't "loud, young and fun"; it's just that the owners have decided to keep the quality high enough so that foodies say, "It's the best of the trendy sushi restaurants in Manhattan." Which makes it the perfect place to take out-of-town-ers for that glam New York City evening (and good eats as well).

Japanese | Informal | Expensive | greenwich village | 6 Bond St. | 212-777-2500 | www.bondstrestaurant.com | Dinner daily

Casa Mono   89.5

This tapas restaurant was Mario Batali's first foray outside of the Italian kitchen, and we are happy to report that the small plates cuisine of Spain seems to have survived Batali-azation. Sure, the food that chef de cuisine Andy Nusser serves is not quite as authentic as what you will find at some of the other tapas specialists in town, but if you are looking for a casual meal between dinners at the city's top restaurants, Casa Mono is a good choice. Negatives are that it's "loud, cramped and crowded," plus they don't allow you to BYOB. But "if you can shoehorn into a seat," you will find "food that is consistently delicious."

Tapas | Informal | Moderate | gramercy | 125 E. 17th St. # 1 | 212-253-2773 | www.casamononyc.com | Lunch & Dinner daily

db Bistro Moderne   89.5

"It's the burger, stupid!" No, James Carville hasn't become a restaurant critic; that's just our way of telling you that more than half the people who rated this restaurant recommended it for the famous db burger (filled with braised short ribs and black truffle) alone. It's "a true New York signature dish," according to one reviewer, who has "been there several times but never ordered anything other than the burger." We did get a more adventurous soul to admit that "the other food – bacon-veiled salmon with gnocchi, brussels sprouts and trompette mushrooms – is pretty tasty, too." The restaurant fills a niche in the culinary no-man's-land between Grand Central Terminal and the Theater District.

French | Casual | Moderate | midtown west | 55 W. 44th St. | 212-391-2400 | www.danielnyc.com | Open daily

Dévi   89.5

A while back, Suvir Saran came up with a concept that, at the time, was unique for Indian cuisine: Start with the artisanally sourced ingredients used at the city's top restaurants, but prepare them so that their fine, innate qualities aren't masked by spice mixtures and marinades. The concept turned out to be a hit, resulting in tandoori lamb chops that are medium rare (not well done) and tandoori fish preparations that are moist and juicy. Other standout dishes, like Manchurian cauliflower and chicken schnitzel Marsala, demonstrate an understanding of culinary technique that extends well beyond the typical Indian kitchen.

Indian | Informal | Moderate | flatiron | 8 E. 18th St. | 212-691-1300 | www.devinyc.com | Dinner daily, Lunch Mon-Fri

EN Japanese Brasserie   89.5

The reason to go to this bright and lively restaurant is to sample the fresh, creamy tofu made in house several times a day. Though "the rest of the food is not up to the same standard," one could build an adequate meal by supplementing this specialty with an assortment of sushi and cooked preparations. While it would probably be more popular if the non-tofu-based dishes were better than "adequate," reviewers are quick to say that the "absolutely delicious" tofu and yuba are "worth a trip on their own."

Japanese | Casual | Moderate | west village | 435 Hudson St. | 212-647-9196 | www.enjb.com | Dinner daily, Lunch Mon-Fri

Fatty Crab   89.5

Zak Pelaccio spent part of his youth in Malaysia, and this restaurant is his homage to that country's cuisine. The Southeast Asian delights include pork belly and beef sliders, spicy barbecue ribs, Lo Si Fun (rice noodles with Chinese sausage and shitake mushrooms), chicken laksa and "chili crabs – yum!" as one eloquent reviewer put it. The place is small, cramped and noisy, as well as super-popular, so be prepared for a significant wait for a table on a weekend night – though, in order to ease the load, they opened a branch on the Upper West Side in 2009.

Malaysian | Informal | Moderate | west village | 643 Hudson St. | 212-352-3592 | www.fattycrab.com | Lunch & Dinner daily

Kanoyama   89.5

When you find yourself in Greenwich Village and you're in the mood for sushi and you don't want to pay the prices of a Jewel Bako or Soto, head on over to this top-flight neighborhood restaurant, which features "fish that is reasonably priced considering the quality you're getting." While there was also praise for the cooked food, like black cod marinated in Saikyo miso, complaints were directed at the "dismal service" (they are often staffed with college students) and a dining room called "small and overcrowded."

Japanese | Informal | Moderate | east village | 175 Second Ave. | 212-777-5266 | www.kanoyama.com | Dinner daily

Keens Steakhouse   89.5

While New York's oldest steakhouse (it opened two years before Peter Luger, in 1885) serves pretty good beef, it's famous for its mutton chop – a triple-cut loin chop that comes with some of the deepest lamb flavor you will ever experience. The rest of the menu is typical steakhouse fare – oysters, salads, grills, Dover sole and lobsters – which can be washed down with one of the city's most famous lists of single malt Scotch. It's all served in an environment that is straight out of old New York; the décor revolves around the restaurant's collection of long, churchwarden pipes smoked by famous people, which covers almost every inch of the walls and ceiling.

Steakhouse | Informal | Expensive | garment district | 72 W. 36th St. | 212-947-3636 | www.keens.com | Dinner daily, Lunch Mon-Fri

Market Table   89.5

This sister restaurant of The Little Owl (see below) offers a more spacious dining room, making it easier to book a table as well as stretch your arms between courses. While Mikey Price prepares an eclectic American cuisine with enough care to make visiting worthwhile – among his offerings are crispy calamari with guacamole and chili crema or grilled lamb t-bones with a gouda gratin – the restaurant lacks the personality of its sibling. "One of the better hamburgers in the city" is available at lunch.

New American | Informal | Moderate | greenwich village | 54 Carmine St. | 212-255-2100 | www.markettablenyc.com | Lunch & Dinner daily

Mercadito   89.5

People always talk about finding a Mexican restaurant that blends authenticity and high-quality local ingredients. Well, it's available at this nondescript venue in the East

Village, which features ceviches like shrimp with pico de gallo, pineapple and jalapeño-tomato broth and guajillo-marinated whole red snapper with a red cabbage tomato salad and chipotle vinaigrette. Garnering comments like "inexpensive and terribly satisfying, with a staff that is impossibly friendly and on their game each and every time," it's a restaurant that should be better known.

Mexican | Informal | Moderate | east village | 179 Ave. B | 212-529-6490 | www.mercaditony.com | Lunch & Dinner daily

Nobu 57   89.5

While it offers a menu similar to the downtown original, Nobu's midtown venue has fallen prey to some of the pitfalls that plague offshoots; some reviewers complained they were "trading on the name." But over the past year and a half we have seen a distinct upturn in the reviews, and now comments are more likely to be positive – for example, "a welcome addition to the Midtown scene" and" some of the best fish dishes around." One major element in the change is a distinctly different ambience from the original's, driven by the "uptown-looking clientele, "which makes for "terrific people-watching."

Japanese | Casual | Expensive | midtown west | 40 W. 57th St. | 212-757-3000 | www.myriadrestaurant-group.com | Dinner daily, Lunch Mon-Sat

Perbacco   89.5

Despite raves from certain members of the local food press, Simone Bonelli's cuisine never really caught on the way we expected it to. Having trained at Osteria Francescana in Modena, Bonelli mixes traditional Italian fare with contemporary creations, like ravioli of prosciutto di Parma and mascarpone that he tops with a carpaccio of cantaloupe or slow-cooked pork belly with caramelized red onion, steamed broccoli rabe and a black pepper honey glaze. Bonelli's skills are still developing – the chef is only 28 years old – but advocates of modern Italian culinary technique insist it's worth a trek downtown, as it's "more inventive than its location and price would suggest."

Italian | Informal | Moderate | lower east side | 234 E. 4th St. | 212-253-2038 | www.perbacconyc.com | Dinner daily, Lunch Sat-Sun

Perry Street   89.5

Reviews are mixed for this Jean-Georges Vongerichten restaurant on the ground floor of architect Richard Meier's building gracing West Street. Some reviewers report that "the creative food matches the coolly elegant atmosphere" and go on to mention dishes like a salad of frisée, goat cheese, peach and wasabi. But critics say the cuisine "lacks inspiration and tastes like it has been prepped [well] ahead of time." The things everyone likes are the price point and the view. No, not the view of the Hudson River, silly; we mean the one of Nicole Kidman eating dinner at the next table.

New American | Casual | Moderate | west village | 176 Perry St. | 212-352-1900 | www.Jean-Georges.com | Lunch & Dinner daily

Primehouse New York   89.5

The B.R. Guest organization has created one of the most attractive steakhouses in the city. The menu is a bit broader than the typical steak restaurant's: Starters like New England clam chowder and Thai shrimp dumplings and mains like Chilean sea bass with chanterelles, grilled corn and roasted heirloom tomato broth complement a full slate of Creekstone Farms steaks. "Much better than I expected," said one reviewer, adding that the food is "sort of corporate but good nonetheless."

Steakhouse | Casual | Expensive | murray hill | 381 Park Ave. South | 212-824-2600 | www.primehouse-nyc.com | Dinner daily, Lunch Mon-Sat

Rao's   89.5

The southern Italian cuisine won't break down any doors – it's the ambience that makes this vintage East Harlem dining room the quintessential New York experience. Unfortunately, they don't take reservations, having pre-assigned the tables to regulars. That means the only way to get in is to befriend someone who owns a table and beg him to either invite you or, even better, give it you for the evening. Is it all worth it? Well, as one reviewer put it, "How good does exclusivity taste? I did not dislike a recent meal, but I'm not dying to return."

Italian | Casual | Expensive | harlem | 455 E. 114th St. | 212-722-6709 | www.raos.com | Dinner Mon-Fri

Scalinatella   89.5

A location close to Midtown and an intimate basement dining room makes this northern Italian restaurant a favorite with celebs – David Crosby, Kate Hudson and Katie Couric are among those spotted over the years. All of the standard fare is on hand, from pastas to grills, along with the occasional more ambitious dish like peppered tuna in a balsamic glaze. There's just one catch: The prices are significantly higher than at similar restaurants, which doesn't seem to be much of a deterrent for the well-to-do crowd that frequents the place.

Italian | Casual | Expensive | upper east side | 201 E. 61st St. | 212-207-8280 | Dinner daily, Lunch Mon-Sat

Strip House   89.5

Though the menu is not much different than at other steakhouses in the city, the cool décor, "part brothel, part 1950s Italian restaurant," adds an extra element to the experience here. Other things in its favor are its location in Greenwich Village, a part of the city that isn't overflowing with good steakhouses, and an adequate wine list. If eating large hunks of beef in a room that feels like Sinatra could be sitting at the next table isn't enough of a draw, you also have the option of bringing your own wine.

Steakhouse | Informal | Expensive | greenwich village | 13 E. 12th St. | 212-328-0000 | www.striphouse.com | Dinner daily

T-Bar Restaurant & Lounge   89.5

Kudos to this restaurant's management for figuring out there are enough people who live on the Upper East Side to support an upscale steakhouse. Now neighborhood residents are happy to be able to save the $15, 15-minute taxi ride to Midtown and still get a high-quality, prime 14-oz. aged New York strip. The rest of the fare is typical for the cow palace category. "It's a welcome addition to the neighborhood" for another reason: The small bar area provides a mingling spot for 40+ singles.

New American | Informal | Moderate | upper east side | 1278 Third Ave. | 212-772-0404 | www.tbarnyc.com | Dinner daily, Lunch Mon-Sat

Txikito   89.5

Having created the New York City tapas craze during their days at Tía Pol, Alex Raij and husband Eder Montero carry on at this venue, serving "the most authentic version of Basque cuisine in the country." Those looking for something more substantial than tapas can call in advance, and Alex and Eder will be happy to prepare a full meal, of the type that a typical Basque family might enjoy for Sunday dinner. There's a reasonably good wine list, and they also offer corkage at this bit of "Bilbao on the Hudson."

Tapas | Informal | Moderate | chelsea | 240 Ninth Ave. | 212-242-4730 | www.txikitonyc.com | Lunch & Dinner Tue-Sat

Balthazar   89.0

With an ambience and décor reminiscent of La Coupole, no other restaurant captures the spirit of 1930s Paris better than Balthazar. As in the brasseries of that bygone era, the mix of people it attracts transcends class, and on the right night the crowd will include tourists, suburbanites who got dressed up and ventured in for a night in SoHo and svelte fashionistas, slurping oysters side by side. The "food can be hit or miss," but everyone agreed it was much better than they'd expected. The service, the welcome and the "delicious bread from Balthazar Bakery" were uniformly praised.

French | Casual | Moderate | soho | 80 Spring St. | 212-965-1414 | www.balthazarny.com | Open daily

Café Sabarsky   89.0

The most European experience in the city is available at this "hidden gem in the Neue Galerie," where Kurt Gutenbrunner serves eggs, smoked meats and Austrian pastries at breakfast before switching to heartier fare like goulash and crepes stuffed with smoked trout and horseradish crème fraîche for lunch. You can cap off the experience with a tour of the gallery's exquisite collection of German abstract and expressionist art – that is, once you've wiped the schlag from the delicious Austrian coffee off your upper lip.

Austrian | Informal | Moderate | upper east side | Neue Galerie | 1048 Fifth Ave. | 212-288-0665 | http://kg-ny.com/Cafe-sabarsky | Breakfast & Lunch Wed-Mon, Dinner Thu-Sun

Colicchio & Sons   89.0

After closing Craftsteak, Tom Colicchio reincarnated this "attractive" space with this new venture. Problem is, instead of crafting a fresh culinary concept, he serves "a cuisine similar in style to his Gramercy Tavern days" – such as pork belly with pepper jam and dandelion greens –"only not as good." Some reviewers feel it "will improve over time," while others say "Colicchio has taken the name of his children in vain" in the process of maintaining his empire.

New American | Casual | Expensive | chelsea | 85 Tenth Ave. | 212-400-6699 | www.colicchioandsons. com | Lunch & Dinner daily

Del Posto   89.0

When this restaurant owned by the Babbo team and Lidia Bastianich first opened in 2005, most of the reviews we collected were highly negative. But over time, the talented Mark Ladner, who wowed diners when he was at Lupa, has figured out how to make his customers happy (if still reluctant to award the place top honors). Billed as haute Italian cuisine, the menu includes dishes like orecchiette with lamb neck sausage, cherry peppers and broccoli rabe, along with wood-grilled lobster with gnocchetti sardi.

Italian | Casual | Expensive | chelsea | 85 Tenth Ave. | 212-497-8090 | www.delposto.com | Lunch & Dinner daily, Sat dinner only

Great NY Noodletown   89.0

If it's the middle of the night and you're in the mood for a bowl of wonton noodle soup or barbecued meats, look no further than this " dingy"Chinatown stalwart, where your fellow diners are likely to include chefs who just finished their dinner service and taxi drivers slurping shrimp dumpling soup before they turn in for the night. The salt-baked chicken with ginger, the signature dish, "should not be missed."

Chinese | Informal | Moderate | chinatown | 28½ Bowery | 212-349-0923 | Lunch & Dinner daily

La Socarrat   89.0

Asturias-born Lolo Manso is one of the true characters of the New York restaurant scene. After his great success at La Nacional, he opened up this narrow restaurant with counter-only seating, serving what is easily the best paella in the city. There are a number of different tapas to start, but the highlight of your dinner will be one of his eight different paellas or fideuas; the last thing the waiter does when bringing the dish to the table is to scrape the caramelized rice, known as the socarrat, off the bottom of the pan, ensuring that "your last few bites will be the best of the meal."

Spanish | Informal | Moderate | chelsea | 259 W. 19th St. | 212-462-1000 | www.socarratpaellabar.com | Lunch & Dinner daily

Le Relais de Venise (L'Entrecote)   89.0

This New York outpost of a legendary Parisian bistro is "possibly the simplest restaurant you will ever eat in." They serve only one thing: a green salad topped with mustard vinaigrette, followed by steak, sliced and served with the house secret sauce ("don't bother asking for ketchup" – or the sauce's recipe), along with some of the best frites on this side of the Atlantic. And if you're still hungry after you finish your portion, they will be happy to offer you seconds; for an extra charge, there are also classic desserts available. "*Je t'aime*" is how one reviewer feels about the restaurant.

French | Informal | Moderate | midtown east | 590 Lexington Ave. | 212-758-3989 | www.relaisdevenise. com | Lunch & Dinner daily

Little Giant   89.0

Prepared from fresh ingredients and served in liberal portions, Julie Taras Wallach's first-rate comfort food features dishes like truffled asparagus with a duck egg and wild mushrooms and dayboat scallops with minted pea purée, toasted hazelnuts and pea tendrils. "Boisterous and friendly" is how one reviewer described the atmosphere, while another noted, "It's amazing what a talented chef can do without a full kitchen." The restaurant has been so successful that Wallach and partner Tasha Garcia Gibson have opened a second restaurant (Tipsy Parsons, not included in our survey) in Chelsea.

New American | Informal | Moderate | lower east side | 85 Orchard St. | 212-226-5047 | www.littlegiant-nyc.com | Lunch & Dinner daily

Maze   89.0

Despite good reviews, this offering from Gordon Ramsay (based on his successful London original) hasn't really caught on. Maybe the awkward space, half restaurant/half bar, has something to do with it, or maybe the fact that it's "a bit pricy for small plates" keeps people away. Those who have tried it recommend dishes like the deconstructed BLT, salmon with watercress and a scrambled egg and a foie gras velouté with twice-cooked poussin.

French | Casual | Moderate | midtown west | London Hotel | 151 W. 54th St. | 212-468-8889 | http://gordonramsay.com | Lunch & Dinner daily

Oriental Garden   89.0

If you want to spot some of the top toques in New York City having dinner on their nights off, head down to this Chinatown institution, where you will find them feasting on a bevy of crustaceans that includes Dungeness crab, Santa Barbara prawns, Australian lobsters and Alaskan king crabs (in season). While the menu stretches beyond fish, reviewers suggest you "stick to the seafood specialties." The English-speaking waiters are friendly and helpful, making it easier to choose among the exotic creatures that are swimming in tanks near the entrance.

Chinese | Informal | Moderate | chinatown | 14 Elizabeth St. | 212-619-0085 | Lunch & Dinner daily

Quality Meats   89.0

While our reviewers typically don't like steak restaurants from the Smith & Wollensky group, they feel differently about this more upscale bi-level offering. Similar to places like BLT Steak, it uses ingredients sourced from artisanal producers, and the food is prepared by trained chefs, in this instance a team led by Park Avenue Summer's Craig Koketsu, who created the concept and continues to supervise the menu. The "strength of the other entrées on the menu" makes this an excellent choice when your party includes non-carnivores.

Steakhouse | Casual | Expensive | midtown west | 57 W. 58th St. | 212-371-7777 | www.qualitymeatsnyc.com | Dinner daily, Lunch Mon-Fri

The Redhead   89.0

The Southern fare that Meg Grace serves at this "under-the-radar" gastropub has earned the place a near-cult following. Grace's menu features dishes like crawfish macaroni and cheese, shrimp grits with andouille sausage and "an amazing fried chicken." An interesting list of beer and cocktails – Redhead Fizz (vodka, elderflower cordial and fresh lemon juice) is a favorite – appeals to the crowd that just got out of work and wants to forget the day with a drink or three while munching on bacon-peanut brittle.

Southern | Informal | Moderate | east village | 349 E. 13th Street | 212-533-6212 | www.theredheadnyc.com | Dinner daily

Resto   89.0

The word of mouth diminished after Resto's original chef Ryan Skeen left, but successor Bobby Hellen is beginning to attract attention for his meat-intensive Belgian cooking. In addition to house-made charcuterie and specialties like roasted halibut with chestnut spaetzle and short ribs carbonnade, a "terrific list of Belgian beers" helps you wash it all down. The "superb côte de boeuf" and poularde that Hellen sources from Four Story Hill Farms are among the most satisfying meat dishes in the city.

Belgian | Informal | Moderate | murray hill | 111 E. 29th St. | 212-685-5585 | www.restonyc.com | Lunch & Dinner daily

The Standard Grill   89.0

We have to tip our hat to Dan Silverman. The "eye-candy is so outstanding" at his Standard Hotel restaurant that even if he put slop on the plates, the place would still be jammed. But true to his training at Lever House and Union Square Café, he offers well-made dishes like chilled avocado soup with peekytoe crab and an organic veal chop from Schiller Farms with a wild mushroom fricassee; there's also a raw bar and a nice selection of charcuterie. Wine-lovers, beware of a "limited list and no corkage policy."

New American | Casual | Moderate | meatpacking district | Standard Hotel | 848 Washington St. | 212-645-4100 | www.thestandardgrill.com | Open daily

Terroir Wine Bar   89.0

After opening two successful restaurants here in town, Marco Canora decided he wanted to do a more casual spot. So, after renting a space just down the block from his first restaurant, Hearth, Canora opened this Italian wine bar where he offers a menu of bar snacks, panini, assorted cheeses, salumi and bruschetta, plus a few large dishes like cotechino sausage with a fried egg and lentils. An "eccentric, esoteric wine list" and "competent food" make it a good spot for late-night charcuterie or post-dinner drinks. It's worked so out so well, he's added a branch in TriBeCa.

Italian | Informal | Moderate | east village | 413 E. 12th St. | 646-602-1300 | www.wineisterroir.com | Dinner daily, Lunch Sun

Second Location: tribeca | 24 Harrison St. | 212-625-9463 | www.wineisterroir.com | Dinner daily, Lunch Tue-Sun

Tía Pol   89.0

This narrow tapas bar came to the attention of the New York dining community when Alex Raij and her husband, Eder Montero, commanded the stoves. Since the pair opened Txikito, we haven't seen as many reviewers here as before, but the place is still super-popular, and comments like "I waited more than 20 minutes for a table" are typical. And they are still serving a menu that features classic tapas fare, like squid in its ink with rice, along with a few dishes that have a more modern touch, like chorizo with bittersweet chocolate.

Spanish | Informal | Moderate | chelsea | 205 10th Ave. | 212-675-8805 | www.tiapol.com | Lunch and Dinner daily, Lunch Tue-Sun

Wu Liang Ye   89.0

Now down to one location after closing their 86th Street branch, this Szechuan restaurant still has a full slate of classics on hand (cold noodles with sesame sauce, double-sautéed pork, sautéed string beans, crispy fish filets with chilis). But the house specialties are dishes served in a Yibin sauce (named after the city in the Szechuan province). It's well known to our reviewers, one of whom told us that "after years of not eating

Chinese, I tasted their delicious food and started eating it again."

Chinese | Szechuan | Informal | midtown west | 36 W. 48th St. | 212-398-2308 | Lunch & Dinner daily

A Voce   88.5

A Voce's reputation was built when chef Andrew Carmellini was at the helm. After he left, the owners raided the kitchen at Spiaggia and hired Missy Robbins to take his place. Robbins continues to serve the style of rich Italian fare for which the restaurant is known, like ravioli filled with foie gras. The downtown location features a lovely patio – a good bet, since some reviewers complained that the dining room is "so loud you can get a headache." The newer uptown location has the look and feel of a chic nightclub.

Italian | Casual | Expensive | flatiron | 41 Madison Ave. | 212-545-8555 | www.avocerestaurant.com | Dinner Mon-Sat, Lunch Mon-Fri |

Second Location: columbus circle | 10 Columbus Circle, 3rd floor | 212-823-2523 | Lunch & Dinner daily

Asiate   88.5

Because the Mandarin Oriental Hotel was the first part of the Time Warner Center to open, its eatery created a lot of buzz at first. But now it has settled into being "a typical hotel restaurant" where the Asian-fusion food – butter-poached lobster with polenta, honshimeji mushrooms and a Kaffir lime emulsion – takes a backseat to non-culinary concerns like the beautiful surroundings and a nice view. The steep prices certainly don't help; some reviewers are quick to say, "It's easy to get a better meal elsewhere for the same money."

Asian | Casual | Expensive | columbus circle | Mandarin Oriental | 80 Columbus Circle, 35th floor | 212-805-8881 | www.mandarinoriental.com/newyork | Lunch & Dinner daily

Bar Masa   88.5

While the prevailing wisdom is that Masa Takayama's second venue offers an inexpensive way to sample the superb ingredients he serves at his namesake flagship next door, the truth is that "Bar Masa has more in common with the average sushi place than with its sister restaurant." Besides sushi, there are also noodle dishes and cooked fare like uni and sweet corn risotto, as well as various cuts of meat and seafood grilled over a hibachi. It's a good place to grab a bite before a set at Jazz at Lincoln Center.

Japanese | Casual | Expensive | columbus circle | Time Warner Center | 10 Columbus Circle, 4th floor | 212-823-9800 | www.masanyc.com | Lunch & Dinner Mon-Sat

Commerce   88.5

With the talented Harold Moore and Snir Eng-Sela in the kitchen, it doesn't surprise us that most visitors to this bustling brasserie say they enjoy the cuisine. What does surprise us is that the positive word of mouth hasn't generated more of a buzz. We wonder if the reports of "stadium-caliber noise" have something to do with it. But those who brave the hubbub always say good things about the inventive brasserie fare, like hand-rolled orecchiette with a ragù of "odd things" (oxtail, trotters and tripe) or roast chicken for two with truffled potatoes and vegetables.

French | Informal | Expensive | west village | 50 Commerce St. | 212-524-2301 | www.commercerestaurant.com | Dinner daily, Lunch Sat-Sun

Delmonico's   88.5

One of the oldest restaurants in the U.S., Delmonico's opened in 1837. It claims to have been the site where a number of well-known dishes were invented, including eggs Benedict (1860s), lobster Newburg (1876), baked Alaska (1867) and, of course, Delmonico steak. Today it's basically a steakhouse, though a few classics remain on the menu, like chicken à la Keene (1880s). It's "full of Wall Street power brokers and their clients" who enjoy eating steaks in "a room that can pass for a gentlemen's club."

Steakhouse | Casual | Expensive | financial district | 56 Beaver St. | 212-509-1144 | www.delmonicosny.
com | Dinner Mon-Sat, Lunch Mon-Fri

Elio's   88.5

The food at this Upper East Side power restaurant is not dissimilar to what you will find at any of the dozen or so other northern Italian venues populating the neighborhood: mozzarella and tomato, pastas, veal chops, grilled fish and the like. But "if you are look-ing to eat your pasta in the same dining room as Barbara Walters or members of the Tisch family" at "commensurately high prices," Elio's is your place. On those terms, it's enjoyable enough, even if the food will never knock your socks off.

Italian | Casual | Expensive | upper east side | 1621 Second Ave. | 212-772-2242 | Dinner daily

Four Seasons Pool Room   88.5

This design masterpiece is worth visiting for the iconic Philip Johnson architecture alone. Unfortunately, as is often the case with restaurants that have a strong non-culi-nary draw, the cooking could be better. It's too bad, because once upon a time – when serving a seasonal menu was a revolutionary concept in the U.S. – the Four Seasons was a trendsetter. But even the best seasonal ingredients can't undo the effects of a cuisine that most consider stale and tired. The "intense prices" (a number of entrées are more than $50) add insult to injury.

Continental | Formal | Very Expensive | midtown east | 99 E. 52nd St. | 212-754-9494 | www.fourseason-
srestaurant.com | Dinner Mon-Sat, Lunch Mon-Fri

Grand Sichuan Eastern   88.5

Some of the best Chinese food in the city is available at this ordinary-looking restaurant within eyeshot of the Roosevelt Island tram. Favorites include tea-smoked duck, "sinus-clearing" sliced fish in a soup of hot bubbling oil and beef filets in hot chili sauce. The vegetable dishes – like sautéed loofah, shredded pumpkin with spicy green peppers and platters overflowing with hot Szechuan peppers – are worth a visit on their own. "Eating there made me feel as if I've experienced authentic Chinese cuisine" is how one reviewer described his experience.

Chinese | Informal | Moderate | midtown east | 1049 Second Ave. | 212-355-5855 | www.thegrandsichuan.
com | Lunch & Dinner daily

Insieme   88.5

After their initial success at Hearth downtown, Marco Canora and Paul Grieco opened this more formal Italian restaurant in the heart of the Theater District. While it has shown the occasional glimpse of brilliance in dishes like cicatelli with a pork ragù, torn mint and Parmegiano, "a lack of inventiveness and refinement in the cooking" results in a rating that falls somewhat short of their ambitions. In fact, a large percentage of reviewers expressed a clear preference for the more rustic cuisine at Hearth.

Italian | Casual | Expensive | midtown west | Michelangelo Hotel | 777 Seventh Ave. | 212-582-1310 | www.restaurantinsieme.com | Dinner Mon-Sat, Lunch Mon-Fri

Le Cirque   88.5

Despite a lower-than-expected rating, driven in part by its reputation as a place where socialites go to blow air kisses rather than eat serious food (do designer-garbed social-ites even eat?), the cuisine here – featuring dishes like foie gras ravioli and a saddle of lamb with mission figs and a goat cheese panisse – is not all that different from the food at a place like Daniel. That isn't particularly surprising, since this restaurant in its original location was in fact the place where Daniel Boulud first became famous (oddly enough, that site now houses Boulud's restaurant Daniel.) The circus-colorful atmo-sphere that attracts diners like Henry Kissinger does nothing for foodies, but it makes it "a perfect dress-up place to celebrate a birthday or anniversary."

French | Formal | Very Expensive | upper east side | 151 E. 58th St. | 212-644-0202 | www.lecirque.com | Dinner Mon-Sat, Lunch Mon-Fri

New Won Jo   88.5

If one were to throw a dart while standing blindfolded on 32nd Street between Fifth and Sixth Avenues, we are certain it would hit a Korean barbecue joint. That our reviewers singled this restaurant out from the pack is a function of three things: the quality of the food, the fact that "they grill your meat over real charcoal" (they do it for you, instead of making you do it yourself) and the warm welcome they offer people who lack Korean blood in their veins. Busy well into the night, it's a perfect place for a late dinner after a sporting event or concert at nearby Madison Square Garden.

Korean | Informal | Moderate | koreatown | 23 W. 32nd St. | 212-695-5815 | www.newwonjo.com | Open 24 hours daily

Porter House New York   88.5

Michael Lomonaco, the chef at Windows on the World at the World Trade Center before 9/11, was fortunate not to be in the restaurant on that fateful morning. After a short absence from the New York dining scene, he reappeared in the Time Warner Center, offering steaks that are "good enough to make this restaurant useful" before a perfor-mance at Lincoln Center or the Rose Theater. A beautiful setting argues in Lomonaco's favor, while "mediocre sides" and an "embarrassingly overpriced wine list" make some reviewers argue against it.

Steakhouse | Casual | Expensive | columbus circle | Time Warner Center | 10 columbus circle, 4th fl. | 212-823-9500 | www.porterhousenewyork.com | Lunch & Dinner daily

'ino   88.0

This tiny wedge of a restaurant is a favorite with many of our reviewers, both for its brunch treats, like truffled egg toast or the frittata of the day, and for panini, like pan-cetta with oven-roasted tomato, arugula and lemon mayo or bresaola, asparagus and pecorino peppato. More than 100 different Italian wines are on offer, including interesting choices from every region of Italy. We thought this comment best described how people feel about the restaurant: "It's our favorite place, so please don't go, as it's too small for the both of us."

Italian | Wine Bar | Informal | greenwich village | 21 Bedford St. | 212-989-5769 | www.cafeino.com | Open daily

Aburiya Kinnosuke   88.0

At this Tokyo-style Japanese izakaya restaurant you can dine in a booth, in a small private dining room or at an L-shaped counter dominated by a robata grill. The menu lists a staggeringly large number of small plates, ranging from seasonal sashimi, noodles, rice and vegetable dishes cooked in a casserole to a vast assortment of meats and fish or cooked over the robata; "superb" tsukune (chopped chicken sausage) is a specialty of the house. A location in "the dining desert around Grand Central" works in its favor.

Japanese | Informal | Moderate | midtown east | 213 E. 45th St. | 212-867-5454 | www.aburiyakinnosuke. com | Dinner daily, Lunch Mon-Fri

Beacon   88.0

Opening a restaurant in Midtown has always been a treacherous proposition for a chef: business can be brisk for lunch but the area empties out at night. Waldy Malouf overcame the odds at this restaurant where the focus is on cooking over an open fire. The long list of items handled in the wood-burning grill and oven – pork belly, oysters, lamb short ribs, meatballs, mac 'n' Roquefort cheese, plus more than a dozen others – has made it "one of the most useful restaurants in the city" for the past dozen years. Especially popular: the small "burger bar" facing the kitchen; open only on weekdays, it serves a grass-fed variety that devotees swear by.

American | Casual | Expensive | midtown west | 25 W. 56th St | 212-332-0500 | www.BeaconNYC.com | Dinner daily, Lunch Sun-Fri

Blue Ribbon Bakery   88.0

This casual offering from the Bromberg brothers attracts hordes of of people who patiently wait to sample the boys' unique combination of European bistro and American comfort fare (for example, shrimp and bacon hash during the day and bone marrow and lamb's tongue by night), as well as some of the best bread in the city. One reviewer wished that the dishes themselves "showed a bit more imagination," but the consensus is that it's a "cozy space that makes for a solid standby in the Village."

French Bistro | Informal | Moderate | greenwich village | 35 Downing St. | 212-337-0404 | www.blueribbonrestaurants.com | Open daily

The Breslin   88.0

Like their first restaurant, The Spotted Pig (see review above), this second offering from April Bloomfield and Ken Friedman is a continuation of the notion of dining as "a celebration of fat." But there's more to creating a successful restaurant than good intentions, and while reviewers are "happy to keep returning" for dishes like onion and bone marrow soup, lamb burgers and a pig's foot large enough to serve two, the restaurant doesn't manage to generate the same level of enthusiasm as its sister gastropub. Perhaps it's the execution; perhaps it's the location in the trendy Ace Hotel. In any event, in this instance the critical complain about "heavy, salty comfort food" that's "not worth waiting in line for."

Gastropub | Informal | Moderate | flatiron | Ace Hotel | 16 W. 29th St. | 212-679-1939 | www.thebreslin.com | Open daily

Chinatown Brasserie   88.0

Rolls filled with Berkshire pork belly and asparagus and wok-fried cod with white and green asparagus are just two of the interesting-sounding creations at Joe Ng's upscale Chinese restaurant. Reviewers are split about the taste: Its advocates call it "the best Chinese food in the country" and point to the various honors bestowed on Ng in his native country. But more critical types describe the fare as "not any better than what you find in Chinatown" – though they admit, "The much nicer atmosphere does make a big difference."

Chinese | Casual | Moderate | greenwich village | 380 Lafayette St. | 212-533-7000 | www.chinatownbrasserie.com | Lunch & Dinner daily

Congee Village Restaurant & Bar   88.0

With 30 types of congee (slow-cooked rice porridge) including exotic versions that include frog meat and pig's liver, this large, bustling Hong Kong–style restaurant lives up to its name. It's "great for big crowds," especially when a member of your party speaks Mandarin so you can order from the Chinese menu. It's also very popular with large Asian families, who crowd the vestibule while waiting for tables – "a chaotic scene" that reminded one reviewer of the Chinese restaurant episode on *Seinfeld*.

Chinese | Informal | Moderate | lower east side | 100 Allen St. | 212-941-1818 | www.congeevillagerestaurants.com | Lunch & Dinner daily

Cookshop   88.0

The dining room in Marc Meyer's place is dominated by a blackboard listing the various purveyors who supply its ingredients. Meyer is from the non-interventionist school of cooking, and some reviewers complain that the cuisine is "too plain" to make Cookshop a special destination. However, the simple fare doesn't seem to have had an impact on its popularity, as the large portions of American comfort food – e.g., the Vermont Lamb Tasting with a chickpea and rice salad and cucumber yogurt – keep packing them in.

New American | Informal | Expensive | chelsea | 156 Tenth Ave. | 212-924-4440 | www.cookshopny.com | Open daily

Craftbar   88.0

Back when Marco Canora and Akhtar Nawab ran the kitchen (certain of their specialties, like pecorino fondue with acacia honey and hazelnuts and veal ricotta meatballs, are still on the menu), the more casual of Tom Colicchio's restaurants had a buzz. But of late, it has become far less popular with our reviewers, causing us to wonder if people are simply tired of Tom and his seeming omnipresence. It doesn't seem to be the food, now supervised by Lauren Hirschberg, since the reviewers who do go have nothing but praise for dishes like Berkshire porchetta with a fried egg, collard greens and polenta.

Mediterranean | Informal | Moderate | flatiron | 900 Broadway | 212-461-4300 | www.craftrestaurant.com | Open daily

Fairway Café & Steakhouse 88.0

The steaks that Mitchell London serves at this no-frills dining room on the second floor of the Fairway grocery store might be the best bargain in the city. The bare-bones environment and a "lack of amenities and no service to speak of" prevent it from being more popular. There are tasty sides, and among the other entrées on offer are chicken schnitzel, braised short ribs and roasted branzino, along with one of the best burgers in the city. It's super-convenient before a show at the Beacon Theater.

Steaks | Brasserie | Informal | upper west side | 2127 Broadway, 2nd fl. | 212-595-1888 | www.fairwaymarket.com/restaurant.html | Open daily

Harrison 88.0

Like its sister, The Red Cat (see below), this New American restaurant serves a purpose for neighborhood residents, but doesn't offer much of an allure to diners outside the environs of TriBeCa. Of course, you wouldn't be able to tell that from the crowds, which on the weekends can swell and produce an "overwhelming" din. Still, one reviewer told us that if you visit Monday through Thursday "It's a nice, comfy place," with food that "isn't ambitious enough to offend anyone."

New American | Casual | Expensive | tribeca | 355 Greenwich St. | 212-274-9310 | www.theharrison.com | Dinner daily

Joe's Shanghai 88.0

In case you've never had a Shanghai soup dumpling, it's a doughy ball, slightly larger than a wonton and stuffed with minced pork or crabmeat. When the dumpling is steamed, a significant amount of liquid is generated and fills the interior, and this delicious "soup" shoots into your mouth when you take a bite. Joe's other fare, like Manila clams, frogs' legs and whole chicken with ginger, is top-notch, but the real attraction here is the "ethereal soup dumplings," which are guaranteed to reward you with a bit of that delicious broth in every bite.

Chinese | Informal | Moderate | chinatown | 9 Pell St. | 212-233-8888 | www.joeshanghairestaurants.com | Lunch & Dinner daily

Second Location: midtown west | 24 W. 56th St. | 212-333-3868 | Lunch & Dinner daily

Mercer Kitchen 88.0

Jean-Georges has had a long run at this boutique hotel on one of SoHo's busiest corners. Opened in 1998, the 200-seat venue is filled with people enjoying Asian-tinged appetizers like soft-shell crab tempura with Napa cabbage and sweet-hot mustard or the contemporary French fare that J-G is known for, like slowly baked salmon with fresh corn pudding and cherry tomato vinaigrette. It's "a good way to get a Jean-Georges fix when you're downtown," and a dining room filled with some of the best-looking people in the city doesn't hurt either,

French | Casual | Expensive | soho | Mercer Hotel | 99 Prince St. | 212-966-5454 | www.Jean-Georges. com | Open daily

Mr. K's 88.0

Most cities can count just one upscale Chinese restaurant among their ranks, but New

York has a good half dozen. Mr. K's is the best of the lot, and reviewers who like eating won ton soup surrounded by Art Deco flourishes say, "The food is very good, the service impeccable and the restaurant elegant." But the contingent that dislikes upscale ethnic dining counters, claiming, "The food is outmoded and pretentious and served in a Western style that is out of touch with the times."

Chinese | Casual | Expensive | midtown east | 570 Lexington Ave. | 212-583-1668 | www.mrksny.com | Lunch & Dinner daily

Otto   88.0

Though the pizza was routinely panned when this Mario Batali and Joe Bastianich restaurant opened, it didn't take long for people to figure out they could eat well if they skipped it and stuck to the delicious salumi and marinated fish and vegetables. Since then, a number of our reviewers have enjoyed the restaurant for the "dependable food" served in a "boisterous atmosphere" – and the pizza has even improved! Don't forget to sample the superb gelato, which comes in traditional flavors as well as more exotic ones like olive oil.

Italian | Informal | Moderate | greenwich village | 1 Fifth Ave. | 212-995-9559 | www.ottopizzeria.com | Dinner daily, Lunch Mon-Fri

Peking Duck House   88.0

According to our reviewers, this restaurant is a "one-trick duckie," as diners are advised to ignore the rest of the menu and stick to the namesake dish. Along with the privilege of eating the tasty little packets of pancake-wrapped roasted meat slathered with hoisin sauce, you get a pre-dinner show when a knife-wielding chef wheels the bird to your table and carves it in front of your eyes – a ritual that "wows the out-of-towners who don't get to eat Chinese food very often."

Chinese | Informal | Moderate | chinatown | 28 Mott St. | 212-227-1810 | www.pekingduckhousenyc.com | Lunch & Dinner daily

Public   88.0

If you're confused about what passes for global cuisine these days, head over to this restaurant where Brad Farmerie combines fried green-lip mussels with shiso, sansho pepper and wasabi-yuzu dipping sauce; beet gnudi with whipped lemon ricotta and a smoked almond and celery leaf pesto; and Berkshire pork with salsify, apple purée, sage shortbread and watercress – all on the same menu. Reviewers say, "It might not be the most revolutionary cuisine in the world, but it's a comfortable downtown spot when dining with a group of friends."

International | Informal | Moderate | little italy | 210 Elizabeth St. | 212-343-7011 | www.public-nyc.com | Dinner daily, Lunch Mon-Fri

Pulino's   88.0

The décor at Keith McNally's Italian trattoria looks like a Roman version of Balthazar. Starting at 8:30 in the morning and continuing until 2:00 a.m. the next day, you can dig into "surprisingly good pizzas," along with platters of antipasto and dishes roasted in a wood oven, like pork rollatini with prosciutto, mozzarella and sage. It's located on one of the busiest corners in the city, and the huge, hip crowds add to the "chaotic atmosphere." But reviewers wonder, "Will the quality of the food change?" now that founding chef Nate Appleman has left.

Italian | Casual | Moderate | nolita | 282 Bowery | 212-226-1966 | www.pulinosny.com | Lunch & Dinner daily

Ramen Setagaya   88.0

Along with Momofuku and Ippudo, this New York branch of a Japanese mini-chain is one of the entrants in the "who serves the best ramen in New York City sweepstakes." That contest won't be decided in this space, but we'll note fans' praise for "broth that is delicate, elegant and subtle," along with "a good range of noodles of various gauges of thickness." Given that this is New York City, it's not surprising to find one blasé commentator who concluded that his bowl of soup was "not bad, especially compared to chicken noodle soup."

Japanese | Informal | Moderate | east village | 141 First Ave. | 212-529-2740 | Lunch & Dinner Wed-Sun

Sakagura   88.0

Despite the "astounding selection of sakes" and an "interesting subterranean space," there's a feeling that the quality of the food at this izakaya specialist has declined over the past few years. The late hours and fun atmosphere work in its favor, as does a high-quality seasonal sashimi plate. But despite its popularity, especially with Manhattan's Japanese community, the consensus is that it's past its prime; one reviewer felt as though he had "arrived at the stadium after the game was over."

Japanese | Informal | Moderate | midtown east | 211 E. 43rd St. | 212-953-7253 | www.sakagura.com | Dinner Mon-Sat, Lunch Mon-Fri

Savoy   88.0

There was a time when Peter Hoffman's restaurant seemed better suited for San Francisco than New York City. But now that market cuisine has become popular, Hoffman's cooking – one part New American, one part Mediterranean and one part Alice Waters, resulting in dishes like grilled Vermont quail with caramelized sunchokes, Meyer lemon vinaigrette, juniper and medjool dates – seems like a perfect fit. An avid supporter of the sustainable food movement, Hoffman organizes a number of theme dinners each year, featuring special guests that who from farmers to visiting chefs.

Mediterranean | Informal | Expensive | soho | 70 Prince St. | 212-219-8570 | www.savoynyc.com | Dinner daily, Lunch Mon-Sat

Scarpetta   88.0

When he won the James Beard Award in 2003, Scott Conant caused a mini-sensation, and the acclaim continued after he opened this restaurant in 2008. But while he has received good notices from the local media, our reviewers are mixed: Some praise the "homey pastas and braises" served in this "airy, more casual space" in the West Village, but critics complain that he's "still serving the same food he was cooking at L'Impero," and "It's not for serious Italian food lovers."

Italian | Casual | Expensive | west village | 355 W. 14th St. | 212-691-0555 | www.scarpettanyc.com | Dinner daily

Spice Market   88.0

While most of our reviewers characterize this place as being more about the drinks and the party than the Southeast Asian food, a fair number of them recommend it, saying things like, "I thought I would hate it, but the food, atmosphere and service were all outstanding." Even though the conventional thinking is that the club-like setting makes it "a better choice for people in their 20s," one of our more mature reviewers told us, "My husband and I went for our anniversary, got a couple of small dishes and entrées to share, and we loved everything."

Asian | Casual | Moderate | meatpacking district | 403 W. 13th St. | 212-675-2322 | www.Jean-Georges.com | Lunch & Dinner daily

Szechuan Gourmet   88.0

This was always considered the weak sister among the Szechuan restaurants that dominate Flushing's Prince Street. But after a Manhattan location opened, a favorable review in a local newspaper catapulted it to the attention of the dining community. They do a good job with things like braised lamb and pork belly, as well as seafood and tofu soup. One reviewer told us, "They use heat to enhance, rather than to kill dishes," which makes them stand out from the swarm of Szechuans populating New York City.

Chinese | Informal | Moderate | murray hill | 21 W. 39th St. | 212-921-0233 | Lunch & Dinner daily

Tomoe Sushi   88.0

Noted for the long lines that extend out its front door and wind down Thompson Street, Tomoe Sushi offers one of the best quality-for-value sushi experiences in the city. "A hole in the wall of a restaurant," it's the only sushi place we know of that doesn't have counter seating. Sushi experts say, "The slicing is rudimentary at best," but fans counter, "The fish is fresh and the portions are generous," which explains the lines.

Japanese | Informal | Moderate | greenwich village | 172 Thompson St. | 212-777-9346 | http://tomoesushi.com | Lunch & Dinner daily

Wolfgang's Steakhouse   88.0

Named after Wolfgang Zwiener, former head waiter at Peter Luger, this is probably the most successful of that legendary steakhouse's clones. But our reviewers are split on it. Some say, "It does the [steak] concept justice," while others go further, calling it "better than the original." Most opinions fall on the side that says, "It never seems to hit the same high notes as its inspiration," while questioning "whether the steaks have 28 days of age on them." At least here, a reservation is not as difficult to snag as at Luger.

Steakhouse | Casual | Expensive | murray hill | 4 Park Ave. | 212-925-0350 | www.wolfgangssteakhouse.net | Lunch & Dinner daily

Second Location: tribeca | 409 Greenwich St. | 212-925-0350 | www.wolfgangssteakhouse.net | Lunch & Dinner daily

Woo Lae Oak   88.0

One sign of an ethnic group's upward mobility is the opening of a restaurant featuring an upscale version of its cuisine. And when the restaurant that most signifies that mobility moves from Koreatown to fashionable SoHo, you know the cuisine has come of age. Of course, along with the niceties found in such a transformation, such as the ability to enjoy "cleaned up versions" of bulgogi and bibimbap to a constant backdrop of chill-out music, you are also guaranteed criticisms like "not authentic" and "too trendy for a Korean restaurant."

Korean | Casual | Expensive | soho | 148 Mercer St. | 212-925-8200 | www.woolaeoaksoho.com | Lunch & Dinner daily

Yakitori Totto   88.0

Knees, necks, breasts, skin, liver, gizzard, tail, heart and a little-known part of the thigh known as the oyster are just some of the chicken parts you can order at this second-floor robata specialist. They also grill up meat, fish and vegetables and offer rice and noodle dishes, but the best way to appreciate the specialty of the house is to sit at the counter and "watch the various skewers go onto the grill and point to the ones that look interesting." "Expect a wait, even after the theater."

Japanese | Informal | Moderate | midtown west | 251 W. 55th St., 2nd fl. | 212-245-4555 | http://tottonyc. com | Dinner daily, Lunch Mon-Fri

ACCEPTABLE

'inoteca   87.5

"It's a mob scene" at this Lower East Side restaurant where salads, platters of salumi, an assortment of bruschetta and a dozen different panini keep the throngs happy. If you want to do more than nibble, you can order an "amazing" pork chop and chicken cacciatorre, which one reviewer called "better than it had any right to be." A "friendly and enthusiastic staff" keeps things moving, though the "expansive" list of Italian wines will make you want to stay and order another platter of affettati misti.

Italian | Informal | Moderate | lower east side | 98 Rivington St. | 212-614-0473 | www.inotecanyc. com | Lunch & Dinner daily

Artisanal   87.5

No, that isn't a pair of old socks – it's the aroma of cheese emanating from one of the best fromageries in the city. The rest of the French brasserie fare, especially the four types of steak frites made with aged prime beef, is surprisingly well prepared considering how busy the place is. Otherwise, it's "excruciatingly noisy, and the service can be wanting." But then, the real draw is the cheese, and whether it's on an assorted platter or in a fondue or a sandwich, it should not be missed.

French | Informal | Moderate | murray hill | 2 Park Ave. | 212-725-8585 | www.artisanalbistro. com | Lunch & Dinner daily

Café Habana   87.5

Though the name suggests Cuban cuisine, the menu at this trendy NoLita restaurant is actually a mix of dishes from Cuba and central Mexico. That means your dinner choices can range from a plate of roast pork to a chicken quesadilla. Brunch is the most popular meal, but truth is, the place is super-popular all day long, so expect a "horrendous wait" for a table. Churros and a Mexican hot chocolate from the small takeout shop next door make the perfect dessert.

Cuban/Mexican | Informal | Moderate | nolita | 17 Prince St. | 212-625-2001 | www.cafehabana. com | Open daily

Dim Sum Go Go   87.5

Back in the days when this restaurant attempted to offer a market-based version of Chinese cuisine, it was considered a trailblazer, and we are certain if we had published a guide at that time it would have received a higher rating than it does currently. But these days reviewers are saying that dishes like pan-fried halibut with scallions and garlic sauce "are not up to the levels of the past." It's a shame, especially given the proliferation of restaurants offering ingredient-based dining over the past 15 years.

Chinese | Informal | Moderate | chinatown | 5 E. Broadway | 212-732-0797 | Lunch & Dinner daily

E.A.T.   87.5

Where else but on New York's Upper East Side could you find a restaurant where lox, eggs and onions are offered alongside potato gratin? The menu also lists three dozen types of salads, along with a dozen and a half sandwiches. It's a great spot for a breakfast or lunch when you're hitting the stores on Madison Avenue or the museums on Fifth, provided you're willing to tolerate the "excruciatingly high prices." Bustling all day long, it's on the quiet side in the evenings.

Cafe | Informal | Moderate | upper east side | 1064 Madison Ave. | 212-772-0022 | www.elizabar. com | Open daily

HanGawi   87.5

Kalbi and bulgogi are replaced by tofu and a variety of mushrooms at this unique, "Zen-like" Korean meat-free restaurant on New York's Kimchee Row. If you're worried about getting full on vegetarian fare, reviewers gurantee that the noodle dishes, porridges, casseroles and sautéed and grilled vegetables will hold you over until your next roast beef sandwich. Still, the experience is noticeably lacking in proteins, causing one reviewer to describe it as" pointless unless you're on a date with a vegan."

Korean | Informal | Moderate | koreatown | 12 E. 32nd St. | 212-213-0077 | www.hangawirestaurant. com | Lunch & Dinner daily

The Little Owl   87.5

Given the terrific word of mouth, one would think Joey Campanero's restaurant would have a higher rating. But it's merely "the ideal neighborhood restaurant." The fare includes a number of special pastas and "a damn good pork chop," but reviewers say the rest of the food lacks that special element that sets the better restaurants apart. Still, you wouldn't be able to tell that from the waiting time, which can be as long as two hours on a weekend night.

New American | Informal | Moderate | west village | 90 Bedford St. | 212-741-4695 | www. thelittleowlnyc.com | Lunch & Dinner daily

Orsay   87.5

Orsay is filled with Upper East Siders who care more about what people at the next table are wearing than they do about the food they are eating. While reviewers said dishes like an appetizer of roasted quail stuffed with foie gras were "serviceable," some of the comments were deadly, like, "Why go to an overcrowded, noisy, snooty place when there are better choices in the neighborhood?" and" It's a good place if you are deaf or plan on becoming deaf!"

French | Casual | Expensive | upper east side | 1057 Lexington Ave. | 212-517-6400 | www. orsayrestaurant.com | Dinner daily, Lunch Sun-Fri

Peasant   87.5

Frank De Carlo loves his wood-burning grill – as do a number of our reviewers, like the one who said the orata that De Carlo stuffed with herbs and charred on the grill was "a cross between dining and aromatherapy." Or how about a few slices of "succulent" spit-roasted leg of lamb with trevisano and polenta? The "hip, dark and sexy" setting attracts a trendy crowd, even if – or perhaps because – it's a bit out of character for a restaurant serving this type of market Italian fare.

Italian | Informal | Moderate | little italy | 194 Elizabeth St. | 212-965-9511 | www.peasantnyc. com | Dinner Tue-Sun

The Red Cat   87.5

Everyone seems to love Jimmy Bradley's cooking. What makes most people choose his restaurant over the competition in Chelsea is a menu with dishes like crispy oyster and watercress salad and a grilled double-cut pork loin with blue cheese tomato gratin. Of course, the location has its advantages too: It's quite convenient after gallery-hopping in West Chelsea, after an event at Madison Square Garden or even after visiting the Javits Convention Center. Of course, some reviewers are keen to point out that while it makes a great choice when in the zone west of Eighth Avenue, it's "not worth a detour" otherwise.

New American | Casual | Expensive | chelsea | 227 Tenth Ave. | 212-242-1122 | www.theredcat.com | Dinner daily, Lunch Tue-Sat

Spigola   87.5

This top neighborhood Italian features Scott Fratangelo in the kitchen doing the cooking while his wife, Heather, is busy running the front of the house. The menu won't yield anything too exciting, but "solid" fare like squid ink fettuccine, brick-roasted chicken and osso buco means that "getting a reservation at a reasonable hour can be a chore." You can dine on the outdoor terrace in good weather, and they let you BYOB.

Italian | Informal | Moderate | upper east side | 1561 Second Ave. | 212-744-1100 | http://spigolonyc.com | Dinner Tue-Sun, Lunch Sat-Sun

Ushiwakamaru   87.5

While some reviewers sing the praises of this venue, calling it "the best sushi restaurant that nobody talks about," the lower-than-expected rating is caused by a lack of consensus, with the negatives rearing their heads in comments like "I fail to see the attraction given the other choices within walking distance." Determining the quality of fish is sort of cut-and-dried, so it's a bit unusual to find

this level of disagreement – even more so because of the restaurant's popularity with young Japanese diners.

Japanese | Informal | Moderate | greenwich village | 136 W. Houston St. | 212-228-4181 | Dinner Mon-Sat

'Cesca   87.0

Kevin Garcia's "homey and hearty" cuisine features crudos like bigeye tuna with chiles; garganelli, house-made chicken sausage, zucchini and tomato; and a heritage pork chop, smoked bacon, heirloom Tuscan beans and fried rapine. The restaurant is large, lively and predominantly filled with people who live on the Upper West Side, although the crowd swells with outsiders before a performance at the nearby Beacon Theater. Numerous reviewers complained about the "high prices" for what they call nothing more than a neighborhood restaurant.

Italian | Informal | Moderate | upper west side | 164 W. 75th Street | 212-787-6300 | www.cescanyc.com | Dinner daily, Brunch Sun

Apiary   87.0

Beginning with Indigo and continuing with a long run during the heyday of the now-defunct Veritas, New York's oenophile community has always been in love with Scott Bryan's cooking. That's because Bryan specializes in the type of luxurious comfort cuisine that pairs well with important bottles of wine. Working against him in this restaurant is an environment that can be "deafening to the point of being unpleasant" and a "no-BYOB policy except for Monday night." But fans say that $35 for a Bryan prix-fixe menu is the "bargain of the century."

New American | Casual | Moderate | east village | 60 Third Ave. | 212-254 0888 | www.apiarynyc.com | Dinner daily

Atlantic Grill   87.0

If you stick to things like oysters and can

get your server to tell you what fish is fresh that day, you can have a good meal at this B.R. Guest restaurant overflowing with tony East Siders, an older singles scene and couples on dates. Fortunately, if you choose wrong, your meal will be no less than ordinary. One reviewer cautions experienced sushi lovers to "stay away from the raw fish," as it isn't at a level of quality that'll make you happy.

Seafood | Casual | Expensive | upper east side | 1341 Third Ave. | 212-988-9200 | www.atlanticgrill.com | Lunch & Dinner daily

Bar Americain   87.0

Since hardcore foodies are quick to write off restaurants helmed by Bobby Flay, we were surprised to see a number of positive comments about this midtown place. Always a good chef, Flay has come up with a dining concept – a stylized version of American comfort food – that his kitchen executes at a level sufficient to attract comments like "I hate celebrity chef restaurants, but for this one I make an exception." It's convenient for a business lunch and for pre- or post-theater dining, too.

New American | Casual | Expensive | midtown west | 152 W. 52nd St. | 212-265-9700 | www.baramericain.com | Lunch & Dinner daily

BLT Fish   87.0

Though they start off with a fairly good product, a kitchen that is "lacking in conception and execution" yields an end result with little relation to a quality dining experience centered on fresh fish. The clientele is predominantly bridge and tunnel, and making matters worse is the cacophony as people try to talk over the ear-splitting music blaring over the sound system. The more formal upstairs dining room is a hair quieter than the downstairs fish shack.

Seafood | Casual | Moderate | flatiron | 21 W. 17th St. | 212-691-8888 | www.bltfish.com | Dinner Mon-Sat

BLT Market   87.0

After success with steak, fish and hamburger restaurants, the BLT gang has added market cuisine to their list of places. This venue in the Ritz-Carlton was described as "overpriced" and "overrun with tourists," and dishes like a $38 pistachio-crusted venison loin with chestnuts and braised red cabbage seem to bear that out. A saving grace is the location – the corner of Sixth Avenue and 59th Street – which offers terrific people-watching from an outdoor terrace.

New American | Casual | Expensive | midtown west | Ritz-Carlton | 1430 Sixth Ave. | 212-521-6125 | www.bltmarket.com | Dinner Tue-Sat

Café d'Alsace   87.0

Owned by Simon Oren (Nice-Matin, Five Napkin Burger, L'Express), this restaurant got off to a rocky start when it opened, but of late chef Philippe Roussel seems to have turned things around. Okay, it still isn't like being in Alsace, but he does a competent job with the classics like choucroute and baeckeoffe of lamb, and the food is "surprisingly good for a neighborhood restaurant." Some people go just to order one of the more than 100 beers on offer; there's even a special beer sommelier to help you choose the right bottle.

French Brasserie | Informal | Moderate | upper east side | 1695 Second Ave. | 212-722-5133 | www.cafedalsace.com | Lunch & Dinner daily

Da Silvano   87.0

When Silvano Marchetto opened this restaurant in 1975, "Italian food" in New York City meant veal Parmigiana and chicken cacciatore. But 36 years later, Tuscan cuisine is ubiquitous, and the cooking here doesn't seem as special as it once did. The food is just what you'd expect: simply done fare like penne arrabiata or a veal chop flavored with sage. The ambience is low-key – a bit surprising, considering the place is a favorite with celebrities in the film industry. It also has what many feel is "the city's best outdoor terrace," which makes for great people-watching.

Italian | Casual | Expensive | greenwich village | 260 Sixth Ave. | 212-982-2343 | www.dasilvano.com | Lunch & Dinner daily

Del Frisco's   87.0

"Large," "over the top" and "overpriced and over-rated" are some of the opinions we received on this Dallas-based steakhouse chainster. But that doesn't stop it from being hugely popular, and despite the "B-quality steaks," the large dining room is brimming with people, so don't be surprised when you learn there is a significant wait for a table. At least there's a good wine list.

Steakhouse | Casual | Expensive | midtown west | 1221 Sixth Ave. | 212-575-5129 | www.delfriscos.com | Dinner daily, Lunch Mon-Fri

Jing Fong   87.0

While San Francisco and Los Angeles specialize in cavernous Chinese restaurants that feed dim sum to thousands each day, there are surprisingly few of that ilk in New York. This multi-floored palace is one of them, and the place can get so chaotic, reviewers say, "There is no earthly way to describe the scene here on the weekend. Think Giants Stadium." Others call it a "good place for dumplings and more traditional dishes," adding it's "not so good for things like chicken feet."

Chinese | Informal | Moderate | chinatown | 20 Elizabeth St. | 212-964-5256 | www.jingfongny.com | Lunch & Dinner daily

Joseph Leonard   87.0

Despite getting off to a shaky start with our reviewers, this offering from Gabe Stulman is now described as "the quintessential neighborhood restaurant" serving "well-done" versions of American bistro cuisine like Atlantic cod with potatoes, mushrooms and cabbage or a crispy braised pork hock with arugula, lemon and crispy capers. Reviewers talk about "perfect portions of great food" and "and a kitchen that knows its limits and cooks to them." A "nice, friendly vibe" certainly helps with what would otherwise seem like "cramped quarters."

American | Informal | Moderate | greenwich village | 170 Waverly Pl. | 646-429-8383 | www.josephleonard.com | Lunch & Dinner Tue-Sun

Le Gigot   87.0

The French bistro fare at this" bite-size restaurant" won't offend anyone. On the other hand, it's not going to inspire anyone either. Let's just say it's handy for a steak frites or a duck confit when you don't want to bother with a fancier place. And of course their namesake dish is the specialty of the house. The prices are "slightly high," and it offers an "indifferent wine list," but that's offset by the ability to bring your own. It's cash only.

French | Informal | Moderate | greenwich village | 18 Cornelia St. | 212-627-3737 | www.legigotrestaurant.com | Lunch & Dinner Tue-Sun

Lupa   87.0

Italophiles used to go wild for Mario Batali's Roman trattoria, which imports many of its ingredients from Italy. An interesting dining format – a series of small plates featuring salumi, crudos, vegetables and cheese, followed by pastas as well as larger plates like skate with clams or crispy duck in an agrodolce sauce – resulted in many of our reviewers saying they preferred the place to Babbo. But after chef Mark Ladner decamped for Del Posto, we immediately started seeing comments like "I had the impression that the quality has sharply deteriorated," and sentiments have yet to turn around.

Italian | Informal | Moderate | greenwich village | 170 Thompson St. | 212-982-5089 | www.luparestaurant.com | Lunch & Dinner daily

Matsuri 87.0

We know many people who make Tadashi Ono's restaurant their top choice when they want to have dinner at a large, trendy, party-style Japanese restaurant. Not only is it "one of the most consistent mega-Asians," the breadth of the menu makes it an easy place for non-sushi lovers to find options. Of course, you can't overlook the party atmosphere, enhanced by a multi-tiered dining room that makes it seem like "The eye candy is in 3-D." A list of more than 200 sakes is guaranteed to make your night all the more lively.

Japanese | Informal | Moderate | chelsea | 369 W. 16th St. | 212-243-6400 | www.themaritime-hotel.com | Dinner daily

Megu 87.0

Some mega Japanese restaurants are all about the party. But Megu is about the flash – as in people flashing large wads of cash so they can order ridiculously expensive platters of fatty tuna followed by Kobe everything. Unfortunately, the food isn't always prepared with the type of care the ingredients deserve. Still, it's a great choice if you want to feel like you're in Vegas without leaving New York, especially since the experience is "guaranteed to empty your wallet."

Japanese | Casual | Expensive | tribeca | 62 Thomas St. | 212-964-7777 | www.megurestaurants ,com | Dinner daily

Second Location: midtown east | 212-964-7777 | www.megurestaurants.com | Lunch & Dinner daily

Mezzaluna 87.0

If you want to eat Italian food elbow-to-elbow with Italian nationals or sit next to Jean-Georges on his night off as he consumes a pizza, make the trek to the "most authentic trattoria in the city," where diners have been enjoying brick-oven-baked pies, pastas and carpaccios since 1984. It also offers a few specials like a whole roasted fish, a lasagna of the day and a meat dish like a veal chop. It's small and cramped, and the no-reservation policy (for parties under five) means you can expect a short wait for a table.

Italian | Informal | upper east side | 1295 Third Ave. | 212-535-9600 | www.mezzalunany.com | Lunch & Dinner daily

Molyvos 87.0

While some of our reviewers are fans of the Livanos family's "high-end taverna with an emphasis on seafood," calling it "the best restaurant of its type in town," the more blasé shrugged, "Though they do a reasonably good job of it, Greek cooking isn't all that exciting to begin with." A decent list of Greek wines argues in its favor, but a "large, loud and noisy dining room" cuts the other way.

Greek | Casual | Expensive | midtown west | 871 Seventh Ave. | 212-582-7500 | www.molyvos.com | Lunch & Dinner daily

Morton's, The Steakhouse 87.0

The show – your waiter brings a cart to your table that acts as a visual menu, displaying every cut of steak and side dish, including potatoes the size of softballs – is great at this link in one of the country's biggest steakhouse chains. Unfortunately, the quality is "merely average," but ultimately it's still a better choice than many of the other chains out there. A pro-BYOB policy gives it another advantage as most of the top steakhouses in the city make you buy wine from their lists.

Steakhouse | Casual | Expensive | midtown east | 551 Fifth Ave. | 212-972-3315 | www.mortons. com | Dinner daily, Lunch Mon-Fri

Ouest 87.0

When he was in charge of the kitchens at Alison on Dominick and Cascabel, his cuisine was among the most vibrant in the city. But so much of the soul has gone out of his cooking that one reviewer asked, "What happened to Tom Valenti?" That doesn't mean his fans have deserted him: They are still enjoying his brand of comfort food, like pan-roasted squab with duck liver risotto, crisp artichokes and Parmesan. But it is worth noting that cooking once "worth traveling for" is now considered merely "good for a neighborhood restaurant."

New American | Casual | Expensive | upper west side | 2315 Broadway | 212-580-8700 | www. ouestny.com | Lunch & Dinner daily

Pam Real Thai   87.0

Diners looking for homestyle Thai cooking where "complexity and subtlety complement the heat" are quick to choose this restaurant. In addition to the standard repertoire, the kitchen gets a bit more inventive with dishes like Thai beef jerky, which you can follow with an assortment of "meat and seafood dishes prepared with great respect." Many reviewers say this is their first choice for Siamese fare in Manhattan, especially when near the Theater District.

Thai | Informal | Moderate | midtown west | 404 W. 49th St. | 212-333-7500 | www.pamrealthai-food.com | Lunch & Dinner daily

Sip Sak   87.0

Along with being "the city's ambassador for Turkish food," Orhan Yegen is one of the true characters of the New York dining scene. He first came to attention in 1991 with the Turkish Kitchen, and after selling it, he spent a decade developing restaurants for other people before finally settling down here in 2004. Along with the usual array of dips, kebabs and moussakas, Orhan's list of daily specials usually includes rarely seen dishes like cow's brains or calf's tongue.

Turkish | Informal | Moderate | midtown east | 928 Second Ave. | 212-583-1900 | www.sip-sak. com | Lunch and Dinner daily

Sparks Steak House   87.0

Some reviewers called Sparks their favorite steakhouse – not just for the wet-aged steaks, but for the terrific wine list that comes complete with friendly pricing. The sometimes notorious place is super-popular with large parties of business diners, too, so seating delays can be significant. But here's a helpful hint: While waiting for a table, ask to see the wine list, order a nice bottle and tell them you would like it decanted. We predict that within moments, a host will lead you to a table in the room that is normally reserved for regulars.

Steakhouse | Casual | Expensive | midtown east | 210 E. 46th St. | 212-687-4855 | www. sparkssteakhouse.com | Dinner daily, Lunch Mon-Fri

August   86.5

When it first opened, this restaurant got off to a quick start. But "the magic is gone," and now it has settled into being a good "homey and cozy" neighborhood place. It's convenient for West Village residents who happily enjoy the "rustic cooking" (everything is prepared in a wood-burning oven) without having to clean up after dinner or for those visiting the area for a film at the nearby IFC Theater or a set at the Blue Note.

Italian | Informal | Moderate | west village | 359 Bleecker St. | 212-929-4774 | www.augustny.com | Lunch & Dinner daily

Benoit   86.5

If you are the type of diner who objects to a celebrity chef (Alain Ducasse, in this instance) buying a famous Parisian restaurant from its original owner, only to exploit its brand name while lowering the quality of dishes like escargots in garlic butter and skate wing grenobloise, make sure to avoid Benoit. If comments like "The food is boring," "The portions are tiny" and" The service is abysmal" aren't bad enough, we can go on tell you about the "poorly stocked wine list." Only the "excellent desserts" drew praise.

French Bistro | Casual | Moderate | midtown west | 60 W. 55th Street | 646-943-7373 | www. benoitny.com | Lunch & Dinner Mon-Sat

Buddakan   86.5

As with many other pan-Asian restaurants, Buddakan is more about the party than the food – with one difference: The food is much better than everyone expects it to be, so much so that a few reviewers actually mentioned individual dishes like "delicious edamame dumplings and frogs' legs." Even so, the cuisine comes second to what's really a cruising bar, with a clientele that probably lives outside of Manhattan. You'll be fine as long as you remember that.

Pan-Asian | Casual | Expensive | chelsea | 75 Ninth Ave. | 212-989-6699 | www.buddakan.com | Dinner daily

Café Katja   86.5

Some restaurants perform above their pay grade, like this simple Austrian that inspired comments like "I'm probably overrating this place, but I don't care. The sausages are hearty and spicy, the charcuterie plate is the same, and the goulash is the best I've had outside of Germany." Another says the "pretzels are outstanding," and notes that it has "an amazing beer menu," while yet a third claims, "It's my favorite neighborhood restaurant – it feels like I'm eating with my hipster family."

Austrian | Informal | Moderate | lower east side | 79 Orchard St. | 212-219-9545 | www.cafe-katja. com | Dinner daily

City Hall   86.5

While the concept of serving a menu based on the cuisine of old New York is clever, it won't turn heads unless you base it on the highest-quality ingredients. So what we have here is a noble effort from Henry Meer, with "consistent food" that appeals to people of all ages but that doesn't rise to the level of going out of your way for. In its favor is a comfortable dining room with well-spaced tables, which makes it "easy to have a conversation" during dinner.

American | Casual | Expensive | tribeca | 131 Duane St. | 212-227-7777 | www.cityhallnewyork. com | Lunch & Dinner daily

Ed's Chowder House   86.5

Heralded for his cooking at the Sea Grill, Ed Brown decided to go out on his own with Eighty One – a place that, after getting off to a good start, was done in by the combination of an upscale dining format, an Upper West Side location and a bad economy. Now Brown has thrown his lot in with the China Grill Group, and his cooking can be enjoyed in a menu that features five types of chowders and herb-crusted skate with horseradish mashed potatoes.

Seafood | Casual | Moderate | upper west side | Empire Hotel | 44 W. 63rd St | 212-956-1288 | www.chinagrillmgt.com | Open daily

Four Seasons Grill Room   86.5

While the Pool Room is where the action is at night, by day the bar area and adjacent dining room of this iconic restaurant host one of the city's top power-lunch scenes, especially for the media crowd. One experienced reviewer sized up the experience by telling us, "I don't know which is more difficult, getting a table (unless you're dining with someone like David Remnick) or being able to afford the $50 entrées (unless you happen to be his guest)."

Continental | Casual | Very Expensive | midtown east | 99 E. 52nd St. | 212-754-9494 | www. fourseasonsrestaurant.com | Lunch Mon-Fri

Michael's   86.5

Once it was popular with discerning New York foodies, but these days it's the media crowd that keeps Michael's jammed at lunch, while it's quiet at dinner – an unusual dynamic for a Midtown restaurant of this stature. Maybe it's the price-per-quality ratio – evening entrées begin at $32 and climb to $45, and a burger costs a whopping $35. Of course, cost doesn't stop the expense-account crowd. And as one reviewer astutely pointed out, "It's one of the few places in New York where you can still get California cuisine."

Californian | Casual | Expensive | midtown west | 24 W. 55th St. | 212-767-0555 | www.michaelsnewyork.com | Dinner daily, Lunch Sun-Fri

Phoenix Garden 86.5

For decades this restaurant was located in Chinatown. But when a large part of its clientele decamped to the suburbs, it also relocated – to a neighborhood where fans can easily hop on a train after dinner. While it's now geared more to banquets and celebratory dinners, which necessarily means the menu's a bit more Americanized, "You can eat well if you stick to the Cantonese fare." In fact, one reviewer claimed, "I would eat there on a weekly basis if I lived in the neighborhood."

Chinese | Casual | Expensive | murray hill | 242 E. 40th St. | 212-983-6666 | www.thephoenixgarden.com | Lunch & Dinner daily

Shun Lee | 86.5
Shun Lee West

Michael Tong's restaurants are probably the most famous upscale Chinese venues in the country. Still, they come in for their share of controversy – some calling them "consistently good," others "over-priced and dumbed down." Perhaps this reviewer offered the definitive assessment: "Growing up in a Chinese household, it's easy for me to dismiss the food as Westernized, but it always tastes good." The debate is moot for gourmet-minded concert-goers, who find the West Side

branch a "handy location for a quick bite near Lincoln Center."

Chinese | Casual | Expensive | midtown east | 155 E. 55th St. | 212-371-8844 | www.shunleepalace.com | Lunch & Dinner daily

upper west side | 43 W. 65th St. | 212-595-8895 | www.shunleewest.com | Lunch & Dinner daily

Stanton Social Club 86.5

Apart from Spanish tapas bars, it's difficult to find a small-plates restaurant that our reviewers are willing to recommend. Stanton Social is close to being the exception, with "cooking that's surprisingly good for such a hip place." The eclectic menu typically strolls from Korean chile- and miso-glazed sea bass satays to charred squid lettuce wraps to the house version of beef Wellington – grilled filet mignon, foie gras mousse and mushroom duxelles wrapped in puff pastry.

Eclectic | Informal | Moderate | lower east side | 99 Stanton St. | 212-995-0099 | www.thestantonsocial.com | Dinner daily, Lunch Sat-Sun

Taboon 86.5

"Neo-Middle Eastern" characterizes this offering from an Israeli chef. Unfortunately, while it's a good idea – an attempt to take everything from hummus to schwarma to a new level – the result is nothing more than simple Mediterranean chow with a Middle Eastern twist. The "pleasant environment" and "location in the middle of nowhere" make it useful for those who need a place to eat while visiting the far reaches of Midtown West.

Mediterranean | Informal | Moderate | midtown west | 773 Tenth Ave. | 212-713-0271 | Dinner daily

Turkish Kitchen 86.5

While reviewers recommend the mezzes and grills at the city's premier Turkish restaurant, the more uncommon cooked dishes, like manti (delicate beef dumplings) and comlek kebabi (lamb baked in a casserole), receive even more acclaim. There's a good selection of cocktails, as well as Turkish wines. Criticism was directed at the service, which was "inconsistent for this caliber of food."

Turkish | Informal | Moderate | murray hill | 386 Third Ave. | 212-679-6633 | www.turkishkitchen.com | Dinner daily, Lunch Mon-Fri

Uncle Nick's   86.5

"Warm, homey, chaotic and good" is how reviewers describe this Greek restaurant. The mezze-style menu allows you to order a greater selection of dishes, like flaming saganaki, grilled baby octopus with balsamic and a slew of different kabobs. There always seems to be a lengthy wait for a table, which is understandable given the "reasonable prices" of "fresh seafood and cheap retsina."

Greek | Informal | Moderate | midtown west | 747 Ninth Ave. | 212-245-7992 | www.unclenicksgreekrestaurant.com | Lunch & Dinner daily

21 Club   86.0

Visiting this old speakeasy is more about the ambience, which includes what seems like an endless supply of wonderful paintings and artifacts, than the food (a "delicious steak tartare," a "rightly famous hamburger" and "an exceptional wine list" aside). Opinions are split between those who call it "the quintessential New York experience" and those who say it's "a clubby hellhole." Regardless of what anyone thinks, however, you will be hard-pressed to find a better power-lunch scene.

American | Informal | Expensive | midtown west | 21 W. 52nd St. | 212-582-7200 | www.21club.com | Dinner Mon-Sat, Lunch Tue-Sat

Candle 79   86.0

Reviewers say, "I'm emphatically non-vegetarian but have found Candle 79 to be a terrific resource when dining with

non-meat-eaters"; "The innovative dishes could instantly turn a carnivore into a plant eater"; "Such good food; it tastes like meat!" Of course, it was a cinch that a contrarian would describe the food as "pretty much tasteless." But most reviews are like the one from this father: "It's one of the only places I can take my daughter to eat and where I actually enjoy my meal as well."

Vegetarian | Casual | Moderate | upper east side | 154 E. 79th St. | 212-537-7179 | www.candle79.com | Lunch & Dinner daily

Casa Lever   86.0

If you can't finagle a lunchtime table at the Four Seasons Grill Room, you will definitely have an easier time just by crossing the street to this restaurant in the other iconic building on Park Avenue. It's run by the team that manages the Sant Ambroeus restaurants, and offers similar northern Italian fare. That means you can enjoy a selection of salads, pastas and simple mains like veal paillard, in a "gorgeous room" filled with a combination of Euro types and executives who work in the neighborhood.

Italian | Casual | Expensive | midtown east | 390 Park Avenue | 212-888-2700 | www.casalever.com | Open Mon-Sat

Celeste   86.0

This small Italian trattoria lorded over by its jovial owner, Carmine, has been packing them in for the past seven years. Part of the reason is a low price point, but "fresh ingredients from Italy," many of them imported by Carmine himself, are the main attraction. Reviewers seem to prefer the pizzas and pastas, especially the linguine with grilled clams, to the entrées. It's a good choice when you have a large party of friends or when family is in town.

Italian | Informal | Moderate | upper west side | 502 Amsterdam Ave. | 212-874-4559 | Dinner daily Lunch Sat-Sun

Chin Chin 86.0

Back before places like Buddakan and Tao were on the scene, a lively, upscale Asian restaurant meant a place like Chin Chin. The dining scene is vastly changed since that time, and many reviewers would agree that "this used to be the place to go for serious higher-end Chinese," but note that "The food hasn't changed in decades." Still, it's highly recommended for those who enjoy dishes like shrimp in a Grand Marnier sauce, Chinese-style.

Chinese. | Casual | Expensive | midtown east | 216 E. 49th St. | 212-888-4555 | www.chinchinny.com | Lunch & Dinner daily

Gahm Mi Oak 86.0

If you're tired of slurping up pho but are still looking for a cathartic experience in which you bury your head in a bowl of soup, check out this spot in the heart of Koreatown that's always filled with people enjoying the house specialty, sul longtang (ox bone broth topped with beef brisket, rice and rice noodles). Purportedly, it can help head off a hangover, which might explain why the predominantly Korean clientele is peppered with the odd Caucasian nursing a bowl after a night of bar-hopping.

Korean | Informal | Moderate | koreatown | 43 W. 32nd St. | 212-695-4113 | Lunch & Dinner daily

Gallagher's Steak House 86.0

Since there's a display case in the window showing numerous cuts of beef aging in the meat locker, one would think the fare at this Theater District classic would be delicious. But, alas," it's just another mediocre steakhouse." In a city where there is so much good stuff to be had, why bother with restaurants offering B- and C-level beef?

Steakhouse | Informal | Expensive | midtown west | 228 W. 52nd St. | 212-245-5336 | Lunch & Dinner daily

Ivo & Lulu 86.0

This teeny-tiny restaurant focuses on serving organic produce along with meat and game from the purveyor D'Artagnan. It's popular with the BYOB crowd (they don't charge corkage), which often fills the restaurant despite the tight space to enjoy dishes like a rabbit and ginger sausage in a carrot-miso cream and duck confit with jerk spices and mango marinade. It's reasonable, too – "You can order the entire menu for under $200," as one reviewer put it.

French | Informal | Moderate | soho | 558 Broome St. | 212-226-4399 | Dinner daily

Kittichai 86.0

This Thai fusion restaurant located in the Thompson Hotel offers a" trendy atmosphere," a "scene-y SoHo crowd in a cool room" and, not surprisingly, "good people-watching." Unfortunately, what it doesn't offer is compelling Thai food, although if you're with a large group of people who want a casual meal in a fun environment before a night of clubbing downtown, you could fare much worse food-wise than dishes like lemongrass-stuffed chicken breast with wild mushrooms and a chili jam drizzle.

Thai | Casual | Expensive | soho | 60 Thompson St. | 212-219-2000 | www.kittichairestaurant.com | Open daily

La Grenouille 86.0

To give you a sense of how long this restaurant has been around, one reviewer wrote of his experiences here as far back as 1962, telling us, "Nothing much has changed over the years, but in the interim, dining standards have changed, and this restaurant feels dated as a result." With a menu loaded with classics like Dover sole in mustard sauce, and a room featuring "spectacular flower arrangements," it makes perfect sense that the place remains popular with older diners, as well as with the ladies who lunch.

French | Formal | Expensive | midtown east | 3 E. 52nd St. | 212-752-1495 | www.la-grenouille.com | Lunch & Dinner Tue-Sat

Mermaid Inn   86.0

This is one of those restaurants our reviewers don't really care for, despite its super-popularity with the dining public: We received cracks about "annoying" service and "blah" food. Maybe that's because fish and seafood are less forgiving than other ingredients – when they aren't the very best quality, they can be difficult to enjoy. Yet it does have proponents, who proclaimed, "The price is right" for the preparations of "good, straightforward seafood" that comes with a "fairly priced wine list."

Seafood | Informal | Moderate | east village | 96 Second Ave. | 212-674-5870 | www.themermaidnyc.com | Dinner daily

Mexicana Mama   86.0

Hungry fans say they are happy to put up with "unbearable waits" and "punishingly uncomfortable banquette seating" for a chance to dine at this "little gem in the West Village." Although it was "more cutting edge" when Julieta Ballesteros was doing the cooking, the "authentic menu" at this simple storefront still includes "the best salsas I've had in my life," one reviewer raves, along with dishes like chicken mole and enchiladas suiza, a flour tortilla filled with chicken, cilantro and onion, baked with a tomatillo-poblano sauce and melted cheese.

Mexican | Informal | Moderate | west village | 525 Hudson St. | 212-924-4119 | Lunch & Dinner Tue-Sat

Parma   86.0

If you want to see the city's top investment bankers, corporate lawyers and other movers and shakers outside of their professional milieu, show up at this veteran Italian restaurant at 7:00 p.m. on a Sunday evening and you will find them dining with their families. On weeknights it's sort of a "B version of Elio's," where the pastas and simple preparations of northern Italian cuisine please a clientele of business diners and locals enough that they keep coming back.

Italian | Casual | Expensive | upper east side | 1404 Third Ave. | 212-535-3520 | Dinner daily

Pylos   86.0

While chef Diane Kochilos has some interesting ideas about modernizing Greek cuisine, like organic boned chicken farci with raisins, rosemary, thyme and Kasseri cheese, ingredients that are not at the same level as other Hellenic eateries (reflected by the low prices) hold this restaurant back. Still, that doesn't stop a strong minority of reviewers from declaring this attractive restaurant "their favorite Greek restaurant" in the city.

Greek | Informal | Moderate | east village | 128 E. Seventh St. | 212-473-0220 | www.pylosrestaurant.com | Dinner Wed-Sun, Lunch daily

Brasserie Ruhlmann   85.5

Even with the talented Laurent Tourondel in the kitchen, reviews of this lively restaurant range from "very good brasserie food and magnificent décor" to "its location is the only thing keeping this overpriced turkey open." Regardless of which side of the argument you take, you will probably agree it's "touristy" – but then, it is in Rockefeller Center, and "it will do in a pinch" if you're in the area and desperate for brasserie fare.

French Brasserie | Casual | Expensive | midtown west | 45 Rockefeller Plaza | 212-974-2020 | www.brasserieruhlmann.com | Lunch & Dinner daily

Chennai Garden   85.5

Many of our reviewers are fond of this vegetarian restaurant in the heart of Curry Hill for its honest version of spicy

South Indian dishes like idli, dosa and uttapam, served with fillings that range from the expected curried potatoes and peas to cheese and fiery hot chiles. Fans praise it as "different than the usual generic Indian offering," while critics call it "seriously lacking when it comes to décor, service and other amenities."

Indian | Informal | Inexpensive | murray hill | 129 E. 27th St. | 212-689-1999 | Lunch & Dinner daily

Hell's Kitchen   85.5

We rarely hear anyone mention this restaurant on the edge of the Theater District, yet whenever we visit there's a lengthy wait for a table. Jorge Pareja serves what is billed as progressive Mexican cuisine, resulting in a menu that offers dishes like duck confit empanadas with cranberry mole and pico de gallo. It's especially busy after the shows let out: You may need to nurse your pineapple-strawberry margarita at the bar for a bit before sitting down.

Mexican | Informal | Moderate | midtown west | 679 Ninth Ave. | 212-977-1588 | www.hellskitchen-nyc.com | Dinner daily

Kefi   85.5

Although it's consistently packed with hungry West Side diners, our reviewers feel that Michael Psilakis hasn't been able to transfer his success at Anthos and Mia Dona to this moderately priced nouveau Greek. "Nothing original, inspiring or even particularly good here," snapped one reviewer, while another called it "not good enough to put up with the crowds and the noise."

Greek | Informal | Moderate | upper west side | 505 Columbus Ave. | 212-873-0200 | www.kefirestaurant.com | Dinner daily, Lunch Tue-Sun

Maya   85.5

When Richard Sandoval first opened this restaurant, enamored gourmands dubbed it the next step in the refinement of Mexican cuisine (a process started by Josefina Howard at Rosa Mexicano). But rather than continuing to evolve over time, Sandoval went all commercial on us and began opening additional branches instead. "The neglect shows," our reviewers say, and this restaurant has fallen off the foodie radar as a result.

Mexican | Casual | Expensive | upper east side | 1191 First Ave. | 212-585-1818 | www.modernmexican.com | Dinner daily

Snack Taverna   85.5

With dishes like veal meatballs with a red wine reduction and a citrus yogurt, this relatively inexpensive West Village Greek is "never brilliant but always tasty." There are a series of small as well as large plates on offer, along with a small wine list that you can supplement with a fair corkage policy. "Small, cramped, fun and casual" sums up the scene.

Greek | Informal | Moderate | west village | 63 Bedford St. | 212-929-3499 | http://snackny.com | Lunch & Dinner daily

Bar Veloce   85.0

Against a backdrop of flat-screen TVs showing a continuous stream of classic Italian films, you can enjoy a glass of some unknown Italian wine, along with a wide assortment of panini, tramezzini and a small plates menu focused on salads, mozzarella and sliced meats. Helpful bartenders and a menu that does a good job of describing the choices make it easy for the "cool, young crowd" that frequents the place to choose a glass that perfectly suits their mood.

Italian | Informal | Inexpensive | east village | 176 Seventh Ave. | 212-629-5300 | www.barveloce.com | Dinner daily

Centrico   85.0

The consensus is that "the food is tastier than it needs to be" at this hot spot in

TriBeCa. Aarón Sanchez is behind the stoves, and his ingredient-based cuisine features dishes like pepita-crusted salmon with corn-summer squash picadillo and basil-cotija cheese pesto, as well as grilled adobo sirloin steak with cactus and rajas. But despite what some call "a high level of cooking," our reviewers agree that "most people seem to be there for the drinks" and the overall scene, rather than the food.

Mexican | Casual | Moderate | tribeca | 211 W. Broadway | 212-431-0700 | http://www.myriadrestaurantgroup.com/centrico | Dinner daily

Churrascaria Plataforma   85.0

You can feast on unlimited amounts of meat at this Brazilian restaurant that is predominantly frequented by tourists and business travelers. "The convivial surroundings add to the grande bouffe experience." But views on the food itself are tougher, with comments like "The meats are poorly grilled" and "The quality is mediocre at best." As one reviewer put it, "I'm still waiting to hear about a restaurant that serves unlimited quantities of high-quality ingredients."

Brazilian | Informal | Moderate | midtown west | 316 W. 49th St. | 212-245-0505 | www.churrascariaplataforma.com | Lunch & Dinner daily

Fresco by Scotto   85.0

The food at this restaurant was more enjoyable before the Scotto family started making regular appearances on *The Today Show*. Since then, what used to be solid Italian fare has become overly fussy: think salmon with Savoy cabbage, radicchio, cippolini onions, duck confit, creamy polenta, apple cider and sherry wine reduction. It's a shame, because they are the nicest people you will ever meet. But their restaurant has been downgraded to nothing more than "a reasonable option for a midtown business lunch." It's especially popular among on-air television and radio personalities

(reflecting *Good Day New York* anchor Rosanna Scotto's relationship to the management).

Italian | Casual | Expensive | midtown east | 34 E. 52nd St. | 212-935-3434 | www.frescobyscotto.com | Dinner Mon-Sat, Lunch Mon-Fri

Minca Ramen   85.0

In the mood for ramen but looking to avoid the prices of a place like Ippudo or Momofuku? Head farther east to this specialist where the "broth is classic," "The noodles are al dente" and "Your lips will be sticky from the thick broth." As one critic characterized it, "While the better-known Japanese noodle restaurants might have an edge, the ramen here is excellent, and I am happy to slurp up every last spoonful."

Japanese | Informal | Inexpensive | east village | 536 E. 5th St. | 212-505-8001 | www.newyorkramen.com | Lunch & Dinner daily

Perilla   85.0

Harold Dieterle was one of the first chefs to leverage his appearance on TV's *Top Chef* into his own restaurant. The cuisine is New American with some Asian touches, like coconut-crusted Montauk fluke with bok choy, wood ear mushrooms, green mung beans and Pandan curry. In a rare occurrence, Perilla actually divided our reviewers on cost, with both "surprisingly affordable" and "very pricy" among the comments we collected.

New American | Casual | Moderate | greenwich village | 9 Jones St. | 212-929-6868 | www.perillanyc.com | Lunch & Dinner daily

Periyali   85.0

Twenty-eight years ago, when the owners of Il Cantinori opened this restaurant, Greek food in this town rarely rose above taverna level. But now refined Greek cuisine, like filets of salmon wrapped in fillo with spinach, has become ubiquitous and is often prepared better elsewhere. Still, places don't last this long without people liking the food. A case in point: One reviewer who's been eating there since the beginning still finds it "as delightful as ever."

Greek | Casual | Moderate | flatiron | 35 W. 20th St. | 212-463-7890 | www.periyali.com | Dinner daily, Lunch Mon-Fri

Pure Food & Wine   85.0

Sarma Melngailis' vegan cuisine includes creations like porcini ravioli with truffle cream sauce, baby white asparagus, pickled ramps, parsley salad and porcini oil. While that might sound delicious, reviewers are split on whether the raw-food focus works, with fans saying "the consistently delicious" and "endlessly creative" dishes "will charm your palate," while foes call it "terribly overpriced for food that isn't even cooked."

Vegan | Casual | Moderate | gramercy | 54 Irving Pl. | 212-477-1010 | www.purefoodandwine.com | Lunch & Dinner daily

Riingo   85.0

With the departure of founding chef Marcus Samuelsson, this Japanese eatery changed gears. Riccardo Traslavina has instituted an Italianish New American cuisine, like a pan-seared tuna steak served with grilled polenta and roasted peppers. Reviewers say the change hasn't caught on, and one consumes the "indifferent food" in an "attractive" but "empty dining room."

New American | Casual | Moderate | midtown east | Alex Hotel | 205 East 45th St. | 212-867-4200 | www.riingo.com | Lunch & Dinner daily

Sea Grill   85.0

Since chef Ed Brown left to open Eighty One, we haven't seen that many reviews of this Rockefeller Center restaurant run by the Patina Group. Maybe it's identity confusion: While the place's maritime name remains, fewer than half the entrées on the menu come from a lake, river or sea. One diner declared, "Post-Brown, the only reason to go here is to impress out-of-towners around tree-lighting time, and even then it isn't worth battling the crowds."

Seafood | Casual | Expensive | midtown west | Rockefeller Plaza | 19 W. 49th St. | 212-332-7610 | www.theseagrillnyc.com | Dinner daily, Lunch Sun-Fri

Smith & Wollensky   85.0

"The first link in what has become nothing more than a chain," this is the epitome of a B-level steakhouse, a status confirmed by reviewers who say, "I could never understand why others rated this place so highly"; "better than most in the second tier, but definitely second tier"; "the TGIF of national steakhouses"; and "Meals here have been average at best."

Steakhouse | Informal | Expensive | midtown east | 797 Third Ave. | 212-753-1530 | www.smithand-wollensky.com | Lunch & Dinner daily

Kouzina by Trata   85.0

Another one of the many Greek seafood restaurants that cropped up after the success of Estiatorio Milos, this one features the same format: lots of "over-priced fish" sitting on ice waiting for someone to throw it on the grill. "They could never charge these prices if the menu listed it as sea bass instead of lavraki," one reviewer carped. On summer weekends, a second location in the Hamptons hosts a jumping single scene and is as much a club as a restaurant.

Greek | Casual | Expensive | upper east side | 1331 Second Ave. | 212-535-5800 | www.trata.com | Lunch & Dinner daily

Tse Yang   85.0

In business for more than 20 years, Tse Yang is filled at lunchtime with expense-accounters, whose ranks are supplemented at dinner by theatergoers and visitors from the various hotels nearby. The service and setting seem "a bit more formal than the other upscale Chinese restaurants in town," and a wine list that includes offerings from producers like DRC and Harlan Estate supports that view. While they're famed for serving solid versions of luxury fare like Peking duck, those in the know opt for the Beggar's Chicken, which must be ordered two days in advance.

Chinese | Formal | Expensive | midtown east | 34 E. 51st St. | 212-688-5447 | Lunch & Dinner daily

OTHER RESTAURANTS MENTIONED

Ed's Lobster Bar   84.5

Considering that Ed McFarland is a veteran of Pearl Oyster Bar, it's not surprising his eponymous eatery seems an imitation of that popular spot. What's disappointing is that it's a "poor imitation." Reviewers suggest you "move on" unless you can't manage the taxi ride to his alma mater, or you find yourself desperate for a lobster roll in SoHo.

Seafood | Informal | Moderate | soho | 222 Lafayette St. | 212-343-3236 | www.lobsterbarnyc.com | Lunch & Dinner daily

Great Jones Café   84.5

More of a bar known for "strong drinks," "a top notch jukebox" and the probability that a notable figure from the New York City rock scene is working behind the bar. The food – an assortment of hamburgers, plus Cajun specialties like seafood jambalaya and roast chicken with a brown sugar glaze – is more than adequate, but it's more about the "fun atmosphere" and "great staff" than the down-home country eats here.

Cajun | Informal | Moderate | greenwich village | 54 Great Jones St. | 212-674-9304 | www.greatjones.com | Dinner daily, Lunch Tue-Sun

Gobo   84.5

A number of reviewers called this "my favorite vegetarian restaurant in New York City," serving "tantalizing, Asian-inspired fare" like hand-wrapped, pan-seared green tea vegetable dumplings and organic king oyster mushroom in sizzling basil black bean sauce. It's popular for takeout and delivery, and on a nice day you can grab a veggie-burger with yam fries and a large wheat grass, carrot, beet, celery and apple juice and enjoy your meal while sitting on a bench in Washington Square Park.

Vegetarian | Informal | Moderate | greenwich village | 401 Sixth Ave. | 212-255-3902 | www.goborestaurant.com | Lunch & Dinner daily

Second Location: upper east side | 1426 Third Ave. | 212-288-5099 | www.goborestaurant.com | Lunch & Dinner daily

JoJo   84.5

"Once the gleam in his eye, now the bastard son at the family reunion": Jean-Georges Vongerichten's first restaurant has clearly fallen on hard times. Not only is the cuisine – including dishes like poached lobster with lemon risotto and caramelized fennel – considered inferior to the master's West Side flagship, the room is so small and the tables so close together that one reviewer joked, "I proposed to my girlfriend there and the woman at the next table accepted."

French | Casual | Expensive | upper east side | 160 E. 64th St. | 212-223-5656 | www.Jean-Georges.com | Lunch & Dinner daily

Landmarc   84.5

Despite their being among the most popular restaurants in the city, these two brasseries from Marc Murphy leave reviewers unimpressed. The fare does not offend, the fact that they serve choice (instead of prime) beef means that many "choose to eat their steak elsewhere." You might do better with the classic brasserie items, like frisée salad, boudin noir and moules prepared several different ways. The "terrific wine program" is a consolation, especially the large selection of well-priced half bottles.

French Brasserie | Informal | Moderate | tribeca | 179 W. Broadway | 212-343-3883 | www.landmarc-restaurant.com | Lunch & Dinner daily

Second Location: columbus circle | Time Warner Ctr., 3rd fl. | 212-823-6123 | www.landmarc-restaurant.com | Lunch & Dinner daily

Mr. Chow   84.5

A few reviewers enjoyed the food at this "upscale Chinese restaurant for socialites having a night out." But those who say things like "overpriced, over-hyped and underwhelmed" are more in tune with the prevailing opinion (and the low score). Service that is "nasty and condescending" and prices that are out of balance with the low-quality food led several to slam it as "a very expensive rip-off."

Chinese | Casual | Expensive | upper east side | 324 E. 57th St. | 212-751-9030 | www.mrchow.com | Dinner daily

Second Location: tribeca | 121 Hudson St. | 212-965-9200 | www.mrchow.com | Dinner daily

Pastis   84.5

The focus is a bit more on the scene at this Balthazar spin-off, which isn't all that surprising considering its location in the heart of the Meatpacking District. The food attracted a few positive comments, but most people said it was a step or two below its sister restaurant; instead, the draw here is the "incredible eye candy" that comes in all shapes, sizes, genders and orientations and that populates the restaurant morning, noon and well into the wee hours of the night.

French Brasserie | Informal | Moderate | meatpacking district | 9 Ninth Ave. | 212-929-4844 | www.pastisny.com | Open daily

Rosa Mexicano   84.5

With guacamole made tableside and a double-thick pork chop grilled and served in a spicy adobo sauce, Josefina

Howard's restaurant played a prominent role in introducing American diners to upscale Mexican dining. But fame brought expansion, and now that there are multiple locations, Rosa Mexicano has become "nothing more than a chain restaurant" whose quality deteriorates in proportion to the number of branches it opens. In other words: Once a trendsetter, it is now considered merely trendy.

Mexican | Informal | Moderate | sutton place | 1063 First Ave. | 212-753-7407 | www.rosamexicano.com | Dinner daily, Brunch Sat-Sun

Second Location: upper west side | 61 Columbus Ave. | 212-977-7700 | www. rosamexicano.com | Lunch & Dinner daily

Third Location: flatiron | 9 E. 18th St. | 212-533-3350 | www. rosamexicano.com | Lunch & Dinner daily

Angelica Kitchen   84.0

Looking for an open-face Reuben sandwich made with tempeh and served by a waitress with a stud in her tongue? Like to see a portion of the proceeds from your agrarian salgado appetizer go to the Friends of the Brazilian Landless Workers Movement? That sums up this place that "really knows how to cook vegetarian." Expect a wait, as it seems to always be filled with old hippies and the crème de la crème of the East Village hipster crowd.

Vegetarian | Informal | Moderate | east village | 300 E. 12th St. | 212-228-2909 | www.angelicakitchen.com | Lunch & Dinner daily

Brasserie   84.0

Back in the 1970s, when Americans were still cutting their teeth on the rudiments of fine dining, the Brasserie was an important cog in the contemporary restaurant scene. Being open 24 hours a day back then added to its allure – ah, the cachet of enjoying a bowl of onion soup at 3:00 a.m. seemed especially exotic. But now this subterranean establishment is considered "sub-par," and the main reason to visit appears to be the lack of other places to eat in the neighborhood.

French | Casual | Expensive | midtown east | 100 E. 53rd St. | 212-751-4840 | www.patinagroup. com | Lunch & Dinner daily

Café Evergreen   84.0

"Not the same since the legendary Henry Leung left" is what multiple reviewers said about this old-school Chinese. But some still claim it offers the "best dim sum on the Upper East Side," plus a terrific wine list. Given the location, it has the unusual distinction of being a top place for takeout and delivery for those who are staying or visiting someone at one of the nearby hospitals.

Chinese | Casual | Moderate | upper east side | 1288 First Ave. | 212-744-3266 | http://cafeever-greenchinese.com | Lunch & Dinner daily

Cafe Luxembourg   84.0

Though the food was described as "consistently unimpressive bistro fare," a location that is a short walk from Lincoln Center means this place is often mobbed, especially pre-theater, causing one reviewer to point to dishes like roasted cod grantinée as "evidence of the culinary black hole" known as the Upper West Side.

French Brasserie | Informal | Moderate | upper west side | 200 W. 70th St. | 212-873-7411 | www. cafeluxembourg.com | Open daily

Dylan Prime   84.0

There was praise for a "capable wait-staff," "pleasant décor" and "steaks cooked to the correct temperature," so it's a shame that one of the few choices for beef in TriBeCa couldn't muster a better rating. The comment that puts it all into perspective: "While the steaks are acceptable, acceptable really isn't good enough when it comes to steaks."

Steakhouse | Casual | Expensive | tribeca | 62 Laight St. | 212-334-4783 | www.dylanprime.com | Dinner daily, Lunch Sun-Fri

Five Points   84.0

This is the site of Marc Meyer's first success, which built its reputation by offering diners a market-based, seasonal cuisine (think roast Amish chicken with butter lettuce and roast potatoes) for a reasonable price. The concept was so successful that it eventually allowed him to open Cookshop and Hundred Acres (see reviews above). While this location has its fans, the rating reflects a feeling that Meyer's cooking is so non-interventionist that he "doesn't do enough with the terrific ingredients he sources."

New American | Informal | Moderate | soho | 31 Great Jones St. | 212-253-5700 | www.five-pointsrestaurant.com | Lunch & Dinner daily

Japonica   84.0

It is amazing how many reviewers said their first experience eating sushi after they moved to New York City was at this Village veteran known for its hefty portions. While the quality varies from excellent to ordinary, you can enhance your meal if you request a table in the café window at the 12th Street and University Place end of the restaurant, and "watch the world go by while chewing on those big pieces of fish."

Japanese | Informal | Moderate | greenwich village | 100 University Pl. | 212-243-7752 | www. japonicanyc.com | Lunch & Dinner daily

Live Bait   84.0

Owned and frequented by models and their wannabe boyfriends, Live Bait attracts a crowd more interested in the frozen margaritas than in the Cajun dishes like blackened, farm-raised Delta catfish. The combination of "bad food and a good scene" makes it "a standby if you're in the neighborhood" and need a cold beer and a hamburger while occupying a room filled with tall, blonde women.

Cajun | Informal | Moderate | flatiron | 14 E. 23rd St. | 212-353-2400 | Lunch & Dinner daily

Moustache   84.0

There are constantly long lines for "really cheap, pretty good, Middle Eastern fare" like hummus falafel, chicken kebab and lamb ribs outside this West Village venue. But the specialty of the house is what they call pitza, a series of flatbreads that are topped with everything from ground lamb to shrimp and scallops before being baked in the oven. Based on food alone, it deserves a better rating, some reviewers say, but "the ambience and service left something to be desired." They also operate another location in Brooklyn.

Middle Eastern | Informal | Moderate | west village | 265 E. 10th St. | 212-228-2022 | http://moustachepitza.com | Lunch & Dinner daily

Nice Matin   84.0

With daube, pistou and pissaladière on his menu, Andy d'Amico serves just enough Provençal fare for this eatery (co-owned by restaurateur Simon Oren) to warrant its name. A "welcoming neighborhood restaurant" rather than a destination, its moderate prices make it "a good stop for a post-movie meal," our reviewers declare. They also find it a popular brunch and breakfast spot, *sept sur sept*, as the French say.

French Brasserie | Informal | Moderate | upper west side | 201 W. 79th St. | 212-873-6423 | www.nicematinnyc.com | Open daily

Pampano   84.0

This upscale Mexican seafood restaurant owned by Richard Sandoval has fans and foes. Fans feel they offer "well-prepared, inventive seafood dishes with a Mexican spin," while foes claim the fare is "watered-down in order to appeal to people who are afraid of real Mexican food." At least the rooftop deck is "a lovely place to have a drink" while you're waiting for your table.

Mexican | Casual | Moderate | midtown east | 209 E. 49th St. | 212-751-4545 | www.modernmexican.com | Dinner daily, Lunch Mon-Fri

Patsy's   84.0

When you eat at Patsy's, you step back in time to the 1950s. The southern Italian food hasn't changed very much over the years, and the menu is dominated by classics like linguine with clam sauce, chicken Marsala and veal pizzaiola. In the old days the food worked well enough to make the place a hangout for celebrities like Frank Sinatra, but current reviewers have downgraded it to "Good before the theater, but I would choose a different place for a more leisurely meal."

Italian | Casual | Expensive | midtown west | 236 W. 56th St. | 212-247-3491 | www.patsys.com | Lunch & Dinner daily

Thalassa   84.0

While some reviewers find the seafood fresh at this TriBeCa Greek, others feel the experience is weighed down by "indifferent preparations" and "high prices considering the quality of the food and service." As one reviewer put it," I love the idea but hate the execution." However, the 5,000-bottle wine list goes a long way to helping some diners keep their minds off of the food.

Greek | Casual | Expensive | tribeca | 179 Franklin St. | 212-941-7661 | www.thalassanyc.com | Dinner Daily, Lunch Sun-Fri

Triomphe   84.0

Some 40% of our reviewers rated this restaurant as merely Acceptable, offering comments like "Why go there with db Bistro next door and other good places nearby?" and "Steven Zobel's restaurant has a lot of work to do before we can recommend it." It is popular with the BYOB crowd, however, which might be because the servers treat them as if they had purchased an expensive bottle, and the kitchen exhibits great flexibility in cooking meals that match the wines.

New American | Casual | Expensive | midtown west | 49 W. 44th St. | 212-453-4233 | www.triomphe-newyork.com | Dinner Daily, Lunch Sun-Fri

Water Club   84.0

Until a number of reviewers weighed in on it, we'd never heard of anyone eating here unless they were invited to a wedding or a bar mitzvah. While it might be perfect for such celebratory affairs – it's right on the East River – as a dining experience it's sort of a "B version of the mothership," Brooklyn Café, with a less creative menu and "acceptable" food.

New American | Casual | Expensive | murray hill | East River at 30th St. | 212-683-3333 | www.thewaterclub.com | Lunch & Dinner Tue-Sun

Yama   84.0

"Fine for a neighborhood sushi place" and "great for college kids" characterize the comments about this Gramercy sushi specialist that's been doling out cuts of fish for more than a decade. Part of the problem is the overly liberal hand in the kitchen: "The Maki rolls are large but suffer from ubiquitous spicy mayo that overpowers the fish and rice."

Japanese | Informal | Moderate | gramercy | 122 E. 17th St. | 212-475-0969 | Dinner Mon-Sat, Lunch Mon-Fri

Bottega del Vino   83.5

One would think that a New York branch of a Veronese restaurant would offer better cuisine. But the fare – potato gnocchi with pesto, oven-roasted sea bass in a balsamic glaze or lamb chops with rosemary and thyme – is similar to what you'll find at northern Italian restaurants all over the city, and not even up to the level of many of those. However, it does sport a "very good wine list."

Italian | Casual | Expensive | upper east side | 7 E. 59th St. | 212-223-3028 | www.bottegadelvinonyc.com | Open daily

Brasserie 8½   83.5

What's so hard about serving onion soup and steak frites that people enjoy rather than describe as "boring midtown expense-account fare"? As another reviewer put it, "Below-street-level restaurants must have something unique to compensate for their location – this establishment does not." It's a shame this restaurant in the Solow Building doesn't fare better, as it's so convenient for shoppers and office workers.

French Brasserie | Casual | Moderate | midtown west | 9 W. 57th St. | 212-829-0812 | www.patina-group.com | Dinner Daily, Lunch Sun-Fri

Cafe Español   83.5

If you grew up in New York City during the '60s and '70s, the Spanish dish known as paella meant rice and an assortment of meats or fish cooked in a pot. But even though we now know that a proper paella is cooked in a pan, a number of Spanish restaurants in New York continue to prepare it the old way. And "while the arroz verde might still be the same, unfortunately so is the décor. Good if you want to travel back in time!"

Spanish | Informal | Moderate | greenwich village | 172 Bleecker St. | 212-505-0657 | http://cafeespanol.com | Lunch & Dinner daily

Il Mulino   83.5

This Greenwich Village veteran suffers from a reputation of catering to unsuspecting tourists who can't distinguish between well-made northern Italian fare and poorly made Continental cuisine. If that doesn't deter you, you might want to heed the advice of the reviewer who said, "It's shtick, it's touristy, it's horrendously expensive. Still, they serve the best veal Marsala in the city."

Italian | Casual | Expensive | greenwich village | 86 W. 3rd St. | 212-673-3783 | www.ilmulino.com | Dinner Mon-Sat, Lunch Mon-Fri

Wo Hop   83.5

During the 1970s, a 3:00 a.m. visit to Chinatown meant waiting for a table at a place like Hong Fat, Lin's Garden or Wo

Hop. But with much of Manhattan's old-guard Chinese community having moved to Flushing, Wo Hop is the only one of the three to soldier on. They still serve the same old-school Cantonese fare, like pork lo mein and beef chow fun, which incredibly "taste exactly the way they tasted in the old days."

Chinese | Informal | Inexpensive | chinatown | 17 Mott St. | 212-267-2536 | Lunch & Dinner daily

Les Halles   83.0

It seems like "popularity went to their heads" at this French brasserie, made famous by alum chef Tony Bourdain's depiction in his bestseller, *Kitchen Confidential*. Now, having abandoned any pretense of trying to please discriminating diners, it's a "cramped, crowded and noisy tourist destination." A reputation of "making people wait for 45 minutes even when they have reservations" puts it squarely on the list of places our reviewers try to avoid.

French Brasserie | Informal | Moderate | murray hill | 411 Park Ave. S. | 212-679-4111 | www.leshalles.net | Open daily

Lure Fishbar   83.0

While blessed with an "exceptionally friendly staff" and a "varied wine list featuring several not-so-common varietals," the food can be hit-or-miss at this swanky SoHo seafooder. Diners are advised to skip the "overpriced and underwhelming" sushi and instead go for "small plates like fried Blue Point oysters or tuna tiradito." It's often mobbed, a result of a location where serious cooking can be difficult to come by.

Seafood | Sushi | Informal | soho | 142 Mercer St. | 212-431-7676 | www.lurefishbar.com | Lunch & Dinner daily

Carlyle Hotel   82.5

How you feel about dining at this hotel restaurant depends on how you feel about eating hotel food. First, we have the usual haters who ask, "What the hell is this place doing on the survey?" Then there are those who talk about the "beautiful setting, excellent service, traditional but well-prepared food and atmosphere that can't be beat." Others say, "You don't go for the cooking; you go in hopes of being seated within earshot of someone like Wallace Shawn so you can eavesdrop on the witty conversation."

French | Formal | Expensive | upper east side | Carlyle Hotel | 35 E. 76th St. | 212-744-1600 | www.thecarlyle.com | Open daily

Frankie & Johnnie's   82.5

Given the popularity of steak restaurants in New York City, we are always surprised when one proves unable to draw enough support to be recommended by our reviewers. That's the case with this "old-school steakhouse," which moved to the Theater District after a decades-long run in Turtle Bay. "The mediocre food and poor service" might have something to do with the low rating, along with incorrect cooking temperatures: One reviewer complained his steak came out "hard and charred when I ordered medium."

Steakhouse | Casual | Expensive | midtown west | 269 W. 45th St. | 212-997-9494 | www.frankieandjohnnies.com | Dinner daily, Lunch Tue-Sat

Morrell Wine Bar & Cafe   82.5

This is another one of those places we just don't understand: You start out with a terrific wine list as a result of your association with the shop that operates under the same name, and you collect numerous comments about "the delicious list of wines by the glass." So why not spend a little bit extra on your chef so that people will enjoy the cuisine? Instead, you end up with reviews that talk about "mediocre food" and "terrible service."

French | Casual | Moderate | midtown west | 1 Rockefeller Plaza | 212-262-7700 | www.morrellwinebar.com | Lunch & Dinner Mon-Sat, Brunch Sun

Pó   82.5

Before becoming a world-famous chef, Mario Batali ran the kitchen at this restaurant. But when he left, the owners didn't take the appropriate steps to replace him, resting on the laurels of his renown instead. They have maintained Batali's style of Italian cuisine, still serving dishes like a grilled pork chop with mashed pumpkin and apple mostarda. Nevertheless, reviewers remain unimpressed; the general feeling among them is, "There's no other way to describe this place but 'past its prime.'"

Italian | Informal | Moderate | greenwich village | 31 Cornelia St. | 212-645-2189 | www.porestaurant.com | Dinner daily, Lunch Wed-Sunr

Heidelberg   82.0

Manhattan's Yorkville neighborhood was once homebase for the city's German population. But its breweries have been replaced by high-rise apartment buildings, and this bar/restaurant is one of the few remnants of a once-thriving community. Unfortunately, the "bland food" tastes like a remnant as well, though one reviewer singled out the sizzling pork shank for praise. Even so, the majority insists that a visit here is more about gemutlichkeit and a place to wear your lederhosen than about enjoying a quality German meal.

German | Informal | Moderate | upper east side | 1648 Second Ave. | 212-628-2332 | www.heidelbergrestaurant.com | Lunch & Dinner daily

Odeon   82.0

While it's full for both lunch and dinner, late night is the favored time to visit this granddaddy of New York City brasseries. Unfortunately, while it serves a purpose for downtown insomniacs or rockers who have just finished their sets at Madison Square Garden, along with those who have been out clubbing, the food is "without any flair or general purpose," although people profess to be fond of the hamburgers. Everyone agrees that "It is a better scene than restaurant."

French Brasserie | Informal | Moderate | tribeca | 145 W. Broadway | 212-233-0507 | www.theodeonrestaurant.com | Open daily

Compass   81.5

Once upon a time, Compass was considered a place worth traveling to from other parts of the city. But it's been "a ship without a captain" ever since chef John Fraser left to open Dovetail (see above). What remains is a quiet place, convenient to Lincoln Center, serving "food that lacks consistency." Given their past success, wouldn't it be worth their while to hire a first-rate culinary captain?

New American | Casual | Moderate | upper west side | 208 W. 70th St. | 212-875-8600 | www.compassrestaurant.com | Lunch & Dinner daily

Blue Water Grill   81.0

The ratings for this seafood restaurant are lower than those garnered by others run by its parent, the B. R. Guest organization, such as Primehouse or the Atlantic Grill (for both, see above). Still, the place does have a few things in its favor, including "good, fresh fish" served in a "civilized atmosphere" and "comfortable outdoor seating" on a terrace that overlooks the dynamic Union Square street scene.

Seafood | Raw | Informal | Moderate | flatiron | 31 Union Sq. W. | 212-675-9500 | www.bluewatergrillnyc.com | Lunch & Dinner daily

Haru   81.0

While B-level sushi is bad enough, a chain of B-level sushi restaurants is one tekka maki too far. Yet in spite of that sentiment (and the low rating), some of our reviewers consider Haru "consistent and convenient" and "useful for takeout on a work night or a quick meal in the neighborhood." Reviewers also say that the "nice atmosphere" goes a long way to offset the quality of the fish.

Japanese | Informal | Moderate | upper east side | 1329 Third Ave. | 212-452-2230 | www.harusushi.com | Dinner daily

Kitchenette   81.0

This place is mostly about breakfast and brunch rather than dinner. One reviewer wrote of "applewood-smoked bacon, creamy savory cheese grits, light and fluffy biscuits and pancakes that are near perfection." Cheap prices and "high-quality baked goods" make it an even more attractive choice for the first meal of the day. The lunch and dinner menus tend to feature salads and sandwiches along with lighter entrées.

American | Informal | Inexpensive | tribeca | 1272 Amsterdam Ave. | 212-531-7600 | www.kitchenetterestaurant.com | Open daily

One If by Land,   81.0
Two If by Sea

This is considered one of New York City's most romantic restaurants and the quintessential reservation to bag for Valentine's Day, but one wonders if the lovers who flock here are too busy fondling each other to actually taste the food. Even the flowers-and-fireplace décor came under criticism – while it's "romantic" according to a few, others dismiss it as merely "cheesy."

American | Casual | Expensive | greenwich village | 17 Barrow St. | 212-255-8649 | www.oneifbyland.com | Dinner daily, Sun brunch

Brick Lane Curry House   80.5

True to the name, they serve British-style Indian food here (Brick Lane is a big Indian-restaurant street in London). Reviews are mixed, with some diners describing the food as "Indian-influenced comfort food that is nicely spiced and well prepared," while others say it's "not measurably better than the much cheaper Indian restaurants around the corner."

British expats seem to enjoy it more than other diners.

Indian | Informal | Expensive | east village | 306-308 E. 6th St. | 212-979-8787 | www.bricklanecurryhouse.com | Lunch & Dinner daily

Capsouto Frères   80.5

More than 20 years ago, the Capsouto brothers opened a restaurant on a deserted street in TriBeCa. Now, while the rest of the 'hood has been gentrified, Washington Street remains deserted, except for the limos lined up outside this friendly bistro. The rating bespeaks the food quality, but the one thing everyone does like are the soufflés.

French Bistro | Informal | Moderate | tribeca | 451 Washington St. | 212-966-4900 | www.capsoutofreres.com | Dinner daily, Lunch Tue-Fri

Ditch Plains   80.5

We find it a bit of a head-scratcher when opinions are split as drastically as they are with this restaurant. How can it be that there are reviewers who say, "Nice casual downtown option for solid seafood," while others complain, "I do not understand the popularity of this dive or what it's doing in the Village. The bar is bad, and the food is awful. Stay away." A few feel "it's worth the trip for the wine alone" (like its Landmarc siblings).

Seafood | Informal | Moderate | greenwich village | 29 Bedford St. | 212-633-0202 | www.ditchplains.com | Lunch & Dinner daily

Barolo   80.0

"The best garden space in New York," a "plentiful, yet pricy wine list," a "touristy, Euro crowd" and "food that is an afterthought" make this attractive restaurant "the epitome of a SoHo eatery." Given the many other choices nearby that serve better food in a chic setting, the only reason to go here has to be to watch the beautiful people eat non-authentic dishes like homemade squid-ink bowtie pasta with asparagus and smoked salmon.

Italian | Casual | Expensive | soho | 398 W.
Broadway | 212-226-1102 | www.nybarolo.com |
Lunch & Dinner daily

Il Cantinori   80.0

This Tuscan restaurant, a magnet for
celebrities, has fallen on hard times,
attracting comments like "I grew up eating here, but it has slipped to the bottom
rung," "The food can be pedestrian and
the service hurried, yet not sharp," and
our favorite: "Seriously, I'll duel with anyone who recommends this place. "

Italian | Casual | Expensive | greenwich village
| 32 E. 10th St. | 212-673-6044 | www.ilcantinori.
com | Dinner daily, Lunch Mon-Fri

Old Homestead   80.0

How do you square comments like "as
one of New York's oldest steakhouses,
it should be on a par with Peter Luger or
Keens, and it's just not" with "the oldest
and still the best steak restaurant in the
city. Do not miss the creamed spinach
as a side to any one of several excellent
steak selections"? Easily – when you're
talking about a place that's big with
the bridge and tunnel crowd but that
Manhattanites steer clear of. Ultimately
"high prices that border on silly and a
service attitude that drips with disdain"
tilt opinion squarely against it.

Steakhouse | Casual | Expensive | chelsea | 56
Ninth Ave. | 212-242-9040 | www.theoldhome-
steadstekhouse.com | Lunch & Dinner daily

Asia de Cuba   79.5

Comments about this Morgans Hotel hot
spot (the first opened by Ian Schrager)
were actually more favorable than the
low score would indicate – provided that
you dispense with the notion that you're
there to eat well. The whole point is to
take advantage of the "terrific people-
watching" and to enjoy a menu that
allows groups to share plates of Asian

fusion cuisine in a party-like atmosphere.

Asian Fusion | Casual | Moderate | murray hill
| 237 Madison Ave. | 212-726-7755 | www.chi-
nagrillmgt.com | Dinner daily, Lunch Mon-Fri

Le Perigord   79.5

If you're 50 years old and want to be
the youngest person in the room, or you
want "French food circa 1975," head over
to this Sutton Place war horse, still serving such delicacies as fricassee of escargots with hazelnut butter and medallions
of veal in a morel sauce. "It's a relic of the
past," said one reviewer, who added that
a recent change in chefs means the place
"isn't quite as dusty as it once was."

French | Casual | Expensive | midtown east |
405 E. 52nd St. | 212-755-6244 | www.leperigord.
com | Dinner daily, Lunch Mon-Fri

Maloney & Porcelli   79.5

The Smith & Wollensky gang felt that
carnivores of Irish and Italian descent
needed representation, so they opened
this offshoot that also caters to expense-
accounters. We're somewhat puzzled as
to why they couldn't open a place that
was at least as good as the mothership.
"There are too many steakhouses to
bother with anything but the best meat
or the best value, and this isn't either."

Steakhouse | Casual | Expensive | midtown east
| 37 E. 50th St. | 212-750-2233 | www.maloneyand-
dporcelli.com | Dinner daily, Lunch Mon-Fri

MarkJoseph   79.5

This was the first of the Peter Luger spi-
noffs. It got off to a quick start, but after
a number of other Luger copycats came
onto the scene, they were overtaken by
places like Ben & Jack's and Wolfgang's.
Aside from the convenience of getting a
steak in the Financial District, "why go
here when the food is better elsewhere?"

Steakhouse | Casual | Expensive | financial dis-
trict | 261 Water St. | 212-277-0020 | www.mark-
josephsteakhouse.com | Dinner daily, Lunch Mon-Fri

El Quijote   78.0

Walk into this old-school Spanish restaurant in the notorious Chelsea Hotel (which has hosted Sid Vicious, Janis Joplin, Allen Ginsburg and Robert Mapplethorpe, to name just a few) and you have entered a culinary time warp, where the paella is made in pots and not pans, and where the chef doesn't have any qualms about adding flour to thicken the sauces. Aside from the fact that it's fun to have this kind of meal once every five years, the "huge portions of food served at reasonable prices" ensure that the place is constantly jammed.

Spanish | Informal | Moderate | chelsea | 226 W. 23rd St. | 212-929-1855 | www.elquijoterestaurant. com | Lunch & Dinner daily

Ninja   78.0

"How has this restaurant survived so many years?" is what reviewers ask about this Japanese eatery described as "more of a spectacle than a restaurant." The expected lineup of luxury ingredients are present, from black cod to Berkshire pork belly to an assortment of exotic rolls, but other than "going for some oddly entertaining antics on the part of the staff," the "food is unremarkable."

Japanese | Casal | Expensive | tribeca | 25 Hudson St. | 212-274-8500 | www.ninjanewyork. com | Dinner daily

Spring Street Natural   75.0

It's been 38 years since Spring Street started serving dishes like tempeh black bean chili and southwestern grilled organic chicken salad on what is one of SoHo's busiest corners. Problem is, the food is "the definition of disappointment," and "Someone forgot to tell the crowds the food was tasteless." On the other hand, "at least the food attempts to be healthy."

Vegetarian | Casual | Moderate | soho | 62 Spring St. | 212-966-0290 | www.springstreetnatural.com | Open daily

Cheap Eats

UNIQUELY DELICIOUS

Katz's Delicatessen   8.9

Walking into Katz's is like going back in time. The interior, which includes a sign sporting their famous slogan "Send a salami to your boy in the Army," hasn't changed since the '40s. What sets it apart from other delis is an exceptional pastrami sandwich, sliced by hand and served steaming hot. Ordering is part of the fun: There are four slicing stations, and after you tell your slicer whether you prefer your pastrami juicy or lean, he will offer you a few slices to sample. One taste will send you into a state of ecstasy, causing you to nod your head in approval, after which he will slice enough meat for a sandwich 3 or 4 inches high. Besides the "ethereal pastrami," the "Hot dogs have a nice crispy skin," and "The turkey sandwich is always solid," but most find the corned beef underwhelming. If you can't stomach the lines there is waiter service along the back wall.

Delicatessen | Inexpensive | lower east side | 205 E. Houston St. | 212-254-2246 | www.katzdeli. com | Open daily

Bánh Mì Saigon Bakery   8.4

This Little Italy hole-in-the-wall is the crème de la crème of the Vietnamese sandwich places that have cropped up in New York over the past decade. Reviewer comments range from "my mouth waters just thinking about it" to "I enjoy it so much that this is one of the few places that I prefer not to tell other people about." There are nine banh mis on offer, including pork, chicken, meatball and one made with sardines (unusual for these parts). Unfortunately, visiting means eating the food at home, the office or on a park bench as, despite a recent move to larger digs, it's still takeout only.

Vietnamese | Inexpensive | chinatown | 198 Grand St. | 212-941-1541 | Open daily

Ess-a-Bagel   8.3

It's rare that our reviewers single out a bagel bakery, but the specimens at Ess-a-Bagel are too "chewy, dense and delicious" to go unheralded. In fact, it's developed an international reputation, so don't be surprised to hear the countermen speaking Japanese to their customers. Although some feel the smoked fish doesn't hold up against that of other classic appetizing shops, one reviewer claims a sandwich of smoked salmon, sable, vegetable cream cheese and tomato on a toasted onion bagel is "as close to heaven as it gets." Insider's tip: "Ask them to scoop out the inside of the bagel so your sandwich is not so messy."

Delicatessen | Inexpensive | midtown east | 831 Third Ave. | 212-980-1010 | www.ess-a-bagel.com | Open daily

Clinton Street Baking   8.0 Company & Restaurant

With "I waited an hour and a half for brunch and it was well worth it" typical of the comments we read, it's obvious that our reviewers adore this breakfast specialist. Reason: "the best pancakes in New York," along with praiseworthy eggs Benedict, crab cakes and "some of the best baked goods in the city." One person recommended checking it out on a weekday when the lines are usually shorter. Lunch and dinner bring savory dishes like fried chicken and shrimp and grits, but the fact that they serve blueberry pancakes all day is proof that breakfast's the thing.

Bakery | Inexpensive | lower east side | 4 Clinton St. | 646-602-6263 | www.clintonstreetbaking.com | Open daily except Sun dinner

Keste Pizza & Vino   8.0

Robert Caporuscio's restaurant is an enigma wrapped in Neapolitan-style pizza dough. Some of our most experienced reviewers claim it offers the best pizza they ever had, calling it "as close to being in Naples as you will find in the U.S." But we also have critics who dislike this style of pie, complaining about "pastry-like dough that is too soft in the center." There are a few salads and appetizers on offer, plus a calzone that some say "sets the standard for all other versions" and that "shouldn't be missed."

Pizzeria | Inexpensive | greenwich village | 271 Bleecker St. | 212-243-1500 | www.kestepizzeria.com | Lunch & Dinner daily

Momofuku Milk Bar   8.0

After the amazing success of his other restaurants, David Chang decided to focus his attention on a bakery. Fortunately, he had a secret weapon in the person of Christina Tosi, who is talented enough to create a dessert experience that's quirky enough to match Chang's cuisine. On any given evening, lines of people are waiting for unusual creations like crack pie or compost cookies, as well as four flavors of soft-serve ice cream. One reviewer characterized the offerings as "thoughtful, ingenious desserts, which you can't find anywhere else," while another (one obviously addicted to the place) said, "I always try to stop in if I'm anywhere nearby."

Bakery | Inexpensive | east village | 251 E. 13th St. | 212-254-3500 | www.momofuku.com | Open daily

RECOMMENDED

Bouchon Bakery   7.8

Though it doesn't get the same type of raves as his other restaurants, this casual offering from Thomas Keller packs them in just the same. You start out with "what might be the best baguette in the city" and continue with lighter fare like the quiche du jour or chicken and dumpling soup. Or you can recharge with "some of the best macarons ever" after a day of shopping in the Time Warner Center. A number of people seemed shocked by the "high prices"; obviously, they didn't see the letters TK engraved into the food.

Bakery | Inexpensive | columbus circle | 10 columbus circle | 212-823-9366 | www.bouchon-bakery.com | Lunch & Dinner daily

Jacques Torres Chocolate   7.8

Looking for a place to have dessert after a movie or dinner elsewhere? There was a time when New York was full of places that fit that description. But time hasn't been kind to the dessert specialists (calorie-watching might have something to do with that), which makes this "quaint chocolate shop" from Le Cirque pastry chef Jacques Torres extremely useful. The assortment of delights on offer ranges from chocolates, chocolate chip cookies, pithiviers and the house hot-chocolate blend, available either plain or laced with hot chiles.

Dessert | Inexpensive | west village | 350 Hudson St. | 212-414-2462 | www.mrchocolate.com | Open daily

Hampton Chutney Co.   7.7

The menu at these sandwich shops revolves around a rice and lentil crepe known as the dosa. Some of the fillings are traditional, like peas and curried potatoes, while others are decidedly less so, like sautéed spinach, roasted onions and jack cheese or smoked turkey, arugula and roasted tomatoes. There's also a soup of the day, as well as dal and a number of subcontinental-inspired beverages like cardamom iced coffee, orange blossom lemonade and mango lassis.

Sandwiches | Inexpensive | soho | 68 Prince St. | 212-226-9996 | www.hamptonchutney.com | Lunch & Dinner daily

Second Location: upper west side | 464 Amsterdam Ave. | 212-362-5050 | www.hamptonchutney.com | Lunch & Dinner daily

Kyotofu   7.7

"A hint of Kyoto in New York" is how one reviewer described this restaurant where all of the "elegant, subtly sweet and satisfying desserts" are made of tofu. Offerings include matcha green tea crème brûlée, warm sweet potato cake, vegan Valrhona chocolate cake or violet and other "unusual flavors" of soft-serve ice cream. The restaurant also serves a short menu of savory snacks that nobody seems to like, which holds it back from an even higher rating.

Dessert | Inexpensive | midtown west | 705 Ninth Ave. | 212-974-6012 | www.kyotofu-nyc.com | Lunch & Dinner daily

Shake Shack   7.7

The road to success in the food industry is traveled by restaurateurs who have correctly calculated that people will gladly pay more for an ordinary item if the quality is substantially improved. In starting Shake Shack, Danny Meyer felt that he could charge a premium for a fast food–style hamburger, served from a stand in Madison Square Park, if he used a higher-quality grind of meat. Well, he was right, and a few short years later, you can now enjoy those "juicy and beefy-tasting burgers" at five locations (both in- and outdoors) around the city. The Shack also offers hot dogs and bratwursts, plus beer, wine and frozen custard.

Hamburgers | Inexpensive | flatiron | Madison Square Park | 212-889-6600 | www.shakeshack-nyc.com | Lunch & Dinner daily

Big Wong   7.6

"Big Wong indeed – it's restaurants like this that make Manhattan so well-endowed when it comes to Chinese food!" Feast on congee, noodle soups and what might be the best Chinese-style roast duck in the city at this bustling Chinatown lunch place. There's also a full menu of Cantonese fare. On weekdays the clientele is a mix of locals and people from the nearby courtroom buildings, but weekends bring large Chinese families whose numbers are exceeded only by the number of plates on their tables.

Chinese | Inexpensive | chinatown | 67 Mott St. | 212-964-0540 | Breakfast & Lunch daily

ChikaLicious 7.6

Designed by the architect responsible for the Momofukus and Soto, this "adorable" restaurant is where Chika Tillman and an assistant serve a three-course dessert tasting, along with an assortment of exotic teas and wines by the glass. The desserts are appropriately minimalist and on a given night will likely include the "rightly famous" fromage blanc cheesecake. Chika's husband Don supervises the dining room, which holds a mere eight at the counter and another ten at the tables.

Dessert | Inexpensive | east village | 203 E. 10th St. | 212-995-9511 | www.chikalicious.com | Dinner Thu-Sun

burger joint at Le Parker Meridien 7.4

Located behind an unobtrusive curtain just off the the reception area in the Parker Merdien Hotel, this simple burger, fries and milkshake spot has risen to near-cult status among New York City diners. "A great hole-in-the-wall find, not gourmet, but juicy, greasy and tasty" is how one reviewer described it. However, some caution it has become too popular – you can spot it by the lines extending out the door – and "not as good as it was when it first opened."

Hamburgers | Inexpensive | midtown west | Le Parker Meridien | 118 W. 57th St. | 212-708-7414 | www.parkermeridien.com | Lunch & Dinner daily

Ferrara 7.4

They began serving canolis, sfogliatelle, baba-rhum and Italian cheesecake at this Little Italy classic in 1892. Once people thought of it as "too commercial," but now that so many pasticcerias in the neighborhood have met that big baker in the sky, many reviewers see this old-timer in a new light: "Walking up to Ferrara after a meal in Chinatown makes for a perfect end to an evening."

Desserts | Informal | little italy | 195 Grand St. | 212-226-6150 | www.ferraracafe.com | Open daily

Porchetta 7.4

It's worth the journey downtown for what's been dubbed "the most luscious sandwich in New York City." It's nothing but slices of pork, crunchy cracklings and fat stuffed between crusty bread slices, but it's "so good you want to die." In addition to being the source of be-all and end-all of porchetta, Sara Jenkins' closet-sized restaurant also serves soups and a vegetable dish of the day, like turnip tops or carrots with feta cheese. Our reviewers give just one caution: "You will need to take Lipitor if you visit this place on a regular basis."

Italian | Inexpensive | east village | 110 E. 7th St. | 212-777-2151 | www.porchettanyc.com | Lunch & Dinner daily

Zabar's Café 7.4

A short walk from the West Side museums, this conveniently placed coffee bar/lunch counter serves a number of items from the landmark delicatessen next door, like tasty breads, baked goods and coffee made from Zabar's famous blend. One downside is seriously cramped quarters; "Presumably the discomfort is to move customers through as quickly as possible," one reviewer theorized.

Café | Inexpensive | upper west side | 2245 Broadway | 212-787-2000 | www.zabars.com | Breakfast & Lunch daily

A Salt & Battery 7.3

By serving what our reviewers describe as "very nice fish and chips," "really good fish and chips" and even "great fish and chips," the two Brits who own this place have their fellow expats jumping with joy over portions of pollock, sole, haddock and whiting, all served with greasy, salty piles of you-know-what. Servers are "gruff but friendly," and reviewers say "it's worth putting up with them for one of the best/cheapest meals in the city."

British | Inexpensive | greenwich village | 112 Greenwich Ave. | 212-691-2713 | www.asaltandbattery.com | Lunch & Dinner daily

Amy's Bread   7.3

The reason to visit this pair of West Side bakery-cum-casual restaurants is the nearly 30 different types of homemade breads – organic miche, rustic Italian, whole wheat, oat pecan with golden raisins and prosciutto and black pepper twist, to name a few – "which do a terrific job of enhancing what's inside your sandwich" (serviceable ingredients like roast turkey or tuna salad). Okay, okay, we know that some of you also go there for the tasty pastries and other baked goods.

Bakery | Inexpensive | chelsea | Chelsea Market | 75 Ninth Ave. | 212-462-4338 | www.amysbread.com | Open daily

Barney Greengrass   7.3

Feast on Formica at this ancient Jewish-style appetizing store where you enjoy dishes like lox, eggs and onions and platters of smoked fish in a cramped dining room. But note: There have been grumblings about "fish that isn't as fresh as it used to be since Moe Greengrass passed away and his nephew took over." Still, it offers the classic New York Jewish power breakfast, and come Saturday and Sunday morning, you will find many of the city's top honchos brunching on lox, eggs and onions with their families.

Delicatessen | Inexpensive | upper west side | 541 Amsterdam Ave. | 212-724-4707 | www.barneygreengrass.com | Breakfast & Lunch Tue-Sun

City Bakery   7.3

Though our reviewers liked the breakfast pastries and the simple lunch fare of

sandwiches, salads and savory dishes like mac 'n' cheese, this restaurant's renown stems from what is commonly felt to be "the best hot chocolate in the city," made from a blend of various melted chocolates and cream. Some may find the libation "too rich," but sipped through the homemade marshmallow on top, it really hits the spot on a cold winter's day. A combo pretzel/croissant is a close second to the hot chocolate in popularity.

Bakery | Inexpensive | flatiron | 3 W. 18th St. | 212-366-1414 | www.thecitybakery.com | Breakfast & Lunch daily

Motorino   7.3

In the current competitive artisanal pizza environment, this popular Brooklyn pizzeria figured it'd gain an advantage by grabbing the idle oven left behind by Pizzeria Napoletana (which moved to San Francisco). Still, reviewers are split on Motorino, offering comments that range from "a good pizza and a comfortable environment" to "yummy but not particularly impressive. Crust was wayyyy too doughy and soft."

Pizzeria | Inexpensive | east village | 349 E. 12th St. | 212-777-2644 | www.motorinopizza.com | Lunch & Dinner daily

Taim   7.3

One of life's great choices awaits you at this simple Israeli restaurant: Should you order the falafel or the sabich sandwich, both of which come with an assortment of toppings ranging from hot sauce to feta cheese? "The new gold standard for falafel," said one reviewer, while another mentioned it in the same breath as the iconic L'As du Fallafel in Paris. They also serve "an exceptionally silky hummus," and the fries with the garlic aioli have "just the right amount of kick."

Israeli | Inexpensive | greenwich village | 222 Waverly Place | 212-691-6101 | www.taimfalafel.com | Lunch & Dinner daily

V & T   7.3

During the '60s and '70s, pizza culture in
NYC meant grabbing a slice at your local
pizzeria. When families wanted a fancier
place for dinner, they often chose a place
like V & T, which offered a full menu of
Italian fare and sold pizza only by the
pie. While that style of southern Italian
restaurant has virtually disappeared, V &
T has managed to hang on, and they are
still serving the same "thick, juicy pies" to
local residents and students and faculty
from nearby Columbia University.

Pizzeria | Moderate | morningside heights | 1024
Amsterdam Ave. | 212-666-8051 | www.vtpizzeri-
arestaurant.com | Lunch & Dinner daily

Crif Dogs   7.2

Unless a hot dog emporium makes its
own sausages, it rarely stands out. But
Crif's uniqueness factor comes from its
toppings and condiments, like a bacon-
wrapped hot dog with lettuce, tomato
and mayo, or the dog that comes with
tomato-molasses ketchup and deep-
fried mayo, named the Wylie Dufresne
(many of the creations are inspired by,
and named for, local chefs). A cool way
to consume them is with cocktails at the
PDT Bar next door – the dogs are passed
through an interior window.

Hot Dogs | Inexpensive | east village | 113 St.
Mark's Pl. | 212-614-2728 | www.crifdogs.com |
Lunch & Dinner daily

'wichcraft   7.1

When Tom Colicchio decided he wasn't
making enough money roasting meats
and vegetables at Craft, he opened these
upscale sandwich shops. The chef making your meatloaf sandwich probably
has a degree from a culinary school, and
when you add superior ingredients to the
mix, you end up with a better product
than the competition's. It's "a bit expensive" for what it is, but most people seem
to like the experience, except for the

waits, which can be as long as 30 minutes when they get super-busy.

Sandwiches | Inexpensive | midtown west |
Bryant Park | 11 W.40th St. | 212-780-0577 |
www.wichcraftnyc.com | Lunch daily

Adrienne's Pizzabar   7.0

The dearth of good places to eat in lower
Manhattan is an eternal problem, so
one can imagine the welcome afforded
this purveyor of "the best pizza in the
Financial District." Pies come in two
different types: 10-inch circular pies or
old-fashioned square ones, both available with toppings like sausage or broccoli rabe. It's so popular and perpetually
crowded that one reviewer recommended those who want pizza for lunch "call at
10:30 a.m. and reserve a few pies."

Pizzeria | Informal | Inexpensive | financial dis-
trict | 54 Stone St. | 212-248-3838 | www.adrien-
nespizzabar.com | Lunch & Dinner daily

"Co."   7.0

This is yet one more artisanal pizzeria
– this time from Sullivan Street Bakery
owner Jim Lahey. Fans say a "flavorful
crust" and" good combinations" (one
reviewer recommends the bianca with
a side of ricotta) offset long waits for
a table and high prices. But those who
don't like the style say that "the crust
that tastes like pastry dough" puts this
place somewhat lower on the pizza totem
pole, especially given the city's numerous
options for artisanal pies. In its favor are
a large, comfortable space with a broader
menu of starters and "much better service than the other pizzerias in town."

Pizzeria | Inexpensive | chelsea | 230 Ninth Ave.
| 212-243-1105 | www.co-pane.com | Lunch &
Dinner Tue-Sun

Hummus Place   7.0

To American diners, a bowl of hummus is
merely an appetizer that you dip pieces
of pita bread into. But it has a much

deeper meaning to Israeli nationals, who are happy to make it the focus of their meal. Hence these restaurants that serve the oily, garlicky chickpea spread with an assortment of different toppings, along with a handful of other vegetarian dishes like shakshuka.

Middle Eastern | Inexpensive | east village | 109 St. Marks Pl. | 212-529-9198 | www.hummusplace.com | Lunch and Dinner daily

Second Location: upper west side | 305 Amsterdam Ave. | 212-799-3335 | www.hummusplace.com | Lunch and Dinner daily

Third Location: West Village | 71 Seventh Ave. So. | 212-924-2033 | www.hummusplace.com | Lunch and Dinner daily

Mamoun's Falafel Restaurant   7.0

This Middle Eastern icon serves "the best falafel sandwich in the city." Open until 5:00 a.m., it typically attracts a long line of hipsters, NYU students, taxi drivers and others jonesing for a falafel fix. They also serve various spreads and grills, including a combo of hummus, falafel and "damn good schwarma" that's available in a platter or a combo sandwich.

Middle Eastern | Inexpensive | greenwich village | 119 Macdougal St. | 212-674-8685 | http://mamouns.com | Lunch & Dinner daily

Shopsins   7.0

Even though the namesake owner (immortalized in a *New Yorker* profile by Calvn Trillin) is in his 60s and the spring is gone from his step, the menu at Kenny Shopsin's Lower East Side lunch counter is still the same unusual mix of American luncheonette fare and regional dishes ranging from tacos to Thai curry. It's "an indescribable experience," and we're not sure how much longer Kenny will be able to keep at it, so we suggest you visit sooner than later.

Coffee Shop | Inexpensive | lower east side | 120 Essex St. | www.shopsins.com | Lunch Wed-Sun, Breakfast Wed-Sat

OTHER PLACES MENTIONED

Hill Country   6.9

Texas native Marc Glosserman was tired of not being able to find good barbecue in New York, so he quit his job in the telecommunications industry and opened Hill Country. Like its inspiration, Kreuz Market in Lockhart, Texas, it offers a number of smoked meats, but the focus is on the smoked brisket made by pit master Elizabeth Karmel (which begs the question of whether they have female pit masters in red states). You wait in line to order at a counter and then eat the food off brown butcher paper – without plates. Glosserman has been so successful he's recently opened Hill Country Chicken a few blocks away.

Barbecue | Inexpensive | chelsea | 30 W. 26th St. | 212-255-4544 | www.hillcountryny.com | Lunch & Dinner daily

Penelope   6.9

"Better than almost every diner in the city" is what one reviewer said about this breakfast and brunch specialist that features fare like pumpkin waffles and homemade granola. Lunch and dinner bring comfort-food classics such as mac 'n' cheese, chicken pot pie and burgers. It's super-popular, so expect a wait, especially on Saturday and Sunday mornings, when it's "flooded with recent college grads nursing their hangovers."

Coffee Shop | Inexpensive | murray hill | 159 Lexington Ave. | 212-481-3800 | www.penelopenyc.com | Open daily

Popover Café   6.9

This neighborhood restaurant, sort of "a poor man's Sarabeth's," is getting a bit worn around the edges. Specializing in the type of comfort cuisine that was popular with New Yorkers a generation ago, the menu features dishes like crab cake fritters and chicken "pop" pie (chicken pot pie in a popover). It's popular at breakfast, probably because the popovers are fresh from the oven, ready to be slathered with strawberry butter.

American | Inexpensive | upper west side | 551 Amsterdam Ave. | 212-595-8555 | www.popovercafe.com | Open daily

Amy Ruth's   6.8

Dig into the Ludicris (fried chicken wings) or the Melva Smith (savory jerk shrimp) at this Harlem classic where the dishes are named after celebrities. For breakfast there are waffles with an assortment of savory sidekicks ranging from smothered pork chops to chicken livers, while lunch and dinner bring sandwiches and heartier fare like stews. "A step up from Sylvia's [see below], if only a small one; it's possible to have a good meal here."

Southern | Inexpensive | harlem | 113 W. 116th St. | 212-280-8779 | www.amyruthsharlem.com | Open daily

Blue Smoke   6.8

Danny Meyer and Kenny Callaghan's ode to American barbecue offers a variety of different styles, including ribs prepared à la Memphis, Kansas City or Texas. Those seeking more refined fare can opt for entrées like seared salmon with grilled tomatillo-roasted almond sauce or a filet mignon with chipotle-béarnaise sauce. "It's not the best barbecue in the city," said one reviewer, "but the combination of good-enough food plus better service and amenities make it worth visiting."

Barbecue | Inexpensive | murray hill | 116 E. 27th St. | 212-447-7733 | www.bluesmoke.com | Lunch & Dinner daily

John's Pizzeria   6.8

While Lombardi's (see below) predates it by more than 20 years, John's was the pizzeria that made coal-oven pizza famous, and during the '80s and '90s, visiting meant long waits for a table. Now coal-oven pizzerias are everywhere, but many of our reviewers continue to prefer

John's, deeming it "still one of the best pizza joints in the world" and "a reference point for New York pizza."

Pizzeria | Inexpensive | greenwich village | 278 Bleecker St. | 212-243-1680 | www.johnsbrickoven-pizza.com | Lunch & Dinner daily

Patsy's Pizzeria   6.8

While its brick oven has been turning out crusty pies since 1933, this East Harlem legend vaulted in popularity in the 1970s – when many Manhattanites considered traveling up to Harlem a dangerous proposition – after the *New Yorker* mentioned it in a profile on music industry legend Ahmet Ertegun. Since then, however, numerous pizzerias in town have installed a coal oven, so now the only reason to venture uptown is to experience a "classic pie in a classic atmosphere."

Pizzeria | Inexpensive | east harlem | 2287 First Ave. | 212-534-9783 | www.thepatsyspizza.com | Dinner daily, Lunch Sat-Sun

J. G. Melon   6.7

One of the most famous burgers in New York can be found at this "cherished bar and grill" that is a holdover from the 1970s. It's always crowded, so expect a short-to-medium wait for a table. They also offer simple pub fare like salads and steaks, but we would guess that 75% of the people order the burger.

Hamburgers | Inexpensive | upper east side | 1291 Third Ave. | 212-744-0585 | Lunch & Dinner daily

Nicky's Vietnamese   6.7
Sandwiches

Nicky's is OAD's number two among the various banh mi places in the city. Those who prefer a more authentic street-food scene said, "It's too gentrified compared to the competition," while others complained about "bread that could be better." On the other (positive) hand, "either of the pork sandwiches are quite tasty," especially when washed down with a

Vietnamese iced coffee.

Vietnamese | Inexpensive | east village | 150 E. 2nd St. | 212-388-1088 | www.nickyssandwiches. com | Lunch & Dinner daily

Chop't Creative Salad Company   6.6

"They turn a salad into an art form" at this casual spot so popular that the line at lunchtime often snakes out the door. One reviewer told us,"It's easy to make yourself a nice healthy lunch – or you can say screw it and tell them to throw in the fried chicken and blue cheese." They also offer a full slate of sandwiches like the Kebab Cobb: chopped grilled chicken, feta cheese, red onions and pita chips.

Salad | Inexpensive | flatiron | 24 E. 17th St. | 646-336-5523 | www.choptsalad.com | Dinner daily, Lunch Mon-Fri

Papaya King   6.6

In 1932, after falling in love with papaya juice while on vacation in Miami, Gus Poulos introduced New Yorkers to the delights of tropical drinks. Three years later, Gus took a German bride and added frankfurters to his menu. The rest is culinary history. Now, nearly 80 years later, you can hardly walk by his stand without seeing a line of people waiting to order "a combo" (a pair of hot dogs with sauerkraut and a 16-oz. drink).

Fruit Drinks/Hot Dogs | Inexpensive | upper east side | 179 E. 86th St. | 212-369-0648 | www. papayaking.com | Open daily

Second Avenue Deli   6.6

In an era in which kosher delis have steadily disappeared, this Lebewohl-family-owned icon holds the fort, even if it has moved from its historic Lower East Side locale to a Murray Hill side street. The new quarters are a bit clean and shiny for those craving a retro experi-ence, but they have managed to transfer enough haimishkeit from the downtown

location to make a visit worthwhile when you're in the mood for a corned beef sandwich or a bowl of cabbage borscht.

Delicatessen | Inexpensive | murray hill | 162 E. 33rd St. | 212-689-9000 | www.2ndavedeli.com | Open daily

Viand   6.6

Despite the basic diner fare, they pay-enough attention to the food to warrant a mention. Roast turkey's the specialty, and the burgers are a step up from those at other coffee shops. The unusually nar-row space comes with a hilarious owner reminiscent of the Greek diner owner in the old *Saturday Night Live* skits.

Coffee Shop | Inexpensive | upper east side | 673 Madison Ave. | 212-751-6822 | Open daily

Second Location: upper east side | 1011 Madison Ave. | 212-249-8250 | Open daily

Westville   6.6

This trio of coffee shops offers eclectic menus featuring everything from egg salads, burgers and hot dogs to larger plates like grilled pork chops smothered with onions and mushrooms. Always packed with neighborhood types (Village yuppies on the West Side and hipsters on the East Side), each makes for "a great neighborhood spot" but not much more.

Coffee Shop | Inexpensive | west village | 210 W. 10th St. | 212-741-7971 | www.westvillenyc.com | Open daily

Second Location: east village | 173 Avenue A | 212-677-2933 | www.westvillenyc.com | Open daily

Third Location: chelsea | 246 W. 18th St. | 212-924-2133 | www.westvillenyc.com | Open daily

Alice's Tea Cup   6.5

Given that the Alice referred to is the one from Wonderland, it isn't unusual for our reviewers to include the word "cute" in their comments – as in "what a cute little spot" and "a cute place for breakfast or brunch" to "a sometimes too-cute atmosphere." There are "terrific scones," and in addition to providing "exquisite people-watching," it makes for a good place to take out-of-town guests. The one drawback is the lines: Waits can be up to two hours on the weekends.

Tea Salon | Inexpensive | upper east side | 156 E. 64th St. | 212-486-9200 | www.alicesteacup.com | Open daily

Second Location: upper west side | 102 W. 73rd St. | 212-799-3006 | www.alicesteacup.com | Open daily

NoHo Star   6.5

A strange mélange of dishes are offered at this bustling restaurant that serves continuously throughout the day, with the menu of omelets, salads and light entrees supplemented by Chinese fare in the evenings. Reviewer comments were all over the map, but it drew praise for a "user-friendly menu", along with "one of the best hamburgers in the city." It's the only place we know outside New England that serves Indian pudding and ginger ale made with freshly grated ginger root.

American/Chinese | Inexpensive | greenwich village | 330 Lafayette St. | 212-925-0070 | www. nohostar.com | Lunch & Dinner daily

5 Napkin Burger   6.4

After the hamburger they were serving at Nice Matin (see above) caused a mini-sensation, that restaurant's owners opened this burger-centric offshoot. The "slightly gamey flavor" indicates that skirt steak or tenderloin is included in the grind, and there's also a veggie burger as well as patties made from tuna, turkey and lamb. The Theater District location makes it useful as a place to grab a casual meal before the curtain goes up.

Hamburger | Inexpensive | midtown west | 630 Ninth Ave. | 212.757.2277 | www.5napkinburger. com | Lunch & Dinner daily

Second Location: upper west side | 2315 Broadway | 212-333-4485 | www.5napkinburger.com | Lunch & Dinner daily

Carnegie Deli   6.4

Immortalized in Woody Allen's 1984 film *Broadway Danny Rose*, this institution hasn't been the same since owner Leo Steiner's untimely death in 1987, as evidenced by comments about the once-cherished pastrami that is now considered "strictly for tourists." The environment hasn't changed, but as one reviewer put it," when Leo died, "the tam [Yiddish for taste] did, too."

Delicatessen | Inexpensive | midtown west | 854 Seventh Ave. | 212-757-2245 | www.carnegiedeli. com | Open daily

Daisy May's BBQ USA   6.4

Having made a name serving some of the best steaks in the city at the Penthouse Executive Club, Adam Perry Lang now has "carved himself a niche" by serving real pit barbecue on Manhattan's far West Side. He's a nice Jewish boy from Long Island (who got the barbecue bug while attending university), so it shouldn't surprise anyone that brisket is the best cut.

Barbecue | Inexpensive | midtown west | 623 11th Ave. | 212-977-1500 | www.daisymaysbbq.com | Lunch & Dinner daily

Gray's Papaya   6.4

When it comes to New York City tropical drink/hot dog emporiums, Gray's plays Avis to Papaya King's Hertz. It also offers orange, grape, piña colada and banana daiquiri drinks, as well as the skinny hot dogs that one reviewer described as "salty, meaty and so good." While the concept isn't as unique as it once was, reviewers admit that "It's hard to walk by without stopping in for a dog and some type of juice."

Fruit Drinks/Hot Dogs | Inexpensive | upper west side | 2090 Broadway | 212-799-0243 | Open daily

Lombardi's   6.4

Having equipped his restaurant with the

first coal-fired pizza oven in the U.S. back in 1905, Lombardi's founder Gennaro Lombardi could be called the father of American pizza. Unfortunately, when it comes to his venue today, reviewers say "a historic site" is not enough and offer comments like "nice crust but little flavor" and "yet another sub-par, touristy place." But despite those comments – and the presence of numerous other pizzerias in the 'hood – you will always find a "significant wait for a table" here.

Pizzeria | Inexpensive | little italy | 32 Spring St. | 212-941-7994 | www.firstpizza.com | Dinner daily, Lunch Sat-Sun

Artie's Delicatessen   6.3

From the 1960s to the 1990s, every New York City neighborhood with a Jewish population had a kosher delicatessen. Artie's, unlike other holdovers from that era, is run by a younger generation and is considered "part theme park, part deli." Though the food is nothing more than the type of commercial fare you can find all over the city, people pretty much agree that "having an agreeable deli in your neighborhood" isn't such a bad thing.

Delicatessen | Inexpensive | upper west side | 2290 Broadway | 212-579-5959 | www.arties.com | Open daily

Norma's   6.3

This breakfast and brunch specialist has one of the most amazing-looking menus you will ever read – including a $1,000 omelet with caviar (which they "dare you to put on your expense account"). Unfortunately, ingredients that are only "slightly better than what a diner would serve" hold it back from being more highly rated. Add "atrocious waits" to the mix, even on weekdays, when the restaurant is full of hotel guests and people having business meetings at breakfast.

American | Casual | Moderate | midtown west | Le Parker Meridien | 118 W. 57th St | 212-708-7460 | www.normasnyc.com | Breakfast & Lunch daily

Sarabeth's Kitchen   6.3

We guess that the people waiting on the excruciatingly long lines for weekend brunch at this mini-chain haven't heard that the "the quality of food got worse" when Sarabeth Levine sold her interest in the restaurants to concentrate on her prepared-foods business. Nominally at least, the menu hasn't changed, however: It's the same mix of baked goods and egg dishes for breakfast and light entrées for lunch and dinner.

American | Inexpensive | upper east side | 1295 Madison Ave. | 212-410-7335 | www.sarabeths.com | Open daily

Second Location: upper west side | 423 Amsterdam Ave. | 212-496-6280 | www.sarabethswest.com | Open daily

Third Location: midtown west | 40 Central Park South | 212-826-5959 | www.sarabethscps.com | Open daily

Serendipity 3   6.3

A tourist attraction that's built its reputation on its Frrrozen Hot Chocolate. But to show you how irrelevant the food is, we didn't know they served anything else until we read the comments by our reviewers! One told us, "It's the perfect place to take your high-school sweetheart after a movie or a show, provided you're still in high school."

Dessert | Inexpensive | upper east side | 225 E. 60th St. | 212-838-3531 | www.serendipity3.com | Lunch & Dinner daily

Bubby's Pie Company   6.2

Being kid-friendly and being open 'round the clock are definitely among the reasons for the unbelievable popularity of this place. But these features aren't enough for our reviewers: "Every dish – from the appetizers to the entrées to the desserts – is mediocre, and the service is generally no better than average."

Coffee Shop | Inexpensive | tribeca | 120 Hudson St. | 212-219-0666 | www.bubbys.com | Open daily

Corner Bistro   6.2

Though its reputation borders on the national, our reviewers are less than impressed by "the most overrated burger in the world, let alone New York City." Still, the place is jammed, often with drunken students – which might explain its popularity; one reviewer told us, "The burgers taste much better after you consume massive quantities of alcohol."

Hamburgers | Inexpensive | west village | 331 W. 4th St. | 212-242-9502 | www.cornerbistro. ypguides.net | Lunch & Dinner daily

Joe's Pizza   6.2

Since the proliferation of upscale coal- and brick-oven pizzerias, it's become difficult to find good pizza by the slice. Joe's serves a classic example, described by one reviewer as "up there with the very best old-style New York pizzerias." Many of our Village-based reviewers are regulars; one of them often drops by for a slice on the way home, even after he has eaten a full meal at another restaurant.

Pizzeria | Inexpensive | greenwich village | 137 Seventh Ave. | 718-398-9198 | Lunch & Dinner daily

P. J. Clarke's   6.2

Though it was once considered to have one of the best hamburgers in the city, these days our reviewers say things like "The burger has gone way downhill," and burgers are "cooked to order, so long as your order is well-done." Adding insult to injury, "Even the beer is bad."

Hamburgers | Inexpensive | midtown east | 915 Third Ave. | 212-317-1616 | www.pjclarkes.com | Lunch & Dinner daily

BLT Burger   6.1

This simple burger joint in the heart of the Village started out with a bang. But like everything else in the BLT chain, the quality has diminished over time. "Tacky décor" doesn't help, and the experience caused one reviewer to call the restaurant "a slight on the name of chef Laurent Tourondel" (who, by the way, is no longer associated with the BLT group).

Hamburger | Inexpensive | greenwich village | 470 Sixth Ave. | 212-243-8226 | www.bltburger. com | Lunch & Dinner daily

Le Pain Quotidien   6.1

Considering how many locations this Belgian-owned chain operates, we're always surprised at the high standards the restaurants are able to maintain. In the morning, they serve up a variety of pastries (croissants, pains au chocolat), which you can supplement with a soft-boiled egg, granola or oatmeal and wash down with steamy bowls of café au lait. Lunch tends to run toward soups, salads and sandwiches, many served on the delicious baguettes they sell at the front of the store.

Bakery | Inexpensive | upper east side | 1131 Madison Ave. | 212-327-4900 | www.lepainquoti-dien.com | Breakfast & Lunch daily

Second Location: flatiron | 38 E. 19th St. | ABC Carpet & Home | 212-673-7900 | www.lepainquo-tidien.com | Breakfast & Lunch daily

Third Location: upper west side | 60 W. 65th | 212-721-4001 | www.lepainquotidien.com | Breakfast & Lunch daily

Check website for additional locations

Tea & Sympathy   6.1

Ever come across a shop in a foreign city that specializes in selling American food products? Well, this is a British equivalent for this country, offering dishes like Welsh rarebit and tweed and kettle pie that "make you feel like you're dining at a pub in London." In the afternoon you can drop in for a spot of tea and crumpets, and the small grocery next door allows the truly homesick to stock up on necessities like a tin of mushy peas.

British | Inexpensive | west village | 108-110 Greenwich Ave. | 212-989-9735 | www.teaandsym-pathy.com | Lunch & Dinner daily, Breakfast Sat-Sun

Dinosaur Bar-B-Que 6.0

While the food at this bustling Harlem restaurant is perfectly acceptable, it is "nowhere as good" as the 'cue served at the Syracuse original. Oddly enough, the "cheesy atmosphere" and" no-frills environment" are considered pluses by our reviewers, as are the three different microbrews on tap. A location under the West Side Highway makes it convenient for commuters on their way home to Westchester or northern New Jersey.

Barbecue | Inexpensive | chelsea | 700 W. 125th St. | 212-694-1777 | www.dinosaurbarbque.com | Lunch & Dinner daily

Zum Schneider 6.1

Lots of beer, lots of links, lots of wursts and lots of people hung over the next morning from drinking beer into the wee hours. While it's a lot of fun, nobody likes the food much, and someone even called "the beer selection disappointing." Still, it's a good place for a party – just not a dinner party.

German | Inexpensive | east village | 107 Avenue C | 212-598-1098 | www.zumschneider.com | Dinner daily, Lunch Sat-Sun

Veselka 6.0

One doesn't usually associate hipsters with Ukrainian food, but the unusual combo defines this East Village luncheonette. Go and witness waitresses with Polish accents serving pierogi, blintzes, goulash and Hunter's Stew to a combination of fellow countrymen and young diners sporting spiky hair, the latest tattoos and immense appetites.

Ukrainian Coffee Shop | Inexpensive | east village | 144 Second Ave. | 212-228-9682 | www.veselka.com | Open daily

Stage Deli 5.9

What you will find here is the same commercial, kosher-style delicatessen available all over the city, the difference being that the sandwiches are named after celebrities who eat there – like the Howard Stern (pastrami, brisket and Muenster cheese – can we say bleah?) or the Adam Sandler (Nova Scotia salmon, sturgeon and onions). It will do in a pinch, but ultimately eating here is more about the restaurant's connection to show business than about delicious food.

Delicatessen | Inexpensive | midtown west | 834 Seventh Ave. | 212-245-7850 | www.stagedeli.com | Open daily

Hallo Berlin 5.8

The menu is dominated by sausages and beer at this very casual restaurant in Clinton. In addition to appetizers like the eight types of sausages on offer, there are herrings, soups and potato pancakes, along with entrées like goulash and schnitzel. Some think the food is on the bland side, but as one reviewer told us, "You could do wurst" when you're in the mood for German food.

German | Inexpensive | midtown west | 626 Tenth Ave. | 212-977-1944 | www.halloberlinrestaurant.com | Lunch & Dinner daily

Pop Burger 5.8

Order a hamburger at this venue and you'll be seeing double. That's right – an order comes with two slider-size burgers that you can supplement with "the best fries in the world" and a creamy shake. A bonus is the "bizarre atmosphere," a function of the shop's hyper-modern design and the graphics on display.

Hamburgers | Inexpensive | upper east side | 14 E. 58th St. | 212-991-6644 | www.popburger.com | Lunch & Dinner daily

RUB BBQ 5.8

Paul Kirk is a Kansas City barbecue legend, but his restaurant hasn't caught on with our reviewers. If we had to put our finger on their dissatisfaction, we would say it was meat dried-out from being smoked too long. There were also complaints about the "cafeteria-style space that offers few or no amenities." The one item that attracted praise: the "superb Kansas City–style burnt brisket ends."

Barbecue | Inexpensive | chelsea | 208 W. 23rd St. | 212-524-4300 | www.rubbbq.net | Lunch & Dinner daily

Sylvia's   5.8

What is arguably the best-known soul food restaurant in the country has turned into a tourist attraction that is "a shadow of its former self." As one disappointed diner put it, "Sylvia might be an icon, but sadly, the food at her eponymous landmark isn't worthy of her name."

Southern | Inexpensive | harlem | 328 Lenox Ave. | 212-996-0660 | www.sylviassoulfood.com | Lunch & Dinner daily

Two Boots   5.7

While a minority claims this pizza chain is underrated, the consensus is that Two Boots is now "a case study in the pitfalls of over-expansion. What used to be funky, soulful and tasty is now just a gimmicky sham on top of flavorless crust."

Pizzeria | Inexpensive | greenwich village | 42 Avenue A | 212-254-1919 | www.twoboots.com | Lunch & Dinner daily

Veniero's   5.7

It's the "yummy Italian cheesecake," both regular and Sicilian style, that's drawing them to this cafe that dates back to a long-gone era. The rest of the pastries (cookies, sfogliatelle, canolis, etc.), which are also available for take out, are "no different than what you find at dozens of Italian bakeries around the city."

Dessert | Inexpensive | east village | 342 E. 11th St. | 212-674-7070 | www.venierospastry.com | Open daily

Eisenberg Sandwich Shop   5.6

While everyone loves the depression-era

décor, there is a lack of consensus about this classic luncheonette. Fans recommend it for sentimental reasons, praising fare that "dates back to a time when no one had heard of arugula."

Coffee Shop | Inexpensive | flatiron | 174 Fifth Ave. | 212-675-5096 | www.eisenbergsnyc.com | Open daily except closed Sat-Sun dinner

Duke's   5.4

This place opened when finding ribs, chicken and pulled pork wasn't so easy. But "now that the city has a plethora of real barbecue, where does Duke's fit in?" They serve "serviceable food," at best, in a "noisy, frat-house setting."

Barbecue | Inexpensive | gramercy | 99 E. 19th St. | 212-260-2922 | Lunch & Dinner daily

Ben's Deli   5.3

This Garment District kosher deli is not particularly popular with reviewers. While a number of them expressed their displeasure with it, the one comment that stood out was "dreck – it doesn't even deserve the designation of deli."

Delicatessen | Inexpensive | garment district | 209 W. 38th St. | 212-398-2367 | www.bensdeli.net | Lunch & Dinner daily

Friend of a Farmer   5.3

This transplant from Roslyn should really be called Friend of a Commercial Farmer, as the ingredients are basically the same stuff served at just about every mundane diner in the metro area. Some applaud the "hearty, homey fare," but others complain that "It's as if someone airlifted a restaurant from Long Island and dropped it in the middle of Manhattan."

Breakfast | Inexpensive| gramercy | 77 Irving Pl. | 212-477-2188 | www.friendofafarmernyc.com | Open daily

Stand   5.2

While it's a terrific concept and a terrific

space, our reviewers are not especially impressed by this hamburger restaurant. A "better-than-average list of sides," like sweet potato fries and mac 'n' cheese, cuts in its favor, but that wasn't enough to stop some from opining that it is "overpriced and underwhelming."

Hamburgers | Inexpensive | greenwich village | 24 E. 12th St. | 212-488-5900 | www.standburger. com | Lunch & Dinner daily

Fanelli's Café   5.1

One of the few remaining old-school corner bars (it's been there for more than a century) in Manhattan is populated by frat boys, tourists and locals. There is "reasonably good pub food," including "greasy burgers" served in a "timeless atmosphere. It's always jam-packed, especially on weekend evenings.

Hamburger | Inexpensive | soho | 94 Prince Street | 212-226-9412 | Lunch & Dinner daily

Max Brenner: Chocolate   5.0
by the Bald Man

"Overly sweet," "overly crowded" and" overly hyped" is how reviewers described this dessert emporium. They serve dinner entrées, but one reviewer claimed that's "a ploy to get unsuspecting diners to order the cloyingly sweet desserts." Another who gave it a rating of must avoid said, "If I have to explain this rating, you deserve to go to the restaurant."

Dessert | Inexpensive | east village | 841 Broadway | 212-388-0030 | www.maxbrenner.com | Open daily

Sarge's Deli   5.0

While they serve a full assortment of Jewish-style sandwich meats at this 24-hour delicatessen, a Murray Hill institution, our reviewers have so little respect for the food that someone told us "I would prefer to starve" rather than eat here. Those who feel differently find it a convenient place to grab a corned beef

sandwich or chicken in the pot if they happen to get hungry at 4:00 a.m.

Delicatessen | Inexpensive | murray hill | 548 Third Ave. | 212-679-0442 | www.sargesdeli.com | Open daily

Wildwood Barbeque   5.0

What does the B. R. Guest organization do when it has to fill an empty space on Park Avenue South? Well, it steals a pit master from Hill Country and creates a thematic restaurant based on Texas-style barbecue. At best, they do an acceptable job of it, but "The barbecue's a bit watered down" and there's a feeling that the crowd isn't filled with the type of diehard 'cue lovers that other places nearby (i.e., the aforementioned Hill Country) attract.

Barbecue | Inexpensive | gramercy | 225 Park Ave. S. | 212-533-2500 | www.wildwoodbbq.com | Lunch & Dinner daily

Jackson Hole   4.8

Eight locations around the city operate under the Jackson Hole name, but this is the original. Their contribution to our dining culture is the "big blob of meat" that, after being formed into a patty, is cooked under a metal ice-cream-sundae cup. If you like "enormous and very greasy burgers," this is your place.

Hamburgers | Inexpensive | upper east side | 232 E. 64th St. | 212-371-7187 | www.jacksonholeburgers.com | Lunch & Dinner daily

Rare Bar & Grill   4.6

This place has the perfect name for a restaurant that specializes in hamburgers, yet a number of our reviewers find the patties to be among the worst in the city. "It's a great concept, but the quality of the meat just doesn't cut it" is how many in our survey described the experience.

Hamburgers | Inexpensive| murray hill | 303 Lexington Ave. | 212-481-1999 | www.rarebarandgrill.com | Lunch & Dinner daily

New York City: Outer Boroughs NY

AN IMPORTANT DESTINATION

Peter Luger   96.1

When it comes to places to eat corn-fed beef, anyone who tells you they know a restaurant that serves better steak than Peter Luger doesn't know what they are talking about. Whenever a shipment of prime short loins arrives at any of the top meat wholesalers in New York City, Luger is given "first pick," meaning that their buyer is allowed to walk through the wholesaler's cold box and choose the ones that look the best. Of course, that doesn't mean every steak is perfect, but the exceptionally high rating for a steakhouse is a good indication of how often the system works correctly.

In addition to the "ethereal porterhouse steaks," the menu offers quirky starters and side dishes, from hot-house tomatoes that one slathers with a sickly sweet steak sauce and horseradish to hash brown potatoes, that round out what is a uniquely American regional dining experience. Reservations are tough to come by, making lunch a good option; that's also when they serve one of the city's best hamburgers, made from the trimmings of 28-day-aged steaks and priced at an über-bargain $9.50.

Steakhouse | Informal | Expensive | williamsburg | 178 Broadway | 718-387-7400 | www.peterluger.com | Lunch & Dinner daily

RECOMMENDED

The Kitchen at Brooklyn Fare   91.5

By day, it's a commercial kitchen that services a grocery/gourmet shop; at night, it turns into a restaurant where 18 lucky diners sit at the kitchen pass and watch the Bouley-trained César Ramirez turn out a dinner of 18–20 small-plate courses that change daily. Ramirez's menu is heavy on fish and seafood dishes, which is not all that surprising given his training. The comments were almost uniformly positive: The Kitchen was described as a cuisine that is "creative yet tethered to traditional technique" and a "friendly price point," plus a BYO-only policy makes it "one of the best quality-to-price ratio" meals you will find in the New York metropolitan area.

New American | Informal | Expensive | downtown brooklyn | 200 Schemerhorn St. | 718-243-0050 | www.brooklynfare.com | Open daily

SriPraPhai   91.3

This is easily the best Thai restaurant in New York – and along with places like Lotus of Siam in Las Vegas and Jitlada in Los Angeles, a contender for the best in the country. People from every part of the city regularly ride the subway out to Woodside for the delicious soups, noodle dishes and vast assortment of curries along with pastries from an on-premises bakery. One reviewer opined that what sets SriPraPhai apart is "a menu with tons of choices where they aren't using the same five sauces over and over again." No wonder the place is always jammed with a combination of Thai nationals, hipsters and foodies who are searching for the perfect bowl of tom yum. The legendary banana sticky rice has been known to cool a palate that has been exposed to the most incendiary of dishes.

Thai | Informal | Moderate | woodside | 64-13 39th Ave. | 718-899-9599 | www.sripraphairestaurant.com | Lunch & Dinner Thu-Tue

Dressler   91.0

Before coming here, Polo Dobkin toiled in the kitchens of Gramercy Tavern. The time he spent there shows in his New American menu, which features dishes like house-smoked black cod with a potato galette and horseradish and black sea bass with white asparagus, Jerusalem artichoke, fingerlings and black trumpet mushroom vinaigrette. The upscale décor is more in keeping with a restaurant in TriBeCa than Brooklyn, as is the cost of the entrées, which were described as "Manhattan prices in Williamsburg." An added bonus is a location on Broadway, which makes it a good backup choice if the wait is too long at Luger or The Diner.

New American | Casual | Moderate | williamsburg | 149 Broadway | 718-384-6343 | www.dresslernyc.com | Dinner daily, Brunch Sun

Al Di La   90.9

Brooklyn residents will point to numerous restaurants that are worth a trip to their borough, and one that Manhattanites are quick to agree about is this no-reservation Italian in Park Slope. The Venice-inspired menu includes dishes like malfatti (gnocchi made from Swiss chard and ricotta), squid ink risotto "that will make you feel like you're sitting alongside the Grand Canal" and entrées like hake filet baked with cherry tomatoes or a grilled balsamic-glazed skirt steak. The warm and friendly service is most welcome, especially since you need something to cheer you up after your long wait for a table.

Italian | Informal | Moderate | park slope | 248 Fifth Ave. | 718-783-4565 | www.aldilatrattoria.com | Dinner daily, Lunch Wed-Mon

Prime Meats   90.8

When the two Franks of Spuntino fame (see below) decided to expand beyond Italian small plates, they went down the block and opened this German-influenced steakhouse that serves "well-made, farm-to-table versions of German specialties" like sauerbraten and pork schnitzel. Those who are really hungry can roll up their sleeves with a 36-day-aged côte de boeuf or a Belle Rouge chicken that has been brined in pickle juice before being roasted. Other than one person who said the No-reservation and no-credit card policy means the aggravation factor is as high as the quality," we have yet to find a reviewer who didn't enjoy the place.

German/Steakhouse | Informal | Expensive | carroll gardens | 465 Court St. | 718-254-0327 | www.frankspm.com | Open daily except lunch Fri-Sun

Roberta's   90.6

Local hipsters and the occasional straggler from out of town are quick to crowd into this converted warehouse in Brooklyn's Bushwick section for "top-flight wood-burning-oven pizzas," many of which are offered with unusual toppings like ramps with sausage or double garlic, mushrooms, jalapeños and sopressata picante. But savvier diners note that while the pizzas are delicious, "The focus should be on Carlo Mirachi's creative cuisine." Mirachi's dishes – which include oysters with Meyer Lemon sorbet and his own take on fried chicken – are so tasty that it is common to hear reviewers say "He's a young chef to watch" and "His cooking is as exciting as anywhere in the city"

Italian | Informal | Moderate | bushwick | 261 Moore St. | 718-417-1118 | www.robertaspizza.com | Lunch & Dinner daily

The Diner   90.2

Well before Williamsburg was overflowing with places to eat, the people who run this restaurant had the vision to take an old broken-down diner and open a market-driven restaurant in it. A dozen years later, reviewers are still enjoying the "incredible ingredients," while offering comments like "a perfect spot for all meals. The pork breakfast hash was revolutionary in my dining life. Great steaks, yummy mussels, outstanding cocktails. Always, always good" and "The setting is warm, welcoming and interesting, the beer and wine selection great; the food is consistently prepared with care and precision, and on top of that the wait staff is friendly, knowledgeable and relaxed."

New American | Informal | Moderate | williamsburg | 85 Broadway | 718-486-3077 | www.dinernyc.com | Lunch & Dinner daily

TOP LOCAL CHOICE

Blue Ribbon Sushi   89.5

There's a split of opinion about this sushi duo (the other's in SoHo) from the Bromberg brothers. One fan called the SoHo location "one of my favorite downtown restaurants," while another countered with "It's difficult to recommend B-quality sushi." Many frequenters favor the more gimmicky fare, like rolls of yellowtail with straw mushrooms or lobster, shiso and caviar. Still, even if it's not a serious sushi experience, it's handy if you're in the neighborhood, especially this branch in Park Slope, which suffers from a shortage of adequate raw fish experiences.

Japanese | Informal | Moderate | park slope | 119 Sullivan St. | 212-343-0404 | www.blueribbonrestaurants.com | Lunch & Dinner daily

Frankies Spuntino   89.5

"Not pretentious, just delicious" is what reviewers say about the "simple, honest Italian-inspired cooking" at this Carroll Gardens favorite. The two chefs who run the place (both named Frank) are among the most entertaining owners you will meet, and they offer diners "a dazzling array of small plates," including sweet potato and sage ravioli in a parmesan broth and pork braciola marinara. Beloved by people who live in the neighborhood, it has transcended being just another local joint and become a destination for many diners.

Italian | Informal | Moderate | carroll gardens | 457 Court St. | 718-403-0033 | www.frankiesspuntino. com | Lunch & Dinner daily

The Grocery   89.5

There was a time when finding contemporary cooking prepared by a trained chef in this area of Brooklyn meant – traveling into Manhattan. But Sharon Pachter and Charles Kiely changed that in 1999 when they opened this restaurant. And while the Boerum Hill-Carroll Gardens area is now bustling with good places to eat, they are still serving the unique mix of farm-to-table and Mediterranean cuisine they picked up when they were working for Peter Hoffman at Savoy. Reviewers say the "highly accomplished food" served in a setting described as "informal in a good way" makes it one of the top spots on Smith Street.

Mediterranean | Informal | Moderate | carroll gardens | 288 Smith St. | 718-596-3335 | http://thegroceryrestaurant.com | Dinner Tue-Sat, Lunch Thu-Sat

Marlow & Sons   89.5

Like its better-known sibling, The Diner (see above), located directly next door, this bodega/wine bar/oyster bar/tavern is always packed. The "sparse menu" includes a handful of main dishes, which happy diners wash down with "out-of-this-world cocktails." Some panned the cuisine as being "overhyped farm-to-table," but one person told us, "The glibness of it all – the décor, the wait staff, etc.– bothers me to no end, yet I keep going back to this place for their excellent brick chicken and market salad."

New American | Informal | Moderate | williamsburg | 81 Broadway | 718-384-1441 | http://marlowand-sons.com | Open daily

Ping's Seafood   89.5

Aficionados of the cuisine will tell you that the best Chinese cooking in the city can be found at this corner restaurant in Elmhurst. What sets Ping's apart are the unique dishes created by its chef/owner, like a casserole of lobster and taro cake sautéed in X.O. sauce or a steamed Dungeness crab served atop a bed of chow fun with a fresh garlic sauce. The culinary prowess on display is a step up from other Chinese restaurants, as evidenced by a top New York City chef pronouncing the cooking "amazingly clean." Note: They operate a Manhattan location, but the cooking is not as compelling there.

Chinese | Informal | Moderate | elmhurst | 83-02 Queens Blvd. | 718-396-1238 | Lunch & Dinner daily

Saul   89.5

After working with David Bouley and Eric Ripert, Saul Bolton abandoned the bright lights of haute cuisine for the friendly confines of Boerum Hill, where his French-inspired menu features seared Hudson Valley foie gras with sweet and sour prunes and caramelized Block Island swordfish with kale, chorizo and a pine-nut condiment. The level of cooking is "surprisingly high for a Brooklyn location," and more than one reviewer claims it's "the best of the numerous restaurants in the area."

New American | Casual | Moderate | cobble hill | 140 Smith St. | 718-935-9844 | www.saulrestaurant.com | Dinner daily

Asian Jewels   89.0

Valet parking is the first sign that this Hong Kong-style seafooder is more upscale than your typical Chinese restaurant. The second: The tanks of fish that are filled with jumbo shrimp, king crab, giant Australian lobsters and what the waiter calls Hong Kong snapper, which tilts the scales at $80 a pound. During the day they serve "some of the best dim sum in the city," but the most fun can be had in the evening when a party of six to eight can slowly spin the lazy Susan in the middle of the table, sampling from platters holding those giant crustaceans.

Chinese | Informal | Moderate | flushing | 133-30 39th Ave. | 718-359-8600 | Lunch & Dinner daily

General Greene   89.0

With its small plates menu featuring dishes like salt and pepper pork ribs with sumac yogurt, roast cod with creamed grits and a center-cut pork chop with Italian hot peppers and escarole, "There's something for everyone to eat at this unusual restaurant," which is typically brimming with young couples who have moved to Fort Greene. No visit would be complete without a quick stop at the small grocery store in back, where they sell locally made ingredients (as in, made in Brooklyn).

Eclectic | Informal | Moderate | fort greene | 229 DeKalb Ave. | 718-222-1510 | www.thegeneralgreene.com | Open daily

Locanda Vini e Olii   89.0

This funny little trattoria located in an old corner pharmacy does its best to make you feel you're in Italy. The food is quirky – starters include tuna salami and lamb prosciutto – and the owners use D.O.C.G. ingredients whenever they can. The wines are just as unusual as the food. There were some complaints about the size of the portions, with one person opining "when they said they were small plates they really meant it" and another complaining of "second-class treatment" unless you're friends with the owner.

Italian | Informal | Moderate | fort greene | 129 Gates Ave. | 718-622-9202 | www.locandany.com | Dinner Tue-Sun

Noodle Pudding   89.0

Reviewers shower praise on this "solid pan-Italian" that features the cuisine of both northern and southern Italy. The trattoria-style menu includes classic pasta dishes like angel hair with pomodoro or lasagna Bolognese, while mains might be osso buco or rabbit braised with tomatoes, garlic and herbs. The no-reservation policy and a price point that's 15% lower than similar restaurants in the neighborhood mean you can expect to wait for a table if you don't get there before the dinner rush.

Italian | Informal | Moderate | brooklyn heights | 38 Henry St. | 718-625-3737 | Dinner Tue-Sun

River Café   89.0

The current state of the River Café must surely make New York foodies sad. Because of its rich, 34-year history at the forefront of the New American cuisine movement, including having had the likes of Larry Forgione, Charlie Palmer, David Burke and Rick Moonen in charge of the kitchen, it pains us to read comments like "If it weren't for the views no one would go there." People do still praise the Sunday brunch (maybe the bar is lower when it comes to eggs Benedict). Otherwise, the reviewer who said, "Have a drink and enjoy the view, and then jump on the subway and eat someplace else" seems to be on the right track.

New American | Casual | Expensive | dumbo | 1 Water St. | 718-522-5200 | www.rivercafe.com | Lunch & Dinner daily

Applewood   88.5

David Shea's New American market cuisine features dishes like veal sweetbreads with English pea purée and chili oil or grilled Vermont pork with braised collard greens and bacon smoked with the wood the restaurant is named after. Brooklynites assure us, "It's worth the trek from Manhattan" to eat at his charming restaurant. Meanwhile, Manhattanites counter with "It might be a neighborhood gem" and "a good choice when visiting the Brooklyn Museum or BAM," but it's not necessarily a destination.

New American | Informal | Moderate | park slope | 501 11th St. | 718-788-1810 | www.applewoodny.com | Dinner Tue-Sat, Lunch Sat-Sun

Chestnut 88.5

Daniel Eardley's place is probably the least well-known of the restaurants on Smith Street. The menu features crispy squash blossoms with curried chickpeas and a smoked pork chop with escarole and hibiscus jus. One reviewer compared the food to nearby Applewood (see above), adding, "They don't take the farm-to-table movement anywhere near as seriously and are merely interested in serving good food." The menu changes regularly, but a core of entrées – like hanger steak with a red wine sauce – are always available.

New American | Informal | Moderate | boerum hill | 271 Smith St. | 718-243-0049 | www.chestnuton-smith.com | Dinner Tue-Sun, Lunch Sun

ACCEPTABLE

Elias Corner 87.5

This restaurant once held cult status with the Cheap Eats community. But after moving across the street to a larger space, its following abandoned it. We always found the situation puzzling as the quality of the fish there wasn't any different. Whatever it was, reviewers still think it's a good choice for "super-fresh fish" at "ridiculously low prices," though one reviewer cautions, "You get what you pay for, even in Astoria."

Greek | Informal | Moderate | astoria | 24-02 31st St. | 718-932-1510 | http://eliascorner.com | Dinner daily

Joe's Shanghai 87.5

If you have never had a Shanghai soup dumpling, it's a doughy ball, slightly larger than a wonton and stuffed with pork or crabmeat. Upon steaming, a significant amount of liquid fills the interior, and this delicious "soup" shoots into your mouth when you take a bite. The other fare (Manila clams, frogs' legs, chicken with ginger) is top-notch, but the real attraction remains the "ethereal dumplings," which are guaranteed to reward you with a bit of that delicious broth in every bite.

Chinese | Informal | Moderate | flushing | 136-21 37th Ave. | 718-539-3838 | www.joeshanghairestaurants.com | Lunch & Dinner daily

Piccola Venezia 87.5

They have been slinging red sauce at Piccola Venezia for nearly 40 years. And while it's merely a neighborhood restaurant, it's fancy enough to be a place where local families celebrate special occasions and other big nights out. The fare is what you expect for Italian in the boroughs: stuffed eggplant, rigatoni Bolognese and thick veal chops, along with one of the better wine lists in the city. Popular with the local business community, it motivated one regular to tell us, "I always get the feeling that the Godfather's about to walk in."

Italian | Casual | Moderate | astoria | 42-01 28th Ave. | 718-721-8470 | www.piccola-venezia.com | Lunch & Dinner daily

Dominick's 87.0

Given that they have been serving large portions of pasta, like linguine with red sauce and shrimp and baked ziti, along with entrées like chicken Parmigiana and broiled pork chops topped with hot vinegar peppers, for more than 55 years, it's easy to see why no other Italian restaurant is more closely associated with the Arthur Avenue section of the Bronx than Dominick's. While some reviewers say the food was better when the old man ran the place (his son-in-law is now in charge), it's still packed with people "seated elbow to elbow" enjoying "copious portions" of "inexpensive food" – especially before Yankees home games, when there's always a packed house.

Italian | Informal | Moderate | belmont | 2335 Arthur Ave. | 718-733-2807 | Lunch & Dinner Wed-Mon

Spicy & Tasty 87.0

This is probably the most famous and popular of the Flushing Szechuan restaurants; some even claim it's the best in the city, including the reviewer who told us, "the tasty fare makes it worth enduring the 80-minute subway ride from my home." They do a good job with cold dishes, and they probably have "more parts of the pig on offer" than any other Chinese restaurant in New York. The atmosphere's a bit sterile, due to its relocation to a storefront in a newish office building a few years back.

Chinese | Informal | Moderate | flushing | 39-07 Prince St. | 718-359-1601 | Lunch & Dinner daily

Uncle Jack's Steakhouse 86.5

It used to be impossible to find a 28-day-aged prime steak in Queens. But William Jack Degel felt a location near the Rail Road station in Bayside could support a restaurant where people would pay Manhattan prices for a steak. That was back in 1996, and thousands of strips and porterhouses later, Degel has been able to open two Manhattan branches and is about to open another in Glen Head (Nassau County). The "surprisingly good" steaks are similar to those proffered at any of the national chains.

Steakhouse | Casual | Expensive | bayside | 39-40 Bell Blvd. | 718-229-1100 | www.unclejacks.com | Dinner daily, Lunch Mon-Fri

Queen 86.0

While classic Italian restaurants are disappearing at a steady rate, the Vitiello brothers are serving their third generation of guests. The place was opened by their father in 1958. By day it serves as a hangout for politicos and judges who work in the nearby courts and offices, while at night it attracts a crowd that is happy to eat the retro-style food. "Worthy of your patronage" is how one reviewer described it, adding, "The only

drawback is that service can be slow – the consequence of everything being made to order."

Italian | Informal | Moderate | brooklyn heights | 84 Court St. | 718-596-5955 | www.queenrestaurant.com | Lunch & Dinner daily

OTHER PLACES MENTIONED

Water's Edge 81.5

One of the most outstanding views of the New York City skyline is countered by some of the most mundane food you will ever eat. The ambience is even nicer in the summer months, when you can take in the sights while sitting at an outdoor table. One reviewer said, "It's harmless. Check it out when you're in Long Island City." But you know things are bad when another reviewer says, "Great views. Just don't look at your plate."

Seafood | Casual | Expensive | long island city | East River & 44th Dr. | 718-482-0033 | www.watersedgenyc.com | Dinner Mon-Sat

Cheap Eats

UNIQUELY DELICIOUS

Di Fara's 8.7

This ordinary-looking pizzeria has risen to cult status in recent years. Dominic De Marco shuns the modern-day conveniences that other pizzerias rely on, like pre-made dough or sauces, resulting in pies that our older reviewers say, "taste like the pizza I used to eat in Brooklyn when I was growing up." Comments that do a good job of capturing the experience say, "The place is a dump, the wait is ridiculous, and the price is exorbitant, but getting to eat that pizza after watching him make it is worth it" and "There are long lines, long waits and an impossible-to-figure-out ordering process, but man, the pies here are to die for."

Pizzeria | Moderate | flatbush | 1424 Ave. J | 718-258-1367 | http://www.difara.com | Lunch & Dinner Wed-Sun

Mile End 8.0

New York and Montreal Jews fight about two things: Which city has better bagels, and if New York pastrami is as good as Montreal smoked meat. And since Noah Bernamoff opened this Montreal-style delicatessen, enthusiasts have been shuttling between Boerum Hill and the Lower East Side on a quest to find the definitive answer. Like other culinary pioneers who are interested in recreating, while respectfully updating, the cuisine of their youth, Bernamoff takes an artisanal approach, and his smoked beef has a "longer and more complex finish" than the deli fare most people are used to eating. There are other Jewish delicacies on hand, like shmaltzed radish and tongue polonaise, as well as a house version of the Quebecois classic, poutine (a mixture of smoked meat, cheese curds and gravy on fries – whose combination of dairy and meat clearly is a nod to assimilation).

Delicatessen | Inexpensive | boerum hill | 97A Hoyt St. | 718-852-7510 | www.mileendbrooklyn. com | Breakfast & Lunch Mon-FriDinner Wed-Sun

RECOMMENDED

Egg 7.9

There are a number of Southern-style dishes on offer at this narrow breakfast spot off Bedford Avenue, like biscuits and gravy or organic grits and eggs, which diners supplement with tasty sides like candied bacon or Col. Bill Newsom's "absolutely delicious" country ham. Lunch and dinner bring savory fare like fried chicken or a grilled-cheese sandwich made with organic bread. Although the place is filled with hipsters from the neighborhood, it also attracts visitors from the other side of the river. As one Manhattan-based reviewer told us, "It's worth making a trip over the Williamsburg Bridge" to eat here.

Southern | Inexpensive | williamsburg | 135 N. 5th St. | 718-302-5151 | www.pigandegg.com | Breakfast & Lunch daily, Dinner Wed-Sun

Benfaremo, the Italian Ice King 7.8

They have been filling little white paper cups with slushy ices for over 60 years at this retro-looking spot in Corona's old Italian neighborhood. They offer 40 flavors, ranging from classics like lemon to more unusual offerings like cotton candy and vanilla chocolate chip. It's a favorite with many of our reviewers, one of whom declared, "If the lemon ices are king, then the pistachio ices are the Pope." Expect a line during the warm weather.

Dessert | Inexpensive | corona | 5202 108th St. | 718-699-5133 | http://thelemonicekingofcorona. com | Lunch & Dinner daily

Franny's 7.7

Most reviewers recommend the wood-fired pizzas at this popular Italian restaurant where the crusts are "thin, blistered, and have the perfect amount of bounce and chew." Though one said that "toppings are minimal," there are ten types of pies on offer with numerous decorations, including clams, chiles and parsley, as well as tomatoes, provolone picante and onions. You can choose from one of four pastas if pizza isn't your thing, and start with various salumi or other appetizers.

Pizzeria | Inexpensive | park slope | 295 Flatbush Ave. | 718-230-0221 | www.frannysbrooklyn.com | Dinner daily, Lunch Sat-Sun

Totonno's 7.7

Back in 1924, Anthony "Totonno" Pero, known as one of the best "pizziaolos" in the city, installed a coal-burning brick oven at his Coney Island shop. He made pies until he ran out of dough, and if you happened to be waiting on line at the time – tough luck to you. Like his beloved Dodgers, Totonno is no longer with us. But his family is still sliding pies into his oven, and people are still lining up.

Pizzeria | Infexpensive | coney island | 1524 Neptune Ave. | 718-372-8606 | www.totonnos.com | Lunch & Dinner Wed-Sun

Trattoria Zero Otto Nove   7.5

While the Bronx has always had a number of thriving Italian neighborhoods, it used to be that if you wanted pizza from a wood-burning oven, you had to head to Manhattan — until, that is, Roberto Paciullo installed a wood-burning oven in this Arthur Avenue trattoria. And with some help from his neighbor, a cheese shop named Casa de Mozzarella, he turns out pies so authentic that one reviewer, who recently returned from Italy, told us, "I couldn't tell the difference between the pizza on the Amalfi Coast and the pizza I ate in the Bronx."

Pizzeria | Moderate | bronx | 2357 Arthur Ave. | 718-220-1027 | www.roberto089.com | Lunch & Dinner Tue-Sat

L & B Spumoni Gardens   7.4

We've always been puzzled as to why this place in the Gravesend graveyard has "spumoni" in its name when it's actually more of a classic Brooklyn-style pizzeria, with square-shaped slices of Sicilian pies a specialty of the more than 70-year-old house. Of course, when you're done eating your pizza or hero sandwich, you can feast on spumoni cakes for dessert, ranging from 7 to 12 inches in size. (For the uninitiated, spumoni is an Italian dessert made of layers of ice cream, whipped cream, candied fruit and nuts.)

Pizzeria | Inexpensive | gravesend | 2725 86th St. | 718-449-1230 | www.spumonigardens.com | Dinner daily, Lunch Sat-Sun

Grimaldi's Pizza   7.0

In 1990 the Grimaldi family, of Patsy's Pizza in East Harlem, decided to take advantage of what had become a valuable asset by opening this coal-fired, brick-oven pizzeria underneath the Brooklyn Bridge. Almost immediately, long lines formed, and they continue to this day. There are only a few toppings to choose from, and it's cash only. "Be prepared for a wait no matter what time of day," although the blistered pies come out fast and the turnover is quick.

Pizzeria | Inexpensive | dumbo | 19 Old Fulton St. | 718-858-4300 | www.grimaldis.com | Dinner daily, Lunch Sat-Sun

OTHER PLACES MENTIONED

Brooklyn Ice   6.9
Cream Factory

For decades this 1920s fireboat house built sat idle. But a few years ago, someone figured out it would be a good location to sell ice cream. Now there are long lines stretching out the door, with people waiting to order the "creamy and delicious" cold stuff. Super-convenient when visiting Grimaldi's Pizza (directly across the street; see above) or when driving back to Manhattan after dining at a restaurant in Park Slope or Carroll Gardens.

Dessert | Inexpensive | dumbo | Corner of Old Fulton and Water Sts. | 718-246-3963 | www.brooklynicecreamfactory.com | Open daily

DuMont Burger   6.8

The "big and juicy" burger here is served in a space called "small, intimate, friendly and focused." There are a few other dishes on offer, including "a smashing mac 'n' cheese." Some "mean fries and onion rings" plus a "limited number of artisanal beers on tap" do a good job of complementing the tasty patties. Arguing against it is "meat that is seasoned," something that offends purists who prefer their burgers cooked au naturel.

Hamburger | Inexpensive | williamsburg | 314 Bedford Ave. | 718-384-6127 | www.dumontburger.com | Lunch & Dinner daily

Fette Sau   6.6

This Southern-style barbecue from the people who brought you DuMont Burger (see above) is among the best in the city, thanks to its "rotating array of carefully prepared meats" along with a "better than average American craft beer list."

NEW YORK CITY: OUTER BOROUGHS

The barbecued meats, like brisket and pork, are preferred to the ribs. A few people criticized the setting, saying it's fine for the hipsters who populate the neighborhood but "a bit bare bones" for visitors making a trip from Manhattan.

Asian | Inexpensive | williamsburg | 354 Metropolitan Ave. | 718-963-3404 | www.fettesaubbq.com | Dinner daily, Lunch Sat-Sun

Pio Pio   6.6

With a whole chicken cooked a la brasa going for a meager $10, this chain of Peruvian restaurants might offer the best deliciousness-to-price ratio in the city. They also have other Peruvian fare, including ceviche, avocado salad and a typical seafood platter, along with sides of rice, beans and both green and sweet plantains. "Awesome chicken, great ceviche, even better prices."

Peruvian | Inexpensive | rego park | 62-30 Woodhaven Blvd. | 718-458-0606 | www.piopio.com | Lunch & Dinner daily

Second Location: jackson heights | 84-02 Northern Blvd. | 718-426-4900 | www.piopio.com | Lunch & Dinner daily

Fatty 'Cue   6.3

Zak Pelaccio's interesting way of blending American and Southeast Asian barbecue results in dishes like coriander bacon with steamed yellow curry custard and Brandt Ranch beef brisket with chili jam, aioli, red onion and bone broth. The lower-than-expected rating is a result of what one reviewer described as "food that is culturally confused" and environs that are deemed "loud and boisterous." Another reviewer, who's actually a fan of Pelaccio's other restaurants, lamented that the food here was "too expensive, too fatty and too bad."

Southeast Asian Barbecue | Moderate | williamsburg | 91 S. 6th St. | 718-599-3090 | www.fattycue.com | Lunch & Dinner daily

Junior's   6.3

A location at the head of the downtown Brooklyn shopping district meant Junior's was historically one of the busiest restaurants in Brooklyn. Then in 1973, *New York Magazine* anointed its cheesecake the best in the city and it got even busier. While the food is not any different than at other coffee shops and they now operate locations in Manhattan, we still get the occasional reviewer who says it's "worth the trip to Brooklyn" for a piece of that cheesecake.

Dessert | Inexpensive | downtown brooklyn | 386 Flatbush Ave. Ext. | 718-852-5257 | www.juniorscheesecake.com | Open daily

Nathan's Famous   6.3

There was a time when people spoke of Nathan's in hushed tones. Now it's a chain and "long past its prime." Still, there is some value to visiting the original Coney Island location, and a number of reviewers are quick to admit that the hot dog and thickly cut French fries are "fast food classics" and "still rank among the best in the city."

Hot Dogs | Inexpensive | coney island | 1310 Surf Ave. | 718-946-2705 | www.nathansfamous.com | Open daily

Donovan's Pub   5.0

This classic pub in the heart of Woodside's Irish neighborhood was propelled to citywide attention when a number of publications determined that it served the best hamburger in the city. Unfortunately, only half of our reviewers agree: Those in favor say it offers "consistently great food served in a warm and friendly atmosphere," while those against it say, "Cheap isn't the same as good."

Hamburgers | Inexpensive | woodside | 5724 Roosevelt Ave. | 718-429-9339 | Lunch & Dinner daily

Northern New Jersey NJ

HIGHLY RECOMMENDED

Elements   94.3

Sometimes timing is everything. At the same moment that owner Steve Distler decided the Princeton area could sustain an establishment offering serious dining, the Garden State was undergoing an artisanal farming boom. Scott Anderson, who had worked with Craig Shelton at the Ryland Inn, turns those terrific ingredients into dishes like a soup of local asparagus with a soft-poached egg and summer truffles or diver scallops harvested from the Jersey Shore and served with ham, split peas and morels. And if you're lucky, Anderson's rice-less mushroom risotto – finely diced mushrooms, mushroom broth, tomato, parmesan and white truffles – will be on the menu when you visit. Comments were effusive: "Absolutely a top-notch dining experience driven by creativity and a dedication to acquiring the best product"; "have eaten at the chef's table several times, and the creative and flavorful food prepared is always delightful"; and "this is the most creative restaurant between New York and Washington, D.C., by far, and absolutely worth a special trip."

New American | Casual | Expensive | princeton | 163 Bayard Ln. | 609-924-0078 | www.elementsprinceton.com | Dinner Daily, Lunch Sun-Fri

Pluckemin Inn   93.0

When Juan Jose Cuevas first took over the kitchen at this restaurant in the heart of New Jersey horse country, his menu was geared to the local clientele. But after six months he struck up a relationship with Three Meadow Farms and began serving the style of food he was known for when he was cooking at Blue Hill in New York City. The superb vegetables that Cuevas uses turn up in dishes like grilled kampachi and roasted brussels sprouts served in a grapefruit and Sauternes broth infused with garden chile and lemon thyme, or Griggstown chicken with basmati rice, sunchoke and broccoli rabe. "The flavors were delicate, and most dishes were accompanied by a spoon for enjoying flavorful broths or sauces" is how one reviewer described his meal. BYO is allowed, although they also offer one of the best wine lists in the Garden State.

New American | Casual | Expensive | bedminster | 359 Rte. 206 S. | 908-658-9292 | www.pluckemininn.com | Dinner daily, Lunch Mon-Fri

RECOMMENDED

Scalini Fedeli   91.6

If you favor New York-style, northern Italian dining, Michael Cetrulo's restaurant does its best to bring the standards used at the top European restaurants to a cuisine that, too often in the U.S., is prepared by chefs without formal training. Cetrulo puts his own abilities to good use with inventive offerings like pappardelle in a sauce of venison and hare finished with Barolo wine and bitter chocolate or a juniper- and black-pepper-crusted venison chop with a port and balsamic vinegar sauce. The dining room is "ornate and showy," which explains the well-dressed clientele and the fancy cars in the parking lot.

Northern Italian | Casual | Expensive | chatham | 63 Main St. | 973-701-9200 | www.scalinifedeli.com | Dinner Mon-Sat, Lunch Mon-Fri

Shumi 91.0

Show us a suburb that counts multi-million-dollar homes among its ranks and we will show you a suburb where people are willing to pay large sums of money for high-quality raw fish. That's the case at this restaurant in a "hidden location – blink and you will miss it," where chef Ike doles out piece after piece of "pristine sushi" to a cadre of fans who are happy to travel long distances for the experience. Maybe the most important recommendation comes from the area's local chefs, who all swear, "It's the only place I will eat sushi outside of Manhattan."

Japanese | Informal | Expensive | somerville | 30 S. Doughty Ave. | 908-526-8596 | Dinner Tue-Sun, Lunch Tue-Sat

Ninety Acres at Natirar 90.5

Though its "proprietary-farm-to-table" concept is similar to that of places like Blue Hill at Stone Barns and the Herbfarm, this "beautiful, upscale venue" offering "amazing views" from "a location on the top of a hill in a 90-acre park" is not all that well known to diners. David Felton's mission is to utilize ingredients that are raised right on the property, resulting in "fresh and delicious dishes" like a stew of pasture-raised veal flank with peppers or chicken potpie with root vegetables and tasso ham. What has become a popular Sunday brunch allows diners to take advantage of the lovely setting even during the winter months.

New American | Casual | Moderate | peapack-gladstone | 2 Main St. | 908-901-9500 | http://ninetyacres.com | Dinner Tue-Sun, Brunch Sun

TOP LOCAL CHOICE

The Bernards Inn 89.5

Serving guests since 1907, this archetypical inn dates from a time when this horsey area was more of a weekend retreat than a suburb. Despite the fact that it features soothing piano music on its website (rarely a good sign), reviewers like Corey Heyer's "pricy" New American cuisine, which includes dishes like peekytoe crab salad with chilled cantaloupe soup and filet mignon of buffalo with fried green tomatoes and poblano mole sauce. The dining rooms have been "lovingly restored," and the "high-end atmosphere" makes it "perfect for those who like to dress to impress." One of the best wine lists in the state offers more than 1,500 bottles.

New American | Casual | Expensive | bernardsville | 27 Mine Brook Rd. | 908-766-0002 | www.bernardsinn.com | Dinner Daily, Lunch Sun-Fri

Blu 89.5

In writing about Blu, one of our more experienced reviewers told us, "Quite often restaurants located in the suburbs of major cities are overrated by the locals. But the cooking here" – like a duck breast, braised red cabbage, caramelized turnips and a red wine fig emulsion – "was surprisingly good, and I will go as far as to say that the chef is good enough to make it in New York City." It's super-convenient for diners who are headed for a concert at the Wellmont Theater, just down the street.

New American | Informal | Moderate | montclair | 554 Bloomfield Ave. | 973-509-2202 | www.restaurant-blu.com | Dinner Tue-Sun

David Burke Fromagerie   89.5

With restaurants in New York, Connecticut and Chicago, you would think that David Burke would be busy enough. But the master of whimsy is at it again at this restaurant in the northern tip of Monmouth County, where the slate of unusual creations includes a Hot and Angry Lobster Cocktail, pretzel-crusted crab cake and cheesecake lollipops. It does appear that Burke has toned it down a bit compared to the offerings at his big-city locations. But the locals seem happy enough.

New American | Casual | Expensive | rumson | 26 Ridge Rd. | 732-842-8088 | www.fromagerierestaurant.com | Lunch & Dinner Tue-Sun

Rat's   89.5

The main reason most people visit this restaurant is to wander through J. Seward Johnson's sculpture garden, which was inspired by Monet's garden at Giverny and which features 250 contemporary works. After a stroll through the grounds, they enjoy Shane Cash's "better-than-average" compositions of the plate; carefully sourced ingredients are molded into dishes like a tasting of Colorado lamb with saffron or raisin cous cous with harissa oil. There's a good wine list, and lots of choices for vegetarians. But the "idyllic setting" dominates the comments.

New American | Casual | Expensive | hamilton | 16 Fairgrounds Rd. | 609-584-7800 | www.ratsrestaurant.org | Lunch & Dinner Tue-Sun

Doris & Ed's   89.0

Ten years ago, this was one of the most revered restaurants in New Jersey. It built its reputation by offering diners two different menus: contemporary seafood preparations, like a sautéed filet of East Coast halibut with baby turnips, green beans, roasted figs and almond purée, and old-fashioned seafood-house fare, like flounder stuffed with king crab, jumbo lump crab or lobster. The "great seafood" comes with a "great waterfront location," making it "still one of the best places to eat at the Shore."

Seafood | Casual | Expensive | highlands | 348 Shore Dr. | 732-872-1565 | www.dorisandeds.com | Dinner Wed-Sun

CulinAriane   88.5

It was difficult getting a reservation at this "tiny Montclair gem" before chef Ariane Duarte became famous as a contestant on *Top Chef*. But now that it's become even more difficult, we suggest that if you want to enjoy her New American cuisine (featuring dishes like caramelized onion, potato and white cheddar cheese pierogi with braised rabbit or a trout "BLT" with oven-toasted tomato, wilted arugula and crispy prosciutto), you are advised to call at least a week in advance.

New American | Informal | Moderate | montclair | 33 Walnut St. | 973-744-0533 | culinariane.com | Dinner Wed-Sun

Stage Left   88.5

Convenient when visiting the State Theater, Stage Left offers New American cuisine, with starters like seared dayboat scallops with maitake mushrooms and sweet pea purée; pastas like beet, mint and goat cheese risotto served with wild mushrooms; and a full slate of steaks and chops, like a Berkshire pork chop accompanied by Peruvian and Yukon Gold potato salad with Nueske's bacon. They also serve what some say is the best hamburger in the state. The wine list offers a "cross section of interesting bottles" from regions around the world.

New American | Casual | Expensive | new brunswick | 5 Livingston Ave. | 732-828-4444 | www.stageleft. com/sl/dine/ | Dinner daily

Blue Bottle Café   88.0

It's to the Philipsons' benefit that their "magical restaurant that emphasizes local ingredients" is located in the heart of an area that is experiencing an artisanal farming boom. Besides "the delicious produce" that Aaron Philipson features in his cuisine (multiple reviewers mentioned the chicken and quail from nearby Griggstown Quail Farms), diners are warned to "save room for Rory Philipson's delicious desserts." Reviewers praised it as "one of my favorite contemporary restaurants in the area" and "a hidden treasure that not many people know about."

New American | Informal | Moderate | hopewell | 101 E. Broad St. | 609-333-1710 | www.thebluebottle-cafe.com | Dinner Tue-Sat, Lunch Wed-Fri

ACCEPTABLE

Acacia   87.5

The second choice for an upscale yet casual meal in Mercer County can be found at this "solid restaurant," which one reviewer claimed "is a major accomplishment compared to most other restaurants in the area." The menu is a type of heavy New American fare – potato-wrapped shrimp alongside a mushroom spinach pancake with brandy cream – that restaurants outside of major American cities seem to specialize in. Add service and ambience that is "just okay," and you end up with the type of dining experience one comes to expect in the suburbs.

New American | Casual | Expensive | lawrenceville | 2637 Main St. | 609-895-9885 | www.acaciacuisine.com | Dinner Tue-Sun, Lunch Tue-Fri

Ajihei   87.5

Say you are visiting Princeton for a conference or have a meeting at one of the area's pharmaceutical companies. You decide you want sushi, but you're not up for the 40-mile round trip to Shumi (see above). Odds are you will end up here. Unfortunately, the other amenities do not stack up against the fresh fish: The "space is so tiny it's difficult to seat parties larger than three," resulting in "horrendous waits during peak hours," and the "service and atmosphere are both horrible." Yet reviewers still say it's their number one choice for sushi in Princeton.

Japanese | Informal | Moderate | princeton | 11 Chambers St. | 609-252-1158 | Dinner Tue-Sun, Lunch Tue-Fri

Cucharamama   87.0

Among the dishes you can sample at Maricel Presilla's pan-South American restaurant are arepas from Venezuela, potatoes and salt cod fritters from Brazil and spinach-and-walnut cannelloni in the style of those enjoyed in Argentina's River Plate region. There's a "lively and sexy bar scene," but some people think it's "a bit pricy" compared to what they are used to paying for ethnic food on the Hoboken side of the river.

Pan-Latin | Informal | Moderate | hoboken | 233 Clinton St. | 201-420-1700 | www.cucharamama. com | Dinner Tue-Sun, Lunch Sun

The Frog & the Peach   87.0

Bordering the counties of Mercer and Somerset, Middlesex is the poor relation. Not surprisingly, it's difficult finding a good high-end meal there. But locals tell us that "The F & the P is the best restaurant in the New Brunswick area," featuring an eclectic menu of dishes like crispy calamari with frisée lettuce and jalapeño jelly, which diners can enjoy in a dining room that features a large atrium ceiling. A number of reviewers mentioned the $32 Frugal Farmer prix-fixe menu featuring ingredients like Griggstown Quail Farm chicken meatballs.

New American | Casual | Expensive | new brunswick | 29 Dennis St. | 732-846-3216 | www.frogandpeach.com | Dinner daily, Lunch Mon-Fri

Origin   86.5

Somerville seems to be the go-to spot for upscale ethnic food in central New Jersey. The predominantly Thai menu, with a few French dishes thrown into the mix, means you can choose between Massaman Curry or breast of Muscovy duck in a Grand Marnier sauce. Being able to bring your own wine makes it one of the area's more popular restaurants in the area.

Thai | Casual | Moderate | somerville | 25 Division St. | 908-685-1344 | www.originthai.com | Dinner Tue-Sun, Lunch Tue-Sat

Fascino   86.0

When the kitchen is on at this northern Italian/New American restaurant at the foot of downtown Montclair, the food can be tasty. But "getting a good meal is hit or miss," and that's what's driving the low-ish rating. It's BYOB policy and "the above average glassware" are huge pluses but reviewers aren't sure that's enough to compensate for the inconsistent cooking,

Italian | Informal | Moderate | montclair | 331 Bloomfield Ave. | 973-233-0350 | www.fascinorestaurant.com | Dinner Wed-Sun

Amanda's   85.5

The American cooking – like sea scallops with a savory corn purée, grilled aspara-gus and bacon and tomato vinaigrette – is fine enough, although the real reason to come here is the town-house setting, complete with a working fireplace and "cozy ambience." It's not a bad choice if you happen to be on this side of the river, but the food isn't worth paying the $1.75 fare on the PATH train to Hoboken.

New American | Informal | Moderate | hoboken | 908 Washington St. | 201-798-0101 | www.amandasrestaurant.com | Dinner daily, Lunch Sat-Sun

Blue Pointe Grill   85.0

Opinions are split about this Princeton seafooder. Those in favor say: "It's flat out underrated. The fresh seafood is well prepared, and the BYOB policy means it's one of my go-to restaurants in the area." Meanwhile, the nays counter: "This is a pretty standard seafood-type place, and there is nothing particularly creative about the cooking." Some reviewers say they prefer buying fish in the adjacent shop and cooking it at home.

Seafood | Informal | Moderate | princeton | 258 Nassau St. | 609-921-1211 | www.jmgroup-princeton.com | Dinner daily

Serenade   84.0

With a number of dishes priced at $35, you would think you were dining in Manhattan rather than a town 25 miles west. Alas, the prices are the only cosmopolitan thing about it. Reviewers say dishes like a grilled venison chop with red cabbage are in keeping with the restaurant's suburban location. Adding insult to injury are comments like "It's slipped a bit over the past few years" and "The kitchen doesn't always express its full potential."

New American | Casual | Expensive | chatham | 6 Roosevelt Ave. | 973-701-0303 | www.restaurantserenade.com | Dinner daily, Lunch Mon-Fri

Nicholas   83.5

This is one of those strange ones. A number of reviewers nominated Nicholas and Melissa Harary's restaurant for the honor of best restaurant in New Jersey. But others said, "My meal was awful" and "I'm not sure why this is highly rated." One reviewer tried to explain his negative feelings, telling us "They ruin the food by trying to make it too fancy."

New American | Casual | Expensive | middletown | 160 Rte. 35 S. | 732-345-9977 | www.restaurant-nicholas.com | Dinner daily

Park & Orchard   83.0

While appearing to be a casual place frequented by the local business crowd, this restaurant offers an unusual feature: one of the best, and most fairly priced, wine lists in the country. Unfortunately, the food leaves a lot to be desired.

Italian | Informal | Moderate | east rutherford | 240 Hackensack St. | 201-939-9292 | www.parkandorchard.com | Dinner Mon-Sat, Lunch Mon-Fri

Cheap Eats

RECOMMENDED

DeLorenzo's Tomato Pies   7.4

This old-timer has been serving pizza since 1947. You can order a basic pie, along with any of 15 toppings (priced at $1 per topping). They also serve what they call Clam Tomato Pies. "Crispy,

thin, sweet and delicious – hands down the best pizza ever, and I will go as far as to say in the world," one fan raved. An heirloom tomato salad starter shows that they have kept abreast of the times, though they insist on clinging to an unusual policy of not providing grated cheese on request.

Pizzeria | Inexpensive | robbinsville | 2350 US Highway 33 | 609-341-8480 | www.delorenzostomatopies.com | Dinner daily, Lunch Tue-Fri

OTHER PLACES MENTIONED

Tick Tock Diner   5.2

Given the dozens of diners in New Jersey, it's hard for one to stand out. This eatery somehow manages to differentiate itself, in spite of the fact that "Most of the food they serve is the same as any other diner in Jersey." Maybe it's the classic diner architecture, which dates from 1948. Or maybe it's the impossible-to-miss location on Route 3. Whatever the reason, it's a reasonable place to stop when you need a BLT sandwich to hold you over until the next meal.

Diner | Inexpensive | clifton | 281 Allwood Rd./Rte. 3 W. | 973-777-0511 | www.theticktockdiner.com | Open daily

Westchester County / Upstate New York / Fairfield County CT

WORTH PLANNING A TRIP AROUND

Blue Hill at Stone Barns   98.4

With the help of the Rockefeller family, Dan Barber is on his way to creating the country's first sustainable restaurant. Not only does Blue Hill at Stone Barns grow most of its produce, it also raises chickens, turkeys, geese and Berkshire pigs right on the property. In fact, in the hands of Barber the concept of sustainability knows no bounds. He supervised the construction of a slaughterhouse, and reduced heating and fuel bills by 75% by recycling the restaurant's compost. Fortunately, Barber's cuisine is as ambitious as his efforts at sustainability. But rather than invoking the Chez Panisse model of cooking pristine ingredients in the simple manner of a regional restaurant, Barber has incorporated the modern culinary techniques that can be found in some of the most cutting-edge kitchens in Europe.

The tasting menu (the only option) always begins with an array of bite-size vegetables, followed by an assortment of homemade salamis, hams and terrines. Then back to vegetables for a more serious expression of the best of the season, like a service of a half dozen varieties of heirloom tomatoes, which arrive in guises ranging from simply sliced to gently sautéed, or as an intensely flavored sorbet. Fish is often paired with a gentle reduction of fresh fruit or vegetables, and the meat course can range from Stone Barns chicken (the best in the country according to numerous reviewers) to various cuts of Berkshire pork to baby lamb that Barber sources from Vermont. The wine list is worthy of the food, although a one-bottle limit on BYOB is a bit of a hassle for true oeneophiles. Not to be outdone by the delicious eats, the setting – the Stone Barns were built in the 1920s and are reminiscent of a Hollywood movie set – is absolutely magnificent.

New American | Formal | Expensive | pocantico hills | 630 Bedford Rd. | 914-366-9600 | www.bluehill-stonebarns.com | Dinner Wed-Sun, Lunch Sun

TOP LOCAL CHOICE

Dressing Room – A Homegrown Restaurant   89.5

Along with lemonade, popcorn and salad dressing, this is yet another business that the late Paul Newman had a hand in creating. The American fare based on locally raised ingredients is split into small, medium and large plates – "simple, casual fare" like kettle macaroni and cheese with farmstead cheddar, cured pork belly and breadcrumbs –that is "prepared with a minimum of fuss." One of Connecticut's best, and priciest, hamburgers ($12) can be found here, and the location next to the Westport Country Playhouse means that it's difficult to snag a table before the curtain goes up.

New American | Casual | Expensive | westport | 27 Powers Ct. | 203-226-1114 | www.dressingroomhome-grown.com | Lunch & Dinner daily, closed Sun lunch

Pasta Nostra   89.5

Mention this restaurant to Norwalk-area residents and they immediately break into smiles. Thirty years ago, Joe and Susan Bruno opened a restaurant based on homemade pasta, and they are still serving a full slate of such dishes, like spaghetti with clam sauce, gnocchi Bolognese and fettuccine Alfredo, along with homemade sausages and entrées like steak pizzaiola. Despite its popularity, we did find a few reviewers who claimed, "It's slipped a bit in recent years."

Italian | Informal | Moderate | norwalk | 116 Washington St. | 203-854-9700 | www.pastanostra.com | Dinner Wed-Sun

Xaviars at Piermont   89.5

Once you cross the Hudson River from Westchester into Rockland County, quality dining experiences are at a premium. Fortunately, Peter Kelly's "small, excellent restaurant with a well-trained staff and a focus on local cuisine" stands ready to save those who cross that divide. The New American menu features dishes like creamy lobster soup with Santa Barbara uni custard, petits croutons and coral froth, accompanied by a wine list that features "a good representation of French and German bottles." Booking in advance is imperative as they have only about a dozen tables.

New American | Casual | Expensive | piermont | 506 Piermont Ave. | 845-359-7007 | www.xaviars.com | Dinner Wed-Sun, Lunch Fri, Sun

ACCEPTABLE

Coromandel   86.5

With locations from New Rochelle to the suburbs of New Haven, this restaurant chain is a main source of Indian food for the population that lives along the Merritt Parkway. A number of reviewers claim the Darien location "is the best of them all," adding that "they serve region-al dishes you won't find elsewhere," like halibut stewed in a Tranvancore sauce. Of course, the suburban locations inspired comments from cosmopolites like "might be the best Indian in Fair-field County, but still a far cry from New York City."

Indian | Informal | Moderate | darien | Good Wives Shopping Center | 25-11 Old Kings Hwy. N. | 203-662-1213 | www.coromandelcuisine.com | Lunch & Dinner daily

Tarry Lodge   86.5

This Batali-Bastianich venue gets a low rating, despite the fact that the talented Andy Nusser is running the kitchen. Unfortunately, with Nusser also in charge of the stoves at Casa Mono (see above), this restaurant seems to suffer from "absentee-chef-itis." The one element of the menu that did get good reviews were the "tasty pizzas," some with unusual toppings like guanciale, black truffles and sunnyside-up egg.

Italian | Casual | Moderate | port chester | 18 Mill St. | 914-939-3111 | www.tarrylodge.com | Lunch & Dinner daily

Ching's Kitchen   86.0

This one falls into the category of "a pleasant meal, provided you aren't look-ing to break new ground." The pan-Asian menu includes everything from spring rolls to clay pot casseroles to crispy red snapper with Penang curry. Residents of Fairfield County tell us the "buzzy atmo-sphere" and "efficient service" make it "a good choice before or after the movies"

or for "a Sunday evening family dinner."

Asian | Informal | Moderate | darien | 971 Post Rd. | 203-656-2225 | Lunch & Dinner daily

Aberdeen   85.0

When Westchester Chinese families want dim sum and the 25-mile journey to Chinatown is a bridge or tunnel too far, they end up at what is probably the most "authentic" Chinese restaurant between New York and Boston. Reviewers say, "The décor is as plain as it comes, and the staff is pleasant and works hard. While I haven't yet found a signature dish that is a must-have, I haven't found a dish you need to avoid either."

Chinese | Informal | Moderate | white plains | 3 Barker Ave. | 914-288-0188 | Lunch & Dinner daily

Crabtree's Kittle House   83.0

One of the greatest wine lists in the country – nearly 6,000 varietals – can be found at this unusual restaurant located in a building that dates from 1790 and that "seems better suited for a small town in Virginia than the suburbs of New York City." The food? It's American/ Continental and decidedly ordinary considering the majesty of the wine list, especially with Blue Hill having raised the bar in the area. But despite the very ordi-nary food, the wine list makes it a must go for sophisticated wine lovers.

American | Casual | Expensive | chappaqua | 11 Kittle Rd. | 914-666-8044 | www.kittlehouse.com | Dinner daily, Lunch Sun-Fri

OTHER PLACES MENTIONED

Match   81.5

This is one of those restaurants that thrives in the suburbs and smaller cities, but would never last if it were located in Manhattan. The menu has a bit of every-thing on it, from pizza to tuna tartare to pastas to blackened swordfish, but as usual, "More effort is spent on being hip than serving good food." At least it's "not a bad place for some drinks and snacks."

New American | Casual | Expensive | south nor-
walk | 98 Washington St. | 203-852-1088 | www.
matchsono.com | Open daily

Jack's Oyster House   80.5

In 2013, they'll be celebrating the 100th
birthday of this institution that has func-
tioned as a hangout for members of the
New York State Legislature ever since
it opened. While there's a "great, old
New York vibe," customers are advised
to stick to plain broiled fish and meats,
as the food is mediocre at best (some
say, not unlike the statesmen it serves).
"Forty years ago it was elegant dining,"
said one reviewer, "but while times have
changed elsewhere, it might as well still
be 1970 at Jack's."

American | Casual | Expensive | albany | 42
State St. | 518-465-8854 | www.jacksoysterhouse.
com | Lunch & Dinner daily

Cheap Eats

UNIQUELY DELICIOUS

Dinosaur Bar-B-Que   8.5

John Stage's restaurant defies the common wisdom that there isn't any good
barbecue in the Northeast. The key to
Stage's success is the high-quality smok-

ers he invested in, which, according to
several reviewers, "turn out some of the
best barbecue anywhere." There's brisket, pork and chicken, but the big ticket
item is the St. Louis–style ribs. Sides
include everything from mashed potatoes with gravy to mac 'n' cheese, and on
weekend evenings they offer live blues
music. One reviewer noted, "The food
here is surprisingly better than at the
New York City location."

Barbecue | Inexpensive| syracuse | 246 W. Willow
St. | 315-476-4937 | www.dinosaurbarbque.com |
Lunch & Dinner daily

RECOMMENDED

Super Duper Weenie   7.3

Whether ordering a New Englander (sauerkraut, bacon, mustard, sweet relish and
raw onion) or a Cincinnatian (chili with
cheddar cheese and chopped onions),
reviewers say they "love that weenie"
when talking about the roadhouse Gary
Zemola opened in 1992. The fries are
made with potatoes from the Hudson
Valley, and the shakes with fresh fruit.
The result is a hot dog stand that one
reviewer described as "the real deal and
the best dog around, hands down."

Hot Dogs | Inexpensive | fairfield | 306 Black
Rock Turnpike | 203-334-DOGS (3647) | superdup-
erweenie.com | Lunch daily, Dinner Fri-Sun

San Francisco, Northern California & the Pacific Northwest

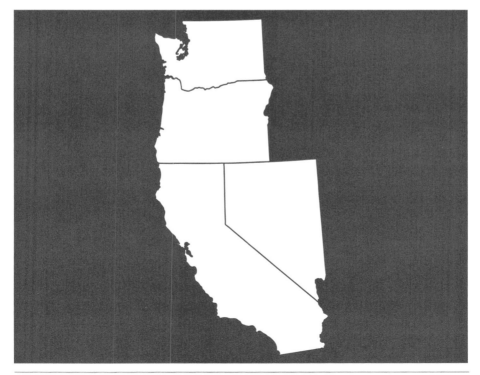

Carmel and Monterey Peninsula CA

AN IMPORTANT DESTINATION

Marinus   95.1

Some chefs wow their customers with culinary technique that, in another context, might seem like mere sleight of hand. But others are just plain good cooks. The latter describes Cal Stamenov, a veteran of numerous top venues, including Masa and Citrus. Over the years, Cal has acquired a dedication to precision cooking, and his kitchen at this elegant lodge located deep in the Carmel Valley sends out dish after dish of food so perfectly made that one reviewer described it as "a wonderful expression of high-quality ingredients," and another said, "While the cuisine is not groundbreaking, the preparations are exquisite."

True to the spirit of lodge cuisine, Stamenov's menu focuses on hearty fare like game, mushrooms and truffles, along with vegetables and herbs from a garden on the grounds of the Bernardus Winery. While most people travel to the region during the summer, late fall/winter is actually a great time to visit; it's truffle season, and Cal offers dishes like lightly smoked and grilled duck served atop a black truffle risotto. Even pastry chef Ben Spungin gets into "black diamond" mode with truffle ice cream coated in a truffle caramel. Mark Jensen manages one of the country's best wine lists, which includes a "staggeringly good selection" of red and white Burgundies.

New American | Casual | Expensive | carmel valley | Bernardus Resort | 415 Carmel Valley Rd. | 831-658-3595 | www.bernardus.com | Dinner Wed-Sun

HIGHLY RECOMMENDED

Aubergine   94.9

When chef Walter Manske left the kitchen, some felt this intimate, 12-table dining room would never recover. But what they didn't count on was little-known Christophe Grosjean. After working at several top restaurants in France as well as serving as chef de cuisine at Marinus, he arrived at Aubergine and quickly returned it to one of the top dining destinations on the Central Coast. Dishes like Monterey spot prawns with yuzu and a fennel purée emulsified with olive oil or capon and salsify with a duxelle of black trumpet mushrooms combine a sturdy foundation of classical French technique and the light touch that characterizes contemporary French haute cuisine. A 4,500-bottle wine list means you won't have much of a problem finding something interesting to drink with the tasty cuisine. *Note: Justin Cogley, a veteran of Charlie Trotter's, recently replaced Grosjean as chef de cuisine after our survey closed.*

French | Casual | Expensive | carmel | L'Auberge Carmel | Monte Verde St. at 7th | 831-624-8578 | www.laubergecarmel.com | Dinner daily

RECOMMENDED

Sierra Mar   91.7

Even if you're not ready to plop down an average $1,000 a night for a hotel room at this luxury resort, you can still enjoy the lovely views of Big Sur from its dining room by reserving a table for lunch or dinner. While dishes like heirloom tomatoes with Buffalo mozzarella and pesto and grilled rib eye with gruyère potato gratin suggest that Craig von Foerster's New American menu doesn't take many chances, that doesn't seem to deter reviewers from calling the experience "a treat for all of the senses" and "worth the drive if you are anywhere close to the area."

New American | Casual | Expensive | big sur | Post Ranch Inn | Post Ranch/Hwy. 1 | 831-667-2800 | www.postranchinn.com | Lunch & Dinner daily

Anton and Michel 90.0

If you're the type of diner who still enjoys food once marketed as "Continental cuisine," head on over to this mainstay of the Monterey Peninsula where they have been serving escargots in puff pastry and chateaubriand carved tableside for over 30 years. The "attentive service" is in keeping with the style of dining, as is "a wine list offering more than 800 different bottles," priced in a way that wine lovers will find appealing. While it's been surpassed by other places, some say "it's still one of the best in the Carmel area," though acknowledging "it could use a bit of revamping."

Continental | Casual | Expensive | carmel-by-the-sea | Mission St. (bet. Ocean Ave. & 7th) | 831-624-2406 | www.carmelsbest.com | Lunch & Dinner daily

Passionfish 90.0

Two important things to note, before we discuss the quality of the food at this very pleasant restaurant: The first is that they use only sustainable fish; the second is that the extensive wine list is priced at or near retail. Only then do we get to Ted Walter's cuisine, which features dishes like Monterey squid in a spicy cilantro-citrus sauce and striped bass with potato gnocchi, gremolata broth and shittake mushrooms. Though on the younger side, the staff is "courteous," and Walters also offers a few meat dishes, like duck confit or grass-fed rib eye, for those who are pescaphobic.

Seafood | Casual | Expensive | pacific grove | 701 Lighthouse Ave. | 831-655-3311 | www.passionfish.net | Dinner daily

TOP LOCAL CHOICE

Casanova 89.0

Here you'll find solid Belgian, Italian, and French dishes like spaghetti with steak tips, halibut with a corn and tomato relish and a rack of lamb in a pistachio croute. While the food is traditional and lacks innovation, it's prepared with enough love and care to make this "a reasonable place for a casual dinner after a hard day of shopping the Carmel art galleries and boutiques" or "after losing 25 balls to the ocean at Pebble Beach." A lovely wine cellar stocked with more than 30,000 bottles also goes a long way to help ease a golfer's pain.

Belgian | Casual | Expensive | carmel | Fifth Ave. (bet. Mission & San Carlos) | 831-625-0501 | www.casa-novarestaurant.com | Lunch & Dinner daily

Fandango 88.0

With a menu that offers everything from cassoulet to sand dabs to veal piccata to the house version of paella, along with an assortment of daily specials cooked over a wood-burning grill, calling this restaurant "old-school" is an understatement. Always full of families, it's "a hangout for many locals," and we garnered many comments like "I have been coming here since the '80s and I've never been disappointed." In keeping with the dining style, don't be surprised when Pierre Bain stops by your table to see if you're enjoying yourself.

Continental | Casual | Moderate | pacific grove | 223 17th St. | 831-372-3456 | www.fandangorestaurant. com | Lunch & Dinner daily

ACCEPTABLE

The Sardine Factory   86.5

Though some reviewers dismiss this restaurant as a tourist trap, others say it's worth visiting for a seafood-based menu that is "plain but solid." There are several different dining rooms, each decorated in a 19th-century style that one reviewer described as "over the top." Fish on offer include local abalone, swordfish and Petrale sole, along with various shellfish sourced from the East, and there is a complete menu of corn-fed, prime-aged beef. Capping it all off is a wine list of 1,500 bottles.

Seafood | Casual | Expensive | monterey | 701 Wave St. | 831-373-3775 | www.sardine factory.com | Dinner daily

Pacific's Edge   86.5

While this restaurant's picture windows offer one of the most spectacular views of the Pacific, reviewer after reviewer commented on contemporary California cuisine that was "good enough" but didn't live up to the setting. A "superb wine list" argues in its favor, yet as one reviewer put it, "The reason you go is for the experience of watching the sun set over the Pacific." Can it be that difficult to hire a chef whose cuisine can stand up to the view?

Californian | Casual | Expensive | carmel | Hyatt Carmel Highlands | 120 Highlands Dr. | 831-622-5445 | www.pacificsedge.com | Dinner daily

Mendocino CA

RECOMMENDED

Café Beaujolais   90.0

Anyone who makes the long trip up the Pacific coast to this secluded town without having at least one meal at this legendary restaurant is probably fasting. True to its California roots, the menu features dishes like local Dungeness crab cakes with Asian slaw, crispy noodles and Petaluma duck two ways, with caramelized onion buttermilk spatzle, wilted kale and wild huckleberry sauce – all consisting of "fresh, high-quality ingredients prepared competently if not inspirationally." A "lovely cottage décor" and "pretty good wine list" bolster the appealing combination of location and cuisine.

Californian | Informal | Expensive | mendocino | 961 Ukiah St. | 707-937-5614 | www.cafebeaujolais.com | Dinner daily, Lunch Wed-Sun

Paso Robles CA

TOP LOCAL CHOICE

Artisan   89.0

One would have to drive 100 miles in either direction of the vast expanse known as California's Central Coast to find a restaurant on a par with Artisan. Chris Kobayashi is in love with the ingredients grown in this fertile region, and "a nice mix of California, French, and Italian ideas" is on display in dishes like yellow fin tuna with fried green tomatoes, black olive aioli and frisée lettuce, or local farm-raised chicken with chanterelles, potatoes and espelette peppers. The vibe is "young and hip" and "the wine list features an array of unusual bottles from local wineries."

New American | Casual | Moderate | paso robles | 1401 Park St. # 105 | 805-237-8084 | www.artisanpasorobles.com | Lunch & Dinner daily

Bistro Laurent   88.0

"Fine renderings of French classics with accents from the local larder" is how one reviewer described Laurent Grangien's restaurant. Many reviewers said they preferred it to the more widely heralded Artisan. The French bistro menu includes both lighter fare, like a warm salad of lobster with orange vinaigrette, and heartier dishes, like a rib-sticking dish of braised beef with baby carrots in a red wine sauce. And you can drink the best local varietals, making it a perfect place to recharge after a long day of wine-tasting.

French Bistro | Informal | Moderate | paso robles | 1202 Pine St. | 805-226-8191 | www.bistrolaurent. com | Lunch & Dinner Tue-Sat

Portland OR

HIGHLY RECOMMENDED

Castagna   93.5

Though he's not well-known among American diners, drop the name Adoni Aduriz during a conversation with serious foodies and you will immediately get their attention. And if you want to experience food prepared by one of the Spanish master's star pupils, you can pocket the cost of the flight to San Sebastian and book a table at this delightful restaurant. After spending a year and a half working for Aduriz at Mugaritz, Matt Lightner decided that he wanted to come home to Portland; fortunately, Monique Siu was looking to reinvent her restaurant at the same time, and she hired Lightner to give the New American cuisine a more progressive spin. The result is "the most innovative (yet still delicious) food in Portland," featuring dishes like squid with almond milk; charred leeks, lemon and almonds; and wild ginger ice cream with parsley root, gingerbread and marshmallow (Lightner forages the ginger himself). A number of reviewers compared Castagna favorably to progressive places like McCrady's in Charleston and the Town House in Virginia, and we expect it to be promoted to the ranking of Important Destination in future guides.

Progressive | ·Casual | Expensive | hawthorne | 1752 S.E. Hawthorne Blvd. | 503-231-7373 | www.castagnarestaurant.com | Dinner Wed-Sun

RECOMMENDED

Le Pigeon   91.6

All you need to know about Gabiel Rucker's cuisine is that his restaurant's motto is "In Foie Gras We Trust." Rucker is the kind of chef who's never met a slab of bacon he didn't like, and he finds countless ways to use it. Along with two assistants, Rucker offers dishes like foie gras bacon served with brioche and a farm egg or a smoked pork chop served atop a stew of fennel and white beans. "The most interesting and inventive food in Portland" manages to be "so well-balanced that even the richest dishes don't seem heavy." Rucker's reach extends to "over-the-top desserts" like profiteroles stuffed with foie gras or corn bread topped with maple ice cream that's been showered with cubes of maple syrup-soaked bacon. Rucker's partner, Andy Fortgang, previously the beverage director at Craft in NYC, has organized a wine list that has surprisingly good depth for a restaurants of this size.

French | Informal | Expensive | kerns | 738 E. Burnside St. | 503-546-8796 | www.lepigeon.com | Dinner daily

Beast   90.9

Following in the footsteps of chefs like Gabrielle Hamilton and April Bloomfield, Naomi Pomeroy is a woman who loves her meat. After making a name for herself at a number of local restaurants, she finally found her calling at this bare-bones dining room dominated by two communal tables and an open kitchen. Each Wednesday Naomi posts a menu that is served through Saturday evening. The six-course meal always features a charcuterie plate that might include a foie gras bon bon with Sauternes gelée or a pig's head terrine with parsley and lemon. And your main course might be braised Rainshadow El Rancho goat with gnocchi and roasted beets. Reviewers called it "fine dining without the fuss" and "sexy food from sexy ladies."

French | Informal | Expensive | alberta arts district | 5425 N.E.30th Ave. | 503-841-6968 | www.beastpdx.com | Dinner Wed-Sun, Lunch Sun

Pok Pok   90.8

Andy Ricker's cooking is so compelling that we are comfortable mentioning his name in the same breath as David Chang's. The well-deserved plaudit is a result of Ricker's obsession with Southeast Asian cuisine, manifested in a menu of "dishes you won't see elsewhere." Those looking for staples like pad Thai should try a different restaurant; but if catfish marinated in turmeric and sticky rice juice or fried chicken wings doused in caramelized Phu Quoc after being marinated in fish sauce and palm sugar is the type of thing that appeals to you, we suggest you immediately buy a plane ticket marked destination PDX. Even the décor – it's designed to look like a shack in Thailand – has an authentic feel to it.

Thai | Informal | Moderate | clinton | 3226 S.E. Division St. | 503-232-1387 | http://pokpokpdx.com | Lunch & Dinner daily

Biwa   90.0

The "best izakaya in town, and maybe the West Coast" offers yet one more outlet for Portland's super produce. Bowls of udon and ramen are laced with various toppings, and there are 14 different items grilling on the robata, including chicken breast, thigh, liver and heart, as well as the tender chopped-chicken meatball called tsukune. Reviewers love it all, saying "Eight stars. Order everything and anything. It's great," "If it says pork belly, order it," and "Their only-after-10:00 p.m. burger is one of the best ever!" An "amazing sake list" and a late-night menu make it "a favorite with local chefs" after they finish the dinner service.

Japanese | Informal | Moderate | buckman | 215 S.E. Ninth Ave. | 503-239-8830 | www.biwarestaurant. com | Dinner daily

Higgins Restaurant and Bar 90.0

In 1984, well before it was fashionable, Greg Higgins brought local and sustainable cuisine to Portland's Heathman Hotel. He opened his own restaurant in 1994, and 17 years later, he's still holding true to his principles, serving dishes like baked Virginia oysters with nettle pesto, parmesan cheese and garlic breadcrumbs or a Tuscan "whole pig" plate that includes fennel sausage, braised belly, ribs and crepinette served with a cranberry bean stew. As is to be expected when a restaurant has been around this long, there are claims that it's "living on its reputation." But many more reviewers call it "a must for those who want to experience Pacific Northwest dining at its best."

New American | Casual | Moderate | downtown | 1239 S.W. Broadway | 503-222-9070 | http://higgins-portland.com | Dinner Daily, Lunch Mon-Fri

TOP LOCAL CHOICE

Beaker and Flask 89.5

Would it surprise you if we said that the focus of this restaurant was the cocktails? Most reviewers mentioned them ahead of the food, as in: "some of the best and most inventive cocktails we have ever had," "It's worth going just to have the very talented bartender mix you something unique," and "acclaimed for their cocktails, justifiably so." But we also read comments like "amazing cocktails and even better food" in praise of Ben Bettinger's cooking, which features dishes like mustard grilled rabbit with bacon, chanterelle crispy pork and an apple crepe.

New American | Casual | Moderate | buckman | 720 S.E. Sandy Blvd. | 503-235-8180 | www.beakerandflask.com | Dinner Mon-Sat

Laurelhurst Market 89.5

Portland is so dominated by hipsters that there's even a steakhouse that caters to them. Run by the Simpatica Dining Hall team, Laurelhurst offers cuts of beef from Creekstone Farms, Niman Ranch and Strube for less than $25. Or if steak's not your thing, there's Afton Fields chicken with Anson Mills polenta or a champagne-braised choucroute garnie. To say the place is popular is an understatement. As one reviewer told us, "All of you who are now making me wait for two hours for a table at this establishment, kindly go somewhere else. This perfectly cooked steak is MINE!"

Brasserie | Informal | Moderate | laurelhurst | 3155 E. Burnside St. | 503-206-3097 | www.laurelhurstmarket.com | Dinner daily

Nostrana 89.5

Looking for San Francisco–style Cal-Ital in Portland? Check out Kathy Whims' menu, featuring Scamorza cheese with shiitake mushrooms, eight different types of pizza and rosemary-and-mascarpone–stuffed chicken breast with roasted Brussels sprouts and ciabatta. A wood-fired stove is the focus of the dining room, both physically and because of the prevalent aroma of burning wood. They also offer a late-night happy hour menu – after 9 p.m. it's $5 for an "amazing pizza margherita!"

Italian | Informal | Moderate | southeast | 1401 S.E. Morrison St. | 503-234-2427 | http://nostrana.com | Dinner Daily, Lunch Mon-Fri

Simpatica Dining Hall   89.5

Imagine the type of bare-bones dining room, dominated by a long, communal table, that you would find at a dining hall in Amish country. Add a bit of elegant hipsterishness to the décor and you've got Simpatica. In keeping with dining-hall tradition, meals are served family style, and an evening's menu includes a mishmash of foods that can range from salt cod and potato brandade to a jambalaya of Dungeness crab and duck. "Beautiful setting, amazing dishes and lingering diners seated family style." They also serve "the best brunch in Portland."

New American | Informal | Moderate | southeast | 828 SE Ash St. | 503-235-1600 | www.simpaticacatering.com | Dinner Fri-Sat, Sun brunch

Urban Farmer   89.5

In other cities, steakhouses might be limited to chains like Morton's or Ruth's Chris. But in Portland, they are a celebration of farmers, foragers and purveyors. At Urban Farmer you can start your meal with Pacific oysters on the half shell or a salad of Dungeness crab, hearts of palm and carrot, then continue with cuts from ranchers like Brandt, Painted Hills and Niman Ranch, as well as Piedmontese beef from Montana Ranch Brand and wagyu from Strube Ranch. You'll enjoy your dinner in a "unique and classy environment" that is "quiet, yet spacious and welcoming."

New American | Informal | Moderate | southeast | 525 S.W. Morrison St. | 503-222-4900 | www.urbanfarmerrestaurant.com | Open daily

Wildwood   89.5

Cory Schreiber, considered (along with Greg Higgins) the founder of Portland's local and sustainable cuisine movement, opened Wildwood in 1984. Schreiber left tin 2007, but Dustin Clark carries on the tradition of serving dishes like skillet-roasted Totten Inelt mussels and house-cured, fire-roasted ham with creamed sauerkraut, dried fruits and apple butter. Reviewers say, "While it's not what it once was," the "fresh, local produce and fish are always prepared with attention to detail." The prices are somewhat high for Portland, which might explain why the dining room is populated with an older crowd.

New American | Casual | Moderate | northwest | 1221 N.W. 21st Ave. | 503-248-9663 | wildwoodrestaurant.com | Dinner daily, Lunch Mon-Sat

Andina   89.0

Nuevo Peruvian is not a cuisine we come across very often, we have to admit, but after importing chefs from her native country as consultants, Doris Rodriguez de Platt has created a restaurant one reviewer characterizes as "inventive food with an exceptional wine and cocktail list." Begin your meal with the ceviche of the day or crispy golden prawns breaded with quinoa and served with a salsa agridulce, and continue with pisco-brined Draper Valley chicken "escabeche" style and sweet potato served two ways: crispy quinoa croquettes and huacatay-cotija cheese gratin.

Peruvian | Casual | Moderate | pearl district | 1314 N.W. Glisan St. | 503-228-9535 | www.andinarestaurant.com | Lunch & Dinner daily

Café Castagna   89.0

If you want to sample a more casual version of Matt Lightner's cooking, check out this restaurant located next door to its big brother, Castagna. The menu mixes simple bistro and trattoria fare, like duck confit with a Port reduction, with orecchiette with cauliflower, garlic, anchovies, chili flakes and breadcrumbs. One reviewer sang its praises by saying, "Café Castagna, we love thee. Such a fabulous patio experience when the weather is good, the cozy dining room when it's not, and arancini without the long flight to Italy. Always great service, almost like old friends. Don't ever change."

New American | Casual | Moderate | southeast | 1758 S.E. Hawthorne Blvd. | 503-231-9959 | http://castagnarestaurant.com | Dinner daily

Caffé Mingo   89.0

The terrific foodstuffs grown around the city usually go onto the menus of Pacific Northwest eateries. But there's no law that says other restaurants can't benefit from the regional bounty, too. Case in point: Caffé Mingo, which uses Portland-area produce in traditional recipes from the Boot. When locals want a well-made bowl of pasta or a slab of Italian-style meatloaf with mashed potatoes and caramelized onion sauce, this is where they go. In addition to the "good food and nice atmosphere," "tables crowded close together and a noisy open kitchen" give it a "big-city trattoria feel."

Italian | Informal | Moderate | uptown | 807 N.W. 21st Ave. | 503-226-4646 | http://www.barmingonw.com/caffemingo.html | Dinner daily

Clyde Common   89.0

"Proof that Portland is a great restaurant city" is on display at this restaurant that advertises itself as a tavern, but whose menu is a dead ringer for a London-style gastropub's. Pull up a chair at a communal table and dig into chicken-fried chicken livers with watercress, cucumber and lemon aioli or a crispy confit pork shank with braised cabbage and smoked apples. The "convivial space" is "filled with hipsters sporting beards and hats." Late-night dining is available at what may be "the best bar in Portland."

Gastropub | Informal | Moderate | southwest | 1014 S.W. Stark St. | 503-228-3333 | www.clydecommon.com | Dinner Daily, Lunch Mon-Fri

Hiroshi   89.0

Portland might be good at a lot of things, but sushi isn't one of them. For locals in a city that brims with high-quality, inexpensive places to eat, throwing down $10 or more for a single piece of fish seems a bit out of character. Within a limited field, Hiroshi Ikegaya runs the "city's best sushi restaurant," complete with "delicious food and a lovely atmosphere." As with sushi places everywhere, the best experience is at the counter, and reviewers recommend you "sit back and let chef Ikegaya take you for a ride."

Japanese | Casual | Expensive | pearl district | 926 N.W. 10th Ave. | 503-619-0580 | Dinner Mon-Sat, Lunch Tue-Fri

Park Kitchen   89.0

Don't be fooled by the "casual and relaxed atmosphere." In a city where chefs are obsessed with sourcing high-quality ingredients, Scott Dolich might be the most obsessed of all. Working out of a storefront in a historic building on the edge of the Pearl District, he wrings every last bit of flavor out of his local, sustainable ingredients, creating dishes like spinach soup with sesame oil and feta cheese, nettle fettuccini with cardoncello mushrooms and shaved goat cheese or pan-seared, first-of-the-season Alaskan halibut served atop a fondue of spring leeks.

American | Informal | Moderate | pearl district | 422 N.W. 8th Ave. | 503-223-7275 | www.parkkitchen. com | Dinner Mon-Sat, Lunch Mon-Fri

Toro Bravo   89.0

No matter what their cuisine, Portland's best chefs manage to feature the wonderful local ingredients. Some do it by tweaking traditional recipes, while others add new presentations to a traditional menu. John Gorham takes the latter approach, and the result means that a Basque piperade peacefully co-exists with lamb bacon on grilled bread with apple butter. As Toro Bravo is extremely popular, a 45-minute wait isn't uncommon, but that means you can relax with a glass or two of sherry until your table is ready.

Spanish | Informal | Moderate | boise-eliot | 120 N.E. Russell St. | 503-281-4464 | www.torobravopdx. com | Dinner daily

Country Cat Dinner House and Bar   88.0

By taking a "light and seasonal approach" with dishes like braised Sweet Briar Farms beef with hand-cut egg noodles, wild mushrooms and a roasted vegetable ragout, this blend of Southern and Pacific Northwest cuisine results in one of Portland's most popular neighborhood restaurants. The "lively environment" and "enthusiastic wait staff" add to the experience, and the "family-friendly atmosphere" means that it's full of parents and children in the earlier hours of the evening. The $12 Beer 'n' Burger Mondays are a "must go for the onion rings alone."

American | Informal | Moderate | southeast | 7937 S.E. Stark St. | 503-408-1414 | www.thecountrycat.net | Open daily

Paley's Place   88.0

Fans of Vitaly Paley's restaurant often speak of it in hushed tones. It dates back to 1995 and was one of the city's original proponents of local ingredients. We weren't surprised to read comments like "elegant and simple Northwest cuisine" and "great spot, great service, great food." But a full one-third of our reviewers don't rate it anywhere as highly, saying, "At one time this might have been 'the place' to go in Portland, but it's no longer top dog in the city" and lamenting that it's "in serious need of some new life."

New American | Casual | Moderate | northwest | 1204 N.W. 21st Ave. | 503-243-2403 | www.paleysplace. net | Dinner daily

Ping   88.0

It didn't take Andy Ricker very long to capitalize on his success at Pok Pok. However, Ping is more of a place for drinks and snacks, with food that revolves around grilled skewers of pork collar, short rib, chicken butt and lamb satay, along with an assortment of Thai snacks and a few noodle dishes. Comments run from the ecstatic – "Andy Ricker is God" – to the more considered: "unusual cocktails, great bites off the grill, creative small and large plates. The only thing to watch out for is how your bill adds up because you want to try everything."

Thai | Informal | Moderate | Chinatown | 102 N.W. 4th Ave. | 503-229-7464 | www.pingpdx.com | Dinner Mon-Sat, Lunch Mon-Fri

ACCEPTABLE

Carafe 87.5

Portland's most popular French bistro comes with an air of authenticity. The menu is filled with dishes like escargots, moules à la crème, crispy duck leg confit and choucroute garnie, and the décor features café-style tables and chairs and a lovely outdoor patio. The result: a bit of "Paris in Portland" that's "worth going to if you're a Francophile." Of course, this is Portland, with all those terrific fresh, local ingredients, so the Gallic classics all come with a distinctly local flair.

French Bistro | Informal | Moderate | downtown | 200 S.W. Market St. | 503-248-0004 | www.carafebistro.com | Dinner Mon-Sat, Lunch Mon-Fri

3 Doors Down Café 87.0

Only in Portland do the simplest of neighborhood restaurants serve dishes like Silvies Valley Ranch grass-fed beef carpaccio with micro-greens, shaved parmesan and garlic aioli or a grilled Carlton Farms pork chop with caraway-braised red cabbage, mashed potatoes and demi-glace. Fans say it's "a great restaurant that uses fresh, local produce and fish, and the kitchen pays attention to the details" and claim "the pastas are delicious and the vodka penne is justly popular."

New American | Informal | Moderate | hawthorne | 1429 S.E. 37th Ave. | 503-236-6886 | www.3doorsdowncafe.com | Dinner Tue-Sun

Clarklewis 87.0

In another city, this type of restaurant – a trendy-looking warehouse with a refined industrial vibe – would be more about the flash than the food. But in Portland, it's a proud member of the city's local and sustainable movement, serving dishes like turkey noodle soup with trofie and sage or grilled Cattail Creek lamb with borlotti beans, radicchio and Persephone squash. Reviewers say it's "not as great as it once was, but it remains a great space with great energy and good food."

New American | Casual | Moderate | industrial district | 1001 S.E. Water Ave. | 503-235-2294 | www.clarklewispdx.com | Dinner Mon-Sat, Lunch Mon-Fri

Dundee Bistro 87.0

(26 miles southwest in Dundee)

Every wine-growing region needs a restaurant like Dundee Bistro (Mustards Grill in the Napa Valley would be an equivalent). The menu is the typical wine country mishmash based on local ingredients, like a starter of beignets of sweet yellow corn and applewood-smoked bacon and mains like wild Petrale sole with cauliflower and lemon-caper cream. Add a "casual vibe" and a "top-notch list of local wines" and you have "a favorite for lunch or before driving back to Portland after a day of tasting."

New American | Informal | Moderate | Dundee | 100-A S.W. Seventh Street | 503-554-1650 | www.dundeebistro.com | Lunch & Dinner daily

Joel Palmer House 87.0

(33 miles southwest in Dayton)

His family had run the iconic Joe's Tavern in Redding, Pennsylvania, since 1916, but 80 years later, Joe Czarnacki picked up stakes and moved operations to the Willamette Valley after deciding that the Redding area could no longer support fine dining. Now his son Chris Czarnacki serves the family's signature recipes, many of which revolve around wild mushrooms, like Heidi's Three Mushroom Tart and Joe's Wild Mushroom Soup. While some reviewers enjoyed themselves here ("How many delicious things can you do with mushrooms!"), more critical types derided "a heavy hand in the kitchen," adding that the "prices would be too high at half the cost."

Continental | Casual | Expensive | dayton | 600 Ferry St. | 503-864-2995 | www.joelpalmerhouse.com | Dinner Tue-Sat

Navarre   87.0

The food is sourced from a local Community Supported Agriculture scheme, and they pour 50 wines by the glass at this rustic-looking restaurant that could be mistaken for a taverna in the Basque region of Spain. The menu is printed on scraps of recycled paper; you check off the dishes you want and hand the list to your server. Most of the items come in tapas-size portions, and on any given day the list of large plates might include a paté of country pork with prunes, trout baked in parchment or buffalo flank steak.

Mediterranean | Informal | Moderate | kerns | 10 N.E. 28th Ave. | 503-232-3555 | navarreportland.blogspot.com | Dinner daily, Lunch Fri-Sun

Bluehour   86.5

More bar than restaurant, this "Pearl District icon" is a place to "dress up and be seen," reviewers say. When you're not paying attention to the crowd, you can delve into a charcuterie platter, gnocchi topped with shaved Oregon black truffles or Draper Valley chicken with chestnut dumplings and local mushrooms. The New American fare, a list of "wonderful cocktails" and "an excellent rotating selection of cheese" make this a more serious dining experience than people give it credit for.

New American | Casual | Expensive | pearl district | 250 N.W. 13th Ave. | 503-226-3394 | www.bluehouronline.com | Dinner daily, Lunch Sun-Fri

EaT: An Oyster Bar   86.5

Given how fertile the waters are and how many varieties of oysters are raised in the Pacific Northwest, it pains us to report that this is a New Orleans–style restaurant rather than a straightforward expression of the region's best bivalves – though in all fairness, they do offer a selection of local oysters on the half shell. Reviewers say it's "a comfortable place to hang out" and enjoy dishes like black-

ened catfish, frog's legs and jambalaya.

Cajun | Informal | Moderate | boise-eliot | 3808 N. Williams Ave. | 503-281-1222 | http://eatoysterbar.com | Lunch & Dinner daily

Painted Lady   86.0

(24 miles southeast in Newberg)

Though highly touted by the local food press, Allen Routt's cuisine did not similarly enrapture our reviewers. Routt's dining room is populated with local celebrities (one reviewer wrote of dining next to the governor), but despite the setting, comments mentioned "a dated approach to the cuisine," including "sauces that I could do a better job with at home." It does have its fans, who say, "consistent, great Wine Country dining always."

New American | Casual | Expensive | newberg | 201 S. College St. | 503-538-3850 | www.thepaintedladyrestaurant.com | Dinner Wed-Sun

Typhoon   86.0

Even in hipsterish Portlandia, you can find an upscale version of Thai cuisine. The menu here includes a list of what they call Chef's Fave Raves, like grilled beef with grapes in a spicy-garlic lime dressing or Fish on Fire, filet of halibut drizzled with choo chee curry sauce and rum and served flambé. Reviewers say there's "somewhat of a corporate feel to the place, but the food is quite good" and note the "fancy setting, fabulous servers – perfect for guests."

Thai | Casual | Moderate | southwest | 410 S.W. Broadway | 503-224-8285 | www.typhoonrestaurants.com | Open daily

Lauro Kitchen   85.5

David Machado digs deep into his roots with dishes like Cataplana-roasted mussels with chouriço and a tagine of chicken with winter squash and couscous. But depending on who you ask, Lauro Kitchen is "Portland's best Mediterranean restaurant" or "just another neighborhood restaurant with okay food." One reviewer did his best to split the middle saying, "It's good, really good, but it's not the be-all, end-all."

Mediterranean | Informal | Moderate | southeast | 3377 S.E. Division St. | 503-239-7000 | www.laurokitchen.com | Dinner daily

Noble Rot   85.5

The term "noble rot" describes grapes afflicted with botrytis, a condition that increases sugar content to the extent that it practically turns the dry Semillon grape into a Sauternes. So what better name to give a "hip" wine bar where a glass comes with some of the best views in the city? And if you must eat while you sip, there are sandwiches like a ham and cheddar panino with mango chutney or a pork chop with red rice, roasted root vegetables and Fuji apples.

Wine Bar | Informal | Moderate | northeast | 1111 E. Burnside, 4th floor | 503-233-1999 | www.noblerotpdx.com | Dinner Mon-Sat

Heathman   85.0

It's a shame that this lovely 1927 hotel, which celebrates its location next to the Portland Center for the Performing Arts with a fine art collection, doesn't have a better restaurant. It was renowned when Greg Higgins ran the kitchen back in the '80s. Now, while it still subscribes to Portland's local and sustainable move-ment, "solid" was the best thing anyone said about Philippe Boulot's French cook-ing. Breakfast is an option, especially if you're in the mood for a Hangtown Fry, made of Willapa Bay oysters, eggs, bacon, peppers, onions and Parmesan.

French | Casual | Expensive | downtown | Heathman Hotel | 1001 S.W. Broadway | 503-790-7752 | www.heathmanhotel.com | Open daily

OTHER PLACES MENTIONED

Portland City Grill   84.5

Every metropolis needs a place like the Portland City Grill. Set on the 30th floor of an office building, it offers tried-and-true New American fare like Dungeness crab cakes with a shaved fennel salad and an entire slate of steaks and chops along, with a handful of entrées like a garlic herb grilled pork tenderloin. But no one goes for the food; they go for "the best views in the city" and a happy hour described as a "meet market."

New American | Casual | Expensive | downtown | 111 S.W. Fifth Ave., 30th fl. | 503-450-0030 | www.portlandcitygrill.com | Dinner Daily, Lunch Mon-Fri

Jake's Famous Crawfish   84.0

This 110-year-old Portland institution was considered a "tourist location" even before it was taken over by the McCormick & Schmick's chain. A few people enjoyed the "fresh fish" in a "warm environment," but the comment that best sums it up is "overpriced, average seafood in a classic old-school setting. Jake's is the place your parents always thought of as the best place in town. It hasn't changed, but the world has moved on."

Seafood | Casual | Expensive | downtown | 401 S.W. 12th Ave. | 503-226-1419 | www.mccormickandschmicks.com | Dinner daily, Lunch Mon-Sat

Veritable Quandry   84.0

Open since 1971, this "classic Portland spot" does a good job with familiar items, but doesn't offer anything outside the typical American food experience. It's popular for special occasions on a year-round basis, but especially in summer, when guests can enjoy a "beautiful gar-den patio." The combination of a "safe menu" and the ability to dine outdoors in the middle of the city makes it a "perfect place to take your parents after a tour of the city."

New American | Casual | Moderate | downtown | 1220 S.W. 1st Ave. | 503-227-7342 | www.veritablequandary.com | Lunch & Dinner daily

¡Oba!   83.0

In Portland, even the Nuevo Latino restaurants use organic ingredients. But that doesn't stop reviewers from describing dishes like the Puerto Rican shrimp fried rice and ancho-crusted ahi tuna as "tired Latin fusion cuisine." Still, it works on those special nights that require a restaurant with a "romantic dining room," and numerous people mentioned the "great happy hour"; one person said it's "worth going for the mojitos alone!"

Latin | Casual | Expensive | pearl district | 555 N.W. 12th Ave. | 503-228-6161 | www.obarestaurant.com | Dinner daily

Cheap Eats

UNIQUELY DELICIOUS

Olympic Provisions   8.5

Of all of the noble professions in the culinary world, the one of salumist is certainly a rarity in the U.S. So what are the odds that two of the country's premier salumists would be situated in the Pacific Northwest? That's been the case since 2009, when Elias Cairo started to fabricate "the best cured meats around" – among them, a dozen different types of dried salami, including the award-winning Saucisson d'Arles – on the second floor of a converted cereal mill in Portland's Warehouse District. (Salumi Artisan Cured Meats, in Seattle, is the other.) If you make it through the charcuterie course and still have an appetite, they offer a menu of gastropub-style fare like a roasted chicken thigh with shallots, cream and cremini mushrooms.

Delicatessen | Inexpensive | southeast | 107 S.E. Washington St. | 503-954-3663 | www.olympicprovisions.com | Lunch & Dinner Mon-Sat

RECOMMENDED

Bunk Sandwiches   7.5

On a per capita basis, no other city in America might have as many quality cheap-eats spots as Portland. Bunk is at the top of the heap, with "creative sandwiches put together by folks who know what it takes to make a good one." One reviewer waxed poetic about a "fried egg sandwich that's perfection – firm and greasy on the outside, liquid gold on the inside." Another simply asked why it must be so "delicious"?

Sandwiches | Inexpensive | southeast | 621 SE Morrison St. | 503-477-9515 | www.bunksandwiches.com | Breakfast & Lunch Mon-Sat

Stumptown Roasters   7.5

What started out as a single location in 1999 has grown into a business with branches as far away as New York City. But the original location on Division Street is "still the standard-bearer for the indie Portland coffee scene." Absolutely beloved by the locals, it garnered kudos like, "The original when it comes to origin, farming practice and roasting along with a damn good cup of coffee," "Who doesn't love Stumptown?" and "These guys always knew their beans – now everyone, everywhere knows them."

Dessert | Inexpensive | old town | 4525 S.E. Division St. | 505-230-7702 | www.stumptowncoffee.com | Open daily

Ken's Artisan Pizza   7.1

While Apizza Scholls is the best known of Portland's various pizzerias, reviewers say they prefer the pizza at Ken's. "If you are making the grand tour of great pizza places in the country, you should include Ken's. It's consistently good, and the Neapolitan-style pizza is well executed every time." Of course, that type of recommendation means "there's always a line and never a table available." And because they're open only from 5 p.m. to 10 p.m., showing up at "off" hours isn't an option.

Pizzeria | Inexpensive | southeast portland | 304 S.E. 28th Ave. | 503-517-9951 | www.kensartisan.com | Dinner daily

Little T American Baker   7.0

You'll find the "best baguette in Portland" at this bakery, along with breakfast pastries that range from a typical pain au chocolat (albeit with pralines) to rarer varieties like the orangiata, a Grand Marnier–flavored citrus brioche. Lunch could be ham and cheese on a seeded hoagie or bread salad with mozzarella, tomato and basil. Even the space was complimented for its "large plate glass windows" that allow one to gaze out onto the local street scene while ruminating over a cup of espresso.

Bakery | Inexpensive | southeast portland | 2600 S.E. Division St. | 503-238-3458 | www.littletbaker.com | Breakfast & Lunch daily

Screen Door   7.0

This restaurant's dedication to a pan-Southern cuisine means a menu that includes everything from Low Country–style shrimp 'n' grits to Texas-style BBQ brisket to brunch specialties like a praline bacon waffle. On the plus side, the food is made with Portland's terrific local ingredients. "Dress warmly as you will likely wait outside for an hour" sums up the downside. One Texas-born reviewer praised it for serving "the best fried chicken and Southern-style veggies in the Northwest!"

New American | Inexpensive | queen anne | 2337 E. Burnside St. | 503-542-0880 | www.screendoor-restaurant.com | Dinner daily, Lunch Sat-Sun

Voodoo Doughnut   7.0

In 2003, two friends who at the time knew nothing about making doughnuts opened this unique spot on what looks like Portland's version of Skid Row. Visit on the weekend and you are guaranteed to find yourself in a long line of locals and tourists who are waiting for a chance to sample kooky creations like the Loop (vanilla icing and Fruit Loops), Mango Tango (mango jelly and vanilla frosting), the Diablos Rex (icing in the shape of a pentagram), Cock-N-Balls (shaped like you-know-what) and their most famous offering – the Bacon Maple Bar, in which an actual slice of bacon stretches across the maple icing. They serve Stumptown Coffee, or you can stick with the classic accompaniment, a cold glass of milk.

Dessert | Inexpensive | downtown | 1501 N.E. Davis St. | 503-235-2666 | www.voodoodoughnut. com | Open daily

OTHER PLACES MENTIONED

Bijou Café   6.8

While it's just a simple checkered-tablecloth type of place, with a menu that offers eight different types of omelets; buckwheat and buttermilk pancakes; French toast made from whole wheat bread, cinnamon bread or brioche; and hash made with oysters, roast beef or mushrooms (the vegan-friendly version), Bijou is where Portlandians go for power breakfasts. The most popular item might be the Hangtown Fry, an omelet-like dish that combines oysters and bacon.

Coffee Shop | Inexpensive | downtown | 132 S.W. 3rd Ave. | 503-222-3187 | Breakfast & Lunch daily

Apizza Scholls   6.3

We were surprised at the low rating of this nationally known pizzeria. In one corner are fans who argue that "The thin, chewy, charred pizza crust is the best in the country," and has "rightfully earned a place among the top American pizzas." Those opposed counter that the crust is "too charred" and say that "While they are passionate about making pizza, somehow the fine ingredients and care taken in preparing them do not produce excellent results."

Pizzeria | Inexpensivel | southeast | 4741 S.E. Hawthorne Blvd. | 503-233-1286 | www.apizzascholls.com | Dinner daily

Pine State Biscuits   6.1

"Tall, flaky," "buttery and crumbly"

biscuits serve as the anchors for sandwiches with fillings like fried chicken, grits cakes or flank steak; there's also "classic style" (that is, covered with gravy and topped with an egg). "Get there early before the hipsters wake up" in order to avoid the line for "stick-to-your-bones comfort food" that offers "the perfect cure for a hangover."

Southern | Inexpensive| southeast | 3640 S.E. Belmont St. | 503-236-3346 | www.pinestatebiscuits.com | Breakfast & Lunch Daily

Mother's Bistro & Bar   6.0

Considering that the Deep South couldn't be farther away from Portland, it's amazing how many restaurants serve Southern cuisine. At Mother's, the combination of "comfortable surroundings," "friendly wait staff," "yummy comfort food" and "sunlight streaming through the windows into the dining room" make it the perfect place to take your, er, mother for a mac 'n cheese.

Southern | Inexpensive| downtown | 212 S.W. Stark St. | 503-464-1122 | www.mothersbistro.com | Lunch & Dinner Tue-Sat, Sun lunch only

Papa Haydn   6.0

It's been 33 years of cakes and pastries with names like Autumn Meringue, Boccone Dolce, Georgian Peanut Butter Mousse and White Chocolate Mint Torte at this café that pays tribute to the owner's favorite composer. They offer a full menu of savory fare for lunch and dinner, but most people go for the "amazing desserts." Indulging yourself here is "a popular way to end an evening," though be prepared for waits of up to 90 minutes on Fridays and Saturdays.

Dessert | Inexpensive | southeast | 701 N.W. 23rd Ave. | 503-228-7317 | www.papahaydn.com | Lunch & Dinner daily

San Francisco, Marin County & the East Bay CA

AN IMPORTANT DESTINATION

COI   96.7

In a town overrun with Chez Panisse clones and restaurants serving Cal-Ital cuisine, Daniel Patterson is striving for something different. Although the self-taught Patterson first attracted national media attention at Elisabeth Daniel in 2000, it wasn't until he opened this 28-seat, North Beach dining room in 2006 that his career really began to take off. Relying on a subtle use of modern technology and a diverse selection of locally grown organic ingredients, Patterson crafts what is easily the city's most progressive cuisine, one that we think will appeal to those who lean toward contemporary cooking; yet, as one reviewer put it, Patterson's fare is "surprisingly not as molecular as everyone said it was going to be."

Patterson's menu emphasizes a minimalist, vegetable-oriented approach to cuisine described as "interesting without sacrificing flavor," like his Earth and Sea (new harvest potatoes, cucumber, borage, sea beans and ice plant flowers) or morels served with burnt rice, ash, smoke and pine. And when he does utilize meat in a dish, it's in a subtle way, like a dish of bone marrow with caviar and beetroot purée or a fried chicken consommé served with artichokes, fava beans, radish and green garlic. Patterson is still young and still developing, so if you go now you can follow the culinary evolution of someone who has the potential to be an important chef in years to come.

Progressive | Casual | Very Expensive | north beach | 373 Broadway | 415-393-9000 | www.coirestaurant.com | Dinner Tue-Sat

Quince   96.2

It's hard for a Cal-Ital chef to set himself apart from the pack in San Francisco, where the cuisine dominates the culinary landscape. But with "a dedication to refining the Cal-Ital experience" that is unique, combined with "a command of culinary technique rarely seen in an Italian restaurant," Michael Tusk does just that. In fact, shortly, after Quince opened to rave reviews in 2003, one of the top chefs in the Bay Area told us it was "only a matter of time before Tusk's cuisine earned an even higher rating." Well, his prediction came true, and the restaurant has been so successful that in 2010 it moved from its original Pacific Heights location into much larger quarters in Jackson Square.

Everyone raves about Tusk's handmade pastas – one reviewer told us there are days when as many as ten different types are on offer – which turn up in dishes like spaghetti with clams, melon and espresso and which are supplemented with starters like octopus (Tusk tenderizes it by massaging it by hand) and mains like Liberty duck with a blood orange glaze and fennel mostarda. The lovely ambience and the warm welcome offered by Lindsay Tusk and her staff also drew positive comments, with one person praising her for "greeting her guests as if they were coming to her home for dinner."

Italian | Casual | Expensive | downtown | 470 Pacific Ave. | 415-775-8500 | www.quincerestaurant.com | Dinner daily

Sushi Ran   95.9

As a marker for how successful this restaurant has been during the reign of Okinawa native Yoshi Tome, its number of seats has expanded from 26 to 90 since he purchased the place in 1986. And while it might fly under the radar in terms of national attention, many of our San Francisco–based reviewers are happy to travel to Sausalito to eat at what is considered the best Japanese restaurant in the Bay Area. (Tip: Take the ferry from downtown, as it's only a short walk from the terminal.)

A stickler for the best possible fish, Tome is quick to shun items that other restaurants are happy to carry (like frozen fugu); the vast majority of his seafood is flown in from Tokyo's Tsukiji Market. In addition to the delicious sushi, Tome offers an excellent range of innovative and tasty cooked dishes, a 300-bottle wine list featuring both New and Old World wines, and a "great list of sakes," with more than 30 selections.

Japanese | Informal | Expensive | sausalito | 107 Caledonia St. | 415-332-3620 | www.sushiran.com | Dinner Daily, Lunch Mon-Fri

Commis   95.3

No, it isn't Heston Blumenthal or Andoni Aduriz. It isn't even a speeding bullet. It's super-chef James Syhabout, who after years of working as the sous-chef at Manresa (interspersed with stints for the chefs named above), has finally gone out on his own. While initial reports included reviews like "The chef is still finding his way" and "definitely a chef to watch, though he's not quite there yet," now we are more likely to see comments like "wonderful ingredients" and "technically perfect," along with the pithy "amazing, simply amazing."

Given his résumé, one would have thought that Syhabout's first effort would be more of a grand restaurant. Instead, he chose a simple dining room in North Oakland where walls washed in a light gray serve as a backdrop for bare wooden tables. The simplistic décor belies the sophistication of the cuisine, exemplified by a slow-cooked egg served with Medjool dates and onion cream ("an explosion of synergistic flavors") or a water-cress soup with oysters enveloped in milk skin or a corned pork jowl that one reviewer dubbed "the best piece of swine to ever cross my lips." We suggest you reserve one of the six seats at the counter, where you can "just tell James to work his magic."

New American | Informal | Expensive | north oakland | 3859 Piedmont Ave. | 510-653-3902 | www.commisrestaurant.com | Dinner Wed-Sun

Chez Panisse   95.2

Back in the 1970s, when agricultural conglomerates were forcing independent farmers out of business, Alice Waters opened a restaurant that used only ingredients raised naturally. Given what people were used to eating – dishes prepared with mass-marketed ingredients raised in a manner that allowed them to be shipped across country – there were many who argued that her efforts would be in vain. But Waters realized that diners wanted something more, and in the process of devising a cuisine that they would like, she defined the contemporary American dining experience so clearly that we propose that when she retires, the restaurant, with its lively Arts and Crafts décor, be moved to the Smithsonian Museum and showcased next to Julia Child's kitchen.

The storied history of Chez Panisse complicates the way the dining community views the restaurant. Some adore the loving and respectful manner in which the pristine ingredients are prepared, while others say the cuisine is nothing more than what is offered at dozens of regional restaurants in France and Italy, and now in many American restaurants. A third camp factors its reputation into the equation, offering comments like "I voted 'Must Go' for its significance in terms of modern culinary history, but I would give it a lower rating if it had opened recently." There is a nice list of small-producer wines, with an emphasis on bottles from southern France, although a few reviewers claim it has been picked over.

Provençal | Casual | Expensive | berkeley | 1517 Shattuck Ave. | 510-548-5525 | www.chezpanisse.com | Dinner Mon-Sat

HIGHLY RECOMMENDED

Gary Danko   93.7

This is one of the most controversial restaurants in our survey: Some 90% of our reviewers recommend it, with 20% rating it as Must Go, while 10% absolutely slam the place, calling it "overrated and coasting on its reputation." As with most disagreements, the truth lies somewhere in between, and we suspect that if you enjoy eating at what we call "big city, upper middle restaurants," you will enjoy the cooking here, which features dishes like risotto with lobster, rock shrimp, asparagus, morels and stinging nettles, and roast loin of bison with king trumpet mushrooms, glazed cipollini and herb spatzle. There's a spectacular wine list offered, it must be said, at spectacular prices. It's super-popular, so much so that a number of people complained of experiencing "long waits for a table despite reservations."

New American | Casual | Expensive | fisherman's wharf | 800 N. Point St. | 415-749-2060 | www.garydanko.com | Dinner daily

Masa's   93.2

As the years pass, it is typical for a restaurant to lose relevance within the fine-dining community. But Gregory Short has given Masa's a second life. A French Laundry alumnus, Short has re-energized the restaurant by introducing the type of long, multi-course tasting menu his former employers are known for, causing one reviewer to refer to his cuisine as "French Laundry light." The four and seven-course menus feature dishes like a beggar's purse of fall vegetables or a tasting of spring lamb from Elysian Fields Farms served with a San Marzano tomato marmalade, baby artichokes and squash blossoms. Alan Murray's wine list is packed with hard-to-get cherries, as well as the types of older wines that reflect the length of time the restaurant has been in business.

Seafood | Casual | Expensive | union square | 648 Bush St. | 415-989-7154 | www.masasrestaurant.com | Dinner Tue-Sat

Ritz-Carlton Dining Room   93.2

There's a split of opinion about this restaurant, which features former French Laundry second Ron Siegel at the helm. Fans praised the "precise cooking with luxurious ingredients," especially in the Chef's Tasting Menu, which features dishes like lobster with black truffles, sunchoke purée and red beet essence and hot foie gras with huckleberries, brioche and Rome apple juice with long pepper. In contrast, foes feel "It was better when he first arrived back in 2005," adding "The chef now lives on his reputation." Putting that debate aside, the place does offer bonuses in the form of fair pricing (the tasting menu is $125 for seven courses) and a "spacious room along with large tables," which makes this "one of best places in the city to have a conversation over dinner."

New American | Formal | Very Expensive | nob hill | Ritz-Carlton | 600 Stockton St. | 415-296-7465 | www.ritzcarlton.com | Dinner Tue-Sat

Swan Oyster Depot   92.8

They have been shucking fresh oysters since 1912 at this restaurant that some find reminiscent of Barcelona's Cal Pep. Besides oysters, there are clams and other assorted shellfish on offer, along with chowder, seafood salads and seasonal specialties like Dungeness crab. And if the idea of a large pile of sparkling-fresh shellfish isn't enough of a lure, the countermen are total characters. As the entire place consists of a mere 20 stools, you can expect a line that stretches out onto Polk Street and a 20- or 30-minute wait. However, we suggest you think twice about going if counters filled with large piles of empty shells make you squeamish.

Seafood | Informal | Moderate | polk gulch | 1517 Polk St. | 415-673-1101 | Open daily

Kiss Sushi   92.6

When it comes to sushi, San Francisco has always lagged behind Los Angeles in terms of quality establishments. But many of our reviewers say this "pocket square of a restaurant (it seats a mere 12 people, including five at the counter)" offers the best sushi in the city, with "expertly prepared cuts of fish" kept in "pristine condition." Add an amiable staff to the mix (one reviewer referred to Naka-San and his wife as "the adorable couple who run this place") and we understand why one reviewer told us, "I hesitate to recommend this restaurant because . . . I don't want to create unnecessary demand." However, a few folks complained of "poor value" due to "high prices" and a "limited selection of fish that never changes."

Japanese | Informal | Moderate | japantown | 1700 Laguna St. | 415-474-2866 | Dinner Tue-Sat

La Folie   92.5

Every city has a number of French expat chefs who soldier on despite the declining popularity of traditional French cuisine. Roland Passot is among those who carry that torch
in the Bay Area, and he keeps the local Francophile community happy with a tortellini
of foie gras in a duck and oxtail consommé, a terrine made with warm pig's feet, sweetbreads and lobster, and a pancetta-wrapped venison loin served with an apple-studded
potato galette. While the food is described as "rich and intense," the service occasionally comes under fire for being "fussy," "pretentious" and "overbearing," though one
reviewer found the persnickety quality "perfect when you're in the mood for a classic,
romantic, whimsical and delicious meal."

French | Casual | Expensive | russian hill | 2316 Polk St. | 415-776-5577 | www.lafolie.com | Dinner Mon-
Sat

Benu   92.3

This restaurant from former French Laundry executive chef Corey Lee was one of the
most highly awaited openings of 2010. While everyone loved his cooking in Yountville,
Lee has yet to attract the same level of enthusiasm here. Of Korean heritage, Lee mixes
dishes like risotto with sea urchin, butternut squash, celery and black truffle with such
offerings as beef braised in pear, so it's not surprising to hear the restaurant referred
to as "the Asian French Laundry." But the consensus among reviewers is best reflected
in comments like "precise, over-theorized, over-exercised," "technically perfect but
lacking character" and "Despite the precise technique and perfect execution, the food
hasn't quite settled into its vision yet."

New American | Casual | Expensive | soma | 22 Hawthorne St. | 415-685-4860 | www.benusf.com |
Dinner Tue-Sat

Ame   92.2

We can't think of another restaurant that serves both Japanese and Italian cuisine.
Not a fusion of the two, but offerings that reflect, in turn, the ethnic backgrounds of its
husband and wife owners, Hiro Sone and Lissa Doumani. The mix-and-match menu
affords the rare opportunity to start your meal with miso-glazed pork ribs before being
transported to Italy and a ragout of rabbit atop a polenta cake. (Is this how they eat
at the Japanese embassy in Rome?) Doumani was praised for her delicious pastries,
and more than a few people have noted that things in the dining room have been going
more smoothly since she began supervising the service.

Italian/Japanese | Casual | Expensive | soma | St. Regis Hotel | 689 Mission St. | 415-284-4040 | www.
amerestaurant.com | Dinner daily

Chez Panisse Café   92.2

You come away feeling as if you have visited a shrine when you've eaten at this, the
more informal of Alice Waters' dining rooms, which is probably as close as you can get
to casual European-style dining in the U.S. There's not much to the menu other than
perfect ingredients prepared with love and care, like Cannard Farms rocket served with
artichokes and hand-stretched mozzarella, Monterey Bay squid roasted in a wood-
burning oven and served with aioli, and grilled leg of Magruder Ranch veal with fried
spring onions, wild spinach and porcini mushrooms. There's the same quirky wine list

as at the more formal downstairs restaurant – or corkage, if you prefer.

Provençal | Casual | Moderate | berkeley | 1517 Shattuck Ave. | 510-548-5525 | www.chezpanisse.com | Dinner Mon-Sat

Boulevard   92.1

While many of the restaurants that opened during the height of the California cuisine craze have either shut their doors or have dwindled in popularity, Boulevard remains a sought-after standard-bearer. On most evenings Nancy Oakes' place is full of diners who still enjoy dishes like seared Sonoma foie gras with root beer jelly, vanilla sour cherries and toasted whole grain bread from Berkeley's renowned Acme Bakery or prime rib of Berkshire pork roasted in a wood-burning oven and served with mashed potatoes and caramelized cauliflower. The wine list is packed with gems bottled just up the road in Napa and Sonoma.

Californian | Casual | Expensive | embarcadero | 1 Mission St. | 415-543-6084 | www.boulevardrestaurant.com | Dinner Daily, Lunch Mon-Fri

RECOMMENDED

Jardinière   91.8

After honing her chops at Rubicon (which unfortunately closed three years ago), Traci des Jardins partnered with Pat Kuleto to open this restaurant. While some of our reviewers find the cuisine too safe and corporate for their taste, the place always seems to be bustling with loyal diners, especially when the symphony or the opera is in season. Des Jardins' menu features dishes like Wolfe Ranch quail wrapped in bacon served with lentils, oranges and Niçoise olives, along with a selection of a half-dozen cheeses that have been aged in-house. There's an extensive wine list, but its "less than friendly" pricing constitutes a huge negative for some reviewers.

French | Casual | Expensive | civic center | 300 Grove St. | 415-861-5555 | www.jardiniere.com | Dinner daily

Saison   91.7

Josh Skenes is back. After making a name for himself at Chez TJ, he took a few years off to go surfing. But in 2009 he opened this "gorgeous space" with a goal of "redefining the concept of a fancy meal." An important part of Skene's strategy is a wood-burning grill situated on the restaurant's patio. But he's not content with just cooking food on the grates. Skenes puts ingredients right in the ash or sets them next to a pile of flaming logs. One reviewer recommended it as being "in the Manresa/Arpege mode" adding, "the food will be great one day," while another called his experience "one of the most eye-opening meals of the year."

New American | Casual | Expensive | mission | 2124 Folsom St. | 415-828-7990 | www.saisonsf.com | Dinner Tue-Sun

Canteen   91.0

Having worked at some of the great Parisian restaurants, Dennis Leary wasn't on track to be running what is in essence a high-end diner. But he does such a good job of it that you will find significant competition when trying to book one of the 20 seats here.

The menu changes daily, and on the night you visit, Leary might be serving a polenta and goat cheese clafoutis with roasted chanterelles or pork schnitzel with a poached egg and chicory. The one complaint we kept hearing was about a "closet-size kitchen" that "sometime takes its toll on his cooking," but overall that doesn't seem to have had much of a negative impact.

New American | Informal | Moderate | nob hill | 817 Sutter St. | 415-928-8870 | www.sfcanteen.com | Lunch & Dinner Wed-Sun, Tue dinner only

Dopo   90.8

While other Cal-Ital offerings grab a lot of attention, Jon Smulewitz's restaurant seems to fly under the radar. But reviewers who know it well were quick to tell us it's the top restaurant of its type. In fact, one esteemed European chef told us his visit "was my favorite meal of my trip" – and that was after he spent two weeks eating at every top restaurant in the Bay Area. What he was raving about are "miraculous" homemade salumi, "crusty, crusty pizzas," agnolotti of lamb with mint and pecorino and a hen leg stewed with artichokes and Gaeta olives and topped with Parmesan. They don't take reservations, so "go early" if you don't want to wait on "lines that can be a pain."

Cal-Ital | Informal | Moderate | oakland | 4293 Piedmont Ave. | 510-652-3676 | www.dopoadesso.com | Dinner Mon-Sat, Lunch Mon-Fri

Acquerello   90.7

Acquerello isn't as widely known as other places, but those familiar with it claim it serves the best straightforward Italian cuisine in San Francisco. Suzette Gresham-Tognetti's no-nonsense creations are on the richer side, like a Parmesan budino topped with a fresh arugula salad or risotto made with prawns, bay scallops, caviar and Prosecco or lightly smoked sturgeon served with shredded oxtail and a red wine drizzle. The place is a favorite with the local BYOB crowd, even though Giancarlo Paterlini (arguably the greatest host in town) supervises a primo wine list.

Italian | Casual | Expensive | polk gulch | 1722 Sacramento St. | 415-567-5432 | www.acquerello.com | Dinner Tue-Sat

Prospect   90.7

Most successful chefs open additional locations as fast as they can. But Nancy Oakes waited 17 years to branch out. Debuting in 2010, Prospect reflects the changes that have occurred in dining during the last two decades, both in terms of décor – this is a sleek "modernistic room," instead of the Belle Epoque setting of Boulevard – and cooking. Oakes' California cuisine has been updated to New American dishes like Petaluma organic chicken with a foie gras emulsion, sweet potatoes and Himalayan truffles. The "large, beautiful" eatery is typically brimming with young diners, causing reviewers to describe it as "a happening place" serving "food that shows flashes of brilliance."

New American | Casual | Expensive | soma | 300 Spear St. | 415-247-7770 | www.prospectsf.com | Dinner daily, Lunch Sun

Yank Sing   90.6

The best known of the big-three dim sum specialists in the metro area claims to offer 100 different types of small plates, including dumplings filled with lobster, broccoli and tobiko or – in the case of the Goldfish Dumpling – crunchy shrimp, bamboo-shoot tips and cilantro in a translucent wrapper. But the house specialties are the cooked dishes: shrimp wrapped in bacon or a crab claw that's encased in a seafood mousse before hitting the deep fryer. The single most popular dish might be the tinfoil chicken – thighs doused in a delicious barbecue sauce, then wrapped in foil and roasted.

Chinese | Informal | Moderate | soma | Rincon Center | 101 Spear St. | 415-957-9300 | www.yanksing.com | Open daily

Hog Island Oyster Bar   90.5

Oysters on the half shell come in quantities of 6, 12 or 24 at this outlet of a company that cultivates oysters in Tomales Bay. If you prefer them cooked, they come casino style, barbecued, with tarragon or in a stew. If bivalves aren't your thing, there are salads, sole and a grilled-cheese sandwich made with fromage from Cowgirl Creamery. While the Ferry Terminal Market location means you can slurp your oysters while enjoying the beautiful views of San Francisco Bay, it also means long lines of people.

Seafood | Informal | Moderate | embarcadero | Ferry Building Marketplace | 1 Ferry Bldg. | 415-391-7117 | www.hogislandoysters.com | Dinner Mon-FriLunch daily

Zuni Café   90.5

The cultural importance of Judy Rogers' restaurant merits its mention in the same breath as places like New York's Union Square Café and La Coupole in Paris. The food is nothing fancy, just a selection of oysters and starters like the house version of a Caesar salad, and mains like Petrale sole with sauerkraut in a Riesling butter sauce or what is easily the most famous roast chicken in the country, cooked in a brick oven and served with a warm bread salad, red mustard greens, scallions, currants and pine nuts. There's a short wine list, but also corkage; we suggest wine lovers bring their own.

Mediterranean | Informal | Moderate | hayes valley | 1658 Market St. | 415-552-2522 | www.zunicafe.com | Lunch & Dinner Tue-Sun

Bar Crudo   90.4

There's a preference for the raw over the cooked at this hip little seafood bar. Order the crudo platter and you get to taste one of everything. But the dishes reviewers mentioned most often were butterfish with a quail egg, Arctic char with creamy horseradish and wasabi tobiko and scallops with a fava bean purée. "About as fresh as fish gets in this city" is the way one person described the quality, although he quickly added, "which isn't all that difficult considering that we're talking about San Francisco." A "relaxed atmosphere" and an "interesting beer list" make this small restaurant above the Stockton tunnel all the more appealing.

Seafood | Informal | Moderate | nob hill | 655 Divisadero St. | 415-409-0679 | www.barcrudo.com | Dinner Tue-Sun

Range   90.4

Phil and Cameron West's restaurant is a great example of the type of dining experience that San Francisco excels at: a mid-priced place with solid food made from fresh local ingredients. It's small and the tables are close together, but dishes like soft-shell crab with avocado and jalapeño vinaigrette and a pan-roasted bavette steak with creamed spinach and porcini mushrooms are consistently well prepared, offering good value for the money. They also serve what some argue is the best roast chicken in the Bay area. The "inventive, seasonal cocktails" come highly recommended, too.

New American | Informal | Moderate | mission | 842 Valencia St. | 415-282-8283 | www.rangesf.com | Dinner daily

Frances   90.3

Melissa Perello has put her years cooking at notable Bay Area restaurants like Charles Nob Hill and the Fifth Floor to good use. Here the small menu offers only four choices of appetizers and entrées, like spugnole pasta with cotechino sausage, black trumpet mushrooms and Fiore Sardo pecorino and a Liberty Farms duck leg with butter beans, endives and Sicilian olives. But despite the limited choices, Perello gets much love from our reviewers, who say things like "exceptional comfort food in a neighborhood setting," "typical San Francisco fare but it's done absolutely right" and "It's worth the month-long wait for a table."

New American | Casual | Moderate | castro | 3870 17th St. | 415-621-3870 | www.frances-sf.com | Dinner Tue-Sun

One Market   90.3

Not generally as well-known or well-respected as its neighbor Boulevard, One Market gets dismissed as just a place where the after-work crowd hangs out. But a top Bay Area chef told us that this reputation is undeserved; he says that Mark Dommen's unfussy California fare, featuring dishes like olive oil–poached black cod with eggplant, leek ash and tomato-ginger broth, is vastly underrated and that this is his favorite place for New American cuisine in the city proper. A plus is a well-organized wine list full of the hard-to-find bottles that winos expect to find in a restaurant at the corner of Market Street and the Embarcadero, aka the heart of San Francisco.

New American | Casual | Expensive | embarcadero | 1 Market St. | 415-777-5577 | www.onemarket.com | Dinner Mon-Sat, Lunch Mon-Fri

Spruce   90.3

Tired of eating with hipsters or the young crowds that flock to the numerous Cal-Ital restaurants dominating the Bay Area dining scene? Head up to Pacific Heights and dine among the well-heeled at this New American place that clearly "isn't the usual San Francisco dining experience." Mark Sullivan's menu focuses on luxury ingredients, like seared and preserved foie gras with Riesling-poached apples and butter-poached lobster with braised lettuces and golden potato gnocchi. A number of reviewers felt it was "overpriced," but others say the "great service adapted to San Francisco's laid-back attitude" and a "spectacular wine and spirits list" mitigate the high prices.

New American | Casual | Expensive | pacific heights | 3640 Sacramento St. | 415-931-5100 | www. sprucesf.com | Dinner Daily, Lunch Mon-Fri

Kokkari Estiatorio   90.2

Given San Francisco's fondness for Cal-Ital restaurants, it was only a matter of time until someone adapted the Cal-Ital approach to Greek cuisine. While Erik Cosselmon's menu features Hellenic classics like moussaka and various spit-roasted meats, he also turns organic market ingredients into zucchini cakes with cucumber and mint or grills spring lamb organ meats with potatoes and lemon-oregano vinaigrette. The place is praised for "not being kitschy like other Greek restaurants"; even the wine list goes well beyond the usual retsina, with numerous interesting choices from European and domestic winemakers.

Greek | Informal | Moderate | downtown | 200 Jackson St. | 415-981-0983 | www.kokkari.com | Dinner Daily, Lunch Mon-Fri

Rn74   90.1

It says something about Michael Mina's cooking when our reviewers prefer this wine bar that features bistro-style fare to the fancier stuff he serves at his eponymous restaurant. Part of the allure is a wine list "full of wonderful things." Unfortunately, reviewers note that "unless you're wealthy you won't be able to afford them," and the "inexpensive offerings on the list are not as interesting." As for the food, dishes like a consommé with sautéed foie gras, oxtail and Burgundy onions and coq au vin "Moderne" are "good enough," but the place is "more of a wine lover's dream" than anything else.

French | Casual | Moderate | soma | 301 Mission St. | 415-543-7474 | www.michaelmina.net/rn74 | Dinner Daily, Lunch Mon-Fri

Fifth Floor   90.0

This restaurant attracted national media attention when the chef was Laurent Gras (formerly of Peacock Alley in New York City and currently at L2O in Chicago). After he left, Melissa Perello kept things going until the place was taken over by the group that runs Aqua. These days David Bazirgan is at the helm, and his menu features dishes like octopus with a pimenton marinade, parsley and a cryo-pickled pepper salad; minute smoked Kobe beef sashimi with carrot yogurt sauce; and a crepinette of rabbit with grilled sword leaf lettuce, walnut, fava and rabbit jus. Comments offered by reviewers ranged from "a hip, upscale vibe with good-quality food" to "it hasn't come close to hitting the heights it hit when Gras was at the helm."

French | Casual | Expensive | soma | Hotel Palomar | 12 4th St. | 415-348-1555 | www.fifthfloorrestaurant.com | Dinner Mon-Say

Piperade   90.0

Through his use of organic ingredients, Gerald Hirigoyen brings local sensibilities to his native Basque cuisine in dishes like piquillo peppers stuffed with goat cheese and raisins and Pacific snapper with fried garlic vinaigrette. Hirigoyen offers a classic Basque dish of the day, like calamari sautéed in its own ink, while the restaurant's namesake, finished with a poached egg and a slab of Serrano ham, is always on the menu. They emphasize Basque wines when they can. "Hirigoyen's cooking is as precise as it is soulful. Basque meets California in top-shelf ingredients and bold flavors."

Basque | Casual | Moderate | downtown | 1015 Battery St. | 415-391-2555 | www.piperade.com | Dinner Mon-Sat, Lunch Mon-Fri

R & G Lounge   90.0

Popular with local Chinese families as well as tourists, this classic Cantonese restaurant is considered by more than one of our reviewers to have "the best food in Chinatown."

It's a bit more upscale than other choices in the neighborhood, even more so if you eat in the upstairs dining room, where a myriad of dishes will be served on a tablecloth. But the food is so tasty that one reviewer told us, "I don't care which room I eat in, as long as I eat." It's especially popular during Dungeness crab season (roughly from mid-November through March), when you will see the crustacean done up in a variety of styles (the universal favorite is fried with salt and pepper).

Chinese | Informal | Moderate | chinatown | 631 Kearny St. | 415-982-7877 | www.rnglounge.com | Lunch & Dinner Daily

TOP LOCAL CHOICE

Campton Place   89.5

One would have to point to Chez Panisse to cite a Bay Area restaurant that has had as much impact on the local culinary scene as Campton Place (its roster of past chefs includes Bradley Ogden, Jan Birnbaum and Daniel Humm). But when the Taj chain took over, they decided to find someone who could combine indigenous cuisine with the culinary elements of the historic Spice Route. Enter Srijith Gopinathan who, after training at England's Manoir aux Quat'Saisons with Raymond Blanc, has hit the trail with dishes like hand-picked Dungeness crab with apple gelée and royal sterling Osetra caviar.

Indian | Formal | Expensive | downtown | Taj Campton Place | 340 Stockton St. | 415-955-5555 | www.camptonplace.com | Open daily

Delfina   89.5

The simple neighborhood air of this restaurant notwithstanding, ask a dozen people who serves the best Cal-Ital cuisine in the city and one-third to one-half of them will say Delfina. Craig Stoll's obsession with the local terroir shows up in dishes like a house-made wild boar sausage with a lentil salad, paccheri pasta with blue-nosed sea bass or wild nettle pasta (when nettles are in season), and mains like sand dabs in acqua pazza with tomatoes and olives. It's extremely popular, and since it's on the smaller side, you will need to book well in advance of your visit.

Cal-Ital | Informal | Moderate | mission | 3621 18th St | 415-552-4055 | www.delfinasf.com | Dinner daily

Epic Roasthouse   89.5

This upscale steakhouse from Jan Birnbaum and Pat Kuleto features modern décor, a terrific wine list that includes a number of unique Napa offerings and Birnbaum's "gutsy but refined cuisine," which includes dishes like gingersnap-crusted pork porterhouse with crispy Anson Mills grits cake and Montmorency sour cherries and cornmeal-crusted jalapeño rings. However, there are those who see it as a commercial steak restaurant and not much more, and think the "killer views" come with "mediocre food at stratospheric prices."

New American | Casual | Expensive | embarcadero | 369 Embarcadero | 415-369-9955 | www.epicroasthousesf.com | Dinner Daily, Lunch Mon-Fri

Luce   89.5

Given dishes like Dungeness crab with satsuma gel and salad, trout caviar and cucumber consommé or guinea hen with foie gras hollandaise and a stew of mushrooms, most diners think that Dominique Crenn has overcome the usual curse of hotel restaurants on high floors. Complimenters call the cuisine "precise cooking, French deconstruction-ist in spirit, with lots of thought and good execution." The worst thing anyone said was "just another very good hotel restaurant – unobjectionable, unsurprising, unexciting."

French | Casual | Expensive | soma | InterContinental San Francisco Hotel | 888 Howard St. | 415-616-6566 | www.lucewinerestaurant.com | Open daily

Oliveto   89.5

If one were to map the genealogy of the Cal-Ital movement, Oliveto would be at the base of the family tree. It was opened by Paul Bertolli, after he left Chez Panisse, who spent 11 years behind the restaurant's stoves before turning them over to Paul Canales. The menu, a prototype for restaurants in the genre, teems with delicious pastas, hand-crafted salumi (in fact, Bertolli left to make salumi under the Fra Mani label) and meats that are braised until they are fork-tender. Each year Oliveto holds a number of now-famous theme dinners, based on tomatoes, on truffles, or on – their most celebrated ingredient – whole hog, which draw chefs and foodies from all over the country. The fairly priced wine list emphasizes top regional wines rather than collector's items.

Cal-Ital | Informal | Moderate | oakland | 5655 College Ave. | 510-547-5356 | www.oliveto.com | Dinner Daily, Lunch Mon-Fri

Shalimar   89.5

Indian food fanatics in San Francisco are willing to brave the "scary location" on Jones Street for the "spectacular, wonderfully fresh North Indian cuisine" at this restaurant. All of the expected tandoori and curry dishes are here, along with a few unusual items like lamb masala and goat Karahi. Reviewers offered comments like "my favorite Indian in the city," "the food is less spicy than in most Indian places but no less flavorful" and "too greasy for me, but my vegetarian and lamb-eating friends love it."

Indian | Informal | Moderate | tenderloin | 1409 Polk St. | 415-776-4642 | www.shalimarsf.com | Lunch & Dinner daily

Slanted Door   89.5

Had this guide been published in the late '90s, Charles Phan's California-ized Vietnamese restaurant would have earned a much higher rating. Back then, it was the Momofuku of its day. But after it relocated to the Ferry Building in 2004, the food was "adapted to satisfy the tourist trade," most reviewers feel. Nevertheless, "one of the best lists of small-grower wines in the country" and "spectacular views of San Francisco Bay" make it a venue that is "still good enough to waste a meal on," especially at lunch on a sunny afternoon.

Vietnamese | Casual | Moderate | embarcadero | Ferry Building Marketplace | 1 Ferry Bldg. | 415-861-8032 | www.slanteddoor.com | Lunch & Dinner daily

SPQR   89.5

The A 16 team has brought us the cuisine of the "great, talented young chef" Matthew Accarrno, whose take on the Cal-Ital genre includes ricotta fritters with smoked maple syrup, hand-cut tagliatelle with sea urchin, spicy tomato sauce and green onion and Sonoma rabbit with Bosc pear, chestnut, parsnip, dandelion and mustard. Add "low checks" and Shelley Lindgren's "exceptional wine list" and you have "an experience that stands out from others in the city," even though "Accarrino adheres to the Italian principal of good ingredients and simple preparations."

Cal-Ital | Informal | Moderate | pacific heights | 1911 Fillmore St. | 415-771-7779 | www.spqrsf.com | Dinner Daily, Brunch Sat-Sun

Yoshi   89.5

What started as a small sushi bar run by Yoshie Akiba and two friends has morphed into a 330-seat jazz club that serves a full menu of Japanese fare. In addition to sushi, chef Sho offers small plates like Kobe beef tataki along with mains like miso-marinated black cod and Kurobuta prime pork loin. The only time people seem to eat here is when they are also going to a show. Or as one reviewer put it, "decent Japanese food, great club."

Japanese | Informal | Moderate | oakland | 1330 Fillmore St. | 415-655-5600 | http://sf.yoshis.com/sf/restaurant | Dinner daily

Yuet Lee   89.5

This old-school Cantonese restaurant on the corner of Broadway and Stockton offers all sorts of Cantonese specialties, with a special emphasis on seafood. It's open until the wee hours of the morning, which means you have a good chance of running into local chefs enjoying exotic fare like Sampan-style rice soup (pig skin, baby shrimp, chicken, pork stomach and peanuts) or chomping down on fresh fish dishes like sea bass in a scallion and ginger sauce. It's famous for its salt and pepper shrimp, and the salt and pepper Dungeness crab, offered in season, is a cheap-eats masterpiece.

Chinese | Informal | Moderate | chinatown | 1300 Stockton St. | 415-982-6020 | Lunch & Dinner daily

À Côté   89.0

Reviewers talk about the "great food for a great price" at this "trendy bistro" in Oakland. Matt Colgan is most famous for the mussels he roasts in a wood oven before finishing them with a splash of Pernod, but he also serves mains like duck Bolognese, rabbit boudin blanc, pork osso buco and seared sturgeon, all for $18 or less. There's also a "great bar scene" and "excellent cocktails" to go with your dinner. Though most reviewers recommend it, one dissenter called it "just another trendy bistro that doesn't live up to the hype."

French | Informal | Moderate | oakland | 5478 College Ave. | 510-655-6469 | www.acoterestaurant.com | Dinner daily

Aziza   89.0

Mourad Lahlou is attempting to do for Moroccan food what David Chang did for Korean and Johnny Monis for Greek: create a contemporary version of an ethnic cuisine through the use of artisanal ingredients and modern cooking techniques. On first blush Lahlou's menu seems to have more in common with sophisticated places like COI than with an authentic ethnic restaurant, but starters like lima beans with ras-el-hanout or lamb sausage with harrisa-spiked goat yogurt and mains like beef with a carrot-tomato stew are firmly rooted in the Moroccan tradition. However, Melissa Chou's "interesting desserts" are purely modern creations that steer clear of Mideastern influences.

Moroccan | Informal | Moderate | outer richmond | 5800 Geary Blvd. | 415-752-2222 | www.aziza-sf.com | Dinner Wed-Mon

Flour + Water   89.0

San Francisco seems to be able to absorb an endless number of pizza and pasta specialists. But despite the fact that Flour + Water is just one of many, reviewers are more
than happy to devote an evening here, eating pizzas like the Osso – bone marrow,
rapini, fontina and horseradish – as well as pastas like Aleppo pepper maltagliati with
rabbit sausage and mustard greens. The "place is a madhouse," and while it's a tough
reservation to come by, they have a "cute community table and a bar."

Italian | Informal | Moderate | mission | 2401 Harrison St. | 415-826-7000 | http://flourandwater.com |
Dinner daily

Globe   89.0

One of the original Cal-Ital restaurants is still serving up king salmon with bocconcini
pasta and rapini and braised Niman Ranch lamb shoulder with ruby crescent potatoes
and artichokes. Comments range from "I keep going over and over for the amazing
pastas" to "acceptable only late at night." Speaking of that, it's not as popular as it used
to be, except with the hipster crowd, which we assume comes from having a downtown
location and a 1:00 a.m. closing time.

Cal-Ital | Informal | Moderate | downtown | 290 Pacific Ave. | 415-391-4132 | Dinner Daily, Lunch Mon-Fri

Koi Palace   89.0

Some people argue that the best dim sum in the country is to be found at this massive
restaurant located near the airport. The extensive list of small plates includes rarely
seen dishes like abalone shu mai, shark's fin dumplings served in broth and puff pastry
filled with durian paste. You can also take advantage of a full menu of Hong Kong–style
cuisine like a clay pot of taro, pumpkin and stewed prawns. It's extremely popular, and
the waits on weekends can be substantial, despite the cavernous size of the place. An
Asian staff adds to the authentic feel.

Chinese | Informal | Moderate | daly city | 365 Gellert Blvd. | 650-992-9000 | www.koipalace.com |
Lunch & Dinner daily

Michael Mina   89.0

Many of our reviewers believe Michael Mina's flagship is the most overrated restaurant
in San Francisco. To be more specific, they find the execution of his signature dishes
– like Maine lobster pot pie or the "Five Seas" tasting of Japanese fish with nishiki rice
and a ginger vinaigrette – to be formulaic. The service is attentive and the wine list
extensive, but when push comes to shove, it all "sounds and looks better than it tastes."
Unfortunately, you wouldn't be able to tell that from the high prices.

New American | Casual | Expensive | downtown | 252 California St. | 415-397-9222 | www.michaelmina.
net | Dinner Daily, Lunch Mon-Fri

Orson   89.0

After her success at Citizen Cake, Elizabeth Falkner has delved into progressive savory
fare. After imbibing some inventive cocktails, those in a modern mood can order a
starter of an explosive Caesar salad and follow it with a dish of salmon, farro, carrots,
parsnip and black truffle. But reviewers say that "too many of the dishes seem to be

experimental for the sake of experimenting," and they suggest you "stick to more straightforward fare" like pizza or a burger with duck fat fries.

Progressive | Casual | Moderate | soma | 508 4th Street | 415-777-1508 | www.orsonsf.com | Lunch & Dinner Tue-Sat, Lunch only Sun

Ozumo   89.0

Though it comes with "a nice ambience and a good bar scene," Ozumo is yet one more San Francisco Japanese restaurant that reviewers consider "good but not great." Besides a full menu of sushi and all sorts of cooked preparations, they offer a full robata menu and a sake lounge. One reviewer said the cooking is "surprisingly competent for such a trendy location," but unfortunately "prices are sky-high" for the quality.

Japanese | Informal | Moderate | embarcadero | 161 Steuart St. | 415-882-1333 | www.ozumo.com | Dinner daily, Lunch Mon-Fri

Perbacco   89.0

The rating for this restaurant puts it in the middle of the Cal-Ital pack, as a number of our more experienced reviewers just haven't warmed up to the place. Those who feel differently recommend dishes like veal tartar with lardo bruschetta, hand-cut tagliatelle topped with five-hour pork sugo and a grilled Berkshire pork chop served with smoked pancetta and slow-cooked Romano beans. Its fans say that a "warm atmosphere" makes it "a solid choice if you're in the area."

Cal-Ital | Casual | Moderate | downtown | 230 California St. | 415-955-0663 | www.perbaccosf.com | Dinner Mon-Sat, Lunch Mon-Fri

A 16   88.5

Named after the autostrada that stretches from Naples to Canosa, Liza Shaw presents you with a menu featuring snapshots of the food you'd find along that route. Included among the offerings are some of the best wood-burning-oven pizzas in the city, house-cured meats like bresaola and coppa di testa, and pastas like the signature ricotta gnocchi. Shelley Lindgren's 500-bottle list, which specializes in unusual offerings from a region that extends from Rome all the way to Sicily, allows for perfect pairings with the food. While it's been a favorite with locals ever since it opened, its tables became even more scarce after its original chef, Nate Appleman, won the James Beard Award.

Cal-Ital | Informal | Moderate | marina | 2355 Chestnut St. | 415-771-2216 | www.a16sf.com | Dinner daily, Lunch Wed-Fri

Absinthe   88.5

It's the terrific brunch menu – featuring scrumptious creations such as warm biscuits, fried eggs and buttermilk-sausage gravy, and a Dungeness crab-salad sandwich with hot house tomatoes and Benton's bacon – that drives the ratings at this restaurant. The fare at dinner is more conventional, like French onion gratinée and cinnamon-braised lamb shank served with couscous. It's an understatement to use the word "stupendous" to describe the wine list – page after page of well-priced bottles from producers that don't turn up in restaurants all that often.

French | Casual | Moderate | hayes valley | 398 Hayes St. | 415-551-1590 | www.absinthe.com | Lunch & Dinner Tue-Sun

Foreign Cinema   88.5

Modern movie classics like Chinatown or La Cage aux Folles play in the background at this super-hip restaurant in the Mission District. A raw bar features a dozen types of oysters, and the rest of the eclectic Cal-Mediterranean menu, like sautéed risotto galettes with asparagus and lemon oil and harissa roast pork tenderloin with mint and tomato chutney, matches the unusual atmosphere. Unfortunately, the best comment we read about the food was "good but unexceptional," with most reviewers agreeing the main draw was the "cool space and atmosphere."

Mediterranean | Informal | Moderate | mission | 2534 Mission St. | 415-648-7600 | www.foreigncinema. com | Dinner Daily, Lunch Mon-Fri

La Mar   88.5

In his native Peru, Gastón Acurio is a living legend. And as part of a global expansion, he's brought his ceviches, anticuchos, causas and platos grandes to the Embarcadero – so you no longer have to buy a plane ticket to Lima to experience his cuisine. Problem is, rather than opening an intimate restaurant where his disciples mix the tiraditos in front of your eyes, he has opened a "large, commercial restaurant" located in Pier 1.5 that's "a factory for birthday and graduation parties."

Peruvian | Casual | Moderate | embarcadero | Pier 1.5 (at Washington St.) | 415-397-8880 | www.lamarsf. com | Lunch & Dinner daily

Rivoli   88.5

The Cal-Ital dining experience has spread to Berkeley. Wendy Brucker's menu features a filo tart of shrimp, Monterey Bay squid, roasted peppers and feta cheese, gnocchi made with Bellwether Farms ricotta and served with roasted pears and fig marmalata and a Moroccan spiced-roasted chicken breast with apricot, cherry jus, couscous with pistachios, mint and garlic yogurt. Roscoe Skipper oversees the dining room, along with a wine list that has "too many interesting bottles costing less than $100" to count.

Cal-Ital | Informal | Moderate | berkeley | 1539 Solano Ave. | 510-526-2542 | www.rivolirestaurant.com | Dinner daily

Ton Kiang   88.5

The most artisanal of the big-three dim sum restaurants (everything is made in-house, including the sauces), Ton Kiang is to well-prepared vegetarian fare as Koi Palace is to unusual dumpling preparations and Yank Sing is to fried dishes. They also specialize in the cuisine of China's Hakka region, including rarely seen clay pot casseroles, like Pacific oysters with ginger and scallions, sizzling onion chicken and braised oxtail with carrot and celery.

Chinese/Dim Sum | Informal | Moderate | outer richmond | 5821 Geary Blvd. | 415-752-4440 | www. tonkiang.net | Open daily

Bar Jules   88.0

About this place that features "very good ingredients" that are "starkly cooked" and "served in big portions," it's not surprising to hear reviewers say, "If the French bistronomique concept were to be translated to San Francisco, its name would be Bar

Jules." The typical daily menu includes just nine or ten dishes, like seared sea scallops with grilled rapini and a hard-cooked egg or baby goat braised overnight with chick peas, artichoke hearts and preserved lemon. A "cozy ambience" perfectly matches the "simple fare."

French | Informal | Moderate | hayes valley | 609 Hayes St. | 415-621-5482 | www.barjules.com | Lunch & Dinner Wed-Sat, dinner only Tue

Fleur de Lys   88.0

While there was a time when Fleur de Lys was a contender for the best dining experi-ence in the city, the style of French cuisine (featuring dishes like veal sweetbread meniere with morels) that Hubert Keller serves is much less popular than it used to be. A loyal older following manages to keep the rating fairly high, but some of the com-ments were absolutely brutal, with people saying things like "all that I fear in French food – heavy sauces that look like they're congealing on the plate" and "my one visit was memorable for all the wrong reasons."

French | Formal | Expensive | downtown | 777 Sutter St. | 415-673-7779 | www.fleurdelyssf.com | Dinner Tue-Sat

Nopa   88.0

File this one under the heading Cal-Med. Dishes from the wood-burning oven include flatbread of spicy fennel sausage and black cod with Manila clams, celery root cream and maitake mushrooms. One reviewer explained the restaurant's popularity: "Interesting, well-chosen wine list; great burgers; large but comfortable space with a great bar and communal table, along with late-night hours." Another couldn't disagree more, saying, "sloppy execution and a patented cooler-than-thou vibe – I just don't understand the overwhelming adoration for this place."

Mediterranean | Informal | Moderate | western addition | 560 Divisadero St. | 415-864-8643 | www.nopasf.com | Dinner daily, Lunch Mon-Fri

O Chamé   88.0

For the past 18 years, David Vardy's restaurant has been the number one choice for East Bay residents looking for Japanese comfort food. Start with an order of seared hamachi with braised leeks and horseradish sauce and continue with "light and crunchy" tempura or "toothsome" noodles in broths with "plenty of tasty meat" floating in the soup bowls. Or if protein's your thing, you can dig into a grilled skirt steak with green chard, edamame beans and Portobello mushrooms.

Japanese | Informal | Moderate | berkeley | 1830 4th St. | 510-841-8783 | www.themenupage.com/ochame.html | Lunch & Dinner daily

ACCEPTABLE

César   87.5

Whether for a casual meal out or just for drinks before visiting nearby Chez Panisse, César is uniformly praised by our reviewers. Maggie Pond's menu, a bit more ambitious than the typical tapas bar, includes preparations like squid stuffed with chorizo, Alaskan halibut à la plancha and vegetarian paella studded with wild mushrooms, asparagus, cauli-flower, garbanzos, zucchini, peas, favas and piquillo peppers. There's an empha-sis on small-grower and artisanal wines. The same tasty cuisine is available at a second location in Oakland, César Latino.

Tapas | Informal | Moderate | berkeley | 1515 Shattuck Ave. | 510-883-0222 | www.barcesar.com | Lunch & Dinner daily

Second Location: oakland | 4039 Piedmont Ave. | 510-985-1200 | www.barcesar.com | Lunch & Dinner daily

Fringale   87.5

This is where Gerald Hirigoyen first made his name (he's still an owner, though these days he cooks at Piperade). The cuisine at Fringale attempts to cover the French side of the Basque region. Utilizing "great ingredients that are carefully prepared," it includes dishes like bacon-wrapped pork tenderloin with braised Savoy cabbage and duck confit with lentils in a red wine sauce.

Basque | Casual | Moderate | soma | 570 4th St. | 415-543-0573 | www.fringalesf.com | Dinner Tue-Sun, Lunch Tue-Fri

Incanto   87.5

At Incanto, owner Mark Pastore often tells his guests that the food represents "a part of Italy that just happens to be called California." Chris Cosentino's menu features squash blossoms with ricotta and basil, handkerchief pasta with pork ragù and a combination of Boccalone sausage and smoked escolar. The menu can be "offal-centric" at times, and the lower-than-expected rating is driven by reviewers who complain about consistency, saying things like "One meal soars, and then the next is ordinary."

Cal-Ital | Informal | Moderate | noe valley | 1550 Church St. | 415-641-4500 | www.incanto.biz | Dinner Wed-Mon

Thanh Long   87.5

While our reviewers often have mixed feelings about upscale Asian restaurants, they did recommend a few things at this Vietnamese from the An family of Crustacean fame. One reviewer suggested eating "as much crab and garlic noodles as possible," while another raved about the clay pot of sizzling seafood. But the best way to experience the restaurant is to reject the printed menu altogether and "ask them to serve you dishes from the An family's private menu."

Vietnamese | Casual | Moderate | outer sunset | 4101 Judah St. | 415-665-1146 | www.anfamily.com | Dinner Tue-Sun

BayWolf   87.0

Open for over 20 years, BayWolf would be better known if it weren't for its location (though the lower rent of the area is reflected in the price of the entrées, most of which cost less than $20). Local culinary sensibilities are on display in a salad of roasted peppers, grilled corn and arugula with buttermilk blue cheese, while mains might be sole with cilantro, cumin, lime and marinated vegetables or Liberty Ranch duck with corn cakes and balsamic-soaked cherries.

Californian | Casual | Moderate | oakland | 3853 Piedmont Ave. | 510-655-6004 | www.baywolf.com Dinner Tue-Sun, Lunch Tue-Fri

Chaya Brasserie   87.0

Chaya was all the rage back in the day. And while fare like pappardelle with Kobe beef Bolognese and truffle oil is still popular with a few of our reviewers, most of them have moved on to newer, more extravagant versions of the Asian party restaurant. Still, a typical comment was from a reviewer who was "always surprised by how much I like this place," despite the fact that it is "always filled with suits and other corporate types" hanging out at the bar.

Asian | Casual | Moderate | embarcadero | 132 Embarcadero | 415-777-8688 | www.thechaya.com | Lunch & Dinner daily

Greens   87.0

With an arsenal of 11 top-selling cookbooks, Deborah Madison is one of the country's preeminent vegetarian chefs. But success seems to have gone to her head, and the comments her place attracts these days include "It's become a bit tired over the years" and "If you are going to claim to be a high-class vegetarian restaurant, the food should be better." The Fort Mason Center location, complete with lovely views of the bay and Alcatraz Island, adds to the experience.

Vegetarian | Informal | Moderate | marina | Fort Mason Ctr. | 415-771-6222 | www.greensrestaurant.com | Dinner daily, Lunch Tue-Sun

Harris'   87.0

Like sushi, steakhouses are not this city's thing. But if you get a hankering for a slab of beef after trudging up and down those hills all day, this "old-school fancy" restaurant offers "some of the best steaks in the area." Those who like their meat gussied up can order classics like steak Diane or tournedos Rossini. The wine list offers an "exceptional selection of reds from Northern California."

Steakhouse | Casual | Expensive | polk gulch | 2100 Van Ness Ave. | 415-673-1888 | www.harrisrestaurant.com | Dinner daily

Le Colonial   87.0

A good choice for those who prefer a French-colonial ambience to a native Vietnamese one. The experience comes complete with the option to dine on an outdoor terrace while sipping drinks with funny names, a DJ blasting music and food (like pan-roasted halibut with wilted spinach, served with a ginger soy beurre blanc and a Dungeness crab salad) that is "tasty, though a little bit dated."

Vietnamese | Casual | Moderate | downtown | 20 Cosmo Pl. | 415-931-3600 | www.lecolonialsf.com | Dinner daily, Lunch Mon-Fri

Sebo   87.0

Only in sushi-poor San Francisco could some people claim that "a restaurant run by two white guys" is a contender for the honor of the best sushi in the city. Not known for their traditional preparations but described as serving a "cuisine with traditional roots," the creative duo working behind the counter keeps reviewers happy with "some of the freshest fish in the city," along with an izakaya menu featuring dishes like Okinawan simmered spareribs and kelp. They don't take reservations and seating is limited, so it's a good idea to get there on the early side.

Japanese | Informal | Moderate | hayes valley | 517 Hayes St. | 415-864-2122 | www.sebosf.com | Dinner Tue-Sat

Farallon   86.5

Mark Franz and Pat Kuleto opened Farallon in 1997, in an era when this type of sleek, highly stylized, multi-seat place was in vogue. The Union Square location makes it a convenient stop for tourists and locals after a busy shopping day, and "the beautiful Captain Nemo under-the-sea setting plays a major role in the experience." While Franz's New American seafood cuisine has its admirers, the general feeling is that the food is a bit corporate and nowhere as extraordinary as the décor.

Seafood | Casual | Expensive | downtown | 450 Post St. | 415-956-6969 | www.farallonrestaurant.com | Dinner daily

Murray Circle   86.5

There may not be a better example of the gulf between big city and suburban dining than the difference in quality between restaurants in San Francisco and those in Marin County. But if you're hungry, and you happen to find yourself on the wrong side of that divide, check out this restaurant with a "nice view, competent cooking and a good wine list." Set in a remodeled U.S. Army building that is well appointed and quiet, it's blessed with spectacular views of the Golden Gate

Bridge that abound from almost any-where in the place.

Californian | Casual | Moderate | sausalito | Cavallo Point Lodge | 601 Murray Circle | 415-339-4750 | www.murraycircle.com | Open daily

Town Hall   86.5

A spot where the ex-frat-boy crowd goes after work, Town Hall is popular and crowded, with "food that is excessively rich and a clientele that is excessively noisy." The casual American fare, like biscuits with country ham and red pepper jelly or duck enchiladas with tomatillo salsa, is full of bold flavors intended to appeal to the youngish clientele. It's recommended for a large, boozy gathering after a long day of physical labor or for people on a first date.

New American | Informal | Moderate | soma | 342 Howard St. | 415-908-3900 | www.townhallsf.com | Dinner Daily, Lunch Mon-Fri

Kuleto's   86.0

With notables like Boulevard and Jardinière in his portfolio, Pat Kuleto co-owns some of the Bay Area's best-known, and has lent his name to this Union Square shopping district venue. Robert Helstrom's San Francisco-ized Italian fare begins with a menu of house-made salumi and extends to dishes like Liberty Farms duck breast with chestnut polenta, braised red cabbage and grappa-soaked cranberries. "Always acceptable, often very good, but not cutting-edge" sums up reviewer comments.

Italian | Casual | Expensive | union square | 221 Powell St. | 415-397-7720 | www.kuletos.com | Open daily

Silk's   86.0

Once an important training ground for a host of now-famous chefs, including Ken Oringer and David Kinch, Silk's was also a groundbreaker in the Asian fusion genre that was in style more than a decade ago.

These days executive chef Rick Bartram offers dishes like sustainable salmon tartare with avocado, Thai basil and yuzu dressing, and while the restaurant offers a romantic environment, an air of "high-quality hotel restaurant" hangs over it.

Californian | Casual | Expensive | downtown | 222 Sansome St. | 415-986-2020 | www.mandarinoriental.com | Dinner daily, Lunch Tue-Sat

Hong Kong Flower   85.5
Lounge (15 miles south in Milbrae)

If you have a few hours to kill before or after a flight at SFO, you can practically walk to this restaurant where local Chinese families gather to enjoy dim sum by day and specialties like double-boiled shark's fin soup with abalone or oysters baked with XO sauce in the evening. They've been at it for more than 20 years, and some reviewers say, "Its best days have already passed, but you can still always get a pretty good meal here."

Chinese | Informal | Moderate | milbrae | 51 Millbrae Ave. | 650-692-6666 | www.mayflowerseafood.com | Lunch & Dinner daily

Kyo-ya   85.5

It's a shame that in sushi-starved San Francisco one of the few nods to upscale Japanese dining is described as "corporate dining with a Japanese accent in the impersonal setting of the Palace." There are raw fish and noodle soups and mains like rock cod simmered in a sweet soy sauce or tuna belly steak with apple purée and eringi mushrooms. But "Safe is the best compliment one can pay this place." Guess hotel food is hotel food regardless of the ethnicity.

Californian | Moderate | Expensive | soma | Palace Hotel | 2 New Montgomery St. | 415-546-5090 | www.sfpalacerestaurants.com | Lunch & Dinner Mon-Fri

L'Osteria del Forno   85.5

Despite displaying all the indications of

an authentic osteria, this restaurant is geared toward tourists rather than serious Italophiles. But as one reviewer said, it's "one of the better options in North Beach, which given the paucity of good places to eat in the area, really is damnation through faint praise. It's a red-checkered tablecloth, jug of Chianti, tomato sauce made with canned tomatoes type of place masquerading as an authentic Italian" restaurant. Others say, "You're best off if you stick to simpler fare like the pizza."

Italian | Informal | Moderate | north beach | 519 Columbus Ave. | 415-982-1124 | www.losteriadel-forno.com | Lunch & Dinner Wed-Mon

Millennium   85.5

We get mixed reports about this vegan-centric restaurant in the Hotel California, where Eric Tucker attempts to make those who are craving meat forget it's been left off the menu by serving unusual creations like Indonesian tempeh and yuba roulade with seared shitake mushrooms. Fans talk about the "many innovative vegetarian and vegan preparations," while foes counter with "I have never had an impressive meal in several visits." A nice list of biodynamic wines and unusual cocktails complements the "interesting food."

American | Casual | Expensive | soma | Hotel California | 580 Geary St. | 415-345-3900 | www. millenniumrestaurant.com | Dinner daily

supperclub   85.5

You get to eat Caesar salad while wearing latex gloves or have a tin labeled "dog food which is filled with meat loaf" at this import from Amsterdam – causing some to call it more of an entertainment concept than a restaurant. But if you're in the mood for an interesting night out, it might strike you as it did this reviewer: "Amazing experience. Went with a group of six women and spent the night dancing and dining. Food was great and the

vegetarian menu was one of the best I;ve had in the city."

Eclectic | Casual | Expensive | civic center | 657 Harrison St. | 415-348-0900 | www.supperclub. com | Dinner daily

Tadich Grill   85.5

It was just over 150 years ago, while the California Gold Rush was still going strong, that they started serving Dungeness crabs and other local seafood at this restaurant located near the Market Street cable car turntable. While some reviewers claim "they are mostly trading on their reputation," plenty still enjoy the simply prepared specialties like cioppino, rex sole, sand dabs and a Hangtown Fry (an oyster and bacon frittata) in an environment described as "true old San Francisco."

Seafood | Informal | Moderate | downtown | 240 California St. | 415-391-1849 | www.tadich-grill.com | Lunch & Dinner Mon-Sat

Blowfish Sushi to Die For 85.0

Most cities have a party-style Japanese restaurant. In San Francisco, Blowfish fills that slot, and the experience evoked comments like, "I guess if you really must have fusion sushi in a trendy atmosphere with a large group, this would be the place to go," and "trendy sushi surrounded by anime at top volume and even louder patrons. It's what I would imagine living in a pinball machine must feel like."

Japanese | Casual | Moderate | mission | 2170 Bryant St. | 415-285-3848 | www.blowfishsushi. com | Dinner Daily, Lunch Mon-Fri

Hayes Street Grill   85.0

Twenty-five years ago, this restaurant was up near the top of the list of places that diners had to visit when in San Francisco. Now it's just a "famous place that had its day in the sun, with both the food and the room feeling dated." They still do their best to serve the best of the

Pacific Northwest catch – wild salmon from Half Moon Bay, local swordfish, salmon from the Columbia River and Ft. Bragg Petrale sole. It's convenient before the symphony or the opera.

Seafood | Casual | Moderate | civic center | 320 Hayes St. | 415-863-5545 | www.hayesstreetgrill. com | Dinner Daily, Lunch Mon-Fri

Sutro's at the Cliff House 85.0

This gorgeous spot, built just after the Gold Rush, evoked comments like "great location, OK food," "Come for the view, have a glass of wine, but eat dinner elsewhere," "It's a historical landmark but the food is meh," "Go at sunset for best effect," and "only for a hamburger and the view." Speaking of the view, in addition to watching the tide crash on the rocks, you can also watch the seals do a bit of sunbathing.

American | Casual | Expensive | outer richmond | 1090 Point Lobos Ave. | 415-386-3330 | www. cliffhouse.com | Lunch & Dinner daily

OTHER RESTAURANTS MENTIONED

Buckeye Roadhouse 84.5

You will probably find this ode to California comfort cuisine, including dishes like calamari with tomatillo salsa and chili-lime "brick" chicken with avocado and stuffed pasilla pepper, either "fun with good enough food" or "gimmicky with poor food." Regardless of how you feel about the fare, the venue – a building that dates from 1937 – is a "fun spot for drinks while looking out over the Bay."

Eclectic | Informal | Moderate | mill valley | 15 Shoreline Hwy. | 415-331-2600 | www.buckeyeroadhouse.com | Lunch & Dinner daily

Woodward's Garden 84.5

They are selling "charm, charm and more charm" at this Mission District restaurant named after the amusement park that stood on the site until 1891. The fare is out of the Chez Panisse playbook, like

pork osso buco with faro risotto, asparagus, fava beans and spring peas. As one person put it, "It's nothing more than your typical San Francisco restaurant, but they seem to do it with a bit more care than the others." And then there's all that charm.

Californian | Casual | Moderate | mission | 1700 Mission St. | 415-621-7122 | www.woodwardsgarden.com | Dinner Tue-Sat

Cafe Jacqueline 83.5

Dining takes a backseat to romance at this North Beach classic, where the menu is limited to an appetizer of soup, salad or snails, followed by a variety of soufflés with savory fillings like prosciutto or lobster and then followed by dessert versions in standard flavors like Grand Marnier and chocolate. Everyone agrees it's one of those hokey places that is "clichéd and tired," but that doesn't stop people from going at least once.

French | Casual | Moderate | north beach | 1454 Grant Ave. | 415-981-5565 | Lunch & Dinner daily

Doña Tomás 83.5

Upscale Mexican is always tricky. While there are fans who say things like "tasty enough to be on the list of places to try if opportunity presents itself," others say, "incredibly disappointing. We left after the appetizers and had dinner elsewhere." At least the cocktails are "perfectly mixed."

Mexican | Informal | Moderate | oakland | 5004 Telegraph Ave. | 510-450-0522 | www.donatomas. com | Dinner Tue-Sat

North Beach Restaurant 83.5

Before the Cal-Ital movement swept this city, the traditional Italian restaurants that populate North Beach predominated. Few people mention them anymore, except for this place, which has been tossing pasta in sauce since 1970. Comments range from "tasty Italian food in an atmosphere that feels a lot like Italy itself" to "Italian food from my father's era, and the only reason to go is when he comes to visit."

Italian | Casual | Expensive | north beach | 1512 Stockton St. | 415-392-1700 | www.northbeachres-taurant.com | Lunch & Dinner daily

Sam's Grill and Seafood Restaurant   83.5

Like its seafood soul brother, the Tadich Grill, this classic seafood house that dates back to 1867 has kept its follow-ing over the years; it's the kind of place where you sit in a curtained booth and knock back a few Cosmopolitans, fol-lowed by dishes like filet of sole à la Marguery or pan-fried calamari steak à la Sam. You know a restaurant has been around for a long time when it doesn't even bother with website.

Seafood | Casual | Moderate | downtown | 374 Bush St. | 415-421-0594 | Dinner Mon-Sat, Lunch Mon-Fri

Teatro ZinZanni   83.5

You can have a little bit of dinner while watching the cabaret show at this restau-rant that serves something approximat-ing northern Italian cuisine. Reviews of the overall experience range from "a lot of fun" to "cheesy," but the best com-ment the food attracted was "adequate." At least they let you bring your own wine.

Italian | Casual | Moderate | embarcadero | Pier 29, The Embarcadero | 415-438-2668 | www.zinzanni.org | Dinner Thu-Sat

House of Prime Rib   82.5

It's only right that in the world's most liberal city, there has to be one restau-rant where your grandparents from the Midwest, as well as members of British gentlemen's clubs, will feel comfortable. This old-school palace of beef, with its four different cuts of prime rib, fits the bill nicely. One reviewer recommends

that you "go for the king cut."

Steakhouse | Casual | Expensive | nob hill | 1906 Van Ness Ave. | 415-885-4605 | http://houseofprimerib.ypguides.net | Dinner daily

Cheap Eats

UNIQUELY DELICIOUS

Una Pizzeria Napoletana   8.9

True to its namesake, this restaurant aims to recreate the perfect Neapolitan-style pizza, a goal they support by caring for their dough with a "monk-like devo-tion" while attempting to use only DOCG ingredients whenever they can. The result: Numerous reviewers claimed this was "the best pizza" they ever had. One went to the trouble of specifying: "The ingredients are of the highest quality – the sauce has a delicate acidity nicely balanced by the creaminess of the buf-falo mozzarella, while the dough, from a wild yeast culture and never refrigerated, has a complexity you can't find in other pizza dough." Speaking of dough, they bake pies until that day's supply runs out, so we suggest you arrive early.

Pizzeria | Moderate | mission | 210 11th St. | 415-861-3444 | www.unapizza.com | Dinner Wed-Sun

Humphry Slocombe   8.6

Jake Godby is a genius. He took what must be the simplest food in the world – ice cream – and, by using the principles of molecular gastronomy, created what he calls "a challenging ice cream shop." The day's flavors are likely to include chocolate-smoked sea salt, duck fat pecan pie, "Red Hot" banana, hibiscus beet and a bourbon and corn flakes combo that goes by the name of Secret Breakfast. Or maybe he will be serving foie gras ice cream sandwiches that day. As to be expected when it comes to experimental cuisine, the "unsual fla-vors usually, but don't always, translate to great enjoyment." One reviewer put things into perspective when he said, "Not everything is brilliant. But what is brilliant is shockingly brilliant."

Dessert | Inexpensive | mission | 2790 Harrison St. | 415-550-6971 | www.humphryslocombe.com | Open daily

Tartine Bakery and Café   8.4

People just love Elisabeth Pruett and Chad Robertson's bakery. In fact, reviewers were so enthusiastic that comments like "This is the only bakery in the U.S. that can be compared with those in Paris," and "The baked goods were better than at many of Europe's finest bakeries" were commonplace. In addition to the breakfast treats, which include "an almond croissant to die for" and a *pain au jambon* called "possibly the single best morning pastry made in the U.S.," there are hot pressed sandwiches, like Humboldt Fog goat cheese on walnut bread and delicious pastries like éclairs and a lemon meringue cake rectangle.

Bakery | Inexpensive | mission | 600 Guerrero St. | 415-487-2600 | www.tartinebakery.com | Open daily

Dynamo Donut   8.3

If it were solely up to us, we would give this bakery an even higher rating. But since it isn't, we'll simply agree with the reviewer who said, "awesome doughnuts, fantastic texture, mildly sweet flavor, very fresh-tasting." The only other thing you need to know: the incredible range of flavors, which include chocolate rosemary almond, banana de leche, caramel de sel, apricot cardamom, candied orange blossom, lemon pistachio and, apparently everyone's favorite, maple-glazed bacon apple. Drinks are limited to coffee and an espresso made with beans that come from Four Barrel Coffee.

Bakery | Inexpensive | mission | 2760 24th St. | 415-920-1978 | www.dynamodonut.com | Open Tue-Sun

Mama's on Washington Square   8.3

Known for serving San Francisco's best breakfast, Mama's varied menu extends to rarely seen dishes like a Dungeness crab omelet or French toast made with fat-free apple yogurt cinnamon bread. But there's a catch: You have to be willing to wait an hour and a half for a table. Most people are put off by the lines, with one person telling us, "There's the food, and there's the wait, and I'm not sure they are even close to being in balance." It's less crowded at lunch, when you can order one of the city's best hamburgers, along with salads and a number of dishes geared toward vegetarians

Coffee Shop | Inexpensive | north beach | 1701 Stockton St. | 415-362-6421 | www.mamas-sf.com | Breakfast & Lunch Tue-Sun

4505 Meats   8.2

A food stand wouldn't normally make a guide like ours. But this isn't your ordinary food stand. After giving up a career as a chef, Ryan Farr and wife Cesalee opened an artisanal butcher shop, though it's less a shop than a kitchen that churns out the hot dogs, bacon, chicharrones and all types of sausages that the Farrs sell at a stand at the Ferry Building Marketplace on Thursday and Saturday mornings. But what most people are lining up for is "one of the best hamburgers in the country," made from a "complex blend of cuts" and including "lots of dry-aged flavor." As one reviewer put it, Farr's "kicking butt and not asking for forgiveness."

Cafe | Inexpensive | embarcadero | Ferry Building Marketplace | www.4505meats.com | Lunch Thu & Sat

Pizzetta 211   8.1

With comments like "the best pizza in the Bay Area" and "head and shoulders above other pizzerias in the city," there's not much more to say about this tiny place. As with most everything that's good to eat in this city, artisanal ingredients – in this instance, wonderful vegetables, meats and cheeses that are sparsely placed on "remarkably thin crusts that allow the ingredients to shine" – are fundamental to its excellence. It's beloved by our reviewers (the lowest rating anyone gave it was Highly Recommended); one went gaga over the "crave-worthy" lamb sausage and runny egg pizza. There are only ten seats, so expect a wait if you don't get there early.

Pizzeria | Moderate | outer richmond | 211 23rd Ave. | 415-379-9880 | www.pizzetta211.com | Dinner daily, Lunch Wed-Sun

Blue Bottle   8.0

James Freeman is one of those great American success stories. He began serving his coffee at a local farmer's market, and his various roasts of beans became so popular that he now occupies a prime piece of real estate in the Ferry Building while also operating locations in faraway places like Brooklyn. As for explaining why his coffee is so popular, our prose couldn't possibly do it the same justice as these comments: "cult coffee," "The coffee is quite exceptional," "yummers" and "Close your eyes and you're in Italy."

Cafe | Inexpensive | embarcadero | Ferry Bldg. Marketplace | 1 Ferry Bldg. | 415-983-8030 | www.bluebottlecoffee.net | Breakfast & Lunch daily

Second Location: soma | SFMOMA | 151 3rd St. | 415-495-3394 | www.bluebottlecoffee.net | Breakfast & Lunch daily

Third Location: soma | Mint Plaza | 66 Mint St. | www.bluebottlecoffee.net | Breakfast & Lunch daily

Fourth Location: oakland | 300 Webster St. | www.bluebottlecoffee.net | Breakfast & Lunch daily

Pizzeria Delfina   8.0

After Craig Stoll had so much success at Delfina, he opened this shop next door and started serving "a slightly modern-ized take on the Neapolitan-style pizza." You can start with a half-dozen antipasti like deep-fried rice balls, move onto daily specials such as meatballs en sugo and end your meal with a pizza with "good, crusty dough and spare toppings" like clams and Pecorino or radicchio and egg.

Pizzeria | Moderate | mission | 3621 18th St. | 415-552-4055 | www.delfinasf.com | Dinner daily

RECOMMENDED

Saigon Sandwich   7.9

Everyone loves San Francisco's most famous Vietnamese sandwich joint, where "they stuff baguettes with delicacies so mouthwatering they should write the letters U-M-A-M-I on the top of the sandwich." It's just a hole in the wall, but the banh mi "are certified delicious," including a vegetarian version that appeals to the numerous hipsters who frequent the place.

Vietnamese | Inexpensive | tenderloin | 560 Larkin St. | 415-474-5698 | Breakfast & Lunch daily

La Taqueria   7.9

What sets this place apart from the other taquerias that span Mission Street between 26th and 29th Streets are tacos and burritos "stuffed to the gills with juicy meats" and served in an "impeccably clean space" at a price that makes it "hard to believe they make any money selling them." An added attraction is the cool working-class neighborhood, populated by an unusual combination of Latinos, hipsters and other folks going about their business, which makes visiting what someone described as "the Cadillac of taquerias" even more fun. It doesn't hurt that you can finish your meal with desserts from either Humphrey Slocombe or Dynamo Donut, both within walking distance.

Mexican | Inexpensive | mission | 2889 Mission St. | 415-285-7117 | Lunch & Dinner daily

Cheese Board Pizza Collective 7.5

Opened as a cheese shop during the Bay Area food revolution of the mid-70s, the Collective expanded into "pizza for Tuesday lunch" in 1985. The then-novel artisanal pizza caused a sensation, and the Collective (based on the principles of an Israeli kibbutz) opened a full-time restaurant. Of the contemporary pizzeria, our reviewers say, "The pizza, served on a thin sourdough crust topped with up-market vegetarian ingredients, is always solid," and "The ability to order by the slice is unique for a place that sells arti-sanally styled pizzas."

Pizzeria | Inexpensve | berkeley | 1512 Shattuck Ave. | 510-549-3055 | www.cheeseboardcollective. coop | Lunch & Dinner Tue-Sat

Bette's Oceanview Diner 7.4

Expect a wait at this quirky diner in the heart of the Fourth Street shopping dis-trict. Bette's is famous for its pancakes and scones (they come in six different flavors), so it's no wonder that breakfast and brunch are the most popular meals of the day. While the expanded menu is "a step up from ordinary diner fare," the ingredients aren't artisanal, with the result that ultimately it's more of diner-like experience than some reviewers would like it to be.

Coffee Shop | Inexpensive | berkeley | 1807 Fourth St. | 510-644-3230 | www.worldpantry. com/bettes | Breakfast & Lunch daily

In-N-Out Burger 7.3

In-N-Out has a cult following, which is not so easy for a chain with close to 200 locations. Part of the mystique has to do with what used to be a secret menu, known only to the faithful but now avail-able to everyone on the Internet. Fans feast on creations like the 2 x 4 (two pat-ties and four pieces of cheese), the 3 x 3 or the monstrous 4 x 4. They even serve a burger for the gluten-intolerant, in which the bun is replaced with a lettuce wrap. The rest of the fare – fries, sodas, shakes – is more conventional.

Hamburgers | Inexpensive | fisherman's wharf | 333 Jefferson Street | 800-786-1000 | http://in-n-out.com | Open daily

Second Location | daly city | 260 Washington Street | 800-786-1000 | http://in-n-out.com | Open daily

Sears Fine Food 7.1

Open since 1938, this iconic coffee shop in the heart of Union Square earned its reputation by serving "eighteen perfect, tiny, greaseless Swedish pancakes" – and until 3:00 p.m., too. The rest of the breakfast and lunch fare is typical for a diner, but the pancakes are so popular that the line of people waiting to get in extends well down the block.

Coffee Shop | Inexpensive | downtown | 439 Powell St. | 415-986-0700 | www.searsfinefood. com | Open daily

OTHER PLACES MENTIONED

Gott's Roadside 6.2

There's a mom-and-pop feel to the St. Helena location of Gott's, which offers daily specials like a sandwich of home-made mozzarella with heirloom toma-toes. Conversely, the big-city branch feels like it has more in common with In-N-Out Burger. Still, it's a noticeable step up from most fast-food restaurants, and if you can bear the excruciatingly long lines, a burger, shake and fries make for a pretty good meal when you're visit-ing either the Ferry Building Marketplace or Wine Country.

Hamburgers | Inexpensive | embarcadero | Ferry Building Marketplace | 1 Ferry Bldg. | 415-318-3423 | www.gottsroadside.com | Open daily

These are some of the things our reviewers do to kill time in-between meals
(continued)
....

Mathematician, Emergency Room Doctor, Sociologist, Politician, Pop Music Critic, Real Estate Attorney, Investment Banker, Art Dealer, Environmentalist, Paint Factory Owner, Private Investigator, Headhunter, Insurance Litigator, Political Consultant, Retired Businessman, Bookstore Owner, Economist, Geneticist, Law School Student, Waiter, Sports Statistician, Food Writer, Winemaker, Anesthesiologist, Publicist, Business Consultant, Gadfly, Food Photographer, Banker, Personal Injury Attorney, Heiress, Commercial Baker, Internet Marketing Consultant

....

Join their ranks by signing up to participate in our 2012 Dining Survey. Who knows, maybe the thing you do to kill time in-between meals will show up on next year's list.

www.opinionatedabout.com

San Francisco South Bay CA

Manresa   100.0

While most of the dining public discovered it only a few years ago, many of our review-ers have been fans of David Kinch's restaurant since it opened in 2003. Kinch, who turns 50 this year, learned the ropes working for Barry Wine at New York's Quilted Giraffe, which he followed with a stint at Silk's. Then, after working in kitchens in Japan, Burgundy and San Sebastián, Kinch returned to San Francisco with the goal of creating an American equivalent of the regional dining experience found in France and Spain. The concept attracted a strong following with both locals and foodies, but it was only after Kinch partnered with Cynthia Sandberg at Love Apple Farms in 2006 and started growing his own produce for the restaurant that Manresa developed the strong national reputation it enjoys today.

Beloved by the locavores in our survey, the delicious vegetables Kinch raises turn up in dishes like Into the Vegetable Garden (inspired by Michel Bras' gargouillou) or a riceless risotto made with root vegetables, mushrooms and Parmigiano-Reggiano. A master with fish – whether in simple preparations like sea bream with olive oil and chives, or more complex dishes like a winter tidal pool with abalone, sea urchin, foie gras, shellfish and mushroom – Kinch handles the raw ingredients as if he had trained with the top sushi chefs in Japan. One reviewer commented that what makes the restaurant special is Kinch's "almost perfect sense of how to utilize modern culinary technique in order to maximize the flavor aspect of a dish."

New American | Casual | Very Expensive | los gatos | 320 Village Ln. | 408-354-4330 | www.manresarestaurant.com | Dinner Wed-Sun

Sawa Sushi   93.4

Sushi restaurants aren't usually controversial (except for their prices), but for some reason Steve Sawa's place stirs up a storm. It has a number of rabid fans, and it isn't unusual for them to go wild for its high-quality sashimi dishes. Comments included, "I can't argue with the fish, which is among the best I've had anywhere" and "Steve isn't a chef; he's a procurement officer and it just so happens he's the best one on the planet." But there is an opposition team, one that isn't enamored with Sawa's slicing skills, and that says things like "overrated, overhyped, overpriced" and "expensive for the worst sushi I have ever had." The location – a storefront with a tacky interior in a hard-to-find, strip mall – fans the flames of the heated debate.

Japanese | Informal | Moderate | sunnyvale | 1042 E. El Camino Real | 408-241-7292 | sawasushi.net | Lunch & Dinner Mon-Sat

Baumé   92.0

When this restaurant was first slated to open, people weren't optimistic about its chances – the site had hosted a series of failed ventures. But Bruno Chemel, who ran the kitchen at Chez TJ after Joshua Skenes and Chris Kostow, proved the doomsayers wrong, and Baumé is now considered "a notch below the very best in the Bay area." Chemel describes the food as "French cuisine moderne with a Zen touch," which boils down to cuisine based on the principles of molecular gastronomy but with a focus on ingredients rather than the technique – like a dish of leeks, Burgundy truffle, Gigha halibut and shiso or lantern scallops with lichee, Lilikoi and chocolate. More than one reviewer was surprised that the restaurant isn't more popular with visiting foodies.

Progressive | Casual | Very Expensive | palo alto | 201 S. California Ave. | 650-328-8899 | www.baumerestaurant.com | Dinner Wed-Sun, Lunch Fri

RECOMMENDED

Evvia   90.4

This cousin of Kokkari Estiatorio is one of the best choices in the South Bay. You begin with the house pita bread topped with olives, tomatoes, mizithra cheese and caramelized onions before moving on to dishes like beets that chef Stavros Pappas roasts in a wood-burning oven and tops with skordalia and dill. The lunch menu offers lighter fare, like pita wrapped around albacore tuna, red bell pepper and caramelized onions, while dinnertime customers enjoy heartier preparations like goat braised with tomatoes and served with orzo and herb feta.

Greek | Casual | Moderate | palo alto | 420 Emerson St. | 650-326-0983 | www.evvia.net | Dinner daily, Lunch Mon-Fri

TOP LOCAL CHOICE

Le Papillon   89.5

Working his way up from dishwasher to chef, Scott Cooper has updated the menu at this restaurant, which, at age 34, was considered a dowager by Silicon Valley locals. And from the rating, it appears that Cooper has succeeded with a menu that includes dishes like foie gras with maple Blis and miso butterscotch, and grilled buffalo with syrah jus, parsnip purée and cocoa nibs. Cooper's food, "a tranquil dining room, efficient service" and a reputation as "a wine drinker's destination" all explain why Le Papillon still flutters the wallets of so many business types for dinner.

Contemporary French | Casual | Very Expensive | san jose | 410 Saratoga Ave. | 408-296-3730 | www.lepapillon.com | Dinner daily, Lunch Fri

Amber India   89.0

San Francisco is not particularly known for its Indian restaurants, but if you have a jones for a bowl of curry, this four-restaurant mini-chain with headquarters in Mountain View serves "the best and most consistent Indian food in the Bay Area." The menu is fairly traditional, but dishes like curried scallops, paneer made from fresh goat cheese, and sea bass tikka give the cuisine a progressive edge. Note: If you like your Indian fare fiery, be forewarned that this "tame, slightly whitewashed" version won't satisfy.

Indian | Informal | Moderate | Mountain View | 2290 W. El Camino Real | 650-968-7511 | www.amberindia.com | Lunch & Dinner daily *Check website for other locations*

Kaygetsu   89.0

Surprisingly, given the large number of people of Japanese and Korean descent who live in the Bay Area, there is a dearth of quality sushi restaurants. Two of the better choices are located in the South Bay, and a number of reviewers say this Menlo Park place serves "the best sushi on the Peninsula." While most guests choose to order a kaiseki menu, regulars say that the food is better if you take a seat at the sushi bar and simply tell the chef to slice away to his heart's content.

Japanese | Informal | Moderate | menlo park | 325 Sharon Park Dr. | 650-234-1084 | www.kaygetsu.com | Dinner Tue-Sun, Lunch Tue-Fri

231 Ellsworth   88.0

Isaac Miller is the latest in a string of chefs who have cooked at this San Mateo restaurant. While his cuisine shows an ambitious side, with dishes like Foie Gras Three Ways and locally sourced halibut with green garlic risotto, artichokes, truffle aioli and preserved lemon, an assessment of the place as "good if you're in the area, but otherwise unexceptional" sums up the general sentiment. There's a deep wine list that includes an especially good selection of Napa Valley Cabs dating back to the 1970s.

New American | Casual | Expensive | san mateo | 231 S. Ellsworth Ave. | 650-347-7231 | www.231ellsworth.com | Dinner Mon-Sat, Lunch Tue-Fri

ACCEPTABLE

Bistro Elan   86.0

The clientele at the "other top restaurant in Palo Alto" is a unique mix of local families, Silicon Valley business diners, Stanford professors and alums. The menu is replete with bistro classics prepared with organic ingredients, like heirloom broccoli with buffalo mozzarella and green garlic or a slow-roasted Niman Ranch lamb shoulder served with peas, carrots, fingerlings, oyster mushrooms and cipollini onions. It's lively and noisy, and the carefully thought-out wine list is short but fairly priced.

New American | Casual | Moderate | palo alto | 448 S. California Ave. | 650-327-0284 | www.bistroelan.com | Dinner Tue-Sun, Lunch Tue-Fri

Mayflower Restaurant   85.5

If you find yourself in the South Bay and you're just dying to eat authentic Chinese food, head on over to this Hong Kong–style restaurant, sister to Hong Kong Flower Lounge in Millbrae. It's a similar scene: local Chinese families love to gather to enjoy dim sum by day and specialties like double-boiled shark's fin soup with abalone or oysters baked with XO sauce in the evening. Expect long waits if you get there around lunchtime.

Chinese | Informal | Moderate | milpitas | 428 Barber Ln. | 408-922-2700 | www.mayflower-seafood.com | Open daily

Blowfish Sushi to Die For 85.0

Most cities have a party-style Japanese place. Blowfish fills that slot in a city that can't even count a Sushi Samba among its ranks of restaurants, and the experience evoked comments like, "I guess if you really must have fusion sushi in a trendy atmosphere with a large group, this would be the place to go" and "trendy sushi surrounded by anime at top volume and even louder patrons. It's what I would imagine living in a pinball machine must feel like."

Japanese | Casual | Moderate | san jose | 2170 Bryant St. | 415-285-3848 | www.blowfishsushi.com | Dinner daily, Lunch Mon-Fri

OTHER RESTAURANTS MENTIONED

Navio   84.5

If you're anywhere between Palo Alto and San Francisco and are tired of eating the terrific, locally raised produce that's served at almost every restaurant in that corridor and prefer hotel food instead, book a table at this spot in the Ritz-

Carlton on Half Moon Bay. Of course, "hotel-quality service" comes with the hotel-quality food. At least you can enjoy the "lovely views over the Pacific" from the dining room.

New American | Casual | Expensive | half moon bay | Ritz-Carlton | 1 Miramontes Point Rd. | 650-712-7040 | www.naviorestaurant.com | Open daily except Sun Lunch

Tamarine   84.5

With its "standard fancy ethnic cuisine," Tamarine is the low man on the totem pole of Palo Alto dining. The upscale Vietnamese fare includes dishes like rosemary chicken skewers, lemongrass-blackened bass and honey-miso–seared duck. While the food is tame compared to that of more authentic Vietnamese restaurants, it's a popular choice for Silicon Valley business dinners, making it a difficult reservation to get.

Vietnamese | Informal | Moderate | palo alto | 546 University Ave | 650-325-8500 | www.tamarinerestaurant.com | Dinner daily. Lunch Mon-Fri

Viognier   84.0

This casual restaurant in Draeger's Market turns high-quality ingredients into California comfort cuisine like rack of lamb with golden raisin, chorizo and

pine nuts. There's a great wine selection (courtesy of the market), and while it's not a destination, it's "a reasonable lunch stop if you have a long layover at the San Francisco airport." You can also take advantage of one of the top gourmet markets in the country and pick up some goodies for the trip home.

Californian | Informal | Moderate | san mateo | Draeger's Market | 222 E. Fourth Ave. | 650-685-3727 | www.viognierrestaurant.com | Dinner daily

Chez TJ   82.5

They keep losing their chef at this beleaguered restaurant. The last one was Scott Nishiyama whose experience at places like the now-defunct Cello and the French Laundry showed up in dishes like Morrow Bay sablefish cooked sous vide with Yukon Gold potatoes, Manila clams, Oregon black truffles and smoky ocean broth. Suzanne Chowla manages a list full of Old World wines, always a plus in a part of the country where most of the cellars are California-centric.

New American | Casual | Expensive | mountain view | 938 Villa St. | 650-964-7466 | www.cheztj.com | Dinner Tue-Sat

Seattle WA

AN IMPORTANT DESTINATION

The Herbfarm (18 miles northeast in Woodinville)   95.0

No other restaurant rated this highly evokes comments that highlight such a drastic split between the cuisine and the rest of the experience. Nearly everyone who reviewed The Herbfarm derided it for the pre-dinner festivities, which include a tour of the herb garden, and an introduction to every person working in the kitchen, calling the peripheral goings-on "ridiculous" and a "dog and pony show." And those reviewers who didn't criticize what diners have to endure before dinner lambasted the restaurant for the way they serve the meal: Everyone in the 50-seat dining room is served at the same time; one reviewer described the "off-putting mass-dining style" as "catering."

On the other hand, with a menu overflowing with amazing local ingredients, which on any given night might include perch from Puget Sound, reef-netted sockeye salmon from Lummi Island, and beef and lamb raised in Oregon, complemented by amazing produce from the restaurant's farm, the menu reads like a primer on the ingredients of the Pacific Northwest. Nearly everyone agreed with the reviewer who described a nine-course dinner, based on "seriously fresh ingredients," as "far exceeding my expectations." Arguing in its favor are a wine list with 4,200 selections; arguing against it is a "horrid cancellation policy" whereby you are charged the full price of a meal.

New American | Casual | Very Expensive | queen anne | 14590 NE 145th St. | 425-485-5300 | www.theherbfarm.com | Check Opening Hours for theme dinners

HIGHLY RECOMMENDED

Canlis   93.4

The physical setting of some restaurants is so magnificent that the room becomes an integral part of the dining experience. That's the case at this "Mid-Century Modern masterpiece," built for $50,000 in 1950. But while all agree on the décor, feelings about the cuisine are more mixed: Jason Franey, who worked with Daniel Humm at Eleven Madison Park, is responsible for keeping two sets of diners happy: regulars who demand that the food taste the way it has since the '50s, and younger diners in search of more modern preparations. The result is a menu on which contemporary dishes like Muscovy Duck roasted with plums, prunes and Marco Polo black tea coexist alongside stalwarts like Peter Canlis prawns in a butter and vermouth sauce. Happily, the "polished service," an "exquisite wine cellar stocked with 18,000 bottles" and the "magnificent views of Lake Union" go a long way to overcome food that can be delicious but is all too often described as "carefully crafted not to offend or challenge."

New American | Casual | Expensive | queen anne | 2576 Aurora Ave. N. | 206-283-3313 | www.canlis.com | Dinner Mon-Sat

Rover's   93.1

Given how French restaurants seem to be pilloried on a regular basis, we were pleasantly surprised to see the reaction to this restaurant and its "slightly modernized version of French cuisine." Our reviewers hail it for being one of the best restaurants in Seattle. Well-known for wearing a Borsalino hat while working behind the stoves, Thierry Rautureau creates "wonderful, rich sauces" that turn up in traditional dishes like crispy sweetbreads with squash, morels and Marsala jus or in more modern preparations like spot prawns in a light shellfish nage with fennel. "A polished, professional restaurant that serves well-made food using often great ingredients" is how one reviewer described it, while others mentioned a "warm reception," a "stylish setting" and an "excellent wine list."

French | Casual | Expensive | capitol hill | 2808 E. Madison St. | 206-325-7442 | www.rovers-seattle.com | Dinner Tue-Sun, Lunch Fri

Crush   92.0

While many chefs serve their personal version of Pacific Northwest cuisine, no one has raised it to as high a level as Jason Wilson. From a small Tudor house at the foot of East Madison Street's restaurant row (Rover's and Nishino are down the block), Wilson serves dishes like hand-rolled potato gnocchi and Dungeness crab with brown butter, honey crisp apples, wild mushrooms and arugula or 48-hour braised Painted Hills beef short ribs with Yukon potato purée, bacon and sage-scented baby carrots. There's a "well-thought-out and well-stocked" wine list covering almost every region in the world, and the combination of "intimate space and delicious food" has made Crush a "top choice for celebrating a special occasion."

New American | Casual | Expensive | capitol hill | 2319 E. Madison St. | 206-302-7874 | www.chefjasonwilson.com | Dinner Tue-Sun

Nishino   91.6

After cutting his teeth at Matsuhisa, Tatsu Nishino opened this lively restaurant near Madison Park in 1995. More than 15 years later, it's still the place where Seattle's elite go to have sushi. Given his mentor, it isn't surprising that there are two aspects to Nishino's menu: traditional Japanese dishes, which include pristine cuts of high-quality fish, and more progressive fare like snow crab tempura on a creamy wasabi sauce or curried halibut cheek with sautéed mushroom, swiss chard and cilantro aioli. The "smartly decorated" dining room always seems to be full, and there are so many tasty-looking dishes on the menu that one reviewer suggested you "work up a big appetite" by taking a walk through the beautiful Washington Park Arboretum before dinner.

Japanese | Informal | Expensive | capitol hill | 3130 E. Madison St. | 206-322-5800 | www.nishinorestaurant.com | Dinner daily

Spinasse   91.3

Of all of Italy's regional cuisines, Piemontese might be the least familiar to American diners. But don't tell that to Jason Stratton, whose dedication to reproducing it as faith-fully as possible results in a fully booked restaurant from the moment it opens until closing time. At the heart of Stratton's cooking are his homemade pastas, and if you sit at the chef's counter and order a tasting menu, it will likely include tortellini in broth, tagliatelle with pork shoulder that has been braised in milk and what one reviewer called "the best tajarin I've had outside of Italy," lightly tossed with butter and sage. A "small and decent list" of northern Italian wines and "friendly service" make a visit here one of the most delightful evenings in the city.

Italian | Informal | Expensive | capitol hill | 1531 14th Ave. | 206-251-7673 | www.spinasse.com | Dinner Wed-Mon

Lark   90.8

While many Seattle restaurants strive for a big-city feel, John Sundstrom's venue, with its "outstanding selection of innovative small dishes" based on the "highest-quality, locally sourced ingredients," feels more like the type of casual farm-to-table place you tend to find in Portland. Sundstrom does Pacific Northwest cuisine with a few twists, like Penn Cove oysters with a spicy tomato granite, potato rösti with clabber cream and paddlefish caviar or braised lamb shoulder with emmer papardelle, zucchini and chard. One reviewer told us, "The best small plates restaurants make you want to keep on ordering until you cannot eat anymore. Lark is that kind of place."

New American | Informal | Moderate | capitol hill | 926 12th Ave. | 206-323-5275 | www.larkseattle.com | Dinner Tue-Sun

Café Juanita (16 miles northeast in Kirkland)   90.5

Though Italy is nearly 6,000 miles away, Holly Smith does such a good job of capturing the spirit of its cuisine that her restaurant might as well be located outside of Bologna. Smith utilizes the bounty of the Northwest in starters like Madhatcher squab breast with escarole, walnut oil and aged balsamico; maltagliati with Cattail Creek lamb sugo, minted green beans and honeyed ricotta; and rabbit braised in Arneis wine with a Ligurian chickpea crepe, pancetta and porcini. Beloved by a number of our reviewers, the place garnered comments like "super-high-quality ingredients and owners who really care" and "the best Italian restaurant in the Seattle area; nothing else comes close."

Italian | Casual | Moderate | kirkland | 9702 NE 120th Pl. | 425-823-1505 | http://cafejuanita.com | Dinner Tue-Sun

Campagne   90.0

Despite the fact that Campagne is "one of the best addresses in Seattle for Francophiles," our reviewers tell us they are "surprised at how easy it is to get a table" at this "wonderful restaurant with welcoming interiors and a lovely menu." The kitchen turns seasonal ingredients into bistro classics like a sweet onion gratin with Parmesan and asparagus or crispy pork shoulder with brown butter, capers and fingerling potatoes. The "offbeat wine selections" and "excellent service" make this a good choice for dinner near the Pike Place Market, an area whose restaurants are more likely to cater to non-discerning tourists rather than to gourmands.

New American | Informal | Moderate | belltown | Pike Place Market | 1600 Post Alley | 206-728-2233 | www.campagnerestaurant.com | Open daily

TOP LOCAL CHOICE

Tilth   89.5

Though Maria Hines has a national reputation for serving "high-quality locavore cuisine," our reviewers have mixed feelings about her restaurant. Those in favor call it "a good showcase for local ingredients" and claim it serves a "high-quality meal in a homey environment." But others say that Hines "takes the organic gimmick to the extreme," adding that "A number of dishes don't work" because she is "hamstrung by her commitment to organic ingredients." All of the dishes on the menu are available in half portions, giving small parties the ability to craft their own tasting menus.

New American | Informal | Moderate | wallingford | 1411 N. 45th St. | 206-633-0801 | www.tilthrestaurant.com | Dinner daily, Lunch Sat-Sun

Le Pichet   89.0

With "superb" locally made charcuterie and possibly "the best roast chicken in the city," this French bistro located on one of the busiest corners of downtown gets kudos like "a destination" and "a must-visit for any foodie." "Small, crowded and noisy," it makes for the perfect place to relax with a casse-croûte, a plat du jour, a platter of cheese or just a cup of coffee after spending a day of shopping or a few hours touring the stalls in the Pike Place Market.

French | Informal | Moderate | downtown | 1933 First Ave. | 206-256-1499 | www.lepichetseattle.com | Open daily

Ray's Boathouse   89.0

If you want to impress out-of-town guests at a place with a nice view, check out this converted boathouse; the "top-notch fresh fish and seafood make it a memorable spot for either lunch or dinner." The menu trends toward Pacific Northwest with an Asian tinge, best evidenced by sablefish that's available either smoked with a horseradish sabayon or in a sake kasu with honey soy and scallion oil. Sticklers for sustainability, they do their best to help preserve fish species for future generations.

Seafood | Casual | Expensive | ballard | 6049 Seaview Ave. NW | 206-789-3770 | www.rays.com | Dinner daily

Sitka & Spruce   89.0

From the perspective of the physical plant, there might be no other restaurant in the country that more closely resembles the gastropubs you find all over the U.K. than Sitka & Spruce. "Cozy" is the best way to describe this place, set inside the Melrose Market and with most seating at a large, wooden communal table. Chef/owner Matt Dillon's menu – dishes like chicken liver paté with chanterelles and huckleberries, clams with celery root and horseradish and charcoal-grilled chicken with chickpeas, yogurt and harissa – ensures you have not just a pub but a gastropub experience.

Mediterranean | Informal | Moderate | capitol hill | 1531 Melrose Ave. E. | 206-324-0662 | www.sit-kaandspruce.com | Lunch & Dinner Tue-Sat, Mon lunch only

Dahlia Lounge   88.0

When Tom Douglas opened this place in 1989, few restaurants served a refined version of Pacific Northwest cuisine. He has opened seven additional places since then, but at his flagship he's still serving dishes like Rogue Creamery Echo Mountain blue cheese with Chioggia beets, as well as Dungeness crab cakes with smoked paprika and roasted pepper hash. But 22 years is a long time in the restaurant business, and while most reviewers use adjectives like "solid" and "tasty" when describing the food, there is also the sentiment that "It seems about ten years out of date."

New American | Casual | Expensive | belltown | 2001 Fourth Ave. | 206-682-4142 | tomdouglas.com | Lunch & Dinner daily

Harvest Vine, The   88.0

It is doubtful you will find a tapas chef with a more appropriate name than Joseba Jiménez de Jiménez. And it is even more fitting that his menu is filled with dishes like red and golden beets with olive oil, sherry vinegar and garlic, lightly scrambled eggs with duck confit and cream and pan-roasted monkfish with bluefoot mushrooms, Serrano ham and hazelnuts. One reviewer called it "among the top three restaurants in the city," while another raved about the desserts prepared by the chef's wife, Carolin Messier de Jiménez, like blue cheese tart with roasted grapes and white wine sauce.

Spanish | Informal | Moderate | madison park | 2701 E. Madison St. | 206-320-9771 | www.harvestvine.com | Dinner Daily, Lunch Mon-Fri

How to Cook a Wolf   88.0

Ethan Stowell does his best to channel M.F.K. Fisher at this small plates restaurant in the Queen Anne District. The menu offers 18 types of dishes, including a soft-boiled egg with hot coppa and anchovy aioli, escolar crudo with avocado, Serrano chili and lime and half of a poussin with fingerling potatoes, Taggiasca olives and capers. Plus there are four pastas, including cavatappi with pancetta, onion and tomato. The combination of "high-quality food" and a "low price point" means "it's difficult to get in."

Mediterranean | Informal | Moderate | queen anne | 2208 Queen Anne Ave N. | 206-838-8090 | ethanstowellrestaurants.com | Dinner daily

ACCEPTABLE

Flying Fish   87.5

Rather than rely on attracting customers because of her Lake Union setting, Christine Keff cooks as though her room doesn't have a view. Keff's seafood-intensive menu focuses on local fish, in dishes like an open-face razor clam sandwich with tartar sauce and slaw or Columbia River Spring Chinook salmon with a vegetable tabbouleh and charmoula. Entering its 16th year, Flying Fish is still good enough to evoke comments like "one of the best places for seafood in a city that is notable for its seafood restaurants."

Seafood | Casual | Moderate | lake union | 300 Westlake Ave. N. | 206-728-8595 | http://flying-fishrestaurant.com | Dinner daily, Lunch Mon-Fri

Metropolitan Grill   87.5

Set in a building that dates from 1903, the city's top beef palace earns kudos like "classic steakhouse atmosphere. I had the sense I was in good, competent hands with the staff: The waiters were on top of their game. The steak was perfectly executed and presented at the right moment and temperature." Given that the same group owns Elliott's Oyster House (see below), it's a bit disappointing that Metropolitan doesn't offer a complete raw bar, however. We guess they want to encourage people to visit both restaurants.

Steakhouse | Casual | Expensive | downtown | 820 Second Ave. | 206-624-3287 | www.themetro-politangrill.com | Dinner daily, Lunch Mon-Fri

Salish Lodge Dining Room 87.5

(28 miles west in Snoqualmie)

It would be great if restaurants that possessed an idyllic setting were required to supply idyllic cuisine as well. But, alas, so many are like this venue, where "a beautiful setting with superb service" is offset by "mediocre food." It's too bad: It would be delightful if you could truly enjoy dishes like their version of chicken and waffles (organic-farmed chicken breast, Washington sweet onion waffle, wilted greens, and a rhubarb-fireweed honey syrup), while overlooking majestic Snoqualmie Falls.

New American | Casual | Expensive | snoqualmie | Salish Lodge | 6501 Railroad Ave. SE | 425-888-2556 | www.salishlodge.com | Lunch & Dinner daily

Wild Ginger   87.5

Despite the fact that pan-Asian cuisine is "sort of passé these days," Seattle-based diners are still enjoying Nathan Uy's place. There are a dozen or so different variations of satays on offer, ranging from traditional skewers like chicken to more exotic preparations like young mountain lamb. The extensive list of cocktails, wine and beer goes a long way to enhance the spicy food. The "decent" fare is served in a "serene environment in a convenient downtown location."

Pan-Asian | Casual | Moderate | downtown | 1401 Third Ave. | 206-623-4450 | www.wildginger.net | Lunch & Dinner daily

Elliott's Oyster House   87.0

Too often seafood restaurants located harborside turn out to be tourist traps, but this bivalve specialist, serving "the most extensive selection of Northwest oysters I have found anywhere," is an exception to the rule. On some days there are more than 40 varieties available, including some rarely seen outside this region, like Pickering Passage and Jorstad Creek. Unfortunately, the cooked fare is not up to the quality of the oysters – otherwise this "enormous, loud, friendly" site would have a higher rating.

Seafood | Informal | Moderate | downtown | 1201 Alaskan Way, Pier 56 | 206-623-4340 | www.elliottsoysterhouse.com | Lunch & Dinner daily

Etta's Seafood   87.0

All the fruits of the Northwest seas are on offer at a touristy location a block from the Pike Place Market: Stellar Cove oysters baked with bacon horseradish jam, Dungeness crab from the waters near Bellingham and the signature "Rub with Love" cold smoked Alaskan Wild King salmon served with cornbread pudding. Comments ranged from "simple cooking done very well" to "surprisingly good, considering it's part of a five-restaurant empire owned by Tom Douglas."

Seafood | Informal | Moderate | downtown | 2020 Western Ave. | 206-443-6000 | www.tom-douglas.com | Lunch & Dinner daily

Restaurant Zoë   87.0

Considered the toast of Belltown when it opened, Scott Staples' restaurant now garners split opinions. Fans talk about a "fun, relaxed" environment and a "finely prepared" menu utilizing local ingredients. But another contingent says it's "coasting on its reputation" and questions everything from the style of the cuisine to the freshness of the ingredients. A "lovely corner location" with large glass windows argues in its favor, while a "noisy dining room" cuts the other way.

New American | Informal | Expensive | belltown | 2137 Second Ave. | 206-256-2060 | www.restaurantzoe.com | Dinner daily

Chez Shea   86.5

Located on the second floor of Pike Place Market, this small French bistro is evocative of the type of place you would stumble upon while strolling around Paris' Marché aux Puces. The "fine French

food" is complemented by "charming service" and "a romantic atmosphere." Dishes like pan-seared Alaskan black cod with cipollini onions, baby cauliflowers and a Meyer lemon beurre blanc demonstrate that the kitchen takes full advantage of the market down below.

French Bistro | Informal | Expensive | downtown | Pike Place Market | 94 Pike St. | 206-467-9990 | www.chezshea.com | Dinner Tue-Sat

Daniel's Broiler   86.5

The value added at this steakhouse run by the Schwartz brothers comes from two things: the "beautiful views" overlooking Lake Union and an "extensive wine list" featuring "a superb selection of bottles from the Pacific Northwest." Otherwise, the "decent steaks" are the same as those at any upscale steakhouse chain. There's not even the token surprise dish or two that many a modern cow palace offers in an effort to be different; like the beef, the menu here is cut and dried.

Steakhouse | Casual | Expensive | lake union | Leschi Marina | 200 Lake Washington Blvd. | 206-329-4191 | www.schwartzbros.com | Dinner daily

El Gaucho   86.5

While the name suggests a restaurant revolving around a parrillada, or Argentine grill, this place turns out to be merely a North American steakhouse with a pseudo-'30s Latino vibe (embodied in entrées like the Flaming Swords of lamb and beef). Being "overpriced" and having "a decent wine list" makes it a perfect expense account restaurant, especially since reviewers are "happy to pay more for the theatrical setting."

Steakhouse | Casual | Expensive | belltown | 2505 First Ave. | 206-728-1337 | www.elgaucho.com | Dinner daily

Poppy   82.0

After spending 17 years as executive chef of The Herbfarm, Jerry Traunfeld decided that firing up the tandoor was preferable to cooking in a Bonnet oven – hence, this Thali-style restaurant. Problem is, Traunfeld tones down the traditional Indian spicing, perhaps in an effort to appeal to mainstream western palates, and "The result is that the food is tame and uninteresting. It bears no resemblance to Indian food other than the arrangement on the plate."

Indian | Informal | Moderate | capitol hill | 2505 First Ave. | 206-728-1337 | www.elgaucho. com | Dinner daily

Palisade   77.5

There's not much love for this kitchen among our reviewers, who slammed the food as "tragic" – "It made me long for the Cheesecake Factory," one panelist admitted. Still, this can be "a great place to take people to admire the lovely view over Elliott Bay." Another option: going at happy hour, when "good martinis" and "a nice atmosphere" combine with the vistas for a pleasant start to the evening.

Seafood | Casual | Moderate | magnolia | Elliott Bay Marina | 2601 W. Marina Pl. | 206-285-1000 | www.palisaderestaurant.com | Lunch & Dinner daily

Cheap Eats

Salumi Artisan   8.6
Cured Meat

You know the saying "Like father, like son." Well, the reverse is true in this case. In 1999, after 31 years in the aviation industry, Armandino Batali – dad to the famous Mario – traded in his Excel spreadsheets for a Berkel meat slicer and began making what some feel is the best salumi in the country. On Tuesdays through Fridays you will find a line of people waiting to order a sandwich made from one of a dozen sausages or hot sandwiches filled with meatballs or porchetta. Reviewers show their love with comments like "Lines out the door, but worth it. Portions were huge yet disappeared" and "The balance of meat, cheese, and condiments is just perfect."

Italian | Inexpensive | pioneer square | 309 Third Ave. S. | 206-621-8772 | www.salumicuredmeats. com | Lunch Tue-Fri

Macrina Bakery and Café   8.0

While Macrina sounds like a take on the name of owner Leslie Mackie, it actually belongs to a fourth-century Greek saint and mystic who preached the concept of living a simple, self-sufficient life. In keeping with the saint's teachings, every morning Mackie helps the residents of Seattle sustain themselves on breads and pastries like a raisin brioche twist, a lemon and sour cherry coffeecake or a Parmesan and rosemary ham biscuit. You can eat in or take out; one reviewer who visits the city on a regular basis said, "I always buy a sandwich and breads for the long plane ride home."

Bakery | Inexpensive | belltown | 2408 First Ave. | 206-448-4032 | www.macrinabakery.com | Breakfast & Lunch daily

Beecher's Handmade   6.6
Cheese

If you love the smell of burnt cheese, get on the line at this combination fromagerie and tourist attraction located across from the Pike Place Market where "The kids can watch them turn curds into cheddar," and then enjoy the finished product in an assortment of sandwiches, mac 'n' cheese and the house specialty, grilled cheese on rye.

Sandwiches | Informal | belltown | 1600 Pike Pl. | 206-956-1964 | www.beechershandmadecheese. com | Breakfast & Lunch daily

Serious Pie   6.4

Part of a three-eatery complex (Dahlia Lounge and Dahlia Bakery are the others), this pizzeria operated by Tom Douglas gets raves from locals: "The crust alone makes it worth going." But those who eat pizza in other American cities on a regular basis say Douglas' attempt to replicate the style of pie topped with artisanal ingredients offered by Los Angeles's Pizzeria Mozza "falls short" and ask, with so much good pizza available these days, "Why eat here?"

Pizzeria | Moderate | belltown | 316 Virginia St. | 206-838-7388 | http://tomdouglas.com | Lunch & Dinner daily

Wine Country, including Napa & Sonoma Counties CA

WORTH PLANNING A TRIP AROUND

French Laundry, The   100.0

Thomas Keller's landmark is the country's ultimate dining destination. A full 65% of our reviewers traveled from outside the state in order to eat here. By far the most famous chef America has ever produced, Keller can claim multiple accomplishments, including creating a number of signature dishes that are on par with top dishes by European chefs, as well as redefining the art of fine dining for American sensibilities. But beyond the lengthy list of his creations, it's his second-to-none attention to detail that makes eating here a special experience. And the amazing thing is that, despite the fact that it's more than 15 years since French Laundry began to win acclaim, we still find the same commitment to excellence and detail that was exhibited on the day it opened.

We could use the entire space allotted to this review to write about the signature dishes, which include Oysters and Pearls (a creation of poached oysters with pearl tapioca in an egg sabayon sauce that's probably the best-known dish ever created by an American chef); white truffle custard with truffle debris; cauliflower panna cotta topped with Sevruga caviar; and Peas and Carrots (butter-poached lobster tail in a ginger carrot sauce). Such dishes are mandatory eating for anyone who wants a proper education in haute cuisine. The rest of your meal will feature impeccably sourced ingredients that end up in dishes like a wood pigeon roasted with fig leaves (the aroma of vanilla wafts through the dining room when it's served, as the waiter lifts the lid of the pot it was cooked in). Of course, some people are critical, saying things like "the food has become too formulaic" or complaining about "a wine list with excessive pricing." Then there are those who mutter that Mr. Keller no longer does the cooking himself. But we see those as minor bumps in the road and suggest that this is a trip everyone should take at least once, if not 40 or 50 times (like some of our reviewers).

French | Casual | Very Expensive | yountville | 6640 Washington St. | 707-944-2380 | www.frenchlaundry.com | Dinner daily, Lunch Fri-Sun

The Restaurant at Meadowood   98.4

Of all the chefs whose restaurants earned a rating of Worth Planning a Trip Around in our survey, Chris Kostow is probably the least well-known. That's partly because he's relatively new to the food scene, compared to others on this level – and partly due to an erratic career path. After working under a trio of terrific mentors (Daniel Patterson, Trey Foshee and Daniel Humm, to be specific), Kostow took his first position as the executive chef at Chez TJ in Mountainview. Almost immediately, the local food press anointed him as one of the top toques in the Bay Area. Local foodies flocked to the restaurant, and Kostow was on his way to becoming a household name. But before anyone who lived elsewhere had a chance to visit, Kostow quit – the culinary version of leaving them at the altar.

But now he's back, and in the three short years since he established residence at this luxurious resort in St. Helena, he has taken full advantage of the wonderful ingredients grown in these lush surroundings. Kostow's culinary sensibility shows in a composition of green garlic, bergamot, Marcona almond and root vegetables, fluke steamed en cocotte with summer squash, chorizo and squid or a lamb shank that he roasts with vaudovan, eggplant, date and pickled carrots. Already he's earned some of the highest ratings in this guide, along with comments like "his cooking is only going to get better." Yet many diners still aren't familiar with his cuisine. Let's hope that changes the next time they visit Wine Country – provided, of course, that Kostow stays put this time.

New American | Casual | Expensive | st. helena | Meadowood Napa Valley | 900 Meadowood Ln. | 707-967-1205 | www.meadowood.com | Dinner Mon-Sat

Cyrus   97.3

For years, Napa County consistently outpaced Sonoma when it came to high-end dining destinations. But in 2006, Douglas Keane and Nick Peyton felt that a place like Healdsburg could handle the type of culinary sophistication found in the neighboring county, and so they created a significantly more formal venue. The evening's festivities begin with a Champagne and caviar cart – five types of caviar that might range from American paddlefish to Iranian Golden Osetra – followed by Keene's luxurious, Asian-tinged French cuisine.

The five- and eight-course tasting menus emphasize luxury ingredients, like Thai-marinated lobster with avocado and mango or wagyu beef with burdock and shiso in an oxtail consommé. Even the vegetable dishes, which include silken tofu with kombu, scallions and yuzu or porcini mushrooms with spring onions, fava beans and smoked carrots, have a luxurious feel to them. There's an amazingly well-stocked wine list, making for some of the best pairings offered in the county. Complaints were usually directed at non-culinary matters like "an out-of-the-way location," "tables that are too close together" and "heavy-handed pricing."

French | Casual | Expensive | healdsburg | 29 North St. | 707-433-3311 | www.cyrusrestaurant.com | Dinner Thu-Mon

Ubuntu   96.1

If we told you that one of the best restaurants in the country shared a space with a yoga studio and served only vegetarian fare, you would probably say we were nuts. But we promise that if you try Aaron London's cooking at this attractive restaurant in the heart of downtown Napa, you will consider us completely sane – and savvy as well. Don't believe us? How about Forono beet leaves served as a borscht with red-veined sorrel, cracked potato, horseradish, crème fraiche and pickled quail eggs or an Ubuntu steam bun stuffed with burrata and coated with sunchoke "dirt."

Saying that London has taken vegetarian cuisine to a new level sounds like a cliché, but comments like "well-executed and inventive fare with enough richness to satisfy omni-vores," "so hearty and flavorful that you probably won't realize you're eating vegetarian cuisine" and "a vivid demonstration that cuisine can revolve around the vegetable and that meat is only a sidekick in the game" should convince you that we are not exaggerating. We also dare someone to find a vegetarian restaurant with a better wine list. The dining room is a tribute to all things natural: Everything from the flooring to the furniture has been designed with an eye toward reducing the toll on Earth's resources.

Vegetarian | Casual | Expensive | napa | 1140 Main St. | 707-251-5656 | www.ubuntunapa.com | Dinner Daily, Lunch Mon-Fri

Auberge du Soleil   93.3

The main draw at this Wine Country mainstay is "an idyllic setting" that includes the option to dine on a patio overlooking the Napa Valley. Add Robert Curry's French cuisine and the "expert service" to the mix and you have one of the area's most popular spots. Curry's cuisine has an Asian tinge to it these days, as in a dish of poached Hopper shrimp with green papaya, grapefruit, cilantro and curry or Liberty Farms duck with philo apples, glazed chestnuts, bacon, cocoa nib and an anise sauce. The lovely setting wasn't lost on our reviewers, who offered comments like "gorgeous restaurant, amazing food, very elegant – recommended for a long, leisurely lunch," "Beautiful views over the vineyards make for a magical meal" and "You can't go wrong with a platter of oysters and a glass of Champagne while watching a spectacular Napa Valley sunset."

French | Casual | Expensive | rutherford | 180 Rutherford Hill Rd. | 707-963-1211 | www.aubergedusoleil.com | Lunch & Dinner daily

RECOMMENDED

ad hoc   91.8

This fixed-menu, family-style affair from Thomas Keller shouldn't be underestimated. A typical evening's menu might include a Cobb or Caesar salad, Texas-style barbecue or Southern-fried chicken, followed by a cheese course and dessert, all for the bargain-basement price of $52 a person. A "limited wine list" makes it the perfect place to bring that special bottle you picked up at a winery tasting. While a few people complained about not being able to choose their own meals, most were effusive, saying things like, "We were there on the day they served 48-hour braised short ribs, and I hope this is what they serve in heaven!"

American | Informal | Moderate | yountville | 6476 Washington St. | 707-944-2487 | www.adhocrestaurant.com | Dinner daily, Lunch Mon-Fri

Bouchon   91.4

While Thomas Keller's attention to detail and commitment to excellence are clearly in evidence, diners expecting the "French Laundry light" are barking up the wrong tree. Instead, you will find an excellent raw bar and user-friendly French bistro cuisine, like pan-seared tuna with ratatouille and roast chicken with red rice and lardons, served by a friendly staff in a lively environment. "Solid food with excellent ingredients; they stick to the middle road, but the execution is flawless" sums it up best. It's one of the few places in the Valley that offers late-night dining, making it useful for those who need to sleep off a long day of wine-tasting before dinner.

French Bistro | Casual | Moderate | yountville | 6534 Washington St. | 707-944-8037 | www.bouchonbistro.com | Lunch & Dinner daily

Terra   91.1

Set in a 100-year-old stone building on a St. Helena side street, Terra has historically received raves. But it opened at a time when the dining options in the Wine Country were more limited than they are today, and now, facing more competition and with another restaurant to run in San Francisco, Hiro Sone and Lissa Doumani are receiving more mixed reviews. As one long-term customer summarized it: "Still good, but it has lost a bit of focus since they opened Ame." Sone's cuisine combines Asian and Mediterranean styles, and his menu ranges from dishes like Kampachi carpaccio with hijiki, cucumber, radish and ponzu to a grilled Kurobuta pork chop with broccoli di'Ciccio and ricotta gnocchi.

Asian-Mediterranean | Casual | Expensive | st. helena | 1345 Railroad Ave. | 707-963-8931 | www.terrarestaurant.com | Dinner Wed-Mon

Redd   91.0

Richard Reddington's resumé reads like a Who's Who of famous chefs – he's cooked under Alain Passard, Roger Vergé and Daniel Boulud – which he's supplemented with stints as executive chef at Auberge du Soleil and Masa's. In 2005, he went out on his own and opened Redd, where he features New American fare like rabbit mole with soft polenta, cheddar cheese and jícama, Petrale sole with chorizo, calamari and a saffron curry sauce and Niman Ranch pork osso bucco in a pine nut crust with green garlic potato purée. Redd is literally a stone's throw from the French Laundry; if the cancellation you've been waiting for there doesn't materialize, this is "clearly the next-best fine dining option in Yountville."

New American | Casual | Expensive | yountville | 6480 Washington St. | 707-944-2222 | www.reddnapavalley.com | Lunch & Dinner daily

Bottega   90.3

Having had success as the chef at Tra Vigne before he moved onto projects like the website NapaStyle, a Food Network television show, Consorzio Oils and his own vineyard, Michael Chiarello decided it was time to open this Italian restaurant down the street from the French Laundry. While it exhibits all the indicia of a place that takes advantage of tourists, some reviewers applaud the "wine-friendly take on Italian cuisine" that features "great pastas" like papardelle with veal, pork and porcini Bolognese, along with many different types of grilled and wood-roasted meats. But others dismiss Chiarello's return to restaurateuring, muttering about "bused-in tourists who are attracted to the flame of the chef's TV fame like moths."

Italian | Informal | Moderate | napa | V Marketplace | 6525 Washington St. | 707-945-1050 | www.botteganapavalley.com | Dinner daily, Lunch Tue-Sun

Bistro Jeanty   90.0

When you're tired of eating contemporary fare prepared by chefs with names like Keller, Reddington and Chiarello, saunter over to what is an old standby for many of our reviewers and kick back with some unfussy French comfort food. The menu at Bistro Jeanty includes every classic bistro dish you can think of, including sole meunière, quenelles de brochet in lobster sauce (rarely seen these days), coq au vin and tarte Tatin. The wine list is short, but true to the low-key ostentation the Wine Country is known for, you can still quaff a bottle of Screaming Eagle for $2,100 if you're in that kind of a mood.

French Bistro | Informal | Moderate | yountville | 6510 Washington St. | 707-944-0103 | www.bistro-jeanty.com | Lunch & Dinner daily

Cole's Chop House   90.0

While Napa is overrun with collectors who would love to enjoy a large hunk of beef with a special bottle of California Cab scored at a tasting earlier that day, the Valley has always lacked for high-quality steak restaurants. Cole's does its best to fill that niche, and the "big steaks, big drinks, and big side dishes" will save many a wine lover from having to make the trip back into San Francisco to enjoy the combination. "Easygoing service" and "a nice outdoor patio" make the combination taste all the better.

Steakhouse | Casual | Expensive | napa | 1122 Main St. | 707-224-6328 | www.coleschophouse.com | Dinner daily

Madrona Manor   90.0

If you owned a Victorian mansion that featured an elaborately decorated dining room, what type of cuisine would you serve? New American, of course. At least that's what Jesse Mallgren does at this "small romantic" Healdsburg venue. Mallgren's menu includes dishes like scallops sashimi served with uni, borage, Meyer lemon and fresh wasabi or suckling pig with Anson Mills polenta, corn, morels and truffle. Comments included "super-fresh and creative" and "a lovely place to have a special dinner," but reviewers weren't so kind to the wine list, calling it "weak and overpriced" (unusual for a restaurant in Wine Country).

New American | Casual | Expensive | healdsburg | 1001 Westside Rd. | 707-433-4231 | www.madrona-manor.com | Dinner Wed-Sun

TOP LOCAL CHOICE

étoile   89.5

"If only the food were as exquisite as the surroundings," our panelists sigh about this "romantic venue" on the grounds of the Domaine Chandon winery. Perry Hoffman's menu features dishes like California white sea bass with burdock root, baby corn, shrimp mousse and Kaffir lime broth, and most of the dishes are paired with glasses of Champagne made within walking distance of the dining room. Lunch is the most popular meal, as it allows diners to view the vineyards while sipping their bubbly.

New American | Casual | Expensive | yountville | 1 California Dr. | 707-944-2892 | www.chandon.com | Lunch & Dinner Thu-Mon

La Toque   89.5

Ken Frank became a Wine Country mainstay when he opened a second incarnation of his legendary Sunset Strip eatery, La Toque, in Rutherford in 1998. Now ensconced in the Westin Verasa Hotel complex just outside downtown Napa, Frank specializes in contemporary French fare that still makes diners happy – for example, dayboat scallops with baby fennel, artichokes and squid ink aioli or a boneless lamb loin with cumin-scented carrot purée and chickpea fries. The terrific wine list has "an especially good selection of Burgundies," unusual in an area where local varietals usually dominate.

French | Casual | Expensive | napa | 1314 McKinstry St. | 707-257-5157 | www.latoque.com | Dinner daily

Oenotri 89.5

There are reviewers who say you can find "the best Italian food in the Napa Valley" at this new addition to the downtown dining scene. There are 17 types of salumi on offer, along with dishes like grilled Monterey Bay squid salad with Rangpur lime relish and Niman Ranch flatiron steak pizzaiola with Parmigiano and fried kale. The "setting is hip, the ingredients fresh, the pizza well-done and the pastas fantastic," and "The rustic Italian cuisine is presented with flair from solid professionals who know their way around a wood-fired oven." The wine list offers good value.

Italian | Informal | Moderate | napa | 1425 First St. | 707-252-1022 | www.oenotri.com | Dinner daily

Farmhouse Inn and Restaurant 89.0

This restaurant makes for a good choice in an out-of-the-way part of Sonoma County that isn't exactly overflowing with top restaurants. Steve Litke's ingredient-based Cal-Med cuisine — roasted Berkshire pork tenderloin medallions with herb-roasted Yukon Gold potatoes and warm sherry bacon vinaigrette — is simply prepared, and the décor is cozy and romantic. An added bonus is a "solid California wine list devoid of price gouging," and a "lovely 18-room inn" allows guests to enjoy the wines from the nearby Russian River area without having to drive afterward.

Californian | Casual | Expensive | forestville | 7871 River Rd | 707-887-3300 | www.farmhouseinn.com | Dinner Thu-Mon

Mustards Grill 89.0

You have reached the heart of Wine Country when you arrive at Cindy Pawlcyn's iconic restaurant. The menu is filled with dishes that helped define the California dining experience: crispy calamari with curried slaw, smoked Sonoma duck with mustard seed fruit conserva and the famed Mongolian pork chop with sweet and sour red cabbage. Unfortunately, the quality of the cooking isn't what it once was, and the focus seems to be on keeping tourists happy (those who know little about food, that is), rather than turning out a quintessential version of California cuisine.

Californian | Informal | Moderate | st. helena | 7399 St. Helena Hwy./Hwy. 29 | 707-944-2424 | www.mustardsgrill.com | Lunch & Dinner daily

Cindy's Backstreet Kitchen 88.5

Everyone seems to love this casual little restaurant on a St. Helena side street, where small plates hold piquillo peppers stuffed with cumin-braised beef, while larger plates include mushroom tamales with creamy grits and chard. You can also order a burger or what one reviewer called "an adult grilled cheese sandwich" if you want a lighter meal. It's perfect as a stop between tastings, and don't be surprised if the winemaker from your last appointment is sitting at the table next to you. We note that one person did complain about the portions, saying that "They were too large."

Californian | Informal | Moderate | st. helena | 1327 Railroad Ave. | 707-963-1200 | www.cindysbackstreetkitchen.com | Lunch & Dinner daily

Syrah 88.5

Josh Silvers' restaurant is one of the few good places to eat in this part of Sonoma

County. The menu mixes the cooking of France and California, and the result is dishes like a brandade of crispy cod and potato served with olive caponata and a piquillo pepper coulis or an herb-brined poussin that Silver complements with mascarpone grits and bacon-braised calvo nero. There's "a thoughtful use of local ingredients," and it's not surprising that the "large, wonderful wine list" is filled with local bottlings of syrah, petite sirah and an assortment of New World Rhone wines.

Californian | Informal | Moderate | santa rosa | 205 Fifth St. | 707-568-4002 | www.syrahbistro.com | Dinner daily

Willi's Wine Bar   88.5

If you don't want a heavy meal after a day of tasting but do want to keep drinking, you might want to check out this Healdsburg wine bar. The small plates menu includes flatbread with chanterelle mushrooms, melted leeks, goat cheese crème fraîche and blood sausage as well as Liberty Farms barbecue pulled duck with white cheddar polenta. One way to utilize the "extensive wine list" is to try a flight of a particular varietal: $10 gets you an assortment of Sauvignon Blancs or Bordeaux blends from different regions.

Eclectic | Informal | Moderate | healdsburg | 4404 Old Redwood Hwy. | 707-526-3096 | www.williswinebar.net | Dinner daily, Lunch Tue-Sat

Zazu   88.5

Just a roadhouse on the outskirts of Santa Rosa, Duskie Estes and John Stewart's restaurant should be high on your list if you like quirky places. The menu features sandwiches like turkey meatballs Parmesan or pork cheek with salsa verde, and larger plates like duck confit hash with a fried egg on top or cocoa nib foie gras with rhubarb gastrique. There's even a breakfast pizza with a fried egg and sausage. It's always filled with locals who appreciate a place that uses local and sustainable ingredients and a "low-key, farm-chic atmosphere."

California | Informal | Moderate | santa rosa | 3535 Guerneville Rd. | 707-523-4814 | www.zazurestaurant.com | Dinner Wed-Mon, Brunch Sun

ACCEPTABLE

Angèle   87.5

As a foodie stop, the town of Napa has always played second fiddle to other Valley villages with more famed venues. Set on the riverfront, Angèle's is popular with those who live in the Valley, but visitors don't seem to be as impressed with what they describe as "ordinary bistro fare," such as onion soup, stuffed quail, poulet Provençal and beef Bourguignon. There's a tasty little wine of both domestic and French wines.

French Bistro | Informal | Moderate | napa | 540 Main St. | 707-252-8115 | www.angelerestaurant.com | Lunch & Dinner daily

Brix   87.5

Brix has always occupied a lovely space, but the food has never lived up to the surroundings. Now Anne Gingrass, one of the doyens of California cuisine, is behind the stoves preparing the interesting blend of Italian, Mediterranean and California culinary concepts you can find all over the region. Gingrass's menu features dishes like a Sonoma duck breast with creamy faro, fava beans and morels. "One of the nicest patios in Napa" is a lovely place to have lunch.

Californian | Informal | Moderate | st. helena | 7377 St. Helena Hwy./Hwy. 29 | 707-944-2749 | www.brix.com | Lunch & Dinner daily

Go Fish   87.5

Cindy Pawlcyn's fish restaurant is not as well-liked as her other establishments. Reviewers suggest you stick to the "glistening fresh sushi" and offerings from the raw bar, while avoiding "exorbitantly priced" dishes, like Alaskan halibut with porcini, asparagus and Calabrian chiles and cioppino; one reviewer described the cooked fare as "poorly executed." There were also complaints about "uncomfortable seating" and "uppity service," but our favorite was "sushi and sole almondine on the same menu?"

Seafood | Informal | Moderate | st. helena | 641 Main St. | 707-963-0700 | www.gofishrestaurant. net | Lunch & Dinner daily

Rutherford Grill   87.5

If it looks like a Houston's, feels like a Houston's and smells like a Houston's, it must be a Houston's – even if it's called something else. Having said that, some folks did praise the "very simple, unpretentious American fare," like barbecued ribs and Caesar salad, in "a friendly environment that is a step above a diner." Given the location, the wine list is surprisingly "indifferent," but corkage is offered. Yet the place is excessively popular, causing one reviewer to quip, "maximum burgers, maximum lines."

American | Informal | Moderate | rutherford | 180 Rutherford Hill Rd. | 707-963-1211 | www.hillstone.com | Open daily

Tra Vigne   87.5

"They prey on tourists" is how one reviewer described this St. Helena classic, while another said, "I was shocked at how ordinary this was. If you can't serve ingredients-based Italian food when you are located in the Napa Valley, you have to be doing something wrong." Still, others like it as a simple place to stop for lunch during an afternoon of wine shopping. But our advice is to stick to the Pizzeria Tra Vigne (see below) by day

and to eat your serious meals elsewhere.

Italian | Informal | Moderate | st. helena | 1050 Charter Oak Ave. | 707-963-4444 | www.travignerestaurant.com | Lunch & Dinner daily

Wine Spectator Greystone 87.5

This casual spot on the campus of the Culinary Institute offers eclectic choices like a soft-shell crab BLT with chipotle aioli, lamb kefta with falafel, tzatziki and baba ghanoush and pan-roasted ling cod with prosciutto, broccolini, butter bean-olive relish and smoked paprika vinaigrette. It comes with a "stunning setting" and "cheap wine prices." Try to eat on the terrace during warm weather.

American | Informal | Moderate | st. helena | Culinary Institute of America | 2555 Main St. | 707-967-1010 | www.ciachef.edu | Lunch & Dinner daily

Cafe La Haye   87.0

When you don't want to spend hundreds of dollars for dinner, check out this "cute little place" off the square in Sonoma. The California-inspired menu includes a Dungeness crab cake with lemon aioli and a glazed pork chop with cider-braised cabbage and grilled onion over basmati rice. One reviewer described the cuisine as "gutsy," while another who's a regular customer claimed, "The food keeps getting better and better."

California | Informal | Moderate | sonoma | 140 E. Napa St. | 707-935-5994 | www.cafelahaye.com | Dinner Tue-Sat

Cook St. Helena   87.0

What do you do when you get hungry after a few hours walking around downtown St. Helena? Well, you stop in at this casual restaurant to fill up on some handmade mozzarella with arugula pesto and Meyer lemon oil or stuffed red trout with fingerling potatoes, fennel and puttanesca vinaigrette. The "chef and staff are friendly and helpful." The only downside of its "great price to value ratio" is that

"When it's full it can be too noisy."

New American | Informal | Moderate | st. helena | 1310 Main St. | 707-963-7088 | www.cooksthelena.com | Lunch & Dinner Mon-Sat, Sun dinner only

Dry Creek Kitchen   87.0

Charlie Palmer's Healdsburg offering got off to a fast start, but over the past year the opinions seem to have cooled. "Sometimes the food's wonderful, other times just okay" is a sentiment we heard often, with the inconsistency being blamed on a series of chef changes. On the bright side, corkage is free if you bring any bottle of wine that was made in Sonoma County.

New American | Casual | Expensive | healdsburg | 317 Healdsburg Ave. | 707-431-0330 | www.hotelhealdsburg.com | Dinner daily, Lunch Fri-Sun

The Girl and the Fig   86.5

The lack of good places to eat in the area makes this bistro, adjacent to the Sonoma Hotel and open from brunch through dinner, one of the more popular choices in the county. The ingredients are sourced from the local farmer's market, and there is an extensive list of local cheeses, as well as a quirky wine list that focuses on Rhone varietals. Most consider it a better choice for a casual daytime meal of a soup or salad than for the heavier fare they serve in the evening.

French Bistro | Informal | Moderate | sonoma 110 W.Spain St. | 707-938-3634 | www.thegirlandthefig.com | Lunch & Dinner daily

Mirepoix   86.5

If you're looking for a good meal in the Santa Rosa area, join the winemakers who are digging into Matthew Bousquet's French bistro cuisine here. Mirepoix offers "the best quality-to-price ratio in the area," and dishes like Egg in a Hole (brioche, frisée, onions and brie) or sweetbreads, potatoes and horseradish are so popular that Bousquet moved the

restaurant into new, larger quarters.

French Bistro | Informal | Moderate | windsor | 275 Windsor River Rd. | 707-838-0162 | www.restaurantmirepoix.com | Dinner Wed-Sun

Bistro Don Giovanni   85.5

Often frequented by the locals, this Italian seems "run of the mill" to our reviewers, who ask, "Why would anyone who is visiting want to eat there, given the other choices nearby?" Well, for the scene and the al fresco dining or for the "reasonable corkage policy" or for a simple bowl of pasta, if that's what you're craving. Otherwise, you're better off moving on to one of the many other choices offered in Napa these days.

Italian | Informal | Moderate | napa | 4110 Howard Ln. | 707-224-3300 | www.bistrodongiovanni.com | Lunch & Dinner daily

John Ash and Co.   85.0

Despite a beautiful setting amid the vineyards of the Ferrari-Carano Winery, this nearly 30-year-old restaurant is best suited to non-foodie couples celebrating a special occasion, rather than those who have traveled to the Wine Country to feast on local ingredients prepared with respect and care. Though John Ash's name is still attached to the restaurant, Thomas Schmidt now does the cooking. If weather permits, try to eat on the patio.

Californian | Informal | Moderate | santa rosa | 4330 Barnes Rd. | 707-527-7687 | www.johnashrestaurant.com | Dinner daily

OTHER PLACES MENTIONED

K and L Bistro   84.5

Quality bistro fare is available at this "out of the way" venue in Sebastopol. Dungeness crab cakes and a fritto misto of rock shrimp, calamari and zucchini are favorites with a number of our reviewers, who like K and L's combination of high standards, good value and unpretentious setting. A diverse wine list, featuring choices that extend well beyond Sonoma County bottlings, adds to the experience.

Californian | Informal | Moderate | sebastapol | 119 S. Main St. | 707-823-6614 | www.klbistro.com | Lunch & Dinner Mon-Sat

Press   83.0

Wine Country always seemed short a steakhouse until Leslie Rudd (of winery fame) opened this attractive restaurant, where he serves grilled and roasted versions of meats from purveyors like Creekstone Farms and Hudson Ranch. Given the location, there's "the obligatory superb wine list," and if you want a lighter meal, a bar menu features items like a Kobe burger and roast chicken frites.

Steakhouse | Casual | Expensive | st. helena | 587 St. Helena Hwy. | 707-967-0550 | www. presssthelena.com | Dinner Wed-Sun

Hurley's   81.5

A standard slate of California comfort fare – including Sugar Pie pumpkin risotto and tamarind- and chipotle-glazed buffalo short ribs – is on hand at this restaurant that's described as either "a good choice if you're locked out of the Yountville biggies" or a "tourist trap." Whatever your point of view, it's "one of few casual dining spots in the county."

American | Informal | Moderate | yountville | 6518 Washington St. | 707-944-2345 | www.hurleysrestaurant.com | Lunch & Dinner daily

Cheap Eats

RECOMMENDED

Bouchon Bakery   7.8

Though it doesn't get the same raves as his other restaurants, this casual offering from Thomas Keller packs them in just the same. You start out with "what might be the best baguette in the region" and continue with lighter fare like the quiche de jour or the chicken and dump-

ling soup. Or you can recharge with "an espresso and some of the best macarons ever." A number of people mentioned "high prices," but they obviously didn't see the letters TK engraved into the food.

Bakery | Inexpensive | yountville | 6528 Washington St. | 707-944-2253 | www.bouchon-bakery.com | Breakfast & Lunch daily

Pizzeria Tra Vigne   7.5

Everyone seems to be fond of this wood-burning-oven pizzeria. While it offers salads and pastas, the main attraction is the four thin-crust pizzas with toppings that range from the typical to the more exotic, like Gulf shrimp and chicken apple sausage. Considering that many Napa restaurants get away with underperforming for less-than-knowledgeable tourists, one reviewer stated, "There is no reason for the pizza to be as good as it is here, but it really does hit the spot."

Pizzeria | Inexpensive | st. helena | 1016 Main St. | 707-967-9999 | www.travignerestaurant.com | Lunch & Dinner daily

Gott's Roadside   6.2

There's a mom-and-pop feel to the St. Helena location of Gott's, which includes daily specials like a sandwich of home-made mozzarella with heirloom toma-toes, while the big-city version feels like it has more in common with In-N-Out Burger. Still, it's a noticeable step up from most fast-food restaurants, and if you can bear the excruciatingly long lines at lunch, a burger, shake and fries make for a pretty good meal when you're visiting Wine Country. They also operate a second location in the Oxbow Public Market, which is just a stone's throw from downtown Napa,

Hamburgers | Inexpensive | st. helena | | 933 Main St | 707-963-3486 | www.gottsroadside.com | Open daily

Second Location: napa | Oxbow Public Market | First St. | 707-224-6900 | Open daily

Yosemite CA

Erna's Elderberry House   91.0

Some traditional dining settings come off as stodgy and old-fashioned, while others seem totally charming. Erna's is a case study for the latter, in large part because Karsten Hart's menu, featuring dishes like diver scallops with a Pecorino risotto or a braised duck foie gras strudel, fits the environment like a glove. With comments like "The setting is gentle and the service wonderful, with excellent food and a wine list par none," it's easy to see that it holds a special place for a number of our reviewers. But keep in mind what one reviewer told us: "I had a great time, but I kept expecting the von Trapp family singers to jump out from the behind the curtains."

European | Formal | Expensive | 48688 Victoria Ln. | 559-683-6800 | www.elderberryhouse.com | Dinner daily, Lunch Sun

Washington DC & the Mid-Atlantic States

Annapolis MD

RECOMMENDED

Joss Cafe & Sushi Bar   90.3

We sat up and took notice when one of our reviewers said he thought that the Joss Cafe serves "the best sushi on the East Coast outside of NYC," a comment promptly followed by this from a chef who used to work in the area: "I would stop in after dinner service two or three times a week, it was that good." We are usually skeptical about these things, so we checked it out ourselves, and we have to say we agree with them both. You can go classic and sit at the counter and ask for an omakase that will include cuts like escolar and rockfish, or get a bit more inventive with a hand roll of Kobe beef minced with garlic chips.

Japanese | Informal | Moderate | 195 Main St. | 410-263-4688 | Dinner daily, Lunch Mon-Sat

TOP LOCAL CHOICE

Jimmy Cantler's Riverside Inn   88.5

Chesapeake Bay blue crabs reign supreme at this Annapolis institution, situated on sedate Mill Creek, where you can begin with crab dip, crab Caprese or two different types of crab soup before moving on to soft-shell crabs, crab cakes, baked lump crab imperial or the house special crab boil, which includes three crabs, mussels, clams, shrimp, corn on the cob and coleslaw. Of course, traditionalists can stick to a basic crab boil. All that's left to order is the ice-cold beer. There's a full menu of seafood if crab's not your thing, but why else would you be here?

Seafood | Informal | Moderate | 458 Forest Beach Rd. | 410-757-1311 | www.cantlers.com | Lunch & Dinner daily

Atlantic City NJ

TOP LOCAL CHOICE

Chef Vola's   88.0

Chef Vola's has been open since 1921 and under the command of the Esposito family for close to 30 years. Set in the basement of a private house just off the Boardwalk, it kept for many years an unlisted number and you needed an introduction from a regular to get a table. Now they have loosened things up, but food-wise, it's still a true throwback: all sorts of antipasti, pastas doused in red sauce and entrées that range from meatballs to veal parmigiana to gigantic prime steaks served with a char crust. Most of the people who dine here have been doing so for at least a quarter-century. It's about "as old school and quirky as it gets" – and "should not be missed" if you are going to be in Atlantic City.

Italian | Informal | Expensive | 111 S. Albion Pl. | 609-345-20221 | www.chefvolas.com | Dinner Tue-Sun

ACCEPTABLE

Gallagher's Steakhouse   86.0

While some reviewers described this outpost of the New York original as "classic," the prevailing opinion seems to be, "I can't recommend it in New York, and I can't recommend it here either." Realists remarked, "While there are too many alternatives [in NYC] to bother with this mediocre establishment, AC is not filled with good places to eat, which causes it to move a rung up the ladder."

Steakhouse | Casual | Expensive | 1133 Boardwalk | 609-340-6555 | www.gallagherssteakhouse.com | Dinner daily

Cheap Eats

UNIQUELY DELICIOUS

White House Sub Shop   8.0

"Could be the best subs we ever had" is how one reviewer described this sandwich shop's fare. The menu offers endless combinations of Italian cold-cut sandwiches, but their hot offerings, including the cheese steak and the chicken cacciatore, are not to be underestimated. The classic American ambience (not retro – it genuinely dates from the 1940s), which includes seating in booths or at the counter, adds a refreshing element. The place sells so many sandwiches that they get a delivery of freshly baked bread every 30 minutes, which is, incidentally, about how long you will wait for a table on a weekend afternoon.

Sandwiches | Inexpensive | 2301 Arctic Ave. | 609-345-1564 | Lunch & Dinner daily

Baltimore MD

HIGHLY RECOMMENDED

Charleston   92.4

With starters like shrimp and andouille with grits, and shellfish bisque laced with tarragon oil and a fried green tomato "sandwich" with a lump crab hash, "haute Low Country" is the best way to describe North Carolina native Cindy Wolf's cooking – for the starters, at least. Mains, like pan-roasted king salmon with squash blossom beignets and basil mayonnaise or duck breast with a rhubarb and bing cherry compote and port wine reduction, slant more toward New American cuisine. Wolf's husband and partner, Tony Foreman, lords over a 600-bottle wine list, which includes a superb selection of Burgundies, along with numerous cherry-picked varietals from every other important wine region. That, along with a dining room described as "stylish and elegant" with a "lovely view overlooking the harbor," makes this a contender for the best restaurant along the Acela route between NYC and D.C.

New Southern | Casual | Expensive | harbor east | 1000 Lancaster St. | 410-332-7373 | www.charlestonrestaurant.com | Dinner Mon-Sat

RECOMMENDED

Prime Rib   91.1

You still have to wear a jacket and tie to dinner at this "throwback to the steakhouses of the '40s and '50s." Besides the "hefty cuts of prime rib," there are strips, rib eyes, filet mignons and an assortment of other steaks and chops, all of a quality that's considerably higher than the national steak chains. To be honest, we can't remember the last time we had to get dressed up to have dinner at a steakhouse, but then again, we can't remember the last time a restaurant listed broccoli florets on its menu, either. Things are more casual at lunch, when you can eat *sans cravate*, though "Wearing a jacket is still *de rigueur*."

Steakhouse | Formal | Expensive | mount vernon | 110 N. Calvert St. | 410-539-1804 | www.theprimerib.com | Dinner daily

Joss Cafe & Sushi Bar   90.3

We sat up and took notice when one of our reviewers said he thought that the Joss Cafe (sister to the Annapolis original) serves "the best sushi on the East Coast outside of NYC," a comment promptly followed by this from a chef who used to work in the area: "I would stop in after dinner service two or three times a week, it was that good." We are usually skeptical about these things, so we checked it out ourselves and we have to say we agree with them both. You can go classic and sit at the counter and ask for an omakase that will include cuts like escolar and rockfish, or get a bit more inventive with a hand roll of Kobe beef minced with garlic chips.

Japanese | Informal | Moderate | mount vernon | 195 Main St. | 410-263-4688 | Lunch & Dinner Mon-Sat, Sun dinner onl

Woodbury Kitchen   90.0

With a menu filled with dishes like Rappahannock oysters, Richfield Farms corn soup or Marvesta sizzling shrimp and Springfield Farm chicken 'n' biscuits and Liberty Farms beef stew on house-made egg noodles, it seems clear that no other chef is as committed to serving the ingredients of the Mid-Atlantic as Spike Gjerde. Set in a renovated mill building, his restaurant is "a pleasant surprise in the no-man's land of Baltimore dining." Another reviewer claims, "Gjerde's cooking would be better-known if he was cooking in a different city." We happen to agree with that sentiment, and as more people learn about the restaurant, we expect to see Gjerde rewarded with a higher rating.

New American | Casual | Moderate | hampden | 2010 Clipper Park Rd., No. 126 | 410-464-8000 | www. woodberrykitchen.com | Dinner daily, Brunch Sun

TOP LOCAL CHOICE

The Black Olive   89.5

In other cities, this type of Greek seafooder might be just another fish in the culinary sea; but in Baltimore it's one of the best places in town. Small, family-owned and set in a converted row house, it applies "Greek and Mediterranean flair" to the daily selection of "fresh fish" that includes Dover sole, dorade, rockfish and turbot, along with a selection of grilled meats like rack of lamb and filet steak. An "excellent wine list" and a "charming setting" add to its appeal. Only "a lack of innovation to the cooking" holds it back from a higher rating.

Greek | Informal | Expensive | brooklyn | 814 S. Bond St. | 410-276-7141 | www.theblackolive.com | Lunch & Dinner daily

Petit Louis Bistro   88.5

Every city needs a restaurant that is "always filled with regulars" enjoying "solidly prepared bistro food" in a "cozy and comfortable setting." Offering a menu that seems to include every Gallic classic dish imaginable (think croque monsieur at lunch, magret de canard roti at dinner), Cindy Wolf and Tony Foreman's contribution to the genre attracts comments like "close to perfect for what it's trying to be." Foreman is in charge of the restaurant's wine list, and you get to wash down your oysters and steak frites with "a nice selection of French wines by the glass."

French Bistro | Informal | Moderate | downtown | 4800 Roland Ave. | 410-366-9393 | www.petitlouis.com | Dinner Tue-Sun, Lunch Tue-Fri

Helmand   87.0

Off the top of our heads, we can't think of another Afghan restaurant with a national reputation other than this 20-year-old Mount Vernon veteran featuring "authentic cuisine," "attentive service" and "subdued elegance." Then again, we can't think of another Afghan restaurant owned by the brother of Afghan president Hamid Karzai either. There's an emphasis on vegetarian dishes like roast pumpkin with garlic sauce, but the specialty of the house is a marinated and lightly spiced rack of lamb that goes by the name of Chopan.

Afghan | Informal | Moderate | mount vernon | 806 N. Charles St. | 410-752-0311 | www.helmand. com | Dinner daily

Obrycki's   87.0

As the experience at this granddaddy of Baltimore crab houses comes complete with butcher paper, mallets, greasy hands and dirty faces, the only other thing you need is a cold pitcher of beer (or two). It used to have more of an allure for destination diners, but for some reason "They lost their touch a number of years ago," and now many of our reviewers say they would rather make the 40-minute drive to Annapolis to eat at Cantler's and they go here "only in a pinch."

Seafood | Informal | Moderate | brooklyn | 1727 E. Pratt St. | 410-732-6399 | www.obryckis.com | Lunch & Dinner Mar-Oct

Tio Pepe   86.5

A generation ago, this restaurant was important to American diners. It served a cuisine that presented itself as Spanish but that was actually Continental with Castilian overtones. As the years passed, rather than updating their cuisine, management held firm to this tradition. The kitchen still prepares out-of-date concoc-tions like filet of sole with bananas and hollandaise sauce. And while not without charm, the descriptions are geared to the inexperienced: Paella, for example, is called "a typical Spanish rice dish."

Continental | Casual | Expensive | mount vernon | 10 E. Franklin St. | 410-539-4675 | Dinner daily, Lunch Mon-Fri

Lebanese Taverna   85.0

It seems that Baltimore has one reasonable example of each kind of ethnic cuisine, and this Lebanese restaurant in the Inner Harbor has assumed that role for Middle Eastern food. This is its fifth location (the original opened in 1979 in Arlington, Virginia). The menu lists every mezze, kibbe and kabob imaginable, as well as a full range of grilled meats, fish and gently simmered stews. They also offer a good list of Lebanese wines.

Middle Eastern | Casual | Moderate | 2641 719 S. President St. | 410-244-5533 | www.lebanesetaverna.com | Lunch & Dinner daily

Cheap Eats

Attman's   6.5

One expects to see the extended family from the film *Avalon* throwing back a few tasty dogs with 'kraut and mustard at this Jewish deli, open since 1915 and located in East Baltimore's Corned Beef Row. Of course, when it comes to Jewish delis, the issue is whether they can measure up to a New York City standard; one of our reviewers was willing to certify that Attman's is "capable of playing in the same league as delis up north."

Delicatessen | Inexpensive | east baltimore | 1019 E. Lombard St. | 410-563-2666 | www.attmansdeli.com | Open daily

Atwater's   6.3

Peasant wheat, cranberry pecan, chili cheddar and a raisin pumpernickel that's made with cocoa powder, coffee and molasses and goes by the name of Flatulent Goblin are but four of the 17 breads made daily at this "wonderful place to have lunch and people-watch." There are soups like Moroccan vegetable with couscous and sultanas, "a really good chicken salad" and sandwiches like a vegetarian banh mi with grilled lemongrass tofu served on ciabatta bread.

Sandwiches | Inexpensive | belvedere square | 529 E. Belvedere Ave. | 410-323-2396 | www.atwaters.biz | Dinner daily Mon-Sat

Faidley Seafood 6.2

This crab cake specialist in Lexington Market is not as legendary as some of Baltimore's crab houses, but it moved a few of our reviewers to say they serve "arguably the best crab cakes on the planet." Side dishes include coleslaw, collard greens and house-made pickled beets. "Just order a big lump platter and life is good."

Seafood | Inexpensive | downtown | 203 N. Paca St. | 410-727-4898 | www.faidleyscrabcakes.com | Breakfast & Lunch Mon-Sat

Cape May NJ

TOP LOCAL CHOICE

Ebbitt Room 88.0

Seemingly situated at the end of the world, Cape May is New Jersey's answer to Key West, full of Victorian houses converted into hotels or bed-and-breakfasts. Within this 19th-century setting, the Virginia Hotel offers guests an experience that's more modern than most – as Lucas Manteca's menu offers dishes like short rib and shrimp basil ravioli or grilled Duroc pork with spicy polenta that reviewers deem "pricy but worth it." The Ebbitt Room also features "a nice setting" along with a "good wine list," causing reviewers to say "it's worth the two-hour trek to eat there on special occasions."

American | Casual | Expensive | Virginia Hotel | 25 Jackson St. | 609-884-5700 | www.virginiahotel.com | Dinner daily

Fredericksburg VA

HIGHLY RECOMMENDED

Volt 94.8

If you want to see what media exposure can do for a talented young chef, book a table at Bryan Voltaggio's bustling restaurant.Virtually unknown before he became a runner-up on *Top Chef* to his brother Michael, Voltaggio converted an old mansion into what is probably the most attractive restaurant in the entire region. The place offers three dining options. The main room features dishes like red wattle pork with brussels sprouts, Hernandez sweet potato and preparations of red cabbage that are served à la carte, while the chef's dining room features a tasting menu of the day. Then there is Table 21, eight counter seats that look into the kitchen, where diners enjoy a 21-course extravaganza that includes cutting-edge creations like Chicken Parmesan – Parmesan broth noodles topped with tomato and basil dipping dots and fried chicken. "The food finds that sweet spot between creative and tasty," say our reviewers, though there are some who bemoan the fact that the cuisine in both dining rooms, while hardly old-fashioned, is more traditional than at Table 21.

Progressive | Casual | Expensive | 228 N. Market St. | 301-696-8658 | www.voltrestaurant.com | Lunch & Dinner Wed-Sun

Philadelphia PA

Vetri   93.1

Some of the best cooking in Philadelphia can be found at Marc Vetri's intimate Center City town house. While the food is technically classified as rustic Italian, Vetri and executive chef Jeff Benjamin impose contemporary sensibilities on the cuisine, creating dishes like pastrami foie gras with fruit mustards, roasted sweetbreads with a carrot crema and cipollini onions, pigs' foot ravioli with fennel pollen and orange zest and slow-roasted baby goat with soft polenta. It's one of the few restaurants in the city to have a liquor license, and there's a full, if expensive, wine list. Diners looking to have the complete Vetri experience should note that the degustazione menu is available only on Friday and Saturday evenings and must be ordered in advance.

Italian | Casual | Expensive | washington square | 1312 Spruce St. | 215-732-3478 | www.vetriristorante.com | Dinner Mon-Sat

Morimoto   92.0

Before he became famous as an Iron Chef, Masaharu Morimoto was the number two in Nobu's kitchen, so we aren't the least bit surprised when people refer to his cuisine as "Nobu light." But he distinguishes himself from his mentor at the omakase bar, where the chefs (including Morimoto himself on some nights) dole out tasting menus that start at $250 per person and quickly spiral upward if items are supplemented with luxury ingredients like Kobe beef or truffles. If that sounds a bit steep, the dishes served in the main dining room, like eight-spice lobster and yosedofu, a tofu dish made tableside and served with various dipping sauces, should keep you happy. It's a fun dining environment, made even more festive by the décor, including an interior that slowly changes colors every few minutes – one of the more attractive installations we've seen.

Japanese | Casual | Expensive | washington square | 723 Chestnut St. | 215-413-9070 | www.morimoto-restaurant.com | Dinner daily, Lunch Mon-Fri

Amada   91.4

Jose Garces has done an excellent job of capturing the Spanish tapas experience at Amada. There are cured meats and sliced cheeses; classic tapas like garlic shrimp and ham croquetas; nine different vegetarian tapas like Hen-of-the-Woods mushrooms, asparagus with thyme and roast peppers with eggplant; and meats and fish, like lamb chops, chipirones and king salmon grilled à la plancha. Larger plates, intended for the entire table to share, include paella with lobster or suckling pig. There is a short list of Spanish wines, cavas and sherries, and the cocktails, like the Tie Me Up, Tie Me Down (a lemon rosemary martini) are all named after the films of director Pedro Almodóvar.

Spanish | Informal | Moderate | old city | 217 Chestnut St. | 215-625-2450 | www.amadarestaurant.com | Dinner daily, Lunch Mon-Sat

Le Bec-Fin   91.0

Georges Perrier is trying hard to rekindle interest in his Rittenhouse Square institution, "a phenomenon during the 1980s," by offering an à la carte menu as well as several prix fixe options, ranging from $80 to $185, and small-plates of bistro fare in the more casual Bar Lyonnais. Despite the noble attempt at a comeback, there's a broad consensus that the restaurant – once the best in Philadelphia – has seen better days. There is nothing on the menu that you haven't tasted before, and the elegant, old-world ambience, which includes a dining room dominated by three gigantic chandeliers and two servers per table, is a throwback to a bygone era of dining. Even so, some people still find the classic French cuisine and service "charming." "It's a dinosaur," said one of our reviewers, "but a friendly one." *Note: The restaurant was slated to close in spring 2011, but a public uproar convinced Perrier to remain open.*

French | Formal | Very Expensive | rittenhouse square | 1523 Walnut St. | 215-567-1000 | www.lebecfin.com | Lunch & Dinner Tue-Sat

Lacroix at the Rittenhouse   90.9

Though it bears his name, Jean-Marie Lacroix no longer runs this kitchen. Problem is, neither do the host of chefs who followed him. Jon Cichon is the latest to try to stabilize things, and his unfussy New American fare includes dishes like sweetbreads with coconut and truffle or a veal chop with Belga lentils, baby carrots and pomegranate. There a "terrific wine list" with more than 500 different bottles, but the restaurant's cause isn't helped by prices called "insulting." Oenophiles prefer it on Mondays, when they can enjoy the eight-course tasting menu with a bottle from their own cellars.

New American | Formal | Expensive | rittenhouse square | 210 W. Rittenhouse Square | 215-790-2533 | www.lacroixrestaurant.com | Open daily

Fountain Restaurant   90.0

From our perspective, this restaurant wouldn't exist if it weren't subsidized by a hotel chain. Having said that, some of our reviewers have warm feelings for this spot in the Four Seasons, where the French/Continental cuisine includes dishes like savory winter squash soup with duck confit and cranberry bread pudding or grilled center-cut beef fillet with wild mushrooms and melted leek ragout. The environment is appropriately "hushed," and the service is exactly what one expects in this setting. As for comments, the one that seems to describe it best said, "It's great, but still a Four Seasons."

Continental | Formal | Expensive | logan square | Four Seasons Hotel | 1 Logan Sq. | 215-963-1500 | www.fourseasons.com/philadelphia/dining/fountain_restaurant/ | Dinner daily, Lunch Mon-Sat

TOP LOCAL CHOICE

Bibou   89.5

With Le Bec-Fin in decline, Bibou – run by one of Le Bec-Fin's former executive chefs – has become the French restaurant in Philadelphia that many of our reviewers prefer. That could be because Pierre Calmels' postage-stamp-size dining room has more to do with a bistro than a grand dining experience, and fare like a ragout of snails and fava beans with chanterelles and tarragon or mains like a braised pig's foot stuffed with foie gras and French lentils fit the environment perfectly. Comments range from the glowing ("Food execution was superb") to the non-complaint complaint like "I wish they offered more than five entrées."

French | Informal | Moderate | bella vista | 1009 S. 8th St. | 215-965-8290 | www.biboubyob.com | Dinner Wed-Sun

Chifa   89.5

After his success at Amada, Jose Garces decided to inject an Asian influence into
Peruvian cuisine. The result: dishes like a seafood platter in an aji Amarillo sauce or salt-
baked shrimp that you can dip into srirachi mayo. There are also various Peruvian- and
Nikkei-style ceviches, as well as steamed buns filled with hoisin-glazed pork belly and
empanadas filled with crab meat. Surprisingly, it all works, with one reviewer saying
"Garces' other restaurants might have more pizzazz, but this one offers flavors that are
not easily duplicated."

Peruvian | Informal | Moderate | society hill | 707 Chestnut St. | 215-925-5555 | www.chifa-restaurant.
com | Dinner daily, Lunch Mon-Fri

Friday Saturday Sunday   89.5

When a restaurant described as "a neighborhood standby for over 37 years" enters
the Top Local Choice category, we can't help but take notice. Part of the attraction is
the "solid comfort food," like the house special, a cream of mushroom soup laced with
cognac, or a herb-grilled, double-thick pork chop with a roasted garlic-Roquefort sauce
and whipped potatoes. Another selling point is a wine list featuring bottles at $10 above
the restaurant's cost. "It's not the most adventurous cooking," but being "reliable and
consistent" and "tiny and romantic" obviously counts for more with our reviewers.

New American | Casual | Moderate | rittenhouse square | 261 S. 21st St. | 215-546-4232 | www.frisatsun.
com | Dinner Daily

Tria   89.5

This popular wine bar celebrates three different results of fermentation: wine, beer and
cheese. Our reviewers called it "the best unique wine and beer selection ever," served
by a "staff that is incredibly knowledgeable." Between sips, you can enjoy cheese in
various guises, including a bruschetta of pistachio herbed ricotta with lavender honey, a
smoked chicken and Lancaster bacon salad with Black River blue cheese, or a smoked
salmon and herbed goat cheese sandwich on a grilled brioche. Complaints were generally reserved for "a menu on which the food offerings rarely change."

Wine Bar | Informal | Moderate | rittenhouse square | 123 S. 18th St. | 215-972-8742 | www.triacafe.com
| Lunch & Dinner daily

Zahav   89.5

The son of Israelis, Michael Solomonov (formerly of Marigold Kitchen) has gone back
to his roots with this restaurant that pays homage to Israel's culinary heritage. The
mezze include house-smoked sable with challah, fried egg and garlic, shipudim (skewers cooked over charcoal) of short ribs with celery root, dates and apples, and a slow-
cooked lamb shoulder that one reviewer described as "the Jewish version of the Ssam
Bar pork butt." The opportunity to eat "lots of wonderful courses for a very reasonable
amount of money" has reviewers wondering, "Who could ask for more?"

Israeli | Informal | Moderate | society hill | 237 Saint James Pl. | 215-625-8800 | www.zahavrestaurant.
com | Dinner daily

Barclay Prime   89.0

This Rittenhouse Square steakhouse from restaurateur Stephen Starr allows diners to choose the weapon of their choice (that is, a steak knife from an assortment presented at your table) along with the beef it'll cut, including a host of Kobe steaks like the Tajima Kobe, described as "the best steak around." There are "fresh" East Coast oysters, a "solid beef tartare" and "revelatory Kobe sliders." The usual steakhouse sides are on hand, and the setting is a "bit more upscale" than your usual big city cow palace.

Steakhouse | Casual | Expensive | rittenhouse square | 237 S. 18th St. | 215-732-7560 | www.barclay-prime.com | Dinner daily

Bistro 7   89.0

Described as "more elegant than your standard BYOB," Michael O'Halloran's New American restaurant has a menu that reads like a list of what was available at the farmer's market that morning. Starters include a salad of pickled red and yellow beets and Lancaster County strawberries with fresh goat's cheese, while your main might be fried squash blossoms stuffed with lump crab, served atop a rock shrimp risotto studded with sweet peas, summer squash, fresh-cut corn and basil. Some criticize O'Halloran's cuisine for being "a little too fussy," but those comments are offset by the ones that mention "fair pricing."

New American | Casual | Moderate | old city | 7 N. 3rd St. | 215-931-1560 | www.bistro7restaurant.com | Dinner Tue-Sun

Marigold Kitchen   89.0

One of the most popular BYOBs in the city when Steve Cook and Michael Solomonov were the owners, Marigold Kitchen is still blooming (unlike many other restaurants that floundered when the founders departed). Having worked at a slew of top progressive restaurants, including Alinea, Hugo's and Binkley's, chef Robert Halperin seems to have things under control. His New American menu features dishes like Maine day-boat cod with a sourdough-egg crust, fingerling potatoes, bacon-braised Napa cabbage and a ham nage. No wonder a number of reviewers claim this "inventive and fun" place is their favorite in Philadelphia.

New American | Informal | Moderate | university city | 501 S. 45th St. | 215-222-3699 | www.marigold-kitchenbyob.com | Dinner Wed-Sun, Lunch Sun

10 Arts   88.0

Eric Ripert's offering in the Ritz-Carlton manages to overcome the odds of a celebrity chef operating a successful restaurant in a remote location. In part it succeeds because the menu (executed by chef Jennifer Carroll) "doesn't take many chances" but is still daring enough to offer dishes like Loch Duart salmon poached in duck fat with artichokes and a citrus emulsion. A few reviewers complained about "an unusual space that is merely part of the lobby cordoned off into a restaurant," but most were happy with the "three solid meals a day" prepared by a *Top Chef* finalist.

New American | Casual | Expensive | center city | Ritz-Carlton | 10 Avenue of the Arts (S. Broad St.) | 215-523-8273 | www.10arts.com | Dinner Tue-Sat, Lunch Mon-Fri

Osteria   88.0

What would you do if you owned the most successful Italian restaurant in Philadelphia (Vetri, see above) and wanted to cash in on your accomplishment? You would open a place where you can offer an inexpensive version of your cuisine. Hey, that sounds just like what Mario Batali did when he opened Otto a few blocks away from Babbo in Manhattan, and maybe that's why numerous reviewers called Marc Vetri's restaurant "the Philly version of Otto." The large space is full of people sitting at tables covered with various antipasti, pizza, pasta and wines served by the quartino.

Italian | Informal | Moderate | fairmont | 640 N. Broad St. | 215-763-0920 | www.osteriaphilly.com | Dinner daily, Lunch Thur-Fri

ACCEPTABLE

Distrito   87.5

Opinions are somewhat split over Jose Garces' foray into Mexican fare, with those on the pro side saying, "It's not your usual taco stand," while the cons say, "It's a fun place, but I thought it was just too expensive for Mexican food." The size of the restaurant might have something to do with it: 250 people can enjoy a chicken ropa vieja or a quesadilla of skirt steak, washing the food down with a cerveza or a variety of different takes on the margarita.

Mexican | Informal | Moderate | university city | 3945 Chestnut St. | 215-222-1657 | www.distrito-restaurant.com | Lunch & Dinner daily

Jake's   87.5

One of the few restaurants in central Philly that is not a BYOB (though they do offer corkage on Sunday and Monday evenings), Jake's has been in business for more than 20 years. The American fusion cuisine features dishes like duck spring rolls with orange, blackberry and mustard sauces and porcini-crusted lamb sirloin with an English pea and pearl onion risotto. Opinions split sharply, ranging from "overrated" to "an old soldier still doing a very good job."

American | Casual | Moderate | roxborough | 4365 Main St. | 215-483-0444 | www.jakesrestaurant.com | Dinner daily

Southwark   87.0

While the experience is mostly about the "knowledgeable bartenders" dispensing "a great selection of spirits," Sheri Waide's "food should not be overlooked." Waide utilizes ingredients from the region's best suppliers in a house-made sausage with seasonal accompaniments or a braised pork shank served with roasted vegetables and a white wine mustard broth. The restaurant is "cramped and crowded," and it's "difficult to get a seat," especially during what reviewers say is "one of the best happy hours in the city."

New American | Informal | Moderate | south philly | 701 S. 4th St. | 215-238-1888 | www.southwarkrestaurant.com | Dinner Tue-Sun

Fork   86.5

Fourteen years is a long run for a Philadelphia bistro. Terence Feury's résumé lists Le Bernardin and the late Striped Bass, which means that dishes like pan-seared Pocono trout with local white sweet potato frites, pickled cauliflower, Serrano chiles and a lime-curry rémoulade are prepared with an experienced hand. Reviewers say, "It was always good, and with chef Feury now in the kitchen, the flavors are even more pronounced, assertive and bold."

New American | Casual | Moderate | old city | 306 Market St. | 215-625-9425 | www.forkrestaurant.com | Dinner daily, Lunch Mon-Fri

Matyson   86.0

Included in the comments we collected about this Rittenhouse Square restaurant were "very good BYOB," "one of the best BYOBs in Center City" and "probably the best BYOB in the city." But while the chefs have recently changed, reports say that the New American fare – like ahi tuna tartar with avocado, cucumber, melon and coconut-poblano pepper emulsion or grilled chile-rubbed pork chop with crispy chipotle grits, queso fresco and bacon-red onion marmalade – hasn't altered a bit.

New American | Casual | Moderate | rittenhouse square | 37 S. 19th St. | 215-564-2925 | www.matyson.com | Dinner Mon-Sat, Lunch Mon-Fri

Buddakan   85.0

As with many other Asian Fusion restaurants, Buddakan is more about the party than the food – with one difference: The food here is much better than everyone expects it to be, so much so that a few reviewers actually mentioned individual dishes like "delicious edamame dumplings or frogs' legs." As long as you remember it's essentially a cruising bar and focus on the "amazing atmosphere that will definitely put you in a good mood," you'll be fine.

Asian Fusion | Casual | Moderate | old city | 325 Chestnut St. | 215-574-9440 | www.buddakan.com | Dinner daily, Lunch Mon-Fri

City Tavern   85.0

"Dining in the Revolutionary War era was kind of fun" says one reviewer about his experience at this restaurant where waiters dressed in 18th-century period garb serve traditional American fare. "Good pepper pot soup" is the best comment we could dig up about the food. Still, the "cozy, rustic setting" is nice "for lunch on a winter's day," and of course, "the show" is ideal for "for taking out-of-town guests" craving colonial culture.

American | Casual | Moderate | old city | 138 South 2nd St. | 215-413-1443 | www.citytavern.com | Lunch & Dinner daily

Lee How Fook   85.0

The most popular restaurant in Philly's small Chinatown gets mixed reactions from our reviewers. Fans talk about "fabulous authentic food and staff that remembers you from month to month," while those who are less enamored say "There must be someplace better to eat in Chinatown." It's a good choice for the budget conscious; aside from the Peking duck, which is priced at $27 and serves two people, the most expensive dish on the menu costs $13.95.

Chinese | Informal | Inexpensive | downtown | 219 N. 11th St. | 215-925-7266 | www.leehowfook.com | Lunch & Dinner Tue-Sun

OTHER RESTAURANTS MENTIONED

Tinto   84.5

Given his success at Armada, one would think that Jose Garces would have an easier time impressing our reviewers at this wine bar/restaurant that takes its inspiration from the pinotxo restaurants in the Basque region of Spain. The "smallish menu" ranges from bocadillos to brochettes cooked over charcoal, and if you're really hungry you can knock down a New York strip steak. Reviewers say, "Great take on Basque tapas, but the place has a corporate feel."

Spanish | Informal | Moderate | rittenhouse square | 114 S. 20th St. | 215-665-9150 | www.tintorestaurant.com | Lunch & Dinner daily

Continental   84.0

With a vibe straight out of '60s Las Vegas, this restaurant launched Stephen Starr's empire. The comments about the quirky food, like teriyaki filet mignon and lobster mashed potatoes, are to be expected: "Everything is good, nothing is great" and "a place for having something to eat with your drinks." As for the ambience, "cool Rat Pack vibe" and "perhaps the loudest restaurant in the country" pretty much sum it up.

Eclectic | Informal | Moderate | old city | 138 Market St. | 215-923-6069 | www.continentalmartinibar.com | Lunch & Dinner daily

La Famiglia 83.0

At the other end of the spectrum from Philly's BYOB dining scene is this grand Italian venue, where they have been dousing thick veal chops in rich white wine sauces since 1976. The "voluminous wine list" includes many vintages bottled before the restaurant opened its doors. Comments about "good service" and "a pleasant dining experience" were fairly consistent. On the negative side, however, most people agree that both food and wine are overpriced.

Italian | Casual | Moderate | old city | 8 S. Front St. | 215-922-2803 | www.lafamiglia.com | Dinner Mon-Sat, Lunch Tue-Fri

Cuba Libre 82.0

Pre-Castro Havana lives on at this restaurant, where dishes like ceviche, camarones, enchiladas and vacas frita share the spotlight with mojitos, piscos and other specialty cocktails. A lively bar scene adds to the festivities, and the concept is so popular they have opened additional branches around the U.S. The food isn't bad, but one reviewer warned diehard foodies that the place is "more about the salsa playing on the stereo system than the salsa on your plate."

Pan-Latin | Casual | Moderate | old city | 10 S. 2nd St. | 215-627-0666 | www.cubalibrerestaurant.com | Lunch & Dinner daily

Alma de Cuba 82.0

At this spot, one of the first of Stephen Starr's concept restaurants, the major attractions are the "faux Havana ambience" and a "good bar scene." The menu hasn't changed a bit over the ten years it has been open, resulting in "Pan-Latin food that can be somewhat out of date," the critical claim. But others say that doesn't matter since the "Major focus is on the scene, not the food."

Pan-Latin | Casual | Moderate | rittenhouse square | 1623 Walnut St. | 215-988-1799 | www.almadecubarestaurant.com | Dinner daily

Sang Kee Peking Duck House 81.0

They say there are two things worth consuming at this Chinatown stalwart celebrating its 30th birthday this year: won ton noodle soup and Peking duck. Yes, we know the rating is on the low side, but "Forget the other fare – mediocre Peking duck is still worth eating."

Chinese | | Informal | Moderate | downtown | 238 N. Ninth St. | 215-925-7532 | www.phillychinatown.com/sangkee.htm | Lunch & Dinner daily

Jack's Firehouse 75.0

Though Jack McDavid (a true character) has sold the restaurant, he still acts as a consultant to this place, which offers contemporary Southern fare – think cornflake-crusted shrimp with hot and sour pepper sauce – served in an old, converted firehouse. Ultimately, most reviewers think the food "lacks consistency," making it "just not good enough," considering the other options in Philly.

Southern | Informal | Moderate | fairmont | 2130 Fairmount Ave. | 215-232-9000 | www.jacksfirehouse.com | Lunch & Dinner daily

Cheap Eats

UNIQUELY DELICIOUS

John's Roast Pork 8.1

Philadelphia is serious about its sandwiches, and the sandwich the city's residents are most serious about is found at this funny little building in a part of South Philly known as Pennsport. After waiting on a long line, you get to watch the counterman make your sandwich. First he splits an Italian loaf down the middle, then he scoops slices of pork that have been soaking in an Italian-style gravy onto the bread, and he finishes the sandwich with slices of sharp provolone cheese and a few forks of rapini. You grab a seat on one of the benches outside of the restaurant and enjoy "the best sandwich in the city, cheese steaks included" while the semis and dump trucks roll by. Some reviewers also swear by their cheese steaks, but it's not called John's Cheese Steaks, now, is it?

Sandwiches | Informal | pennsport | 14 E. Snyder Ave. | 215-463-1951 | www.johnsroastpork.com | Open Mon-Fri

Tony Luke's Old Philly Style Sandwiches   7.7

Not as well known as Pat's or Geno's, this is the "cheese steak of choice" for many of our reviewers when they find themselves in South Philly. The menu, a bit more diverse than other famous joints', includes a roast pork sandwich with sharp provolone and Italian greens that someone described as "the bomb," along with the vegetarian-friendly egg, pepper and potato hoagie. The lines can be monumental, especially when the Phillies are in town, and veterans advise that the best way to beat the lines is to "call ahead and place your order."

Sandwiches | Inexpensive | south philly | 39 E. Oregon Ave. | 215-551-5725 | www.tonylukes.com | Open Mon-Sat

Pho 75   7.6

"It's the place to go for Pho" claim the reviewers who frequent this Philly link in a mini-chain that serves 17 variations on the dish. The décor is as bare bones as it gets. But one thing is sure: You are bound to find "a busy dining room" where a number of people are having "a cathartic experience" with a bowl of soup.

Vietnamese | Inexpensive | south philly | 1122 Washington Ave. | 215-271-5866 | Open daily

Taqueria La Veracruzana   7.5

At this, "the best of the South Philly taquerias," you can enjoy carnitas made with "good-quality meat" and al pastor made "in the authentic style." Get there

early and you can breakfast on scrambled eggs with green sauce and cheese; go in the evening and you can enjoy shrimp sautéed with tequila, jalapeños, pepper and garlic.

Sandwiches | Inexpensive | bella vista | 908 Washington Ave. | 215-465-1440 | Open daily

Pat's King of Steaks   7.3

Expect to encounter a long line at this triangular fast-food stand in South Philly where Pat Olivieri is credited with inventing the cheese steak sandwich back in 1930 and where, to their credit, "they still turn out a decent sandwich." The controversy at Pat's has always been their policy of limiting the cheese toppings to Cheese Whiz. But that hasn't reduced the length of the lines. Being open 24 hours a day clearly adds to the allure.

Sandwiches | Inexpensive | south philly | 1237 E. Passyunk Ave. | 215-468-1546 | www.patskingof-steaks.com | Open daily

Geno's Steaks   6.5

Because of the unusual angles of the streets, the buildings that occupy the corners of 9th and Passyunk are triangular in shape. One corner is taken up by Pat's, another by Geno's, and there's a never-ending debate about who makes the better cheese steak. Those who give the edge to Geno's often do so because they prefer their sandwich with provolone rather than Cheese Whiz. You can fill up on greasy fare at 4:00 a.m. if you're awake and hungry at that time of night.

Sandwiches | Inexpensive | south philly | 1219 S. 9th St. | 215-389-0659 | www.genosteaks.com | Open daily

Honey's Sit 'n' Eat   6.0

One would think that a restaurant that combines "Jewish with southern hipster" fare would be located in a place like Atlanta or Charleston. But here it is right in Philly, and the odd combination means you can get your eggs with a side order of potato latkes and grits. Reviews are mixed: Some reviewers recommend dishes like chicken-fried steak and Maui tacos, while others say "The combination's sum is less good than its parts."

Coffee Shop | Inexpensive | northern liberties | 800 N. 4th St. | 215-925-1150 | www.honeys-restaurant.com | Open daily except Sun dinner

Jim's Steaks   5.9

The low rating for this infamous South Street eatery likely has something to do with the large pile of steak on the griddle that you see when you walk into the restaurant: It has been sitting around for too long, and the meat is overcooked. If you aren't in the mood for leathery beef, they serve a variety of hoagies that run the gamut from ham and cheese to tuna.

Sandwiches | Inexpensive | south st. district | 400 South St. | 215-928-1911 | www.jimssteaks.com | Lunch & Dinner daily

Famous Fourth   5.7
Street Delicatessen

They have been slicing and stuffing corned beef and pastrami into sandwiches since 1923 at this narrow corner restaurant. Also available: a complete menu of Jewish fare, ranging from stuffed cabbage to chicken in the pot. The food comes with a side of "some of the best people-watching in the city," especially at Sunday brunch, when the dining room is full of local celebs and families busily fressing on bagels and lox. One reviewer told us he had so much fun that it was "worth the heartburn I got afterward."

Delicatessen | Inexpensive | south st. district | 700 S. 4th St. | 215-922-3274 | http://famous4th-streetdelicatessen.com | Open daily

Dalessandro's   5.3

What used to be one of Philly's best cheese steaks has "gone way downhill since the family that owned it sold the place." Now we get complaints about "quality that is inconsistent," including sandwiches made with "overcooked, dried-out meat." It's a bit of schlep to get there, and midtowners mutter there seem to be "much better and closer options."

Sandwiches | Inexpensive | south roxborough | 600 Wendover St. | 215-482-5407 | dalessandros.com | Lunch & Dinner daily

Philadelphia Suburbs PA

HIGHLY RECOMMENDED

Talula's Table   92.9

This restaurant located in a popular gourmet store only has one table – for 8 to 12 people – and it books up a year in advance. You read that correctly. Every morning at 7:00 a.m., they take reservations for exactly one year from that date. What's the fuss about? Well, this is where the owners of the popular Django decamped to, and each night one lucky table of diners gets to enjoy "the best food in the Philly region." The menus are based on the bounty of the day's market, like a sweet corn tart or Amish pasture chicken with chicken chorizo mole and toasted almonds. Everyone praises the food, but the difficulty in getting a reservation creeps into every comment, from "Hands-down the best meal in the city . . . there's a reason people wait a year for reservation" to "they do an excellent job, but is it worth waiting a year for a reservation? Hell no."

New American | Informal | Expensive | kennett square | 102 West State St. | 610-444-8255 | www.talulastable.com | Open daily

RECOMMENDED

Birchrunville Store Cafe   91.4

One of the best restaurants in the Philadelphia area happens to be located 35 miles from Center City. On its face, the food doesn't look much different from what you can order elsewhere, but the standards of the cooking are so high that dishes like a goat cheese soufflé with a mache salad and sun-dried tomato vinaigrette or a veal chop porterhouse with chanterelles, cognac and mustard taste quite a few steps up in quality. Surprisingly, it's not very well known, but close to 50% of the reviewers who navigated the back roads of Chester County to eat here used the word "outstanding."

French | Casual | Expensive | birchrunville | 1403 Hollow Rd. | 610-827-9002 | www.birchrunvillestore-cafe.com | Dinner Wed-Sat

TOP LOCAL CHOICE

Blackfish   89.5

It's "small and cramped" and "noisy at times," but if more people tried eating at Chip Roman's Conshocken place, they would know about the "excellent food at reasonable prices." The seafood-heavy menu includes blue crab salad with pickled cantaloupe and rose geranium or line-caught tuna with corn and soybean succotash. Reviewers describe it as "the 'burbs' best BYOB and, arguably, the best in the entire Delaware Valley," telling those with wine cellars, "Time to break out your best bottles, friends."

Seafood | Casual | Moderate | conshocken | 119 Fayette St. | 610-397-0888 | www.blackfishrestaurant.com | Lunch & Dinner Tue-Fri, Sat-Sun dinner only

Restaurant Alba   89.0

Sean Weinberg's entry into the sweepstakes for the best BYOB in the Northeast suburbs is not the most popular with our reviewers. The cuisine is on the Italian side of New American, and the best-selling dishes, like octopus with lemon-oregano vinaigrette and hanger steak served with a Tuscan tomato-bread salad, come out of the restaurant's wood-burning grill. "Sort of Italian, sort of locovore food – execution can be a bit sloppy, but when the ingredients are good, the food can rise above the cooking."

New American | Casual | Moderate | malvern | 7 W. King St. | 610-644-4009 | www.restaurantalba.com | Dinner Tue-Sat, Thu-Fri lunch

ACCEPTABLE

Nectar   87.5

There were no shortage of complaints about Patrick Feury's restaurant being "the most expensive dining in the 'burbs." Feury mixes French and Asian concepts to create dishes like a duo of braised short ribs and petit filet mignon served with Yukon Gold potatoes and Thai chili hollandaise. Though it's lauded as "one of the better Asian Fusion restaurants around" by some, others feel that "You're better off going downtown unless you're on an expense account."

Asian | Casual | Expensive | west chester | 1091 Lancaster Ave. | 610-725-9000 | www.tastenectar.com | Dinner daily, Lunch Sun-Fri

333 Belrose   87.0

Given the general state of suburban dining, residents of Delaware County are fortunate to have Carlo deMarco's restaurant as one of their local choices. The eclectic menu features dishes like spinach and aged Gouda tortelloni or pan-blackened rainbow trout with smoked bacon cheese grits. Reviewers praise "seasonally changing menus" and "food that's always fresh and well presented." There's "quite a bar scene catering to the divorced crowd" as well.

New American | Casual | Expensive | radnor | 333 Belrose Ln. | 610-293-1000 | http://333belrose.com | Dinner daily, Lunch Mon-Fri

Dilworthtown Inn   87.0

Some habits die hard – in this instance, the propensity for restaurants located in pre-Revolutionary War buildings to serve Continental cuisine. It makes one wonder if this is the kind of place where George and Martha snuck off for a quick veal Oscar during their winter in Valley Forge. While some modern fare has been added to the menu, it hasn't made a dent in the general opinion that "Eating here is more about the ambience than the food. "

Continental | Casual | Expensive | west chester | 1390 Old Wilmington Pike | 610-399-1390 | www.dilworthtown.com | Dinner daily

Gilmore's   86.0

Gilmore's is a rare example of a suburban restaurant that approaches the heights of the top BYOBs in downtown Philadelphia. The reason? Peter Gilmore spent 22 years as the chef de cuisine at Le Bec-Fin before moving to West Chester. Gilmore's French menu includes starters like a spring risotto with morels and porcini, and mains like mahi mahi dusted with porcini powder and Poulet Wellington, in puff pastry with mushroom duxelle and sauce Perigourdine.

French | Casual | Moderate | west chester | 133 E. Gay St. | 610-431-2800 | www.gilmoresrestaurant.com | Dinner Tue-Sun

Yangming   85.5

What are the odds of finding an upscale, well-regarded Chinese restaurant in a swanky suburb? Not very good, and Michael Wei's restaurant is no exception. Comments like "mediocre food in a nice setting," "overpriced Chinese; the food is acceptable but you can do as well or better in Chinatown in the city" and "filled with local college students and their parents" sum up the experience.

Chinese | Casual | Moderate | bryn mawr | 1051 Conestoga Rd. | 610-527-3200 | www.yangmingrestaurant.com | Dinner daily, Lunch Mon-Sat

OTHER PLACES MENTIONED

Sola   84.0

Unlike northern Montgomery County, which is overrun with quality BYOB restaurants, the Bryn Mawr area suffers from a drought dining-wise. Sola, one of the best of the bunch along the Main Line, offers fare like Jersey corn soup with Maine lobster salad and pork tenderloin stuffed with caramelized onions. There is better-than-usual stemware, a $2 corkage policy and an "excellent value prix fixe menu on weekdays."

New American | Casual | Moderate | bryn mawr | 614 W. Lancaster Ave. | 610-526-0123 | www.solabyob.com | Dinner Tue-Sun

Savona   83.0

"Ouch" is what one reviewer said about Andrew Masciangelo's restaurant, where you can plop down $40 for a porcini-dusted rack of lamb. Not even a "great wine program run by Philly's first master sommelier, Melissa Monosoff" can save the place from a thrashing. Bar Savona, newly remodeled and retooled, offers "a more affordable option."

Italian | Casual | Expensive | gulph mills | 100 Old Gulph Rd. | 610-520-1200 | www.savonarestaurant.com | Dinner daily

Margaret Kuo   82.0

We have to admit that the rationale for Chinese décor downstairs and Japanese upstairs is a bit unclear to us. But while they do their best to prevent the cultures from cross-pollinating, they haven't imposed territorial restrictions on the actual food, allowing for a true pan-Asian experience in which your Peking duck

dinner can be preceded by a platter of sushi and sashimi.

Chinese | Casual | Moderate | wayne | 175 E. Lancaster Ave. | 610-688-7200 | www.margaret-kuos.com | Lunch & Dinner daily

Washington Metropolitan Area DC

WORTH PLANNING A TRIP AROUND

Minibar   98.2

If you are looking to have the El Bulli experience without the cost of a plane ticket to Spain, reserve one of the six counter seats at José Andrés' Penn Quarter restaurant. Each weekday evening, Andres offers two seatings in which diners are dazzled with a menu right out of the Ferran Adria playbook. Aside from the interesting and tasty food, the close proximity to the kitchen allows you to watch the chefs prepare your meal right in front of your eyes with a sleight of hand usually reserved for Las Vegas magicians. It's the ultimate in dining as theater, and as one of our reviewers said, "All dining should be this much fun!"

The 26-dish menu features linguine made with feta cheese water and gelatin, sweet pea "caviar," conch fritters with a a liquid center and foie gras that appears as cotton candy as well as in a warm foie gras soup with cold foie gras foam. Champagne goes well with this type of meal, and one of the benefits of sharing space with Café Atlantico (see below) is that the wine list has a good selection of small-grower Champagnes. Dinner is "one of the most unusual dining experiences in the country" and "certain to challenge any preconceived notions about presentation, taste, or texture."

Progressive | Casual | Very Expensive | penn qtr | 405 8th St. NW | 202-393-0812 | http://cafeatlantico.com/minibar | Dinner Tue-Sat

AN IMPORTANT DESTINATION

Komi   95.6

Before Komi, in terms of complexity and the application of sophisticated technique, Greek fare hadn't seen the type of advancement that has taken place in other European cuisines. True, people tried to modernize it and often your swordfish would be more expertly grilled – but it was still grilled, which is basically the same way it would be cooked in a tavern. But then Johnny Monis came along and, by employing some culinary methods used by the top progressive and molecular chefs, succeeded where others failed, creating a version of Greek cuisine that is distinctly modern while maintaining its Hellenic soul.

Savvy diners know the best way to experience Monis' cooking is to order the 12-course menu degustazione, which bombards them with a series of mezze, then an assortment of raw-fish dishes, salads that have been deconstructed and reassembled – like Monis' "Caesar," with a single crouton encased around a liquid center that tastes of the salad – succulent pastas featuring luxury ingredients like mushrooms, sea urchin and foie gras and a grand finale of fork-tender, roast baby goat that comes with five dipping sauces. Reviewers describe it as "a post-modern trendsetter that has only gotten better, more sophisticated and more wise with age, without losing any of the edge that has long made it special."

Greek | Casual | Expensive | dupont circle | 1509 17th St. NW | 202-332-9200 | Dinner Tue-Sat

Sushi Taro   95.1

A second-generation Japanese-American, Nobu Yamazaki grew up in the Washington D.C. area, the heir to a popular sushi restaurant in Dupont Circle. But Nobu wanted to be an omakase chef, so he went back to Japan to learn how to slice fish at the highest level. His return to the States was celebrated with a complete renovation of his family's restaurant, which now includes a special omakase room featuring a six-person sushi counter lorded over nightly by Nobu himself.

Each night he offers diners what is truly the best of the daily market, with delicacies running from unusual vegetables and mushrooms to various cuts of high-quality fish to a shabu shabu of octopus so fresh that it is still moving (we're not kidding) before it's submerged in the steaming broth. As a result, Sushi Taro has "gone from average to excellent," says one reviewer, while another places it "at the level of sushi restaurants in New York City or Los Angeles." Unfortunately, the uptick in quality means that prices have also gone up, causing one longtime customer to grouse, "I understand the food is exceptional, but now I can't afford it."

Japanese | Informal | Expensive | dupont circle | 1503 17th St. NW | 202-462-8999 | www.sushitaro.com | Lunch & Dinner Mon-Fri, Sat dinner only

HIGHLY RECOMMENDED

Citronelle   94.1

Michel Richard's restaurant in the Latham Hotel has been one of the top formal dining experiences in the capital for more than a decade. Richard is a former second to maître pâtissier Gaston Lenôtre, and you can see his background in the intricately crafted, whimsical takes on classics like Caesar salad and tuna Niçoise, and dessert served as if it were breakfast. And it would be a shame to visit the restaurant without sampling his signature dish: Lobster Begula, pearl-shaped pasta soaked in squid ink – giving it the appearance of fish eggs – served in a caviar tin over chunks of lobster claw. Those who prefer straight-ahead cooking can opt for dishes like abalone from Monterey with caviar cream or chateaubriand with pearl vegetables, a Yukon Gold gratin and a syrah sauce. The wine list, especially deep in Champagnes, is one of the best in the city.

French | Formal | Expensive | georgetown | Latham Hotel | 3000 M St. NW | 202-625-2150 | www.citro-nelledc.com | Dinner Tue-Sun

RECOMMENDED

CityZen   91.5

Back in 2008, when we published the results of our first survey, Eric Ziebold's res-taurant barely fell into the Top Local Choice category. Given his background as a former second to Thomas Keller at the French Laundry, that didn't really make sense; at worst the combination of his talent and training should have yielded a rating of Recommended. There has been a distinct uptick in positive reviews since then, and the restaurant has now finally earned that rating, with comments like "food that is creative and full of flavor – Eric Ziebold is probably the best chef in D.C. now." Ziebold's mentor's influence is evident in dishes like butter-poached lobster with poached currants and toasted pine nuts, while Ziebold's own personality shines in a mille-feuille of prime Midwestern beef with bone marrow bread pudding.

New American | Formal | Expensive | marina | Mandarin Oriental | 1330 Maryland Ave. SW | 202-787-6006 | http://www.mandarinoriental.com/washington/dining/cityzen/ | Dinner Tue-Sun

Rasika   90.9

Whether D.C. residents or out-of-towners, our reviewers agree about this Indian restaurant in the heart of Penn Quarter. Though Vikram Sunderam is a veteran of London's Bombay Brasserie, he left their classic Moghul style cuisine on the banks of the Thames and brought a more modern approach to this nation's capital. You start with "an out-of-this-world" Palaak chat and continue with delicacies like Coogi sweetbreads with balsamic vinegar and spiced quinoa or Sunderam's take on Japanese-style miso-marinated black cod, prepared with fresh dill, honey, star anise and red wine vinegar. There's a "cool wine list with lots of interesting choices." One reviewer ended his comments by saying, "I am going back soon, and you should go, too!"

Indian | Casual | Expensive | penn qtr | 633 D St. NW | 202-637-1222 | www.rasikarestaurant.com | Dinner Mon-Sat, Lunch Mon-Fri

Palena   90.8

When it comes to bistro-style dining, Frank Ruta runs what many consider the best restaurant in the capital. The charcuterie, made in-house, plays a big part in the menu, both in starters like Cotechino sausage with raviolini of kabocha squash and shaved goat cheese and mains like a Columbia River sturgeon wrapped in house-made pancetta served with choucroute and a mustard emulsion. The roast chicken is legendary, and one person claimed "It's worth the trip to D.C. just to eat Ruta's bar fries." Oh, and did we mention that the Ruta grinds his own meat and bakes his own buns for "the best burger in the city?"

New American | Casual | Expensive | cleveland park | 3529 Connecticut Ave. NW | 202-537-9250 | www.palenarestaurant.com | Lunch & Dinner Tue-Sun

Eve (7.5 miles south in Alexandria)   90.7

Most D.C. area residents will tell you that Cathal and Meshelle Armstrong's Alexandria restaurant is "on the short list of area places worth making a special trip out of the city for." A proponent of ingredients sourced from the region's small farmers, Armstrong uses beef from the Ruppersberger Co-op and pheasant from Beaver Creek Farm, as well as locally raised vegetables that appear in dishes like a gratin of local cauliflower served with frisée lettuce and Manni white truffle oil. Bistro offerings range from steak tartare served with pumpernickel baked in house to house-cured pork belly with Jersey cabbage, roasted onions and tournéed potatoes. The excellent wine list has numerous delicious, reasonably priced bottles.

New American | Casual | Expensive | alexandria | 110 S. Pitt St. | 703-706-0450 | www.restauranteve.com | Lunch & Dinner Mon-Fri Sat dinner only

Corduroy   90.0

When Tom Powers' restaurant was located in a Sheraton Hotel, it was the darling of the local foodie community. But now that it's moved into a town house near the city's convention center, people don't seem to be talking about it as much. It's odd, as Powers' cooking hasn't changed, and dishes like a bisque of blue snapper, carpaccio of lobster with drawn butter, and pork cheeks and tarbais beans prepared osso buco style, are as delicious as they were at the old location. It's even more puzzling in light of recent comments that claim, "The new location is simply beautiful, the food is still exemplary, albeit more expensive and the service exquisite. Mr. Powers' restaurant continues to excel."

New American | Casual | Expensive | mount vernon | 1122 9th St. NW | 202-589-0699 | www.corduroydc.com | Dinner Mon-Sat

TOP LOCAL CHOICE

2941   89.5

After a period in which a revolving door of chefs made dining here an adventure, things have calmed down with Bertrand Chemel in charge of the kitchen. He's a veteran of New York City's Café Boulud, and you can see that restaurant's influence in dishes like cocoa-rubbed pork belly confit with house-made chorizo and pancetta-wrapped venison loin with foie gras and toasted wild rice. There was praise for sommelier Matthew Carroll and his 12,000-bottle wine list, as well as kudos for the "striking room, which overlooks a lake," an attempt to make you forget that the restaurant is actually located in an office park.

French | Casual | Expensive | falls church | 2941 Fairview Park Dr. | 703-270-1500 | www.2941.com | Lunch & Dinner Mon-Fri Sat dinner only

Obelisk   89.5

It might not be readily apparent from its name, but Obelisk is one of the top northern Italian restaurants in D.C. The 36-seat room near Dupont Circle features five-course set menus from chef Jerry Corso, consisting of dishes like sweetbread and porcini ravioli, sea bass with peppers, a grilled quail and sausage combo and an expertly roasted leg of lamb. Owner Peter Paston has crafted a small but attractive wine list, while doing a superb job running the dining room, whose décor is dominated by 19th-century French botanical prints. The prix-fixe format makes this one of the best dining bargains in town.

Italian | Casual | Expensive | dupont circle | 2029 P St. NW | 202-872-1180 | Dinner Tue-Sat

Marcel's   89.5

Robert Wiedmaier offers diners four-, five-, and seven-course menus of modern French cuisine, featuring dishes like a gratin of Prince Edward Island mussels, Alaskan ling cod in lemongrass-miso broth, and lamb tenderloins wrapped in phylo and served with a cumin Madeira sauce. The "classic French cuisine in an elegant setting," with "service that is attentive without being overbearing," makes it popular with the diplomatic corps, while a location at the edge of Georgetown makes it convenient before a performance at the Kennedy Center. It's "hard to have anything but a nice time here."

French | Formal | Expensive | georgetown | 2401 Pennsylvania Ave. NW | 202-296-1166 | www.marcelsdc.com | Dinner daily

Charlie Palmer Steak   88.5

This upscale steakhouse from Aureole's Charlie Palmer is like other steakhouses associated with a celebrity chef – a bit on the pricy side – but that drawback is offset by a "lovely setting at the foot of Capitol Hill." The menu offers the type of New American cooking you associate with Palmer, with an emphasis on various cuts of prime beef. Add to the high-quality cow "good sides and generally careful execution" and a "terrific wine list," and the result is "a better choice than the average steakhouse chain."

Steakhouse | Casual | Expensive | capitol hill | 101 Constitution Ave. NW | 202-547-8100 | www.charlieplamer.com | Dinner Mon-Sat, Lunch Mon-Fri

Johnny's Half Shell   88.5

Ann Cashion and John Fulchino's seafood specialist seems to have changed for the worse since it moved to Dupont Circle. Some reviewers still praise the simple seafood fare, like pan-roasted Rappahannock littleneck clams with bacon or a fillet of delicata catfish with lemony shrimp and Andouille sausage risotto, but others say "you're better off stopping at the Taqueria Nacionale," located at the rear of the restaurant, for some fish tacos. A location facing the Capitol rotunda makes it "a popular spot for pols and their staffers."

Seafood | Informal | Moderate | dupont circle | 400 N. Capitol St. NW | 202-737-0400 | www.johnnyshalfshell.net | Lunch & Dinner Mon-Fri Sat dinner only

La Chaumière   88.5

If you're dying for good, old-fashioned Gallic fare, consider visiting this restaurant, which bills itself as a "French country inn in the middle of the city." The menu is full of classic dishes that aren't often seen on menus anymore, like quenelles de brochet, tripes à la mode de Caën, salmon in puff pastry with dill sauce and sautéed calf's brains. Reviewers call it "cozy, rich, grand and unapologetically old school" and "a wonderfully warm and cozy restaurant with incredibly impressive service."

French | Casual | Moderate | georgetown | 2813 M St. NW | 202-338-1784 | www.lachaumieredc.com | Lunch & Dinner Mon-Fri Sat dinner only

Mark's Duck House (8 miles west in Falls Church)   88.5

Opinions are split about this nondescript restaurant in a suburban strip mall that, on the surface, looks like any number of suburban Chinese eateries. Its fans declare "you need to travel all the way to California to find dim sum at this level of quality," while a multitude of detractors call it "overrated." Then there's a third contingent that occupies the middle ground, declaring that regardless of how you feel about the dumplings and small plates, the Chinese-style barbecued meats are nonpareil, particularly the namesake dish, which is "maybe the best roast duck in the U.S."

Chinese | Informal | Moderate | falls church | 6184-A Arlington Blvd. | 703-532-2125 | www.marksduck-house.com | Lunch & Dinner daily

Bistro Bis   88.0

"One of D.C.'s best combinations of reasonable price, ambience and professional service," Jeffrey Buben's restaurant is "recommended for people who want to mix serious conversation with good food." The traditional French fare, which includes dishes like Basque-style chicken and a duet of veal façon grand-mère, is well-executed, and the "well-chosen wine list" enhances the experience. There were complaints about "a dining room with a poor layout – try to steer clear of the tables to the left of the entrance."

French Bistro | Casual | Moderate | capitol hill | Hotel George | 15 E St. NW | 202-661-2700 | www.bistrobis.com | Open daily

Proof   88.0

What is probably the District's best wine list can be found at this Penn Quarter wine bar/restaurant. There is a long list of charcuterie and artisanal cheeses on offer, and the cooked food, which has an Asian flair, features dishes like miso-glazed sablefish with buckwheat noodles, rabbit braised in white wine and a Pineland Farms hanger steak dressed with jalapeño vinaigrette. "Arguably D.C.'s most sophisticated wine program," say reviewers with a "menu that's every bit the booze's match."

Wine Bar | Casual | Moderate | penn qtr | 775 G Street NW | 202-737-7663 | www.proofdc.com | Dinner daily, Lunch Mon-Fri

Kinkead's   88.0

When this New American eatery opened back in 1983, seafood brasseries were rare. Despite the fact that they're now commonplace, Bob Kinkead's restaurant remains a D.C. institution and a favorite with local VIPs. For starters, there's "a terrific raw bar," which you can follow with one of the house signatures, like Yucatan-style tuna soup or pepita-crusted salmon. Or you can stick with the daily catch, simply cooked over a wood-burning grill. A selection of artisanal cheeses is a nice way to finish your meal.

Seafood | Casual | Expensive | foggy bottom | 2000 Pennsylvania Ave. NW | 202-296-7700 | www.kinkead.com | Dinner daily, Lunch Mon-Fri

Vidalia   88.0

Spanning the country, Jeffery Buben's menu ranges from Mid-Atlantic classics, like a pig's trotter from nearby St. Mary's County stuffed with smoked ham hock and collard greens, to southern fare like shrimp and grits with andouille sausage, shellfish cream, and, of course, Vidalia onion. There's "a well-crafted wine list" featuring "many reasonably priced choices" and, adjacent to the wine cellar, a private dining room for 20 people – perfect for a group that wants to eat well while making a dent in that terrific list.

New American | Casual | Expensive | dupont circle | 1990 M St. NW | 202-659-1990 | http://vidaliadc.com | Dinner daily, Lunch Mon-Fri

ACCEPTABLE

Café Atlantico   87.5

It's a shame that José Andrés can't put together a kitchen team that can do a better job at his flagship restaurant. A stagnant menu doesn't help (though first-time diners will find it interesting to read). Still, some dishes, like the duck confit with passion fruit oil glaze, remain tried and true. The Latino "dim sum" brunch that's served on Sundays is popular, because"it features a few of the dishes that Andres serves at Minibar" (see above), one flight up.

Pan-Latin | Casual | Moderate | penn qtr | 405 8th St. NW | 202-393-0812 | www.cafeatlantico.com | Lunch & Dinner Tue-Sun

Old Ebbitt Grill   87.5

This institution opened in 1856 just around the corner from the White House, and every U.S. president has eaten here – in fact, Teddy Roosevelt is responsible for some of the animal heads on display over the bar. The cuisine revolves around simple fare: a raw bar, grilled fish and meats, and the kind of diverse menu usually found at an upscale pub. There's a top-flight wine list, and given the location, the place is "always full of politicos," especially during happy hour.

Seafood | Informal | Moderate | downtown | 675 15th St. NW | 202-347-4800 | www.ebbitt.com | Open daily

Capital Grille   87.5

It's fitting that the most frequently reviewed steakhouse in our nation's capital is named, well, Capital. All the usual cuts of steaks are on hand, with the beef described as "consistently good for a national chain." Famous as "a hangout for many Republican lobbyists," it offers "fun people-watching" in a "loud and boisterous" environment. Add in prompt service" from an "attentive staff" and you see why some reviewers prefer it over other steakhouses in the city.

Steakhouse | Casual | Expensive | penn qtr | 601 Pennsylvania Ave. NW | 202-737-6200 | www. thecapitalgrille.com | Dinner daily. Lunch Mon-Sat

Tabard Inn   87.5

Among the pluses at this 90-year-old hotel are "a wonderful old dining room" and a "delightful garden" during the spring and summer. It's "ideal for a late breakfast or a leisurely lunch," especially with a glass or two of wine. Just bear in mind that, despite a New American menu that features organic ingredients and dishes like braised bison short ribs with English pea ravioli, the consensus is that the food is nothing more than ordinary.

New American | Casual | Moderate | dupont circle | Hotel Tabard Inn | 1739 N St. NW | 202-331-8528 | www.tabardinn.com | Open daily

Zola   87.5

When a restaurant offers chicken with truffle pesto for $39 and beef with winter

vegetables for $35 (we're still trying to work out how chicken can cost more than beef) and it can only muster a rating of Acceptable, comments like, "One can thank tourists and a decent bar scene for this place still being around" don't surprise us. Of course, if you like congregating with lots of good-looking young people for drinks and dinner, this might become your number one choice in D.C.

New American | Casual | Expensive | penn qtr | 800 F St. NW | 202-654-0999 | www.zoladc.com | Dinner daily, Lunch Mon-Fri

Bourbon Steak   87.0

An easy, fast way for a hotel to get into the upscale dining market is to make a deal with a celebrity chef. That's what the Four Seasons did here with Michael Mina, whose "swanky" steakhouse attracted comments like "beautiful space, great service, and well-prepared food." One reviewer, a concierge, told us, "I've gotten a 50-50 good/bad response whenever I recommended it to guests." Another cost-conscious reviewer commented, "It's best when someone else is paying."

Steakhouse | Casual | Expensive | georgetown | 2800 Pennsylvania Ave. NW | 202-944-2026 | www.fourseasons.com | Dinner daily, Lunch Mon-Fri

Hank's Oyster Bar   87.0

This "definition of a neighborhood spot" offers "a nice variety of fresh oysters" amid a "faux fish shack vibe." There's less enthusiasm for the cooked fare, with reviewers complaining "the kitchen has a tendency to overcomplicate things." Still, it's "tasty enough to warrant a visit," and the "good bar scene" makes it popular with vast legions of single locals.

Seafood | Informal | Moderate | dupont circle | 1624 Q St. NW | 202-462-4265 | www.hanksdc.com | Dinner daily, Lunch Sat-Sun

Peking Gourmet Inn   87.0

For those who believe there is a corollary between good Chinese food and Republican politics, we note that one reviewer claimed this "hidden and special place" was "a hallowed haunt of the first President Bush." The Peking duck is obviously the thing – it was mentioned favorably by more than 85% of reviewers, who showered it with adjectives such as "excellent," "amazing" and even "a minor miracle." Be sure "not to miss any dish that includes garlic sprouts."

Chinese | Informal | Moderate | falls church | 6029 Leesburg Pike | 703-671-8088 | www.pekinggourmet.com | Lunch & Dinner daily

Sushiko   87.0
(7 miles northwest in Bethesda)

Every metropolis needs a neighborhood sushi joint, and this pair of venues serves that purpose for D.C.'s northwestern suburbs (Bethesda and Chevy Chase, respectively). Among the oldest sushi restaurants in the area, they are "still one of the most dependable," Sushiko "holds its own," even though there's not much support for raw-fish culture in these parts. Of course, not everyone agrees, especially the reviewer who claimed, "I get better sushi in Columbus, Ohio," adding, "The cooked dishes are better, but not by much."

Japanese | Informal | Moderate | bethesda | 2309 Wisconsin Ave. NW | 202-333-4187 | Dinner daily, Lunch Tue-Fri

Second Location: chevy chase | 5455 Wisconsin Ave. | 301-961-1644 | www.sushikorestaurants.com | Dinner daily, Lunch Tue-Fri

Bistrot Lepic & Wine Bar   86.5

Two restaurants for the price of one. The downstairs is a "traditional French bistro with white tablecloths," while upstairs there's a "cozy wine bar" that can also accommodate groups. The menu is the same at both: a combination of small and large plates like salmon in a potato crust and medallions of beef with polenta and shitake mushrooms. Expect to find "rus-

tic cuisine" being consumed by an "older crowd" in a "nice atmosphere."

French Bistro | Casual | Moderate | georgetown | 1736 Wisconsin Ave. NW | 202-333-0111 | www.bistrotlepic.com | Lunch & Dinner daily

Bombay Club   86.5

When Washington's elite are looking for classic Indian fare in an upscale environment, they head to this "elegant" restaurant run by the team that operates Rasika. "Prices are significantly higher than your typical curry joint's," but reviewers say "it's worth paying a bit more" for the combination of "great food, good service, and a good atmosphere." It's close to the White House and boasts the name of every famous politician of the last ten years on its guest list.

Indian | Casual | Moderate | downtown | 815 Connecticut Ave. NW | 202-659-3727 | www.bombayclubdc.com | Dinner daily, Lunch Sun-Fri

Circle Bistro   86.5

"An unsung hero of D.C. dining," Circle Bistro has long been a humble haven for some of the most consistent, sophisticated yet accessible cooking in town. Ethan McKee is currently in charge of the kitchen, offering dishes like soft-shell crabs with summer squash, basil and brown butter. The combination of "an interesting menu," an "attention to detail" that includes "good service" and an "interesting cheese course" makes you feel you're dining in a much more formal restaurant.

New American | Casual | Moderate | west end | 1 Washington Circle NW | 202-293-5390 | www.thecirclehotel.com | Open daily

DC Coast   86.5

Despite a confusing name (we haven't noticed a coast near D.C. lately), Brendan Cox has turned "good Southern food into something even better" at this downtowner that's popular with the see-and-be-seen business lunch crowd. The New

American cuisine emphasizes local seafood like fried Chesapeake Bay oysters with smoked onion and apple slaw. Even those against it say the fresh ingredients are "decently prepared" and the service "manages to hold its own despite the crowded dining room."

New American | Casual | Moderate | downtown | 1401 K St. NW | 202-216-5988 | www.dccoast.com | Lunch & Dinner Mon-Fri

Jaleo   86.5

There's been grumbling of slippage of qualilty at Jaleo now that José Andrés has become a celebrity chef. Even so, reviewers still enjoy the classic tapas here, as well as more modern creations, like chorizo wrapped in potato or fried pork cheeks served with blood oranges, and those who aren't just grazing can end the savory part of the meal with one of four paellas on offer. The wine list is full of Cavas, a number of different sherries and interesting Spanish wines.

Spanish | Informal | Casual | penn qtr | 480 7th St. NW | 202-628-7949 | www.jaleo.com | Lunch & Dinner daily

BlackSalt   86.0

Some reviewers claim that Jeff Black runs "the best seafood restaurant in the D.C. area," while others say it's "merely average in a city where there are few good choices for seafood." There's a market on the premises, and the "well-sourced fish" ends up in dishes like roast California sturgeon with Guatemalan prawns and a cumin-piquillo broth. Its location in the far-northwestern reaches of the city makes it a popular dinner stop for suburban Maryland commuters.

Seafood | Casual | Moderate | palisades | 4883 MacArthur Blvd. NW | 202-342-9101 | www.black-saltrestaurant.com | Lunch & Dinner daily

L'Auberge Chez Francois   86.0

The Haeringer family has been at the helm of this restaurant since it opened 57 years ago (with a move from D.C. proper to Great Falls in 1975). The classic Alsatian fare hasn't changed very much over the years. With reviewers' comments ranging from "a standby for special occasions" to "vastly overrated," whether you will like it or not seems to depend on whether you find this style of quaint French-country dining charming rather than merely hokey.

French | Casual | Expensive | great falls | 331 Springvale Rd. | 703-759-3800 | www.lauberge-chezfrancois.com | Lunch & Dinner Tue-Sun

Central Michel Richard   85.5

With starters of onion soup, frisée salad and steak tartare and entrées like cassoulet and calves' liver and bacon, all the classics are on hand at the more casual of Michel Richard's two D.C. offerings. And if you're in the mood for a burger, there are five types, ranging from classic to ahi tuna to Richard's signature lobster burger. Reviewers say the "bold, brash flavors are sometimes undermined by a lack of attention to detail."

French | Informal | Moderate | penn qtr | 1001 Pennsylvania Ave. NW | 202-626-0015 | www.centralmichelrichard.com | Dinner Mon-Sat, Lunch Mon-Fri

Firefly   85.0

You can start your evening with a drink at one of the liveliest bars in the city, then move into the dining room for Daniel Bortnick's eclectic American menu, which features everything from chicken matzoh ball soup to a mini pot roast with Yukon Gold mashed potatoes, braised baby carrots and roasted shallot jus. "A cozy restaurant with some fantastic cocktails; even if you're not hungry it's worth stopping by for an after-work drink and a snack."

New American | Casual | Moderate | dupont circle | 1310 New Hampshire Ave. NW | 202-861-1310 | www.firefly-dc.com | Open daily

Fogo de Chão   85.0

This is probably the best of the churrascarias in town, despite the fact that it's a chain with a dozen locations around the U.S. We don't recommend it for the most discerning diners, but if you are in the mood to pig out on a "massive salad bar" and "a plentiful assortment" of meats, you can eat as much as you want until they have to carry you out of the place.

Brazilian | Casual | Moderate | downtown | 1101 Pennsylvania Ave. NW | 202-347-4668 | www.fogo-dechao.com | Dinner daily, Lunch Mon-Fri

Morrison-Clark Inn   85.0

This Victorian-style inn, occupying a building that dates back to 1864, features a "charming setting," "accommodating hosts" and "fine-quality Southern dining" with dishes like panko-breaded East Coast oysters and a grilled pork chop with creamy grits and port mustard sauce. The location near the Convention Center makes it a popular choice with business folk, who are happy to take advantage of the restaurant's garden during the warmer months.

New American | Casual | Moderate | downtown | 1015 L St. NW | 202-898-1200 | www.morrison-clark.com | Dinner daily, Lunch Sun-Fri

Ray's the Steaks   85.0

Large portions of reasonably priced steak and inexpensive wines make this one of D.C.'s most popular places. But despite the crowds, our reviewers point out that "They serve choice, not prime, meat," which allows for the cheaper tabs. Still, fans say, "At $29, the steak is well worth the price, even if the quality isn't as good as at the top steak restaurants in town."

Steakhouse | Informal | Moderate | arlington | 2300 Wilson Blvd. | 703-841-7297 | Dinner daily

Teatro Goldoni   85.0

Some 80% of reviewers offered favorable comments about this restaurant, while the remainder slammed the place. The menu, featuring dishes like an assortment of cornetti filled with different types of fish or salt-cured duck breast with Ligurian black olives, evoked comments that ranged from "the most interesting Italian menu in the city" to "fine for a business lunch, but not much more." The best way to experience the restaurant is from a perch at the kitchen table.

Italian | Casual | Moderate | golden triangle | 1909 K St. NW | 202-955-9494 | www.teatrogoldoni.com | Dinner Mon-Sat, Lunch Mon-Fri

OTHER RESTAURANTS MENTIONED

1789   84.5

Despite the fact that this Georgetowner is owned by the Clyde's chain, D.C. diners seem to have a warm spot in their hearts for it. The "historic and quaint setting" helps, along with a well-stocked wine list that does a good job of complementing the classic – if "no better than competent" – French/American cuisine. The festive atmosphere makes it especially popular during the Christmas season.

French | Casual | Expensive | georgetown | 1226 36th St. NW | 202-965-1789 | www.1789restaurant.com | Dinner daily

Equinox   84.5

Todd Grey offers diners New American creations like sautéed North Carolina shad roe with creamy mascarpone grits and crispy speck (bacon) or maple-brined duck breast with cumin-scented date purée and roasted cipollini onions. Reviewers describe the food as "good and creative for D.C., but not that special from a wider perspective." There isn't much of a wine list either.

New American | Casual | Expensive | downtown | 818 Connecticut Ave. NW | 202-331-8118 | www.equinoxrestaurant.com | Dinner daily, Lunch Mon-Fri

i Ricchi   84.5

The type of classic Tuscan restaurant

every city needs, i Ricchi serves simple, no-nonsense food that is well-prepared in an environment that could well be overlooking San Gimignano. The dining room is always full of locals, some who have been enjoying Chef Ricchi's "Italian comfort food" for the past twenty years. Soups and risottos are among the stand-outs on the menu, and special praise was offered for any of the grilled meats as well as the wine list.

Tuscan | Casual | Moderate | dupont circle | 1220 19th St. NW | 202-835-0459 | www.iricchi.net | Lunch & Dinner Mon-Fri, Sat dinner only

Lebanese Taverna   84.5

Now that they have opened their sixth location, the magic has gone from the Abi-Najm family's Lebanese restaurant, which dates back to 1979: "Mezzes are reliable, not great, and the rest of the menu is acceptable" sums up the comments. On the plus side, the menu does contain every kibbe and kabob imaginable, as well as a full range of grilled meats and fish, plus gently simmered stews. They also offer a reasonably good list of Lebanese wines.

Middle Eastern | Casual | Moderate | woodley park | 2641 Connecticut Ave. NW | 202-265-8681 | www.lebanesetaverna.com | Lunch & Dinner daily

Nora   84.5

Nora Pouillon created a sensation when she became the first D.C. area chef to feature organic ingredients. But these days many people say that she has been coasting on her reputation and that there has been little change to the food since she first opened. Even if their cutting-edge nature has dulled a bit, the bistro-style offerings are still made from first-class, fresh produce and good-quality meats – especially game in season – and there's an interesting wine list.

New American | Casual | Moderate | dupont circle | 2132 Florida Ave. NW | 202-462-5143 | www.noras.com | Dinner Mon-Sat

Oceanaire Seafood   84.5

Half the comments about this chain said "think steakhouse for fish." The décor has a nautical theme, and the service is polished and professional. As for the quality of the food, some praise "an excellent raw bar" and "very large portions of fresh fish," while others report that "Lobbyists love it but foodies shrug."

Seafood | Casual | Moderate | downtown | 1201 F St. NW | 202-347-2277 | www.theoceanaire.com | Dinner daily, Lunch Mon-Fri

Zatinya   84.5

As with sister Jaleo (see above), José Andrés' Middle Eastern small plates restaurant has "lost its oomph" of late. It's a shame because there are a number of interesting-sounding dishes on offer, like roasted cauliflower with sultanas, caper berries and pine nut purée and Kalamata-marinated sirloin served with feta cheese and scallion purée. Another advantage: "a better wine list" than you normally find at ethnic restaurants.

Mediterranean | Informal | Moderate | penn qtr | 701 9th St. NW | 202-638-0800 | Lunch & Dinner daily

Cashion's Eat Place   83.5

While her name is still prominently featured, Ann Cashion sold her interest in this restaurant back in 2007 in order to concentrate on Johnny's Half Shell. Still, everyone agrees that "a hip atmosphere" helps make this a "great spot" in the Adams Morgan neighborhood." But there is disagreement about the food, with fans praising the "constantly changing menu" and critics complaining of "watery sauces" and "everything swimming in butter."

New American | Casual | Moderate | adams morgan | 1819 Columbia Rd. NW | 202-797-1819 | www.cashionseatplace.com | Dinner Tue-Sun

Georgia Brown's   83.5

We are always looking for a Southern/

soul food restaurant that our reviewers can recommend, but with this "D.C. mainstay" attracting comments like "heavy, unbalanced, faux-Southern cuisine" and "Southern schtick on a stick," it seems this eatery isn't it. Not that this "hangout for the city's African-American establishment" doesn't have some points in its favor – especially a "lively environment" that makes it "a wonderful place to take out-of-town visitors."

Southern | Casual | Moderate | downtown | 950 15th St. NW | 202-393-4499 | www.gbrowns.com | Lunch & Dinner daily

Heritage India   83.5

Put this pair of "very good traditional Indian restaurants" in the category of "upscale enough." The Mughal-style menu lists all the classics, from tandooris to "delicious curries," which "they will be happy to spice up upon request." Word has it that the "Dupont Circle location is as good as the Georgetown original," a comment we don't hear about an offshoot very often.

Indian | Informal | Moderate | georgetown | 2400 Wisconsin Ave. NW | 202-333-2100 | www. heritageindiausa.com | Lunch & Dinner daily

Second Location: dupont circle | 1337 Connecticut Ave. NW | 202-331-1414 | www. heritageindiausa.com | Lunch & Dinner daily

TenPenh   83.5

D.C.'s version of places like Spice Market or Buddakan is true to the "corporate-style Asian fusion" concept, offering dishes like Malaysian roti canai, Filipino spring rolls, Korean barbecue ribs and Thai tom yum soup. It's buzzy, it's happening, it's downtown, it's noisy, and it has "great martinis." But while it's "a nice place to have a business lunch," the "Food isn't much better than the corner Thai restaurant."

Pan-Asian | Casual | Moderate | downtown | 1001 Pennsylvania Ave. NW | 202-393-4500 | www. tenpenh.com | Dinner daily, Lunch Mon-Fri

B. Smith's   83.0

It would be great if B. Smith's restaurant were as beautiful as the namesake lady herself or if the food were as magnificent as its environs. Instead, the Union Station location is merely "a grand setting for some seriously shoddy cooking." One reviewer said, "You can eat well if you choose carefully," but comments like "Make sure to take Lipitor before your meal" are more in keeping with the general consensus.

Southern | Casual | Moderate | capitol hill | 50 Massachusetts Ave. NE | 202-289-6188 | www. bsmith.com | Lunch & Dinner daily

Old Angler's Inn   83.0
(14 miles northwest in Potomac)

Few restaurants bill themselves as a place where bikers and hikers can stop for a meal, but that's exactly what this Maryland veteran dating back to 1860 does – as well as advertise its "picturesque location," which can be "very romantic, especially during nice weather." As is often the case with scenic sites, the "Food can be uneven – sometimes wonderful, sometimes not so good."

American | Casual | Expensive | potomac | 10801 MacArthur Blvd. | 301-365-2425 | www.oldanglersinn.com | Lunch & Dinner Tue-Sun

Acadiana   82.5

Reactions to this Cajun restaurant coalesce around three different points of view. One claimed, "It would be good even if it were located in New Orleans," a more conditioned one called it "completely satisfactory," and the third dismissed it as "corporate and stale." We guess whether you want to go will be a function of how badly you want to eat smoked chicken, andouille gumbo and New Orleans–style barbecue shrimp while in the D.C. environs.

Southern | Casual | Moderate | mount vernon | 901 New York Ave. NW | 202-408-8848 | www.acadianarestaurant.com | Dinner daily, Lunch Sun-Fri

Tosca   82.0

This handsome northern Italian restaurant features an ambitious menu filled with dishes like frogs' legs sautéed in white wine, triangle pasta filled with olive oil-poached swordfish in a light lobster sauce and grilled ramp-crusted T-bone lamb chops with a sunchoke timbale. There's a serviceable wine list, good service and two different tasting menus. The Penn Quarter location makes it popular with the expense-account crowd.

Italian | Casual | Moderate | penn qtr | 1112 F St. NW | 202-367-1990 | www.toscadc.com | Lunch & Dinner Mon-Fri Sat dinner only

Clyde's   80.5

Three comments pretty much sum up what this Georgetown restaurant is all about: "perfectly fine Chesapeake Bay food by Georgetown standards," "really a diner in fern-bar clothing, complete with interesting knick-knacks hanging on the walls" and "just awful, everything is bland, blah and fried. I wouldn't go even if I lived in the neighborhood." The criticism doesn't stop it from always being filled with a clientele that's described as "the real Washington."

American | Informal | Moderate | georgetown | 3236 M St. NW | 202-333-9180 | www.clydes.com | Lunch & Dinner daily

Roof Terrace at   79.5
Kennedy Center

While we get to read many a harsh review, few were as blunt as the ones that described this as "a really bad restaurant" – one to visit "only if I'm starving and there isn't time to eat elsewhere." Which nails the problem: restaurant-wise "There aren't many options" that are convenient for a pre-Kennedy Center meal. It offers a "pleasant setting," if that's any consolation.

American | Casual | Moderate | foggy bottom | 2700 F St. NW | 202-416-8555 | www.kennedy-center.org | Dinner on days of major performances

Kafe Leopold   79.5

Fans of this Austrian restaurant located at the base of M Street call it a "great place to go if you're in need of refreshment after shopping in Georgetown," praising the "very nice European-style cakes." But those kudos are countered by critiques like "soggy waffles that tasted as if they came from a packet mix." At least the summertime outdoor seating offers "some of the best people-watching in the District."

Austrian | Informal | Inexpensive | georgetown | 3315 M St. NW | 202-965-6005 | www.kafeleopolds.com | Open daily

Dino   78.0

It's rare that readers regret criticizing a restaurant, but with comments like, "You want to love this place because Dean Gold is so enthusiastic about Italian food and wine, but the food is just not very good," this is one of those exceptions. It seems you're better off dropping by for a drink and snack, as praise was reserved for the "tasty selection of salumi" and "some of the most interesting Italian wines in D.C."

Italian | Informal | Moderate | cleveland park | 3435 Connecticut Ave. NW | 202-686-2966 | www.dino-dc.com | Dinner daily, Lunch Sun

Montmartre   75.0

A number of comments offered about this casual "crowded" restaurant were better than the rating would indicate: "Good, modest, true French cooking by French natives" and "The service is professional, and there's a reasonable wine list with a nice array of mid-tier wines." Unfortunately, some of the more experienced reviewers in our panel still couldn't recommend it, dismissing the place as "just another restaurant serving tired French food."

French Bistro | Informal | Moderate | capitol hill | 327 7th St. SE | 202-544-1244 | www.montmartredc.com | Lunch & Dinner Tue-Sun

Cheap Eats

UNIQUELY DELICIOUS

2Amys   8.2

Our reviewers love visiting this upscale pizza and cured meats specialist, despite having to put up with "the long lines" and a "frenetic atmosphere." Whether it's one of the three pizzas that use D.O.C. ingredients (Naples' official designation of quality) or a more exotic pie like eggplant confit with olives, capers and oregano, devotees claim the fare is "among the best pizzas in the country." We should note that this is Neapolitan-style pizza, with a quiche-like center that strikes the uninitiated unfavorably as a "crust that is soft and floppy." But if you like this type, you'll find 2 Amys "one of the few D.C. places (ethnic or otherwise) that would make a similar impact in other cities."

Pizza | Moderate | cleveland park | 3715 Macomb St. NW | 202-885-5700 | www.2amyspizza.com | Dinner daily, Lunch Tue-Sun

RECOMMENDED

Pho 75   7.6

"It's the place to go for Pho" claim the reviewers who frequent this mini-chain with several locations in the D.C. area. The décor is as bare bones as it gets, and in some locations they only offer communal seating. But one thing is sure: You are bound to find "a busy dining room" where a number of people are having "a cathartic experience with a bowl of soup."

Vietnamese | Inexpensive | arlington | 1721 Wilson Blvd. | 703-525-7355 | Open daily

Second Location: falls church | 3103 Graham Rd. | 703-204-1490 | Open daily

Third location: rockville | 771 Hungerford Dr. | 301-309-8873 | Open daily

Breadline   7.5

Open only for breakfast and lunch, this bakery/café sandwiched between the White House and the World Bank is one of the most popular weekday destinations in the city. Beyond an everyday menu of turkey, tuna, ham and other standard sandwiches, the offerings on the daily menu range from a Reuben to a shrimp po-boy or fried cod with rémoulade and coleslaw. There are also empanadas, falafel, salads and soups of the day, which you can get as part of a combo with a sandwich or salad.

Bakery | Inexpensive | downtown | 1751 Pennsylvania Ave. NW | 202-822-8900 | www.breadline.com | Open Breakfast & Lunch Mon-Fri

Ray's Hell-Burger   7.3
(3 miles west in Arlington)

After Ray's the Steaks moved to a larger space, owner Michael Landrum converted this location into a burger joint. Though it's every bit as popular as its predecessor, the comments reflect a debate similar to the one that revolves around Landrum's steak restaurant: Some call it "the best burger I ever had," while others say that "Choice-grade meat makes for a less juicy burger." They offer a host of "over-the-top toppings," including foie gras and Bordelaise sauce.

Hamburgers | Inexpensive | arlington | 1725 Wilson Blvd. | Lunch & Dinner daily

Ben's Chili Bowl   7.1

Ben's has been the pulse of D.C.'s U Street Corridor since 1958. Though it offers a full coffee shop menu with a soul food emphasis, the main attraction is the hot dogs, including the house special known as the "half smoke with chili" (fondly described as "business development for the association of D.C. cardiologists"). It's a favorite with a host of celebs ranging from Bill Cosby to President Obama, so you can expect to wait on a line that reaches out the door.

Hot Dogs | Inexpensive | u street corridor | 1213 U. St. NW | 202-667-0909 | www.bens chilibowl.com | Open daily except Sun breakfast

OTHER PLACES MENTIONED

Pizzeria Paradiso   6.8

For many years this was considered the top pizzeria in D.C. But it branched out into a mini-chain, and even fans would agree it has become "the second-choice pizzeria" for local diners ("they can be stingy with the toppings," for one thing). But plus points like the "fresh quality ingredients" and "a truly great beer list" mean it's still quite popular – which means it can be an ordeal to get a table.

Pizza | Inexpensive | dupont circle | 3282 M St. NW | 202-337-1245 | www.eatyourpizza.com | Lunch & Dinner daily

Five Guys (3 miles west in Arlington)   6.6

It's a common question among hamburger habitués: "Who's better, Five Guys or In 'N' Out?" Supporters of the former insist, "People don't fully understand how good these burgers are until they try one," while detractors denounce it as having "more grease than class." As usual, the truth lies somewhere in the middle, but if you like fast-food style burgers you'll enjoy this joint.

Hamburgers | Inexpensive | arlington | 1335 Wisconsin Ave. NW | 202-337-0400 | www.fiveguys.com | Lunch & Dinner daily

Florida Avenue Grill   5.5

Not much more than "a greasy spoon" serving a full menu of Southern classics (like "authentic grits and redeye gravy") and basic coffee shop fare. It's "so-so soul food," at best, though at least it "will help pay for the college tuition for your cardiologist's children." Though the neighborhood has been gentrified, a location near Howard University helps it maintain its status as "neighborhood fixture" and "an important social center for the city's black community."

Southern | Inexpensive | u street corridor | 1100 Florida Ave. NW | 202-265-1586 | Open Tue-Sun except Sun dinner

Elevation Burger   5.2

While this mini-chain advertises its use of organic produce and meat, a full one-third of our reviewers can't recommend it. One described its cuisine as "bad food hiding behind a campaign of quality, healthy ingredients." Some reviewers have a soft spot for the milk shakes, available in a multitude of flavors.

Hamburgers | Inexpensive | arlington | 442 S. Washington St. | 703-237-4343 | www.elevation-burger.com | Lunch & Dinner daily

Washington VA

HIGHLY RECOMMENDED

Inn at Little Washington   92.9

Fifteen years ago, this was one of the top restaurants in the country. But these days there is as much speculation about when Patrick O'Connell will retire as there is discussion about his food, which falls into two camps: One complains that the food hasn't changed in years, while the other commends O'Connell for an effective use of local ingredients in dishes like a pullet egg poached in duck consommé with morels and black truffles; shad roe with caviar butter and vodka cream atop black pepper fettuccine; and beef two ways: pecan-crusted, barbequed short ribs and a miniature filet mignon wrapped in Swiss chard. The wine list is one of the best in the country, in terms of both depth and price. However, while everyone praises the service, the antiques-laden dining room has been criticized for being "over-the-top with frills and lace."

New American | Formal | Very Expensive | washington | Middle and Main Streets | 540-675-3800 | www.theinnatlittlewashington.com | Dinner daily

Wilmington DE

RECOMMENDED

Deep Blue   90.9

Despite the proximity to fertile farmland and fish fresh out of the Atlantic Ocean, you could starve looking for a good restaurant while driving the stretch between Philadelphia and Baltimore. That is, unless you time it so you can stop at this seafood specialist in the heart of downtown Wilmington, where Dan Butler sources fish and seafood "that are as good as what you will find at seafood restaurants in major U.S. cities." There's a terrific raw bar, and the New American seafood creations feature dishes like orange-scented steamed Atlantic cod as well as crab cakes with refried garbanzo beans and a spicy avocado sauce. Working against it is "a drab room" – "The décor isn't worthy of the tasty food," reviewers say – though "a lively bar scene" helps.

Seafood | Casual | Moderate | 111 W. 11th St. | 302-777-2040 | www.deepbluebarandgrill.com | Dinner Mon-Sat, Lunch Mon-Fri

Indexes

Alphabetical by Restaurant

Acacia	Lawrenceville	New Jersey	New American
Acadiana	Washington	District of Columbia	Southern
Acme Oyster House	New Orleans	Louisiana	Seafood
Acquerello	San Francisco	California	Italian
ad hoc	Yountville	California	American
Adour	Manhattan	New York	French
Adrienne's Pizzabar	Manhattan	New York	Pizzeria
Agave	Atlanta	Georgia	Southwestern
Ajihei	Princeton	New Jersey	Japanese
AKA Bistro	Lincoln	Massachussetts	French-Japanese
Al Di La	Brooklyn	New York	Italian
Al Forno	Providence	Rhode Island	Italian
Al Vento	Minneapolis	Minnesota	Italian
Al's # 1 Italian Beef	Chicago	Illinois	Sandwiches
Al's Breakfast	Minneapolis	Minnesota	Coffee Shop
Al's Restaurant	St. Louis	Missouri	Steakhouse
Alan Wong's	Honolulu	Hawaii	Hawaiian
Alana's Food & Wine	Columbus	Ohio	New American
Aldea	Manhattan	New York	Portuguese
Alfredo's	Atlanta	Georgia	Italian
Alice's Tea Cup	Manhattan	New York	Coffee Shop
Alinea	Chicago	Illinois	Progressive
Alma	Minneapolis	Minnesota	New American
Alma de Cuba	Philadelphia	Pennsylvania	Pan-Latin
Alon's	Atlanta	Georgia	Bakery
Amada	Philadelphia	Pennsylvania	Spanish (Tapas)
Amanda's	Hoboken	New Jersey	New American
Amber India	Mountain View	California	Indian
Ame	San Francisco	California	Italian (Japanese)
American Hotel	Sag Harbor	New York	American
American Restaurant	Kansas City	Missouri	New American
Amy Ruth's	Manhattan	New York	Southern
Amy's Bread	Manhattan	New York	Bakery
Andina	Portland	Oregon	Peruvian
Angèle	Napa	California	French Bistro
Angeli Café	Los Angeles	California	Italian
Angelica Kitchen	Manhattan	New York	Vegetarian
Angelini Osteria	Los Angeles	California	Italian
Angus Barn	Raleigh	North Carolina	Steakhouse
Animal	West Hollywood	California	Gastropub
Anneke Jans	Kittery	Maine	New American
Annisa	Manhattan	New York	Asian (French)
Anthony's	St. Louis	Missouri	Italian
Anthony's Pier 4	Boston	Massachussetts	Seafood
Antica Posta	Atlanta	Georgia	Italian
Antoine's	New Orleans	Louisiana	Creole
Anton and Michel	Carmel-by-the-Sea	California	Continental
Apiary	Manhattan	New York	New American
Apizza Scholls	Portland	Oregon	Pizzeria
Apple Pan	West Los Angeles	California	Hamburgers
Applewood	Queens	New York	New American
Aquagrill	Manhattan	New York	Seafood
Aquavit	Manhattan	New York	Swedish
Aquitaine	Boston	Massachussetts	French Bistro
Aria	Atlanta	Georgia	New American

Bon Ton Café	New Orleans	Louisiana	Creole
Bond Street	Manhattan	New York	Japanese
Bone's	Atlanta	Georgia	Steakhouse
Bonsoirée	Chicago	Illinois	Progressive
Boqueria	Manhattan	New York	Spanish (Tapas)
Border Grill	Santa Monica	California	Mexican
Bottega	Birmingham	Alabama	Italian
Bottega	Napa	California	Italian
Bottega del Vino	Manhattan	New York	Italian
Boucherie	New Orleans	Louisiana	New Southern
Bouchon	Las Vegas	Nevada	French
Bouchon	Santa Barbara	California	French
Bouchon	Beverly Hills	California	French Bistro
Bouchon	Yountville	California	French Bistro
Bouchon Bakery	Manhattan	New York	Bakery
Bouchon Bakery	Yountville	California	Bakery
Boulevard	San Francisco	California	California
Bouley	Manhattan	New York	French
Bourbon HouseSeafood & Oyster Bar	New Orleans	Louisiana	Seafood
Bourbon Steak	Washington	District of Columbia	Steakhouse
Bradley Ogden	Las Vegas	Nevada	New American
Bradstreet Crafthouse	Minneapolis	Minnesota	Gastropub
Brasa	Minneapolis	Minnesota	Southern
Brasserie	Manhattan	New York	French
Brasserie 8½	Manhattan	New York	French Brasserie
Brasserie by Niche	St. Louis	Missouri	French Brasserie
Brasserie Jo	Boston	Massachussetts	French
Brasserie Ruhlmann	Manhattan	New York	French Brasserie
Bread Garden	Atlanta	Georgia	Bakery
Breadline	Washington	District of Columbia	Bakery
Brennan's	New Orleans	Louisiana	Creole
Bresca	Portland	Maine	Italian
Breslin, The	Manhattan	New York	Gastropub
Brewster Fish House	Brewster	Massachussetts	Seafood
Brick Lane Curry House	Manhattan	New York	Indian
Brigtsen's	New Orleans	Louisiana	Creole
Bristol	Chicago	Illinois	Gastropub
Brix	St. Helena	California	California
Broders' Pasta Bar	Minneapolis	Minnesota	Italian
Brooklyn Ice Cream Factory	Brooklyn	New York	Ice Cream
Brothers at Mattei's Tavern	Los Olivos	California	New American
Bryant & Cooper Steakhouse	Roslyn	New York	Steakhouse
Bubby's Pie Company	Manhattan	New York	Coffee Shop
Buckeye Roadhouse	Mill Valley	California	Eclectic
Buddakan	Philadelphia	Pennsylvania	Asian
Buddakan	Manhattan	New York	Pan-Asian
Buffet Bellagio	Las Vegas	Nevada	Eclectic
Bunk Sandwiches	Portland	Oregon	Sandwiches
Burger Bar	Las Vegas	Nevada	Hamburgers
burger joint at Le Parker Meridien	Manhattan	New York	Hamburgers
Busy Bee Café	Atlanta	Georgia	Southern
Butcher Block, The	Minneapolis	Minnesota	Italian
Butcher Shop	Boston	Massachussetts	Italian
Café Atlantico	Washington	District of Columbia	Pan-Latin

Café Ba-Ba-Reeba	Chicago	Illinois	Spanish (Tapas)
Café Beaujolais	Mendocino	California	California
Café Bizou	Sherman Oaks	California	French Bistro
Café Boulud	Manhattan	New York	French
Café Boulud	Palm Beach	Florida	French Bistro
Café Castagna	Portland	Oregon	New American
Café d'Alsace	Manhattan	New York	French Brasserie
Café du Monde	New Orleans	Louisiana	Dessert
Café Español	Manhattan	New York	Spanish
Café Evergreen	Manhattan	New York	Chinese
Café Habana	Manhattan	New York	Pan-Latin
Café Jacqueline	San Francisco	California	French
Café Juanita	Kirkland	Washington	Italian
Café Katja	Manhattan	New York	Austrian
Café La Haye	Sonoma	California	California
Café Lurcat	Minneapolis	Minnesota	New American
Café Luxembourg	Manhattan	New York	French Brasserie
Café Martorano	Ft. Lauderdale	Florida	Italian (Southern)
Café Martorano	Hollywood	Florida	Italian (Southern)
Café Miranda	Rockland	Maine	Eclectic
Café Pasqual's	Santa Fe	New Mexico	Southwestern
Café Poca Cosa	Tucson	Arizona	Mexican
Café Sabarsky	Manhattan	New York	Austrian
Café Spiaggia	Chicago	Illinois	Italian
Caffè Mingo	Portland	Oregon	Italian
Caiola's Restaurant	Portland	Maine	New American
Cakes and Ale	Decatur	Georgia	Gastropub
California Grill	Orlando	Florida	California
Calumet Fisheries	Chicago	Illinois	Seafood
Cameli's Gourmet Pizza	Atlanta	Georgia	Pizzeria
Camellia Grill	New Orleans	Louisiana	Coffee Shop
Campagne	Seattle	Washington	New American
Campanile	Los Angeles	California	Mediterranean
Campton Place	San Francisco	California	Indian (Mediterranean)
Candle 79	Manhattan	New York	Vegetarian
Canlis	Seattle	Washington	New American
Canoe	Vinings	Georgia	Southern (Contemporary)
Canteen	San Francisco	California	New American
Canters'	Los Angeles	California	Coffee Shop
Capital Grille	Washington	District of Columbia	Steakhouse
Capo	Santa Monica	California	Italian
Capsouto Frères	Manhattan	New York	French Bistro
Carafe	Portland	Oregon	French Bistro
Cardwell's at the Plaza	Clayton	Missouri	New American
Carlos	Highland Park	Illinois	French
Carlyle Hotel	Manhattan	New York	French
Carmen	Boston	Massachussetts	Italian (Southern)
Carnegie Deli	Manhattan	New York	Delicatessen
Carnevino	Las Vegas	Nevada	Italian (Steakhouse)
Casa Lever	Manhattan	New York	Italian
Casa Mono	Manhattan	New York	Spanish (Tapas)
Casa Tua	Miami Beach	Florida	Italian
Casamento's	New Orleans	Louisiana	Seafood
Casanova	Carmel	California	Belgian
Cashion's Eat Place	Washington	District of Columbia	New American

Castagna	Portland	Oregon	Progressive
Cecconi's	West Hollywood	California	Italian
Celeste	Manhattan	New York	Italian
Central Grocery	New Orleans	Louisiana	Sandwiches
Central Kitchen	Cambridge	Massachussetts	French
Central Michel Richard	Washington	District of Columbia	French
Centrico	Manhattan	New York	Mexican
César	Berkeley	California	Spanish (Tapas)
César	Oakland	California	Spanish (Tapas)
Charleston	Baltimore	Maryland	Southern (Contemporary)
Charleston Grill	Charleston	South Carolina	New American
Charlie Gitto's on The Hill	St. Louis	Missouri	Italian (Southern)
Charlie Palmer Steak	Washington	District of Columbia	Steakhouse
Charlie Trotter's	Chicago	Illinois	New American
Charlie's Sandwich Shoppe	Boston	Massachussetts	Coffee Shop
Chase's Daily	Belfast	Maine	Bakery
Chauncey Creek Lobster Pier	Kittery	Maine	Seafood
Chaya Brasserie	San Francisco	California	Asian (French)
Chaya Brasserie	West Hollywood	California	Asian (French)
Cheese Board	Berkeley	California	Pizzeria
Chef Allen's	Aventura	Florida	New American
Chef Mavro	Honolulu	Hawaii	French
Chef Vola's	Atlantic City	New Jersey	Italian
Chennai Garden	Manhattan	New York	Indian (Vegetarian)
Chestnut	Brooklyn	New York	New American
Chez Fonfon	Birmingham	Alabama	French Brasserie
Chez Henri	Cambridge	Massachussetts	French
Chez Panisse	Berkeley	California	French
Chez Panisse Café	San Francisco	California	French
Chez Shea	Seattle	Washington	French Bistro
Chez TJ	Mountain View	California	New American
Chicago Chop House	Chicago	Illinois	Steakhouse
Chifa	Philadelphia	Pennsylvania	Peruvian (Asian)
ChikaLicious	Manhattan	New York	Dessert
Chillingsworth	Brewster	Massachusetts	French
Chin Chin	Manhattan	New York	Chinese.
China Grill	Miami Beach	Florida	Asian
Chinatown Brasserie	Manhattan	New York	Chinese
Ching's Kitchen	Darien	Connecticut	Pan-Asian
Chinois on Main	Santa Monica	California	Asian
Chop't Creative Salad Company	Manhattan	New York	Coffee Shop
Chops Lobster Bar	Atlanta	Georgia	Steakhouse
Chopstix	Atlanta	Georgia	Chinese
Christopher's	Phoenix	Arizona	French
Churrascaria Plataforma	Manhattan	New York	Brazilian
Cindy's Backstreet Kitchen	St. Helena	California	California
Cinque Terre	Portland	Maine	Italian
Circa 1886	Charleston	South Carolina	Southern (Contemporary)
Circle Bistro	Washington	District of Columbia	New American
Citronelle	Washington	District of Columbia	French
Citta Nuova	East Hampton	New York	Italian
City Bakery	Manhattan	New York	Bakery
City Grocery	Oxford	Mississippi	Southern (Contemporary)
City Hall	Manhattan	New York	American
City Market	Luling	Texas	Barbecue

Crofton on Wells	Chicago	Illinois	New American
Crook's Corner	Chapel Hill	North Carolina	Southern
Crossing, The	Clayton	Missouri	New American
Crown Candy Kitchen	St. Louis	Missouri	Coffee Shop
Cru Café	Charleston	South Carolina	Eclectic
Crush	Seattle	Washington	New American
Crustacean	Beverly Hills	California	Asian
Cuba Libre	Philadelphia	Pennsylvania	Pan-Latin
Cucharamama	Hoboken	New Jersey	Pan-Latin
Cuistot	Palm Desert	California	French
CulinAriane	Montclair	New Jersey	New American
Custom House	Chicago	Illinois	New American
Cut	Beverly Hills	California	Steakhouse
Cypress	Charleston	South Carolina	American
Cyrus	Healdsburg	California	French
D'Amico Kitchen	Minneapolis	Minnesota	Italian
Da Silvano	Manhattan	New York	Italian
Daily Catch	Boston	Massachussetts	Italian (Southern)
Daisy May's BBQ USA	Manhattan	New York	Barbecue
Dalessandro's	Philadelphia	Pennsylvania	Sandwiches
Dali Restaurant	Somerville	Massachussetts	Spanish (Tapas)
Dan Tana's	West Hollywood	California	Italian
Daniel	Manhattan	New York	French
Daniel's Broiler	Seattle	Washington	Steakhouse
Dante's Kitchen	New Orleans	Louisiana	New Louisiana
Darrel & Oliver's Café Max	Pompano Beach	Florida	New American
David Burke Fromagerie	Rumson	New Jersey	New American
David Burke's Primehouse	Chicago	Illinois	Steakhouse
David's 388	Portland	Maine	New American
Davio's	Boston	Massachussetts	Steakhouse
db Bistro Moderne	Manhattan	New York	French
DBGB Kitchen & Bar	Manhattan	New York	French
DC Coast	Washington	District of Columbia	New American
Deanie's Seafood	New Orleans	Louisiana	Seafood
Deep Blue	Wilmington	Delaware	Seafood
Degustation	Manhattan	New York	Spanish
Del Frisco's	Manhattan	New York	Steakhouse
Del Posto	Manhattan	New York	Italian
Delfina	San Francisco	California	Cal-Ital
Delmonico Steakhouse	Las Vegas	Nevada	Steakhouse
Delmonico's	Manhattan	New York	Steakhouse
DeLorenzo's Tomato Pies	Trenton	New Jersey	Pizzeria
Deseo	Scottsdale	Arizona	Latin
Dévi	Manhattan	New York	Indian
Di Fara's	Brooklyn	New York	Pizzeria
Dickie Brennan's	New Orleans	Louisiana	Steakhouse
Different Pointe of View	Phoenix	Arizona	New American
Dilworthtown Inn	West Chester	Pennsylvania	Continental
Dim Sum Go Go	Manhattan	New York	Chinese
Din Tai Fung	Arcadia	California	Chinese
Diner, The	Brooklyn	New York	New American
Dino	Washington	District of Columbia	Italian
Dinosaur Bar-B-Que	Manhattan	New York	Barbecue
Dinosaur Bar-B-Que	Syracuse	New York	Barbecue
Distrito	Philadelphia	Pennsylvania	Mexican

Gari	Manhattan	New York	Japanese
Gary Danko	San Francisco	California	New American
Gates Bar-B-Q	Kansas City	Missouri	Barbecue
Gautreau's	New Orleans	Louisiana	New American
Geisha House	Hollywood	California	Japanese
Gene & Georgetti	Chicago	Illinois	Steakhouse
General Greene	Queens	New York	Eclectic
Geno's Steaks	Philadelphia	Pennsylvania	Sandwiches
George's California Modern	La Jolla	California	New American
Georgia Brown's	Washington	District of Columbia	Southern
Georgia Grille	Atlanta	Georgia	Southwestern
Georgian Room at the Cloisters	Sea Island	Georgia	New American
Geronimo	Santa Fe	New Mexico	New American
Giacomo's	Boston	Massachussetts	Italian (Southern)
Gibsons Bar	Chicago	Illinois	Steakhouse
Gilmore's	West Chester	Pennsylvania	French
Gilt	Manhattan	New York	New American
Giorgio Baldi	Santa Monica	California	Italian
Giovanni's on the Hill	St. Louis	Missouri	Italian
Girl and the Fig, The	Sonoma	California	French Bistro
Gjelina	Venice	California	Mediterranean
Globe	San Francisco	California	Cal-Ital
Go Fish	St. Helena	California	Seafood
Gobo	Manhattan	New York	Vegetarian
Good Pie, The	St. Louis	Missouri	Pizzeria
Gordon Ramsay at the London	Manhattan	New York	French
Gordon Ramsay at the London	West Hollywood	California	French
Gotham Bar and Grill	Manhattan	New York	New American
Gott's Roadside	Napa	California	Hamburgers
Gott's Roadside	San Francisco	California	Hamburgers
Gott's Roadside	St. Helena	California	Hamburgers
Graham Elliot	Chicago	Illinois	Progressive
Gramercy Tavern	Manhattan	New York	New American
Grand Sichuan Eastern	Manhattan	New York	Chinese
Gray's Papaya	Manhattan	New York	Hot Dogs
Great Jones Café	Manhattan	New York	Cajun
Great NY Noodletown	Manhattan	New York	Chinese
Green Goddess	New Orleans	Louisiana	Eclectic
Green Zebra	Chicago	Illinois	Vegetarian
Greens	San Francisco	California	Vegetarian
Griddle Café	Hollywood	California	Coffee Shop
Grill 23 & Bar	Boston	Massachussetts	Steakhouse
Grill at the Ritz-Carlton	Clayton	Missouri	New American
Grimaldi's Pizza	Brooklyn	New York	Pizzeria
Griswold Inn	Essex	Connecticut	American
Grocery, The	Brooklyn	New York	Mediterranean
Grotto	Boston	Massachussetts	Italian
Guy Savoy	Las Vegas	Nevada	French
GW Fins	New Orleans	Louisiana	Seafood
Hal's on Old Ivy	Atlanta	Georgia	Continental
Hallo Berlin	Manhattan	New York	German
Hamasaku	Santa Monica	California	Japanese
Hamersley's	Boston	Massachussetts	French Bistro
Hampton Chutney Co.	Manhattan	New York	Indian
Hampton Chutney	Amagansett	New York	Indian

Kingfish Hall	Boston	Massachussetts	Seafood
Kinkead's	Washington	District of Columbia	Seafood
Kiss Sushi	San Francisco	California	Japanese
Kitchen at Brooklyn Fare, The	Queens	New York	New American
Kitchenette	Manhattan	New York	American
Kittichai	Manhattan	New York	Thai
Koi	West Hollywood	California	Japanese
Koi Palace	Daly City	California	Chinese
Kokkari Estiatorio	San Francisco	California	Greek
Komi	Washington	District of Columbia	Greek
Kopp's Frozen Custard	Milwaukee	Wisconsin	Ice Cream
Kouzina by Trata	Manhattan	New York	Greek
K-Paul's	New Orleans	Louisiana	Cajun
Kreuz Market	Lockhart	Texas	Barbecue
Kuleto's	San Francisco	California	Italian
Kuma's Corner	Chicago	Illinois	Hamburgers
Kuruma Zushi	Manhattan	New York	Japanese
Kyma	Atlanta	Georgia	Greek
Kyo Ya	Manhattan	New York	Japanese
Kyotofu	Manhattan	New York	Dessert
Kyo-ya	San Francisco	California	California
L & B Spumoni Gardens	Brooklyn	New York	Pizzeria
L'Absinthe	Manhattan	New York	French
L'Atelier de Joël Robuchon	Manhattan	New York	French
L'Atelier de Joël Robuchon	Las Vegas	Nevada	French
L'Auberge Chez François	Washington	District of Columbia	French
L'Espalier	Boston	Massachussetts	French
L'Etoile	Madison	Wisconsin	New American
L'Osteria del Forno	San Francisco	California	Italian
L20	Chicago	Illinois	French (Seafood)
La Belle Vie	Minneapolis	Minnesota	French
La Casa Sena	Santa Fe	New Mexico	Southwestern
La Chaumière	Washington	District of Columbia	French
La Famiglia	Philadelphia	Pennsylvania	Italian
La Folie	San Francisco	California	French
La Grenouille	Manhattan	New York	French
La Grotta	Atlanta	Georgia	Italian
La Mar	San Francisco	California	Peruvian
La Mer	Honolulu	Hawaii	French
La Morra	Brookline	Massachussetts	Italian
La Petite Folie	Chicago	Illinois	French
La Petite Grocery	New Orleans	Louisiana	New Louisiana
La Super-Rica Taqueria	Santa Barbara	California	Mexican
La Taqueria	San Francisco	California	Mexican
La Toque	Napa	California	French
Lacroix at the Rittenhouse	Philadelphia	Pennsylvania	New American
Lady & Sons	Savannah	Georgia	Southern
Lala Rokh	Boston	Massachussetts	Persian
Lamberts Downtown	Austin	Texas	Barbecue
Landmarc	Manhattan	New York	French Brasserie
Langer's Deli	Los Angeles	California	Delicatessen
Lantern	Chapel Hill	North Carolina	Asian
Lao Sze Chuan	Chicago	Illinois	Chinese (Szechuan)
Lark	Seattle	Washington	New American
Larkspur Restaurant & Bar	Vail	Colorado	New American

Latilla Room	Carefree	Arizona	New American
Laurelhurst Market	Portland	Oregon	Steakhouse
Lauro Kitchen	Portland	Oregon	Mediterranean
Lawry's The Prime Rib	West Hollywood	California	Steakhouse
Le Bec-Fin	Philadelphia	Pennsylvania	French
Le Bernardin	Manhattan	New York	French (Seafood)
Le Cellier Steakhouse	Orlando	Florida	Steakhouse
Le Cirque	Las Vegas	Nevada	French
Le Cirque	Manhattan	New York	French
Le Colonial	Chicago	Illinois	Vietnamese
Le Colonial	San Francisco	California	Vietnamese
Le Coq au Vin	Orlando	Florida	French Bistro
Le Fou Frog	Kansas City	Missouri	French Bistro
Le Gigot	Manhattan	New York	French
Le Pain Quotidien	Manhattan	New York	Bakery
Le Papillon	San Jose	California	French
Le Périgord	Manhattan	New York	French
Le Pichet	Seattle	Washington	French
Le Pigeon	Portland	Oregon	French
Le Relais de Venise	Manhattan	New York	French
Le Vallauris	Palm Springs	California	French
Lebanese Taverna	Baltimore	Maryland	Middle Eastern
Lebanese Taverna	Washington	District of Columbia	Middle Eastern
Lee How Fook	Philadelphia	Pennsylvania	Chinese
Legal Sea Foods	Boston	Massachussetts	Seafood
Les Halles	Manhattan	New York	French Brasserie
Les Nomades	Chicago	Illinois	French
Les Zygomates	Boston	Massachussetts	French Bistro
Let's Be Frank	Culver City	California	Hot Dogs
Levain	Minneapolis	Minnesota	French
LG's Prime Steakhouse	La Quinta	California	Steakhouse
LG's Prime Steakhouse	Palm Desert	California	Steakhouse
LG's Prime Steakhouse	Palm Springs	California	Steakhouse
Lilette	New Orleans	Louisiana	New American
Liluma	St. Louis	Missouri	New American
Lincoln	Manhattan	New York	Italian
Little Giant	Manhattan	New York	New American
Little Owl, The	Manhattan	New York	New American
Little T American Baker	Portland	Oregon	Bakery
Live Bait	Manhattan	New York	Cajun
Lobster Pot	Provincetown	Massachussetts	Seafood
Lobster Roll	Napeague	New York	Seafood
Local 188	Portland	Maine	New American
Locanda Verde	Manhattan	New York	Italian
Locanda Vini e Olii	Brooklyn	New York	Italian
Locke-Ober	Boston	Massachussetts	American
Lodge at Koele Dining Room, The	Lanai City	Hawaii	New American
Lolita	Cleveland	Ohio	Mediterranean
Lombardi's	Manhattan	New York	Pizzeria
Lon's at the Hermosa	Paradise Valley	Arizona	New American
Lorenzo's Trattoria	St. Louis	Missouri	Italian
LoRusso's Cucina	St. Louis	Missouri	Italian
Los Sombreros	Scottsdale	Arizona	Mexican
Lotus of Siam	Las Vegas	Nevada	Thai
Lou	Hollywood	California	Wine Bar

Lou Mitchell's	Chicago	Illinois	Coffee Shop
Louis' Lunch	New Haven	Connecticut	Hamburgers
Luce	San Francisco	California	Italian
Luci Ancora	Minneapolis	Minnesota	Italian
Lucia's	Minneapolis	Minnesota	New American
Lucques	West Hollywood	California	Mediterranean
LudoBites	Los Angeles	California	French
Lula	Chicago	Illinois	Eclectic
Lumière	Newton	Massachussetts	French
Lupa	Manhattan	New York	Italian
Lure Fishbar	Manhattan	New York	Seafood
Má Pêche	Manhattan	New York	Vietnamese
Macrina Bakery and Café	Seattle	Washington	Bakery
Madrona Manor	Healdsburg	California	New American
Magnolia	Charleston	South Carolina	Southern (Contemporary)
Magnolia Grill	Durham	North Carolina	Southern (Contemporary)
Mai Lee	St. Louis	Missouri	Vietnamese
Maialino	Manhattan	New York	Italian
Maine Diner	Kennebunkport	Maine	Coffee Shop
Maloney & Porcelli	Manhattan	New York	Steakhouse
Mama Dip's Country Cooking	Chapel Hill	North Carolina	Southern
Mama's Fish House	Paia	Hawaii	Seafood
Mama's on Washington Sq.	San Francisco	California	Coffee Shop
Mamma Maria	Boston	Massachussetts	Italian (Northern)
Mamoun's	Manhattan	New York	Middle Eastern
Manny's	Chicago	Illinois	Delicatessen
Manny's	Minneapolis	Minnesota	Steakhouse
Manresa	Los Gatos	California	New American
Mansion on Turtle Creek	Dallas	Texas	New American
Mantra	Boston	Massachussetts	French (Indian)
Marcel's	Washington	District of Columbia	French
Marcellino	Scottsdale	Arizona	Italian
Marea	Manhattan	New York	Italian (Southern)
Margaret Kuo	Wayne	Pennsylvania	Chinese (Japanese)
Marigold Kitchen	Philadelphia	Pennsylvania	New American
Marine Room	La Jolla	California	French
Marinus	Carmel Valley	California	New American
Mark's American Cuisine	Houston	Texas	New American
Mark's Duck House	Falls Church	Virginia	Chinese
Market Restaurant and Bar	Del Mar	California	New American
Market Table	Manhattan	New York	New American
MarkJoseph	Manhattan	New York	Steakhouse
Marlow & Sons	Brooklyn	New York	New American
Maroni Cuisine	Northport	New York	Italian
Mary Mac's Tea Room	Atlanta	Georgia	Southern
Mary's Fish Camp	Manhattan	New York	Seafood
Mas	Manhattan	New York	French
Masa	Manhattan	New York	Japanese
Masa's	San Francisco	California	Seafood
Mastro's	Beverly Hills	California	Steakhouse
Mastro's	Scottsdale	Arizona	Steakhouse
Match	South Norwalk	Connecticut	New American
Matsuhisa	Beverly Hills	California	Japanese
Matsuhisa Aspen	Aspen	Colorado	Japanese
Matsuri	Manhattan	New York	Japanese

Momofuku Milk Bar	Manhattan	New York	Dessert
Momofuku Noodle Bar	Manhattan	New York	Korean
Momofuku Ssäm Bar	Manhattan	New York	Asian
Mon Ami Gabi	Chicago	Illinois	French Bistro
Monarch	St. Louis	Missouri	New American
Montagna	Aspen	Colorado	New American
Montmartre	Washington	District of Columbia	French Bistro
Mori Sushi	West Los Angeles	California	Japanese
Morimoto	Manhattan	New York	Japanese
Morimoto	Philadelphia	Pennsylvania	Japanese
Morrell Wine Bar & Café	Manhattan	New York	French
Morrison-Clark Inn	Washington	District of Columbia	New American
Morton's	Chicago	Illinois	Steakhouse
Morton's The	Manhattan	New York	Steakhouse
Morton's, The Steakhouse	Great Neck	New York	Steakhouse
Mosaic	St. Louis	Missouri	Eclectic
Mosaic	Atlanta	Georgia	New American
Mosca's	Avondale	Louisiana	Italian
Mother's	New Orleans	Louisiana	Sandwiches
Mother's Bistro & Bar	Portland	Oregon	Southern
Moto	Chicago	Illinois	Progressive
Motorino	Manhattan	New York	Pizzeria
Moustache	Manhattan	New York	Middle Eastern
Mr. B's Bistro	New Orleans	Louisiana	Creole
Mr. Bartley's Gourmet Burgers	Cambridge	Massachussetts	Coffee Shop
Mr. Beef	Chicago	Illinois	Sandwiches
Mr. Chow	Beverly Hills	California	Chinese
Mr. Chow	Manhattan	New York	Chinese
Mr. K's	Manhattan	New York	Chinese
Mrs. Wilkes' Dining Room	Savannah	Georgia	Southern
Murray Circle	Sausalito	California	California
Musha	Santa Monica	California	Japanese
Musso & Frank's	Hollywood	California	American
Mustards Grill	St. Helena	California	California
N9NE Steakhouse	Las Vegas	Nevada	Steakhouse
Nacional 27	Chicago	Illinois	Latin
Naha	Chicago	Illinois	New American
Nam	Atlanta	Georgia	Vietnamese
Nan Thai Fine Dining	Atlanta	Georgia	Thai
Nana's	Durham	North Carolina	Southern (Contemporary)
Napa Rose	Anaheim	California	California
Nate 'n Al	Beverly Hills	California	Delicatessen
Nathan's Famous	Brooklyn	New York	Hot Dogs
Nava	Atlanta	Georgia	Southwestern
Navarre	Portland	Oregon	Mediterranean
Navio	Half Moon Bay	California	New American
Nectar	West Chester	Pennsylvania	Asian
Neptune Oyster	Boston	Massachussetts	Seafood
New Won Jo	Manhattan	New York	Korean
New York Prime	Atlanta	Georgia	Steakhouse
New Yorker Marketplace & Deli	Atlanta	Georgia	Sandwiches
News Café	Miami Beach	Florida	Coffee Shop
Nice Matin	Manhattan	New York	French Brasserie
Niche	St. Louis	Missouri	New American
Nicholas	Middletown	New Jersey	New American

Ping's Seafood	Queens	New York	Chinese
Pink's Famous Hot Dogs	Los Angeles	California	Hot Dogs
Piñons	Aspen	Colorado	New American
Pinot Bistro	Sherman Oaks	California	French Bistro
Pio Pio	Queens	New York	Peruvian
Piperade	San Francisco	California	Basque
Pizzeria Bianco	Phoenix	Arizona	Pizzeria
Pizzeria Delfina	San Francisco	California	Pizzeria
Pizzeria Mozza	Los Angeles	California	Pizzeria
Pizzeria Paradiso	Washington	District of Columbia	Pizzeria
Pizzeria Tra Vigne	St. Helena	California	Pizzeria
Pizzetta 211	San Francisco	California	Pizzeria
Pluckemin Inn	Bedminster	New Jersey	New American
Pó	Manhattan	New York	Italian
Pok Pok	Portland	Oregon	Thai
Polo Lounge	Beverly Hills	California	American
Pomme	Clayton	Missouri	French
Pop Burger	Manhattan	New York	Hamburgers
Popover Café	Manhattan	New York	American
Poppy	Seattle	Washington	Indian
Porchetta	Manhattan	New York	Italian
Port of Call	New Orleans	Louisiana	Hamburgers
Porter House New York	Manhattan	New York	Steakhouse
Portland City Grill	Portland	Oregon	New American
Prado	Scottsdale	Arizona	Italian
Press	St. Helena	California	Steakhouse
Pricci	Atlanta	Georgia	Italian
Prime	Atlanta	Georgia	Steakhouse
Prime Meats	Brooklyn	New York	German (Steakhouse)
Prime Rib	Baltimore	Maryland	Steakhouse
Prime Steakhouse	Las Vegas	Nevada	Steakhouse
Primehouse New York	Manhattan	New York	Steakhouse
Primo	Rockland	Maine	Italian
Primo	Tucson	Arizona	Italian
Proof	Washington	District of Columbia	Wine Bar
Proof on Main	Louisville	Kentucky	Southern (Contemporary)
Prospect	San Francisco	California	New American
Providence	Hollywood	California	Seafood
Provisions to Go	Atlanta	Georgia	Bakery
Prune	Manhattan	New York	Gastropub
Public	Manhattan	New York	Eclectic
Publican, The	Chicago	Illinois	Gastropub
Pueblo Solis	St. Louis	Missouri	Mexican
Pulino's	Manhattan	New York	Italian
Pump Room	Chicago	Illinois	American
Punch Neapolitan Pizza	Minneapolis	Minnesota	Pizzeria
Pure Food & Wine	Manhattan	New York	Vegetarian
Purple Pig, The	Chicago	Illinois	Gastropub
Pylos	Manhattan	New York	Greek
Quality Meats	Manhattan	New York	Steakhouse
Quang	Minneapolis	Minnesota	Vietnamese
Queen	Brooklyn	New York	Italian
Quince	San Francisco	California	Italian
Quinones Room at Bacchanalia	Atlanta	Georgia	New American
R & G Lounge	San Francisco	California	Chinese

Roof Terrace at Kennedy Ctr.	Washington	District of Columbia	American
Roppongi	La Jolla	California	Pan-Asian
Rosa Mexicano	Manhattan	New York	Mexican
Roscoe's House of Chicken & Waffles	Hollywood	California	Southern
Rosebud	Chicago	Illinois	Steakhouse
Rosemary's	Las Vegas	Nevada	New American
Rover's	Seattle	Washington	French
Rowdy Hall	East Hampton	New York	American
Roy's	Honolulu	Hawaii	Hawaiian
RUB BBQ	Manhattan	New York	Barbecue
Rue de L'Espoir Creative Cooking	Providence	Rhode Island	New American
Rustic Kitchen	Boston	Massachussetts	Italian
Rutherford Grill	Rutherford	California	American
Saam – The Chef's Tasting Room	West Hollywood	California	Progressive
Saddle Peak Lodge	Malibu	California	Continental
Saigon Sandwich	San Francisco	California	Vietnamese
Saison	San Francisco	California	New American
Sakagura	Manhattan	New York	Japanese
Sakura	Minneapolis	Minnesota	Japanese
Salish Lodge Dining Room	Snoqualmie	Washington	New American
Sally's Apizza	New Haven	Connecticut	Pizzeria
Salpicón	Chicago	Illinois	Mexican
Salt Exchange	Portland	Maine	American
Salt Lick	Austin	Texas	Barbecue
Salts	Cambridge	Massachussetts	New American
Salumi Artisan Cured Meat	Seattle	Washington	Italian
Sam's Grill and Seafood Restaurant	San Francisco	California	Seafood
Sanctuary	Minneapolis	Minnesota	New American
Sanford	Milwaukee	Wisconsin	New American
Sang Kee Peking	Philadelphia	Pennsylvania	Chinese
Santacafé	Santa Fe	New Mexico	New American
Santarpio's	East Boston	Massachussetts	Pizzeria
Sapphire Grill	Savannah	Georgia	New American
Sarabeth's Kitchen	Manhattan	New York	American
Sardine Factory, The	Monterey	California	Seafood
Sarge's Deli	Manhattan	New York	Delicatessen
Sasabune	Manhattan	New York	Japanese
Saul	Brooklyn	New York	New American
Savona	Gulph Mills	Pennsylvania	Italian
Savoy	Manhattan	New York	Mediterranean
Sawa Sushi	Sunnyvale	California	Japanese
Scalinatella	Manhattan	New York	Italian
Scalini Fedeli	Manhattan	New York	Italian
Scalini Fedeli	Chatham	New Jersey	Italian (Northern)
Scampo	Boston	Massachussetts	Italian
Scarpetta	Manhattan	New York	Italian
Schwa	Chicago	Illinois	Progressive
Screen Door	Portland	Oregon	New American
SD26	Manhattan	New York	Italian
Sea Change	Minneapolis	Minnesota	Seafood
Sea Grill	Manhattan	New York	Seafood
Sears Fine Food	San Francisco	California	Coffee Shop
Seäsonal	Manhattan	New York	Austrian

Spinasse	Seattle	Washington	Italian
Spoon Thai	Chicago	Illinois	Thai
Sportello	Boston	Massachussetts	Italian
Spotted Pig	Manhattan	New York	Gastropub
SPQR	San Francisco	California	Cal-Ital
Spring Street Natural	Manhattan	New York	Vegetarian
Spruce	San Francisco	California	New American
Sripraphai	Queens	New York	Thai
St. Elmo's Steak House	Indianapolis	Indiana	Steakhouse
St. Paul Grill	St. Paul	Minnesota	Steakhouse
Stage Deli	Manhattan	New York	Delicatessen
Stage Left	New Brunswick	New Jersey	New American
Stand	Manhattan	New York	Hamburgers
Standard Grill, The	Manhattan	New York	New American
Stanton Social Club	Manhattan	New York	Eclectic
Starker's Reserve	Kansas City	Missouri	New American
Stefan's at L.A. Farm	Santa Monica	California	New American
Stella!	New Orleans	Louisiana	New American
Stellina	St. Louis	Missouri	Italian
Stephan Pyles Restaurant	Dallas	Texas	Southwestern
Stoney River Legendary Steaks	Atlanta	Georgia	Steakhouse
Street and Co.	Portland	Maine	Seafood
Strip House	Manhattan	New York	Steakhouse
Stroud's	Kansas City	Missouri	American
Stubb's	Austin	Texas	Barbecue
Stumptown Roasters	Portland	Oregon	Dessert
Sugiyama	Manhattan	New York	Japanese
Sun in My Belly	Atlanta	Georgia	Sandwiches
Super Duper Weenie	Fairfield	Connecticut	Hot Dogs
Superdawg Drive-In	Chicago	Illinois	Hot Dogs
supperclub	San Francisco	California	Vegetarian
Sushi Ann	Manhattan	New York	Japanese
Sushi Den	Denver	Colorado	Japanese
Sushi Nozawa	Studio City	California	Japanese
Sushi of Gari	Manhattan	New York	Japanese
Sushi of Gari 46	Manhattan	New York	Japanese
Sushi Ota	San Diego	California	Seafood
Sushi Ran	Sausalito	California	Japanese
Sushi Roku	Hollywood	California	Japanese
Sushi Roku	Las Vegas	Nevada	Japanese
Sushi Sasabune	West Los Angeles	California	Japanese
Sushi Seki	Manhattan	New York	Japanese
Sushi Taro	Washington	District of Columbia	Japanese
Sushi Wabi	Chicago	Illinois	Japanese
Sushi Yasuda	Manhattan	New York	Japanese
Sushi Zen	Manhattan	New York	Japanese
Sushi Zo	Los Angeles	California	Japanese
Sushiden	Manhattan	New York	Japanese
Sushiko	Bethesda	Maryland	Japanese
Sushiko	Chevy Chase	Maryland	Japanese
SushiSamba	Chicago	Illinois	Japanese
Sutro's at the Cliff House	San Francisco	California	American
Suzanne's Cuisine	Ojai	California	California
Suzuki's Sushi Bar	Rockland	Maine	Japanese
Swan Oyster Depot	San Francisco	California	Seafood

Tony Luke's Old Philly Style Sandwiches	Philadelphia	Pennsylvania	Sandwiches
Tony's	St. Louis	Missouri	Italian
Top of the Hub	Boston	Massachussetts	New American
Top of the Riverfront	St. Louis	Missouri	American
Topolobampo	Chicago	Illinois	New Mexican
Topper's	Nantucket	Massachussetts	New American
Toro	Boston	Massachussetts	Spanish
Toro Bravo	Portland	Oregon	Spanish (Tapas)
Tosca	Washington	District of Columbia	Italian
Totonno's	Brooklyn	New York	Pizzeria
Totoraku	West Los Angeles	California	Japanese
Town Hall	San Francisco	California	New American
Town House	Chilhowie	Virginia	Progressive
Tra Vigne	St. Helena	California	Italian
Trattoria Delia	Burlington	Vermont	Italian
Trattoria Marcella	St. Louis	Missouri	Italian
Trattoria Zero Otto Nove	Bronx	New York	Pizzeria
Trenton Bridge Lobster Pound	Trenton	Maine	Seafood
Tria	Philadelphia	Pennsylvania	Wine Bar
Triomphe	Manhattan	New York	New American
Troquet	Boston	Massachussetts	French Bistro
Tru	Chicago	Illinois	French
Tse Yang	Manhattan	New York	Chinese
Turkish Kitchen	Manhattan	New York	Turkish
Two Boots	Manhattan	New York	Pizzeria
Txikito	Manhattan	New York·	Spanish (Tapas)
Typhoon	Portland	Oregon	Thai
Ubuntu	Napa	California	Vegetarian
Uburger	Boston	Massachussetts	Hamburgers
Uchi	Austin	Texas	Japanese
Umami Burger	Los Angeles	California	Hamburgers
Una Pizzeria Napoletana	San Francisco	California	Pizzeria
Uncle Jack's Steakhouse	Queens	New York	Steakhouse
Uncle Nick's	Manhattan	New York	Greek
Uni	Boston	Massachussetts	Japanese
Union League Café	New Haven	Connecticut	French Bistro
Union Oyster House	Boston	Massachussetts	Seafood
Union Square Café	Manhattan	New York	New American
Upperline	New Orleans	Louisiana	Creole
UpStairs on the Square	Cambridge	Massachussetts	New American
Urasawa	Beverly Hills	California	Japanese
Urban Belly	Chicago	Illinois	Asian
Urban Farmer	Portland	Oregon	New American
Ushiwakamaru	Manhattan	New York	Japanese
V & T	Manhattan	New York	Pizzeria
Valentino	Santa Monica	California	Italian (Northern)
Valentino Las Vegas	Las Vegas	Nevada	Italian
Veni Vidi Vici	Atlanta	Georgia	Italian
Veniero's	Manhattan	New York	Dessert
Veritable Quandary	Portland	Oregon	New American
Vermilion	Chicago	Illinois	French
Versailles	Miami Beach	Florida	Cuban
Veselka	Manhattan	New York	Coffee Shop (Ukrainian)
Vetri	Philadelphia	Pennsylvania	Italian

Wu Liang Ye	Manhattan	New York	Chinese
Wurstküche	Los Angeles	California	Hot Dogs
Xaviars at Piermont	Piermont	New York	New American
XIV	West Hollywood	California	New American
Yakitori Totto	Manhattan	New York	Japanese
Yama	Manhattan	New York	Japanese
Yamashiro	Hollywood	California	Japanese
Yangming	Bryn Mawr	Pennsylvania	Chinese
Yank Sing	San Francisco	California	Chinese
Yoshi	Oakland	California	Japanese
Yoshi's Café	Chicago	Illinois	Asian
Yuca	Miami Beach	Florida	Cuban
Yuet Lee	San Francisco	California	Chinese
Yujean Kang's	Pasadena	California	Chinese
Zabar's Café	Manhattan	New York	Coffee Shop
Zahav	Philadelphia	Pennsylvania	Middle Eastern
Zatinya	Washington	District of Columbia	Mediterranean
Zazu	Santa Rosa	California	California
Zealous	Chicago	Illinois	New American
Zola	Washington	District of Columbia	New American
Zum Schneider	Manhattan	New York	German
Zuni Café	San Francisco	California	Mediterranean

Alphabetical by City

Cambridge, MA	OM	New American
	Rendezvous	Eclectic
	Rialto	Italian
	Salts	New American
	T. W. Food	French
	Tamarind Bay	Indian
	Ten Tables	Mediterranean
	UpStairs on the Square	New American
Cape May, NJ	Ebbitt Room	American
Carefree, AZ	Latilla Room	New American
Carmel, CA	Casanova	Belgian
	Pacific's Edge	California
Carmel Valley, CA	Marinus	New American
Carmel-by-the-Sea, CA	Anton and Michel	Continental
	Aubergine	French
Cave Creek, AZ	Binkley's	New American
Camden, ME	Francine Bistro	New American
Chandler, AZ	Kai	Southwestern
Chapel Hill, NC	Crook's Corner	Southern
	Elaine's on Franklin	Southern
	Lantern	Asian
	Mama Dip's Country Cooking	Southern
	Restaurant Bonne Soirée	French
	Weathervane	American
Chappaqua, NY	Crabtree's Kittle House	American
Charleston, SC	Blossom	Seafood
	Boathouse Restaurant	Seafood
	Charleston Grill	New American
	Circa 1886	Southern
	Cru Café	Eclectic
	Cypress	American
	FIG	New American
	Hank's Seafood	Seafood
	High Cotton	Southern
	Hominy Grill	Southern
	Jestine's Kitchen	Southern
	Magnolia	Southern
	McCrady's	Progressive
	Peninsula Grille	New American
	Slightly North of Broad	French
Chatham, MA	Scalini Fedeli	Italian
Chatham, NJ	Serenade	New American
Chattanooga, TN	212 Market	New American
Chelsea, MA	Tangierino	Moroccan
Chestnut Hill, MA	Oishii	Japanese
Chevy Chase, MD	Sushiko	Japanese
Chicago, IL	Al's # 1 Italian Beef	Sandwiches
	Alinea	Progressive
	Arun's	Thai
	Atwood Café	New American

Chicago, IL	Avec	French
	Avenues	Progressive
	Big Star	Mexican
	Bin 36	New American
	Bistro Campagne	French Bistro
	Blackbird	New American
	Boka	New American
	Bonsoirée	Progressive
	Bristol	Gastropub
	Café Ba-Ba-Reeba	Spanish
	Café Spiaggia	Italian
	Calumet Fisheries	Seafood
	Charlie Trotter's	New American
	Chicago Chop House	Steakhouse
	Crofton on Wells	New American
	Custom House	New American
	David Burke's Primehouse	Steakhouse
	Erwin An American Café & Bar	New American
	Everest	French
	Fogo de Chão	Brazilian
	Francesca's on Taylor	Italian
	Frontera Grill	Mexican
	Gene & Georgetti	Steakhouse
	Gibsons Bar	Steakhouse
	Graham Elliot	Progressive
	Green Zebra	Vegetarian
	Happy Chef Dim Sum House	Chinese
	Honey 1 BBQ	Barbecue
	Hot Doug's	Hot Dogs
	Japonais	Japanese
	Joe's Seafood Prime Steak & Stone Crab	Seafood
	Kuma's Corner	Hamburgers
	L20	French
	La Petite Folie	French
	Lao Sze Chuan	Chinese
	Le Colonial	Vietnamese
	Les Nomades	French
	Lou Mitchell's	Coffee Shop
	Lula	Eclectic
	Manny's	Delicatessen
	Mercat a la Plancha	Spanish
	Mirai Sushi	Japanese
	MK	New American
	Mon Ami Gabi	French Bistro
	Morton's	Steakhouse
	Moto	Progressive
	Mr. Beef	Sandwiches
	Nacional 27	Latin
	Naha	New American
	NoMI	French
	North Pond	New American

Falls Church, VA	2941	French
	Mark's Duck House	Chinese
	Peking Gourmet Inn	Chinese
	Pho 75	Vietnamese
Findlay, OH	Revolver	New American
Forestville, CA	Farmhouse Inn and Restaurant	California
Framingham, MA	Sichuan Gourmet	Sichuan
Fredericksburg, MD	Volt	Progressive
Ft. Lauderdale, FL	Café Martorano	Italian
Glendale, CA	Palate Food & Wine	Wine Bar
Great Barrington, MA	Bizen	Japanese
Great Neck, NY	Morton's	Steakhouse
	Peter Luger Steak House	Steakhouse
Gulph Mills, PA	Savona	Italian
Half Moon Bay, CA	Navio	New American
Hamilton, NJ	Rat's	New American
Healdsburg, CA	Cyrus	French
	Dry Creek Kitchen	New American
	Madrona Manor	New American
	Willi's Wine Bar	Califonia
Highland Park, IL	Carlos	French
Highlands, NJ	Doris & Ed's	Seafood
Hoboken, NJ	Amanda's	New American
	Cucharamama	Pan-Latin
Hollywood, CA	Café Martorano	Italian (Southern)
Hollywood, CA	Geisha House	Japanese
	Griddle Café	Coffee Shop
	Hungry Cat, The	Seafood
	Lou	Wine Bar
	Musso & Frank's	American
	Osteria Mozza	Italian
	Pace	Italian
	Providence	Seafood
	Roscoe's House of Chicken & Waffles	Southern
	Sushi Roku	Japanese
	Yamashiro	Japanese
Holly Hill, SC	Sweatman's BBQ	Barbecue
Honolulu, HI	Alan Wong's	Hawaiian
	Hoku's	Hawaiian
	La Mer	French
	Nobu Waikiki	Japanese
	Roy's	Hawaiian
	Chef Mavro	French
Hopewell, NJ	Blue Bottle Café	New American
Houston, TX	Mark's American Cuisine	New American
Indianapolis, IN	St. Elmo's Steak House	Steakhouse
Ipswich, MA	Clam Box	Seafood
Kamuela, HI	Merriman's	New American
Kansas City, MO	American Restaurant	New American

Kansas City, MO	Arthur Bryant's	Barbecue
	Bluestem	New American
	Gates Bar-B-Q	Barbecue
	Jack Stack Barbeque	Barbecue
	Le Fou Frog	French Bistro
	Starker's Reserve	New American
	Stroud's	American
Kennebunkport, ME	Clam Shack	Seafood
	Maine Diner	Coffee Shop
	Ramp Bar & Grill	American
	White Barn Inn	French
Kennett Square, PA	Talula's Table	New American
Kiawah Island, HI	Ocean Room	Steakhouse
Killington, VT	Hemingway's	New American
Kirkland, WA	Café Juanita	Italian
Kittery, ME	Anneke Jans	New American
Kitterym	Chauncey Creek Lobster Pier	Seafood
La Jolla, CA	A. R. Valentien	New American
	Donovan's Steak & Chop House	Steakhouse
La Jolla, CA	George's California Modern	New American
	Marine Room	French
	NINE-TEN	New American
	Roppongi	Pan-Asian
	Tapenade	French
La Quinta, CA	LG's Prime	Steakhouse
Lanai City, HI	Lodge at Koele Dining Room, The	New American
Las Vegas, NV	Aureole	New American
	B & B Ristorante	Italian
	Bartolotta Ristorante	Italian (Seafood)
	BOA	Steakhouse
	Bouchon	French
	Bradley Ogden	New American
	Buffet Bellagio	Eclectic
	Burger Bar	Hamburgers
	Carnevino	Italian
	Craftsteak	Steakhouse
	Delmonico Steakhouse	Steakhouse
	Emeril's New Orleans	Seafood
	Fleur de Lys	French
	Guy Savoy	French
	Joël Robuchon at the Mansion	French
	L'Atelier de Robuchon	French
	Le Cirque	French
	Lotus of Siam	Thai
	Michael Mina	New American
	Mix	French
	N9NE Steakhouse	Steakhouse
	Nobhill Tavern	American

Listed by Cuisine

Afghan

Helmand	Baltimore, MD
Helmand	East Cambridge, MA

African

Boma – Flavors of Africa	Orlando, FL

American

128 Café	Minneapolis, MN
21 Club	Manhattan, NY
75 Chestnut	Boston, MA
American Hotel	Sag Harbor, NY
Arizona Inn	Tucson, AZ
Balsams	Dixville Notch, NH
Beacon	Manhattan, NY
Belvedere	Beverly Hills, CA
Black Point Inn	Prouts Neck, ME
Bloom	Scottsdale, AZ
Blue Ribbon	Manhattan, NY
City Hall	Manhattan, NY
City Tavern	Philadelphia, PA
Clyde's	Washington, DC
Country Cat Dinner House and Bar	Portland, OR
Crabtree's Kittle House	Chappaqua, NY
Cypress	Charleston, SC
Durgin Park	Boston, MA
Ebbitt Room	Cape May, NJ
Fireplace	Brookline, MA
Griswold Inn	Essex, CT
Hell's Kitchen	Minneapolis, MN
Hurley's	Yountville, CA
Jack's Oyster House	Albany, NY
Jordan Pond House	Bar Harbor, ME
Kitchenette	Manhattan, NY
Locke-Ober	Boston, MA
Millennium	San Francisco, CA
Musso & Frank's	Hollywood, CA
Nicollet Island Inn	Minneapolis, MN
Nobhill Tavern	Las Vegas, NV
NoHo Star	Manhattan, NY
Norma's	Manhattan, NY
Not Your Average Joe's	Beverly, MA

Oar House The	Portsmouth, NH
Old Angler's Inn	Washington, DC
Old Fashioned	Madison, WI
One If by Land	Manhattan, NY
Parker's	Boston, MA
Polo Lounge	Beverly Hills, CA
Popover Café	Manhattan, NY
Pump Room	Chicago, IL
Ramp Bar & Grill	Kennebunkport, ME
Red Lion Inn	Stockbridge, MA
Red Rooster at the Woodstock Inn	Woodstock, VT
Ritz-Carlton Atlanta Grill	Atlanta, GA
Roof Terrace at	Washington, DC
Rowdy Hall	East Hampton, NY
Rutherford Grill	Rutherford, NJ
Salt Exchange	Portland, ME
Sarabeth's Kitchen	Manhattan, NY
Simon Pearce	Quechee, VT
Stroud's	Kansas City, MO
Sutro's at the Cliff House	San Francisco, CA
Top of the Riverfront	St. Louis, MO
Weathervane	Chapel Hill, NC
Wicked Oyster	Wellfleet, MA
Wine Spectator Greystone	St. Helena, CA

Asian

Annisa	Manhattan, NY
Asiate	Manhattan, NY
Ballard Inn, The	Ballard, CA
Benu	San Francisco, CA
Blue Ginger	Wellseley, MA
BluePointe	Atlanta, GA
Chinois on Main	Santa Monica, CA
Crustacean	Beverly Hills, CA
Eurasia Bistro	Decatur, GA
Fatty 'Cue	Brooklyn, NY
Momofuku Ssäm Bar	Manhattan, NY
Nectar	West Chester, PA
Spice Market	Manhattan, NY
Terra	St. Helena, CA
Urban Belly	Chicago, IL
Yoshi's Café	Chicago, IL

Cal-Ital

Cambodian

Chinese

Coffee Shops

Elizabeth's	New Orleans, LA
Five Seasons Beer Company	Atlanta, GA
Frazer's	St. Louis, MO
General Greene	Queens, NY
Green Goddess	New Orleans, LA
Herbie's Vintage 72	St. Louis, MO
Lula	Chicago, IL
Mistral	Boston, MA
Mosaic	St. Louis, MO
Paul's	Atlanta, GA
Public	Manhattan, NY
Rendezvous	Cambridge, MA
Robinhood Free Meeting House	Portland, ME
Stanton Social Club	Manhattan, NY
Vinings Inn	Vinings, GA

French (Contemporary)

Auberge du Soleil	Rutherford, CA
Aubergine	Carmel-by-the-Sea, CA
Avec	Chicago, IL
Bibou	Philadelphia, PA
Bouley	Manhattan, NY
Chaya Brasserie	San Francisco, CA
Chaya Brasserie	West Hollywood, CA
Citronelle	Washington, DC
Clio	Boston, MA
Corton	Manhattan, NY
Cyrus	Healdsburg, CA
Eleven Madison Park	Manhattan, NY
Fifth Floor	San Francisco, CA
French Laundry, The	Yountville, CA
Gordon Ramsay at the London	Manhattan, NY
Gordon Ramsay at the London	West Hollywood, CA
Jardinière	San Francisco, CA
Jean Georges	Manhattan, NY
Josie	Santa Monica, CA
L20	Chicago, IL
La Belle Vie	Minneapolis, MN
La Toque	Napa, CA
Le Bernardin	Manhattan, NY
LudoBites	Los Angeles, CA
Lumière	Newton, MA
Mantra	Boston, MA
Mas	Manhattan, NY
Maze	Manhattan, NY
Mélisse	Santa Monica, CA
Mercer Kitchen	Manhattan, NY
Modern, The	Manhattan, NY
NoMI	Chicago, IL
Nougatine	Manhattan, NY
Palme d'Or	Coral Gables, FL
Patina	Los Angeles, CA
Per Se	Manhattan, NY
Picasso	Las Vegas, NV

Picholine	Manhattan, NY
Rn74	San Francisco, CA
Rover's	Seattle, WA
Tru	Chicago, IL

French (Traditional)

1789	Washington, DC
2941	Falls Church, VA
Adour	Manhattan, NY
Atlas Restaurant	St. Louis, MO
Atmosphere	Atlanta, GA
Birchrunville Store Café	Birchrunville, PA
Bouchon	Santa Barbara, CA
Carlos	Highland Park, IL
Carlyle Hotel	Manhattan, NY
Campagne	Seattle, WA
Central Kitchen	Cambridge, MA
Chef Mavro	Honolulu, HI
Chez Panisse Café	San Francisco, CA
Chillingsworth	Brewster, MA
Christopher's	Phoenix, AZ
Cuistot	Palm Desert, CA
Daniel	Manhattan, NY
Everest	Chicago, IL
Fleur de Lys	Las Vegas, NV
Fleur de Lys	San Francisco, CA
Gilmore's	West Chester, PA
Guy Savoy	Las Vegas, NV
Heathman	Portland, OR
Hungry I	Boston, MA
JiRaffe	Santa Monica, CA
Joël Robuchon at the Mansion	Las Vegas, NV
L'Atelier de Joël Robuchon	Manhattan, NY
L'Atelier de Joël Robuchon	Las Vegas, NV
L'Auberge Chez François	Washington, DC
L'Espalier	Boston, MA
La Chaumière	Washington, DC
La Folie	San Francisco, CA
La Grenouille	Manhattan, NY
La Mer	Honolulu, HI
La Petite Folie	Chicago, IL
Le Bec-Fin	Philadelphia, PA
Le Cirque	Las Vegas, NV
Le Cirque	Manhattan, NY
Le Papillon	San Jose, CA
Le Périgord	Manhattan, NY
Le Pichet	Seattle, WA
Le Vallauris	Palm Springs, CA
Les Nomades	Chicago, IL
Levain	Minneapolis, MN
Marcel's	Washington, DC
Marine Room	La Jolla, CA
Metropolis Café	Boston, MA
Mille Fleurs	Rancho Santa Fe, CA

French Bistro

French Brasserie

Gastropub

Animal	West Hollywood, CA
Bradstreet Crafthouse	Minneapolis, MN
Breslin, The	Manhattan, NY
Bristol	Chicago, IL
Cakes and Ale	Decatur, GA
Clyde Common	Portland, OR
Father's Office	Santa Monica, CA
Holeman & Finch	Atlanta, GA
Olympic Provisions	Portland, OR
Prune	Manhattan, NY
Publican, The	Chicago, IL
Purple Pig, The	Chicago, IL
Spotted Pig	Manhattan, NY
Victory 44	Minneapolis, MN
Village Idiot	West Hollywood, CA

German

Hallo Berlin	Manhattan, NY
Heidelberg	Manhattan, NY
Karl Ratzsch	Milwaukee, WI
Prime Meats	Brooklyn, NY
Zum Schneider	Manhattan, NY

Greek

Avra Estiatorio	Manhattan, NY
Black Olive, The	Baltimore, MD
Elias Corner	Queens, NY
Emilitsa	Portland, ME
Estiatorio Milos	Manhattan, NY
Evvia	Palo Alto, CA
Gardens of Salonica	Minneapolis, MN
Kefi	Manhattan, NY
Kokkari Estiatorio	San Francisco, CA
Komi	Washington, DC
Kouzina by Trata	Manhattan, NY
Kyma	Atlanta, GA
Molyvos	Manhattan, NY
Periyali	Manhattan, NY
Pylos	Manhattan, NY
Snack Taverna	Manhattan, NY
Thalassa	Manhattan, NY
Uncle Nick's	Manhattan, NY

Hamburgers

4505 Meats	San Francisco, CA
5 Napkin Burger	Manhattan, NY
8 Oz. Burger Bar	Miami Beach, FL
8 Oz. Burger Bar	Los Angeles, CA
Apple Pan	West Los Angeles, CA
BLT Burger	Manhattan, NY
Blue Door Pub	Minneapolis, MN
Bobcat Bite	Santa Fe, NM

Burger Bar	Las Vegas, NV
burger joint at Le Parker Meridien	Manhattan, NY
Corner Bistro	Manhattan, NY
Donovan's Pub	Queens, NY
DuMont Burger	Brooklyn, NY
Elevation Burger	Arlington, VA
Fanelli's Café	Manhattan, NY
Five Guys	Washington, DC
Flip Burger Boutique	Atlanta, GA
Flip Burger Boutique	Birmingham, AL
Gott's Roadside	Napa, CA
Gott's Roadside	San Francisco, CA
Gott's Roadside	St. Helena, CA
Hodad's	Ocean Beach, CA
Hut's	Austin, TX
In-N-Out Burger	Daly City, CA
In-N-Out Burger	Los Angeles, CA
In-N-Out Burger	San Francisco, CA
J. G. Melon	Manhattan, NY
Jackson Hole	Manhattan, NY
Kuma's Corner	Chicago, IL
Louis' Lunch	New Haven, CT
P. J. Clarke's	Manhattan, NY
Pop Burger	Manhattan, NY
Port of Call	New Orleans, LA
Rare Bar & Grill	Manhattan, NY
Ray's Hell-Burger	Washington, DC
Shake Shack	Manhattan, NY
Shake Shack	Miami Beach, FL
Stand	Manhattan, NY
Uburger	Boston, MA
Umami Burger	Los Angeles, CA
Vortex	Atlanta, GA

Hawaiian

Alan Wong's	Honolulu, HI
Hoku's	Honolulu, HI
Roy's	Honolulu, HI

Hot Dogs

Ben's Chili Bowl	Washington, DC
Crif Dogs	Manhattan, NY
Gray's Papaya	Manhattan, NY
Hot Doug's	Chicago, IL
Let's Be Frank	Culver City, CA
Nathan's Famous	Brooklyn, NY
Papaya King	Manhattan, NY
Pink's Famous Hot Dogs	Los Angeles, CA
Super Duper Weenie	Fairfield, CT
Superdawg Drive-In	Chicago, IL
Wurstküche	Los Angeles, CA

Sotto Sotto	Atlanta, GA
Spiaggia	Chicago, IL
Stellina	St. Louis, MO
Sweet Basil	Needham, MA
Tarry Lodge	Port Chester, NY
Teatro Goldoni	Washington, DC
Teatro ZinZanni	San Francisco, CA
Tony's	St. Louis, MO
Tosca	Washington, DC
Tra Vigne	St. Helena, CA
Valentino	Santa Monica, CA
Valentino Las Vegas	Las Vegas, NV
Veni Vidi Vici	Atlanta, GA
Vetri	Philadelphia, PA
Via Matta	Boston, MA
Vincenti	Brentwood, CA

Italian (Southern)

Café Martorano	Ft. Lauderdale, FL
Café Martorano	Hollywood, CA
Carmen	Boston, MA
Charlie Gitto's on The Hill	St. Louis, MO
Chef Vola's	Atlantic City, NJ
Daily Catch	Boston, MA
Dominick's	Bronx, NY
Francesca's on Taylor	Chicago, IL
Fresco by Scotto	Manhattan, NY
Giacomo's	Boston, MA
Il Capriccio	Waltham, MA
Irene's Cuisine	New Orleans, LA
L'Osteria del Forno	San Francisco, CA
Marea	Manhattan, NY
Maroni Cuisine	Northport, NY
Mosca's	Avondale, LA
Oscar's Villa Capri	Dunwoody, GA
Pascal's Manale	New Orleans, LA
Patsy's	Manhattan, NY
Piccola Venezia	Queens, NY
Rao's	Manhattan, NY
Roberto's Trattoria	St. Louis, MO
Taranta	Boston, MA

Italian Trattorias

'ino	Manhattan, NY
'inoteca	Manhattan, NY
Al Di La	Brooklyn, NY
Angeli Café	Los Angeles, CA
August	Manhattan, NY
Bar Veloce	Manhattan, NY
Barbuto	Manhattan, NY
Bistro Don Giovanni	Napa, CA
Bresca	Portland, ME
Broders' Pasta Bar	Minneapolis, MN

Butcher Block, The	Minneapolis, MN
Butcher Shop	Boston, MA
Café Juanita	Kirkland, WA
Café Spiaggia	Chicago, IL
Celeste	Manhattan, NY
Citta Nuova	East Hampton, NY
Coppa	Boston, MA
Fascino	Montclair
Floataway Café	Decatur, GA
Flour + Water	San Francisco, CA
Frankies Spuntino	Brooklyn, NY
Il Casale	Belmont, MA
Locanda Verde	Manhattan, NY
Locanda Vini e Olii	Brooklyn, NY
Lorenzo's Trattoria	St. Louis, MO
Lupa	Manhattan, NY
Mezzaluna	Manhattan, NY
Noodle Pudding	Queens, NY
Olio e Limone	Santa Barbara, CA
Osteria	Philadelphia, PA
Osteria Mozza	Hollywood, CA
Otto	Manhattan, NY
Paciarino	Portland, ME
Pasta Nostra	Norwalk, CT
Peasant	Manhattan, NY
Perbacco	Manhattan, NY
Perricone's Marketplace	Miami, FL
Pó	Manhattan, NY
Porchetta	Manhattan, NY
Pulino's	Manhattan, NY
Queen	Brooklyn, NY
Rialto	Cambridge, MA
Ribollita	Portland, ME
Roberta's	Brooklyn, NY
Salumi Artisan Cured Meat	Seattle, WA
Scampo	Boston, MA
Sfoglia	Manhattan, NY
Spigola	Manhattan, NY
Spinasse	Seattle, WA
Sportello	Boston, MA
Teatro	Boston, MA
Terroir Wine Bar	Manhattan, NY
Trattoria Delia	Burlington, VT
Trattoria Marcella	St. Louis, MO

Japanese

15 East	Manhattan, NY
Aburiya Kinnosuke	Manhattan, NY
Ajihei	Princeton, NJ
AKA Bistro	Lincoln, MA
Arigato Sushi	Santa Barbara, CA
Asanebo	Studio City, CA
Bar Masa	Manhattan, NY
Biwa	Portland, OR

Yama	Manhattan, NY
Yamashiro	Hollywood, CA
Yoshi	Oakland, CA

Korean

Gahm Mi Oak	Manhattan, NY
HanGawi	Manhattan, NY
Momofuku Noodle Bar	Manhattan, NY
New Won Jo	Manhattan, NY
Woo Lae Oak	Manhattan, NY

Malaysian

Fatty Crab	Manhattan, NY

Mediterranean

A.O.C.	West Hollywood, CA
Avila	Boston, MA
Blu	Boston, MA
Campanile	Los Angeles, CA
Cleonice Mediterranean Bistro	Ellsworth.ME
Craftbar	Manhattan, NY
Foreign Cinema	San Francisco, CA
Gjelina	Venice, CA
Grocery, The	Brooklyn, NY
How to Cook a Wolf	Seattle, WA
Lark	Seattle, WA
Lauro Kitchen	Portland, OR
Lolita	Cleveland, OH
Lucques	West Hollywood, CA
Michael's Genuine Food & Drink	Miami, FL
Michy's	Miami, FL
Navarre	Portland, OR
Nopa	San Francisco, CA
Oleana	Cambridge, MA
Savoy	Manhattan, NY
Sitka & Spruce	Seattle, WA
Taboon	Manhattan, NY
Ten Tables	Cambridge, MA
Terra	St. Helena, CA
Zatinya	Washington, DC
Zuni Café	San Francisco, CA

Mexican

Barrio Tequila Bar	Minneapolis, MN
Big Star	Chicago, IL
Border Grill	Santa Monica, CA
Café Poca Cosa	Tucson, AZ
Centrico	Manhattan, NY
Distrito	Philadelphia, PA
Doña Tomás	Oakland, CA
Fonda San Miguel	Austin, TX
Frontera Grill	Chicago, IL
Hell's Kitchen	Manhattan, NY
La Super-Rica Taqueria	Santa Barbara, CA
La Taqueria	San Francisco, CA
Los Sombreros	Scottsdale, AZ
Maya	Manhattan, NY
Mercadito	Manhattan, NY
Mexicana Mama	Manhattan, NY
Nuevo Laredo Cantina	Atlanta, GA
Pampano	Manhattan, NY
Pueblo Solis	St. Louis, MO
Rosa Mexicano	Manhattan, NY
Salpicón	Chicago, IL
Tamayo	Denver, CO
Taqueria del Sol	Atlanta, GA
Topolobampo	Chicago, IL

Middle Eastern

Hummus Place	Manhattan, NY
Lebanese Taverna	Baltimore, MD
Lebanese Taverna	Washington, DC
Mamoun's	Manhattan, NY
Moustache	Manhattan, NY
Taim	Manhattan, NY
Zahav	Philadelphia, PA

Moroccan

Tangierino	Chelsea, MA

New American (Expensive)

10 Arts (Expensive)	Philadelphia, PA
1770 House	East Hampton, NY
21 Federal	Nantucket, MA
231 Ellsworth	San Mateo, CA
Abacus	Dallas, TX
American Restaurant	Kansas City, MO
Aria	Atlanta, GA
Aureole	Las Vegas, NV
Aureole	Manhattan, NY
Back Bay Grill	Portland, ME
Bar Americain	Manhattan, NY
Benu	San Francisco, CA
Bernards Inn, The	Bernardsville, NJ
Bertrand at Mr. A's	San Diego, CA
BLT Market	Manhattan, NY
Bluehour	Portland, OR
Bradley Ogden	Las Vegas, NV
Canlis	Seattle, WA
Cardwell's at the Plaza	Clayton, MO
Charleston Grill	Charleston, SC
Charlie Trotter's	Chicago, IL

New American (Moderate)

Bistro 7	Philadelphia, PA
Bistro Elan	Palo Alto, CA
Black Trumpet Bistro	Portsmouth, NH
Blu	Montclair, NJ
Blue Bottle Café	Hopewell, NJ
Blue Room	Cambridge, MA
Blue Spoon	Portland, ME
Boka	Chicago, IL
Brothers at Mattei's Tavern	Los Olivos, CA
Café Castagna	Portland, OR
Café Lurcat	Minneapolis, MN
Caiola's Restaurant	Portland, ME
Cardwell's at the Plaza	Clayton, MO
Canteen	San Francisco, CA
Chestnut	Brooklyn, NY
Circle Bistro	Washington, DC
Compass	Manhattan, NY
Cook St. Helena	St. Helena, CA
Corner Table, The	Minneapolis, MN
Cosmos	Minneapolis, MN
Crofton on Wells	Chicago, IL
CulinAriane	Montclair, NJ
David's 388	Portland, ME
DC Coast	Washington, DC
Dressler	Brooklyn, NY
East Coast Grill & Raw Bar	Cambridge, MA
Erwin An American Café & Bar	Chicago, IL
Firefly	Washington, DC
Fish Out of Water	Santa Rosa Beach, FL
Five fifty-five	Portland, ME
Fork	Philadelphia, PA
Frances	San Francisco, CA
Francine Bistro	Camden, ME
Franklin Café	Boston, MA
Friday Saturday Sunday	Philadelphia, PA
Frog & the Peach, The	New Brunswick, NJ
Front Room	Portland, ME
Fruition	Denver, CO
Hemingway's	Killington, VT
Hil, The	Atlanta, GA
Iris	New Orleans, LA
Jake's	Philadelphia, PA
Jeffrey's	Austin, TX
Joshua's	Wells, ME
Lilette	New Orleans, LA
Liluma	St. Louis, MO
Little Giant	Manhattan, NY
Little Owl, The	Manhattan, NY
Local 188	Portland, ME
Lucia's	Minneapolis, MN
Marigold Kitchen	Philadelphia, PA
Market Table	Manhattan, NY
Marlow & Sons	Brooklyn, NY
Match	South Norwalk, CT
Matyson	Philadelphia, PA
Meritage	Boston, MA
Mezze Bistro & Bar	Williamstown, MA
MiLa	New Orleans, LA
Mirabelle	Austin, TX
Monarch	St. Louis, MO
Morrison-Clark Inn	Washington, DC
Mosaic	Atlanta, GA
Nook	West Los Angeles, CA
OM	Cambridge, MA
one sixtyblue	Chicago, IL
ONE. midtown kitchen	Atlanta, GA
Paces 88	Atlanta, GA
Palace Café	New Orleans, LA
Perilla	Manhattan, NY
Perry Street	Manhattan, NY
Portland City Grill	Portland, OR
Range	San Francisco, CA
Restaurant Alba	Malvern, PA
Revolution	Durham, NC
Riingo	Manhattan, NY
Rioja	Denver, CO
Rosemary's	Las Vegas, NV
Rue de L'Espoir Creative Cooking	Providence, RI
Salts	Cambridge, MA
Sanctuary	Minneapolis, MN
Sapphire Grill	Savannah, GA
Saul	Brooklyn, NY
Screen Door	Portland, OR
Sepia	Chicago, IL
Serpas True Food	Atlanta, GA
Sibling Rivalry	Boston, MA
Simpatica Dining Hall	Portland, OR
Sola	Bryn Mawr, PA
South Congress Café	Austin, TX
Southwark	Philadelphia, PA
Starker's Reserve	Kansas City, MO
Sweet Basil	Vail, CO
Tabard Inn	Washington, DC
Terrene	St. Louis, MO
Town Hall	San Francisco, CA
UpStairs on the Square	Cambridge, MA
Veritable Quandary	Portland, OR
Wink	Austin, TX

Peruvian

Andina	Portland, OR
Chifa	Philadelphia, PA
La Mar	San Francisco, CA
Mo-Chica	Los Angeles, CA
Pio Pio	Queens, NY

Pizzerias

"Co."	Manhattan, NY
2Amys	Washington, DC
Adrienne's Pizzabar	Manhattan, NY
Apizza Scholls	Portland, OR
Black Sheep Pizza	Minneapolis, MN
Cameli's Gourmet Pizza	Atlanta, GA
Cheese Board	Berkeley, CA
DeLorenzo's Tomato Pies	Trenton, NJ
Di Fara's	Brooklyn, NY
Emma's	Boston, MA
Frank Pepe's Pizzeria	New Haven, CT
Franny's	Brooklyn, NY
Fritti	Atlanta, GA
Good Pie, The	St. Louis, MO
Grimaldi's Pizza	Brooklyn, NY
Joe's Pizza	Manhattan, NY
John's Pizzeria	Manhattan, NY
Ken's Artisan Pizza	Portland, OR
Keste Pizza & Vino	Manhattan, NY
L & B Spumoni Gardens	Brooklyn, NY
Lombardi's	Manhattan, NY
Modern Apizza	New Haven, CT
Motorino	Manhattan, NY
Onesto	St. Louis, MO
Patsy's Pizzeria	Manhattan, NY
Pizzeria Bianco	Phoenix, AZ
Pizzeria Delfina	San Francisco, CA
Pizzeria Mozza	Los Angeles, CA
Pizzeria Paradiso	Washington, DC
Pizzeria Tra Vigne	St. Helena, CA
Pizzetta 211	San Francisco, CA
Punch Neapolitan Pizza	Minneapolis, MN
Sally's Apizza	New Haven, CT
Santarpio's	East Boston, MA
Serious Pie	Seattle, WA
Totonno's	Brooklyn, NY
Trattoria Zero Otto Nove	Bronx, NY
Two Boots	Manhattan, NY
Una Pizzeria Napoletana	San Francisco, CA
V & T	Manhattan, NY
World Pie	Bridgehampton, NY

Portuguese

Aldea	Manhattan, NY

Progressive

Alinea	Chicago, IL
Avenues	Chicago, IL
Baumé	Palo Alto, CA
Binkley's	Cave Creek, AZ
Bonsoirée	Chicago, IL
Castagna	Portland, OR
COI	San Francisco, CA
Gargoyles on the Square	Somervile, MA
Graham Elliot	Chicago, IL
Hugo's	Portland, ME
McCrady's	Charleston, SC
Minibar	Washington, DC
Momofuku Ko	Manhattan, NY
Moto	Chicago, IL
Orson	San Francisco, CA
Saam – The Chef's Tasting Room	West Hollywood, CA
Schwa	Chicago, IL
Town House	Chilhowie, VA
Volt	Fredericksburg, MD
WD-50	Manhattan, NY

Sandwiches

'wichcraft	Manhattan, NY
Al's # 1 Italian Beef	Chicago, IL
Atwater's	Baltimore, MD
Beecher's Handmade	Seattle, WA
Bunk Sandwiches	Portland, OR
Central Grocery	New Orleans, LA
Cochon Butcher	New Orleans, LA
Crabby Jack's	New Orleans, LA
Dalessandro's	Philadelphia, PA
Domilise's Po-Boys	New Orleans, LA
Duck Fat	Portland, ME
Geno's Steaks	Philadelphia, PA
Jim's Steaks	Philadelphia, PA
Joan's on Third	West Hollywood, CA
John's Roast Pork	Philadelphia, PA
Johnnie's Beef	Arlington Heights, IL
Kelly's Roast Beef	Revere, MA
Mother's	New Orleans, LA
Mr. Beef	Chicago, IL
New Yorker Marketplace & Deli	Atlanta, GA
Pat's King of Steaks	Philadelphia, PA
Philippe the Original	Los Angeles, CA
Sun in My Belly	Atlanta, GA
Taqueria La Veracruzana	Philadelphia, PA
Tony Luke's Old Philly Style Sandwiches	Philadelphia, PA
White House Sub Shop	Atlantic City, NJ

Seafood

Steakhouse

Swedish

Aquavit	Manhattan, NY

Thai

Arun's	Chicago, IL
Jitlada	Los Angeles, CA
King and I Thai	St. Louis, MO
Kittichai	Manhattan, NY
Lotus of Siam	Las Vegas, NV
Nan Thai Fine Dining	Atlanta, GA
Origin	Somervile, MA
Pam Real Thai	Manhattan, NY
Ping	Portland, OR
Pok Pok	Portland, OR
Spoon Thai	Chicago, IL
Sripraphai	Queens, NY
Tamarind Seed Bistro	Atlanta, GA
Typhoon	Portland, OR

Turkish

Sip Sak	Manhattan, NY
Turkish Kitchen	Manhattan, NY

Vegetarian

Angelica Kitchen	Manhattan, NY
Candle 79	Manhattan, NY
Gobo	Manhattan, NY
Green Zebra	Chicago, IL
Greens	San Francisco, CA
Pure Food & Wine	Manhattan, NY
Spring Street Natural	Manhattan, NY
supperclub	San Francisco, CA
Ubuntu	Napa, CA

Vietnamese

Bánh Mì Saigon Bakery	Manhattan, NY
Le Colonial	Chicago, IL
Le Colonial	San Francisco, CA
Má Pêche	Manhattan, NY
Mai Lee	St. Louis, MO
Nam	Atlanta, GA
Nicky's Vietnamese	Manhattan, NY
Pho 75	Arlington, VA
Pho 75	Falls Church, VA
Pho 75	Philadelphia, PA
Pho 75	Rockville, MD
Pho Grand	St. Louis, MO
Quang	Minneapolis, MN
Saigon Sandwich	San Francisco, CA
Slanted Door	San Francisco, CA
Tamarine	Palo Alto, CA
Thanh Long	San Francisco, CA

Wine Bar

Lou	Hollywood, CA
Noble Rot	Portland, OR
Palate Food & Wine	Glendale, CA
Proof	Washington, DC
Terroir Wine Bar	Manhattan
Tria	Philadelphia, PA

Listed by State

continued **569**

Maryland

Minnesota

continued **571**

New York

Ohio

Oregon

Pennsylvania

continued